AF270263

Exploring

THE GOSPEL OF MATTHEW

THE JOHN PHILLIPS COMMENTARY SERIES

Exploring
THE GOSPEL OF MATTHEW

An Expository Commentary

JOHN PHILLIPS

kregel
PUBLICATIONS

Grand Rapids, MI 49501

Exploring the Gospel of Matthew: An Expository Commentary

© 1999 by John Phillips

Published in 2005 by Kregel Publications, a division of Kregel Inc., 2450 Oak Industrial Dr. SE, Grand Rapids, MI 49505.

All rights reserved. No part of this book may be reproduced, stored in a retrieval system, or transmitted in any form or by any means—electronic, mechanical, photocopy, recording, or otherwise—without written permission of the publisher, except for brief quotations in printed reviews.

Scripture quotations are from the King James Version of the Holy Bible.

ISBN 978-0-8254-3392-4

Printed in the United States of America

7 8 9 10 11 / 29 28 27 26 25 24 23 22 21

CONTENTS

SUMMARY OUTLINE
OF THE GOSPEL ACCORDING TO MATTHEW

More detailed outline points can be found in the text on the pages indicated.

PART ONE: THE KING IS REVEALED (1:1–9:38)

2. The Question of Invoking Law (5:25-26)
3. The Question of Indulging Lust (5:27-32)
4. The Question of Inappropriate Language (5:33-37)
5. The Question of Ineffable Love (5:38-48)
D. The Disciple and His Burdens (6:1-34)
1. Burdens Connected with Worship (6:1-18)
a. The Duties of Life (6:1-4)
b. The Devotions of Life (6:5-15)
c. The Disciplines of Life (6:16-18)
2. Burdens Connected with Wealth (6:19-24)
3. Burdens Connected with Worry (6:25-34)
E. The Disciple and His Behavior (7:1-29)
1. The Fool Exhibited (7:1-5)
2. The Father Extolled (7:6-12)
3. The Future Explained (7:13-14)
4. The Frauds Exposed (7:15-23)
a. Beware of False Prophets (7:15-20)
b. Beware of False Profession (7:21-23)
5. The Foundations Examined (7:24-29)

Section 3: The King's Power (8:1–9:38)   135
I. POWER OVER DESPAIR (8:1-4)
II. POWER OVER DISTANCE (8:5-13)
III. POWER OVER DISEASE (8:14-17)
IV. POWER OVER DISASTER (8:18-27)
V. POWER OVER DEMONS (8:28-34)
VI. POWER OVER DIFFICULTY (9:1-8)
VII. POWER OVER DISDAIN (9:9-17)
A. Social Disdain (9:9-13)
B. Spiritual Disdain (9:14-17)
VIII. POWER OVER DEATH (9:18-26)
IX. POWER OVER DOUBT (9:27-31)
X. POWER OVER DUMBNESS (9:32-34)
XI. POWER OVER DISBELIEF (9:35-38)

PART TWO: THE KING IS RESISTED (10:1–16:12)

Section 1: The Resistance Foretold (10:1-42)   179
I. PREPARATION FOR SERVICE (10:1-15)
A. The Master (10:1)

    B. The Men (10:2-4)
    C. The Mission (10:5-6)
    D. The Message (10:7)
    E. The Miracles (10:8)
    F. The Money (10:9-10)
    G. The Method (10:11-15)
II. PREPARATION FOR SUFFERING (10:16-42)
    A. The Apostles' Foes (10:16-25)
    B. The Apostles' Fears (10:26-39)
    C. The Apostles' Followers (10:40-42)

INTRODUCTION

The Gospel of Matthew presents Christ as King. It was written by a Jew primarily for the Jewish people, whose great hope was for the coming of an oft-promised Messiah. This Messiah would restore the former glories of the kingdom, elevate Israel to the head of the nations, and reign "from the river unto the ends of the earth" (Psalm 72:8). Such a King would put an end to Gentile dominion, restore the world to its Edenic splendor, and bring blessing to all mankind. Jerusalem would be the capital of His global empire and the center of universal worship of Jehovah. Many Old Testament prophecies encouraged these beliefs.

The Jews, however, ignored the spiritual side of those prophecies. They were so enamored of the promises of a Messiah coming to reign that they forgot the promises of a Messiah coming to redeem. They wanted a militant King who would break the power of Rome and inaugurate a new world order based on Judaism and centered in Jerusalem. But God sent them a meek King. The Jews wanted a Sovereign; God sent them a Savior.

The Messianic hope had been aroused in many a Hebrew heart by the spectacular revival ministry of John the Baptist and by the extraordinary teaching and miracles of Jesus. Initially there was speculation that the promised kingdom was about to be established, but the hope quickly soured. As soon as the spiritual dimensions of Christ's ministry became evident, the Jews turned against Him. He was not the kind of King they wanted; He was not the kind of Messiah they had been led to expect.

The religious leaders were in the forefront of the opposition Christ had to face from His own people, for He opposed almost everything those leaders stood for. Obviously a King like Jesus was not going to confirm them in the privileges of their rank or advance them to seats of influence in the kingdom of their dreams. The common people found Him disappointing too, especially after He resolutely rejected their attempts to make Him King. A man like Barabbas, a bold insurrectionist willing to defy the hated power of Rome, was more to their liking.

So, under the cloak of legality, the Jews murdered their God-sent

Messiah, but He refused to stay dead. Soon a new movement was abroad. It began in Jerusalem, swiftly spilled over into the provinces, crossed national frontiers into Samaria, and was now making its impact on the Jewish diaspora as well as making inroads into the Gentile world. Those inroads were astonishing and extremely suspect to the Hebrews.

The man who undertook to explain to the Jews what all these developments meant was Matthew, who was also called Levi. His Gospel reveals that he had a good working knowledge of the Old Testament. Doubtless he was fluent in both Aramaic and Greek, for he had been a tax collector for the Romans in the territory of Herod Antipas. It was while Matthew was sitting in his toll booth near Capernaum on the road from Damascus to the Mediterranean that Jesus had called him to be a disciple. Thereupon he made a feast and invited his fellow tax collectors (a despised fraternity) to come and meet his Master.

Matthew seems to have written his Gospel just before or immediately after the fall of Jerusalem in A.D. 70. By that time Christianity was well established in the world and many of the New Testament books had been written. Matthew's references to "the city of the great King" (5:35), the temple, the holy place, and the impending time of trouble tend to sway the balance in favor of a date just prior to Jerusalem's fall. In that case he probably wrote the Gospel in Palestine, and possibly in Jerusalem itself.

Since Matthew wrote primarily to convince the Jews that Jesus of Nazareth was indeed their promised Messiah, it follows as a matter of course that his Gospel is saturated with the Hebrew Scriptures. There are 129 Old Testament references (53 direct citations and 76 allusions) taken from 25 of the 39 books. Of the 129 references, 89 were made by the Lord Himself (35 citations and 54 allusions). Matthew drew from every part of the Jewish Bible: the Law, the Prophets, and the Writings. Some of the citations were taken from the Hebrew text, but most were taken from the Septuagint, the Greek version of the Old Testament.

One of Matthew's objectives was to show that Old Testament prophecy was fulfilled in Jesus—that He was indeed the Christ. A favorite expression of Matthew was, "All this was done, that it might be fulfilled which was spoken by the prophet" (21:4). Words to that effect occur about sixteen times in his Gospel.

Matthew, as a disciple of the Lord, was able to draw to a large extent on his own recollections of what Jesus had said and done. Perhaps he had made extensive notes as events had unfolded during those extraordinary years he had spent in the company of the Lord Jesus.

About thirty-one passages in Matthew's account are unique to his Gospel. These include a few events connected with the Lord's infancy, ten parables, two miracles, nine discourses, and six events connected with the Lord's death, burial, and resurrection.

Matthew was particularly interested in the church and he was the only Gospel writer to mention it; on two occasions he made a direct and significant reference to the church and he alluded to it on other occasions.

One of the expressions unique to Matthew is "the kingdom of heaven." The phrase occurs thirty-two times and refers to the state of the kingdom while the King is in Heaven. The expression "the kingdom of God," common to the other Gospels, is found in Matthew only five times.

The distinction between the church and the kingdom will become clearer as we proceed with our analysis and interpretation of Matthew's Gospel. The church is not the kingdom; however, the church is in the kingdom. We must always make a difference where God makes a difference.

Although Matthew wrote primarily for Jews, there is no exclusivism in his Gospel. He saw beyond Israel to the church, which was already a power in the world when he wrote. He saw the Gentiles coming into the blessing of God through faith in the Lord Jesus.

Matthew's book, which begins within the narrow limits of Jewish thought, soon opens up, for the second chapter introduces the wise men from the East who came to worship the Christ. And the book ends with the Lord's commission to take the gospel into all the world. When Matthew wrote, he had lived long enough to see that God's purposes in grace were wider than those allowed by the myopia of the Sanhedrin.

PART ONE

The King Is Revealed
Matthew 1:1–9:38

THE KING'S PERSON

(1:1–4:11)

I. THE KING'S ANCESTRY (1:1-17)
A. The Book of the Generation of Jesus Christ (1:1)
1. The Royal Family (1:1a)
2. The Racial Family(1:1b)
B. The Bloodline in the Genealogy of Jesus Christ (1:2-17)
1. The Series (1:2-16)
a. The First Fourteen
The Line of the Patriarchs—The Theocracy (1:2-6a)
(1) Pilgrims in the Land
(a) Abraham
(b) Isaac
(c) Jacob
(d) Judah (Judas) and His Brethren
(e) Pharez (Phares) and Zara, Twins of
Tamar (Thamar)
(2) Parted from the Land
(a) Hezron (Esrom)
(b) Ram (Aram)
(c) Amminadab (Aminadab)
(d) Nahshon (Naasson)
(3) Possessors of the Land
(a) Salmon
(b) Boaz (Booz) of Rahab (Rachab)
(c) Obed of Ruth
(d) Jesse
(e) David the King

  b. The Further Fourteen
   The Line of the Princes—The Monarchy(1:6b-11)
   (1) The First Apostasy
     Apostasy Introduced into the Kingdom
     through the Weakness of Solomon
     (a) Solomon of Bath-sheba
     (b) Rehoboam (Roboam)
     (c) Abijam (Abia)
     (d) Asa
     (e) Jehoshaphat (Josaphat)
   (2) The Further Apostasy
     Apostasy Intensified in the Kingdom
     by the Wife of Jehoram
     (a) Jehoram (Joram)
     (b) Uzziah (Ozias)
     (c) Jotham (Joatham)
     (d) Ahaz (Achaz)
     (e) Hezekiah (Ezekias)
   (3) The Fatal Apostasy
     Apostasy Incurable in the Kingdom
     through the Wickedness of Manasseh
     (a) Manasseh (Manasses)
     (b) Amon
     (c) Josiah (Josias)
   (4) The Final Apostasy
     Jehoiachin (Jechonias) and His Brethren
  c. The Final Fourteen
   The Line of the People—The Dependency(1:12-16)
   (1) The Disrupted Pedigree
     (a) Jehoiachin
     (b) Salathiel
     (c) Zerubbabel (Zorobabel)
   (2) The Declining Peerage
     (a) Abiud
     (b) Eliakim
     (c) Azor
     (d) Zadok (Sadoc)
     (e) Achim

     (f) Eliud
     (g) Eleazar
     (h) Matthan
     (i) Jacob
    (3) The Divine Parentage
     (a) Joseph, the Husband of Mary
     (b) Jesus
  2. The Summary (1:17)

II. THE KING'S ADVENT (1:18–2:23)
 A. The Man (1:18-19)
  1. Joseph's Dilemma (1:18)
   a. His Engagement to Mary (1:18a)
   b. His Estrangement from Mary (1:18b)
  2. Joseph's Decision (1:19)
   a. His Character Revealed (1:19a)
   b. His Compassion Revealed (1:19b)
 B. The Messenger (1:20-23)
  1. All Was Well (1:20)
  2. All Was Wonderful (1:21-23)
   a. The Prospect (1:21)
    (1) Of a Son (1:21a)
    (2) Of a Savior (1:21b)
   b. The Prophecy (1:22-23)
 C. The Marriage (1:24-25)
  1. Joseph's Duty Coincided with His Desire (1:24)
  2. Joseph's Desire Coexisted with His Duty (1:25)
 D. The Magi (2:1-12)
  1. What They Sought (2:1-8)
   a. Their Quest (2:1)
   b. Their Question (2:2)
   c. Their Quandary (2:3-8)
    (1) Herod's Concern (2:3)
    (2) Herod's Counselors (2:4-6)
     (a) The Demand (2:4)
     (b) The Details (2:5-6)
    (3) Herod's Cunning (2:7-8)
     (a) How He Assisted Them (2:7)

          (b) What He Assured Them (2:8)
    2. What They Brought (2:9-12)
      a. They Were Redirected on Their Way (2:9-10)
        (1) The Last of Herod (2:9a)
        (2) The Light from Heaven (2:9b-10)
      b. They Were Reverential in Their Worship (2:11-12)
        (1) Their Goal (2:11a)
        (2) Their Gifts (2:11b)
          (a) Gold—A Tribute to Christ's
             Royalty and Power
          (b) Frankincense—A Tribute to Christ's
             Deity and Priesthood
          (c) Myrrh—A Tribute to Christ's
             Ministry and Passion
        (3) Their Guidance (2:12)
  E. The Massacre (2:13-18)
    1. The Warning from Heaven (2:13-15)
      a. The Divine Precaution (2:13-14)
        (1) Heard (2:13)
        (2) Heeded (2:14)
      b. The Divine Prediction (2:15)
    2. The Wickedness of Herod (2:16-18)
      a. A Diabolical Policy (2:16)
        (1) What Herod Discovered (2:16a)
        (2) What Herod Decreed (2:16b)
      b. A Divine Prophecy (2:17-18)
  F. The Move (2:19-23)
    1. A Change (2:19a)
    2. A Charge (2:19b-20)
    3. A Choice (2:21-23)
      a. Joseph's Steps Ordered of the Lord (2:21-23a)
      b. Joseph's Stop Ordained of the Lord (2:23b)

III. THE KING'S AMBASSADOR (3:1-17)
  A. The Coming of John (3:1-12)
    1. The Period (3:1a)
    2. The Place (3:1b)
    3. The Plan (3:2)

       4. The Prophet (3:3)
       5. The Person (3:4)
       6. The People (3:5-6)
          a. Whence They Came (3:5)
          b. What They Confessed (3:6)
       7. The Proclamation (3:7-12)
          a. The Corruption of Israel's Leaders (3:7-9)
             (1) Their Venom (3:7)
             (2) Their Vanity (3:8-9)
                (a) Religious (3:8)
                (b) Racial (3:9)
          b. The Conquerors of Israel's Land (3:10)
          c. The Coming of Israel's Lord (3:11-12)
             (1) His Might (3:11a)
             (2) His Ministry (3:11b-12)
                (a) A Baptizing Ministry (3:11b)
                (b) A Burning Ministry (3:11c-12a)
                (c) A Blessing Ministry (3:12b)
 B. The Coming of Jesus (3:13-17)
    1. An Exercise concerning That Coming (3:13-15)
       a. The Expostulation of John (3:13-14)
       b. The Explanation of Jesus (3:15)
    2. An Experience Confirming That Coming (3:16-17)
       a. The Anointing of the Spirit (3:16)
       b. The Announcement of the Father (3:17)

IV. THE KING'S ADVERSARY (4:1-11)
 A. Preparing for the Battle (4:1-2)
    1. Where Jesus Was to Go (4:1)
    2. What Jesus Was to Do (4:2)
 B. Prevailing in the Battle (4:3-10)
    1. Tempted along the Line of God's Provision
       Look at You—You have no food! (4:3-4)
       a. What Satan Suggested (4:3)
       b. What Scripture Stated (4:4)
    2. Tempted along the Line of God's Protection
       Look at You—You have no fame! (4:5-7)
       a. The Form of the Temptation (4:5-6)

        (1) The Situation Prepared by Satan (4:5)
        (2) The Suggestion Presented by Satan (4:6)
           (a) The Blatant Trap (4:6a)
           (b) The Biblical Text (4:6b)
    b. The Failure of the Temptation (4:7)
  3. Tempted along the Line of God's Program
     Look at You—You have no fortune! (4:8-10)
    a. The Suggestion Made (4:8-9)
        (1) The Crown (4:8-9a)
        (2) The Cost (4:9b)
    b. The Suggestion Met (4:10)
        (1) The Lord's Will (4:10a)
        (2) The Last Word (4:10b)
C. Proceeding from the Battle (4:11)
  1. Exit the Adversary (4:11a)
  2. Enter the Angels (4:11b)

———❦———

I. The King's Ancestry (1:1-17)

A. The Book of the Generation of Jesus Christ (1:1)

"The book of the generation of Jesus Christ, the son of David, the son of Abraham." What an unusual and, to our minds, uninteresting way to begin a book! Did Matthew know nothing of psychology? Did he not know that a writer must capture the attention of his readers in the first few lines? Of course he did and that is why he began this way.

Remember, Matthew's readers were primarily Jews. When Pilate had pointed to Jesus and said to the Jewish people, "Behold your King!" they had replied with an irony and perversity that beggars description, "We have no king but Caesar" (John 19:14-15). Matthew arrested his audience at once by saying in effect, "Here is Jesus' pedigree. He *was* your King and you will have no other King. The royal line comes to an end in Him."

The Jewish Bible contains the same books as our Old Testament, but they are arranged in a different order—possibly to avoid having the sacred writings terminate with the curse at the end of Malachi. The Hebrews placed the Chronicles at the end, and that arrangement is not without significance, for the first nine chapters of 1 Chronicles are simply long lists of names.

When Ezra the scribe wrote his Chronicles, he had a special audience and special objectives in mind. He wrote for the pioneers who had returned from the Babylonian captivity. They had come to stake a claim in the promised land for the coming of the Messiah who was being so loudly heralded by the prophet Zechariah, but there was an enormous obstacle. The land was still "trodden down of the Gentiles"; Judea was only a small province in the Persian empire. Moreover the repatriated Jews had a mandate to build a temple, not a palace; to set up an altar, not a throne. Thoughtful people were asking, "What has happened to God's promise to David?" Ezra wrote to assure them that although the throne was gone because of their national sins and the debaucheries of their kings, the royal Davidic line was still there.

Then came the silent centuries. For four hundred years—between Malachi and Matthew—God said nothing to His people. Again thoughtful people were asking, "Now what has happened to the royal line of David?" They would look at the Chronicles and realize that the lists of names were incomplete. The promise that the royal line would never lack a man to sit on the throne of David seemed to mock them. The royal line through Solomon had been cursed by Jeremiah because of the sins of Jehoiachin (also called Jechonias, Jeconiah, and contemptuously Coniah). It seemed as though God had forgotten His promise.

But the book of Matthew told the Jews that the royal line was still alive—until it terminated abruptly and permanently in the person of Jesus Christ.[1] Matthew could have found no more compelling opening sentence: "The book of the generation [genealogy, pedigree, lineage] of Jesus Christ, the son of David, the son of Abraham."

"The book of the generation of Jesus Christ" seems to have been the title of the genealogy of Jesus as it appeared in the Jewish records. The expression "the book of the generation" would have interested the Jews for another reason. It occurs twelve times in the Old Testament in the form, "These are the generations of...," and the expression occurs once in the form, "This is the book of the generations of Adam." So the occurrence in Matthew 1:1 is number fourteen.[2] The Jewish readers, used to the significance of numerical patterns in the Bible, could not help being curious.

The Jews would have wondered why the singular "generation" was used in connection with Jesus Christ while the plural "generations" was used throughout the Old Testament. In the Old Testament God was continually starting all over again, first with this family and then with that one. He needed to start over because those old family histories inevitably went from generation to degeneration. But with the coming of Jesus there would come into existence a new generation that would enroll its sons and heirs on the basis of a new principle known as regeneration. The Lord proclaimed this new principle to Nicodemus in John 3:3.

The significance of the word "book" in Matthew 1:1 would not have escaped the Jews. They would have recognized the connection with the "book" of the generations of Adam. In his very first line Matthew was thus saying to the Jewish people, "Here He is, the federal Head of a new family."

"In Adam all die, even so in Christ shall all be made alive" (1 Corinthians 15:22). Adam was the federal head of ruined humanity; Christ is the federal Head of redeemed humanity. "By one man sin entered into the world, and death by sin; and so death passed upon all men, for that all have sinned....As by one man's disobedience many were made sinners, so by the obedience of one shall many be made righteous" (Romans 5:12,19). One would almost think that Matthew had read Paul's Epistle to the Romans, which perhaps he had. The important thing for us is to get our names out of Adam's book and into Christ's.

The significance of the two phrases "the son of David, the son of Abraham" would not have escaped the Jews either. The first phrase showed Christ's link to the Hebrew *royal family;* the second phrase showed His link to the Hebrew *racial family.* No biblically literate Jew could possibly have considered a Messiah who was not a pure Jew or who was unable to establish an unbroken line to David.

Yet after the Jews rejected the true Messiah, they accepted a succession of pseudo-messiahs—and a colorful though sorry lot of impostors they were.[3] One day the Jews will hail a final false messiah and he will be the worst of them all: the antichrist himself (John 5:43).

B. The Bloodline in the Genealogy of Jesus Christ (1:2-17)

1. The Series (1:2-16)

The actual genealogy of the Lord Jesus is divided into three series of fourteen generations (perhaps in some way related to the fourteen generations inherent in the structure of Scripture). This arrangement is evidently a mnemonic device (an aid to memorization) based on the name of David. In Hebrew, "David" would be written *DWD,* the vowels being ignored. Since each letter of the Hebrew alphabet represented a number, "David" would be numerically expressed as 4+6+4 (*D+W+D*); in other words, the numerical value of the name was fourteen, the basis for the numerical arrangement of Christ's ancestry in Matthew 1.

Everyone recognizes the strain required to divide the Lord's ancestry into three equal segments of fourteen names each. Between Jehoram (Joram) and Uzziah (Ozias) for example, the names of Ahaziah, Joash, and Amaziah are deliberately erased from the record (Matthew 1:8). All three died violent deaths. Ahaziah was slain by Jehu (2 Kings 9:27), Joash was murdered by his servants (12:20), and Amaziah was put to death by the people of Jerusalem (14:19). All three kings were wicked.

All three were descendants of Jehoram and his wife Athaliah, the evil daughter of Ahab and Jezebel. As son-in-law of Ahab, Jehoram did not escape God's curse on Ahab and his house. Jehoram "died of sore diseases" (2 Chronicles 21:19). It was through Athaliah that the appalling apostasies introduced into Israel by Jezebel were imported into Judah. In Matthew's omission of Kings Ahaziah, Joash, and Amaziah we see that God's "visiting" for idolatry was literally fulfilled "unto the third and fourth generation" (Exodus 20:4-5). Their names were blotted out according to law (Deuteronomy 29:20).

Similarly the name of Jehoiakim is omitted between the names of Josiah (Josias) and Jehoiachin (Jechonias) (Matthew 1:11). Some think this omission was a copyist's error, since the execrated name of Jehoiachin (Jechonias) was used in both the second and third lists so that each list would have fourteen names. The name of Zedekiah is also left out. Actually Josiah was the last king of Judah as an independent nation; the country came under the control of Egypt after the battle of Megiddo and later Judah came under the control of Babylon.

2. The Summary (1:17)

Matthew concluded his listing with a summary statement:

> So all the generations from Abraham to David are fourteen generations; and from David until the carrying away into Babylon are fourteen generations; and from the carrying away into Babylon unto Christ are fourteen generations.

This statement is not really so in actual fact, but the generations were thus recorded by divine inspiration to show perfection where otherwise all was failure.

We see a similar process of divine selection in the listing of the tribes in the Old Testament. In actual fact there were thirteen tribes, since Joseph was represented by Ephraim and Manasseh. But invariably when the tribes are listed, they are shown as twelve tribes. In the Bible twelve is the number of governmental perfection (for instance the number twelve is prominent in the description of the new Jerusalem in Revelation 21–22); and thirteen is the number of rebellion and apostasy. God sees His people in their perfection, so He lists them as twelve tribes; in actual fact there were thirteen, for in reality they were a rebellious and stiff-necked people.

The genealogy of the Lord Jesus demonstrates the fact that in spite of human failure, God pursued His perfect plans down through the long centuries. Never once did He drop that purple thread. Sometimes it was woven into the fabric of a royal robe; sometimes it was stitched into the sackcloth of a captive slave; sometimes it was found in the homespun of a peasant's smock. But the thread of royal purple was always there.

Five women are found in the genealogy of Jesus. Three of them were women with stained characters: Tamar (Thamar, Matthew

1:3); Rahab (Rachab, 1:5); and Bath-sheba ("her that had been the wife of Urias," 1:6). Tamar was an angered widow who determined to have her rights of Judah even if it meant putting both him and her to open shame (Genesis 38:6-30). Rahab was an abandoned woman, a common harlot of Jericho, but she exercised a faith as great as Abraham's. She married into the royal family of Judah and won honored mention both in Hebrews 11:31 (for her faith) and in James 2:25 (for her works). Bath-sheba was an adulterous wife, but she became a faithful wife to David and fearlessly fought to secure the throne for Solomon. Joseph, the carpenter of Nazareth, was descended from Solomon; and Mary, the mother of Jesus, descended from Nathan, the second surviving son of David and Bath-sheba.

The other two women in Jesus' genealogy were women of sterling character: Ruth the Moabitess (Matthew 1:5) and the virgin Mary (1:16). Ruth was "a virtuous woman," the only woman so described in the Bible (Ruth 3:11). Her portrait is found in Proverbs 31:10-31 (an acrostic based on the letters of the Hebrew alphabet). Mary was the virgin mother chosen by God to be the human vehicle for bringing His Son into the world.

Note whom God deliberately introduced into the genealogy of His Son: sinners of deepest dye; women, when women in Jewish national life were generally regarded as nothing (in his morning prayers a Jewish male habitually thanked God that He had not made him a Gentile, a slave, or a woman); and pagans such as Rahab the Canaanite and Ruth the Moabitess (both members of races cursed by God). Already—on the first page of the New Testament—the Holy Spirit was preparing for a new age. Jew and Gentile, male and female, saint and sinner—all would find new status in the Christ to whom this long list of names leads.

At the end of the list we find the carefully worded statement, "And Jacob begat Joseph the husband of Mary, of whom was born Jesus, who is called Christ" (Matthew 1:16). "Of whom" is a translation of the Greek *ex hēs;* since *ex hēs* is a feminine form, it clearly refers to Mary. "Was born" is a translation of *gennaō.* Up to this point in the chapter, *gennaō* has been used of the father in the usual sense of begetting or engendering. Here suddenly there is a change in the form of the word, since it refers to the mother in the sense of bringing forth into the world. Thus Matthew in his opening genealogy emphasized the fact of the virgin birth and the fact that Joseph was not the father of Jesus.

As Matthew traced the genealogy of Jesus, he kept introducing women's names. He was hinting at something, but would the Jews grasp it? The first promise and prophecy of Scripture foretold the coming of a kinsman-redeemer who would be the seed of the woman (Genesis 3:15). Now He had come, not as the son of Joseph, but as the seed of the woman.

So, simply by listing names, Matthew confronted the Jews with the fact that the One they had murdered was indeed the Son of David—the promised Messiah, the virgin-born seed of the woman, the rightful claimant to David's throne.

The bloodline given by Matthew runs from David through the line of Solomon to Joseph of Nazareth. He might have been a king; instead he was a village carpenter, for all descendants of King Jehoiachin were barred from the throne by divine interdict. Joseph's social status was a silent confirmation of the trustworthiness of Jeremiah's prophecy. Obviously some other son of David, not descended from the accursed Jehoiachin, must be found to sit on the throne. That Son was Jesus, the Son of Mary, descended directly from David through Nathan. Jesus was adopted by Joseph as his legal son and rightful heir upon his marriage to Mary. The two lines thus came together and terminated forever in the person of Jesus Christ.[4]

Down through the centuries of the Judean monarchy, Satan brought his heavy artillery to bear on Solomon's regal line in order to corrupt the royal seed so that God would have to curse it and break faith with David. As we glance back over the genealogy given by Matthew, we can see how Satan went about his business.

Satan's effort to discredit David failed. David sinned in the terrible affair with Bath-sheba, but God's grace and mercy triumphed and David was restored. Moreover Solomon, born to the now-married David and Bath-sheba, was elected by God to be David's heir to the throne.

But Solomon was corrupted by his lust and liberalism and so debauched Jerusalem that the city looked and sounded more like Babylon than the city of God. This time Satan was sure that God would curse David's line. And indeed judgment did fall, but only partial judgment. A prophet was sent to Solomon with the tidings of God's wrath, but out of deference to David the stroke of God was delayed until after Solomon's death. David's throne, much impoverished, was still secured to David's line.

Solomon's son Rehoboam was a fool. In his day and as a result of his folly, the delayed judgment fell. The bulk of the kingdom was severed from the Davidic throne and delivered to a rival aspirant in the north. A rag or two of royalty, however, were spared to Rehoboam in the loyalty of the tribes of Judah and Benjamin. In addition some stragglers from the north resettled in the Davidic kingdom out of conviction and out of protest against the apostasies inaugurated and supported by the new northern king.

After Rehoboam we see a checkered pattern in the royal line: a good king was sometimes followed by a bad king; a bad king was sometimes followed by a good king; a good king was sometimes followed by a good king; a bad king was sometimes followed by a bad king. The fortunes of the Davidic throne seesawed back and forth, but the bad kings became more frequent and the apostasies grew greater and more daring. Good kings like Asa, Jehoshaphat, Uzziah, and Josiah found it harder and harder to effect anything more than surface reforms.

Some of the good kings themselves seemed halfhearted. Jehoshaphat, a victim to his growing fascination with Ahab and Jezebel, went so far as to sanction the marriage of his son Jehoram to their evil daughter Athaliah. No doubt Satan thought he had triumphed there. After the death of Jehoram, Athaliah massacred every possible claimant to the throne on whom she could lay her hands. She almost succeeded in wiping out the royal line—almost! As has been noted, Satan did succeed in having the next three generations expunged from the Holy Ghost-inspired record that Matthew preserved.

Hezekiah did his best to recover the nation, but he was handicapped from the start. His father Ahaz, one of Judah's weakest kings, lived in awe of Assyria all his days and substituted a pagan altar (modeled after one used by the Assyrian kings) for the altar of God. Even Hezekiah's great trust in God and his wholehearted support of Isaiah's revival ministry could not stem the tide of apostasy for long. Hezekiah's greatest mistake was to plead with God to be allowed to recover from a terminal illness; God gave him what he asked for—and sent bitterness into his soul. It was during those added years that "Ezekias [Hezekiah] begat Manasses [Manasseh]," as Matthew so tersely said (1:10). What volumes there are in those three words!

Manasseh was the worst and most wicked of a bad lot. In his day Judah sank into a quagmire of debauchery and idolatry from which the kingdom never recovered. Of all the Judean kings, Manasseh lived longest—so long that even his belated repentance at the end of his life made little impression. He was followed on the throne by Amon, who continued in his father's sins.

Then came Josiah. He and his friend Jeremiah sought to lead the nation back to God, but it was too late. Josiah was cut off in his prime and the succeeding kings turned on Jeremiah and persecuted him as a liar and traitor. Satan must have rubbed his hands with glee as he set about preparing his beloved Babylonians for the coming onslaught on the Davidic kingdom.

With the death of Josiah, the end was in sight. His son Jehoahaz (not even mentioned by Matthew) had had only three months on the throne when he was carried to Egypt as a captive by the pharaoh. Josiah's brother Eliakim (also ignored in the genealogy) was installed as a puppet by the pharaoh, who changed his name to Jehoiakim. He in turn was carried off to Babylon.

Jehoiakim's son Jehoiachin took his place on the throne. In three months and ten days Jehoiachin succeeded in bringing down God's curse on the line of Solomon. No son of Jehoiachin ever sat on the throne. He too was deported to Babylon and his uncle Mattaniah (Zedekiah), another of Josiah's brothers, was installed to preside over the final dissolution of the kingdom.

But while Satan was concentrating his attack on this Davidic line, another line (the one recorded by Luke) was meandering down the back alleys and byways of history, away from the spotlight of the throne. This other line ran from David and Bath-sheba through Nathan to a village maiden named Mary. And of her, not Joseph, was brought forth the promised seed who was at once David's Son and David's Lord.

II. THE KING'S ADVENT (1:18–2:23)

A. The Man (1:18-19)

The story turns to Joseph. It was evident that when the time came for the virgin Mary to become the mother of God's Son, she would need a protector, a husband to shield her from the inevitable process of the Mosaic law. That law would disgrace her even if its full penalty of death for one in her condition were withheld. It was also evident that the holy infant would need someone to fill the role of a father in His early years.

The man God chose was Joseph, a scion of the royal family now fallen on difficult times. A hard-working carpenter living in a despised provincial town in the northern part of the land, he was a most unlikely choice. We would have thought that at the least God's incarnate Son should be raised in a palace, surrounded by the trappings and accouterments of power, and groomed in the art of statecraft and the ways of kings. But Jesus would not need such schooling, for His kingdom was to be fashioned of different fabric.

His kingdom will be imposed upon this world when the right time comes (it could have come two thousand years ago if the Jews had recognized the hour of their visitation), but in the meantime God needed a man to be a father in the home where Mary would raise her Son. Of all the millions of men who have ever lived, God chose Joseph. That Nazareth carpenter must have been a remarkable man.

1. Joseph's Dilemma (1:18)

a. His Engagement to Mary (1:18a)

"Mary was espoused to Joseph." In the Jewish order of marriage there were three stages. First came what we would call the *engagement*. Often this was arranged by the parents; sometimes by official matchmakers. In many cases the engagement was contracted when the bride and groom were still young children. Frequently the engaged couple did not even know each other. The choosing of a life partner was considered far too serious a matter to be left to emotional impulse.

Second came the *betrothal*, the formal ratification of the marriage agreement. The betrothal lasted a year, was completely binding, and enabled the engaged couple to get to know one another. They were regarded as man and wife to the extent that the union could be dissolved only by divorce. The couple, however, were not given the marital rights of man and wife until the third stage: the *marriage*. The marriage ceremony transpired at the end of the year of betrothal and led to the consummation of the marriage. Mary and Joseph's relationship was at the second stage.

During this stage of betrothal came shattering news: Mary told Joseph that she was going to have a baby. He could hardly believe his ears. Nothing he knew about Mary's unblemished character was consistent with such a confession. He was devastated.

Then came an even more astounding announcement. Mary told him that everything was all right; she was still a virgin. An angel had visited her; she had been made pregnant supernaturally by the Holy Spirit; she was going to give birth to Israel's Messiah!

b. His Estrangement from Mary (1:18b)

Frankly Joseph did not believe Mary. If we were in his place, would we believe such a story?

His dilemma was threefold. First, he could not believe that a girl as pure and good and spiritual as his beloved Mary could have done what she must have done if she was indeed pregnant—and the telltale signs were evident before long. He knew perfectly well that he was not the father of the child. Second, Joseph could not believe the story that Mary had told him. It was simply too far-fetched. Third, he did not know what to do about the situation. He had to do something if he was to save his own good name, possibly even his life.

2. Joseph's Decision (1:19)

In the end Joseph came to the conclusion that he would have to terminate the betrothal.

a. His Character Revealed (1:19a)

Giving us one of those rare glimpses into the character of the man chosen by God to be the foster father of His beloved Son, the Holy Spirit calls Joseph "a just man." The expression that is translated "a just man" can also be rendered "a righteous man." The phrase leaves us cold and makes us think of someone hard. Campbell Morgan suggested another rendering: "a straight man, a true man." The idea behind the expression is that Joseph was a man who wanted to do the right thing. He desired to obey God's Word at all costs. There was nothing crooked or devious about him. He could be depended on.

All those fine character traits led Joseph to his decision. He would do what was right. He would simply have to part company with Mary because although he could not believe her to be guilty of immorality, he could not believe her explanation of her condition. Even if it broke his heart and hers, he would have to be guided in this extremity not by his emotional involvement with her, not by any anger or resentment he might naturally feel over being betrayed, but by the Word of God.

When Mary realized her condition, she broke into the hymn we call the Magnificat (Luke 1:46-55), in which she quoted again and again from the Holy Scriptures. When Joseph was faced with her condition, he appealed to the same source for guidance in his hurt and bewilderment. The only Scripture he could think of was Deuteronomy 24:1, which instructed him to "write her a bill of divorcement."

b. His Compassion Revealed (1:19b)

Joseph decided to act as kindly as he could by putting the bill of divorcement in her hand privately instead of exposing her to the shame of a public trial and the danger of an official sentence. He may also have planned to omit any cause in the bill so that there would be no public record to convict her.

Joseph did not have to act at once. We learn from Luke's account that after Mary received the angel's announcement, she left home to visit her cousin Elisabeth, the wife of Zacharias, who was one of the ordained priests of the Lord who ministered in Jerusalem. Mary remained there three months, doubtless glad to be away from the prying eyes and gossiping tongues in her own village. When she returned, Joseph knew it was time for him to act.

B. The Messenger (1:20-23)

1. All Was Well (1:20)

"But while he thought on these things, behold, the angel of the Lord appeared unto him in a dream, saying, Joseph, thou son of David, fear not to take unto thee Mary thy wife: for that which is conceived in her is of the Holy Ghost." What a dream! When Joseph woke up, he realized it was more than a dream. It meant that all his dreams could come true. He could marry his beloved after all. He could marry her with the full approval of Heaven, which far outweighed the disapproval they would face from man. The small-mindedness of small-town people would be sure to make the worst of this hasty marriage.

"The angel of the Lord" who visited Joseph was the Jehovah angel who had first appeared to poor, pregnant, runaway Hagar when she was about to cross the frontier into Egypt and be swallowed up by the "blackness of darkness for ever" (Genesis 16:7; Jude 13). "The angel of the Lord" was none other than the second person of the godhead Himself, who from time to time had appeared in this guise to various children of men in Old Testament times.

The angel hailed Joseph as "thou son of David." The name of David would have reminded Joseph of God's promises to the founder of Israel's royal dynasty (2 Samuel 7:11-16; 1 Chronicles 17:11-14; Psalm 110:1). Incidentally, more Scripture is devoted to David than to any other Bible character and he is the first and last named in the New Testament apart from the Lord Himself.

2. All Was Wonderful (1:21-23)

a. The Prospect (1:21)

(1) Of a Son (1:21a)

The angel told Joseph, "She shall bring forth a son"—not Joseph's son, but God's Son. The second person of the godhead was to be born as a holy child and was to be raised in Joseph's home. He was to be entrusted with the awesome responsibility of overseeing the human growth and development of the Creator of the universe. The task was not to be given to Hillel or Gamaliel or one of the other rabbis. It was not to be given to a rich and influential man such as Nicodemus or Joseph of Arimathaea. God had chosen Joseph the carpenter, an ordinary laboring man of slender means and limited education. He was just as much a chosen vessel as Mary was.

No doubt was left as to the name this Son should be given. The angel instructed Joseph, "Thou shalt call his name Jesus." *Jesus* was an ordinary name borne by hundreds of Jewish boys. It was the same as the Old Testament *Joshua* (*Hoshea* with *Jah* prefixed to it), which means "God our Savior" or "God who is salvation." No more appropriate name could have been chosen. Once that name was associated with God's Son, it ceased to be a common name and became the most wonderful, significant, and glorious name ever uttered by human lips.

(2) Of a Savior (1:21b)

The prospect went beyond that of a Son to that of a Savior. The angel explained that the reason for calling the child *Jesus* was that He would "save his people from their sins." This is the first mention of sin in the New Testament. The angel used the word *hamartia,* which literally means "failure to hit the mark" and clearly refers to failure to keep the law—sin by commission or omission in thought, word, or deed. *Hamartia* is also used (as in Hebrews 10:6) in connection with the sin offering.

Salvation is interwoven with the name *Jesus.* When Peter charged the Sanhedrin with rejecting Christ, he said, "Neither is there salvation in any other: for there is none other name under heaven given among men, whereby we must be saved" (Acts 4:12). Suppose I were to write you a check for a million dollars. You would be no better off, for my name is not good for that kind of money. But if one of the Rothschilds were to write you a check for that amount, you would be a million dollars richer. What makes the difference? The name.

There are people who come to God in their own name, or in the name of Muhammad or the virgin Mary, or in some other name. They are just as lost as they were before, because Muhammad and Mary, for example, are the names of bankrupt sinners. God honors only one name for salvation at the bank of Heaven: the precious name of Jesus.

b. The Prophecy (1:22-23)

The prophecy quoted in Matthew 1:23 was made by Isaiah. In its original context it was made to wicked King Ahaz at the time the Syro-Ephraimitic alliance was forged against him and he in his abysmal folly decided to appeal to the Assyrians for help. He might as well have asked a cat to come and keep peace between a couple of canaries. Isaiah had warned Ahaz against such a suicidal course and had offered him the opportunity to request a sign to encourage his faith. Ahaz had stubbornly refused to request a sign, but he had been given one anyway, the one Matthew quoted (Isaiah 7:14).

Much debate has centered around this prophecy regarding a virgin giving birth to a son. Whatever men may or may not believe about Isaiah's words, the fact that Matthew included them here shows what the Holy Spirit's intention was. He quoted Isaiah's words as a prophecy of the virgin birth of Christ.

The virgin birth of Christ is not an optional article of faith. It is essential to the gospel. If Jesus was not virgin-born, He had a human father. If He had a human father, He was not God. If He was not God, the Bible is false, Jesus Himself was deluded, and we have no adequate Savior from sin. If Jesus was not God manifest in flesh, the life that was surrendered on the cross was only a human life and could never have taken away the sin of the world. As man, He could only have given a life for a life. As God, He laid down an infinite life that was more than sufficient to redeem any number of finite lives.

"They shall call his name Emmanuel," quoted Matthew, "God with us." That should settle the debate. The One who was brought forth into the world by the virgin Mary was God—God manifest in the flesh.

The angel's words must have been music from Heaven in the soul of Joseph. Surely his only regret was that he had ever doubted Mary in the first place. But all doubts were laid to rest now.

C. The Marriage (1:24-25)

With no more delay, Joseph married Mary, his heart's desire. He "did as the angel of the Lord had bidden him, and took unto him his wife" (1:24). *Joseph's duty coincided with his desire.* With a holy fear, he restrained his natural desires until the promised child was born. He "knew her not till she had brought forth her firstborn son" (1:25). *Joseph's desire coexisted with his duty.*

Verse 25 is evidence enough that Mary did not remain a perpetual virgin. We learn from Matthew 12:46-50 and 13:55-56 that a number of naturally born sons and daughters were added to the family. The Roman Catholic edifice built around "the blessed virgin Mary" is founded on a falsehood. Mary, the Lord's mother, did not remain a virgin; she and Joseph entered into a normal husband-wife relationship after the miraculous birth of the Son of God.

In keeping with the angel's word, Joseph named the infant Christ *Jesus.* To countless millions down through the ages, *Jesus* has become the "sweetest name on mortal tongue," the "sweetest carol ever sung."[5]

At the time of Christ's birth, the name Jesus made very little stir on earth. It was not until over a year later that Herod happened to hear about it. True, a few shepherds on the hills surrounding Bethlehem knew about it, and an old man and an old woman in the temple were filled with knowing wonder. But there was no commotion. In Heaven, however, there was quite a stir (Luke 2:13-14). We can imagine the excitement of the angels. "And what are they going to call this wondrous child?" one might ask. "Why, Jesus, of course," another might answer. There was a new name written down in glory, a new name for God. The angels had known Him as Elohim, Jehovah, Adonai, El Shaddai, and Elyon. Now they knew Him in the person of His Son as Jesus.

D. The Magi (2:1-12)

1. What They Sought (2:1-8)

a. Their Quest (2:1)

"When Jesus was born in Bethlehem of Judaea in the days of Herod the king, behold, there came wise men from the east to

Jerusalem." The magi said that in the distant East they had observed a new phenomenon in the sky. The startling tidings of the magi stirred the whole city of Jerusalem, especially King Herod.

Astronomers assure us that two years before the birth of Christ there was indeed a remarkable conjunction of the planets Jupiter and Saturn. In the following year Mars joined the conjunction. This phenomenon occurs only once in every eight hundred years. The renowned astronomer Kepler discovered these facts by observing a similar conjunction in A.D. 1603 and 1604. He noticed that when the three planets came into conjunction, a new, extraordinary, brilliant star was visible between Jupiter and Saturn. Kepler believed that a similar star had appeared under the same circumstances prior to the birth of Christ and that it was this star that was seen by the wise men.[6]

Be that as it may, the magi's attention was arrested by some such sidereal sight—so much so that they determined that a King had been born and they decided to take a long and hazardous journey to find the child. Because the diaspora had spread to all the lands of the East, literate men such as the magi were probably acquainted with the Jewish belief in a coming Messiah. So the wise men undertook their quest.

b. Their Question (2:2)

When their guiding star brought them to Judea, the magi headed straight for Jerusalem, the most likely place for a King to be born. Like a trumpet blast, their question startled the city: "Where is he that is born King of the Jews?"—not prince, but King! Herod's tenure on the throne was ignored in Heaven. The words "born King" must have sent a chill of horror through his evil soul.

That Idumean usurper, known to history as Herod the Great, was sitting on the throne of David when the wise men arrived in Jerusalem. Never had the fortunes of David's royal house fallen lower: its lineal heir was a humble village carpenter and an Edomite was sitting on David's throne. The long struggle between Esau and Jacob was about to come to a head as the serpent's brood of the Edomite Herods set themselves against the Lord's anointed One.

Pompey, the Roman general had captured Jerusalem in 63 B.C., bringing both Jerusalem and Judea under the sway of Rome. Herod, adept at changing sides and improving his position, successfully negotiated the slippery politics of the times as Pompey was defeated by Julius Caesar, as Caesar was murdered, as Mark Antony rose briefly to power, and as Octavius replaced Antony. Soon all

Palestine was in Herod's cruel but capable hands. His reign was one of carnage, bitter hatred, suspicion, and terrible atrocities. Little the Romans cared, as long as the troublesome country of Judea was ruled for them with an iron hand.

Herod filled Jerusalem with foreign mercenaries and the cities of Palestine with spies. No man or woman was safe while Herod reigned. One by one he murdered every rival claimant to the throne. He stamped out the Hasmoneans; he murdered his wife's brother, a lad of seventeen, because he was popular with the Jews; he murdered Mariamne, the beautiful Maccabean princess he had married, because he was suspicious of her, and he murdered both her sons; five days before his death he murdered his son and heir. Herod hacked and hewed his way through life, slaughtering six to eight thousand of the best people in his realm. Caesar Augustus is reported to have cynically said, "I'd sooner be Herod's swine than Herod's son."

Herod's crimes affected his brain. After the murder of Mariamne, he became insane. Storming among his wives, concubines, and female slaves, he would point to this one and that one and shout, "You are not Mariamne!" Then one day as he was walking along the quays at Caesarea, he saw a woman who reminded him of his murdered love. Obsessed by his passion, he seized her. He disregarded the fact that she was a common harlot and later he was struck with a filthy disease. He screamed, "I knew it was Mariamne. She has come back to curse me!" Thereafter a new fire ran through his veins, a fire of madness begotten of the foul infection he had contracted in his besotted state.

This is the man who occupied the throne of David when Israel's rightful King was born and this is the man before whom the magi appeared: a dangerous, suspicious, crafty, unscrupulous tyrant.

c. Their Quandary (2:3-8)

(1) Herod's Concern (2:3)

"Herod...was troubled," we read, "and all Jerusalem with him." The Jews had learned what they could expect when Herod was troubled, especially if the trouble was the kind the magi brought— news of a rival King. Blood would be shed before long. There would be another purge.

A typical afternoon's entertainment for this man was to watch seven or eight hundred of his subjects being crucified on a public platform set up in the middle of the city. He would get drunk with his concubines while he and they enjoyed the gruesome sights. One of his favorite tricks was to enclose his enemies, unarmed, in a narrow place and then send his legionnaires roaring through the doors in full battle array while he urged them on. Every enemy in the place would be slaughtered. And history calls him Herod the Great!

The arrival of the wise men in Jerusalem (instead of Bethlehem) put them in a quandary of which they remained ignorant until it was almost too late. They had aroused a tiger. But with diabolical cunning, he did not roar; he purred.

(2) Herod's Counselors (2:4-6)

Herod wasted no time. He summoned all the chief priests and scribes and posed a theological question. In effect he said, "You people say you are expecting a Messiah. Where would such a One be born?" The answer to that question would enable him to know where he should look for this unwanted King. He also questioned the magi as to when the mysterious star first appeared. Their response would enable him to judge how far back he would need to go in pursuing his inquiries. He would not feel safe as long as anyone was alive who was born between the time the star first appeared and the time the sages showed up in Jerusalem.

Herod's counselors had no trouble telling him where to look for this King. According to Micah 5:2, He was to be born in Bethlehem.

(3) Herod's Cunning (2:7-8)

Once Herod knew where to look for his rival, he resorted to guile. He had questioned the magi "diligently" (accurately, 2:7) and now he told them to search "diligently" (2:8) as they continued on their journey to track down the newborn King. More, he urged them to come back and tell him the results of their search. "I want to go and worship Him too," he said in effect. The word translated "worship" in verses 2 and 8 is *proskenueō*, which means "to pay homage."

2. What They Brought (2:9-12)

a. They Were Redirected on Their Way (2:9-10)

As soon as the wise men stopped trusting in their own reasoning, the mysterious star reappeared and they were redirected on their way. The star led them not only to Bethlehem, which they now knew to be the birthplace, but also to the house where the infant Christ was staying.

The magi's brief excursion into Jerusalem and to the palace had greatly complicated the situation. They did not know it at the time, but they had put the child's life in dire peril. Satan was about to use the monster Herod, whom the magi had unwittingly aroused, to try once more to get rid of the promised seed of the woman.

b. They Were Reverential in Their Worship (2:11-12)

(1) Their Goal (2:11a)

Having been released at last from Herod's menacing presence, the wise men followed the sign in the sky and found their way into the presence of the newborn King. "They saw the young child with Mary his mother, and fell down, and worshipped him." Note that they worshiped Him, not her. Great as our respect for Mary should be, we must be careful not to give her a place God does not give her. In view of the idolatrous worship of Mary in some quarters, this statement needs special emphasis: They worshiped *Him*.

(2) Their Gifts (2:11b)

Many traditions have grown up around the magi. For example it is taken for granted by most people, though the Bible does not say so, that there were three wise men. This idea doubtless developed from the fact that they offered three kinds of gifts to the infant King at whose feet they bowed. One legend says that the wise men were kings. Another says that the magi represented the three races of mankind: the Japhetic, the Hamitic, and the Semitic. According to one tradition the names of the magi were Caspar, Melchior, and Balthazar. Another story pictures one wise man as youthful, one as middle-aged, and one as very old.

F. W. Boreham made an interesting suggestion in his story "The Lost Chronicles of Sufi-Abbas":[7]

One of the three wise men felt sure that what the world needed was a King, one who could rule the nations with authority and power, put down unrighteousness, and bring prosperity and peace to mankind. So, certain that the star would lead them to a King, he brought a royal present, a gift of *gold*, the peculiar treasure of kings.

The second wise man, knowing that the world's ideas of God

were warped, thought that God needed to come down here in human form and show the world what He was really like. So, wanting God to be manifest in the flesh, he brought *frankincense,* a gift for deity since incense was used for worship.

The third hoped that the star would lead them to a Savior. This wise man knew that the world was a sinful place, sadly in need of One who would take on Himself the weight and guilt of the sins of mankind and atone for them. So, convinced that such a great Savior must also be a great sufferer, he brought *myrrh,* a gift for One destined to die since the spice was used to embalm the bodies of the dead.

"They came to Bethlehem," wrote Boreham. "And when they saw that the star had but led them to a baby in a woman's arms, all three were at first overwhelmed with chagrin and dismay."[8] Then they heard Mary sing the song recorded by Luke: "My soul doth magnify *the Lord,* And my spirit hath rejoiced *in God my Saviour…*" (1:46-47, italics added).

"The Lord!" cried the first wise man. "Then I have found my King!" And he presented his gift of gold.

"In God!" exclaimed the second wise man. "Then I have found my God!" And he presented his gift of frankincense.

"My Savior!" chorused the third wise man. "Then I have found my Savior!" And he presented his gift of myrrh.

To say the least, Boreham's story is a lovely idea.

(3) Their Guidance (2:12)

Mission accomplished! The wise men had only one more duty to perform before they returned to their native spheres. They were supposed to go back to Jerusalem and report their findings to the incumbent king so that he too could come and worship the infant Christ. After all, who would not want to worship a King, a God, a Savior? Who would not hasten to pay homage and bring tribute? Surely any right-minded king of the Jews would want to come and lay crown, robe, and scepter at His infant feet. Had not Herod said, "When ye have found him, bring me word again, that I may come and worship him also" (Matthew 2:8)?

Little did the magi know that Herod's plan was to come seeking this rival sovereign with a sword. But God knew. They were "warned of God in a dream" (2:12) and, being wise men, took heed and chose another route home, a road that bypassed Jerusalem and its terrible king.

E. The Massacre (2:13-18)

1. The Warning from Heaven (2:13-15)

a. The Divine Precaution (2:13-14)

There was another warning from Heaven. Joseph was apprised in a dream of the peril in which he and Mary and especially the infant Christ were now placed. God knew Herod's heart and read his secret purpose. The wicked king had "privily" (secretly, 2:7) given his instructions to the wise men. Suspicious of all those around him, he wanted no one to suspect his anxiety and hidden resolve. But he could not hide his innermost thoughts from God.

Having *heard* the warning of immediate peril, Joseph *heeded* the words of the angel of the Lord. Hastily he packed his bags and set out with his little family along the path to Egypt. God plans to bless Egypt during the millennial reign of Christ for sheltering His Son (Isaiah 19:23-25). Often in Scripture Egypt appears as the enemy of God's people, but God will not forget or overlook the asylum it provided for Christ. God is debtor to no man or nation.

b. The Divine Prediction (2:15)

With Herod on the warpath, Egypt was the only safe place for the holy infant. He "was there until the death of Herod" and thus an ancient prophecy was fulfilled, as Matthew was quick to point out to the Jews. Matthew 2:15 refers to what the Lord said through the prophet Hosea: "Out of Egypt have I called my son" (see Hosea 11:1). This statement is invested by the Holy Spirit with prophetic as well as historic significance.

2. The Wickedness of Herod (2:16-18)

The wickedness of Herod came to full flower and fruit. Historians have given us a graphic picture of this ruthless man: A veteran of many of Herod's wars once dared to tell him, "The army hates your cruelty. Have a care, my lord. There isn't a common soldier who doesn't side with your sons, and many of the officers openly curse you." Enraged, Herod had the old soldier stretched on the rack and tortured until he sobbed out meaningless confessions and accusations of treason. Herod urged the torturers on. The wretched man accused more and more officers by name as he was twisted and torn until his joints came apart and his bones cracked. Herod summoned the accused officers and turned a mob loose on them. Livid with rage, he jumped up and down as he screamed for the death of the suspected traitors.

a. A Diabolical Policy (2:16)

"Herod, when he saw that he was mocked of the wise men, was exceeding wroth." Once his suspicions and jealousy were aroused, he could not be deterred even from a massacre of little children. So the dreadful deed was done. He "slew all the children that were in Bethlehem, and in all the coasts thereof, from two years old and under."

b. A Divine Prophecy (2:17-18)

Matthew recalled another prophecy to set before the Jews. He referred them to Jeremiah's allusion to Rama and "Rachel weeping for her children" (Matthew 2:18; Jeremiah 31:15). Jeremiah's prophecy, like so many Old Testament prophecies, had a double fulfillment.

The first and immediate fulfillment was at the time of the Babylonian invasion and the captivity of the Jews. Rama was a town of Benjamin, just five miles north of Jerusalem. When Jerusalem fell, Jeremiah and the other survivors of the siege were taken captive and carried as far as Rama before Nebuchadnezzar ordered Jeremiah's release (Jeremiah 39:11-12; 40:1). At Rama, Jeremiah watched the wretched captives being marched off in chains toward Babylon. He saw their bitter tears. He saw too the misery of the bereaved ragtag and bobtail of the poor who were left behind in a desolated land. Jeremiah prophetically depicted the whole scene as "Rachel weeping for her children," probably because Rachel had died in childbirth. Also the Benjamites (now among the captives) were descended from her. Her tomb was not far away (1 Samuel 10:2).

Jeremiah's vivid imagery of the mother of the tribe rising from her tomb to weep and refusing to be comforted because her children are gone is full of pathos. The prophecy, however, had its further and complete fulfillment in the massacre of the babes of Bethlehem.

F. The Move (2:19-23)

1. A Change (2:19a)

Verse 19 marks a significant change: "Herod was dead."

No more terrible scene is recorded in history than the death of Herod the Great. Gone were his slim good looks. He was coarse, heavy, and almost bald. Three of his front teeth had broken off. Tormented by the horrors of remorse, he would scream out for his loved and murdered wife Mariamne and her murdered sons. Moreover Herod was in the grip of a loathsome disease. His legs had become great stumps, nine inches thick at the ankles. He was covered with sores and full of mortifying wounds horrible to behold. He could not eat without agony. His guards had to be changed frequently because they could not stand the stench emanating from his rotted stomach. His breath smelled like a charnel house. All the crimes of Herod's former years were visited upon his seventy-year-old body. Death worked on the carcass of the living man as though he were already dead.

Even as Herod groaned in the agony of his deathbed, his mind turned to thoughts of murder. He knew the Jews would rejoice at the news of his death, but he would show them! He summoned his mercenaries (Africans, Cilicians, Egyptians, Persians), men who had cold-bloodedly killed off the leaders of the Jews over the years, and commanded them to go into every city, town, and village in Judea, arrest the leading citizens, put them in jail, and guard them well. The prisoners were to be fed and given their comforts, but on the day Herod died, the soldiers were to kill them all. "When I die," he screamed, "the Jews may not mourn me, but by the gods they will mourn." So the leaders of the Jews were shut up in the hippodrome and the countdown to Herod's death began.

Five days before his death his miseries were lightened by one passing ray of Hellish joy. From Augustus, Herod received a letter authorizing the execution of his son Antipater; and the father wasted no time in ordering the son's death.

Another temper tantrum hastened the end and then the news came: Herod is dead. He had reigned for thirty-five years in tyranny and blood. Salome (Herod's sister) and her husband, who were supposed to signal the mercenaries to murder the Jews in the hippodrome, opened the prison doors and set the captives free.

2. A Charge (2:19b-20)

Down in Egypt, Joseph was given a charge. The angel of the Lord conveyed the good news to him and directed his steps back to the land of Israel. Once there, the whole land lay before him. He needed divine guidance as to where he should settle, make his home, and set up his business.

3. A Choice (2:21-23)

Back in the promised land, Joseph heard other news that filled him with fresh fear: Herod's son Archelaus was now on the throne. Herod, by his last will and testament, had divided his realm among three of his sons. Archelaus was to become tetrarch of Judea, Idumea, and Samaria; Antipas was to become tetrarch of Galilee and Perea; Philip was to become tetrarch of Trachonitis, Iturea, Batanea, and Auranitis. The caesar approved the arrangement.

Archelaus, who had spent the night of his father's death carousing with friends, inaugurated his reign by slaughtering three thousand Jews in the temple at the time of Passover. The reason for the slaughter was that the Jews had demanded punishment for those who had committed atrocities during the time of Herod the Great. In response to the massacre, the Jews appealed to Rome with an urgent plea that Augustus remove Archelaus and make Judea a Roman province. After a reign of nine years Archelaus was banished to Vienne in Gaul, where he died in A.D. 6.

After Archelaus, Judea was declared a Roman province and was governed in turn by Quirinius Caponius, Ambivius, Annius Rufus, Valerius Gratus, and Pontius Pilate. The very shadow of the scepter had departed from Judah.

Afraid of Archelaus, Joseph hesitated, again received divine guidance, then headed for Galilee where he settled down in Nazareth. Matthew saw in this choice of location a fulfillment of prophecy: "He shall be called a Nazarene" (2:23). This requires some explanation, since no such direct prophecy can be found in the Old Testament.

The name "Nazareth" is derived from the Hebrew word *netzer,* which means "a sprout." *Netzer* was a term of contempt. When a tree is hewn down, a small green shoot springs up out of the stump. A Hebrew seeing such a shoot would have used the word *netzer.* "It is just a sprout," he would have said. "The tree is gone. Of what use is this shoot?" Similarly Nazareth was just a small town on a hillside hemmed in by fifteen higher hills. It was a town of Galilee, an area that had a mixed population and was often contemptuously called by the Jews "Galilee of the Gentiles."

Scofield says that probably there is a reference in Matthew 2:23 to Isaiah 11:1: "There shall come forth a rod out of the stem of Jesse, and a Branch shall grow out of his roots." "Branch" is a translation of the same word from which "Nazareth" is derived (*netzer*). Thus Jesus the Nazarene is identified not only with Nazareth, but also with a Messianic title in the Old Testament.[9] Jesus, though a Bethlehemite, carried the name of Nazareth with Him, a name that expressed the contempt of those who despised and rejected Him.

Galilee was a land of lush pastures, smiling landscapes, rich farmlands, and a teeming population. Josephus counted 240 towns and villages in the region, each with no fewer than fifteen thousand inhabitants. All the then-known trades flourished there. The lovely sea of Galilee attracted fishermen, and many people lived on its slopes.

Rabbinism was not as deeply rooted in Galilee as in Jerusalem. In rabbinic circles there was a studied contempt for all things Galilean, especially the dialect spoken there, which was despised as being characterized by error and mispronunciation. A common saying among the Jews was "If a person wants to be rich, let him go north; if he wants to be wise, let him come south."

Galilee lay close to the Gentile world. A constant procession of foreigners passed through the area along one of the world's main highways. The region was but a fringe of that greater world, and Nazareth was but a secluded corner of Galilee. In that parochial Nazareth Jesus grew to manhood. He spent about nine-tenths of His early life there, but Matthew passed over the whole period in a single sentence: "He came and dwelt in a city called Nazareth: that it might be fulfilled which was spoken by the prophets, He shall be called a Nazarene" (2:23).

III. THE KING'S AMBASSADOR (3:1-17)

A. The Coming of John (3:1-12)

1. The Period (3:1a)

The silence between Christ's birth and baptism, broken only once, was absolute. There is something awesome about that silence, something that stamps the Gospel record with the signature of God.

Man could not have kept silent about those thirty years in the life of Christ. In fact he hasn't. He has invented the apocryphal gospels and stuffed their worthless pages with prodigies and wonders.

During those thirty years a new generation arose. On August 17, A.D. 14, Caesar Augustus died and Tiberius, having shared the power with his royal stepfather for two years, became sole ruler of the empire. Tiberius was born 42 B.C. and died March 16, A.D. 37. He distinguished himself when a private citizen as an able orator, soldier, and civil servant; when he was the caesar, he showed himself to be lazy, licentious, malicious, cruel, and a master of deceit. In Palestine the cities of Caesarea Philippi and Tiberius were named after him.

In Scripture this period was marked by the coming of John the Baptist, a cousin of the Lord Jesus.

2. The Place (3:1b)

John appeared in the wilderness of Judea, an uninhabitable region running the entire length of the Dead Sea. We would have thought that such a wild place was an unlikely area in which to conduct an evangelistic campaign.

3. The Plan (3:2)

The first word of John that Matthew recorded was "Repent"! Like an Old Testament prophet, John burst upon the national consciousness. The silence of the centuries was broken by an appearance, a proclamation, a rite, and a ministry as startling as Elijah's had been. With that one word all distinctions were destroyed. Priest and publican, rich and poor, Pharisee and Sadducee, learned rabbi and ordinary soldier—all were placed on common ground. As sinners, they had one word from God: "Repent ye: for the kingdom of heaven is at hand."

In the New Testament 119 passages make reference to the kingdom. The kingdom is not the church, although the church is included in it. The Jews were not looking for a church; they were looking for a literal kingdom. Matthew invariably refers to the kingdom as "the kingdom of heaven." Elsewhere it is called "the kingdom of God." To see the reason for this difference, we must digress and look at "the kingdom" as it is presented to us in Scripture, particularly in the New Testament and the Gospel of

Matthew. (The reader will find it helpful to put a bookmark here and refer to the following discussion from time to time.)

It has always been God's intention to set up a kingdom on earth. When He created the earth and made man in His image and after His likeness, He said, "Let them have dominion" (Genesis 1:26). The fall of man resulted in the transfer of that dominion to Satan, who is presented to us as "the prince of this world" (John 12:31; 14:30; 16:11). In that capacity he offered the kingdoms of this world to Christ—at a price (Matthew 4:8-10).

The kingdom was anticipated in the Mosaic law (Deuteronomy 17:14-20). Israel did not sin because they wanted a king, but because they wanted one for the wrong motive and before God's time had come to set up a monarchy on earth (1 Samuel 8).

In due time the kingdom was established in David, with whom God entered into a covenant (2 Samuel 7). Its most important clause stated that from David's seed would come God's true King (7:12-13).

After the death of David and Solomon, declension set in rapidly. The Davidic kingdom was divided and eventually both the northern and southern portions fell to invaders. The kingdom came to an end, but the promise remained. Centuries of silence followed and then John the Baptist came preaching about the kingdom of Heaven.

Matthew's characteristic phrase for describing the kingdom is "the kingdom of heaven" (literally, "the kingdom of the heavens"). The phrase, which he used thirty-one times, is derived from the book of Daniel, where we read that Nebuchadnezzar was made to learn the lesson that "the heavens do rule" (4:26). (Nebuchadnezzar was the king who inaugurated the period of Gentile dominion over Israel known as "the times of the Gentiles" [Luke 21:24].) He had already been told that when Gentile misrule of the earth eventually came to a head during the reign of the antichrist, the "God of heaven" would set up a kingdom on earth (Daniel 2:44-45). Daniel himself was given a confirming vision of this kingdom (7:13-14,27).

The coming millennial kingdom therefore is simply "the kingdom of the heavens," the time when God's rightful King from Heaven will reign over the nations of earth, when Jerusalem will be the capital of a true world empire, and when the tribes of Israel will be administrators under Christ and His apostles (Matthew 19:28; Luke 22:30). The millennial kingdom will also see the restoration of the earth to its Edenic splendor, which was forfeited by Adam's fall (Hebrews 2:5-9). This is a favorite theme of various Old Testament prophets. The coming millennial kingdom then is called "the kingdom of the heavens" because it is the time of the rule of the heavens over the earth.

Two phases of this kingdom are discernible in Matthew. First *the King was presented.* John the Baptist announced that the kingdom was at hand (3:2). The Lord Jesus confirmed this fact as soon as He began His public ministry (4:17).

If the Jews had accepted Jesus as Messiah, national regeneration would have followed. There would have been a swift answer to the prayer that Jesus taught us to pray: "Thy kingdom come. Thy will be done in earth, as it is in heaven" (6:10). No doubt Judas would still have betrayed Christ, but to the Romans, who would have crucified Him. Three days later they would have been faced with a risen King determined to make a quick end of Gentile misrule. The end-time events described by Daniel would have been fulfilled rapidly and the kingdom would have been set up. The Jews, however, rejected the King. Their rejection brought about a change, foreseen by God but not necessarily inevitable. The gospel of the kingdom was no longer preached.

The gospel we preach today (Paul called it "my gospel" in Romans 2:16) is not the gospel of the kingdom, but the gospel of the grace of God, the gospel of Jesus Christ (Acts 20:24; 1 Corinthians 9:17-18; 2 Corinthians 4:4). After the death of Christ the apostles never once alluded to the gospel of the kingdom. But in the Olivet discourse Jesus foretold that the gospel of the kingdom will again be preached prior to the end.

The word translated "end" in Matthew 24:14 is *telos,* which means "the very end." By that time the church will have been removed and God's purposes in this present age of grace will have been accomplished. During the tribulation period the good news will be proclaimed that Satan is about to be deposed and Christ is about to reign. That good news is the gospel of the kingdom. It has reference not directly to salvation by the blood of the Lamb, but to a result of that salvation.

The Jews of Jesus' day rejected their King. Their leaders evidently labored under the mistaken idea that the coming of the kingdom would mean a continuation of the existing Jewish establishment. They were sure that the Messiah would confirm them in their positions and expand their influence and power by setting up a global empire with them as its administrators.

The Jewish leaders were thunderstruck by John's demand that they repent. They certainly were not prepared for the essentially spiritual nature of the new order. Matthew, writing from the other side of the cross and close to the impending destruction of Jerusalem and age-long dissolution of Jewish national life, could clearly see what John and Jesus had been driving at with their devastating word "Repent."

When the Jews officially rejected the King, *the kingdom was postponed* (the second discernible phase of the kingdom of the heavens). Matthew 13 records the mystery parables, which show the relationship of the kingdom to the present age of grace (a parenthesis in God's dealings with the Jewish people as a nation). Several other parables of the kingdom follow (in Matthew 25 for instance), but they have to do with the sphere of Christian profession during the present age.[10]

With the consummation of God's purposes in grace during the present church age, God will resume His direct dealings with the nation of Israel and will bring His kingdom purposes to fruition. The kingdom of the heavens will come, for God's promises of a millennial kingdom have not been canceled; they have just been postponed. God intends to fulfill literally all those "exceeding great and precious promises" that center in the second coming of Christ, just as He literally and historically fulfilled the prophecies that, as we can now see, centered in the first coming of Christ.[11]

The kindred expression "the kingdom of God" needs some comment. It is found only five times in Matthew, but elsewhere is the usual phrase for the kingdom. "The kingdom of God" is a much more comprehensive term than "the kingdom of the heavens," which Matthew alone used, and appropriately so since he was writing primarily for Jews.

Three things can be said about the kingdom of God in contrast to the kingdom of the heavens. First, the kingdom of God is *universal,* including all created beings who willingly own the rule and sovereignty of God: angels; saints from other dispensations; and believers who are saved in this age by the grace of God and are thus baptized by the Holy Spirit into the mystical body of Christ, the church (Luke 13:28-29; Hebrews 12:22-23). In contrast, the kingdom of the heavens is Messianic and millennial and has as its goal the establishment of a literal kingdom of God on this earth.

Since the kingdom of the heavens is the earthly sphere of the universal kingdom of God, the two have much in common. Thus some of the parables that relate to the kingdom of the heavens in Matthew are told in relation to the kingdom of God in Mark and Luke.[12]

Second, the kingdom of God—the subject of apostolic preaching (Acts 28:31)—is *spiritual* and is entered only by way of the new birth (John 3:3-7). The kingdom comes not with outward show

(Luke 17:20), but is inward (Romans 14:17). The kingdom of the heavens, on the other hand, contains carnal and worldly elements, as the parables of Matthew 13 make clear.

Third, the kingdom of God is *eternal.* The earthly phase will come to an end at the close of the millennial age with a universal rebellion against the rule of Christ (Revelation 20:1-10). The kingdom of the heavens will be submerged in the kingdom of God and will be replaced by the eternal state (1 Corinthians 15:24-28).

The kingdom of the heavens has as its goal the restoration of divine authority in the earth, a rebel province in God's universal empire. The restoration will take place in a period of time marked out for that purpose from the endless ages of eternity.

The church is universal, spiritual, and eternal, but it is distinct from the kingdom of God. We get into the church not by birth, but by baptism (1 Corinthians 12:13). Believers today are in both the kingdom of God and the church.

4. The Prophet (3:3)

The voice of John the Baptist broke the silence of four hundred years. He came with the spirit, power, and appearance of Elijah. John, whose coming was foretold by the prophet Isaiah (40:3), claimed to be "the voice of one crying in the wilderness" (Matthew 3:3). No other prophet made the wilderness the scene of his preaching. No mass evangelist today would begin to preach far away from the haunts of men, but John did. He did not go to the people; his magnetism and the power and authority of his message were so great that the people came to him.

Isaiah's prophecy envisioned all obstacles being removed from the path of the oncoming conquering Christ (40:4). No doubt the reference to leveling mountains and filling valleys was moral. And the hundreds of people who came to hear John—the sophisticated suburbanites and the rustic provincials—came to be leveled by the preacher to the same plane of desperate spiritual need.

5. The Person (3:4)

When the people arrived they saw an ascetic, a man clothed in camel's hair. The coarse hair of the camel was usually used for making tents and rough mantles. Elijah wore such clothing as a protest against the Phoenician luxury that in his day was sapping Israel's character. John wore it as a protest against the pervading influence of Greek culture, which had wrought such havoc, especially in the Hellenizing of the upper crust of Israelite society. Around his waist John wore a leather belt. The wealthy of his day wore girdles of costly linen or silk, often wrought with silver or gold. John scorned such embellishments.

He was an Elijah-like prophet who contented himself with eating locusts (clean under the Mosaic law; see Leviticus 11:22) and wild honey. John's days were spent in fasting and prayer, and such food as he ate—the humble fare of the very poor—was another protest against the opulence of the ruling class.

John lived for only one thing: to be a voice thundering at the conscience of his age. There was such a ring of genuineness to his voice and such evidence of sincerity in his life that people responded.

He had been born into the priestly family of the house of Aaron of the tribe of Levi. John, with his drive and convictions, could have forced his way to the top, to the position of high priest of Israel. But early in life he forsook the schools of the rabbis and the rigorous apprenticeship for the priesthood. He decided that what Israel needed was not another priest after the order of Aaron, but a prophet after the order of Elijah. And such he became.

6. The People (3:5-6)

The crowds came from Jerusalem and Judea and from all up and down the Jordan—that is, they came from here, there, and everywhere. John was the talk of town and country. It has been estimated that at least a million people turned out to hear him. Those who came under personal conviction of sin and were persuaded of the imminence of the coming of Christ, he baptized in the Jordan when they confessed their sin.

7. The Proclamation (3:7-12)

Having described the coming of John and the coming of the Jews to hear him, Matthew paused to give us a sample of John's message. It was a threefold proclamation.

a. The Corruption of Israel's Leaders (3:7-9)

(1) Their Venom (3:7)

The first aspect of the proclamation concerned the corruption of Israel's leaders. Calling them a "generation of vipers," John scalded the ears of Pharisee and Sadducee alike. They were people full of venom.

In Matthew 3:7 we find the first mention of these important sects, which were unknown in Old Testament times. The sect of the Pharisees arose in the Maccabean period. They were called separatists by their enemies because they separated themselves from the Hellenizers, the political opportunists and liberals of their day. The Pharisees saw themselves as guardians of the law and its traditions. They were equally zealous regarding the so-called oral law—an ever-growing, burdensome, and virtually useless body of tradition that was fast replacing the Bible in importance to their thinking.

The Sadducees also came into prominence in the time of the Maccabees. They were the aristocrats and politicians among the Jews. The Sadducees, the theological liberals and humanists of their day, would have secularized the Jewish faith, paganized it, and destroyed it if their influence had prevailed. They denied the existence of spirits, the resurrection, and the immortality of the soul and rejected the oral law. Generally they were wealthy persons of high rank, and often they were members of the priesthood. In fact the high priestly families belonged to the party. Having long since yielded to the Hellenizing influence of the Greeks and adopted the principles of Aristotelian philosophy, the Sadducees refused to accept any doctrine they could not prove by pure reason. Their vested interest was the temple.

In the Gospels we see the Pharisees taking the lead in rejecting the Son of God, though both parties were guilty. In the book of Acts we see the Sadducees taking the lead in rejecting the Spirit of God. Both were called "vipers" by John the Baptist. The serpent is a symbol of the devil; indeed Jesus told the Jewish leaders that they were children of the devil (John 8:44). John the Baptist reminded them of the "wrath to come."

(2) Their Vanity (3:8-9)

Many of the Old Testament prophets had warned that the Lord's coming would be accompanied by a visitation of wrath on the wicked, but the Jews comfortably assigned all such visitation to the Gentiles. The self-righteous Pharisees and scornful Sadducees were scandalized to hear this new prophet turn the warning on them. Were they not children of Abraham? Did not that give them automatic status in the kingdom? John took that position by storm: "Think not to say within yourselves, We have Abraham to our father: for I say unto you, that God is able of these stones to raise up children unto Abraham" (Matthew 3:9). Many years later Paul would describe his own "confidence in the flesh" and what one glimpse of Christ did to all his *racial* and *religious* presumptions (Philippians 3:4-9).

b. The Conquerors of Israel's Land (3:10)

The second aspect of John's proclamation concerned the conquerors of Israel's land. There might well be an allusion in Matthew 3:10 to Isaiah 10:33–11:1. In this reference to the hewing down of trees, the Jewish commentators saw a prophecy of the destruction of Jerusalem, which they inferred would immediately precede the coming of the Messiah. More to the point, Zechariah 12:1-14 foretells the end-time disasters that will engulf Jerusalem, and the coming of the Messiah to save the city in its extremity; at that time the Jews will look on Him "whom they have pierced" (12:10).

When Matthew recalled and wrote the ominous words of John the Baptist—"And now also the ax is laid unto the root of the trees"—the land lay desolate under the iron heel of Rome, which was avenging the Jewish revolt. Jerusalem itself was about to be besieged and sacked. The same thing will happen all over again prior to the coming of the King to reign, as Zechariah prophesied. So while John doubtless was aiming at the hardened consciences and the tree-like, soaring, verdant pride of the Jewish leaders, his words also had an ominous prophetic overtone.

c. The Coming of Israel's Lord (3:11-12)

(1) His Might (3:11a)

The third aspect of John's proclamation concerned the coming of Israel's Lord. "He that cometh after me is mightier than I," John said. John was mighty in his own way. He captured the imagination and conscience of the country. He rekindled Israel's Messianic hopes that had lain in the ashes of neglect for centuries.

Between Malachi and Matthew four hundred years of invasion, oppression, persecution, and humiliation had come and gone. The Persians had fallen before the Greeks. The Greek empire had collapsed. The promised land had been a groaning, blood-soaked battleground in the fierce rivalries of the kings of Egypt and Syria. Antiochus Epiphanes had been a veritable antichrist to the Jews. The Maccabees had come—the Hasmoneans had ruled the land and succumbed to the spirit of the age. The Romans had come.

Herod had come. Rabbinic exegetical absurdities had taken root alongside reactionary Hellenistic rationalism.

Now fierce zealots rubbed shoulders with a despairing peasantry. A generation before, there had been a flurry of interest centered on the murderous suspicions of Herod and the rumors of the birth of a King in Bethlehem. But that was thirty years ago; the hopes of the people had come to nothing. The Jews might have said, "Where is the promise of his coming? for since the fathers fell asleep, all things continue as they were from the beginning of the creation" (2 Peter 3:4).

John the Baptist electrified the nation with his proclamation. John was mighty, but the One he proclaimed was mightier far—as the heavens are higher than the earth and as the Creator is mightier than the mightiest of His creatures.

(2) His Ministry (3:11b-12)

John also announced the coming Lord's threefold ministry.

(a) A Baptizing Ministry (3:11b)

Speaking of the Messiah, now about to be revealed, John said, "I indeed baptize you with water unto repentance....He shall baptize you with the Holy Ghost." John himself could have had no idea of what a revolutionary concept in God's dealings with men was involved in that statement.[13] No one had ever been baptized with the Holy Ghost in Old Testament times. People had been inspired by the Holy Spirit, anointed by the Spirit, led by the Spirit, and empowered by the Spirit, but not baptized with the Spirit. The coming King, however, would baptize with the Holy Ghost. That would be one of His ministries.

(b) A Burning Ministry (3:11c-12a)

John said that Christ would also baptize "with fire" (3:11c). The whole Christian age lies between the baptizing and the burning. Matthew understood this concept, but John the Baptist did not, and Matthew was recording John's preaching. Like many Old Testament prophets, John brought the two comings of Christ together for the simple reason that the intervening church age was not revealed either to him or to the Old Testament prophets. If the Jews had accepted Jesus as their Messiah, no church age would have been inserted between the baptism and the burning.

(c) A Blessing Ministry (3:12b)

In addition to His baptizing and burning ministry, the Messiah would have a blessing ministry. The chaff would indeed be cleared away, but the wheat would be gathered into His barn.

B. The Coming of Jesus (3:13-17)

1. An Exercise concerning That Coming (3:13-15)

a. The Expostulation of John (3:13-14)

John's baptism was by immersion, the only kind of water baptism known in the New Testament. The Greek word translated "baptize" is *baptizō*, which is related to another Greek word, *baptō*. *Baptō* is used in the context of a smith tempering a piece of iron by plunging it into a bucket of cold water, or a piece of cloth being dipped into a vat of dye, or a description of a sunken ship. *Baptizō* means "to dip, to immerse." It is never used to mean "to sprinkle"; the Greeks had another word, *rhantizō*, to convey that idea.

John's baptism was instituted by God (John 1:33), just as Christian baptism was later instituted by Christ (Matthew 28:19). John baptized repentant sinners in the Jordan, which in the typology of Scripture is the river of death. From its source high in the mountains of Lebanon, the Jordan flows southward through a tortuous valley until it buries itself in the arid waters of the Dead Sea (about fourteen hundred feet below sea level), from which it has no outlet except by evaporation. It was seventy or eighty miles from Nazareth to the ford of Jordan—the same section of the river that had once opened for the miraculous passage of Israel into the promised land.

Doing what would please the Father (see John 8:29), Jesus came "from Galilee to Jordan" for the express purpose of being baptized by John (Matthew 3:13). Jesus was not acting on impulse; being baptized in the Jordan was part of the "Father's business" (Luke 2:49) that forever occupied the mind of the Lord Jesus. He came as the result of deliberate heart exercise—deliberate meditation, prayer, and sensitivity to the will of God.

John objected at once. Matthew 3:14 says, "John forbad him." The word translated "forbad" is *diakōluō*, which occurs only here. Some have rendered it "was hindering." John, holy man of God that he was, knew he was in the presence of incarnate and absolute holiness. He could not see how One who was "holy, harmless, undefiled, separate from sinners" (Hebrews 7:26) could possibly be immersed in Jordan in a baptism of repentance. John, spiritually sensitive man that he was, felt a deep inner conviction of sin and unworthiness in the presence of Jesus. "I have need to be baptized of thee," he confessed. But the Holy Spirit says that John "was hindering" Jesus. Even the greatest of all God's saints can get in the way. John's expostulation was sin and a hindrance to the working out of "that good, and acceptable, and perfect, will of God" (Romans 12:2).

b. The Explanation of Jesus (3:15)

The explanation of Jesus was gracious but firm: "Suffer it to be so now: for thus it becometh us to fulfil all righteousness." The Lord's baptism was intended to do two things. Its initial purpose was to identify the Savior of sinners with those He came to save. He Himself was sinless, but by accepting a baptism of repentance at the hands of a sinful man, He deliberately identified Himself with Adam's ruined race.

The second purpose of the Lord's immersion in the cold waters of Jordan was to prefigure His eventual immersion in the icy river of death. Later, on His way to Jerusalem for the last time, the Lord would pointedly refer to His death as a baptism (Matthew 20:22-23). Just as He was immersed in the waters of the Jordan, so He would be overwhelmed by His suffering and plunged into death. And just as a person being baptized is brought back up out of the water, so He would rise from the dead.

2. An Experience Confirming That Coming (3:16-17)

So Jesus took His stand in the Jordan, and John immersed Him. As He came back up out of the water, He was given a twofold confirming experience.

a. The Anointing of the Spirit (3:16)

First, the Holy Spirit descended like a dove and came upon Him. This was Christ's anointing for His public ministry. The same Spirit had brooded over "the face of the waters" (Genesis 1:2). And ever since the fall of man, He had been hovering over the sons of men and looking for one on whom He could rest. Noah, after the waters of judgment had abated, sent forth a dove that flew to and fro across the face of the still-receding waters but, finding no rest, returned to the ark. Similarly over centuries of time the Dove of God found no home in the restless seas of humankind until He alighted on God's true Ark, the Lord Jesus Christ.

In coming to rest on Christ, the Spirit anointed Him for the work that now lay ahead. Christ uttered not a single word, took not a single step, made not the slightest move in His public ministry until this holy anointing took place. There never was a time when the Lord Jesus was not filled with the Spirit, but He was anointed at His baptism.

In the Old Testament, priests, kings, and prophets were anointed for their ministry. Their symbolic anointing found its ultimate counterpart in the anointing of the Lord Jesus by the Holy Spirit. The meaning of the name *Messiah* or *Christ* is "the anointed One" and it was in the power of His anointing that He as man performed each facet of His ministry as the Christ of God.

b. The Announcement of the Father (3:17)

The second part of the twofold confirmation was the announcement of the Father. The anointing of the Spirit prepared the Lord for the next three and a half years of ministering to the desperate needs of those with whom He had just identified Himself. But the announcement from Heaven looked back over the past thirty years: "This is my beloved Son, in whom I am well pleased." It was God's public endorsement of the hidden years in that Nazareth home.

God was pronouncing His "well done" as He looked at 10,900 or more days of the Lord's doing always those things that pleased the Father. As a toddler clutching Mary's robe, as a boy playing with His toys, as a youth at the local synagogue school, as a man at the carpenter's bench, He had brought nothing but joy to His Father's heart. In what He did, in what He said, in what He thought, in what He was, Christ had lived in perfect harmony with Heaven. And God announced that He was "well pleased."

Millions of people had already lived on earth and passed under the all-seeing eye of God, but the Father found none other than His Son to be the One in whom was all His delight. He announced the facts of Christ's sinlessness and His sonship to the world. How few there were who had ears to hear!

IV. THE KING'S ADVERSARY (4:1-11)

A. Preparing for the Battle (4:1-2)

Between His birth and His baptism, Jesus spent thirty years being good, kind, loving, happy, peaceful, patient, and submissive. He was perfectly self-controlled because He was perfectly Spirit-controlled. He was a perfectly natural but perfectly good little boy, a perfectly normal but absolutely holy son, brother, neighbor, friend, student, and workman. In other words, He spent His time being what God always intended a human being to be.

Now Jesus was "led up of the spirit into the wilderness to be tempted of the devil" (4:1). The Lord must have had many skirmishes with evil throughout the past thirty years of His life. Maybe there was a school bully to deal with—every school has one. Maybe there was a jealous brother—many homes have one. Maybe there was an opinionated rabbi—many churches have one. Maybe there was a dishonest tradesman—most towns have one. Maybe there was a spiteful neighbor—many communities have one. But moment by moment, step by step, situation by situation, Jesus was filled with the Spirit, and thought, said, and did only what the Father wanted Him to think, say, and do. Jesus made Himself wholly available to God in order to be the channel through which His wisdom, love, and power could be perfectly expressed in terms of a human life.

1. Where Jesus Was to Go (4:1)

The time had now come for Jesus to be tempted in a new and virulent way by none other than the devil himself. Accordingly the first experience Jesus had after His anointing and divine acknowledgment was to be led by the Spirit into the wilderness. The wilderness of Judea was the frightful desolate area that ran back from the western shore of the Dead Sea. It would be hard to imagine a more forbidding landscape. That is where He was to go.

2. What Jesus Was to Do (4:2)

He was to fast in that wilderness for an excessively long period of time: forty days. The Gospel of Mark tells us that during this period of loneliness and isolation, Jesus was with the wild beasts. The accounts in Mark and Luke imply that the whole period was one of temptation, preparing Jesus for the fierce onslaught at the end of the fast. When the devil finally appeared in person, the battle was short but sharp.

Matthew 4:2 says that Jesus "was afterward an hungred." It is said that during a prolonged fast, the feeling of hunger goes away after three or four days, only to return with renewed force at the end of thirty or forty days. This sudden onslaught of recurring hunger became the basis for the first temptation.

B. Prevailing in the Battle (4:3-10)

1. Tempted along the Line of God's Provision (4:3-4)

a. What Satan Suggested (4:3)

The devil began, "If thou be the Son of God…" Satan knew Jesus to be the Son of God, for that truth had recently been publicly proclaimed by the Father at the Jordan. The public ministry of God's beloved Son began and ended with those Satanic words ringing in His ears (Matthew 4:3; 27:40). We can hear the devil's emphasis—"If *thou* be the Son of God"; it was as if he were saying, "You, a poor, starved, emaciated being, famished and perishing with hunger? *You* the Son of God?"

Then came the suggestion, a solution for His hunger: *instant food*. "Command that these stones be made bread," he said. Jesus, of course, could have done that. He could change water into wine. He could multiply a few loaves and fishes and feed thousands. But behind the temptation was the implication that God was being unkind to let Jesus be so hungry for so long.

There was nothing wrong with being hungry and nothing wrong with wanting to satisfy that legitimate craving. The evil in the suggestion was that Christ would have had to act in independence of the Holy Spirit who had led Him into the wilderness, and in independence of the Father who had permitted Him to be deprived of bodily sustenance. Satan was suggesting that Jesus use the resources of His sonship to violate the responsibility of His sonship. The responsibility was never to act in independence of His Father. (Incidentally, a prolonged fast has to be broken gradually, and initially with liquids; solid food can kill.)

b. What Scripture Stated (4:4)

In foiling this temptation, Jesus set what Satan suggested alongside what Scripture stated. The sole resource of the Lord during the entire temptation was the Word of God, the weapon Satan fears more than anything else in this world. Christ said, "It is written" and quoted from Deuteronomy 8:3.

This first ministerial utterance of Jesus, His first utterance after His anointing, showed His absolute confidence in the written Scriptures as the authoritative Word of the living God. The question of errancy or irrelevance never occurred to Him. Those notions are of Satanic origin (Genesis 3:1). In tempting Eve, the devil set out to get her to distrust or distort the Word of God. Jesus picked up and wielded the weapon that she so foolishly neglected in her struggle with the tempter.

When Satan said, "If thou be the *Son of God*," Jesus answered, "*Man* shall not live by bread alone, but by every word that proceedeth out of the mouth of God" (Matthew 4:3-4, italics added). The Lord was in the wilderness to meet Satan's attacks not as God, but as man. Jesus refused to be shaken in His trust in the grace and goodness of His Father or to take any ground other than that found in God's written Word.

This first temptation of Christ represents our temptations to commit sins that have to do with *appetite,* the kinds of sins we associate with lust. These sins are essentially physical. Bodily drives are not wrong; they are necessary to the preservation of life. But they must never be allowed to get out of hand or to control our lives.

2. Tempted along the Line of God's Protection (4:5-7)

a. The Form of the Temptation (4:5-6)

(1) The Situation Prepared by Satan (4:5)

Next the devil transported Jesus to "a pinnacle of the temple"— probably the top of what was known as Herod's royal portico at the southeast corner of the temple enclosure. This pinnacle was the greatest height around the temple and overlooked the Kidron valley, 450 feet below.

(2) The Suggestion Presented by Satan (4:6)

(a) The Blatant Trap (4:6a)

Satan had offered Jesus instant food; now he offered Him *instant fame.* This second temptation was more subtle than the first. The devil said in effect:

> You aren't getting anywhere. Here You are, thirty years of age and You have no audience, no followers, no acclaim. You're not even known. If You listen to me and do what I say, You can be famous instantly, a celebrity overnight. Your name will be on everybody's lips. You'll be front-page news. I'll see that you get the crowds. Now here's the plan: I will set You up, up here on the pinnacle of the temple. You can't get any higher than that here in Jerusalem. The people down there in the temple courts

seem as small as ants. Look! You've already attracted their attention. In a moment You can have their applause. You are now where You should have been years ago—in the public eye. Now then, I have brought You up; You cast Yourself down.

Satan was using his powers of persuasion on Christ, just as he does when he tries to trap us. We need to remember that he can persuade, but he cannot push. He creates the temptation; we create the transgression.

(b) The Biblical Text (4:6b)

Still trying to convince Christ, Satan said in effect:

You must do something daring, something spectacular. You say You trust Your heavenly Father. Well, prove it. Exercise Your faith. Show Your faith by casting Yourself down. Take Your stand on the Word of God. God's Word says, "He shall give his angels charge concerning thee: and in their hands they shall bear thee up, lest at any time thou dash thy foot against a stone." There! That's in the Bible. You reminded me of what the Bible says—now I'm reminding You. You believe the Bible—then do what it says. Put it to the test. The world is waiting to see a man who will go all the way with God, one who behaves as he says he believes.

Satan was urging the Lord to be presumptuous, not trusting. There is a fine line between trusting God and tempting God. It was magnificent faith on Peter's part to step out of that boat at the Lord's express invitation and walk on the waves. It would have been presumption if he had done that under any other circumstances, as some kind of test of God or proof of his faith.

Satan quoted Psalm 91:11-12 not from the original Hebrew manuscripts, but from the Septuagint translation, the same version Jesus had used in defeating the first temptation. In this second temptation the Septuagint was particularly useful to the devil because the translators had added the words "at any time." Satan not only seized on the unwarranted addition; he also was careful to leave something out: "to keep thee in all thy ways." And he omitted Psalm 91:13, which speaks of the Lord treading on the lion and adder and trampling the young lion and the dragon under His feet. Naturally Satan did not even want to think about that verse!

Thus in handling Scripture, Satan used a convenient translation, paraphrased it to serve his own purpose, eagerly accepted an addition, deliberately left something out, and ignored the context. The Lord knew His Bible better than to be taken in by Satan's garbled version of a great and much-loved Messianic Psalm.

b. The Failure of the Temptation (4:7)

The Lord wasted no time arguing with Satan over Bible versions. He Himself used the Septuagint. Jesus countered the devil's attack with another quotation from the book of Deuteronomy: "Thou shalt not tempt the Lord thy God" (6:16). The Lord did not ignore the context, for the next words in that verse ("as ye tempted him in Massah") refer to Exodus 17:7, which speaks of Israel doubting God's presence and care.

The second temptation of Christ represents our temptations to commit sins that have to do with *acceptance,* approval, and applause. The first temptation was along the line of the physical; the second was along the line of the psychological. We all have a legitimate psychological need to be accepted and a desire to be acclaimed. It is surprising what people will do to fulfill the desire. Even a small child will indulge in bad behavior to get attention, to be noticed. Some adults will go to extraordinary lengths to gain the approval of those whose applause is important to them. Psychological needs must never be allowed to get out of hand.

3. Tempted along the Line of God's Program (4:8-10)

a. The Suggestion Made (4:8-9)

(1) The Crown (4:8-9a)

For the third temptation Jesus was transported to a high mountain. From this eminence, Satan as the prince of this world caused the Lord to envision all the kingdoms of this world and their glory—"in a moment of time" Luke 4:5 tells us. (It doesn't take the devil long to exhaust the possibilities of what he has to offer.) Satan had offered the Lord instant food and instant fame; now he offered Him *instant fortune,* the throne of the world without a cross.

(2) The Cost (4:9b)

The glory and pomp of this world's empires were paraded before the Lord: the power of Assyria, Babylon, and Persia; the ancient splendors of Greece; the majesty of imperial Rome. In effect Satan said:

> I gave the world to Alexander; I have given it to caesar. You are a much bigger man than either of them—a better man. Think how the world longs for a King like You. You are a King; all You need is a throne. Think how much good You can do. You can bring in new laws and put Your program into effect. Think of it: carpenter of Nazareth crowned emperor of the world. All of it can be Yours—not just Rome, but beyond the Euphrates, beyond the Nile, beyond the pillars of Hercules.
>
> All I ask is a small pinch of salt on caesar's altar, just one brief bend of the knee. All You have to do is render me one act of homage. Look at You! You have no food, no fame, no fortune. I offer you everything this world contains: the kingdom, the power, and the glory. And no cross!

b. The Suggestion Met (4:10)

(1) The Lord's Will (4:10a)

The Lord had had enough. "Get thee hence, Satan," He said. Jesus did not find anything at all appealing in the devil's program. Christ's holy nature did not find sin attractive; He found it repulsive. He recoiled from every suggestion that He sin—that He act in independence of God.

(2) The Last Word (4:10b)

For the third and last time Jesus appealed to the written Word of God. Quoting Deuteronomy 6:13, He said, "It is written, Thou shalt worship the Lord thy God, and him only shalt thou serve." All His quotations that day were from Deuteronomy 6 and 8. Could it be that the Lord's meditation that morning had been in this portion of God's Word?

The third temptation of Christ represents our temptations to commit sins that have to do with *ambition*. These sins are essentially spiritual, for ambition can quickly generate pride (the original sin, found in Satan himself, see Isaiah 14:12-15) and cause us to exalt some rival to God's throne. Satan offered the world to Jesus in exchange for worship.

The issue is power. Everyone likes to have power, but it is a heady wine. As Lord Acton said, "Power tends to corrupt and absolute power corrupts absolutely." It is not wrong for a person to wish to improve his position, but he needs to beware of why he sets his goals and how he goes about achieving them. I left a promising career in a large business establishment because I felt that the price of success was too high. The institution wanted my soul.

C. Proceeding from the Battle (4:11)

1. Exit the Adversary (4:11a)

Satan had no more to offer. He had tempted Jesus—as he had tempted Eve—with the three great sources of sin: "the lust of the flesh, and the lust of the eyes, and the pride of life" (1 John 2:16). The devil had found the impenetrable armor of Christ's holiness to be impervious to all his temptations. Thoroughly defeated, Satan left.

2. Enter the Angels (4:11b)

The battle was won, but Jesus was exhausted. The temptations had come at a time when He was physically weakened. Satan always seeks to gain the advantage in such a time, for he is wholly without scruples.

Then "angels came and ministered unto him." In the second temptation Satan had suggested to Jesus that He take advantage of those holy ministers; now in God's good time and purpose, they came to Him. It was not part of God's purpose that Jesus should starve to death, or die of exhaustion, or collapse after the strain of the struggle with sin in its most subtle and virulent form.

SECTION 2

THE KING'S PURPOSE

(4:12–7:29)

I. THE KING'S METHOD REVEALED (4:12-25)
   A. The King's Move (4:12-16)
      1. A Sensible Move (4:12)
      2. A Secondary Move (4:13)
      3. A Scriptural Move (4:14-16)
         a. The Prophet (4:14)
         b. The Place (4:15)
         c. The Purpose (4:16)
   B. The King's Message (4:17)
   C. The King's Men (4:18-22)
      1. The Two Who Were on the Shore—
         Casting with Their Nets (4:18-20)
         a. What Christ Observed (4:18)
         b. What Christ Offered (4:19-20)
            (1) The Challenge (4:19)
            (2) The Choice (4:20)
      2. The Two Who Were in the Ship—
         Caring for Their Nets (4:21-22)
         a. How Christ Called (4:21)
         b. How They Came (4:22)
   D. The King's Ministry (4:23a-b)
      1. Walking (4:23a)
      2. Talking (4:23b)
   E. The King's Miracles (4:23c-25)
      1. How Much It Was He Cared (4:23c-24)
      2. How Many There Were Who Came (4:25)

II. THE KING'S MANDATE REVEALED (5:1–7:29)
   A. The Disciple and His Blessings (5:1-16)
      1. The Setting (5:1-2)
      2. The Sayings (5:3-12)
         a. What We Are (5:3-5)
            (1) Poor in Spirit (5:3)
            (2) Pressed in Soul (5:4)
            (3) Patient in Strife (5:5)
         b. Where We Aim (5:6)
         c. Ways We Act (5:7-9)
            (1) When Facing Cruelty (5:7)
            (2) When Facing Corruption (5:8)
            (3) When Facing Conflict (5:9)
         d. What We Accept (5:10-12)
            (1) The Question of Overwhelming Persecution (5:10-11)
            (2) The Question of Overcoming Persecution (5:12)
               (a) Rejoicing through It (5:12a)
               (b) Rewarded for It (5:12b)
      3. The Sequel (5:13-16)
         a. Resisting Decay (5:13)
         b. Removing Darkness (5:14-16)
            (1) The Position of the Light (5:14)
            (2) The Purpose of the Light (5:15)
            (3) The Potential of the Light (5:16)
   B. The Disciple and His Beliefs (5:17-20)
      1. A Personal Appreciation of God's Law (5:17-18)
         a. The Law and Its Fulfillment (5:17)
         b. The Law and Its Future (5:18)
      2. A Personal Application of God's Law (5:19-20)
         a. A Searching Examination (5:19)
         b. A Scathing Denunciation (5:20)
   C. The Disciple and His Bible (5:21-48)
      1. The Question of Injuring Lives (5:21-24)
         a. The Murder and Its Consequences (5:21)
         b. The Motive and Its Consequences (5:22)
         c. The Moral and Its Consequences (5:23-24)

        (1)   Recollection (5:23)

        (2)   Reconciliation (5:24)

  2. The Question of Invoking Law (5:25-26)

    a. A Wise Course (5:25a)

    b. A Woeful Consequence (5:25b-26)

  3. The Question of Indulging Lust (5:27-32)

    a. A Defiled Marriage (5:27-30)

        (1)   God's Condemning Law (5:27)

        (2)   Man's Corrupting Lust (5:28-30)

            (a) A Wrong Look (5:28)

            (b) A Wrong Life (5:29-30)

                i. Dealing with Wrongful Input (5:29)

                ii. Dealing with Wrongful Output (5:30)

    b. A Defaulting Marriage (5:31-32)

        (1)   The Law and Its Position (5:31)

        (2)   The Lord and His Prohibition (5:32)

  4. The Question of Inappropriate Language (5:33-37)

    a. The Danger of a Broken Word (5:33)

    b. The Demand for a Better Way (5:34-37)

        (1)   Swearing Flippantly (5:34-36)

        (2)   Speaking Firmly (5:37)

  5. The Question of Ineffable Love (5:38-48)

    a. The Law of Retaliation (5:38-42)

        (1)   The Law's Way (5:38)

        (2)   The Lord's Way (5:39-42)

            (a) When People Smite Us (5:39)

            (b) When People Sue Us (5:40)

            (c) When People Seize Us (5:41)

            (d) When People Supplicate Us (5:42)

    b. The Law of Reconciliation (5:43-48)

        (1)   The Rule Explained (5:43-44)

            (a) What God Commanded (5:43)

            (b) What God Commends (5:44)

        (2)   The Rule Exemplified (5:45-47)

            (a) A Comparison (5:45)

            (b) A Contrast (5:46-47)

        (3)   The Rule Expanded (5:48)

D. The Disciple and His Burdens (6:1-34)

          (b) Hiding One's Fast (6:17-18a)

              i. There Is to Be No Show (6:17)

              ii. There Is to Be No Sham (6:18a)

       (3) The Question of Applause (6:18b-c)

          (a) The Reality Seen by Our Father (6:18b)

          (b) The Reward Seen by Our Fellows (6:18c)

  2. Burdens Connected with Wealth (6:19-24)

    a. A Choice of Loves (6:19-21)

       (1) One's Hoard (6:19-20)

          (a) Earthly Treasure (6:19)

              i. Where the Moth Ruins (6:19a)

              ii. Where the Rust Rots (6:19b)

              iii. Where the Thief Robs (6:19c)

          (b) Eternal Treasure (6:20)

       (2) One's Heart (6:21)

    b. A Choice of Looks (6:22-23)

       (1) Where Light Is Exalted (6:22)

       (2) Where Light Is Excluded (6:23)

    c. A Choice of Lords (6:24)

       (1) The Choice Explained (6:24a)

       (2) The Choice Exemplified (6:24b)

  3. Burdens Connected with Worry (6:25-34)

    a. Daily Life (6:25-26)

       (1) Its Pressure Acknowledged (6:25a)

          (a) Problems of Diet

          (b) Problems of Dress

       (2) Its Perspective Altered (6:25b-26)

          (a) A New View of Life (6:25b)

          (b) A New Value for Life (6:26)

    b. Divine Logic (6:27-32)

       (1) Our Human Frame (6:27)

       (2) Our Halting Faith (6:28-30)

          (a) The Glory of the Lilies (6:28-29)

              i. Consider Them (6:28)

              ii. Contrast Them (6:29)

          (b) The Glory of the Lord (6:30)

              i. His Utter Dependability (6:30a)

              ii. Our Unworthy Doubts (6:30b)

        (3) Our Heavenly Father (6:31-32)
           (a) A Command (6:31)
           (b) A Comparison (6:32a)
           (c) A Comfort (6:32b)
    c. Different Laws (6:33-34)
        (1) What Must Be First (6:33)
           (a) The Great Priorities of Our Life (6:33a)
               i. The Sphere of God's Rule
              ii. The Sphere of God's Righteousness
           (b) The Great Promises of Our Lord (6:33b)
        (2) What Must Be Fought (6:34)
           (a) Tomorrow's Worries (6:34a)
           (b) Today's Wickedness (6:34b)
E. The Disciple and His Behavior (7:1-29)
  1. The Fool Exhibited (7:1-5)
    a. A Word of Reason (7:1-2)
        (1) What the Critic Does (7:1)
        (2) What the Critic Deserves (7:2)
    b. A Word of Ridicule (7:3-4)
        (1) The Farcical Question (7:3)
        (2) The Foolish Quest (7:4)
    c. A Word of Rebuke (7:5)
  2. The Father Extolled (7:6-12)
    a. The Father's Love Revealed (7:6-11)
        (1) A Warning Word (7:6)
        (2) A Wondrous Word (7:7-11)
           (a) The Invitation Extended (7:7)
           (b) The Invitation Expanded (7:8)
           (c) The Invitation Explained (7:9-11)
               i. The Goodness of a Human Father
                   (7:9-10)
                   a. Will He Give a Stone? (7:9)
                   b. Will He Give a Snake? (7:10)
              ii. The Goodness of Our Heavenly
                   Father (7:11)
                   a. The Comparative (7:11a)
                   b. The Superlative (7:11b)

    b. The Father's Love Reproduced (7:12)
      (1) The Golden Rule (7:12a)
      (2) The Great Revelation (7:12b)
  3. The Future Explained (7:13-14)
    a. The Road to Hell (7:13)
    b. The Road to Heaven (7:14)
  4. The Frauds Exposed (7:15-23)
    a. Beware of False Prophets (7:15-20)
      (1) What False Prophets Pretend (7:15)
        (a) How Deceptive They Are (7:15a)
        (b) How Destructive They Are (7:15b)
      (2) What False Prophets Produce (7:16-20)
        (a) Their Fruits (7:16-18)
          i. The Curse Emphasized (7:16)
          ii. The Contrast Emphasized (7:17-18)
            a. Unexchangeable Life (7:17)
            b. Inescapable Law (7:18)
        (b) Their Future (7:19-20)
          i. Damnation (7:19)
          ii. Discrimination (7:20)
    b. Beware of False Profession (7:21-23)
      (1) A Test (7:21)
      (2) A Tragedy (7:22-23)
        (a) What the Lost Will Claim (7:22)
          i. The Gift of Proclaiming Prophecy
            (7:22a)
          ii. The Gift of Practicing Exorcism
            (7:22b)
          iii. The Gift of Performing Miracles
            (7:22c)
        (b) What the Lord Will Condemn (7:23)
          i. His Ignorance of the Lost
            Declared (7:23a)
          ii. Their Ignorance of the Lord
            Denounced (7:23b)
  5. The Foundations Examined (7:24-29)
    a. The Application of the Message (7:24-27)

        (1) The Sure Foundation
             The Lord's Words Are the Basis for
             Everything (7:24-25)
             (a) The Completion of the Structure (7:24)
             (b) The Coming of the Storm (7:25)
        (2) The Sandy Foundation
             The Lord's Words Are the Basis for
             Nothing (7:26-27)
             (a) The Completion of the Structure (7:26)
             (b) The Coming of the Storm (7:27)
    b. The Astonishment of the Multitudes (7:28-29)
        (1) At the Content of the Sermon (7:28)
        (2) At the Contrast with the Scribes (7:29)

I. THE KING'S METHOD REVEALED (4:12-25)

A. The King's Move (4:12-16)

1. A Sensible Move (4:12)

John the Baptist's ministry lasted somewhere between four and eighteen months, during which time he accomplished the mission to which God had called him. He caught the attention of the nation, awakened its conscience, and baptized and introduced the Messiah. John also stirred up the wrath of Herodias and Herod by denouncing their illegal marriage.

Now the heralded Messiah was preaching and the Baptist was in prison—a most unlikely end, he must have thought, to his fearless ministry. No move was made to secure his release. He was incarcerated in the fortress of Machaerus on the eastern side of the Dead Sea. Matthew said more about all this later, but here he mentioned the imprisonment in order to show the effect it had on Christ: He left Judea for Galilee, putting Himself outside the reach of Herod. It was a sensible move.

John's ministry was over, but he was not abandoned. Soon he would earn a martyr's crown and enter into his eternal reward. Christ had not come to battle the Herods of this world on their terms. Jesus had the power to blast Herod, his fortress, and every soldier in his army into oblivion, but He had not come to do those kinds of things—this time.

2. A Secondary Move (4:13)

When Jesus arrived in Galilee, He made a second move. He left His boyhood home in Nazareth and moved to Capernaum on the sea of Galilee. We can visualize Him handing over the family business to His brothers, kissing His mother goodbye, hugging His sisters, saying His farewells at the local synagogue to neighbors, friends, and customers. We can see Him taking one last look at the valley that had been home to Him for so long.

Much had happened since He had gone south to be baptized in the Jordan by John the Baptist. The apostle John filled in the details in his Gospel. John told of the Lord's preliminary activities in Galilee: the calling of the disciples, the first miracle in Cana, and the first visit to Capernaum (John 1:35–2:12). John went on to tell of the Lord's early Judean ministry, His first Passover after His anointing, the cleansing of the temple, the talk with Nicodemus, the Lord's baptism of His disciples, and the loyalty of John the

Baptist (2:13–3:36). And the apostle told of the Lord leaving Judea for Galilee, His short stop in Samaria, and His encounter with the woman at the well (4:1-42).

Tidings of such events must have caused the people of Nazareth to talk, and great must have been their surprise when the now-famous local boy arrived home only to announce that He was moving to Capernaum. Their gossip may have taken on a malicious note edged with resentment and small-town pettiness.

Capernaum was much more important than Nazareth as a base for reaching Galilee. Situated on the shore of the sea of Galilee, Capernaum was about twenty-five miles from Nazareth and ten miles from Tiberias, an important city not mentioned in the New Testament. The Romans had a famous spa at Tiberias; its hot baths attracted many sick people.

Galilee was cut off from the theological bastion of Jerusalem. The district had never been wholly Jewish, for Solomon had given twenty Galilean cities to Hiram, king of Tyre. Constant invasions and settlement by Gentiles gave the area a mixed population; the western shore of the sea of Galilee was dotted with numerous towns and fishing villages occupied by large numbers of Gentile people. The more racially pure cities of Judea looked with scorn on Galilee and ridiculed the Galilean accent. By leaving Judea and settling in Galilee, Jesus made a significant gesture. It was an indication of His worldwide purpose, always present in His thinking even when He was ministering to "the lost sheep of the house of Israel."

Galilee was crossed by military highways north to south and by ancient caravan routes east to west. In this busy international corridor one could as easily meet a Roman courier or a Greek architect as a quisling Jewish tax collector or a Hebrew peasant.

The sea of Galilee is no more than a lake ringed by mountains. On the western shore the mountains were fertile and covered with orchards, farms, and villages in Jesus' day. Across the lake rose the forbidding ramparts of the desert, which are part of a range that keeps pace with the Jordan all the way south to the Dead Sea and on to the gulf of Aqaba. To the north were the mountains of Lebanon, dominated by majestic Hermon, the summit of which is never free from snow. The sea of Galilee, some 680 feet below sea level, lies in a tropical climate.

In Jesus' day nine cities bordered the lake and a busy life went on all around it. Township ran into township about the feet of the green western hills, and along the shore there were docks and harbors. Farmers elbowed fishermen; dockworkers jostled coopers and ship-wrights. Fishing and fish curing were big business, employing thousands of families and making Galilee famous in the Roman world long before the Gospels were written. An intricate system of aqueducts carried water to the farms and orchards. There were dyeworks at Magdala and pottery kilns and shipyards at Capernaum. Presiding over the whole scene was the regal city of Tiberias with its magnificent Herodian palace, where Greek sculptures shone in the sun and reminded the Jews that their land was in the hands of the Gentiles.

Walking the roads of Galilee, a Jew would meet long caravans heading south to the fords of Jordan. He would meet Rome's marching cohorts encased in iron, and their officers richly arrayed in armor adorned with purple and gold. He would meet Phoenician merchants bringing the treasures of lands across the sea to the bazaars and markets of a hundred towns. He would see chariots of the wealthy, troops of gladiators, and bands of roving entertainers coming to play before the cosmopolitans of Caesarea, Tiberias, and Decapolis. This was "Galilee of the Gentiles" (Matthew 4:15), as the proud Judeans contemptuously termed it. This was where Jesus chose to live.

One of Galilee's busy centers of activity was Capernaum, where Peter and Andrew lived, not far from James and John. There Matthew had plied his trade as a publican, a traitor tax-collector for the Gentile overlords of the land.

3. A Scriptural Move (4:14-16)

a. The Prophet (4:14)

The move to Capernaum was Scriptural—"that it might be fulfilled which was spoken by Esaias the prophet." Matthew appealed to Isaiah 9:1-2, where the prophet had pinpointed the place where the Messiah would live.

b. The Place (4:15)

The location was the tribal territory of Zebulun (Zabulon) and Naphtali (Nephthalim) toward the Mediterranean and the territory beyond Jordan—in other words, the territory of the northern kingdom of Israel, which broke away from the throne of David after the death of Solomon. From the start, the northern kingdom took the lead in idolatry and apostasy.

This particular region was the first to feel the hand of divine displeasure. Wars with Syria and Assyria were followed by the fall of

Samaria and the deportation of the tribes (1 Kings 15:20; 2 Kings 15:29; 17:6; 1 Chronicles 5:26). The Assyrians brought in foreigners to repopulate the denuded land.

c. The Purpose (4:16)

Isaiah had foretold judgment and he had also promised that this ravaged region would come into the glorious light of the Messiah. Remembering Isaiah 9:2, Matthew wrote, "The people which sat in darkness saw great light; and to them which sat in the region and shadow of death light is sprung up." "Galilee of the Gentiles" was soon ablaze with the light of another world, with the shekinah glory of God now dwelling among them in the person of Jesus Christ.

The Lord's move to Capernaum placed Him right in the middle of all the bustle of a world where Hebrew and heathen met and mingled as nowhere else in the promised land.

B. The King's Message (4:17)

John was in prison and Jesus was in Capernaum. "From that time," Matthew said, "Jesus began to preach, and to say, Repent: for the kingdom of heaven is at hand." Herod had silenced one voice and now a far more powerful voice was heard. That voice began exactly where the other had been stopped. The message was the same.

The Herods of this world can never silence the voice of God. They can kill the preacher, but they cannot kill the preaching. As the old American abolitionists put it, "His truth goes marching on."[1]

It will be the same in a coming day. The antichrist will eventually silence the two witnesses (Revelation 11) only to discover that now instead of two witnesses, he has to contend with 144,000 witnesses.

Rumors that the Messiah whom John had proclaimed had indeed come must have penetrated the halls of the rich and powerful. The cleansing of the Jerusalem temple had caused a considerable stir, as it had challenged the vested interests of the influential Sadducees. Now came the tidings that the Messiah was boldly preaching John's message and we can be sure that Herod was alarmed over this new voice in the North.

C. The King's Men (4:18-22)

The day had come for the Lord to begin to gather to Himself those who were to be His disciples on terms of fulltime commitment. We know from John 1:35-42 that John, Andrew, and Peter had already spent time with Jesus, but they had not yet learned that following Him was to be no on-again, off-again affair. On this day, the day of their call, all three, together with John's brother James, were busy about their fathers' business.

God always calls busy people. The Lord's work is no place for lazy individuals. A slothful minister of the gospel is a disgrace to the high calling of God. All such should make a careful study of Eli (1 Samuel 1:9; 3:2-4; 4:13). We meet this Old Testament character three times. The first time he is propped up against one of the posts of the tabernacle; the second time he is in bed and a little boy has to keep waking him up to tell him that someone is calling; the third time Eli is sitting on a chair by the side of the road—upon hearing bad news, he fell off that chair and broke his neck.

We can picture the Lord Jesus walking along the shore of Galilee. The scene that met His gaze was at once peaceful and busy. The sun made the pear-shaped lake sparkle like a sapphire amid the surrounding hills, which rose from six hundred to a thousand feet. A gentle breeze carried the scent of fire and fish to people who were hurrying here and there, going about their business. The air was laden with sounds ranging from expressions of satisfaction to cries of anger, from snatches of Psalms to curses, from whines of beggars to commands of centurions.

1. The Two Who Were on the Shore—Casting with Their Nets (4:18-20)

a. What Christ Observed (4:18)

Resolutely Jesus made His way to a couple of brothers, "Simon called Peter, and Andrew." The kind of net they were using was an *amphiblestron,* a circular, bell-shaped draw net, which was thrown in such a way that it spread out over the surface of the water and trapped everything beneath it as it sank.

b. What Christ Offered (4:19-20)

(1) The Challenge (4:19)

Jesus did not rebuke Peter and Andrew for returning so readily to their regular business. It was far better than being idle. The time had come, however, for them to make a life commitment to the Master. "Follow me, and I will make you fishers of men," He challenged, using their occupation as an illustration of the kind of work in which henceforth they were to be engaged.

(2) The Choice (4:20)

The two men needed no further persuasion. They had already seen enough of Jesus to be convinced that He was indeed the Messiah. It was the chance of a lifetime to be called to be charter members of the impending kingdom. At that time they had no idea that the Lord was headed not toward a throne, but toward a tomb; they did not know that what lay ahead of Him was a cross, not a crown.

2. The Two Who Were in the Ship—Caring for Their Nets (4:21-22)

Farther down the lake were James and John, the sons of Zebedee. Zebedee was a prosperous fisherman with a number of men on his payroll (see Mark 1:20). From the fact that John seems to have known Annas the high priest (see John 18:15), we can infer that the family was quite well-to-do. Matthew 4:21 is the only place in Scripture where we meet Zebedee in person. He raised no objection to his two sons' leaving the family business—walking right off the job, never to come back to it—in order to follow the carpenter from Nazareth who claimed to be Israel's Messiah. What a noble man he must have been!

We meet his wife Salome several times. She once asked Jesus to give her two sons honored places in His kingdom (Matthew 20:20-21); she was present at the crucifixion (Mark 15:40); she was one of the women who went to the sepulcher (Mark 16:1). Some think that Salome and the Lord's mother were sisters (John 19:25). If so, Salome and Zebedee were the Lord's aunt and uncle, and James and John His cousins. And that might help explain why Zebedee was so willing to let his two boys go. He would have known all about the miraculous circumstances of Jesus' birth.

Like Andrew and Peter, James and John wasted no time in responding to the Lord's call to fulltime service. Perhaps it is significant that Simon and Andrew were casting their nets when they were called and James and John were mending theirs. Andrew and Peter became great soul-winners; James and John—especially John—were more the pastor-teacher type. (James was martyred early in the history of the church; see Acts 12:2.)

D. The King's Ministry (4:23a-b)

1. Walking (4:23a)

Matthew wrote, "Jesus went about all Galilee." From north to south, Galilee was about sixty-three miles long and from east to west, about thirty-three miles wide. According to Josephus, its population was about three million.

2. Talking (4:23b)

The Lord concentrated on the synagogues. This innovation in Jewish religious life arose out of the exigencies of the Babylonian exile, when regular Old Testament worship, which was dependent on the sacrifices and the sanctuary, was interrupted with the destruction of Solomon's temple. The new form of worship was imported into Palestine after the captivity and soon synagogues were everywhere, at home and abroad. According to the Talmud there were 480 in Jerusalem before its destruction (T. J. Megillah 73d). Some claim this count to be an exaggeration, but Edersheim confirmed that there were hundreds.[2]

In the synagogues Jesus proclaimed "the gospel of the kingdom," the good news that the kingdom age had dawned, that the millennial promises so common in the Old Testament were now ripe for fulfillment. The people flocked to the services.

E. The King's Miracles (4:23c-25)

1. How Much It Was He Cared (4:23c-24)

The Lord's ministry was accompanied by miracles of an extraordinary character, not only in their nature but also in their number. He healed "all manner of sickness and all manner of disease," Matthew said. Jesus was besieged by the sick, the demon-possessed, and the insane. The word translated "lunatick" is a form of *selēniazō*, which means "to be moonstruck"; perhaps the reference is to epileptics, since in Bible times epilepsy was supposed to be influenced by the moon. "He healed them" is Matthew's simple testimony.

Only thirty-five miracles of Jesus are recorded in the Gospels—an average of less than one a month for the three and a half years of the Lord's public ministry. Jesus obviously performed many more than that, as Matthew's summary statement proves, but the Bible is sparing in recording miracles. A faith founded on miracles is rarely a robust faith. God normally shuts us up to His written Word.[3]

The miracles of the Lord Jesus immediately distinguished Him from John the Baptist, who did no miracles. But John's witness to Christ was powerful and effective (John 10:41-42), a significant testimony to the value of the Word. Jesus came performing marvelous miracles, but that did not prevent the people from turning against Him and crucifying Him in the end.

2. How Many There Were Who Came (4:25)

For the time being, however, the accrediting miracles of the Lord Jesus ensured Him a large following. Matthew said they came "from Galilee, and from Decapolis, and from Jerusalem, and from Judaea, and from beyond Jordan." Decapolis (literally "the ten cities") was a district lying east, southeast, and south of the sea of Galilee.[4] The cities of the Decapolis, which are believed to have been originally colonized by veterans from the army of Alexander the Great, retained their Greek character. Ptolemy is said to have organized them into a governing unit. The district "beyond Jordan" began at the southern line of Galilee and ran down to the old Moabite boundary about the middle of the east shore of the Dead Sea. It is commonly called Perea.

II. THE KING'S MANDATE REVEALED (5:1–7:29)

We have now come to the famous sermon on the mount. There is nothing to compare with it in all the literature of the world. Even the greatest of the world's moral, religious, and philosophical statements blush and stammer in the presence of this sublime declaration.

By the time Christ formulated this great sermon, the Greek philosophers had come and gone, leaving the world as morally bankrupt as they had found it. The religions of the East had likewise had their day. They left men groping in utter darkness, hoping for the ultimate bliss of total nothingness or a better deal in some fancied future incarnation. Their philosophers did nothing but add religious burdens to lives already bowed down with care. The so-called sacred books of the East—the Vedas of the Brahmans, the Pinanas of Sivna and Vishnu, the Koran of the Muslims, the Zend-Avesta of the Parsees, the Tripitaka of the Buddhists—all fail and come far short of the sermon on the mount. As for the Talmud, Edersheim said:

> Who, that has read half-a-dozen pages successively of any part of the Talmud, can feel otherwise than by turns shocked, pained, amused, or astounded? There is here wit and logic, quickness and readiness, earnestness and zeal, but by the side of it terrible profanity, uncleanness, superstition, and folly. Taken as a whole, it is not only utterly unspiritual, but anti-spiritual....It is so utterly and immeasurably unlike the New Testament, that it is not easy to determine which, as the case may be, is greater, the ignorance or the presumption of those who put them side by side.[5]

The sermon on the mount was addressed to people with heavenly rather than earthly hopes. The discourse, while embodying the laws of the kingdom as the Mosaic code embodied the national laws of Israel, was not meant for Jews as Jews. It was meant for people who had been regenerated by the Holy Spirit. No natural man—however sweetly dispositioned, however zealous and sincere, however well-motivated and well-intentioned—can keep the sermon on the mount. Only Jesus did that.

Jesus took the Mosaic law, passed it through the prism of His glorious mind, and broke the light of the law into its primeval colors. Then He lifted everything from the earthly to the heavenly, from the natural to the spiritual, and placed it far beyond all human reach. "That is how people are to live in the kingdom," He said in effect. Obviously only people born again of the Holy Spirit, people indwelt and empowered by the Holy Spirit, can live that kind of life. "Christ in you, the hope of glory" is the key (Colossians 1:27).

The genius of the gospel lies in the fact that as Christ once gave His life *for* us, He now gives His life *to* us. He lived the life Himself for thirty-three and a half years and now continues to live that life in the lives of surrendered believers. During the millennial age when the precepts of the sermon on the mount will be the legal code of the world, people will still need to be regenerated in order to put them into practice.

While it is true that the sermon on the mount has millennial overtones, it belongs in its primary application to those to whom it was addressed: the Lord's people in this age. This is evident from the instructions for those facing persecution (Matthew 5:11-12). No one is going to be persecuted during the millennium.

The sermon was given to the Lord's disciples, the same disciples who were the nucleus of the church in the upper room on the day of Pentecost. In His discourse Christ did not state the laws of salvation; He stated the laws of behavior for those who have been saved. He gave a complete code of conduct for all who desire to please God. Many people consider these laws to be impractical, but the Lord's commands are always accompanied by His enabling power.

A. The Disciple and His Blessings (5:1-16)

The sermon begins with the beatitudes (5:1-12), a series of statements invoking happiness on those who embody the characteristics described.

1. The Setting (5:1-2)

The sermon seems to have been delivered on the slopes above Capernaum. The enormous throngs attracted to Jesus by His miracles followed Him up the mountainside. They were in for a shock, for the kind of kingdom He was about to describe had never entered their wildest dreams. Following the custom of Jewish teachers, Jesus sat down and began to speak. The sermon was directed to His disciples, but it was heard by all. His words rang across the slopes with an authority that was wholly lacking in the pettifogging ramblings of the rabbis. He conveyed concepts that, though unmistakable, soared far beyond the highest aspirations of his eager listeners. "The sermon on the mount," it has been said, "was spoken into the ear of the church and overheard by the world."

2. The Sayings (5:3-12)

Parts of this address are found elsewhere in the synoptic Gospels, notably in Luke. Luke's record, however, consists of only about 30 separate verses (Matthew's has 107) and makes no claim to repeat either the sayings in their chronological order or the sermon in its entirety.

The sayings in Matthew 5:3-12 comprise eight beatitudes, which are in stark contrast to the eight curses that bring the Lord's public ministry to a close (Matthew 23).

a. What We Are (5:3-5)

The first three beatitudes deal essentially with what we are. What we are is infinitely more important than what we do. We do what we do because we are what we are. The word "blessed," which introduces each beatitude, is a translation of *makarios,* which literally means "happy." Here then is the Lord's recipe for a happy life, a happy death, and a happy eternity. His words strike at the roots of all human philosophy. The unregenerate person is unable to understand how the truths expressed in these beatitudes can be the basis for happiness.

(1) Poor in Spirit (5:3)

At the beginning of the beatitudes we read, "Blessed are the poor in spirit: for theirs is the kingdom of heaven." The first demand then is for genuine humility, for the sense of utter spiritual destitution that is awakened by the Holy Spirit when a person sees his nothingness before God. Isaiah cried, "Woe unto them," when he poured the passion of conviction on Israel (Isaiah 5:8-23), but when he found himself in the presence of a holy God he cried, "Woe is me" (6:1-5). A sense of God's presence deals instantly with the haughty spirit that is so much admired by the world.

If believers did not have such changed natures, the malignant evils of the present social order would simply be reproduced in God's kingdom. So on the threshold of the sermon on the mount the Lord placed the gate of humility.

(2) Pressed in Soul (5:4)

While the first beatitude has to do with what we are in our spirits when the Holy Spirit begins His work and leaves us stripped and humbled in the presence of God, the second one has to do with what we are in our souls when our spiritual nakedness and bankruptcy are revealed. We are plunged into sorrow for sin. The sorrow is for our sin and the sin we see all around, sin that breaks God's heart as well as His laws, sin that breaks our hearts too. Those who thus mourn are promised comfort.

(3) Patient in Strife (5:5)

The third beatitude indicates that there is a blessing in store for those who are patient in relation to their circumstances: "Blessed are the meek: for they shall inherit the earth." Meek—not weak. Moses was meek (Numbers 12:3). The Lord Jesus was meek (Matthew 11:29). No one would describe either as weak. To be meek means to be gentle, patient, not given to anger or resentment. The

Lord manifested meekness when He rode in triumph into Jerusalem on an ass's colt instead of on a war horse.

Meekness is a quality not much admired by the world. The world thinks that a meek man is spiritless, spineless, and servile. But Jesus promised the meek that "they shall inherit the earth." When the earth becomes the visible sphere of the Lord's triumph during the millennial age, the meek will be its aristocracy. Augustine warned, "Do you wish to possess the earth? Beware then lest it possess you." In God's wisdom the cross comes before the crown—and that kind of wisdom is foolishness to men (1 Corinthians 1:18-20).

b. Where We Aim (5:6)

The fourth beatitude tells us that we are to aim at being righteous. We are to "hunger and thirst after righteousness." A person who is desperately hungry or thirsty can think of nothing else. Hunger and thirst are the most basic and demanding drives of our physical nature. No one can ignore them for long. Happy is the man who has an equally strong desire to be like God.

None of the world's religions can satisfy the human craving to be good. It is not in man's fallen nature to be righteous, and all religion can do is cultivate his fallen nature. We are made righteous practically by the Holy Spirit.

According to the Epistle to the Romans, righteousness is first revealed, then required, then received, and only after that, reproduced. (The word *righteousness* occurs in thirty-three verses in Romans.) We are constituted righteous positionally by receiving as ours the righteousness of Christ. Our standing before God is thereby made perfect. We are made righteous practically—and righteousness is the key to practical Christianity—by the work of the indwelling Holy Spirit, who imparts to us the divine nature and enables us to overcome our old Adamic nature. This work deals with our state, which is all too often imperfect. Our standing and state will be in perfect harmony when we receive our resurrection bodies. Then we will be like Him for all eternity.

In the meantime the regenerated individual hungers and thirsts after righteousness in the happy anticipation that this desire is not going to be left unfulfilled. One of the horrors of Hell is the fact that God will ultimately say to the lost, "He that is unjust [unrighteous], let him be unjust [unrighteous] still" (Revelation 22:11). Lost people will crave righteousness with utter hopelessness. Not one drop of the water of life will be able to reach them where they are.

c. Ways We Act (5:7-9)

The fifth, sixth, and seventh beatitudes deal with how we act when facing cruelty, corruption, and conflict.

(1) When Facing Cruelty (5:7)

When facing cruelty, injustice, injury, and wrong, we should remember the fifth saying: "Blessed are the merciful: for they shall obtain mercy." Justice was the heart and soul of the law; mercy is the heart and soul of the gospel. He who shows no mercy destroys the bridge over which he himself must pass. Outside the Bible, Shakespeare best extolled mercy, especially in Portia's great speech to Shylock. Shylock demands a literal pound of flesh of Antonio, and Portia tries to persuade the implacable moneylender to be merciful:

> The quality of mercy is not strain'd,
> It droppeth as the gentle rain from heaven
> Upon the place beneath: it is twice bless'd;
> It blesseth him that gives and him that takes:
> 'Tis mightiest in the mightiest: it becomes
> The throned monarch better than his crown.
> . . . .
> It is an attribute to God himself.[6]

(2) When Facing Corruption (5:8)

The sixth beatitude says, "Blessed are the pure in heart: for they shall see God." Jesus was teaching not just purity of life, but purity of heart as well. How rare a flower such purity is! We are to be pure within, where all the mainsprings of life are to be found. We are to be able to look out at life with all its corruption and decay, and remain uncontaminated. Making a heart pure calls for a greater miracle than cleansing a leper or raising the dead.

Medieval monks fled from the corruption of the world to monasteries and cloisters, often built in lonely, inaccessible places and ruled by rigid ascetic laws. The quest for holiness along such lines was doomed before it was begun, for the monks took the corruption of their own hearts with them.

Separation in the Bible is not isolation, but insulation. Jesus lived a completely insulated life. He was in the world, but He was not of the world. He was in touch with the need of the world and in touch with the power of Heaven. There was no short circuit of that power, because He was insulated in impenetrable holiness. For us, purity of heart is impossible apart from saving, sanctifying grace and the reality of Christ's indwelling presence in the person of the Holy Spirit.

The pure in heart shall see God. Only the pure in heart can stand the burning brightness of His holiness. T. Binney expressed the thought in the following verse of song:

Eternal Light, Eternal Light, how pure the soul must be;
When placed within thy searching sight,
It shrinks not, but, with calm delight,
Can live and look on Thee.

(3) When Facing Conflict (5:9)

When facing conflict, we are to act as peacemakers. "Blessed are the peacemakers: for they shall be called the children of God," the seventh beatitude says.

Sin introduced conflict into this world. The first sin separated man from God; the second sin, Cain's murder of Abel, separated man from man. Jesus came to bring peace. One of His Messianic titles is "The Prince of Peace" (Isaiah 9:6). When He was born, the herald angels sang across the Judean hills, "On earth peace, good will toward men" (Luke 2:14). When He comes again, it will be to beat "swords into plowshares" and "spears into pruning hooks" (Isaiah 2:4) and to bring in a reign of peace. In the meantime those who have become partakers of the divine nature do what they can to bring men back into harmony with Heaven through the gospel, and into peace with one another in all the various arenas where hot passions stir up wrath and strife.

A peacemaker is not a pacifist. A pacifist wants peace at any price. Neville Chamberlain's attempts to pacify Hitler give us a graphic example of the folly of appeasement. World peace cannot be achieved apart from the presence of the Prince of Peace. Even He will not achieve world peace apart from battle, judgment, and the rule of the nations with "a rod of iron" (Psalm 2:9).

True peace is based on righteous principles. Genuine peace between man and man can be achieved only when there is peace between man and God in human hearts. So the goal of the peacemaker is to get people right with God; then they will quickly get right with one another.

d. What We Accept (5:10-12)

The eighth beatitude has to do with accepting persecution.

(1) The Question of Overwhelming Persecution (5:10-11)

The Lord Jesus was a realist. He knew that His program would be unpopular. He knew it would lead to His own death and to bitter hostility toward His followers. The Lord certainly did not envision His program bringing about a gradual evolution of love, joy, peace, goodness, and Christian spirit among the nations over the centuries until society was at last perfected. That postmillennialist's dream is not based on the facts of history or the forecasts of Scripture. What the Lord foretold was hostility, hatred, and bitter persecution for His people. Instead of being astonished at the world's reaction to the gospel and its hatred of God's people, we are to expect it.

(2) The Question of Overcoming Persecution (5:12)

When persecution comes our way, we must not react, but rejoice! "Great is your reward in heaven," Jesus declared.

The Lord will one day triumph in the arena of His rejection. All appearances to the contrary notwithstanding, His persecuted people will come into their own, "for theirs is the kingdom of heaven" (5:10). The kingdom of the heavens has its metropolis on high in the heavenly Jerusalem, the glorious city that will yet rule over the nations of the earth. That rule will come not by evolution, but by revolution. Christ's government will be imposed on mankind by God when "the times of the Gentiles" have run their course (Luke 21:24). Then those who have suffered with Him will reign with Him (2 Timothy 2:12). This is the uniform teaching of the prophetic Word.

3. The Sequel (5:13-16)

In the sequel to the beatitudes the Lord gave two illustrations to show how what we are will have an impact on what others do. We who are "the salt of the earth" and "the light of the world" are living in a world of decay and darkness, and we are to have an impact on both conditions.

Note that the Lord said we are the salt of the *earth* and the light of the *world.* His intellectual supremacy enables us to count unquestioningly on His absolute accuracy in the use of two different words here, and we should not mix them up. We are not the salt of the world and the light of the earth; we are the salt of the earth and the light of the world.

a. Resisting Decay (5:13)

Our function as salt is to resist decay. Salt is aseptic. It cannot change corruption into incorruption, but it does prevent corruption from spreading. It is used to hold decay and putrefaction at bay. Before the days of refrigeration, it was the most commonly used preservative.

Salt is a miracle. It is chemically composed of sodium and chloride. Pour a little hydrochloric acid on your hand and it will be burned away in half a minute. Drink hydrochloric acid and you will die in agony in a few minutes. Add sodium to hydrochloride and you will have salt, one of the most common, most useful substances on earth, a substance essential to life itself. Similarly, when God pours His grace into the hydrochloride of our lives, the result is a miracle: a regenerated person placed in the world for the blessing of all mankind.

Jesus said, "Ye are the salt of the earth." The word translated "earth" is *ge*, which refers to the earth as distinct from Heaven. *Ge* is a parochial word also suggesting one special land or country as distinct from other countries. *Ge* suggests the soil as well and conveys the idea of the material side of life. People are viewed as of the earth and Christians are the salt of the earth. Where we live, surrounded by people who are occupied with material things and earthly considerations, we are to be salt. We are to have an arresting effect on the general corruption of society.

The earth, as divorced from Heaven, is corrupt. We are to be the medium through which the heavenly side of things exerts its influence on the earthly side of things. We are to live as a heavenly people in an earthly environment. Just as salt adds tang and flavor to food, we are to exert our godly influence in a pungent, attractive way. We often give a wrong impression of Christianity. Oliver Wendell Holmes—American physician, poet, and humorist—once remarked, "I might have entered the ministry if certain clergymen I knew had not looked and acted so much like undertakers."

Jesus added a warning: "If the salt have lost his savour, wherewith shall it be salted? it is thenceforth good for nothing, but to be cast out, and to be trodden under foot of men." This statement of course refers not to losing one's salvation, but to losing one's testimony and influence. If ever there was a day when the earth needed Christians to keep their testimony and influence, it is this day of the X-rated home movie, internet pornography, and the marching sodomite.

b. Removing Darkness (5:14-16)

We are also to function as light. While salt deals with the moral, light deals with the spiritual. Salt relates to our character, but light relates to our conduct. Salt deals with what a person is; light deals with what a person does. We know what light does—it removes darkness. But we do not know what light is. Light is a miracle.

Jesus said, "I am the light of the world" (John 9:5). He also said, "Ye are the light of the world" (Matthew 5:14). Taken together, the two statements mean that we are to be like Him.

The word translated "world" here is *kosmos,* which relates to the whole created order of things. The root of *kosmos* means "to carve, plane, polish" and implies both order and beauty. In our function as light, we are to make people aware of their relation to the created order and aware of the harmony and beauty of the created universe as subject to the throne of God. Educators have buried this truth in their infatuation with the God-denying, soul-destroying, man-debasing, truth-ignoring theory of mechanistic evolution.

We are to remind people of the existence and authority of God by living in the will of God and by being like Jesus. Just as "a city that is set on an hill cannot be hid," our testimony for God must be consistent, continuous, and conspicuous.

The Lord used two illustrations to explain our function as light: a lamp and a city. The city illustrates our impact on the great outdoors; the lamp illustrates our influence on what goes on indoors. The lamp indicates individual testimony. The city, lit up at night by all the individual candles shining in Christian homes, indicates corporate testimony, the aggregate of all the little individual candles.

Above all, regardless of the scope of its influence, a lamp is intended to shine. No one puts a lamp under a bushel basket. If the lamp is to do any good, it must be put in a place where it can be seen. Luke 8:16 uses the companion illustration of putting a lamp under a bed. The bushel and the bed make a perfect pair. Putting a light under a bushel (the basket used by merchants and farmers for their wares) suggests the world of labor. We can get too busy to shine for Jesus. Putting a light under a bed suggests the world of leisure. We can be too lazy to shine for Jesus.

Incidentally, the illustrations of salt and light have one thing in common. Both salt and light exert their influence silently. We are not heard for our "much speaking" (Matthew 6:7).

The Lord concluded this section of His sermon by saying, "Let your light so shine before men, that they may see your good works, and glorify your Father which is in heaven" (5:16). No one ever exemplified this verse better than the Lord Jesus Himself.

B. The Disciple and His Beliefs (5:17-20)

1. A Personal Appreciation of God's Law (5:17-18)

a. The Law and Its Fulfillment (5:17)

As the Lord continued His sermon, He turned His attention to the Mosaic law—the foundation of Jewish national life and the moral, ceremonial, and religious code under which He lived. First He stated His personal appreciation of God's law. He had not come to destroy the law, but to fulfill it.

The Jews counted 613 separate edicts in the Mosaic law and there never was a single moment when the Lord Jesus did not absolutely fulfill in every detail every commandment. As a baby and as a boy, as a teenager and in the prime of life, at home, at school, at work, at play, as a son and as a brother, as a neighbor and as a friend, as a village carpenter, as an itinerant preacher, in secret and in public, when surrounded by family and friends and when confronted by formidable foes—at all times, in all places, in all ways, He kept the law of God. He kept it in letter and in spirit. He kept the law in its injunctions and in its intentions. He kept it because it was His nature to keep it. He would never dream of not keeping it. It was His Father's will and Jesus always did those things that please the Father (see John 8:29).

In Old Testament times the most sacred object connected with Israel's richly symbolic system of worship was the ark of the covenant that stood within the holy of holies, which was behind the veil. Inside that ark was an unbroken copy of the Mosaic law. Upon that ark rested, as upon a throne, the shekinah glory cloud, the visible token of the presence of God. That ark represented Christ; in His heart resided God's unbroken law; upon Him rested the enthroned Spirit of God, now present on earth in a marvelously new way.

"I saw the Spirit," said John the Baptist. That statement was unique, for in His essence the Holy Spirit cannot be seen; He is eternal and invisible. But the Baptist said, "I saw the Sprit descending from heaven like a dove, and it abode upon him" (John 1:32). The word translated "abode" is *meno,* one of the favorite words of the apostle John. He used it forty-one times in his Gospel, where it is rendered "abide" or "abode" twenty-two times, "dwell" five times, "remain" or "remaining" five times, "continue" three times, "endure" once, "abide still" once, "tarry" three times, and "be present" once. In his Epistles he used *menō* twenty-six times.

It was that visible coming of the Holy Spirit to abide upon the Lord Jesus that identified Him to John the Baptist as the Son of God. The Baptist said, "I knew him not: but he that sent me to baptize with water, the same said unto me, Upon whom thou shalt see the Spirit descending, and remaining [*menō*] on him, the same is he" (John 1:33). The Holy Spirit could enthrone Himself upon Jesus because of the unbroken law hidden in Jesus' heart (Psalm 119:11). In the heart of this One, and this One alone, God's Word could be found intact and unbroken.[7]

God's law had two parts: the moral law and the ceremonial law. In His amazing life the Lord Jesus fulfilled the demands of the moral law. In His death He fulfilled the details of the ceremonial law, which was chiefly concerned with sacrifices and offerings.

He fulfilled the rich symbolism of the sin offering, the trespass offering, the meal offering, the peace offering, and the burnt offering. Jesus was the goat that was slain on the day of atonement, whose blood was taken into the holy of holies; and He was the scapegoat upon which were laid the sins of the people before it was led away into "a land not inhabited" (Leviticus 16:22). He was the bird that the cleansed leper brought to be slain in his stead; and He was the other bird that the cleansed leper brought to be dipped in the blood of the first bird before being set free to fly heavenward for home. Jesus was the unleavened bread of the Passover, and He was the paschal lamb. His were the ashes of the red heifer, and His was the blood that was shed for sin. The red rivers that poured from ten thousand times ten thousand sacrifices were but a feeble type of His precious blood.

Well could He announce: "Think not that I am come to destroy the law, or the prophets: I am not come to destroy, but to fulfil" (Matthew 5:17).

Jesus fulfilled the prophets as well as the law. The prophets in glory must have been overjoyed at the life Jesus lived on earth. "I wrote about His suffering," Isaiah might have cried, reciting Isaiah 53, "and look how He has fulfilled my words to the letter!" David might have added, "Yes, and Psalm 22 as well, and Psalm 69." And Zechariah: "He has also fulfilled my prophecy." God would have commented, "This is my beloved Son," and the angels would have gazed down in wonder, for these are "things the angels desire to look into" (1 Peter 1:12).

b. The Law and Its Future (5:18)

Jesus said He had come to fulfill the law, then added, "Till heaven and earth pass, one jot or one tittle shall in no wise pass from the law, till all be fulfilled." The jot was the smallest letter in the alphabet and the tittle was the smallest part of any letter, sometimes merely the mark that distinguished one letter from another (as in the English alphabet a *c* is distinguished from an *e* by a small horizontal line).

The same almighty Word that spoke the heaven and earth into being spoke the Mosaic law into being. The edicts of the law are as exact, infallible, and timeless as the edicts that hold the stars in space, spin the earth on its axis, and take the earth on its annual march around the sun. God's moral laws are as true and timeless as His material laws.

There are going to be changes in the heaven and earth (Revelation 21:1), but not until their present purpose is fulfilled. That there have already been changes in the Mosaic law is evident from the New Testament, but those changes did not come until the original law in all its parts and sum was fulfilled. First God had to demonstrate that His law was "holy, and just, and good" (Romans 7:12) and that it could be kept in the life of a human being (8:3-4). Once Jesus had fulfilled the law, changes could be made.

The law as a system was repealed. The law as a standard remained—except that it was reduced to two commandments, both comprehended in the word *love:* "Thou shalt love the Lord thy God....Thou shalt love thy neighbour as thyself" (Matthew 22:37-40; Romans 13:8-10).

Such was the Lord's personal appreciation of the law. It was God's delightful demand, Heaven's irreducible minimum, a code of conduct rooted in the character of a holy, loving, all-wise, and impartially just God.

2. A Personal Application of God's Law (5:19-20)

a. A Searching Examination (5:19)

Woe to those who break the least of the commandments, and woe to those who lead others to do so. The Lord exposed the folly of the Pharisees who spent their time dividing the Mosaic law into "great commandments" and "least commandments." They were the same Pharisees who enlarged the borders of their garments (see Matthew 23:5). They had learned nothing from the law.

They must not have read Numbers 15:32-41 thoughtfully. The passage tells of a man who evidently considered the fourth commandment to be the least of the commandments and decided it could be safely disregarded. He soon discovered his folly, for when he went out on the sabbath day to gather sticks, he was stoned to death by direct order of God.

Immediately after this sobering event the Hebrews were instructed to wear a fringe and a "ribband of blue" on the borders of their garments. The fringe was to remind them of all the commandments of God. The threads were of equal length and very close to each other, symbolizing the fact that the divine precepts were closely knit and of equal importance. The blue "ribband" was a reminder of the heavenly origin of the law in all its parts.

b. A Scathing Denunciation (5:20)

Having put the law back into perspective as the rule of life for the nation to whom it was given, the Lord demanded that our righteousness exceed that of the scribes and Pharisees. He introduced His statement with the authoritative "I say unto you." The expression occurs fourteen times in the sermon on the mount (5:18,20,22,26,28,32,34,39,44; 6:2,5,16,25,29).

Our righteousness must exceed theirs both in degree and in kind. (The apostle Paul expanded this theme in his Epistle to the Romans, where the key word is *righteousness*.) Our natural self-righteousness, the kind of righteousness displayed by the scribes and Pharisees, has to be repudiated. In its stead the righteousness of Christ is imputed to us when we believe; it is implanted in us and imparted to us by the indwelling Holy Spirit. No unregenerate person, however religious and righteous he may be in his own eyes or however impressive his reputation as a holy man may be, can produce the kind or degree of righteousness demanded by Christ. In kind, it is His kind; in degree, it is what mathematicians would call "the nth degree." It is beyond calculation. Without His kind of righteousness, no one will enter the kingdom of heaven.

The rest of the sermon on the mount is a commentary on Matthew 5:20.

C. The Disciple and His Bible (5:21-48)

"Ye have heard," said Jesus.

When the Jews returned from Babylon, the common people had forgotten their own language. They could no longer read the Bible in the original Hebrew, so the scribes and rabbis monopolized the teaching of the Scriptures instead of translating the Scriptures into Chaldee or Aramaic for the benefit of the people. Anyone who wanted to know the Bible had to go to the scribes and rabbis, and they handled the Scriptures to suit themselves. Thus the people who listened to the sermon on the mount had *heard* the Law, but they had not read it for themselves. Often they were unable to differentiate between what the Bible said and what the rabbis said it said—between the pure Word of God and the adulterated traditions and commentaries of the religious leaders. The Law had been greatly corrupted by rabbinic interpretation.

The Lord with His authoritative "but I say unto you" swept away the accumulated exegetical rubbish of centuries.

1. The Question of Injuring Lives (5:21-24)

a. The Murder and Its Consequences (5:21)

The consequence of murder was capital punishment—death. The Lord here quoted the law, not as given by Moses—Exodus 20:13; 21:12-14; Numbers 35:17-21; Deuteronomy 19:11-13, where the sin of murder is set forth as a crime against the Creator—but as it was taught by the scribes and Pharisees. They reduced the crime to the act itself, something to be taken up by earthly courts alone. In so doing they left the impression that only the outward act was sinful, and they removed the terror of God's judgment in the life to come.

b. The Motive and Its Consequences (5:22)

The Lord immediately restored the commandment to its original intent. He traced murder to its source or motive: anger. The anger that produces murder, He pointed out, is as great a sin as murder itself. Even though no human court can deal with such anger, it will be treated as seriously as murder at God's assize.

The Lord underlined three degrees of hatred that expose a person to judgment as a violator of the sixth commandment. First is anger "without a cause," an expression not found in some of the manuscripts and considered by many to be a translator's error. (Some have suggested a deliberate gloss to accommodate the hot-tempered King James.) To harbor inward resentment toward another person, Jesus said, puts one "in danger of the judgment"— a reference to the lower court, the council of three in a local synagogue who had jurisdiction over lesser offenses.

The second degree of hatred is demonstrated by the outward expression of dislike. One who says "Raca" conveys the idea of scorn, disdain, contempt. Jesus said that the man who allows his emotions so to carry him away is "in danger of the council"—a reference to the supreme court, the Sanhedrin.

The third degree of hatred results in an even more forceful expression of dislike. To say "Thou fool" is to call a man a reprobate or a rebel, a serious charge. The word translated "fool" here is related to the Hebrew *mōros,* a term that was deeply lodged in the Jewish mind and retained even after the language became Aramaic. There was an unforgettable connection with a sad but significant incident in the life of Moses during which "he spake unadvisedly with his lips" (Psalm 106:33). He used the word *mōros* when he said, "Hear now, ye *rebels;* must we fetch you water out of this rock?" (Numbers 20:10, italics added). For that outburst of temper Moses was kept out of the promised land.

Jesus said that to speak in such a way puts one "in danger of hell fire." Literally, the reference was to the fiery valley of Hinnom just outside Jerusalem, where the refuse of the city was dumped and bodies of criminals were burned. No greater shame could be imagined by a Jew than to be so cremated.

So Jesus took three common phases of Jewish legal procedure— the lower court, the supreme court, and the fires of Hinnom—and invested them with deeper significance. In terms of the new spiritual significance, Jesus was saying that if we become angry, we are instantly in peril. We are not yet haled to judgment, but we are in danger of it; we are on the path that leads there. If we use a term of contempt in speaking of another person, we will have to deal with a higher court. If we utter the ultimate insult, we are in danger of the ultimate punishment: being cast out of the kingdom to the place where refuse is burned. Jesus stressed that we are "in danger."

The Lord did not deal with the actual sin of murder. There was no need for that, for even the scribes and Pharisees agreed on capital punishment for murder. Jesus went behind the murder to the mood, for if we are never angry, we will never kill. So Jesus made anger itself a penal offense.

c. The Moral and Its Consequences (5:23-24)

The moral is simple: We are to get right with those we have wronged, those who have something against us, those with whom we have been angry. Reconciliation is so important that Jesus said it must even take precedence over our worship of God.

The Lord took his illustration from the law of the trespass offering. (The Old Testament sin offering had to do with the principle of sin; the trespass offering had to do with the practice of sin.) When a person brought a trespass offering to the Lord, he was required first of all to go and put things right with the one he had wronged. If he had stolen, he had to give back the full amount plus an additional 20 percent (Leviticus 5:16). In the sermon on the mount the Lord applied this principle to all worship. We cannot look for God's blessing on us or expect Him to accept our offerings if we have injured someone and not bent over backward to put things right.

2. The Question of Invoking Law (5:25-26)

The Lord next used an illustration from Roman law, which of course took precedence over Jewish law in Palestine in those days. On the way to a hearing, both parties to a dispute could settle out of court—by far the most sensible thing to do. As soon as matters were in the hands of a judge, such an amicable settlement was no longer possible; both parties were then subject to the decision of the court.

Law cases are always precarious, so the Lord was advising us to avoid them. He went further and implied that we should put things right with people who think they have been injured by us even when we believe ourselves to be innocent.

As we walk along the highway of life, we have the opportunity to settle disputes among ourselves and make reparation so that the issues will not have to be reviewed by the Judge. If a case is not settled out of court, there is little problem for the believer if the assize in view is that of the great white throne, since only the unsaved will appear there. Such offenders will never be able to pay their debts and will remain prisoners forever.

If the judgment seat of Christ is in view, then the problem of interpretation is more difficult. What is meant by the "officer," the "prison," and paying the "uttermost farthing"? Roman Catholics have built their dogma of purgatory on Matthew 5:25-26, even though the Bible makes it clear that no such place or prospect exists for the child of God. First John 1:7 says, "The blood of Jesus Christ

[God's] Son cleanseth us from all sin." The penal consequences of our sins are fully covered by the finished work of Christ.

Believers are arrayed in the righteousness of Christ, but the Bible still warns us about the judgment seat of Christ. There is abundant evidence in Scripture that our works are to be judged, that we can suffer loss, and that the consequences of our behavior will be reviewed. (Much of the New Testament teaching on this subject relates to the coming kingdom age.) Christians as a rule are far too lenient on themselves and take a far more placid and optimistic view of the judgment seat of Christ than is warranted by the revelation that we have on the subject. Paul mentioned the "judgment seat of Christ" in the same breath as the "terror of the Lord" (2 Corinthians 5:10-11).

We are all on our way to judgment: the sinner to the terrifying judgment of the great white throne, and the saint to the sobering judgment seat of Christ. Jesus said, "Agree...whiles thou art in the way."

3. The Question of Indulging Lust (5:27-32)

Jewish teachers each had a customary phrase to introduce their teaching. The typical phrase of the prophet was "Thus said the Lord." The characteristic phrase of the scribes and Pharisees was "There is a teaching that..." The Lord's identifying phrase was "I say unto you," often linked with "Verily, verily." The prophets appealed to divine authority; the rabbis to this, that, or the other noted scholar. Jesus appealed to His own authority. He quoted the law in order to restate it and lift it to higher ground—on His own authority as the Word made flesh.

Now the Lord spoke with His customary authority regarding the sacredness of marriage. God instituted marriage long before He instituted either the law or the church.

a. A Defiled Marriage (5:27-30)

The background of the Lord's teaching about marriage was the prevalent permissiveness and immorality of the Judeo-Greco-Roman world in which He lived—a world much like the one in which we live.

Among the Jews, two voices were raised to interpret the Mosaic teaching on divorce (Deuteronomy 24:1): the voices of Shammai and Hillel. The school of Shammai heeded the prophet Malachi, who recorded God's voice ringing down the centuries, "I hate divorce." The King James translation reads, "The God of Israel, saith that he hateth putting away" (Malachi 2:16). Hillel's school, on the other hand, was liberal in the extreme, teaching that a man could divorce his wife for almost anything he found displeasing in her, while a woman had no rights at all. Jewish divorce laws, according to this interpretation, were one-sided and chauvinistic.

The Greeks expected a respectable woman to live in seclusion and never to appear on the streets unchaperoned or take part in social life. A Greek man demanded absolute moral purity in his wife, but he granted himself the utmost license to be as immoral as he pleased. He saw nothing wrong with visiting houses of ill-repute, nothing wrong with the employment of a thousand harlots as priestesses in the temple of Aphrodite at Corinth. If he wanted to divorce his wife for any reason, he simply had to dismiss her in the presence of a couple of witnesses and return her dowry.

The Romans started well. Their religion and society were originally founded on the home and the authority of the father in the home. For five centuries divorce was virtually unknown and harlots were viewed with contempt. Then Rome conquered Greece militarily, and Greece avenged herself by conquering Rome morally. Rome plunged into the quagmire of Greek moral pollution. The historian Lecky wrote of the "frantic depravity" that followed Roman contact with Greece. Among the Romans, marriage became "nothing more than an unfortunate necessity."

In cultures outside the Bible world, matters were as bad. We know how Hinduism has debased women and how the raw paganism of other religions has reduced women to the status of childbearing beasts of burden.

Against such a background, Jesus raised His voice with His authoritative "But I say unto you" (Matthew 5:28).

The naked statement of the Mosaic law was clear enough: "Thou shalt not commit adultery" (5:27). But Jesus went straight for the heart. We are not even to look with lust, He said. The word translated "looketh" in 5:28 is *blepō*, which means "to look, to keep on looking, to observe closely and with desire." The first involuntary glance is not the culprit. It is the second glance—the deliberate act that feeds the impulse and turns the glance into a lustful look—that Jesus said puts us in peril. He went behind the outward sin to the source. There would be no adultery, no fornication, no whoredom, no uncleanness of any kind, without that lustful look.

That lustful look, that secret unexpressed desire, constitutes us guilty. So serious is this guilt that Jesus recommended, "If thy right eye offend thee, pluck it out....If thy right hand offend thee, cut it off" (5:29-30)—strong language indeed. The Lord's words were an indication of how deep His feelings were about moral purity and protecting the home. The eye generates the desire, and the hand generates the deed, so Jesus said in effect, "Don't look and don't touch." The Lord was not telling us to cripple ourselves, but to control ourselves.

b. A Defaulting Marriage (5:31-32)

Here the Lord touched briefly on the question of divorce. Again His standards are the highest and holiest.

(1) The Law and Its Position (5:31)

The law of Moses made provision for divorce because of uncleanness. The Pharisees, following the lying liberalism of Hillel, made a great parade of obeying the Mosaic rule regarding the actual bill of divorcement. The Talmudic writers paid but scant attention to the justice of the divorce, but made a great fuss about the form and wording of the bill; they insisted, among other absurdities, that it be written in exactly twelve lines, neither more nor less.

(2) The Lord and His Prohibition (5:32)

Jesus declared that only one sin dissolves marriage in the sight of God: fornication or moral unchastity. Moses conceded to divorce on such grounds, but did not command it.

The Lord's teaching on divorce in the sermon on the mount agrees with His later definitive statement on divorce in Matthew 19:3-12. In both passages divorce is allowed on the ground of marital unchastity ("except it be for fornication"). Such a divorce dissolves the marriage completely and leaves the innocent party free to remarry. Divorce on other grounds leaves neither party free to remarry. In Matthew 19 the Lord took into account the fact that such a lofty stand on divorce cannot be received by everyone (19:10-11). He also took note of the choices open to the divorced person in the matter of remarriage (19:12). Certainly we have no right to enforce harsh, legalistic rulings on people who are divorced on Scriptural grounds nor to treat an innocent party (whose marriage is dissolved by the immoral conduct of his or her partner) as though he or she were the guilty person.

In Matthew 5 the Lord Jesus was dealing in absolutes. He made statements in terms of black and white with no shades of gray because He was giving the laws of the kingdom, the laws of God. He was teaching the law as seen by One in whom is no variableness, neither shadow caused by turning. The sermon on the mount is the law not just in letter, but in spirit as well; the law not as interpreted by the rabbis, but as interpreted by the sinless Son of God. The religious leaders of His day (as so often in our day) saw things in terms of relative morality. Jesus saw things in terms of Heaven's absolutes.

4. The Question of Inappropriate Language (5:33-37)

a. The Danger of a Broken Word (5:33)

The law said, "Thou shalt fear the Lord thy God, and serve him, and shalt swear by his name" (Deuteronomy 6:13). This statement was backed by the warning of the third commandment: "The Lord will not hold him guiltless that taketh his name in vain" (Exodus 20:7).

b. The Demand for a Better Way (5:34-37)

(1) Swearing Flippantly (5:34-36)

The Old Testament permitted people to take an oath by God's name if an oath was necessary. Thereafter the oath was binding. The Pharisees with wicked casuistry said that since the law stipulated that oaths made in the name of the Lord had to be performed, other oaths were not binding. As a result people found themselves obliged to confirm even the most trivial promises by invoking Jehovah's name. To avoid that, they invented all kinds of oaths to add weight to their statements and promises without putting themselves in danger of being held guilty if they broke their word. They swore for instance by Heaven, by the earth, by the holy city, by their heads.

Jesus swept all such oaths aside. He showed that ultimately they all referred to God, for Heaven is God's throne, the earth is His footstool, Jerusalem is the city of the great King, and their heads were made by Him. Man cannot make a single hair black or white to crown the head of youth or old age.

(2) Speaking Firmly (5:37)

"Don't swear at all," Jesus said in effect. "Just say yes or no." All contracts and promises must be kept. Our word should be our bond. We should be marked by total integrity in commitment because our word is backed by total integrity of character. We are to do what we say we will do, whether the commitment is great or small, convenient or inconvenient (Psalm 15:4), because we would not dream of doing otherwise.

We have all been put on guard by people who feel they have to preface their remarks with oaths. They are always saying, "I swear," or "This is the honest truth." We instinctively begin to wonder if they are lying.

The Lord's prohibition regarding oaths does not seem to include judicial oaths (although our courts allow a person to affirm his truthfulness rather than swear it). The Bible says that God swore by Himself (Genesis 22:16-17; Hebrews 6:13; 7:21), that Paul made an oath to the Corinthians (2 Corinthians 1:23), and that Jesus answered under oath when before the Sanhedrin (Matthew 26:63-64).

5. The Question of Ineffable Love (5:38-48)

a. The Law of Retaliation (5:38-42)

(1) The Law's Way (5:38)

Justice is the cardinal principle of government. It is supremely expressed in Israel's law, "An eye for an eye, and a tooth for a tooth." The law is based on a righteous principle not of revenge, but of weighed and measured justice.

Legislatures could not repeal such laws without creating anarchy. The sermon on the mount is not a code for government in a world of crime and armed conflict or for people in an infidel society. It is impossible in such a society to restrain crime and deter aggression by turning the other cheek. In the sermon on the mount the Lord was not legislating for the world of the unregenerate, but for the church and for His kingdom in the millennial age.

(2) The Lord's Way (5:39-42)

For His people, the Lord repealed the Old Testament law of retaliation—"eye for eye, tooth for tooth" (Exodus 21:24; Leviticus 24:20; Deuteronomy 19:21)—which the Pharisees had debased into a license for outright revenge. Instead the Lord promulgated the law of love.

(a) When People Smite Us (5:39)

A slap on the face has been regarded as a highly provocative insult for countless ages, but when people smite us, we are to turn the other cheek. The Lord illustrated in His life what He meant by this rule. When He was smacked in the face, He did not literally turn the other cheek. But although He had omnipotent power at His command and could have hurled His assailant alive into Hellfire, He acted with sublime restraint and contented Himself with a mild reproach (John 18:22-23). The idea is not that we must always passively suffer the assault of the assassin, the bully, or the thief. However, when the interests of Christ's kingdom demand that we turn the other cheek, we should.

(b) When People Sue Us (5:40)

When people sue us, we are to give more than is demanded by the plaintiff. According to the Mosaic law, a man could not be deprived of his outer garment, which doubled as a blanket for him at night; it could be held in bail only when not needed by the defendant (Exodus 22:26-27). The Lord told His disciples to give up not only their inner coats, which could be legally taken from them, but also their cloaks, which as outer garments were exempt from seizure under the law. We too are to be ready to give up that which cannot be taken by law.

A professing Christian of my acquaintance ran up enormous debts in his business. When he saw that his creditors were closing in, he transferred as many assets as he could to his wife and filed for bankruptcy. Protected from his creditors by lenient bankruptcy laws, he was able to shake off most of his debts. He exclaimed to another of my friends, "I had a very profitable bankruptcy!"

Evidently he had never taken the sermon on the mount seriously. The Lord would have had him beggar himself, not bankrupt himself. The Lord would have had him face his creditors on moral grounds, not merely legal grounds; treat them according to the law of love; work his fingers to the bone in order to pay back in full all that his creditors saw fit to demand. In other words, the Lord would have had him give his cloak as well as his coat. As it was, he kept both his cloak and his coat. His creditors had to be satisfied with a few cents on the dollar. Before long he was back in a similar line of business and piling up new debt.

(c) When People Seize Us (5:41)

In the Lord's day the Romans had the right to press both men and beasts into compulsory service when the interests of the government required it. Simon the Cyrenian for example was seized by the Romans and compelled to carry Christ's cross to Calvary (Luke 23:26). The British navy in bygone days had a similar right to seize able-bodied men in time of war and hale them off to sea to serve their country on starvation wages. The press gang was dreaded in all seaport towns. In modern society the courts have the right to impanel juries taken at random from the ranks of the people.

The Jews greatly resented this kind of compulsory service, but the Lord taught that it is our duty to help those who rule over us, to do so cheerfully, and to go beyond the call of duty. When people seize us, we are to go the second mile.

Quite contrary to the Spirit of Christ is the spirit of the age, which espouses marches, demonstrations, and civil disobedience; settles disputes with strikes and confrontation; and fosters disaffection for and defiance of authority.

(d) When People Supplicate Us (5:42)

No Hebrew was obliged to lend money except for charitable purposes. In such cases he was to charge no interest, and all debts of any kind whatsoever were canceled by law every seven years (Leviticus 25:1-28). So there was legislation for charity among the Hebrew people. But Christians are not to stop there; love will not let us. When people supplicate us, we are to respond in a positive way.

Jesus said, "Give to him that asketh thee, and from him that would borrow of thee turn not thou away" (Matthew 5:42). The apostle John, who had sat at Jesus' feet, said, "Whoso hath this world's good, and seeth his brother have need, and shutteth up his bowels of compassion from him, how dwelleth the love of God in him?" (1 John 3:17) Believers should be eager to help relieve the wants and woes of the unfortunate of this world.

So the law of retaliation is obsolete, as is the whole system of *dos* and *don't*s mandated by the Mosaic law. All is changed by the advent of love. The Lord elaborated on the change by stating the law of reconciliation.

b. The Law of Reconciliation (5:43-48)

(1) The Rule Explained (5:43-44)

(a) What God Commanded (5:43)

The law had said, "Thou shalt not avenge, nor bear any grudge against the children of thy people, but thou shalt love thy neighbour as thyself" (Leviticus 19:18). The Pharisees, with callous disregard for the spirit of the law, had taken up the clause "thou shalt love thy neighbour," drawn a wicked inference, and added "and hate thine enemy." Referring to their addition, Jesus said, "Ye have heard that it hath been said, Thou shalt love thy neighbour, and hate thine enemy" (Matthew 5:43).

The Pharisees were without excuse for their blatant distortion of God's Word. In more than one passage in the Law, even the adversary in a lawsuit is described as a neighbor (Exodus 20:16; 22:9) and the same concept is clearly taught elsewhere in the Old Testament (Proverbs 24:28; 25:18).

(b) What God Commends (5:44)

Cutting all ground from beneath the feet of the Pharisees, the Lord said, "But I say unto you, Love your enemies, bless them that curse you, do good to them that hate you, and pray for them which despitefully use you, and persecute you."

(2) The Rule Exemplified (5:45-47)

Jesus Himself provided the supreme example of returning good for evil when He prayed for those who nailed Him to the tree, and died loving them with an everlasting love.

(a) A Comparison (5:45)

The Lord's reason for demanding such loving conduct from us is that we have been born into God's family and we are to be like our heavenly Father. Since He shows unwearying kindness to all men, so should we. He does not discriminate between the evil and the good when in His providential dealings He sends the sunshine and the rain.

(b) A Contrast (5:46-47)

There is no particular virtue in loving those who love us or in giving a cheerful greeting to those who greet us. Why, the publicans did that! Among the Jews of Jesus' day, the publicans were regarded as the lowest of the low. They were the hated tax collectors who worked for the occupying Roman power. No one likes paying taxes, but paying taxes to a foreign conqueror is galling in the extreme. No man who had any self-respect or any regard for his reputation would accept the odious job of publican. As a result, the office was left in the hands of unscrupulous people, most of whom lined their own pockets handsomely in the process of collecting taxes— adding to the fury of their victims.

The Lord taught that our Christianity is of little worth if it generates no loftier love than that displayed by publicans and sinners—and this teaching was recorded by a man who had once been a publican himself!

(3) The Rule Expanded (5:48)

What is the bottom line? "Be ye therefore perfect, even as your Father which is in heaven is perfect." Perfection is impossible to achieve, but it is our goal. In other words, our goal is to be like Jesus. The apostle Paul wrote, "Not as though I had already attained, either were already perfect: but I follow after, if that I may apprehend that for which also I am apprehended of Christ Jesus" (Philippians 3:12).

From the moment of our new birth we are accounted perfect as to our *standing*. God puts us "in Christ" and thereafter sees us as perfect and as righteous as He is. As to our *state*, there remains much land to be possessed (see Joshua 13:1). We struggle to achieve our goal of perfection until we get to glory and receive our resurrection bodies. Then our state and standing will be the same. "We shall be like him; for we shall see him as he is" (1 John 3:2). In the meantime our task is to cooperate with the indwelling Holy Spirit of God so that we will daily become more like God's beloved Son—perfect.

D. The Disciple and His Burdens (6:1-34)

The Lord turned His attention to almsgiving, prayer, and fasting—three areas where wrong motives can easily enter in, especially the desire for the praise or approval of men. The Roman Catholic Church, Buddhism, and many other religions place a lot of emphasis on these exercises. The false prophet Muhammad taught his followers that prayer would carry a man halfway to paradise, fasting would bring him to its gates, and almsgiving would gain him admittance. The Lord showed that these practices as mere religious works are useless.

1. Burdens Connected with Worship (6:1-18)

a. The Duties of Life (6:1-4)

The word translated alms here is often rendered "righteousness," but almsgiving is the subject of the Lord's admonition. Giving alms (giving money, food, or other help to the poor) is a commendable work—only it must be done in secret and not just to win the applause of men. J. B. Phillips rendered 6:2 in his usual graphic style: "When you do good to other people, don't hire a trumpeter to go in front of you—like those play-actors in the synagogues and streets who make sure that men admire them."[8]

"They have their reward," Jesus added. The word translated "they have" here is *apechō,* which was used by the Greeks to refer to a formal receipt. So Jesus was saying that those who trumpet and parade their good works receive their reward the moment someone applauds them. They get what they have been looking for; there is nothing more to come. Today many people give to charities simply to secure a tax advantage. There is nothing wrong in claiming all one's legitimate deductions at tax time, but if a person's motive for giving is to secure a tax-deductible receipt, that is what he gets. He gets what he wanted.

There is no question in the Lord's teaching here about helping the poor. It is taken for granted that Christians will help the needy. Jesus did not say, "*If* you give alms, *if* you pray, *if* you fast." His admonitions are for *when* you give alms, *when* you pray, *when* you fast. These works are part and parcel of one's worship and one's love for Christ. The Lord takes it for granted that we will be so much in love with Him that we will help the impoverished, spend time in prayer, and bring our lives under control. He expects these practices to be an instinctive part of our Christian behavior—manward, godward, and selfward.

The concern is not about *when* we give, pray, and fast, but *why.* What starts out as a *desire* to be all that God wants us to be can degenerate into a *duty;* and what degenerates into a duty can soon degenerate further into an empty *display.* That is what had happened to the Pharisees.

b. The Devotions of Life (6:5-15)

This passage, the Lord's great treatise on prayer, is not only piercing, but also intensely practical. It tells us how to pray, and it tells us how not to pray. Here we have exact instructions about a vital but often neglected area of life.

(1) The Parody of Prayer (6:5)

The kind of prayer that is intended to impress other people is a parody. While it is not part of our culture to stand on a street corner, strike a posture, and pray as the hypocrites in 6:5 did, we can and often do try to impress people when we are called on to pray at church or at some other public function. This is an example of how not to pray.

(2) The Place of Prayer (6:6)

The Lord recommended a private or secret place for prayer. We can pray in secret almost anywhere: in an unused room at home, in a car in a parking lot, in a public conveyance, at a busy intersection while we are waiting for the traffic light to change. Jesus' habit was to rise a great while before daybreak and go off to a desert place or a lonely hillside, for during the day people would never leave Him alone.

Paul said he prayed "without ceasing." Presumably he maintained a constant attitude of prayer so that everything that came his way was turned into an unexpressed thought of supplication, intercession, thanksgiving, or worship. Probably he prayed during the long hours spent plying the needle when making tents and during the long days spent on the road when traveling here and there with the gospel. Since God is omnipresent, we can transform any corner into a cathedral and pray—silently if in a crowd or out loud if we prefer when we are alone.

(3) The Principle of Prayer (6:7-8)

We are not to use "vain repetitions" (6:7). The Lord must have been acutely aware of the danger of taking even the sample prayer in 6:9-13 and parroting the words. He forbade the practice of saying the same words over and over again, as for instance the Buddhist does with his interminable *Om mani padme aun* or the Catholic does with his *Pater Nosters* and *Ave Marias*.

Every pilgrim who goes to Rome visits the pontifical shrine of the holy stairs, the *Scala Sancta*. These it is said were the stairs of Pilate's house that Christ ascended and descended on the day of His condemnation to death; His back was bleeding from His scourging and His blood dripped on the steps. According to medieval tradition the empress St. Helena had the staircase brought from Jerusalem to Rome. Catholics who ascend the twenty-eight steps on their knees, all the while meditating on the passion of Christ, receive from the Church a plenary indulgence on certain holy days and a partial indulgence on other days, provided they have confessed their sins, received holy communion, and prayed for the pope's intentions. As these pilgrims climb, they recite repetitious prayers. They begin:

> My Jesus, through the sorrow you suffered in being separated from your dear Mother and your beloved disciples, have mercy on me.

> > Holy Mother, pierce me through
> > In my heart each Wound renew
> > Of my Savior Crucified.

They go on to the next step and say:

> My Jesus, through the distress of mind you suffered when betrayed by Judas, have mercy on me.

> > Holy Mother, pierce me through
> > In my heart each Wound renew
> > Of my Savior Crucified.

Painful step follows painful step. Ritual prayer follows ritual prayer. Any time you go to Rome you will see the deluded climbing those stairs—you will see Church dignitaries and laymen, young and old, rich and poor, great and small, little girls with holes in their stockings and grown men with pant legs rolled up. All this is done in the name of Christ and in defiance of the Lord's teaching in the sermon on the mount.

(4) The Pattern of Prayer (6:9-15)

(a) What the Lord Recommended (6:9-13)

The sample prayer is, as we might expect, a masterpiece. But note that the Lord did not say, "Pray these words." He said in effect, "Pray this way." When we pray we should pay attention to the Father's person, purpose, provision, pardon, pathway, protection, power, and permanence.

i. The Father's Person (6:9)

We should begin by showing appreciation for God's person: "Our Father which art in heaven." That's the address on the envelope, so to speak, and what an intimate and comforting address it is. We address our prayer to our Father. The greatest name for God in the Old Testament is *Jehovah*—the God of covenant who makes "exceeding great and precious promises" to His people and keeps those promises. But the greatest name of all for God is *our Father,* a name that implies relationship, resources, and responsibilities beyond "all that we ask or think."

Our Father's home is in Heaven, and His home is going to be our home one of these days. Abraham understood this truth. There was a time in his early pilgrimage when he pitched his tent so that Bethel was to the west and Hai was to the east (Genesis 12:8). When he looked east, he was looking back over the way he had come, back toward the sunrise of his life. Looking back, he saw the town called *Hai,* which means "a heap of ruins." He saw a picture of this world of human homes, through which time drives its careless plowshare.

When he looked west toward the setting sun, he remembered that "swift to its close ebbs out life's little day; / Earth's joys grow dim, its glories pass away."[9] Looking west, he saw the town called *Bethel,* which means "the house of God." Abraham saw beyond the sunset to God's eternal home and "called upon the name of the Lord." Jesus taught us to catch this heavenly vision and pray, "Our Father which art in heaven." The Lord wanted to direct our thoughts toward home.

Then He told us to add, "Hallowed be thy name." We may use the name *Father* for God, but there must be no careless familiarity. His is a high and hallowed name, one to be employed with reverence and awe.

ii. The Father's Purpose (6:10)

Before we focus on our own interests, we are to give our attention to God's will and pray that it be done: "Thy kingdom come. Thy will be done in earth, as it is in heaven." Jesus had come from a land where ten thousand times ten thousand angels stand in rapture around the throne of His Father, hang on His words, and rush to do His will. Jesus had come to a world where His kingdom is barely known and where only very rarely, and even then only very imperfectly, does anyone do God's will. Satan could point to the kingdoms of this world, boast that they were his, and offer them as bait to the Son of God. Jesus had come to recover those kingdoms and restore them to God.

The book of Revelation begins in Heaven and ends in Heaven, but in the interval the scenes alternate between Heaven and earth. A scene on earth is followed by a scene in Heaven, and a scene in Heaven is followed by a scene on earth. The reason is that in the Apocalypse we find the full answer to the Lord's prayer. We see God's will being decreed in Heaven and then done on earth.[10]

iii. The Father's Provision (6:11)

In the model prayer there is just one brief mention of our physical and material needs: "Give us this day our daily bread." We do not have to dwell on our needs because God knows all about them. Analysis of our own prayers will often reveal preoccupation with the material side of life; we pray mostly about how we are to be fed, where we are to live, what we are to wear, Aunt Suzy's illness, Uncle Joe's need for a better job. We should not stop praying about these topics. The Lord taught us to include them in our prayers; but material requests are to be kept in their right place and proportion.

iv. The Father's Pardon (6:12)

Next we are to beg for God's pardon: "Forgive us our debts, as we forgive our debtors." This is the prayer not of a sinner, but of a saint. The prayer of a sinner begins and ends with "God be merciful to me a sinner" (Luke 18:13). His cry is a plea for pardon from an offended God, a plea for judicial forgiveness. In Matthew 6:12 the plea is that of a child of God who has grieved his heavenly Father by some wrong attitude, thought, word, or deed and needs parental forgiveness.

The Lord taught the principle that mercy must beget mercy.

Mercy received must be mercy reproduced. How can we logically, consistently, or morally ask God to forgive us if we ourselves are harboring an unforgiving spirit?

v. The Father's Pathway (6:13a)

Focusing our attention on God's pathway, Jesus prayed, "Lead us not into temptation." The Lord knew from personal experience what He was talking about (see Matthew 4:1). God does not tempt us (James 1:13), but He can permit us to be led into temptation—or He can protect us from it. He will only allow temptation that He knows we can withstand (1 Corinthians 10:13; 2 Peter 2:9). God tests us; Satan tempts us.

We are living in a perilous world and we are made of highly flammable material (James 1:13-14). No wonder the Lord urged us to ask God to lead us in His paths and keep us out of the way of temptation (Psalm 23:3).

vi. The Father's Protection (6:13b)

We are also to pray for God's protection from Satan: "Deliver us from evil [the evil one]." The book of Job illustrates what happens when Satan goes after us. We find another example in Luke 22:31-32; the Lord warned boastful Peter, "Satan hath desired to have you, that he may sift you as wheat: But I have prayed for thee, that thy faith fail not."

Paul too knew what it meant to be the subject of direct Satanic attack. He wrote, "Lest I should be exalted above measure through the abundance of the revelations, there was given to me a thorn in the flesh, the messenger of Satan to buffet me" (2 Corinthians 12:7). Whatever Paul's affliction was (epilepsy, bad eyes, or the like), the fact is that he had his "thorn in the flesh" and he called it "the messenger [*angelos,* angel] of Satan." Probably Satan, the prince of darkness, assigned one of his fallen angels to harass the apostle. His ever-active foe assailed him constantly, doubtless with evil thoughts, discouragement, and fear. Three times Paul prayed to be delivered from this harassment, and each time he was told that God's grace was his sufficiency. With such a dread evil spirit ever at his side, the apostle would be safe only as he prayed without ceasing.

Few of us could withstand such temptation, such constant personal attention from Satan and his agents. We are directed by the Lord to pray that we be led in safer pathways and that we be kept under direct protection.

vii. The Father's Power (6:13c)

As we read the closing of the prayer, our thoughts are again directed to God's throne and His interests, and we are reminded of God's power: "Thine is the kingdom, and the power, and the glory." Some scholars think this statement should be deleted, but the overwhelming number of codices contain it.

We have just been taught to ask for protection from the rebel prince of the power of the air, from the ominous prince of this world, a world that denies or defies God's kingdom, God's power, and God's glory. But now we are reminded that Satan is a usurper, that the kingdom is God's, that His power is omnipotent, that Satan is impotent before that power, and that God's glory will yet be displayed in this world. In other words, as the prayer draws to its conclusion, it reaffirms God's intention to set up His kingdom here in the millennial age when "all the earth shall be filled with the glory of the Lord" (Numbers 14:21).

viii. The Father's Permanence (6:13d)

The final phrase of the prayer, "for ever," teaches us to think of God's permanence. Well might we borrow the language of the hymn: "Change and decay in all around I see; / O Thou who changest not, abide with me!"[11]

(b) What the Lord Reiterated (6:14-15)

In an appendix to the prayer, the Lord picked up one of the petitions—the request for forgiveness—and expounded it. It is the only petition so treated.

The Lord presented the truth of verses 14-15 both positively and negatively so that there could be no mistake in interpreting it. "If ye forgive...If ye forgive not..." Unless we are willing to forgive others, and unless we are glad we have the opportunity of extending in some small degree the mercy and forgiveness of which we stand in such great need ourselves, we are not really penitent and therefore cannot receive pardon. God's grace is sufficient to bring us to such penitence.

c. The Disciplines of Life (6:16-18)

(1) The Question of Appetite (6:16a)

The only fast imposed by law on the Jews was that of the day of atonement (Leviticus 16:31). There are, however, other notable Old

Testament examples of fasting, often as a means of expressing national repentance. The whole nation fasted after the civil war with Benjamin (Judges 20:26). Samuel made the people fast after they had gone after the false god Baal (1 Samuel 7:6). In the time of Nehemiah the Jews fasted because of their sins (Nehemiah 9:1). Moses fasted for forty days to prepare himself for a fresh revelation of divine truth from God (Exodus 34:28). The Lord Jesus fasted for a like period prior to His confrontation with the devil (Matthew 4:2).

The Lord did not command us to fast, but neither did He discourage the practice. It is taken for granted in the sermon on the mount that we will fast.

(2) The Question of Appearance (6:16b-18a)

When we feel it necessary to curb our appetites, to impose on ourselves the discipline of denial, to bring the physical under the restraint of the spiritual, we must be careful not to let it show. As Campbell Morgan put it, "We are to have perpetual Lent in our souls and everlasting Easter in our faces." If our fasts are in any way designed to attract the praise of men, our self-denials are in vain.

(3) The Question of Applause (6:18b-c)

Fasting has its place, but we must observe two rules: beware of personal extravagances and beware of public exhibition. The classic example of a man who broke both rules is Simeon Stylites (A.D. 390-459). He did a series of astonishing things to bring his body under control and was canonized by the Roman Catholic Church for his incredible feats of asceticism. Once he had himself walled up in a monastery for the entire period of Lent. He devised all kinds of fiendish means of self-torture and he ended up on top of a pole.

His life on a pole began when he moved to a hillside not far from his monastery and perched on a pillar six feet high. There he sat with an iron collar around his neck, chained to his pole. Periodically the height of the pillar was raised until it was fifty feet high. His disciples had to climb a ladder to bring him such scraps of food as he would condescend to eat. Throughout the bitter cold of thirty Syrian winters and the burning heat of thirty Syrian summers, disdaining any shelter from wind or rain, frost or sun, he sat on his pole and in the end was rewarded by his church with sainthood.

To such excesses men will go. But when we fast, we are to make sure it is a secret between us and God.

2. Burdens Connected with Wealth (6:19-24)

The next theme of this great sermon is the desire for wealth. So many people are burdened not by the spiritual demands of life—almsgiving, praying, and fasting—but by such secular distractions of life as accumulating riches. The desire for material things is strong and subtle. After all, we live in a material world. We are surrounded by material things. We have to handle them. The key to acquiring them seems to be money; it can buy so much. Whether or not we will be distracted by money will be determined by certain choices we have to make.

a. A Choice of Loves (6:19-21)

We can set our affection on things on the earth, or we can set our affection on things above, where Christ sits at the right hand of God (Colossians 3:1-2). We can lay up treasure on earth, or we can lay up treasure in Heaven (Matthew 6:19-20). The Lord laid it down as a principle that our heart will be where our treasure is (6:21).

In Bible times much of what was treasured was in the form of costly fabrics—purple, and fine twined linen. Alongside that, the Lord laid the word "moth." Other treasure was in the form of costly metal. Alongside that, the Lord laid the word "rust." People put their treasures in safe places. Alongside that precaution, the Lord laid the word "thieves." When accumulating earthly treasure, we must beware of that which rots, that which rusts, and that which robs.

The Lord did not condemn all desire to accumulate treasure. He said, "Lay up for yourselves treasures." But He also said, "Lay not up for yourselves treasures." What He condemned is the useless practice of laying up treasure for oneself on earth.

The passion for possessions is not reviled but redirected. The Lord told us to lay up for ourselves "treasures in heaven." We do that by giving our time, talent, and "treasure" to forward God's interests on earth and promote the coming of His kingdom.

So we have a choice of loves. We can be taken up with things earthly or heavenly, and the Lord told us which of the two He would have us choose.

b. A Choice of Looks (6:22-23)

The Lord enlarged on His teaching about treasure by drawing our attention to the eye, which He said can be "single [clear]" (6:22) or "evil [out of order]" (6:23).

Most of my life I have suffered from astigmatism, a problem with the lens of the eye that causes rays of light to fail to converge in one point. As a result my vision is blurred. The Lord was saying that it is possible to have spiritual astigmatism. It is possible not to have things clearly in focus in our spiritual vision. He urged us to have a "single" eye, an eye that does not see blurred images, an eye that sees through the folly of laying up treasure on earth and keeps the next world in proper focus.

c. A Choice of Lords (6:24)

"No man can serve two masters....Ye cannot serve God and mammon," said Jesus. "Mammon" simply means "riches." The word translated "serve" is *douleuō,* akin to *doulos,* which means "slave." The word translated "masters" is *kurios,* which means "lord, absolute owner." So Jesus was saying that no one can be a slave to two owners. We cannot be a slave to material possessions and at the same time own the lordship of Christ in our lives. No compromise is possible. We have to decide which world we are going to live for and which master we are going to serve.

3. Burdens Connected with Worry (6:25-34)

Those who have wealth have one problem; those who have little or nothing of this world's goods carry quite a different burden. The former tend to be concerned with accumulating more and more; the latter are desperately trying to make ends meet. Wealth and worry are opposite problems, but they can be equally distracting to spiritual life.

a. Daily Life (6:25-26)

(1) Its Pressure Acknowledged (6:25a)

The vast majority of the Lord's people are beset on every hand by distracting worry in their daily lives. But He said, "Take no distracting thought" (6:25), for that is the real force of His words. Obviously we have to give some thought to our material needs; food and raiment are necessities. But we are not to be full of care about these things.

(2) Its Perspective Altered (6:25b-26)

We are not to be improvident; neither are we to be anxious. Three times the Lord commanded His people not to be anxious.

The first time (6:25) He said anxiety is unnecessary; the second time (6:31) He said it is unworthy; the third time (6:34) He said it is unprofitable.

The Lord's graphic illustration in 6:26 points us to the birds of the air. They do not plow and plant, sow and reap, and store up provisions in barns, yet God provides for them. There is not a millionaire in the world who could afford to feed all the birds for just one day, but God never stops feeding them. We are of much more value than the birds. God cares for them and of course He cares for us.

b. Divine Logic (6:27-32)

(1) Our Human Frame (6:27)

The Lord used two more illustrations to bring the divine logic into focus. First He said that no one can change his "stature" by being anxious. One rendering of this thought is that a man who is not as tall as he would wish to be cannot add a foot and a half to his height by worrying. Another rendering is that a man cannot add any time to his allotted life span by being anxious about it.

The only person who succeeded in increasing his life span was King Hezekiah. Fifteen years were added to his life and during that time Manasseh, his son and heir, was born to him. But when Hezekiah saw what Manasseh was like, he doubtless wished he had died at God's appointed time (Isaiah 38:1-5; 2 Chronicles 33:1-10).

(2) Our Halting Faith (6:28-30)

In the second illustration the Lord pointed to the common lilies of the promised land, gorgeous wildflowers equally at home in a cultivated garden or among the rankest weeds. These lovely lilies do not toil or spin, yet not even Solomon in all his glory ever wore such robes. If our heavenly Father can so richly array a wayside flower that is here for a moment and then gone forever, why can't we trust Him to take care of our material needs?

(3) Our Heavenly Father (6:31-32)

"O ye of little faith," the Lord had exclaimed in 6:30, as though astonished that any of God's children could doubt for a moment their heavenly Father's tender care. Now Jesus gave a command and offered comfort. "Don't worry about what you are going to wear" was the gist of the command (6:31). Then came the reassuring words: "Your heavenly Father knowcth that ye have need of all these things" (6:32).

c. Different Laws (6:33-34)

(1) What Must Be First (6:33)

"But seek ye first the kingdom of God, and his righteousness," Jesus said, "and all these things shall be added unto you." The things that God knows we need and that He has promised to provide are, when all is said and done, just things. What we are to seek is the kingdom of God. (This is the first of five times that Matthew used the expression "the kingdom of God"; also see 12:28; 19:24; 21:31,43.) If we are to be anxious about anything, it should be the affairs of God's kingdom.

(2) What Must Be Fought (6:34)

Here the Lord told us not to worry about tomorrow. Tomorrow may not come. Before tomorrow we may be taken home to Heaven. And even if tomorrow does come, God will sovereignly arrange its affairs. We are not to add tomorrow's cares to those of today.

"Sufficient unto the day is the evil thereof." The Greek word translated "evil" here embraces not only the calamities and afflictions of life, for the word's roots point to the origin of these things in sin. As long as we are in a sinful world, we will be beset by difficulties. God does not promise that tomorrow will not have its problems, but tomorrow, just as today, is in His capable hands. The Lord would not have us be careless or improvident or foolish in taking no thought for tomorrow; rather He would have us be trustful and take no anxious thought. He would have us live one day at a time. We should pray with the hymn writer:

> Lord, for tomorrow and its needs
>   I do not pray;
> Keep me, O Lord, from stain of sin,
>   Just for today.

There is an old fable about a clock that stood in the corner of a room, busily ticking away the hours. The clock, beginning to think and worry, said to itself: "I tick once every second. There are sixty seconds in a minute and sixty minutes in an hour. That means I have to tick 3,600 times every hour and 86,400 times every day. Then there's tomorrow and the day after that; days and weeks and months lie ahead. In a year I will have to tick 31,536,000 times."

The clock became discouraged and as it added the burden of unborn days to the burden of the present moment of time, it began to run more and more slowly until it almost came to a stop. Then the clock had an encouraging thought. "After all," it said to itself, "it's only a tick at a time." With that flash of insight, the clock gathered strength and carried on with its allotted task—measuring the passing moments a tick at a time.

E. The Disciple and His Behavior (7:1-29)

1. The Fool Exhibited (7:1-5)

Here the Lord forbade a censorious spirit. It is the height of folly to be critical of other people's sins and shortcomings, because all we do is invite them to pounce on our own. Besides, a critical spirit is foreign to that of our Father in Heaven.

a. A Word of Reason (7:1-2)

In 7:1 we are told not to judge other people. The principle needs to be understood in the light of other Scripture passages that tell us we are to judge certain things. Our understanding is also modified by studying the Lord's choice of words and the context in which the principle is stated.

Other Scripture passages indicate that the Lord's prohibition does not include judgment by civil courts, which are necessary in the control of crime in a sinful world (Titus 3:1-2; Hebrews 13:17; 1 Peter 2:13-15). Neither does the prohibition include judgment by the church of those within its fellowship who are disorderly or embrace false doctrine (Matthew 18:16-17; 2 Thessalonians 3:6,14; Titus 3:10). And the Lord did not forbid individuals to make judgments regarding those who do wrong (Matthew 7:15-16; Romans 16:17; 1 Corinthians 5:11; 1 John 4:1). What the Lord prohibited is censoriousness—a critical, faultfinding spirit that prompts us to condemn people without the facts and without remembering our own vulnerability.

In Matthew 7:1 the word translated "judge" is *krinō*. Since it is translated some ten different ways in the New Testament, context is an important factor in determining the word's significance in a particular passage. We can determine that here the Lord did not say "Judge not" in the sense of forbidding us to distinguish between this or that, for in the same context (7:6) He told us to be discriminating. He used the expression to warn us against coming to adverse conclusions about people in a condemning way. He warned us that if we foster a critical spirit toward others, we will reap what we sow. We can expect to be judged and condemned by others in the same way and to the same extent that we judge and condemn them.

b. A Word of Ridicule (7:3-4)

Using the words "beam" and "mote," our King James text shows its age. A beam is a massive piece of timber used for supporting a roof. A mote is a splinter. The Lord talked about the beam and the mote to ridicule the folly of a man pointing to a small splinter in someone else's eye while having an enormous piece of structural timber in his own.

Whatever fault we see in another person's life may be a mere splinter compared with the massive beam of our own lack of love. There is nothing more un-Christlike than a critical spirit. Once a person gets rid of his useless piece of lumber, he is able to see clearly how to help his brother get rid of the damaging splinter.

c. A Word of Rebuke (7:5)

The Lord rebuked the man with the beam in his eye and called him a "hypocrite." No one can hope to help another person while entertaining a censorious spirit toward him. The power for removing an offending splinter lies not in the ability to detect, expose, and condemn, but in a Christlike love that fills the heart with a desire to be helpful and kind.

2. The Father Extolled (7:6-12)

a. The Father's Love Revealed (7:6-11)

(1) A Warning Word (7:6)

The Lord told us that we are not to be censorious, but that does not mean we are to be gullible. We are to have a discerning spirit. "Give not that which is holy unto the dogs, neither cast ye your pearls before swine," He warned. We learn from the context of Peter's use of this warning (2 Peter 2:22) that we are to discriminate between the true and the false, between the child of God and the false teacher. Peter portrayed in vivid language those who resolutely set themselves against holy things but insinuate themselves in holy places in order to traffic in holy things for unholy reasons.

Both dogs and swine were regarded as unclean animals under the Levitical code (Leviticus 11:1-8). Dogs are ready to devour anything, be it the choicest morsel or the filthiest offal. Swine are more openly unclean, loving to wallow in the mire. By the comparison to dogs and swine, the character of false prophets stands exposed. God's people are sheep, not dogs; doves, not swine.

We are not to entrust spiritual things, valuable things, holy things, to those who have revealed themselves to be apostates, false teachers, false shepherds. Rather, we are to be discerning and withhold from such "dogs" and "swine" any place among God's people "lest they trample [holy things, pearls] under their feet, and turn again and rend [us]." False teachers see nothing of value in pearls (a fitting symbol of Christ's sufferings) or holy things. "Beware of dogs," Paul warned (Philippians 3:2). "Without are dogs," John declared when referring to those who are eternally barred from entering the gates of the holy city (Revelation 22:15).

Down through the centuries the church has been rent and torn by "dogs" and "swine." Constantine gave holy things to dogs when he espoused the cause of Christianity and threw open the doors of the church to the world. Paganism was baptized and Christendom was born.

(2) A Wondrous Word (7:7-11)

The Lord's warning word was followed by a wondrous word of invitation. Both the warning and the invitation revealed the Father's love.

(a) The Invitation Extended (7:7)

The Lord showed us how to know where to draw the line between a critical spirit and a discerning spirit. He knows our frame, so He did not give us a list of rules. He simply said, "Ask…seek…knock."

(b) The Invitation Expanded (7:8)

We can picture Him looking into the incredulous faces of His disciples who wondered how in the world anyone could possibly live the kind of life described in the sermon on the mount. He was well aware that no one had the wisdom or strength to keep His commandments, so He linked our impotence to God's omnipotence.

We must come to God and ask. That is, we must recognize our dependence on God. We must seek. That is, we must bestir ourselves; we must earnestly desire to live the life the Lord described. We must knock (*krouō*). That is, we must be importunate and besiege the battlements of Heaven and strike with determination at God's door (*krouō* is also translated "knock/knocketh" in Luke 11:9-10; 13:25). The Lord urged us to be importunate not because God is hard of hearing or slow to respond, but because we are sluggish and prone to give up. Let us remember that, as Campbell Morgan said, it is not a servant who keeps the door, but our Father.[12] And what a Father He is!

(c) The Invitation Explained (7:9-11)

We can rest assured that our Father will give us what we need. The Lord used the illustration of a *human father,* imperfect as he is, "evil" (7:11) as he is—grudging sometimes, harmful too at times— who knows how to give good things to his children. How much more our wondrous *heavenly Father,* who always knows what is best and always does what is right, hastens to supply our needs!

Would a human father mock his hungry child by giving him a stone instead of bread? (Satan would; he offered Christ a stone for bread in the first temptation.) Would a human father mock his hungry child by putting a harmful serpent on his plate instead of a fish? Of course not. Neither were these lofty principles given to us to mock us. All that we need in order to translate them into practice is available to us on request. We just have to ask our Father in Heaven.

b. The Father's Love Reproduced (7:12)

(1) The Golden Rule (7:12a)

The Father's love thus revealed is to be reproduced, so the Lord laid down what has come to be known as "the golden rule": "Therefore [because all the resources of the Father are available to us] all things whatsoever ye would that men should do to you, do ye even so to them." This statement has been called "the capstone of the whole discourse" and "the Everest of all ethical teaching."

In a negative form, the golden rule is found in the teachings of

Socrates, Aristotle, Confucius, Buddha, and Hillel. These people said in effect, "Don't do to others what you would not have them do to you." It remained for the Lord Jesus to change the rule from the negative to the positive and from the passive to the active—and to enshrine the rule in every thought, word, and action of His matchless life. And the distinctive genius of Christianity is that through the miracle of the new birth and the indwelling of the Holy Spirit, a Christlike life is made possible for the blood-bought believer too.

(2) The Great Revelation (7:12b)

"For this is the law and the prophets" is the Lord's final statement on the subject of the golden rule. Embodied in the Mosaic code and amplified in the prophetic word, the golden rule is the underlying principle of all morality. In modern phraseology, the principle is to put ourselves in the other fellow's place and then direct our conduct accordingly.

3. The Future Explained (7:13-14)

Christians are often accused of being narrow-minded and urged to be more broad-minded. We need to remember that we are to be as narrow-minded as the Lord demands and as broad-minded as He allows. In these verses about the road to Hell and the road to Heaven, the Lord put narrow-mindedness and broad-mindedness in proper perspective in the light of eternity. We are admonished to make the right decision when these roads intersect. Our decision affects the direction and destination of our lives.

a. The Road to Hell (7:13)

The road to Hell is the broad road entered by means of the wide gate. It is a popular road, crowded with the careless throngs of those who are blinded by the world. The broad path offers pleasure, promotion, possessions, power, and piety of a sort; customs and culture; and a varied menu of distractions and delights. Gifted men and great are on this road, as are all kinds of vices, vanities, and violence. Ever amid the violets lurk the vipers.

The broad way gets narrower as it goes along. It is brooded over by a lord whose realm is darkness, whose rule is bondage, and whose reign is characterized by revenge against God—revenge in the form of the ruin and damnation of mankind. This road offers no real joy, no genuine or lasting pleasure, and only fleeting moments of happiness at best.

Joy is found only in the presence of God and pleasures for evermore only at His right hand (Psalm 16:11). Since God is not known on the broad path, the devil can offer only synthetic pleasure. God has a monopoly on the real thing. Ever-increasing dosages for ever-diminishing delights is the devil's formula, as every alcoholic, chain smoker, drug addict, sensualist, and pleasure seeker knows.

The broad path gets narrower still as old age creeps in with its handicaps and limitations. Ill health becomes the norm, faculties begin to fail, friends die, and the way grows increasingly lonely and frightening. Then death comes and those who reach the bitter end of the broad road discover too late that Jesus was right all the time. It "leadeth to destruction." The word translated "destruction" in Matthew 7:13 is *apōleia*, which conveys the idea not of extinction, but of ruin—not the loss of being, but the loss of well-being. Here "destruction" refers to eternal spiritual perdition.

b. The Road to Heaven (7:14)

The road to Heaven is the narrow road entered by means of the narrow gate. The stringent precepts of the sermon on the mount make many think that this path is hopelessly narrow.

A false gospel circulating today is patterned after the slick advertising of Madison Avenue. One is almost led to believe that Jesus would have us mail out four-color brochures proclaiming to prospective tourists that the way to Heaven is one of guaranteed luxury—wealth and health all the way. Preachers urge us to practice "possibility thinking" and invite us to invest in Disney-World-style ventures. The Christian life is presented as a round of fun and frolic—to be poor or sickly is a sign of sin or lack of faith, and God, it would seem, wants us to be like the rich fool who boasted that he was "rich, and increased with goods, and have need of nothing" (Revelation 3:17). Such teaching is a Laodicean gospel for a Laodicean church in a Laodicean age.

Not so did the Lord depict the way to Heaven. He said we must begin at the "strait" gate—literally the "narrow" gate. At the entrance there are no giant posters offering material benefits, physical well-being, or escape from peril, persecution, famine, and sword. There is no implied promise that we can have the best of both worlds, no intimation that we can go on living the same old way and still be sure of Heaven.

We cannot enter at the strait gate and walk the narrow way and at the same time be tolerant of sin, expect the praise of men, hold hands with the world, indulge the lusts of the flesh, listen to the lies of the devil, and be in step with the spirit of the age. This world crucified our Savior and will be no friend to those who follow in His steps.

So the road to Heaven is a narrow way, but it broadens out as we grow in grace and increase in the knowledge of God. This road is a path of wonderful friendships—links of love forged with those of like precious faith. The road to Heaven is a path of intellectual challenge, emotional fulfillment, tremendous opportunity, and "joy unspeakable and full of glory" (1 Peter 1:8). The path broadens out and ends in the fullness of eternal life. As Solomon wrote, "The path of the just is as the shining light, that shineth more and more unto the perfect day" (Proverbs 4:18).

There is a narrow road that runs from earth to Heaven, and there is a broad road that runs from earth to Hell. But there is no road that runs from Hell to Heaven (Luke 16:26). The broad road intersects the narrow road at just one place: Calvary. At the cross one can leave the broad road, accept Christ as Savior, and start along the narrow way.

4. The Frauds Exposed (7:15-23)

a. Beware of False Prophets (7:15-20)

Right after warning us of two doors, two directions, and two destinies, the Lord said, "Beware of false prophets" (7:15). False prophets are Satan's emissaries to lure people along the broad road that leads to destruction.

(1) What False Prophets Pretend (7:15)

"False prophets," Jesus said, "come to you in sheep's clothing, but inwardly they are ravening wolves." They come wearing the outward garb of the genuine. They say the right things and do the right things. They do all they can to resemble the sheep in order to gain admittance and win acceptance by the true people of God.

It does not take them long to come. Look at the church at Ephesus for an example. It was founded by Paul on his third missionary journey, which included a three-year stay in Ephesus

(Acts 19:1-20; 20:31). The influence of that church led to the evangelization of numerous nearby cities (Revelation 2–3).

Paul left Ephesus for Europe, spent from three to nine months there (Acts 20:3), returned at length to Philippi (20:6), then went on to Miletus (20:13-17). He summoned the spiritual leaders of the Ephesian church to Miletus for a last conference. Paul had been gone for less than a year, but he could read the signs of trouble ahead. He warned the Ephesian elders:

> Take heed therefore unto yourselves, and to all the flock, over the which the Holy Ghost hath made you overseers, to feed the church of God, which he hath purchased with his own blood. For I know this, that after my departing shall grievous wolves enter in among you, not sparing the flock. Also of your own selves shall men arise, speaking perverse things, to draw away disciples after them (Acts 20:28-30).

Within three years or so Paul was writing to Ephesus, urging the believers to "keep the unity of the Spirit in the bond of peace" and warning them to "be no more children, tossed to and fro, and carried about with every wind of doctrine, by the sleight of men, and cunning craftiness, whereby they lie in wait to deceive" (Ephesians 4:3,14). He was also having to write a letter to the sister church at Colossae, warning the Christians there against the gnostic heretics. The wolves in sheep's clothing were already in the fold, and they were there to deceive and to destroy.

(2) What False Prophets Produce (7:16-20)

The ultimate test of a false prophet is not the attractiveness of his personality, the persuasiveness of his eloquence, or the size of his following, but his doctrine and manner of life.

We do not see the fruit of the Spirit in false prophets. As Paul reminded the Ephesians, "The fruit of the Spirit is in all goodness and righteousness and truth" (Ephesians 5:9). And as Paul reminded the Galatians, who were also being torn by wolves in sheep's clothing, "The fruit of the Spirit is love, joy, peace, long-suffering, gentleness, goodness, faith, Meekness, temperance: against such there is no law" (Galatians 5:22-23). False prophets are corrupt trees bringing forth evil fruit.

The Lord put it this way: "Ye shall know them by their fruits. Do men gather grapes of thorns, or figs of thistles?" (Matthew 7:16). In the end false prophets betray themselves for what they are by their doctrines and by their deeds. They are wolves in sheep's clothing and they produce thorns and thistles.

Thorns and thistles are emblems of the curse (Genesis 3:17-18). False prophets are accursed of God (Galatians 1:8-9). The Lord said they will eventually be "hewn down, and cast into the fire" (Matthew 7:19).

b. Beware of False Profession (7:21-23)

(1) A Test (7:21)

Alongside those who produce notably bad fruit are those who produce no fruit—nothing but leaves. They can be identified not by the religious language they use, but by what they do. It is whether or not a person does what the Lord says that proves whether or not he is a partaker of the kingdom of Heaven. To call on the name of the Lord continually, but never to do what He says is the essence of false profession. The Lord's penetrating question is, "Why call ye me, Lord, Lord, and do not the things which I say?" (Luke 6:46)

(2) A Tragedy (7:22-23)

(a) What the Lost Will Claim (7:22)

It is a tragedy that people who think they are doing the Lord's will in the realm of prophecy, exorcism, and miracles do not realize that Satan is adept at producing counterfeit phenomena. Today many who profess to speak in tongues and to proclaim prophecies are deceiving themselves and others with their so-called gifts.

What is presented as the gift of tongues is patently fraudulent, since the Holy Spirit Himself said that tongues would "cease" (1 Corinthians 13:8). The word translated "cease" here is *pauō*, which means "to stop, to come to an automatic end, to cease in and of itself." What is presented as prophecy is equally suspect. Some of it is extrabiblical and therefore unquestionably false. Some of it is vague rehashing of Biblical statements in or out of context and therefore redundant and deceiving. The Holy Spirit, through Paul, declared that prophecies too would "fail" (*katargeō*).

The word *katargeō* was used significantly by the Lord in His parable of the fig tree. In the story the owner pointed out the utter uselessness of the tree when he said to the dresser of the vineyard, "Why cumbereth [*katargeō*] it the ground?" (Luke 13:7)

Paul used *katargeō* again in 1 Corinthians 13:10, where it is translated "done away": "When that which is perfect is come, then that which is in part shall be done away." Quite evidently the Holy Spirit was indicating that the completion of the New Testament was the "perfect" thing that would render tongues, prophecies, and special knowledge redundant. Those gifts were necessary during the transition period when the Scriptures were being written, but are clearly unnecessary now.[13] How perilous is the position of those who profess to be the Lord's and produce as proof certain sign gifts that were declared by the Holy Spirit to be temporary and of no further relevance.

In Matthew 7:22 the Lord mentioned false claims of prophesying, casting out demons, and doing "many wonderful works" in His name. He repudiated it all. In our generation many make similar claims, but examination of their doctrine (or lack of it) shows them to be highly suspect. Indeed we are face to face today with a massive deception launched against the church by the enemy of souls. This campaign is supported by all kinds of phenomena of an excitable nature, much of which is clearly occult. The New Testament repeatedly warns us about the end-time occult invasion (2 Thessalonians 2:8-11; 1 Timothy 4:1-3; 2 Timothy 4:1-4; 1 John 4:1-3).

(b) What the Lord Will Condemn (7:23)

When warning about the advent of those who use His name, but are not really His at all, the Lord pointed to "that day" (7:22) as the time when they will finally be exposed for what they are: false professors of His name. The expression "that day" anticipates a coming day of judgment. The Lord's verdict will be terrible: "I never knew you: depart from me, ye that work iniquity" (7:23). To claim to have all the sign gifts, but not do what He says is to "work iniquity." The word translated "iniquity" here is *anomia,* which means "lawlessness." Anything done in His name that He Himself has not commanded is simply a form of lawlessness.

5. The Foundations Examined (7:24-29)

a. The Application of the Message (7:24-27)

The application comes in the oft-recalled parable of the wise and foolish builders. The difference between the wise man and the foolish man was not in the men themselves or in their materials. The difference was in their foundations. The story applies to those who are building character. The wise take the sayings of the sermon on the mount at face value and build on them. The foolish are familiar with the sayings, but discount them.

Some evade the application of the sermon. They say, "This teaching is Jewish and not for the church"; or "This counsel of perfection is impractical"; or "This is the rule of conduct for Christ's future kingdom."

Others find the sermon on the mount distasteful for various reasons. It is too confrontational for the timid. It calls for too much strenuous self-denial for the self-indulgent. Its beatitudes expose human nature. Its law of love militates against retaliation, rivalry, and redress of wrongs by legal means. Its path of sorrows, meekly borne, points only to a cross. Its unworldliness strikes at the roots of our pride.

The sermon on the mount is the largest body of Christ's teaching recorded consecutively in Scripture. The sayings have been preserved for us by the Holy Spirit (John 14:26) so that they might be obeyed (Matthew 28:19-20). The essence of the message is repeated in the Epistles. We find prohibition of oaths in James 5:12, nonresistance in 1 Corinthians 6:7, love toward enemies in Romans 12:20, fasting in 2 Corinthians 6:5, the peril of an unforgiving spirit in James 2:13, renunciation of wealth in James 5:1, and the command to seek the kingdom in 1 Thessalonians 2:12.

These sayings of Christ are the rock on which we are to build. When testing comes, the foundation will be everything.

The sayings of men are a foundation of sand on which the foolish build. The philosophies of eastern mystics and the dogmas of Roman pontiffs appeal to many. Principles of Mormonism, psychology, social science, humanism, Darwinism, or Marxism appeal to others. Some who build on sand are noble and sincere, and their religious and philosophical structures seem beautiful—their buildings and deeds are often more attractive than those of many churches. But when the storms come, all systems of doctrine and conduct not founded on these sayings of Christ will fall. We have His word for that. And great will be the fall. Only those structures founded on the rock will stand.

b. The Astonishment of the Multitudes (7:28-29)

The multitudes had never before heard anything like the sermon on the mount. Their rabbis gave wearisome, often false, and often frivolous expositions of the law.

The rabbis constantly referred to what this or that teacher had said. Already in Christ's day the "tradition of the elders" had assumed an authority greater than that of Scripture. According to the Jewish view, God had on mount Sinai given Moses both the written law and the oral law. Hebrew teachers inferred from Exodus 20:1 that along with the Bible, God had given the Mishna, the Talmud, and the Haggada "even to that which scholars would in latest times propound."[14] Traditionalism placed this oral law above the written law.

The rabbis had no system of theology—only a collection of ideas, conjectures, and fancies concerning God, angels, demons, man, his future destiny, his present position, Israel's past history, and her coming glory. Alongside what was noble and pure, the rabbis placed a mass of incongruities, conflicting statements, and debasing superstitions.[15] God's law was made void by rabbinic traditions, and the spirit of the law was crushed under an outward load of ordinances and observances. Judaism was no longer the pure religion of the Old Testament. The common people were oppressed by tradition and confused.

Then Jesus came, and His sermon on the mount blew all the cobwebs of rabbinic tradition away. He spoke with the authority of the living God, and the people could not help but contrast His teaching with that of the scribes. The mumblings heard in the synagogues could not begin to compare with the clear demands of the newly arrived King.

The King's Power

(8:1–9:38)

I. POWER OVER DESPAIR (8:1-4)
A. The Multitude (8:1)
B. The Man (8:2)
   1. The Leper's Condition
   2. The Leper's Coming
   3. The Leper's Confidence
C. The Master (8:3)
   1. He Touched the Leper
   2. He Transformed the Leper
D. The Mandate (8:4)
   1. A "No Talk" Testimony (8:4a)
   2. A "New Walk" Testimony (8:4b-c)
      a. A Revelation to the Priests of the Temple (8:4b)
      b. A Reverence for the Precepts of the Torah (8:4c)

II. POWER OVER DISTANCE (8:5-13)
A. A Noble Roman (8:5-7)
   1. The Place (8:5)
   2. The Plea (8:6)
   3. The Pledge (8:7)
B. A Novel Request (8:8-9)
   1. A Confession (8:8)
      a. Of Unusual Feeling (8:8a)
      b. Of Unusual Faith (8:8b)
   2. A Comparison (8:9)
C. A Notable Response (8:10-12)
   1. The Marvel of the Centurion's Faith (8:10)

        2. The Message of the Centurion's Faith (8:11-12)
        The Lord foresaw how:
          a. The Heathen Would Willingly Receive the Truth (8:11)
          b. The Hebrews Would Wantonly Refuse the Truth (8:12)
    D. A Natural Reply (8:13)
        1. The Healing Promised (8:13a)
        2. The Healing Performed (8:13b)

III. POWER OVER DISEASE (8:14-17)
    A. Peter's House (8:14-15)
        1. The Deadly Sickness (8:14)
        2. The Dynamic Savior (8:15a)
        3. The Devoted Servant (8:15b)
    B. People Healed (8:16)
        1. Power over All Manner of Spirits (8:16a)
        2. Power over All Manner of Sickness (8:16b)
    C. Prophecy Heeded (8:17)
        1. Where the Prophecy Is Found (8:17a)
        2. When the Prophecy Was Fulfilled (8:17b)

IV. POWER OVER DISASTER (8:18-27)
    A. The Setting (8:18)
        1. The Cause for a Move (8:18a)
        2. The Command for a Move (8:18b)
    B. The Scribe (8:19-22)
        1. The Promise Expressed (8:19)
        2. The Price Explained (8:20a)
        3. The Principle Exemplified (8:20b-22)
          a. The Supreme Example (8:20b-c)
            (1) The Rule the Lord Accepted (8:20b)
            (2) The Role the Lord Adopted (8:20c)
          b. The Second Example (8:21-22)
            (1) The Question of a Rival Loyalty Raised (8:21)
            (2) The Question of a Rival Loyalty Rejected (8:22)

    C. The Storm (8:23-27)
       1. The Tempest Stirred (8:23-24)
          a. The Coming of the Storm (8:23-24a)
          b. The Calm of the Savior (8:24b)
       2. The Tempest Stilled (8:25-27)
          a. How the Lord Rebuked the Troubled
             Elect (8:25-26a)
             (1) Their Understandable Fear (8:25)
             (2) Their Undeveloped Faith (8:26a)
          b. How the Lord Rebuked the Tempestuous
             Elements (8:26b-27)
             (1) A Great Calm (8:26b)
             (2) A Great Comment (8:27)

  V. POWER OVER DEMONS (8:28-34)
    A. The Danger (8:28)
    B. The Demons (8:29-32)
       1. Their Plight (8:29)
       2. Their Plea (8:30-32)
          a. A Significant Request (8:30-31)
          b. A Startling Result (8:32)
    C. The Departure (8:33-34)
       1. A Tremendous Story Is Told (8:33)
       2. A Tragic Stand Is Taken (8:34)

 VI. POWER OVER DIFFICULTY (9:1-8)
    A. The Case (9:1-2)
       1. The Place (9:1)
       2. The Paralytic (9:2a-b)
          a. His Friends (9:2a)
          b. His Faith (9:2b)
       3. The Pardon (9:2c)
    B. The Comment (9:3-5)
       1. What Jesus Saw (9:3-4a)
       2. What Jesus Said (9:4b-5)
          a. A Personal Question (9:4b)
          b. A Practical Question (9:5)
    C. The Cure (9:6-7)

      1. The Lord's Power to Cancel Sin (9:6a)
      2. The Lord's Power to Cure Sickness (9:6b-7)
    D. The Crowd (9:8)

VII. POWER OVER DISDAIN (9:9-17)
    A. Social Disdain (9:9-13)
      1. The Publican and His Hospitality (9:9-10)
        a. Matthew—The Willing Disciple (9:9)
          (1) His Doubtful Occupation (9:9a)
          (2) His Delightful Obedience (9:9b)
        b. Matthew—The Wise Disciple (9:10)
          (1) His Love for the Lord (9:10a)
          (2) His Love for the Lost (9:10b)
      2. The Pharisees and Their Hypocrisy (9:11-13)
        a. The Question Asked (9:11)
          (1) Whom They Asked (9:11a)
          (2) What They Asked (9:11b)
        b. The Question Answered (9:12-13)
          (1) By Illustration (9:12)
          (2) By Inspiration (9:13a)
          (3) By Implication (9:13b)
    B. Spiritual Disdain (9:14-17)
      1. The Implication Raised (9:14)
      2. The Implication Refuted (9:15-17)
        The revelation of:
        a. A Coming Dispensational Change (9:15)
          (1) The Bridegroom Present with His Own
              (9:15a)
          (2) The Bridegroom Parted from His Own
              (9:15b)
        b. A Complete Dispensational Change (9:16-17)
        The Lord had come:
          (1) Not to Patch Up the Old Garment—
              Judaism (9:16)
          (2) But to Pour Out the New Wine—
              Christianity (9:17)
             (a) A New Vitality to Be Provided for the
                  Word (9:17a)

(b) A New Vessel to Be Provided for the
Wine (9:17b)

VIII. POWER OVER DEATH (9:18-26)
A. How the Lord Was Revered (9:18-22)
1. A Daring Man (9:18-19)
a. Jairus's Approach (9:18a)
b. Jairus's Appeal (9:18b-19)
(1) The Immense Request (9:18b)
(2) The Immediate Response (9:19)
2. A Desperate Woman (9:20-22)
a. What the Woman Sought (9:20-21)
(1) Her Condition (9:20a)
(2) Her Confidence (9:20b-21)
b. What Jesus Taught (9:22)
(1) A Relationship with Her Lord (9:22a)
(2) A Reward for Her Life (9:22b)
B. How the Lord Was Jeered (9:23-25)
1. The Deluded Crowd (9:23)
2. The Dynamic Christ (9:24)
3. The Dead Child (9:25)
C. How the Lord Was Cheered (9:26)

IX. POWER OVER DOUBT (9:27-31)
A. Two Blind Men (9:27)
1. The Burden of Their Appeal (9:27a)
2. The Basis of Their Appeal (9:27b)
B. Two Believing Men (9:28-30a)
We see:
1. Jesus Testing Them (9:28a)
2. Them Trusting Jesus (9:28b)
3. Jesus Touching Them (9:29-30a)
C. Two Blessed Men (9:30b-31)
1. Their Transformation by His Word (9:30b)
2. Their Transgression of His Word (9:31)

X. POWER OVER DUMBNESS (9:32-34)
A. The Case (9:32a)

B. The Cause (9:32b)
C. The Cure (9:33)
   1. The Release (9:33a)
   2. The Result (9:33b)
   3. The Response (9:33c)
D. The Claim (9:34)
   1. Who It Was Who Spoke (9:34a)
   2. What It Was They Said (9:34b)

XI. POWER OVER DISBELIEF (9:35-38)
   A. Christ's Commission (9:35)
      1. Where He Went (9:35a)
      2. Why He Went (9:35b-c)
         a. To Teach Everyone (9:35b)
         b. To Reach Everyone (9:35c)
   B. Christ's Compassion (9:36)
      He was moved by:
      1. The Multitudes of Mankind (9:36a)
      2. The Misery of Mankind (9:36b-c)
         a. No Real Goals (9:36b)
         b. No Real Guides (9:36c)
   C. Christ's Compulsion (9:37-38)
      1. The Problem (9:37)
      2. The Prayer (9:38)

The sermon was over. The astonished multitudes dispersed and the awed disciples accompanied their royal Master down the mountain toward the lake. Everyone was digesting His new authoritative teaching. Who could He be, this man with such a revolutionary message of love? Could He indeed be the promised King of Israel? John the Baptist had proclaimed Him as such. Yet if He was the King, where was His power? Words were all very well— and His were beautiful, wonderful words. But what Israel needed was not just One who spoke with authority; Israel needed One who acted with power.

Doubts remained in the minds of the Jews, so Matthew brought together in this section of his Gospel a series of mighty miracles performed by the Lord—visible, unmistakable evidence of His kingly power. True, this King did not overthrow the power of Rome. Instead He overthrew the hosts of Hell. Matthew was true to his goal of keeping the messiahship of Jesus before the Jews when he recorded demonstrations of various aspects of the Lord's power.

I. POWER OVER DESPAIR (8:1-4)

A. The Multitude (8:1)

Matthew wrote that "great multitudes followed him." They had been following the rabbis. Some of these masters had embraced the harsh, austere teachings of Shammai and others had embraced the liberal teachings of Hillel. The rabbis told the Jews that the Torah had actually existed in Heaven two thousand years before creation; that the patriarchs (Abraham, Isaac, and Jacob) had known and observed all the ordinances; that Hebrew traditionalism had the same origin as the law itself.

The rabbis taught that the law had been offered by God to the heathen nations; that they had refused it; and that even if they were to repent, they would only prove themselves hypocrites. As for Israel, the Jews were told that although their good deeds might be few, the grand total of all the good deeds of all the Israelites would be a great sum. As for Israel's sins, God would exact payment in the way a man collects his debts from his friends—taking a little bit at a time. Such was the teaching of the rabbis.

No wonder we read that after the sermon on the mount, the multitudes followed the Lord. They wanted to hear more. They had heard enough of the teaching of the rabbis. The rabbis had the synagogues, but Jesus had the crowds. It was a good beginning anyway.

B. The Man (8:2)

The multitude had been gathered to listen to a most remarkable message. Now they were gathered to look at a most remarkable miracle. A leper came to Jesus and they saw the Lord demonstrate His power over the man's despair.

1. The Leper's Condition

Among the Jews, leprosy was regarded as the stroke of God, and not without reason. The cases of Miriam, Gehazi, and Uzziah gave weight to the view. Leprosy was incurable, ending in death. The disease began in a small way but spread inexorably, bringing rottenness to everything it touched. Victims were outcasts, the offscouring of the world. One such man now came to Jesus.

What could Jesus do for a leper? The man was held in the grip of a terrible, loathsome disease that alienated him from all men, forced him outside the camp, and took away all hope of ever being able to draw near to the altars of God. The scribes and Pharisees had nothing to offer him. The priests and Levites could do nothing for him. Neither could the rabbis and rulers. The Sanhedrin and synagogues wanted no part of him. The temple was barred to him and the law legislated against him.

The man's disease illustrated the ravages of sin in a human life. Leprosy symbolized the vile hold of sin, and the Lord had been advocating the highest, holiest, and most heavenly kind of life. What could Jesus do for him? The leper did not need the code of the sermon on the mount. He needed cleansing, and he knew it.

2. The Leper's Coming

Perhaps the leper had stood afar, straining his ears to catch a sentence or two of the new teaching. (The area has remarkable sound-conducting properties.) Perhaps he had heard Jesus say, "Your Father which is in heaven…maketh his sun to rise on the evil and on the good, and sendeth rain on the just and on the unjust" (5:45). Perhaps he had heard Jesus demanding love even for enemies. Perhaps he had heard Jesus say, "If ye then, being evil, know how to give good gifts unto your children, how much more shall your Father which is in heaven give good things to them that ask him?" (7:11) Perhaps he had heard Jesus say, "Give to him that asketh thee.…Turn not thou away" (5:42). Perhaps he had heard

Jesus say, "Ask, and it shall be given you; seek, and ye shall find; knock, and it shall be opened unto you" (7:7). Perhaps he had heard Jesus say, "Whosoever heareth these sayings of mine, and doeth them, I will liken him unto a wise man" (7:24).

Perhaps the leper said to himself, "I'll do it! I'll put those words to the test. I'll go to Him and see if He too, like all the others, will cast me out. He speaks with authority and not as the scribes. I'll put my case in His hands."

Doubtless the crowd saw him coming. They saw the leper's hand covering his lip and heard his terrible cry, "Unclean! Unclean!" Outraged that someone quarantined by law would dare to approach them, and alarmed for their own safety, the people scattered, leaving a wide swath through which the wretched man could pursue his determined course to Jesus.

In defiance of the law that barred him, the man came to Jesus. And wonder of wonders, the Lord did not flee or order him away. For many a long day only fellow lepers had allowed him to come near. And so coming to Jesus, he worshiped Him.

3. The Leper's Confidence

With remarkable faith and insight the leper brought his desperate case to Jesus. He "worshipped him, saying, Lord." (This is the first time Jesus is called *Lord.*) Perhaps the man had heard Jesus talking about those who said, "Lord, Lord," but did not do what He said (Luke 6:46); he was not going to be like them. If He were to send him away, he would go.

Since He had allowed him to come, the leper said, "Lord, if thou wilt, thou canst make me clean" (Matthew 8:2). The man did not say, "If you can, will you?" He said, "If you will, you can."

The leper asked for the impossible: "Make me clean"! He acknowledged how hopelessly defiled he was—through and through, vile beyond words—and prayed, "Make me clean."

C. The Master (8:3)

1. He Touched the Leper

Then Jesus did a lovely thing, something no scribe or rabbi would have done for all the wealth in the world. He touched the leper. No clean man, woman, boy, or girl had touched that poor man since he had become a leper, for to touch him was to be contaminated. If he came too close, people threw stones at him. But in an act of unutterable kindness, Jesus touched him. Here was a demonstration of amazing grace. Here was the golden rule in action.

2. He Transformed the Leper

Jesus said, "I will; be thou clean." Speaking thus, He claimed to be absolutely and altogether God. Our words at best are legislative. We can command and give orders, but we cannot translate them into instantaneous results. The Lord's words are not only legislative; they are also executive. He speaks and it is done. On the morning of creation He said, "Light be!" and light was. He said to the waters, "Bring forth abundantly," and life in myriad forms swarmed through the seven seas (Genesis 1:3,20).

Now "the Word was made flesh" (John 1:14) and He said to the leper, "Be clean." Matthew, who was there when the miracle happened, wrote, "And immediately his leprosy was cleansed" (8:3). Extraordinary! Amazing! The people had never seen anything like it.

D. The Mandate (8:4)

1. A "No Talk" Testimony (8:4a)

First Jesus enjoined silence on the healed leper. The Lord wanted the evidence of his cleansed life to do all the speaking.

2. A "New Walk" Testimony (8:4b-c)

a. A Revelation to the Priests of the Temple (8:4b)

Then Jesus sent the cleansed leper to the priests and told him to "offer the gift that Moses commanded, for a testimony unto them."

We can picture one of the priests returning home that night and saying to his wife: "Something happened to me today that as far as I know has only happened once before in history. A man came to me with two live birds, a piece of cedar wood, a bundle of hyssop, and some scarlet and announced that he was a cleansed leper. And sure enough, he was. He said he had been healed by Jesus of Nazareth. Not since the days of Moses has a cleansed leper presented himself to a priest."

b. A Reverence for the Precepts of the Torah (8:4c)

The ritual for the cleansing of a leper was detailed and lengthy, taking eight days (Leviticus 14:1-32). The wood was from the tallest, proudest tree of the forest, the cedar—speaking of the cutting down of pride. The hyssop was the lowliest shrub—for if pride is at the root of sin, humility is at the heart of its cure. The scarlet indicated that sin is a glaring matter and of the deepest dye. The priest took the wood, the hyssop, the scarlet, and two live birds and dipped them all in living, running water. Water symbolized the Word of God, the agent God uses to show us how desperate our condition is and how remarkable the cure.[1]

One of the birds was then slain over the running water, symbolizing the death of Christ in accordance with the Scriptures. The other bird was dipped in the blood of the dead bird—for identification with it. Along with the live bird, the cedar, hyssop, and scarlet were dipped in the blood—to show that there can be no putting away of sin in any of its forms apart from the shed blood of the Lord Jesus. The blood was sprinkled seven times on the cleansed leper— to convince him of the perfection of the sacrifice and to identify him too with the shed blood, apart from which he could have no acceptance before God. The live bird was then set free to fly heavenward, symbolizing the Lord's resurrection and return to Heaven.

Next the cleansed leper had to wash his clothes to symbolize his cleansing from the vileness of his former lifestyle as a leper and to remove anything remaining from his old life that might contaminate others. He also had to shave off all his hair, which suggested the active growth and natural glory of the flesh. The leper was pronounced clean, but as a special precaution for seven days he had to stay outside of his own tent, although he could remain inside the camp. The ritual reminds us that sin is dangerous and we cannot be too careful to make sure a new convert is truly cleansed before we receive him fully into the fellowship of God's people.

On the eighth day (the day of resurrection) if the man's cleansing was fully established, the remainder of the ritual was enacted. Now a much greater sacrifice was expected, for God looks for rapid growth in those He has cleansed, and a mature comprehension of how much Calvary means.

The healed leper had to bring two male lambs, one ewe lamb, some fine flour mingled with oil, and about a pint of oil to the priest. First the trespass offering was slain and then the sin offering.

The trespass offering had to do with the practice of sin, and the sin offering had to do with the principle of sin. Likewise Calvary takes care of what I do and what I am. The priest was entitled to keep these two offerings for his own use after they were slain and pronounced "most holy" (Leviticus 14:13). Since God had perfectly accepted the sacrifice, the priest could perfectly accept the cleansed offerer.

When the priest slew the trespass offering, he took some of the blood of the animal and put it on the cleansed leper's right ear, right thumb, and right big toe to symbolize a change in behavior. Henceforth the man must listen with a cleansed ear to what God had to say, put a cleansed hand to all his activities, and walk in clean ways pleasing to God. No one can do that unaided, so the priest next took the oil and anointed the man's ear, thumb, and toe to symbolize the fact that it is through the Holy Spirit that a new life becomes possible. But that was not enough. The priest poured the remaining oil on the man's head to symbolize his utter dependence on the outpouring and full anointing of the Holy Spirit to live a Christlike life. (Christ was symbolized by the head.)

Since a sinner usually understands first the seriousness of what he has done and later realizes the truth about what he is, the trespass offering came first and the sin offering later. The priest killed another lamb for the sin offering and afterward offered the meal offering (the flour) and the burnt offering (the third lamb) for the further instruction of the cleansed leper. The meal offering spoke of Christ's flawless life. The burnt offering spoke of His death. After the last offering, the cleansed leper was ready to be received into the full fellowship of God's people.

All this ritual was implied in the Lord's word to the leper in Matthew 8:4: "Go thy way, shew thyself to the priest, and offer the gift that Moses commanded, for a testimony unto them." What a testimony it was of a man cleansed and energized by the Holy Spirit to live as Jesus lived—to live the kind of life indicated in the sermon on the mount!

II. POWER OVER DISTANCE (8:5-13)

The Lord next displayed His power over distance. He does not need to be present physically to accomplish His purposes or to exert His influence and power. That truth should be greatly encouraging to us now that He has gone home to Heaven. Distance means nothing to Him; He can be here as well as there.

A. A Noble Roman (8:5-7)

We now read about a different kind of outcast—not a leper, but a Gentile, a Roman centurion. As far as the majority of Jews were concerned, he might just as well have been a leper, for all they wanted to do with him politically, socially, and religiously. The leper was outside the camp; the centurion was outside the covenant. The Lord responded to both.

We meet the Roman in Capernaum, where the Lord was residing. The centurion (commander of a hundred men, one-sixtieth of a legion) was the officer in charge of the Roman military detachment quartered there. Doubtless he had heard much about Jesus and may even have heard the sermon on the mount, for the mount was not far from where he was stationed. We learn from Luke 7:5 that the centurion had such a love for the Jewish people and such a reverence for Israel's religion that he had built a synagogue for the Jews at Capernaum. He must have been a man of considerable means to have done that. It was this noble Roman who came to Jesus to plead for healing for his servant who was desperately ill.

Disregarding all Jewish taboos about visiting a Gentile home, Jesus at once said, "I will come and heal him" (Matthew 8:7). We note not only the Lord's fine disregard for racial and religious prejudice, but also His marvelous assurance. He did not say, "I'll come and see what I can do." He said, "I will come and heal him."

The Lord's disciples and His Jewish audience must have been astonished at His willingness to touch a leper and visit a Gentile home. They need not have been, for He was simply practicing what He had just preached about love and availability and going beyond the call of duty.

B. A Novel Request (8:8-9)

1. A Confession (8:8)

The centurion, aware of how Jews in general felt about entering a Gentile home, said that he was unfit for the Lord to cross his threshold. Incidentally, he must not have been what the Jews called "a proselyte of righteousness," for as such he would have kept a home that met Jewish kosher standards. As it was, he simply and humbly accepted the fact that most Jews would consider his house defiled and anyone entering it defiled. With remarkable unselfishness as well as dynamic faith, he declined the Lord's offer to come to his home. "Lord," he said, "I am not worthy....Speak the word only."

2. A Comparison (8:9)

Then he compared his authority to that of the Lord and noted the similarity. The centurion was used to obeying and to being obeyed. The Lord also was under authority—perhaps the centurion had heard and understood the Lord's repeated references in the sermon on the mount to His Father in Heaven. And the Lord had authority—one word from Him and leprosy fled. There was no need for Him to come in person. All He needed to do was speak the word of authority and the servant's sickness would be banished.

C. A Notable Response (8:10-12)

1. The Marvel of the Centurion's Faith (8:10)

Jesus, we read, "marvelled" at the centurion's response. In the Gospels there are only two things at which Jesus "marvelled": this man's faith and the unbelief of His own people (Mark 6:6). The Lord admired the centurion's faith, was amazed at the intelligence of it, and commented on it right away.

2. The Message of the Centurion's Faith (8:11-12)

It was a moment of great joy for Jesus. Here was a Gentile believer, one of several in the Gospels whose confidence in Him heralded the coming harvest in the Gentile world. This man's faith was held up by Jesus as a warning to the Jews. If they persisted in refusing the offered heavenly kingdom, the offer would soon be transferred to others who would accept it. Many a Gentile would come from lands beyond the eastern and western boundaries of Israel and sit down with the Hebrew patriarchs in the kingdom of the heavens, while their native-born descendants would be cast into "outer darkness" where there is "weeping and gnashing of teeth" (8:12).

It is not certain whether the "outer darkness" refers to the darkness outside the lighted house of the Father, the darkness of Gehenna, or that place of hopeless, endless night inhabited by those eternally lost. The entrance to Gehenna, which was marked by ever-ascending smoke, was said to be in the valley of Hinnom between the two palm trees beyond the mountains of darkness. Symbolically Gehenna refers to what we call Hell. In 8:12 Jesus spoke of the "outer darkness" as being associated with "weeping and gnashing of teeth." The Jews associated "weeping" with sorrow and "gnashing of teeth" with anger. They thought Gentiles were children of Gehinnom, who could not possibly share in the feast of the Messiah. Jews were children of the kingdom, royal children, children of the upper chamber.[2]

It must have come as a shock to the Jews when the Lord reversed their cherished beliefs. He acknowledged that there were "children of the kingdom" and there was an "outer darkness" of rage and despair. Jesus confirmed that much. But He opened the royal family to all believers; He placed membership in the kingdom within reach of all who would believe, Jew and Gentile alike. And He warned that those who were Jews merely in name were in danger of the "outer darkness."

D. A Natural Reply (8:13)

During the Lord's comments, the Roman centurion stood there, drinking it all in. Then Jesus turned back to him and said, "Go thy way; and as thou hast believed, so be it done unto thee." And so it was. The man headed toward home and "his servant was healed in the selfsame hour."

III. POWER OVER DISEASE (8:14-17)

A. Peter's House (8:14-15)

Matthew called it "Peter's house" (8:14); Mark called it "the house of Simon and Andrew" (Mark 1:29). We would like to know a great deal more about it than we do. We do know that it was a fisherman's home and that Peter's mother-in-law lived there. (So much for Catholicism's championship of celibacy!) Probably Jesus was lodging there.

We learn from Mark 1:21-22,29-34 and Luke 4:31,38-41 that the setting for Matthew 8:14-17 was a sabbath day. The Lord had been to the synagogue, had healed a demoniac, and had evidenced such power that His fame had spread throughout all Galilee. Returning home, He discovered that Peter's mother-in-law did not have the usual festive meal ready; instead she was "sick of a fever." The Lord took the woman's burning hand in

His, "rebuked the fever" (Luke 4:39), and restored her to health. She got up at once, went to the kitchen, and "ministered unto them" (or as some translations put it, "ministered unto him") (Matthew 8:15). What a sabbath meal it must have been!

B. People Healed (8:16)

By now the sun was setting. All day long the news of what had happened in the synagogue and in Simon Peter's house had been filtering up and down the lakeside. As though in a body and by mutual consent, people began to converge on Capernaum. Heading straight for Peter's home, they brought with them demoniacs and diseased relatives, neighbors, and friends. Soon the house was besieged from all sides.

Matthew was there and he told of people healed—"all that were sick"! One word from Jesus and demons fled. One touch of His hand and sickness was banished. The world had never seen such a grand exhibition of power. There was healing for every affliction of body and soul. Not a single person was turned away.

How different are the circuses of today's so-called healers! If the Lord had performed His healing miracles the way modern healers perform theirs, the procedure would have been different indeed. Peter would have been sent into Tiberias to hire the stadium. Posters would have been put up to advertise His coming. There would have been a careful screening and conning of those to be healed. Signals would have been arranged so that His disciples could cue Him in on the kind of case that was coming on stage. There would have been psychological warming up of the crowds and repeated pressure to give liberally in the love offering for the healer and His ministry.

Some candidates for healing would have come forward and been slain in the Spirit, whatever that means. Other candidates, having been worked over psychologically, would have been healed of psychosomatic complaints. Others, not healed at all, would have pretended that they had been. Those who did not pretend would have been told that they had lacked sufficient faith. Some whose symptoms had disappeared would have gone home healed only to discover a few days later that their symptoms were reappearing. If anyone was genuinely healed, it would have been in spite of the healer, not because of Him.

But the Lord did not work miracles that way. He healed people completely. All of them. Permanently. Clinically. Undeniably.

C. Prophecy Heeded (8:17)

1. Where the Prophecy Is Found (8:17a)

Matthew pointed to Isaiah 53:4 and said that the marvelous miracles of healing performed by the Lord Jesus were a direct fulfillment of the prophet's word. "Esaias" said, "Himself took our infirmities, and bare our sicknesses" (Matthew 8:17).

2. When the Prophecy Was Fulfilled (8:17b)

Isaiah 53 is the great chapter on the atonement, the vicarious suffering of Christ on the cross for our sins. In Matthew the Holy Spirit was saying that Isaiah's verse about physical healing was fulfilled by the Lord Jesus in His earthly ministry, but that healing rested solidly on His future redemptive sufferings.

In dying for our sins He dealt with the underlying reason for sickness and suffering. The Lord fully understood that all the physical and mental ills He cured were caused, in the long run, by sin—not necessarily the sin of the individual sufferer (although there were times when that was so), but the sin rooted in the history of the human race. The Lord knew that His right to heal was derived from the fact that He would shortly suffer on the cross, that He would there deal with sin, the root cause of suffering.

In other words, the Lord's power was based on His passion. At Calvary He was going to get at the root, so now He could deal with the fruit. His miracles of healing were in anticipation of the power of the cross to deal with sin, root and branch.

We must be careful when we talk about Christ dealing with the cause of sickness on the cross. It does not mean that immediate physical healing was secured for *us* in the atonement. People who teach that are in error. They are also responsible for inflicting a great deal of mental suffering when they say that healing is always available today and that those who are not healed lack the faith required to receive it. Immunity from death is not our guaranteed right, and neither is physical healing. Ultimately freedom from disease and triumph over death will be ours through the cross—but that awaits what Paul called "the redemption of our body" (Romans 8:22-23).

IV. POWER OVER DISASTER (8:18-27)

As believers we are not exempt from the storms of life any more than we are exempt from sickness and death. The next demonstration of the King's power shows us how we can go through the storms with Him.

A. The Setting (8:18)

Jesus saw the multitudes. We of course would be impressed by that. We are very pleased when crowds of people come to our meetings, buy our books, and support our ministries. All too often we measure our ministries in terms of multitudes. But Jesus was too well informed to be impressed by crowds. When He saw the multitudes, He "gave commandment to depart unto the other side." The command was the first step in another demonstration of power—but it was temporarily interrupted by a scribe.

B. The Scribe (8:19-22)

No doubt the Lord's blunt teaching on discipleship was addressed as much to the curious crowds as to the scribe himself.

A scribe was a man of letters, an educated man, the kind of man considered qualified to teach in the synagogues. Ezra had been a scribe (Ezra 7:12). The priests were the official interpreters of the law, but the scribes, who formed an independent group (religious rather than political), functioned in connection with the development and use of the law by the Sanhedrin and various local courts. The scribes also concerned themselves with the sacred writings of the Jews, both historical and didactic, and were particularly zealous for the ascetic elements in Jewish life that helped seal off the Jews from the Gentiles. Reducing religion to external forms, and appending endless minutiae to the law, the scribes made life a burden for the common people. In the Gospels we often see the scribes siding with the Pharisees. As a class the scribes were in constant conflict with Christ, who sternly denounced them. They liked to be honored by men.

One such scribe, deeply moved by the evident authority of Jesus, now volunteered to become one of His disciples. The Lord did not reject him, but revealed to him the high cost of discipleship. Citing Himself as the supreme example, the living embodiment of that cost, He said, "The foxes have holes, and birds of the air have nests; but the Son of man hath not where to lay his head" (Matthew 8:20). Poverty was part of the curse He bore.

"Son of man" was the Lord's favorite description of Himself. This is the first of eighty-eight occurrences of the title in the New Testament.[3] It is the Lord's Messianic title, His racial name, His claim to kingship over all the earth.[4] "Son of man" occurs first as a title in Psalm 8, where the Lord's coming dominion over the earth is proclaimed. "Son of man" is the Lord's racial name (as the representative man) just as "Son of David" is His royal, Jewish name and "Son of God" is His divine name.

"Son of man" occurs in connection with the Lord's mission (Matthew 11:19), His death and resurrection (12:40; 20:18; 26:2), and His coming again (24:37-44). The title transcends Jewish millennial hopes. When Nathanael confessed Jesus as "the King of Israel," the Lord replied, "Thou shalt see greater things...the angels of God ascending and descending upon the Son of man" (John 1:49-51).

In the first New Testament occurrence of this important title (Matthew 8:20) we see the humility and rejection of the King. He has "not where to lay his head." In contrast, in the last occurrence (Revelation 14:14) He has "on his head a golden crown." The first emphasizes His poverty; the last emphasizes His power. The first brings into focus His first coming; the last brings into focus His second coming.

We are not told how the scribe responded to the way of the cross that the Lord set before him. At this point a man who was already a disciple volunteered for further service. However, he had a rival loyalty in his life. "Suffer me first to go and bury my father," he said (Matthew 8:21). Given the custom and idiom of the time, it is possible that his father was not yet dead. In other words, this man may have been saying, "I cannot leave my father. I have a filial obligation to him." By human standards this sense of duty would be admirable, but when placed in the context of loyalty to Christ, it was a denial of everything.

When a nation conscripts its young men for military service in a time of national emergency, it calls for complete allegiance. The rival claims of father, mother, brother, sister, wife, and children are not allowed to stand in the way of the call of duty. The call of country in time of war is to discipline, self-denial, danger, and death. How dare we offer our heavenly King a lesser allegiance than that which is demanded by our native land?

The Lord rejected this volunteer's terms. "Let the dead bury their dead," He said (8:22). He saw through the man's excuse. In those hot Bible lands the dead were buried the day they died.

Think again of what this volunteer actually said: "Suffer me first to go and bury my father." Now underline two words in that promise: *me first*. There, fully exposed, is the fallacy of his offer and the reason that the Lord was so brusque with him. You cannot say,

"Me first!" and be a disciple. It is an effective denial of the lordship of Christ. What Jesus said in effect to both the scribe and the volunteer was "*Me* first."

C. The Storm (8:23-27)

1. The Tempest Stirred (8:23-24)

The Lord and His disciples boarded a boat, and the Lord curled up on a cushion and fell asleep. He probably occupied part of the low bench in the stern of the vessel where the steersman sat with his hand on the tiller. If this is the same incident as the one recorded by the other Synoptics (Mark 4:37-41; Luke 8:23-25), this is the only time the Gospels record Jesus' being asleep.

He fell asleep and instantly all Hell was let loose on the lake. One of those squalls that arise so swiftly and sweep with such fury over the sea of Galilee came roaring out of the hills. The waves arose, lashed by the violence of the wind. "The ship was covered with the waves," Matthew wrote (8:24). "The waves beat into the ship, so that it was now full" was Mark's graphic description, doubtless drawn from Peter's recollection of the incident (Mark 4:37).

2. The Tempest Stilled (8:25-27)

When a ship is full of water it goes to the bottom—but not that ship!

> No water can swallow the ship where lies
> The Master of ocean, and earth, and skies.[5]

The disciples, however, were scared to death. They awoke the Lord with the fearful cry, "Carest thou not that we perish?" (Mark 4:38) The Lord ignored the insult bred of fear. "He arose, and rebuked the winds and the sea" (Matthew 8:26) just as He rebuked the fever and the demon (Luke 4:39; Mark 9:25). All were His creatures and responsible to obey His will. He said, "Peace, be still" (Mark 4:39)—literally, "Be muzzled."

Like dogs held back by a leash, the howling winds and heaving waves cowered and were still. Thus did the Lord calm the storm, but not until after He rebuked the disciples for their lack of faith. When He demonstrated His sovereign power, they were overawed. They marveled and said, "What manner of man is this, that even the winds and the sea obey him!" (Matthew 8:27) A sense of His deity swept over their souls.

"Why are ye fearful?" He had said to them (8:26). And indeed why are we so fearful when the squalls of life burst upon us? Surely the reason must be that we forget He is with us, come what may, and He is in complete control—even when He seems to us to be fast asleep and unconcerned about our worries, doubts, and fears.

V. POWER OVER DEMONS (8:28-34)

The perilous voyage was over. The vessel had arrived safely at the other side of the lake, probably late the same evening. We can picture the scene with the moon shedding its silvery light over the wild surroundings.

Midway between the north and south ends of the lake and straight across from Magdala was the village of Gergesa. Jesus seems to have landed a little to the south of this village. About sixteen miles to the southeast and about seven miles inland from the lake was the better-known town of Gadara. Still farther to the southeast and about fifty miles from Gergesa was the city of Gerasa. The whole region was known as "the country of the Gadarenes" (Mark 5:1; Luke 8:26) since Gadara was a key town with territory extending to the eastern shore of the sea of Galilee.

A. The Danger (8:28)

Two demoniacs materialized out of the shadows of nearby tombs. They were fierce men who so terrorized the neighborhood that "no man might pass by that way." One of the two seems to have been dominant, for Mark and Luke concentrated on him. Characterized by violence, uncontrollable rage, and suicidal and homicidal frenzies, he was an extreme manifestation of demonic power. These two demon-possessed men were more dangerous than the stormy sea.

B. The Demons (8:29-32)

Demon possession is a terrible reality. In civilized lands it is often confused with insanity. In insanity, the ability to see oneself as a distinct personality with mental, emotional, and volitional powers and moral responsibilities is impaired or lost. In demon possession, another (and evil) intelligence gains control of the person's consciousness. Demon-possessed individuals display more than one consciousness: their own and that of the invading demon or demons.

In ordinary cases of insanity, the power to originate rational responses is lost as a result of disease, vice, shock, or some similar cause. In cases of demon possession, the breakdown of rational behavior is caused by the presence of a superior and intelligent form of evil. The mental faculties and bodily members of the possessed individual are seized by the invading evil spirit. There is often a strange confusion of personalities, a diabolical mixing of the human and the demonic, as in the case of the possessed Gadarenes. Their words and actions sometimes seem to originate from the human source, and sometimes from the demonic source, with both sources being weirdly mixed together.

The dominant demoniac was evidently possessed by many evil spirits. Mark told us that when Jesus commanded him to speak his name and thus reveal himself, he answered, "My name is Legion: for we are many" (5:9). It has been inferred by some that this demented man was the dwelling place of six thousand demons, for a Roman legion had six thousand soldiers. In any case, many evil spirits swarmed in his tortured soul.

1. Their Plight (8:29)

The evil spirits in the two demoniacs recognized Jesus at once. They knew their peril. "What have we to do with thee, Jesus, thou Son of God? art thou come hither to torment us before the time?" they said. The demons knew they were unable to escape from Jesus. They knew His power and trembled at the thought that they were about to be consigned by Him to the eternal torments that awaited them. They knew too that their control over their human victims was about to be terminated by an authoritative word of command from the One before whom they now cowered.

2. Their Plea (8:30-32)

a. A Significant Request (8:30-31)

Knowing that eventually they would be incarcerated in the place of torments, the demons begged to be spared a little longer from their doom. They pleaded for a respite. A large herd of hogs was feeding nearby and the evil spirits requested permission to enter the bodies of those unclean beasts.

Demons appear to have a craving to embody themselves. Fallen angels do not seem to be driven with the same compulsion. We learn from Genesis 6 that certain angels sought to establish liaisons with women of the human race, but that is something different. Those fallen angels seem to have materialized physical bodies (as did the angels who appeared to Abraham and Lot in Genesis 18–19). Demons do not seem to be able to materialize such bodies for their own use, so they try to steal the bodies of human beings, which they thereafter possess. They are like unseen but terrible bacteria that torment their victims.

Why do demons crave embodiment? We are not told. One supposition is that they are actually disembodied spirits of an alien race who at some time in remote and unrecorded history lived on the earth. Because of their extraordinary wickedness they were unclothed of their bodies by an act of divine judgment.[6] That demons are wicked is the uniform testimony of the Bible, of those who have tampered with spiritism, and of those who have confronted demons on the missionfield.

b. A Startling Result (8:32)

So rather than be left unclothed, the foul spirits in Matthew 8 requested permission to possess the bodies of the swine on the nearby hill. The Lord replied in a single word: "Go." Matthew wrote, "And when they were come out, they went into the herd of swine." Preferring death to demon possession, the swine ran into the lake.

This demonstration of the power and authority of earth's rightful King is thought to have taken place about a mile south of Khersa, where a spur of the mountain juts toward the lake and comes within forty feet of the water. The slope is steep and narrow, and a herd rushing down would naturally end up in the lake and be drowned.

C. The Departure (8:33-34)

1. A Tremendous Story Is Told (8:33)

The herdsmen evidently saw the Lord's confrontation with the demoniacs. Being horrified at the destruction of the swine, they "fled, and went their ways into the city, and told every thing."

Doubtless the owners blamed the Lord for their loss. It should be remembered that pigs were unclean animals, proscribed by Mosaic law. The removal of this source of uncleanness was as legitimate as the confiscation and destruction of pornographic literature in a society trying to enforce decent moral standards.

2. A Tragic Stand Is Taken (8:34)

More concerned with the loss of property than with the healing of the demoniacs, the people of the city came to Jesus and asked Him to leave the area. We learn from the accounts of Mark and Luke that the man who once described himself as Legion pleaded with the Lord to be allowed to go with Him. Instead Jesus sent him home to be a witness among his own people.

Matthew assembled tremendous proofs of the Lord's power and as we read them, we say, "It is unlimited." Yet in this present age there is a limitation. Sadly, we may send Him away.

VI. POWER OVER DIFFICULTY (9:1-8)

A number of difficulties are woven into the fabric of the story about the palsied (paralytic) man. There was of course the obvious difficulty of getting the man to Jesus in the first place. There was the difficulty represented by the presence of the Pharisees and doctors of the law; this critical element was not noted by Matthew, but it was recorded by both Mark and Luke. There was the difficulty posed by Jesus to His critics: Is it easier to heal a man of his sickness or to forgive him of his sins?

A. The Case (9:1-2)

1. The Place (9:1)

The Lord returned to Capernaum where He made His home, presumably in Peter's house. We need to look a little more closely at this house. It must have been owned by a moderately well-to-do man, for besides a large family room, it seems to have contained a guest chamber for the Lord as well as accommodations for Peter and his wife and his mother-in-law. Edersheim pictured the Lord "standing in the covered gallery that ran around the courtyard of such houses, and opened into the various apartments. Perhaps He was standing within the entrance of the guest-chamber, while the Scribes were sitting within that apartment, or beside Him in the gallery."[7] The open court was packed with people, and overflow crowds spilled out onto the street.

2. The Paralytic (9:2a-b)

a. His Friends (9:2a)

Mark 2 and Luke 5 fill in details left out in Matthew. Four men, we read, were bringing their desperately ill friend to Jesus. Unable to force their way through the throngs, they carried the man up to the roof, either by climbing an outside stairway or by stepping from one flat roof to another as they moved through the neighborhood on what the rabbis called "the road of roofs." Arriving at their destination, the men wasted no time. They made an opening in the roof directly over where Jesus was teaching and carefully lowered their friend down on his pallet until he lay at Jesus' feet.

We can imagine the commotion caused by the noise on the roof and then the appearance of the paralytic. Doubtless the disturbance was followed by a suspenseful silence. All eyes moved up to the faces peering from above, then down to the pale face of the paralytic, and over to the cheerful face of Jesus. Especially attentive were the Pharisees and doctors of the law who "were come out of every town of Galilee, and Judaea, and Jerusalem." They had come, it seems, to arrive at some kind of decision with regard to this new prophet whose teachings and miracles were creating such a stir.

b. His Faith (9:2b)

Jesus looked into the hearts of all there. He saw the faith— glorious, mountain-moving faith—in the hearts of the paralytic and his friends. He saw the fear in the patient's heart too, fear made more deadly by his conviction of sin and his hopeless condition. The Lord saw the frowns on the faces of the Pharisees and read the critical thoughts of those religious authorities—they were waiting for just one wrong word or act.

3. The Pardon (9:2c)

Jesus looked at the man lying at His feet. "Son, be of good cheer; thy sins be forgiven thee." A literal translation would read, "Your sins have been and are forgiven." Whatever else the startled scribes expected, it wasn't that!

B. The Comment (9:3-5)

1. What Jesus Saw (9:3-4a)

The inner reaction of the scribes was instantaneous: "This man blasphemeth" (9:3). We can date from this point the beginning of the official hostility toward Jesus that developed into a fourfold antagonism and in the end culminated in His death. The fourfold claim of Jesus' enemies was that (1) He was a blasphemer, (2) He made friends with known publicans and sinners, (3) He neglected His religious duties as defined by the rabbis, and (4) He violated the sabbath. Jesus knew their thoughts and went right to the heart of the matter.

2. What Jesus Said (9:4b-5)

He said, "Wherefore think ye evil in your hearts? For whether is easier, to say, Thy sins be forgiven thee; or to say, Arise, and walk?"

The critics seemed to think that the Lord was unable to perform the miracle. *It was one thing for Him to dupe the masses,* they thought, *but now He is talking to the learned men of the land, the custodians of Jewish religion, doctors of the law. He will not be able to hoodwink us. He is trying to save face by resorting to high-flown words. He has exposed Himself for what He is, a blasphemer.*

Jesus knew their thoughts, as He knows ours. He cut right to the bone. Either He was a blasphemer arrogating to Himself the right to forgive sin, or He was God. That possibility they refused to entertain for a moment, even though no other man had ever spoken as He spoke or performed miracles as He did. (The scribes were correct in thinking that only God can forgive sin. He does not share that right with others; it is His own prerogative.)

C. The Cure (9:6-7)

The Lord cured the paralytic of both his *sin* and his *sickness* "that ye may know that the Son of man hath power [authority] on earth to forgive sins" (9:6). Note that the Son of man is the Son of God. He possesses the divine attributes and wields the divine prerogatives. He has the power to forgive sins *on earth;* that is, if sins are to be forgiven at all, they must be forgiven on earth. And He is the One who forgives them. It is no use taking our sins to a priest; we must take them to Jesus. Once we leave this life, it is too late to have our sins forgiven.

Jesus turned to the paralytic. "Arise," He said. The man arose and walked on his own two legs to his house. It was evident that if Jesus could thus authoritatively banish sickness, He could also authoritatively banish sin. Both powers hinged on His anticipated death on the cross. Jesus had proved His point. He had power on earth to forgive sins; He was not a blasphemer.

D. The Crowd (9:8)

The multitudes marveled. We are not told what the reaction of the authorities was at the time, but we know that they were soon to have new opportunities to become hardened in their unbelief and to become the Lord's unyielding foes.

VII. POWER OVER DISDAIN (9:9-17)

Matthew next gave two examples of the growing disdain that the Pharisees and their kind harbored in their hard and unbelieving hearts. The first example is of social disdain (9:9-13) and the second is of spiritual disdain (9:14-17). The first example was connected with Matthew's call, and the second grew out of his conversion. The Lord proved Himself to be Master over this kind of religious snobbery.

A. Social Disdain (9:9-13)

1. The Publican and His Hospitality (9:9-10)

a. Matthew—The Willing Disciple (9:9)

(1) His Doubtful Occupation (9:9a)

The Hebrews hated tax collectors because the collectors were Jews so lost to honor that they stooped to serve the hated Romans. There were two classifications of tax men: the ordinary tax collector; and the customhouse official called the *douanier.* The Jews especially despised the latter.

The office of *douanier* gave the appointee great power to enrich himself, vent his spite on people, play favorites, and inflict hardship. The customs official could force merchants to stop their journeys, unload their beasts, and open every bale and package; he could rifle through it all, read private letters, exact his dues, and generally make life miserable. Taxes and tolls were levied against rich and poor. There were bridge tolls, road taxes, harbor dues, property taxes—as many assessments as rapacious ingenuity could invent.

Matthew, a publican of the hated *douanier* class, had his toll booth at Capernaum. The synagogue of course was closed to him, but doubtless he had often seen Jesus elsewhere. Matthew had probably heard Him speak, seen His miracles, witnessed His grace and love, and longed to be set free from his chains so that he could follow such a Master. Certainly he knew Peter, James, John, and the other fishermen and shipowners of Capernaum, but there was no way such respected men would associate with him.

(2) His Delightful Obedience (9:9b)

Then suddenly Heaven opened up before Matthew. Jesus approached his toll booth and said: "Follow me"! That was all. There were no preliminaries, no prolonged appeals, no invitation to think it over. Jesus knew His man, read his heart, understood his longings, and issued His challenge. Glory filled Matthew's soul "and he arose, and followed him." That was that. As a result we have in our hands today the Gospel that bears his name.

b. Matthew—The Wise Disciple (9:10)

Matthew exhibited *his love for the Lord* and *his love for the lost.* The converted tax collector arranged a party and invited his former friends—those classified contemptuously by the Pharisees as "publicans and sinners"—to come and meet his new Master and His friends. What a sensible thing to do! All new converts should follow his example. Such parties would soon put distance between them and undesirable companions as well as give former friends the opportunity to become followers of Jesus too.

2. The Pharisees and Their Hypocrisy (9:11-13)

a. The Question Asked (9:11)

(1) Whom They Asked (9:11a)

Observing Matthew's party, the Pharisees were sure they had been right in the matter of the paralytic. No self-respecting religious Jew would consort with "sinners." It was suspicious enough that this so-called Messiah's disciples were an odd assortment of fishermen and other "unlearned and ignorant men" (Acts 4:13), but the choice of a publican was the last straw. With calculated cunning the Pharisees approached not Jesus, of whom they were in awe, but His disciples, who they thought were easy prey.

(2) What They Asked (9:11b)

"Why eateth your Master with publicans and sinners?" the Pharisees demanded. The disciples didn't know what to say. It may well be they were doubtful about the matter themselves. The sermon on the mount had not yet taken deep root in their thinking.

b. The Question Answered (9:12-13)

(1) By Illustration (9:12)

The Lord, however, was ready for His critics. In one of His classic utterances He said, "They that be whole need not a physician, but they that are sick." In other words, the great physician demanded, "If a doctor only had patients who enjoyed good health, what kind of doctor would he be?" A doctor goes where sick people are. The reason he's a doctor is to help the sick.

(2) By Inspiration (9:13a)

"Go ye and learn," the Lord added, applying a well-known rabbinic formula used by Jewish teachers when confronted with superficial knowledge. His critics thought they knew so much about the law, and Jesus said, "Go ye and learn"! He directed them to Hosea 6:6 and repeated the gist of it: "I will have mercy, and not sacrifice."

(3) By Implication (9:13b)

The reference to Hosea was appropriate, for that book deals with spiritual adultery and harlotry. The burden of the book grew out of the tragedy in Hosea's family life, and the prophet's task was to show Israel the heart of God, broken over their hardness and sin. God was saying to Israel, "You bring Me sacrifices as though I had some need for them. What I want is to show you mercy."

Jesus, talking to those who thought they were teachers, was saying, "Go and learn the heart of God. Then you will understand why I sit with publicans and sinners." Summarizing His answer to the hypocritical Pharisees, the Lord said, "I am not come to call the righteous, but sinners to repentance" (Matthew 9:13).

B. Spiritual Disdain (9:14-17)

The next challenge came from an unexpected quarter. The disciples of John the Baptist approached the Lord with a question that was troubling them. Their problem lay in the fact that John was an ascetic. His life was almost one continual fast; he ate only Spartan fare—locusts and wild honey. Naturally then, John's disciples thought that asceticism was the way to a truly holy life. In this they had the support of the Pharisees, who placed a great deal of spiritual stock in fasting.

1. The Implication Raised (9:14)

John's followers asked Jesus, "Why do we and the Pharisees fast oft, but thy disciples fast not?" They were implying, as so many religious people do, that there is something suspicious about a belief that makes a person happy. Religion, they think, ought to be gloomy, a matter of stern discipline and self-denial.

2. The Implication Refuted (9:15-17)

The Lord answered with an illustration drawn from the marriage customs of the Jews. The "children of the bridechamber" (9:15) were the bridegroom's friends who went with him to the bride's house, where they were entertained with a seven-day feast. How inappropriate it would have been for the bridegroom's friends to pour cold water on this festive time by announcing that they were fasting and ought not to make merry—they would fast, not feast.

a. A Coming Dispensational Change (9:15)

Along with the illustration, the Lord revealed to John's disciples that a change was coming. The Bridegroom would not always be present; He was to be taken away. The Lord foretold the removal of His visible presence, the coming change in the dispensations, and the dawning of an age during which the Lord would be absent. "Then shall they fast," He added, indicating that fasting would be more appropriate to our age than to John's day. But He did not command fasting. The apostolic church knew nothing of fasting. Arranged fasts become formal and burdensome, a religious duty of no value.

b. A Complete Dispensational Change (9:16-17)

The Lord had not come to patch up the old garment of Judaism. John's disciples thought Jesus had come to reform their religion, but they were wrong. Judaism was obsolete. It was to be rent as a veil is rent. The new cloth of the kingdom was too strong to be patched onto the tatters of rabbinic Judaism. The two were incompatible. It made no sense to tear the new dispensation to pieces to try to salvage the old. The disciples had already shown how easily holes could be torn in Judaism, just by not fasting.

Jesus had come to pour out the new wine of Christianity. Men do not "put new wine into old bottles," He said (9:17). In His day wine was stored in containers made of skin, usually goat skin. New containers had a measure of elasticity and could expand as the pressure of the fermenting wine within increased. Old containers became stiff and lost their resilience; it would be foolish to put new wine in them. This illustration was the Lord's clear declaration that the old dispensation was to be replaced by the new.

The old was right for its day and age. But now it was time for the new—a new dispensation, a new covenant, a new dynamic, new principles, new life, new methods, a new "container."

Christianity was to replace Judaism altogether. The church is not Israel, but something entirely new and unique in God's dealings with men. Those who would equate the church with Israel introduce Judaistic forms, ceremonies, and rules into Christianity. The result of trying to make a patchwork quilt of Judaism and Christianity is confusion. The outcome of such a misconception of Christianity is Christendom with its priests, sacraments, feasts, fasts, holy days, rituals, calendars, and liturgies. The Lord envisioned no such thing. He gave the disciples of John a lot to think about as they went away.

VIII. POWER OVER DEATH (9:18-26)

Next Matthew recorded one of the Lord's greatest miracles: the resurrection of Jairus's daughter. Jesus raised three people from the dead during the course of His ministry and each of the four evangelists recorded at least one miracle of resurrection. The Lord

raised Jairus's daughter, who had just died; a young man on his way
to burial; and Lazarus (the only one named), who had been dead
four days and whose body in that hot climate had already begun to
decay.

A. How the Lord Was Revered (9:18-22)

1. A Daring Man (9:18-19)

a. Jairus's Approach (9:18a)

The Lord was greatly respected by one of the Jewish rulers in
Capernaum. Mark and Luke gave his name as Jairus. Possibly he was
the ruler of the Capernaum synagogue in which the Lord must have
spoken often—with his consent and by his invitation. Into the life
of Jairus had come a great sorrow: his little girl was desperately ill.
The other Gospels tell us she was twelve years old (Mark 5:42; Luke
8:42), the technical age at which a Jewish boy became a man and a
Jewish girl matured. After twelve years of sunshine, death was
casting its dark shadow.

Jairus made up his mind to approach Jesus. We wonder why it
took him so long, why he waited until the last minute when death
was already coming in at the door. We wonder why so many wait
so long to come to Jesus, why so many never come at all. Perhaps
the ruler of the synagogue was afraid of being criticized by his
colleagues. Perhaps he was intimidated by the fact that the tide
of official opinion was beginning to turn against Jesus. But at last
he swallowed his pride, banished his fears, summoned his faith,
and went to Jesus. Perhaps his wife had said something to urge
him on.

b. Jairus's Appeal (9:18b-19)

(1) The Immense Request (9:18b)

"My daughter is even now dead," Jairus said, "but come and lay
thy hand upon her, and she shall live." We learn from the other
Gospels that at this point the little girl was still alive. The distraught
father, however, had left her dying and had no doubt that by now
she was already dead. He had sat by too many deathbeds to have any
illusions about the terminal nature of his daughter's disease or to
cherish any hope that she could survive the death struggles that had
already started when he rushed out of the house.

(2) The Immediate Response (9:19)

The Lord needed no urging. "Jesus arose, and followed him, and so did his disciples," wrote Matthew. ("His disciples" now included Matthew, for he recorded his conversion in 9:9.)

Hope sprang up in the ruler's heart, only to be dashed. There was an interruption and how the distracted father must have fretted at the delay! Anyone with an ounce of imagination can picture the despair on this father's face and read the new fears and frustrations that besieged his heart.

2. A Desperate Woman (9:20-22)

The woman who caused the interruption intended to do no such thing. The last thing she wanted was to draw attention to herself. All she wanted was to sidle up to Jesus, experience His blessing, then melt quietly and quickly away into the throng.

It was the Lord who caused the delay. Perhaps He wanted to rebuke Jairus for his delay in coming. Doubtless He wanted to address the poor woman. Perhaps, as in the case of Lazarus (John 11:6,15), He delayed going so there would be no doubt that He had actually raised the dead.

a. What the Woman Sought (9:20-21)

(1) Her Condition (9:20a)

The woman had an incurable hemorrhage. It had plagued her for twelve years. I think that the Holy Spirit would have us compare the twelve years of joy associated with Jairus's daughter and the twelve years of misery associated with the desperate woman.

The other Gospels add details regarding the woman's condition. She had spent all her money trying to find a cure. Luke, who was a doctor, said that no physician had been able to heal her (8:43). Mark, looking at the case from a layman's point of view, was more caustic; he said that she "had suffered many things of many physicians...and was nothing bettered, but rather grew worse" (5:26). The doctors had taken her money, treated her inadequately, caused her unnecessary pain, built up her hopes, dashed them, and left her worse than they had found her. Now she made up her mind to come to the great physician who never lost a case and never charged a fee.

The woman's disease rendered her ceremonially unclean and,

according to Mosaic law, excommunicated her (Leviticus 12:1-7). Everything she touched was considered unclean (15:19-33). The same Levitical law gave the husband of such a woman the right to divorce her (Deuteronomy 24:1).

Here then was a wretched woman whose case was in many respects as bad as that of a leper. She had lost everything worth having in life: religious consolation, family care, social standing, financial security. No wonder Jesus took time to minister to her in such a special way.

(2) Her Confidence (9:20b-21)

We can understand the woman's anxious desire not to be seen. Not only was there the Levitical curse of defilement; there was also a natural reticence that would make it hard for her to mention her condition to Jesus in front of strangers. Her sole desire was to "touch his garment" (Matthew 9:21). She had no doubt that if she did, she would be made whole. And so she "touched the hem of his garment" (9:20).

Jesus of course dressed like other Jews. His headdress was similar to that worn by Arabs in the Middle East today; it descended over the back of His neck and shoulders. His shoes were sandals and His inner garment was a close-fitting tunic, the seamless robe for which the soldiers gambled at Calvary. Around the middle of the tunic was a girdle and over it was a square outer garment with customary fringes demanded by the Mosaic law (Numbers 15:37-41; Deuteronomy 22:12). The fringes were originally blue, the color of heaven, to remind Israel of their high and heavenly calling among the nations. It was one of those fringes that the woman touched.

b. What Jesus Taught (9:22)

(1) A Relationship with Her Lord (9:22a)

The woman was seeking to lose herself in the crowd when Jesus called to her. Seeing the fear, alarm, and dismay on her face, He said a lovely thing: "Daughter." She was ostracized by her family, but He put her in His family.

(2) A Reward for Her Life (9:22b)

The Lord continued, "Be of good comfort; thy faith hath made thee whole." Matthew wrote, "And the woman was made whole from that hour." She was instantly healed. Mission accomplished!

B. How the Lord Was Jeered (9:23-25)

1. The Deluded Crowd (9:23)

The other Synoptics tell us that at this point news was brought to Jairus that his daughter had died. The Gospel of Matthew hurries us on to his house.

By the time Jairus and the Master arrived at the house, it was crowded with mourners, for everyone in town knew the ruler of the synagogue. Funerals were not delayed in that hot climate. Mourning began at the moment of death and was always noisy. There were frantic demonstrations of sorrow. To the loud lamentations and genuine grief of the bereaved were added the wailings of professional mourners and the doleful music of hired flute players.

2. The Dynamic Christ (9:24)

Jesus took it all in with one glance. "Give place," He said. In other words, "Get out!" If the mourners were startled by that, they were even more astonished by what He said next: "The maid is not dead, but sleepeth." Matthew recorded the reaction of the crowd: "They laughed him to scorn." Luke added, "…knowing that she was dead" (8:53). When the Lord had arrived, the people were lamenting. Two minutes later they were laughing—at Him. He ignored their rudeness. He simply evicted them all; He bundled them unceremoniously out of the house. (Some people simply have to be put out if we are to expect the Lord to do anything.)

Then Jesus performed the miracle. The parallel Scriptures reveal that only five people witnessed it: the parents, Peter, James, and John. But the reality of it was soon known to all.

3. The Dead Child (9:25)

Jesus had said that the little girl was asleep, but He was referring of course to the sleep of the body in death. The soul never sleeps. It never gets tired. It is made in the deathless, tireless image of God and is engineered for eternity. The child's body was dead, but Matthew said that the Lord "went in, and took her by the hand, and the maid arose."

Once when D. L. Moody was asked to speak at a funeral, he

thought he would use one of the Lord's funeral messages as his topic. But he couldn't find one. Moody discovered that Jesus broke up every funeral He attended.

According to Mark and Luke, Jesus did say something at the funeral for Jairus's daughter. Mark 5:41 says, "He took the damsel by the hand, and said unto her, Talitha cumi; which is, being interpreted, Damsel, I say unto thee, arise." Literally translated, Jesus said, "Little lamb, I say unto thee, arise." How inexpressibly lovely!

C. How the Lord Was Cheered (9:26)

Matthew added a footnote: "And the fame hereof went abroad into all that land."

IX. POWER OVER DOUBT (9:27-31)

A. Two Blind Men (9:27)

Two blind men followed the Lord from the house of Jairus to the house of Simon Peter. All the way they had one persistent cry: "Thou son of David, have mercy on us." Their appeal emphasized their belief that Jesus was indeed the Messiah.

Perhaps one reason He did not heal them at once lay in the fact that they believed in His messiahship. It was a delight to His heart to find two people who really and truly believed. So many were only half convinced, in spite of all He had said and done. Even though the crowds were excited about the raising of Jairus's daughter, they still had no real conviction that Israel's promised Messiah had at last come. So He let the two blind men proclaim their message— He let the physically blind tell the spiritually blind that He was the Son of David. The blindness of the milling multitudes was far greater than the blindness of the two men; otherwise all of them would have been proclaiming Him the Son of David.

Jesus is called the Son of David because He was promised directly to David (2 Samuel 7:12,16) and because He was heir to David's throne. The title occurs nine times in Matthew, first in the genealogy of Jesus. Matthew was determined to convince the Jews that the One they had murdered was indeed their Messiah. The second occurrence is in 9:27; here Matthew picked up the words of the blind men and wrote them down in his Gospel for poor blind Israel (Romans 11:25). In the end Jesus used the title Himself to silence unbelievers (Matthew 22:42-46).

B. Two Believing Men (9:28-30a)

In this portion of Scripture the movement is threefold: testing, trusting, touching. Here we see the faith of the blind men.

Doubtless the two men could not understand why Jesus did not stop on the way and heal them, but they were made of sterner stuff than to give up. The good steel of their faith had been tempered and made strong by their need. Probably the crowd tried to silence them because their clamor was getting on their nerves, but the blind men refused to be quiet. In the teeth of opposition and in defiance of their critics, they continued to cry for mercy from the Son of David.

Still echoing their persistent cry, the blind men forced their way into Peter's house. Jesus at last turned to them. Having allowed them to pour out their hearts, He put them to the test: "Believe ye that I am able to do this?" (9:28) When performing His earlier miracles, Jesus had not been so insistent about testing the petitioner. But now that proofs of His claims were accumulating, He demanded a more definite statement of faith. From the blind men, the answer was forthcoming instantly. They had no doubt. If He could raise the dead, He could cure blindness. "Yea, Lord," they eagerly responded. Touching their eyes, He said, "According to your faith be it unto you" (9:29).

C. Two Blessed Men (9:30b-31)

When Jesus spoke that transforming word, the believing men became blessed men. "Their eyes were opened; and Jesus straitly [strictly, sternly] charged them, saying, See that no man know it" (9:30). The danger was that now they might start talking about the miracle instead of the Messiah. In the Lord's view the miracle was not worth talking about. He never did place much stock in miracles. He seemed to be saying, "It is not the miracle that must fill your thoughts. Your thoughts must be filled with Me." The Lord's charge is an important word for our day too, as there seems to be such a hankering after healing miracles.

Sad to say, the blind men fell into the trap. There is almost a note of impatience in Matthew's record: "But *they*, when *they* were departed, spread abroad his fame in all that country" (9:31, italics added).

X. POWER OVER DUMBNESS (9:32-34)

"As they went out, behold, they brought to him a dumb man possessed with a devil" (9:32). The *case* and the *cause* went hand in hand. The man was unable to speak; his inability was caused by a demon who possessed him. The Bible makes no apology for statements like the one in 9:32. The fact was that the man's problem was not caused by some organic deficiency, but by a hostile alien intelligence that had seized him and held him in bondage.

Modern man has little patience with such an explanation. To him everything has to have a nonsupernatural physical or psychological cause. It would never do for him to admit the existence of demons, except in fiction or sensational horror movies. But demons are real enough and so is demon possession.[8]

It was the men who had been healed of blindness who brought the dumb man to Jesus "as they went out" of Peter's house. This poor man was too far gone to come himself. Jesus did not question him or ask for a word of faith. We just read of the *cure*. The Lord took no notice of the symptoms; He went straight to the cause of the problem and summarily dealt with the demon.

The devil was cast out and the man spoke. We cannot help wondering what he said. Matthew just told us what others said. The common people responded with amazement. "The multitudes marvelled, saying, It was never so seen in Israel" (9:33).

But the Pharisees did not marvel. Instead they made a terrible *claim:* "He casteth out devils through the prince of the devils" (9:34). If the statement had been made by a Gentile pagan, it would have been bad enough. But the words were spoken by the religious leaders of Israel, those who were on the conservative side in matters of faith and morals—the fundamentalists! Jesus ignored them.

Verse 34 is Matthew's first clear-cut indication of the way things were going in Israel. The healing of the dumb man is the last in a series of miracles he cited to prove the power of the King. And what was the response? The Pharisees attributed the power to Satan. Later on (chapter 12) Matthew showed what happened when at the final crossroads they did it again. In chapter 9 he simply noted the dreadful statement as evidence of the obdurate unbelief of the Jewish leaders even when faced with incontrovertible evidence that Jesus was both Lord and Christ.

This last miracle in the series—the speaking of the dumb man as soon as the demon had been expelled—prefigures the future great deliverance when the Lord will cast Satan himself and all his hosts out of this world. Then the dumb earth, which has withheld its praise from its Creator and moaned its agonies in a minor key for so long, will break into joyous song (Romans 8:19-22).

XI. POWER OVER DISBELIEF (9:35-38)

In the Lord's first circuit of Galilee (Matthew 4:23-25), He was accompanied by some of His disciples. In the second (8:5–9:1), He was accompanied by all twelve, who were also with Him as apostles. We come now to His third circuit, in which the twelve were sent out to supplement His ministry.

A. Christ's Commission (9:35)

1. Where He Went (9:35a)

Jesus went everywhere and to all classes of Jewish people. He made His way to the cities where great numbers of people faced the problems of urban living. Jesus went to these centers of government, finance, higher education, industry, art, sports, science, religion, entertainment—and crime. He also went to the villages, the little out-of-the-way hamlets where a man's world was his cottage, his cow, and his field of corn. Those places were just as important to Jesus as the cities.

Nobody was too sophisticated for Jesus; nobody was too parochial. He was just as much at home with cultured and educated Nicodemus as He was with outcast Zaccheus. The Lord visited the home of Simon the leper as willingly as he visited the home of Simon the Pharisee and that of Simon Peter. All men were equally on His heart.

2. Why He Went (9:35b-c)

a. To Teach Everyone (9:35b)

Jesus was attracted to the synagogues, for they were natural gathering places. There He could meet the people who came to worship, sing Psalms, and hear Scripture. There He could teach and preach the gospel of the kingdom to everyone who came.

b. To Reach Everyone (9:35c)

He healed everyone who came His way with a need. Matthew repeated the word "every": "Jesus went about…healing *every* sickness and *every* disease" (italics added). (Let all so-called faith healers take note.) It was vitally important to reach everyone. The leaders were hardening their hearts, but the common people were still undecided. The time had come to increase the scope of His ministry.

B. Christ's Compassion (9:36)

The Lord saw *the multitudes of mankind* and He was moved by *the misery of mankind.* His heart went out to one and all. They were weary—"they fainted," Matthew wrote. (The word translated "fainted" is sometimes rendered "were harassed.") They "were scattered abroad, as sheep having no shepherd"—they were lost, lonely, in peril, and defenseless. The Lord was stirred by their plight. His response was not merely an intellectual assessment of the situation of the earth's millions. His response was that of a tender Shepherd, the great Shepherd of the sheep. The blind men had called Him the Son of David and so He was; but David, though the author of the twenty-third Psalm, was not as great a shepherd as his distant Son is.

The Lord saw lost people as having *no real goals.* They were "scattered abroad"—like sheep. Sheep are neither strong, nor smart, nor swift. They are somewhat stupid, having a propensity to go astray and wander aimlessly farther and farther away. Lost sheep have no goal, no instinctive sense that will bring them back to the fold. Jesus saw lost people as sheep wandering here and there through life, with no sense as to where it all leads and where it all ends.

He also saw them as having *no real guides,* "as sheep having no shepherd." What did they have? They had the Pharisees, Sadducees, scribes, and rabbis. But those men were as lost as the people they were attempting to lead.

The world is the same today. People blinded by communism and humanism are wandering in a spiritual wilderness. Millions will perish cherishing the false creeds of Buddhism, Hinduism, and Islam or wander into eternal darkness listening to false teachings within Christendom. No wonder we read of the Lord's compassion.

Each man, woman, boy, and girl living on earth is an object of His heartfelt concern. He could not see a poor woman struggling in loneliness and growing despair for twelve years with a debilitating and distressing disease without wanting to help her. He could not see a poor demoniac unable to speak for himself and not do something about it. He could not look down from Heaven at lost humanity and not say to His Father, "Here am I; send me." He yearns over all the children of men and so should we.

C. Christ's Compulsion (9:37-38)

1. The Problem (9:37)

The Lord crystallized the problem. "Then saith he unto his disciples, The harvest truly is plenteous, but the labourers are few." They still are. To the crying shame of the church, untold millions are still untold. Even now thousands of language groups are without a single verse of Scripture and thousands more have only the barest minimum of Bible texts in their tongue.

2. The Prayer (9:38)

What was the Lord's solution to the problem? "Pray ye therefore the Lord of the harvest, that he will send forth labourers into his harvest." The Lord of the harvest is the Holy Spirit. It is His work to send—ours is to go. It would be better to stay at home than to go without being sent (see Acts 13:13 for the classic New Testament example, John Mark). The Lord of the harvest is to be implored that *He* will send forth laborers. He is only too willing to grant that kind of request, but let the petitioner beware—he may be the first to be sent. If the Holy Spirit sends, it is far better to go than to stay at home.

PART TWO

The King Is Resisted
Matthew 10:1–16:12

The Resistance Foretold

(10:1-42)

I. PREPARATION FOR SERVICE (10:1-15)
  A. The Master (10:1)
    1. His Lordship over His Disciples
    2. His Lordship over Harmful Demons
    3. His Lordship over Human Diseases
  B. The Men (10:2-4)
    1. How the Lord Commissioned Them (10:2a)
    2. How the Lord Coupled Them (10:2b-4)
      a. The Brothers (10:2b-c)
        (1) Simon, called Peter; and Andrew (10:2b)
        (2) James and John, the Sons of Zebedee (10:2c)
      b. The Friends (10:3a-b)
        (1) Philip; and Bartholomew (Nathanael) (10:3a)
        (2) Thomas; and Matthew the Publican, Also
            Called Levi the Son of Alphaeus (10:3b)
      c. The Unknowns (10:3c)
         James the Son of Alphaeus; and Lebbaeus, Whose
         Surname Was Thaddaeus and Who Was Also
         Called Judas the Brother of James
      d. The Opposites (10:4)
         Simon the Canaanite, Called Zelotes; and Judas
         Iscariot, "Who Also Betrayed Him"
  C. The Mission (10:5-6)
    1. Limited (10:5)
    2. Localized (10:6)
  D. The Message (10:7)
  E. The Miracles (10:8)

1. There Was to Be No Failure (10:8a-d)
    a. The Diseased (10:8a)
    b. The Doomed (10:8b)
    c. The Dead (10:8c)
    d. The Demoniacs (10:8d)
2. There Was to Be No Fee (10:8e)
F. The Money (10:9-10)
    1. The Apostles' Resources Prohibited (10:9-10a)
    2. The Apostles' Remuneration Promised (10:10b)
G. The Method (10:11-15)
    1. Where They Should Live (10:11-13)
        a. The Sole Requirement (10:11)
        b. The Spiritual Reward (10:12-13)
    2. Why They Should Leave (10:14-15)
        a. The Cause (10:14a)
        b. The Curse (10:14b-15)
            (1) A Solemn Act (10:14b)
            (2) A Sobering Fact (10:15)

II. PREPARATION FOR SUFFERING (10:16-42)
    A. The Apostles' Foes (10:16-25)
        1. The Lord's Exhortation (10:16)
            a. Their Danger (10:16a)
            b. Their Discernment (10:16b)
            c. Their Disposition (10:16c)
        2. The Lord's Expectation (10:17-23)
            a. Enmity (10:17-18)
                (1) From Hebrew Rabbis (10:17)
                (2) From Heathen Rulers (10:18)
                    (a) The High Rank (10:18a)
                    (b) The Highest Reason (10:18b)
            b. Enlightenment (10:19-20)
                (1) Supernatural in Its Source (10:19)
                (2) Sublime in Its Force (10:20)
            c. Endurance (10:21-23)
                (1) Execration (10:21-22a)
                    (a) No Peace at Home (10:21)
                    (b) No Place to Hide (10:22a)

       (2) Exhortation (10:22b)
       (3) Explanation (10:23)
          (a) A Deliberate Policy (10:23a)
          (b) A Divine Purpose (10:23b)
  3. The Lord's Example (10:24-25)
    a. The Rule for Us (10:24-25a)
       (1) In Principle (10:24)
       (2) In Practice (10:25a)
    b. The Rejection of Him (10:25b-c)
       (1) How Appalling It Was (10:25b)
       (2) How Applicable It Is (10:25c)
B. The Apostles' Fears (10:26-39)
  1. A Call for Courage (10:26-33)
    a. Moral Courage: Daring to Speak (10:26-27)
       (1) The Divine Rule to Be Remembered (10:26)
       (2) The Divine Revelation to Be Received (10:27)
    b. Physical Courage: Dying for Christ (10:28)
       (1) The Wrong Person to Fear (10:28a)
       (2) The Right Person to Fear (10:28b)
    c. Spiritual Courage: Drawing on God (10:29-33)
       (1) God's Omnipresence (10:29)
       (2) God's Omniscience (10:30)
       (3) God's Omnipotence (10:31-33)
          (a) Relative Values (10:31)
          (b) Real Values (10:32-33)
             i. What to Seek (10:32)
            ii. What to Shun (10:33)
  2. A Call to Comprehend (10:34-36)
    a. The Realistic Warning (10:34)
    b. The Revealed Word (10:35-36)
       (1) A Solemn Prospect (10:35a)
       (2) A Similar Prophecy (10:35b-36)
  3. A Call for Commitment (10:37-39)
    a. Love on the Altar (10:37)
    b. Life on the Altar (10:38-39)
       (1) The Prospect (10:38)
       (2) The Principle (10:39)
C. The Apostles' Followers (10:40-42)

1. The Process of Receiving (10:40)
   a. Receive the Man and You Receive the Master (10:40a)
   b. Receive the One Who Saves and You Receive the One Who Sends (10:40b)
2. The Promise of Reward (10:41-42)
   a. A Question of Identity (10:41)
      (1) Identification with One of God's Servants (10:41a)
      (2) Identification with One of God's Saints (10:41b)
   b. A Question of Indemnity (10:42)
      (1) How Small the Token (10:42a)
      (2) How Sure the Truth (10:42b)

The Pharisees had blasphemously accused Christ of performing miracles in the power of Satan (9:34). The common people, though enthusiastic about His miracles, were still undecided about who Christ was. It was evident that there was not going to be a national movement in the Lord's favor. The tide had crested. Soon the ebb flow would begin and it would climax in the cross. The Lord was well aware of opposition even as He began to commission the twelve. As He sent them forth, He foretold the resistance to the King. Thus in this opening section of Part Two we have both preparation for service and preparation for suffering.

I. PREPARATION FOR SERVICE (10:1-15)

A. The Master (10:1)

Our attention is drawn first to the Master's absolute lordship over His disciples, over demons, and over disease. He now empowered the disciples to display the same mighty works that He had been displaying. They too were to minister solely to the nation of Israel. This is important. Signs were essentially for the Jews both in the days of the Lord and later in the days of the apostles (1 Corinthians 1:22). In particular, signs were for unbelieving Jews (1 Corinthians 14:21-25).[1]

As Matthew 10 begins, the kingdom was still being offered to Israel by the Lord. To extend the call, He commissioned His disciples and sent them forth to proclaim the kingdom by sermons and by signs.

B. The Men (10:2-4)

1. How the Lord Commissioned Them (10:2a)

Matthew called the men "apostles" and this was the first time the title was applied to them. They were now more than disciples. They were the King's ambassadors, whose business was to represent Him, to speak His word, and to present the credentials of power He had given them.

2. How the Lord Coupled Them (10:2b-4)

There are four lists of the twelve apostles in the New Testament: three in the Gospels (Matthew 10:2-4; Mark 3:16-19; Luke 6:14-16) and one in Acts (1:13,26). The order of the names varies. However, they are always given in three groups, and the first name in each group is always the same: Peter, Philip, and James the son of Alphaeus. The other names vary in order, but are always in the same group.

The Lord put them in pairs because He was going to send them out two by two (Mark 6:7). For example Peter was linked with his brother Andrew. James was linked with his brother John. Simon Zelotes was linked with Judas Iscariot.

Doubtless the Lord was wise in putting this one with that one, but I wonder how Simon Zelotes got along with Judas Iscariot. Perhaps Simon was made of sterner stuff than Judas and was chosen to keep him company for that reason. What did they talk about, those two? Maybe when we get to Heaven, Simon will tell us.

a. The Brothers (10:2b-c)

(1) Simon, called Peter; and Andrew (10:2b)

There were two sets of brothers, the first pair being Peter and Andrew. Peter's name appears first in all four lists of the apostles and he was the most prominent of the Lord's disciples. A native of Bethsaida and the son of a man named Jonas, he was originally called Simon (John 1:42,44; 21:15). Peter took an early lead in the infant church and was given the keys to open the door of Christianity first to the Jews and then to the Gentiles (Acts 2; 10). However, the idea that he had primacy over the other apostles and in the church is a Roman Catholic myth (1 Peter 5:1-4). The apostle Paul did not hesitate to put him in his place when the situation demanded it (Galatians 2:9-14).

Peter was brought to Christ by his brother Andrew, a lovable kind of man. We see Andrew achieving a degree of prominence on three occasions in the Gospels; each time he was bringing someone to Jesus.

(2) James and John, the Sons of Zebedee (10:2c)

James and John, the second set of brothers, were sons of Zebedee and cousins of the Lord. What a pair of firebrands! Jesus once called them "sons of thunder" (Mark 3:17). Their dynamic impact is evident from the fact that Herod executed James early on and made him the first of the apostles to earn a martyr's crown (Acts 12:2). John outlived all the other apostles—he is reputed to have died at

Ephesus at the age of ninety-four. We are indebted to him for a magnificent Gospel, three Epistles, and the book of Revelation.

b. The Friends (10:3a-b)

(1) Philip; and Bartholomew (Nathanael) (10:3a)

Like Peter and Andrew, Philip came from Bethsaida (John 1:44). (The deacon/evangelist in the book of Acts is not the same person as this Philip.) His friend Bartholomew is usually identified with Nathanael, his full name being Nathanael Bar Tolmai. The Lord described Nathanael as "an Israelite indeed, in whom is no guile!" (John 1:47) We can paraphrase the description as "an Israelite indeed, in whom is no Jacob!"

Philip was the one who brought Nathanael to Jesus. When Philip first told him that they had found the Messiah and that His name was Jesus of Nazareth, Nathanael was skeptical. But once Nathanael met Christ, he acknowledged Him instantly as the Son of God and King of Israel (John 1:49).

Nathanael spoke slightingly of Nazareth, even though he was a Galilean and Nazareth was a town in Galilee. He knew the town well because he lived in the neighboring village of Cana. The persistence with which the Lord's enemies added the epitaph *the Nazarene* to His name suggests that an unusual measure of ill will was directed toward the town. Nazareth was the first town to offer violence to Jesus, and that on only one day's acquaintance with His claims.

(2) Thomas; and Matthew the Publican (10:3b)

Matthew humbly described himself as "the publican," thus acknowledging the matchless grace that put him in the ministry. What a contrast between the money-loving publican and the miracle-working apostle! He was also called "Levi the son of Alphaeus" (Mark 2:14). This description has led some to assume that Matthew and James the son of Alphaeus were brothers, but that is only speculation since *Alphaeus* was a common Jewish name.

Thomas has the word *Didymus* linked to his name in John's Gospel. This Greek word means "twin," so some have supposed that since Matthew and Thomas are mentioned together in Matthew 10:3, they were more than friends—possibly they were twins. Thomas is prominent in the Gospels for his pessimism and skepticism as well as for his loyalty to the Lord.

c. The Unknowns (10:3c)

The next pair listed are James (the son of Alphaeus) and Lebbaeus (whose surname was Thaddaeus). The name *Alphaeus* and the name *Cleophas* (John 19:25) come from the same Hebrew root (*halphah*). James the son of Alphaeus is also called James the Less to distinguish him from James the brother of John. Perhaps James the Less was younger than John's brother James. James the Less is also to be distinguished from the Lord's brother James, whom we meet in Acts.

Little is known of James the Less's partner, Lebbaeus Thaddaeus. He is also called Judas the brother of James (Luke 6:16; Acts 1:13) and Judas not Iscariot (John 14:22).

d. The Opposites (10:4)

Simon the Canaanite and Judas Iscariot make an interesting pair of opposites. Simon, also called Zelotes (Luke 6:15), was a Zealot.

The Zealots formed a fourth party in Israel, the other three being the Pharisees, the Sadducees, and the Essenes. Zealous for the law, Simon's party cited the example of Phinehas (Numbers 25:7-8) and Elijah (1 Kings 18:40) as their authority for taking the law into their own hands. They punished and lynched people they considered offenders. As the time approached for the fall of Jerusalem, the Zealots went to great lengths to enforce their will and, perhaps more than any others, brought about the destruction of the city. They refused to give anyone the title of king. They were willing to face any kind of torture or death for their cause; neither did they shrink from seeing their loved ones die in the struggle for freedom. In their ambition to rid their country of Roman rule, the Zealots were prepared to assassinate anyone.

If Matthew had met Simon the Zealot before they both met Christ, Simon would have been quite prepared to kill him.

Jesus linked this Simon with Judas Iscariot, the man who betrayed Him. Luke 6:16 calls Judas "the traitor," John 6:71 identifies him as "the son of Simon [no relation of Simon the Zealot]," and John 12:6 describes him as "a thief." John added that he kept "the bag" and took charge of what was in it. The word translated "bag" is *glōssokomon,* which refers to a bag for keeping the tongues or reeds of wind instruments. Perhaps before becoming a disciple Judas had been a shepherd in Kerioth, the hilly district of southern Judah (*Iscariot* may have been derived from the Hebrew for "a man of Kerioth"). The bag might have held the pipes so much enjoyed by eastern shepherds. In any case, Judas Iscariot was the only Judean in the Lord's band of disciples. All the rest were Galileans. He was also the only traitor.

C. The Mission (10:5-6)

These twelve men were now commissioned by Jesus to go forth and tell the Hebrew people that Messiah had come. Their mission was *limited* and *localized.* They were forbidden to go beyond the boundaries of Israel: "Go not into the *way* of the Gentiles, and into any *city* of the Samaritans enter ye not" (10:5, italics added). The Jews regarded even the dust of a heathen highway as defiling. The roads of Samaria were regarded as clean, but as far as any fellowship was concerned, the Samaritans were just as unclean as the Gentiles.

The twelve were to restrict themselves to "the lost sheep of the house of Israel" (10:6). The time had not yet come for the Lord to say, "Other sheep I have, which are not of this fold: them also I must bring" (John 10:16). The mission was strictly Jewish. It was intended to give the Jews one more chance of avoiding the age-long dispersion that awaited them, one more chance to accept the King before the offer of the kingdom was withdrawn for thousands of years.

The commission in Matthew 10 is not the same as ours. Our ministry is not restricted to Jews in Israel. We are not forbidden to go to the Gentiles. We are not forbidden to make normal provision for a journey (10:9-10); this clause was expressly canceled by the Lord (Luke 22:35-36). We are not told to shake the dust of an unreceptive city off our feet (Matthew 10:14). We do not stand in fear of synagogue and Sanhedrin (10:17). This mission then was limited as to place and period.

D. The Message (10:7)

The apostles were to announce: "The kingdom of heaven is at hand." And so it was—then. Had the Jews accepted Christ as Messiah at that time, the visible kingdom would have been set up at once.[2] But the message went unheeded and the immediate offer of the kingdom was withdrawn. A new commission (28:18-20) was given for a new dispensation.

E. The Miracles (10:8)

1. There Was to Be No Failure (10:8a-d)

The apostles were empowered to back their message with miracles—the same kind of miracles that Jesus performed. They were to heal the sick, cleanse the lepers, raise the dead, and cast out demons.

This is not our work. We have no commission to heal the sick miraculously or to raise the dead. Those who claim to have the *gift* of healing today are deceived and in turn deceive others. If they wish to convince us that they have this commission, let them give us clear, unequivocal evidence that they have the power to raise the dead; let them raise the dead. Jesus did. Peter did. Paul did. When the gospel was still being backed by signs as a last call to the Jewish nation, healing, exorcism, and resurrection were all in evidence.

At issue here is not divine healing. All healing is from God. It is possible for God to heal us with or without the aid of a doctor. But we have no ground for claiming healing as our right. There are no divine healers today. If there are, let them go to where the sick are— to hospitals. Let them go where the dead are—to cemeteries.

Matthew 10 speaks of a special commission, for a special embassy, to a special people, at a special time, in a special place, and for a special purpose. Miracles were the credentials of the King's ambassadors on the dawn of what could have been the kingdom age. There was to be no failure. The command to perform miracles was authoritative and left no room for hedging, special effects, manipulation, sleight of hand, mass psychology, hypnotism, and fraud.

2. There Was to Be No Fee (10:8e)

Jesus said, "Freely ye have received, freely give." There was to be no love offering for the healer, no charge for admission, no high pressure appeals for money to support the ministry.

F. The Money (10:9-10)

1. The Apostles' Resources Prohibited (10:9-10a)

The Lord expanded on the subject of money. He told the apostles to get up and go, then and there, just as they were. They were to make no provision for their mission: "Provide neither gold, nor silver, nor brass [copper] in your purses [money belts], Nor scrip for your journey, neither two coats, neither shoes, nor yet staves [walking sticks]." According to Luke they were also told to take no bread (9:3). The "scrip" (*pēra,*) was a beggar's bag in which he put the charity he collected. The apostles were neither to pay their own way nor beg.

2. The Apostles' Remuneration Promised (10:10b)

The Lord would provide. He would use people to supply the disciples' needs, but behind those who gave would be the Lord Himself. There were other factors in this same equation: the twelve were Jews, moving among Jews, a people with a worldwide reputation for taking care of their kind; the apostles were armed with powers calculated to win the respect and gratitude of their countrymen; and the mission, being essentially Jewish, would not readily stir up Jewish prejudices.

G. The Method (10:11-15)

1. The Sole Requirement (10:11)

a. The Sole Requirement (10:11)

The Lord explained to the apostles that when they entered a city, they should make inquiries as to who was worthy and ask that person for hospitality. Once they settled on a place, they were to remain there for the duration of their stay and not move to other places that perhaps offered better advantages.

b. The Spiritual Reward (10:12-13)

The host and his house would be rewarded spiritually, for the apostles were to pronounce a benediction on the home. The Lord promised to honor such a draft drawn on Himself, and He is no man's debtor.

2. Why They Should Leave (10:14-15)

Not everyone would welcome the apostles with open arms. If they came to a house or city that would not receive them, they were not to argue. They were to shake off the dust of the place as they left. Shaking off the dust of a city put that city on a par with Gentile cities, which Jews considered unclean.

Such a city was put under a curse by the King Himself. Solemn was His warning: "Verily I say unto you, It shall be more tolerable for the land of Sodom and Gomorrha in the day of judgment, than for that city" (10:15). As it happened, nothing saved the cities of Palestine from the avenging Romans, and the day of judgment has not even come yet.

II. PREPARATION FOR SUFFERING (10:16-42)

In this passage the commission is broadened somewhat. Although the interpretation is still Jewish, the principles and warnings have an application to the church age. Those who are faithful to the Lord and His Word in any age can expect hate and hostility from the world. Down through the Christian era "the blood of the martyrs has been the seed of the Church."[3] All that, however, is envisioned here only in a secondary sense. The context is first and foremost a Jewish Messianic mission.

Christ warned the twelve of opposition from the Jews: "I send you forth as sheep in the midst of wolves....When they persecute you in this city, flee ye into another: for verily I say unto you, Ye shall not have gone over [through] the cities of Israel, till the Son of man be come" (10:16,23). But seemingly all went well, so in what sense then was His warning true?

Even the best of commentators have hedged badly on this question. Campbell Morgan for instance said that the warning refers to "His coming in judgment at the fall of Jerusalem, which took place in A.D. 70." That simply will not do. It is contrary to prophecy to say that the Son of man came in A.D. 70.

By application the warning has secondary reference to the preaching of the gospel during our age, but by interpretation the warning looks ahead to the time of the great tribulation. After the rapture of the church, God will raise up His 2 witnesses (Revelation 11) and His 144,000 witnesses (Revelation 7). Then the Jewish mission originated in Matthew 10 will be resumed. The terrible persecutions of that era (another era of miracles) are envisioned in the Lord's warning to the apostles. As is so often the case with pre-Pentecost prophecy, the church age is passed over either very lightly or entirely.

A. The Apostles' Foes (10:16-25)

1. The Lord's Exhortation (10:16)

Having prepared the apostles for special service, the Lord began to prepare them for suffering. His envoys were to anticipate *danger*. "Behold," He said, "I send you forth as sheep in the midst of wolves." Sheep are defenseless before wolves. Those in all ages who have dared to challenge "the system" have been bitterly persecuted by their foes. Because of the danger, *discernment* is needed, so the Lord commanded, "Be ye therefore wise as serpents." Also needed is a certain *disposition,* so He added, "...and harmless as doves." Being wise as a serpent will enable the Lord's ambassador to see trouble coming and to be prepared to handle it if he cannot avoid it. Being harmless as a dove will enable the Lord's servant to display the Spirit of Christ when trouble does overtake him.

2. The Lord's Expectation (10:17-23)

a. Enmity (10:17-18)

(1) From Hebrew Rabbis (10:17)

The apostles would have to face enmity, so the Lord said, "Beware of men: for they will deliver you up to the councils, and they will scourge you in their synagogues." This warning can hardly refer to Jewish persecution of Gentile Christians since the Jews did not have a record of scourging Gentiles in their synagogues. Such highhandedness would never have been tolerated in the Gentile world. This is a case of Jews persecuting the Lord's Jewish ambassadors.

After Pentecost the Jewish segment of the church was persecuted by the Jewish authorities; synagogue and Sanhedrin became enemies of the gospel. At the time the commission of Matthew 10 was given, however, the Lord's ambassadors do not appear to have been persecuted. Therefore the Lord's warning must refer to the coming tribulation, to the days of the antichrist when the gospel of the kingdom will again be proclaimed and the Jewish mission will again be in full force. This mission will be resumed in the period between the rapture of the church and the Lord's return.

Today the Jews are back in the land, so conditions are again ripe for the fulfillment of prophecy. After the rapture of the church the Lord will resume His dealings with the Jews as His representative people. Many Jews will respond at that time to the gospel of the kingdom, but others, including the authorities, will be enamored of the antichrist. Those unbelieving Jews will bitterly persecute their Jewish compatriots for preaching the unwelcome news of the imminent coming of Christ to reign.

(2) From Heathen Rulers (10:18)

The beast and Gentile authorities will also be active enemies of the Lord's ambassadors and their converts during the tribulation. The revived Roman empire, which will be ruling again, will be administered by ten kings. The Lord indicated, "Ye shall be brought before governors and kings for my sake, for a testimony against them."

Of course many of the principles the Lord gave here for coping with persecution could be applied to the church age. Much of the same kind of hostility was met by the apostles and has been met by the church in spreading the Christian gospel. The interpretation of the Lord's words, however, anticipates the tribulation age.

b. Enlightenment (10:19-20)

The enmity the apostles would face would be offset by enlightenment. The Lord promised to give them wisdom that their enemies would not be able to withstand: "It shall be given you in that same hour what ye shall speak. For it is not ye that speak, but the Spirit of your Father which speaketh in you." A classic illustration is found in Stephen's famous defense, which cut the Jews to the heart and resulted in his martyrdom (Acts 7).

c. Endurance (10:21-23)

The apostles could expect terrible betrayals, even by family members. All men would hate the Lord's ambassadors for their witness to His name. There is indeed no more hated name among the Jews than the name of Jesus.

Betrayals have been common in the persecution of Christians in the church age. For instance in China in the days of Mao Tse-tung a nation of nearly a billion people was systematically brainwashed by a ruthless regime, and a diabolical attempt was made to stamp out Christianity through a policy of betrayal. The fact remains, however, that the prophecy of 10:21 focuses on the last days.

The Lord advocated that the persecuted flee from city to city. There will be a special sense of urgency during the great tribulation. When the beast signs his treaty with the state of Israel there will only be seven years left before the end. When he seizes the rebuilt temple and installs his image in the holy place, there will be only three and a half years left before the coming of the Son of man. The call of God's ambassador during this period will be to resist the beast, refuse his mark, and get ready for the coming kingdom. "He that endureth to the end shall be saved" (10:22). The word translated "end" is *telos,* which refers to the very end of the great tribulation. The word translated "shall be saved" can also be translated "shall escape" or "shall be delivered."

There was of course the possibility that the Jews of Jesus' day would accept the mission of the twelve. Otherwise their offer of the kingdom would not have been bona fide. If the Jews had accepted Christ, their leaders would doubtless have closed ranks against Christ, and both synagogue and Sanhedrin would have persecuted the believers. The dispensation would have come to an end, the kingdom would have been set up, and there would have been no church age.

3. The Lord's Example (10:24-25)

Jesus asked, "If they have called the master of the house Beelzebub, how much more shall they call them of his household?" (10:25) The Pharisees had called Him Beelzebub before (9:34) and they would do it again (12:24). The Lord's servants are not to expect better treatment than the Lord Himself received.

We learn from Mark 3:22 that the authorities, unwilling to recognize the divine source of the Lord's power and unable to explain it any other way, regarded Jesus as permanently possessed by the prince of demons. Instead of acknowledging Him as the Son of God, they regarded Him as the incarnation of Satan. The kingdom He had come to offer did not fit their formula or their taste. Once they arrived at their terrible conclusion, all the rest followed as a matter of course. "The disciple is not above his master," said the Lord (10:24).

B. The Apostles' Fears (10:26-39)

1. A Call for Courage (10:26-33)

In this segment of the commission the Lord concentrated on the natural shrinking of all normal people from suffering, pain, and persecution. Again and again He said, "Fear not," and called for courage.

a. Moral Courage: Daring to Speak (10:26-27)

The enemies of the gospel may do their dread deeds in darkness, but God sees them, and His people are to be bold in speaking out against the wickedness of the age. They are not to speak in whispers; the wickedness they unmask is to be shouted from the housetops. Daring to speak calls for moral courage.

b. Physical Courage: Dying for Christ (10:28)

The Lord called for physical courage to be willing to die for Him: "Fear not them which kill the body, but are not able to kill the soul: but rather fear him which is able to destroy both soul and body in hell."

An example of the need for physical courage is found in the Apocalypse. In Revelation 13:15-18 we read that an ultimatum will be issued requiring everyone to receive the mark of the beast and worship his image or be killed. God will respond by sending an angel with this message:

> If any man worship the beast and his image, and receive his mark in his forehead, or in his hand, The same shall drink of the wine of the wrath of God, which is poured out without mixture into the cup of his indignation; and he shall be tormented with fire and brimstone in the presence of the holy angels, and in the presence of the Lamb: And the smoke of their torment ascendeth up for ever and ever (14:9-11).

In other words, the beast will say, "Receive that mark or die," and God will say, "Receive that mark and be damned."

c. Spiritual Courage: Drawing on God (10:29-33)

Spiritual courage is daring to stake all in God because He will win in the end. That kind of courage can be developed by thinking of His attributes: His *omnipresence,* His *omniscience,* and His *omnipotence.*

We find courage and comfort in the statement in 10:29: "Are not two sparrows sold for a farthing? and one of them shall not fall on the ground without your Father." God attends the funeral of a single sparrow! There is a similar statement in Luke 12:6: "Are not five sparrows sold for two farthings, and not one of them is forgotten before God?" A comparison of the two verses reveals a tremendous truth. One farthing would buy two sparrows, and two farthings would buy not four, but five sparrows. Sparrows were of such little value that when two farthings were paid, an extra bird was thrown in to make a bargain. Yet even that one did not die unattended by our Father.

How much more will He attend to His martyrs! He is present in all His glory at their funerals. Stephen's martyrdom furnishes us with just one example (Acts 7:55-56).

2. A Call to Comprehend (10:34-36)

Jesus warned, "Think not that I am come to send peace on earth: I came not to send peace, but a sword" (10:34). He will impose peace on this planet, but not until He comes to set up the kingdom after the enemies of the faith have had their final fling.

The conversion of a person from a non-Christian home all too often turns his family against him. A man's foes may indeed be "they of his own household" (10:36). These words of Jesus have always been true and will be even more so in the coming age when fear of the beast and his gestapo will make cowards of everyone but those who have staked their all in God.

3. A Call for Commitment (10:37-39)

a. Love on the Altar (10:37)

In view of the enormous issues that swing in the balance, all fear must be set aside and a commitment must be made. Human love must be placed on the altar. Father, mother, son, daughter, all human relationships—sacred as they are, solemn as they are, sweet as they are—must be given up at a time such as the one envisioned by the Lord in Matthew 10 if that is the only way to be loyal to Him.

b. Life on the Altar (10:38-39)

Human life must be placed on the altar. A man must take up his cross, however heavy. He must be prepared to lose his life in order to find it again; if he hoards it, he will only lose it at the last. Those are stern words. They have perennial application, but will come fully into their own in the days just prior to the Lord's return.

C. The Apostles' Followers (10:40-42)

As the Lord drew this distinctive commission to a close, He talked to the apostles about their followers. These last words brought them back to the actual situation they faced as they prepared to leave on their mission. The situation will be the same prior to His coming back as the Son of man.

1. The Process of Receiving (10:40)

Receiving one of the King's men could be costly if not dangerous in a time of public disapproval or official displeasure. Many in Israel knew by now that the Lord was not popular with the nation's leaders. It would cost something to be identified with His apostles.

The opposition will be a thousandfold worse in the time of the great tribulation. To show any kindness to one of the King's men will be to invite betrayal, arrest, deportation, torture, death. But the Lord will say in effect, "Remember, you are not just receiving My messenger; you are receiving Me. And not only Me, but Him that sent Me." What could be a greater privilege?

2. The Promise of Reward (10:41-42)

The receiving and the rewarding go hand in hand. To be daringly identified with one of the King's ambassadors will be to receive an ambassador's reward. Here is compensation commensurate with the deed.

How great the reward, and how small the deed that earns it! "Whosoever shall give to drink unto one of these little ones a cup of cold water only in the name of a disciple, verily I say unto you, he shall in no wise lose his reward" (10:42). "In the name of a disciple" is a Hebraism meaning "because he is a disciple." Just giving a drink of cold water to one of the Lord's own ensures a reward. This teaching is amplified later in the Lord's parable of the sheep and the goats (25:31-46).

So the apostles were armed and forewarned. Off they went two by two to fulfill their commission. How we would love to know how they were received and what miracles they performed! Did they raise the dead? Did two of them go to Nazareth? Who took them in? Who turned them away? Matthew did not say. The answers are part of the unwritten story. All Matthew did was to go on describing the mounting resistance and opposition to the Lord. Israel had crossed another line in its march toward doom.

SECTION 2

THE RESISTANCE FELT

(11:1-30)

I. THE MINISTRY OF JOHN (11:1-15)
  A. John's Spiritual Struggle (11:1-6)
    1. His Question Asked (11:1-3)
      a. What He Heard (11:1-2)
      b. What He Hoped (11:3)
    2. His Question Answered (11:4-6)
      a. The Hard Evidence Presented by Jesus (11:4-5)
        (1) The Special Miracles (11:4-5a)
        (2) The Spiritual Miracle (11:5b)
      b. The Happy Evaluation Proposed by Jesus (11:6)
  B. John's Splendid Stature (11:7-9)
    1. Described by Way of Contrast (11:7-8)
      a. There Was Nothing Weak about Him (11:7)
      b. There Was Nothing Womanish about Him (11:8)
    2. Described by Way of Comparison (11:9)
  C. John's Scriptural Status (11:10-15)
    1. The Prophecy of Malachi (11:10)
    2. The Proclamation of the Messiah (11:11-12)
      a. The Greatness of the Baptist (11:11a)
      b. The Greatness of the Believer (11:11b)
      c. The Greatness of the Battle (11:12)
    3. The Pregnancy of the Moment (11:13-15)
      a. For the Fulfillment of the Word of God (11:13)
      b. For the Fruition of the Work of God (11:14-15)
        (1) A Chance for All to Be Fulfilled (11:14)
        (2) A Challenge for All to Be Forewarned (11:15)

197

II. THE MINISTRY OF JESUS (11:16-30)
   A. The Illustration (11:16-19)
      1. A Very Significant Illustration (11:16a)
      2. A Very Simple Illustration (11:16b-17)
         a. Playing an Emotional Scale (11:16b-17b)
            (1) Weddings (11:16b-17a)
            (2) Funerals (11:17b)
         b. Producing an Emotional Silence (11:17c)
      3. A Very Suitable Illustration (11:18-19)
         How that generation responded to:
         a. The Stern Fasting of John (11:18)
         b. The Sweet Fellowship of Jesus (11:19)
   B. The Indictment (11:20-24)
      1. The Cause (11:20)
      2. The Curse (11:21-24)
         a. The First Curse (11:21-22)
             (1) The Present (11:21a)
            (2) The Past (11:21b)
            (3) The Prospect (11:22)
         b. The Further Curse (11:23-24)
             (1) The Present (11:23a)
            (2) The Past (11:23b)
            (3) The Prospect (11:24)
   C. The Invocation (11:25-27)
      1. The Mystery of the Divine Process (11:25-26)
         a. An Inevitable Process (11:25)
             (1) Truth Concealed from the Sophisticated (11:25a)
            (2) Truth Revealed to the Simple (11:25b)
         b. An Infallible Process (11:26)
      2. The Mystery of the Divine Person (11:27)
         a. He Is Invincible (11:27a)
         b. He Is Inscrutable (11:27b-c)
             (1) The Exclusive Relationship (11:27b)
            (2) The Expanded Relationship (11:27c)
   D. The Invitation (11:28-30)
      1. The Call for Salvation (11:28)

    a. The Plea (11:28a)
    b. The Pledge (11:28b)
  2. The Call for Service (11:29-30)
    a. The Appeal (11:29)
      (1) Our Decision—"Take" (11:29a)
      (2) Our Development—"Learn" (11:29b-c)
        (a) The Teacher (11:29b)
        (b) The Topic (11:29c)
      (3) Our Discovery—"Find" (11:29d)
    b. The Assurance (11:30)

I. THE MINISTRY OF JOHN (11:1-15)

Having commissioned the apostles and sent them on their errand, the Lord continued His own tour in the cities around Capernaum. During the time of the Lord's Galilean ministry, Herod Antipas seems to have been in his Perean domains. His power embraced Galilee, which was west of the Jordan river and the sea of Galilee, and Perea, which was east of the Jordan but farther south. This evil and treacherous man had two palaces in Perea, one at Julias and the other at Machaerus, where he imprisoned John the Baptist.

The ministry of the twelve seems to have reached Perea and attracted Herod's attention. It is likely that this as much as anything terminated the mission of the apostles and caused them to return to Jesus. About the same time, John the Baptist suffered a terrible depression and sent two of his disciples to question Jesus.

Matthew, in writing his Gospel, was continuing to trace for his Jewish readers the development of the national resistance to Christ and His men. Almost as serious as the Jews' rejection of the ministry of Jesus was their rejection of His forerunner. So in 11:1-15, Matthew reviewed the ministry of John the Baptist, a ministry that was extolled by Jesus Himself. John had been popular enough with the rank and file of the people, but the Jewish leaders, having been rebuked by him for their hypocrisy, were his enemies.[1]

A. John's Spiritual Struggle (11:1-6)

1. His Question Asked (11:1-3)

John the Baptist was deeply distressed. He had triumphantly heralded the coming King, had introduced Him to the people at the Jordan, had seen God's Spirit descend on Him, and had given up some of his best disciples to Him. Then John had been thrown in prison by Herod for daring to condemn his marriage to Herodias—and Jesus had done nothing about it. Worse still, the proclaimed Messiah was certainly not doing much to establish the kind of earthly kingdom that John had expected. He began to have second thoughts. "Art thou he that should come," he asked, "or do we look for another?" (11:3) Had he been mistaken?

2. His Question Answered (11:4-6)

a. The Hard Evidence Presented by Jesus (11:4-5)

The Lord sent the two questioners back, bidding them to recount to John the things that they had heard and seen: "The blind receive their sight, and the lame walk, the lepers are cleansed, and the deaf hear, the dead are raised up, and the poor have the gospel preached to them" (11:5).

b. The Happy Evaluation Proposed by Jesus (11:6)

The Lord added a personal word for His faithful forerunner: "And blessed is he, whosoever shall not be offended [find nothing to stumble at] in me." The signs that Jesus pointed out to John were foretold by the prophet (Isaiah 35:5-6; 61:1). No other miracles would have sufficed as His credentials.

B. John's Splendid Stature (11:7-9)

1. Described by Way of Contrast (11:7-8)

a. There Was Nothing Weak about Him (11:7)

The Lord eulogized John the Baptist to the multitudes who were thronging Him. He defended John against those who might use this incident of doubt to detract from his reputation. John was no vacillating man, no "reed shaken with the wind." Jesus was contrasting him with the tall reeds that skirt the Jordan; they stand twelve feet tall, but with each gust of wind bow down to the earth.

b. There Was Nothing Womanish about Him (11:8)

John was not the kind of man who wore soft raiment. He was not about to make some kind of deal with Herod in order to change his prison for a palace.

2. Described by Way of Comparison (11:9)

John was a prophet "and more than a prophet." The prophets foretold the coming of the Messiah, but John was His personal herald who was sent before Him to announce Him to the nation.

The people reckoned John to be a prophet (21:26), but he was not only a prophet. He was also the subject of prophecy.

C. John's Scriptural Status (11:10-15)

1. The Prophecy of Malachi (11:10)

Malachi had foretold the coming of John the Baptist. Matthew was referring to Malachi 3:1 when he wrote, "This is he, of whom it is written, Behold, I send my messenger before thy face, which shall prepare thy way before thee." And John had indeed prepared the way.

2. The Proclamation of the Messiah (11:11-12)

a. The Greatness of the Baptist (11:11a)

By every measure, John was a great man. Jesus said, "Among them that are born of women there hath not risen a greater than John the Baptist." The Lord was paying tribute to his sterling character, moral fiber, natural ability, spiritual stature, and unflinching resolve. Born into the priestly line, John had renounced a career in the priesthood to become a lonely, ascetic, wilderness prophet. He was a true visionary, a spiritual giant.

b. The Greatness of the Believer (11:11b)

"Notwithstanding," Jesus added, "he that is least in the kingdom of heaven is greater than he." The Lord was anticipating the dispensational change.

God was introducing a new order, different from and superior to the old one. God's Old Testament people were essentially an earthly people with earthly hopes, blessings, and promises. God's New Testament people are essentially a heavenly people with heavenly hopes, blessings, and promises. His earthly people had their sights set on a promised land, a world empire, a millennial kingdom, with only occasional and general overtones pointing to the eternal. His heavenly people are seated with Christ in the heavenlies and will be heirs of the celestial city, the new Jerusalem.

The new order is the kingdom of heaven. He that is least in that kingdom is greater than John, the last and greatest of the Old Testament heralds of the coming King. Similarly, the smallest child is greater than the strongest lion because one belongs to the animal kingdom and the other is a human being, a member of a different order.

The Lord still intends to set up the earthly kingdom envisioned by the Old Testament prophets and heralded by John. But as the sermon on the mount made clear, the fundamental laws and life of the kingdom will be spiritual, not worldly.

The earthly kingdom would have been established two thousand years ago if the Jews had accepted Jesus as their Messiah. The Jews, however, rejected Jesus and the new order, made necessary by their unbelief, was introduced to fill in the unsuspected time gap between the two comings of Christ. The church age was introduced by God as a parenthesis in His dealings with Israel and the nations.[2]

Those who belong to this new order have a heavenly calling that is far higher than Israel's earthly one. They are no longer reckoned among them that are "born of women," but among them who have been "born of God."

c. The Greatness of the Battle (11:12)

The Lord then said something that has puzzled many people and been the subject of considerable controversy: "From the days of John the Baptist until now [a period of about three years] the kingdom of heaven suffereth violence, and the violent [the forceful ones] take it [lay hold of it] by force." The word translated "suffereth violence" here is *biazomai*. Probably it refers to the antagonism of the enemies of the kingdom.

The parallel passage in Luke 16:16 reads, "The law and the prophets were until John; since that time the kingdom of God is preached, and every man presseth [*biazomai*] into it." *Biazomai* is a form of *biazō*. W. E. Vine said that *biazō* in the middle voice means "to press violently or force one's way into" and that in Luke 16:16 *biazomai* "indicates the meaning as referring to those who make an effort to enter the Kingdom in spite of violent opposition."[3]

Another view is that the expression "suffereth violence" in Matthew 11:12 means that the kingdom was forcing itself upon men's attention and that forceful ones were laying hold of it. In other words, the kingdom was being preached with convincing power, starting with John the Baptist. Although he did not belong to the kingdom, he had announced its imminence. His forceful appeals had aroused the whole country.

Now the King and His ambassadors were laying siege to the consciences of the Jewish people with convincing words and deeds. Truly the kingdom was forcing itself on everyone's notice. So great was the impact that all who had any strength of mind were being compelled to reveal themselves. Some were daring any opposition to become part of the kingdom; others were trying either to discredit it and destroy the King or to make it serve their own ends.

An example of people's reaction to the preaching of the kingdom surfaced after the feeding of the five thousand. The apostle John wrote:

> Then those men, when they had seen the miracle that Jesus did, said, This is of a truth that prophet that should come into the world. When Jesus therefore perceived that they would come and take him by force, to make him a king, he departed again into a mountain himself alone (6:14-15).

They had entirely wrong views of the kingdom. They wanted to force the pace. As the context in Matthew 11 shows, there is a sense in which John the Baptist too was wanting to force the kingdom.

3. The Pregnancy of the Moment (11:13-15)

a. For the Fulfillment of the Word of God (11:13)

The Lord came back to the subject of John the Baptist right away. "All the prophets and the law prophesied until John," He said. The moment was pregnant with blessing or doom for Israel. The Old Testament revelation was in types and prophecy, but now the promised King and kingdom were at hand, actually in their midst (Matthew 12:28; Luke 17:21).

b. For the Fruition of the Work of God (11:14-15)

Drawing His vindication of John the Baptist to a close, the Lord said, "If ye will receive it, this is Elias, which was for to come" (11:14). Jesus added a challenge for intelligent faith: "He that hath ears to hear, let him hear" (11:15). This expression was used fifteen times by the Lord Jesus. He used it seven times while He was on earth (in their proper order, Luke 8:8; Matthew 11:15; 13:9,43; Mark 4:23; 7:16; Luke 14:35) and eight times after He went to Heaven (in connection with the seven churches in Revelation 2–3; and in Revelation 13:9). *The Companion Bible* states, "The words were never used by mortal man. They were heard only from the lips of Him Who spoke with Divine authority."[4] As John 7:46 says, "Never man spake like this man."

In Matthew 11:15 the expression is used to emphasize the importance of John the Baptist's mission. The Lord wanted the people to understand what would have happened if the nation had heeded John and received the kingdom just proclaimed throughout the land by the twelve apostles and forced on their attention by His person and work. John would have been reckoned as Elijah the prophet (Malachi 4:5) in whose spirit and power he came (Luke 1:17).

Had the Jews repented and wholeheartedly hailed Jesus as King, the seventieth seven of years spoken of in Daniel 9:24-27 would have immediately run its course. There would have been no need for the two-thousand-year exile of the Jews. The terrible events predicted for that seventieth week would have swiftly taken place. The true Elijah would have come and effected the "restitution of all things" (Acts 3:21).

But the nation did not repent. Malachi 4:5 still awaits its literal fulfillment. Those who have "ears to hear" will understand.

II. THE MINISTRY OF JESUS (11:16-30)

A. The Illustration (11:16-19)

Moving the spotlight from John to Jesus, Matthew continued the same sad story of resistance. His record shows that the Lord used *a very significant illustration.* Jesus began, "Whereunto shall I liken this generation?" (11:16) Note the expression "this generation." It occurs sixteen times in the New Testament (Matthew 11:16; 12:41,42; 23:36; 24:34; Mark 8:12 (twice); 13:30; Luke 7:31; 11:30,31,32,50,51; 17:25; 21:32). It occurs another nine times with adjectives—"evil," "wicked," "adulterous," "sinful" (Matthew 12:39,45; 16:4; Mark 8:38; Luke 11:29); "faithless," "perverse" (Matthew 17:17; Mark 9:19; Luke 9:41); "untoward" (Acts 2:40). With only one exception (Matthew 24:34), the expression describes the generation that rejected the Messiah. In all cases it refers to a literal generation.

By introducing the phrase "this generation," the Lord began to toll the bell for the Jewish nation. Its day of visitation and judgment was fast approaching. The Lord had accurately assessed the turn of the tide. He had weighed the nation in the balance and found it wanting.

The comparison Jesus made was not only significant. It was *a very simple illustration.* He likened that impossible generation to children who reject every effort to please them. They complain at weddings as well as funerals.

It was *a very suitable illustration*. The ascetic John the Baptist had come shunning the abodes of men, wearing the coarsest clothing, eating the poorest food. And what was the response of that generation? They said, "He hath a devil" (11:18). In other words, "He is possessed by a demon." The Lord had come "eating and drinking" like anyone else—and what was their response? They said, "Behold a man gluttonous, and a winebibber [how appalling to accuse Him of being a drunkard!], a friend of publicans and sinners" (11:19). What could await a people so perverse and blasphemous but judgment?

B. The Indictment (11:20-24)

1. The Cause (11:20)

The Lord turned quickly from the illustration to the indictment. "Then began he to upbraid the cities wherein most of his mighty works were done, because they repented not." They had heard the sermon on the mount, they had seen His miracles, and they had received the witness of John the Baptist and the twelve apostles, but they "repented not." Jesus had lived and loved and labored in those cities. There He had done His mightiest works; there the light was brightest; there the evidence was irrefutable. They had been first-hand witnesses of the reality of His claims, yet they had refused to change their minds about the nature of the kingdom, the nearness of the King, and their need for repentance.

Those cities were representative of the whole. If He was rejected by them, there was no need to go any farther. The reception would be the same everywhere in Israel. So let the woes come. They were inevitable. People who would find fault with John the Baptist and the Lord Jesus did not deserve the kingdom; they deserved judgment and they could not avoid it.

2. The Curse (11:21-24)

a. The First Curse (11:21-22)

(1) The Present (11:21a)

The first curse concerned two great Galilean cities, Chorazin and Bethsaida. Little or nothing is known of Chorazin, but it is thought to have been a scant two miles from Capernaum at a site now marked by extensive ruins. We have no record of any visit by the

Lord to Chorazin, yet Matthew said it was one of the cities in which "most of his mighty works were done" (11:20). Obviously we know only a small part of the full story. The apostle John wrote, "There are also many other things which Jesus did, the which, if they should be written every one, I suppose that even the world itself could not contain the books that should be written" (John 21:25). He should know, for he (like Matthew) was an eyewitness.

Bethsaida (called Julias by the Romans) was probably a suburb of Capernaum. It was from Bethsaida that Peter, Andrew, and Philip had come in response to the call of the King. To both Bethsaida and Chorazin, the Lord said, "Woe unto thee."

(2) The Past (11:21b)

The Lord contrasted those two great Galilean cities with two great Gentile cities, Tyre and Sidon. He said that if Tyre and Sidon had seen the works done in Chorazin and Bethsaida, "they would have repented long ago in sackcloth and ashes."

Tyre and Sidon were sister cities. Tyre was one of the wealthiest cities of antiquity and her ships bore the commerce of the world. Mighty Carthage on the north coast of Africa had under Hannibal almost conquered Rome, but she was only a colony of Tyre.

(3) The Prospect (11:22)

The Phoenician cities of Tyre and Sidon were powerful, but they were moral sewers and their pagan religions foul. Jezebel came from Sidon. God raised up Elijah to battle the abominations she imported into Israel. "But," said Jesus, "I say unto you, It shall be more tolerable for Tyre and Sidon at the day of judgment, than for you." God measures sin by the light a man, a city, or a nation has been given. The greater the light, the greater the responsibility.

b. The Further Curse (11:23-24)

(1) The Present (11:23a)

The further curse concerned the most privileged of cities, Capernaum. Was any other city ever more blessed? When the King commenced His public ministry, He moved to Capernaum. He made it, so to speak, His temporary capital. Capernaum was His adopted home, the center from which He went forth, and the center to which He always returned from His mission.

Just outside Capernaum He had cleansed the leper. It was the centurion of Capernaum whose servant the Lord had healed. It was the ruler of the Capernaum synagogue whose daughter Jesus had raised from the dead. But Jesus said, "And thou, Capernaum, which art exalted unto heaven, shalt be brought down to hell."

(2) The Past (11:23b)

Jesus went on to contrast that most privileged of cities with the most polluted of cities, Sodom: "If the mighty works, which have been done in [Capernaum], had been done in Sodom, it would have remained until this day." Was there ever a city viler than Sodom? It has given its very name to unnatural vice. In Scripture Sodom is set forth as the supreme example of an overthrow without remedy. God rained down fire and brimstone on Sodom to blot it out and to declare for all time His abhorrence for the homosexual lifestyle it represented.

(3) The Prospect (11:24)

Doubtless the people of Capernaum never groveled in the lusts of Sodom, but Jesus said that their sins were worse. He said to them, "It shall be more tolerable for the land of Sodom in the day of judgment, than for thee." In God's sight, to have lived in the light and privilege given to Capernaum and then to have repudiated that light was a sin worse than Sodom's.

It behooves us to remember that our nation has been given more light than that which was given to Capernaum! We live on this side of the cross. We have a completed New Testament. The Holy Spirit has come. Pentecost has come. The church has been born. In Capernaum's day the Lord's mighty works were largely in the sphere of the physical, but in our land spiritual miracles take place every day. The full light of the gospel has blazed in our cities. Language borrowed from another context reveals the prospect of anyone who rejects the light today:

> Of how much sorer punishment, suppose ye, shall he be thought worthy, who hath trodden under foot the Son of God, and hath counted the blood of the covenant, wherewith he was sanctified, an unholy thing, and hath done despite unto the Spirit of grace? (Hebrews 10:29)

After finishing His illustration and indictment, the Lord turned to His Father for consolation and then, ignoring the nation, appealed to individuals to respond.

C. The Invocation (11:25-27)

Matthew's introductory phrase, "At that time," emphasizes the Lord's rejection (11:25). The cities where He had lived and worked had added their repudiation of Him to all their other sins. His faithful forerunner had sent questions revealing doubt, discouragement, and despair. The Lord's own generation had become childish in its whining unreasonableness. So Jesus turned from men to God. In the face of difficulty the Lord worshiped and gave thanks. He might have said with Jacob, "All these things are against me" (Genesis 42:36). Or like Elijah He might have complained bitterly to God (1 Kings 19:10). Instead He worshiped.

In His prayer we are confronted with two mysteries: the mystery of the divine process and the mystery of the divine person.

1. The Mystery of the Divine Process (11:25-26)

Jesus prayed, "I thank thee, O Father, Lord of heaven and earth, because thou hast hid these things from the wise and prudent, and hast revealed them unto babes" (11:25). He was inferring that the divine process is *inevitable.*

On one side the Lord put "the wise and prudent"—that is, the Pharisees, Sadducees, scribes, priests, rabbis, who thought they knew it all. They were sophisticated and versed in all the rules and rituals of religion and in the endless traditions of the elders. On the other side the Lord put "babes"—that is, His disciples, who were prepared to take the Lord at His word. For the most part they were simple souls, humble fisher folk, described by the intellectuals as "unlearned and ignorant men" (Acts 4:13).

Some people think that because they can figure things out (put two and two together, as we say), they have all the answers. They are hard to reach with the gospel. They are too clever to come to Christ, too good to be guided. On the other hand, some people are still able to see with the wonder and acceptance and faith of a child. To such the gospel appeals. God hides things from those who are wise in their own conceit and reveals them instead to those who will simply take Him at His word. It is the way God works.

Jesus added to His prayer, "Even so, Father: for so it seemed good in thy sight" (11:26). The Lord was content with God's way because it is based on omniscient wisdom. God makes no mistakes. The divine process is *infallible*.

2. The Mystery of the Divine Person (11:27)

a. He Is Invincible (11:27a)

In an exclamation the Lord revealed the mystery of the divine person. He began, "All things are delivered unto me of my Father." The Father has given Jesus all wisdom, all power, all authority, all that is needed to establish the kingdom. God could trust no one else with such an investiture of power; the axiom that power corrupts has been demonstrated in history times without number. But Christ was wholly incorruptible, so all things could be and have been trusted to that glorious Man who works in perfect harmony with His Father.

When Jesus spoke the words recorded in 11:27, it was evident that the kingdom He had come to establish would have to be postponed because of Jewish intransigence and unbelief. But the postponement was by no means the last word. The Lord would build a church. Then He would come back and carry the kingdom through to its full scope and end. The Jews had failed, but He had not failed. He is invincible.

b. He Is Inscrutable (11:27b-c)

(1) The Exclusive Relationship (11:27b)

"No man knoweth the Son, but the Father," Jesus declared, making an undiluted claim to deity. There are depths and mysteries in the person of Christ we will never fathom. In Him we have both perfect deity and perfect humanity. No one can tell where the one ends and the other begins. His nature is inscrutable.

We have formulated our creeds in well-meaning attempts to grasp the nature of Christ's person and to defend the truth against the inroads of heresy. But when we have said it all, we have but touched the hem of His garment. Our sounding lines are far too short to plumb the depths of His glorious being. In the old days when ships sailed in unknown seas, sounding lines were vital. As the ships approached the shallows, the men in the bows took their leads and lines to the forechains, cast them into the sea, and called back their findings: "By the mark five!" or "Deep four!" But what every captain liked to hear was "No bottom with this line!" If we could ever touch bottom in understanding the person of Christ, He would not be God. But He is.

Jesus gave us more to think about: "Neither knoweth any man the Father, save the Son." The gulf between creature and Creator is infinite. No creature, however great his intellectual genius, can comprehend the marvels of God. We cannot unravel all the mysteries of His creation, let alone His character. Between God and man there is a great gulf fixed, an enormous distance in kind. What can we know of the omnipotence, omnipresence, and omniscience of God? We can only play in the shallows of His love, His holiness, His eternal counsels, and His godhead.

The scribes and Pharisees thought they knew God. They knew a bit about God from what He had been pleased to reveal of His mind, heart, and will in the Old Testament. But they had so debated, discussed, and distorted those Scriptures that most of their conclusions about God were wrong.

When Christ said, "Neither knoweth any man the Father, save the Son," He was making another claim to deity. He was claiming to have a mind coextensive with the mind of God, a mind able to think God's thoughts. He was claiming to have a mind that could grasp all the factors of space and time, all the annals of eternity, all the multitudinous details that make up omniscience. Christ was claiming to have a heart that beat in perfect harmony with that of the Father and a will that was able to translate into action the eternal purposes and volition of the infinite. Jesus did not know the Father in the elementary, limited way in which a creature can be said to know Him. Jesus knew the Father even as the Father knew Him—fully, flawlessly. The Lord knew the depths of the Father's being, the complexities of His character, and all the wonders of His person, nature, and personality.

(2) The Expanded Relationship (11:27c)

The Lord added to His statement: "Neither knoweth any man the Father, save the Son, *and he to whomsoever the Son will reveal him*" (italics added). No one can know God apart from Christ. To seek for Him in the teachings of Hinduism, Buddhism, or Islam is to seek for Him in vain. Those teachings do not reveal the Father. To seek Him in creation is equally vain. Creation witnesses to God's eternal power and godhead, but it does not reveal the Father in all the glories of His person and the mysteries of His being. Only Jesus can reveal that. And He does.

When Philip said, "Lord, shew us the Father, and it sufficeth us," Jesus replied, "He that hath seen me hath seen the Father" (John 14:8-9). No such utterance ever fell from the lips of a Hebrew prophet or a Christian apostle. John said, "No man hath seen God at any time; the only begotten Son, which is in the bosom of the Father, he hath declared him" (John 1:18). The word translated "hath declared" here is *exēgeomai,* which means "to lead the way, to make known by expounding." Our word "exegesis" is derived from *exēgeomai.* The Lord Jesus is the exegesis of God.

D. The Invitation (11:28-30)

The nation as a nation had not responded, so the Lord made a personal appeal to the individual. The invitation, coming in a wonderful triplet of verses we know by heart, contains a call for salvation and a call for service.

1. The Call for Salvation (11:28)

The call for salvation consists of a *plea* and a *pledge:* "Come unto me, all ye that labour and are heavy laden, and I will give you rest." What a word picture that was to rabbinic religion and all other religions based on works! Heavy is the load of sin. Laborious and burdensome are man's religious systems with their rites and ceremonies, sacraments and sacrifices, tithes and offerings, rules and regulations, penances and fasts, long prayers and tedious catechisms. Jesus swept those burdens all away.

In the Lord's call, "labour" is countered with "give"; "heavy laden" is countered with "rest." The rest Christ offers cannot be bought or merited or earned. It is a gift. There is nothing to do but come—then rest. Once we have received the gift, we do not have to maintain our salvation by our own efforts. We just rest in Him and in His finished work.

2. The Call for Service (11:29-30)

a. The Appeal (11:29)

Three words sum up the call for service: "take," "learn," and "find." "Take" speaks of our decision; "learn" speaks of our development; and "find" speaks of our discovery.

(1) Our Decision—"Take" (11:29a)

"Take my yoke upon you," Jesus said. Once we are saved, we are called to be harnessed to Him, to work alongside Him. He does not force His yoke on us. The Lord invites us to come and share in His great work in this needy world, to get in step with Him, to be His helpers—as though He needed our help!

What an amazing invitation and how few there are who respond! What greater privilege could there be in all this world than to be yoked to Christ, to be shoulder to shoulder with Him, to take each step with Him? We are given the opportunity to decide to face with Him the unplowed, unplanted field of this world and to leave behind us long furrows in which are planted the precious seed that is able to bring harvests long after our days on earth are done.

(2) Our Development—"Learn" (11:29b-c)

Jesus had just been saying to the common people, who were so religious, and to the leaders of the nation, who were so wrong, "You don't know the Father. I am the only One who knows the Father. If you want to know the Father, you will have to come to Me." We can imagine the reaction: "What arrogance! What conceit!" And we can hear the Lord replying, "On the contrary. I am meek and lowly in heart. What I said about My relationship to the Father is not a manifestation of pride that has overflowed its banks. It is just a statement of the truth. That's the way it is. What I said is a spiritual truth as accurate, unavoidable, and demonstrable as any other kind of truth—be it agricultural, mathematical, or biological."

The Jews rejected Jesus because He was meek and lowly. They did not want a meek King. They wanted a militant King who would smash the power of Rome and make Jerusalem the capital of a new world empire governed by the Jews. They did not want a lowly King. They wanted a lordly King who would humble their enemies in the dust and plant His feet on the necks of Israel's foes.

But the Lord wants us to learn to be like Him. "Learn of me," He said, "for I am meek and lowly in heart." He wants those of us whom He has saved and called into harness to learn the truth about the Father, the truth about the Son, and the truth about ourselves. Our development should be characterized by an ever-growing grasp of the eternal and the infinite.

(3) Our Discovery—"Find" (11:29d)

"Ye shall find rest unto your souls," Jesus pledged. That rest is the secret of true service for the King. True service does not involve feverish anxiety, restless activity, constant pressure, endless deadlines, exhausting haste. True, there is work to be done; there are things to be accomplished for God. But all acceptable service results from our rest in Him.

b. The Assurance (11:30)

The appeal of 11:28-29 leads to the assurance of 11:30: "My yoke is easy, and my burden is light." The Lord will never tax us beyond our strength, never impose a task beyond the ability He gives. He is on the other side of the yoke and He carries all its weight. The responsibility is His. The results are His burden, not ours. The Lord is the kindest, most considerate Master in the world. Come! Take! Learn! Find!

SECTION 3

THE RESISTANCE FOCUSED

(12:1–14:36)

I. THE MALICE OF THE PHARISEES (12:1-50)
  A. Restoring the Sabbath (12:1-14)
    1. A Matter of Hunger on the Sabbath (12:1-8)
      a. Aggravation (12:1)
        (1) The Day
        (2) The Desire
        (3) The Deed
      b. Accusation (12:2-5)
        (1) Its Foundation (12:2)
        (2) Its Folly (12:3-5)
          (a) As to the Deed—The Shewbread (12:3-4)
          (b) As to the Day—The Sacrifices (12:5)
      c. Affirmation (12:6-8)
        (1) Jesus Greater Than the Jewish Sanctuary (12:6-7)
        (2) Jesus Greater Than the Jewish Sabbath (12:8)
    2. A Matter of Healing on the Sabbath (12:9-14)
      a. The Case (12:9-10)
        (1) Where This Incident Took Place (12:9)
        (2) When This Incident Took Place (12:10a)
        (3) Why This Incident Took Place (12:10b)
      b. The Comment (12:11-12)
        (1) How Appropriate It Was (12:11)
        (2) How Applicable It Was (12:12)
      c. The Cure (12:13)
      d. The Council (12:14)
  B. Reaffirming the Scriptures (12:15-24)

1. The Path the Lord Followed (12:15-16)
   a. The Choice He Made (12:15)
      (1) To Withdraw from the Presence of the
          Pharisees (12:15a)
      (2) To Withstand all the Pressure of the
          Pharisees (12:15b)
   b. The Charge He Made (12:16)
2. The Prophecy the Lord Fulfilled (12:17-21)
   a. The Name of the Prophet (12:17)
   b. The Nature of the Prophecy (12:18-21)
      (1) The Marks of the Messiah (12:18)
          (a) His Person (12:18a-b)
              i. He Came to Serve the Living God
                 (12:18a)
              ii. He Came to Satisfy the Living God
                  (12:18b)
          (b) His Power (12:18c)
          (c) His People (12:18d)
      (2) The Method of the Messiah (12:19-20)
          (a) The Dispositional Note (12:19-20a)
              i. The Quietness of His Approach
                 (12:19)
              ii. The Quality of His Appeal
                  (12:20a)
          (b) The Dispensational Note (12:20b)
      (3) The Majesty of the Messiah (12:21)
3. The Prejudice the Lord Fought (12:22-24)
   a. The Miracle of the Lord (12:22-23)
      (1) The Action of the Master (12:22)
      (2) The Acclaim of the Multitude (12:23)
   b. The Malice of the Leaders (12:24)
      (1) Their Bitterness (12:24a)
      (2) Their Blasphemy (12:24b)
C. Refuting the Scorners (12:25-37)
   1. What the Pharisees Said Was Unfounded (12:25-30)
      a. How the Lord Read Their Thoughts (12:25a)
      b. How the Lord Rejected Their Theory (12:25b-30)
         (1) The Consequence of a Divided Kingdom
             (12:25b-27)

(a) The Principle (12:25b)
(b) The Problem (12:26-27)
   i. Made Practical (12:26)
   ii. Made Personal (12:27)
(2) The Confirmation of a Divine Kingdom (12:28-30)
(a) Its Presence (12:28)
(b) Its Power (12:29)
(c) Its People (12:30)
2. What the Pharisees Said Was Unforgivable (12:31-37)
  a. The Nature of Their Sin Exposed (12:31-32)
    (1) Blaspheming the Holy Ghost (12:31)
      (a) Unfathomable Grace (12:31a)
      (b) Unforgivable Guilt (12:31b)
    (2) Belittling the Holy Ghost (12:32)
      (a) The Greatness of God's Mercy (12:32a)
      (b) The Greatness of Their Malice (12:32b)
  b. The Nature of Their Souls Exposed (12:33-37)
    (1) The Source of What We Say (12:33-35)
      (a) A Tree and Its Vintage (12:33)
      (b) A Tongue and Its Venom (12:34)
      (c) A Treasure and Its Value (12:35)
    (2) The Seriousness of What We Say (12:36-37)
      (a) The Everlasting Nature of Our Words (12:36)
      (b) The Evidential Nature of Our Words (12:37)
D. Refusing the Sign (12:38-50)
 1. The National Folly (12:38-45)
  a. The Impertinence of Israel's Peers (12:38-42)
    (1) The Sign Demanded (12:38)
    (2) The Sign Denied (12:39)
    (3) The Sign Discussed (12:40-42)
      (a) A New Factor: The Final Rejection of Jesus by the Hebrews
      (b) A New Focus: The Forthcoming Reception of Jesus by the Heathen
        i. Illustration: The Gentile People Who Sought and Found God's Salvation

    ii. Illustration: The Gentile Princess Who
     Sought and Found God's Sovereignty
  b. The Impenitence of Israel's People (12:43-45)
   (1) A Disturbing Parable (12:43-45a)
    (a) The Demon's Unwilling Departure
     (12:43a)
    (b) The Demon's Unhappy Doom
     (12:43b)
    (c) The Demon's Understandable Decision
     (12:44a)
    (d) The Demon's Unexpected Discovery
     (12:44b)
    (e) The Demon's Unholy Deed
     (12:45a)
   (2) A Dreadful Parallel (12:45b)
 2. The New Family (12:46-50)
  a. The Old Ties Dissolved (12:46-47)
   (1) The Coming of the Lord's Family (12:46)
   (2) The Call of the Lord's Family (12:47)
  b. The New Truth Disclosed (12:48-50)
   (1) Former Relationships Challenged (12:48)
   (2) Future Relationships Changed (12:49-50)
    (a) A New People (12:49)
    (b) A New Principle (12:50)

II. THE MYSTERIES OF THE KINGDOM (13:1-52)
 A. Parables Spoken Publicly (13:1-35)
  1. The Multitudes (13:1-2)
  2. The Mysteries (13:3-35)
   a. The Parable of the Sower—The Message of
    Salvation—Emphasis on the Dispositional
    Aspect (13:3-23)
    (1) The Introduction of the Parable (13:3-9)
     (a) The Sower (13:3)
     (b) The Soil (13:4-8)
      i. The Roadside Soil (13:4)
       The seed's chance for survival:
       a. Little Indeed
       b. Lost Instantly

      ii. The Rocky Soil (13:5-6)
         a. No Depth (13:5)
         b. No Development (13:6)
      iii. The Ruined Soil (13:7)
      iv. The Rich Soil (13:8)
   (c) The Summons (13:9)
(2) The Interruption of the Parable (13:10-17)
   (a) A Word about the Parables (13:10-13)
      i. A Mystery (13:10-11)
      ii. A Method (13:12)
      iii. A Motive (13:13)
   (b) A Word about God's Prophet (13:14-15)
      i. The Man (13:14)
      ii. The Message (13:15)
   (c) A Word about the Disciples' Privilege (13:16-17)
      i. The Discernment That Was Theirs (13:16)
      ii. The Dispensation That Was Theirs (13:17)
(3) The Interpretation of the Parable (13:18-23)
   (a) The Waywardness of Some (13:18-19)
      i. The Word Superficially Received (13:18-19a)
      ii. The Word Satanically Removed (13:19b)
   (b) The Weakness of Some (13:20-21)
      i. Their Initial Response (13:20)
      ii. Their Incomplete Response (13:21)
   (c) The Worldliness of Some (13:22)
      i. Worry Destroys the Seed (13:22a)
      ii. Wealth Destroys the Seed (13:22b)
   (d) The Willingness of Some (13:23)
      i. The Word Comprehendingly Received into the Life (13:23a)
      ii. The Word Consequently Reproduced in the Life (13:23b)

b. The Parable of the Tares—The Malice of
Satan—Emphasis on the Diabolical
Aspect (13:24-30)
   (1) The Sowing (13:24-25)
        (a) The Pure Seed (13:24)
        (b) The Poisonous Weed (13:25)
   (2) The Growing (13:26-28a)
        (a) The Exposure of the Presence of the
             Weeds (13:26)
        (b) The Explanation of the Presence of the
             Weeds (13:27-28a)
   (3) The Mowing (13:28b-30)
        (a) The Proposal (13:28b)
        (b) The Prospect (13:29-30)
              i. Growing Permitted Now (13:29-30a)
             ii. Gathering Promised Then (13:30b)
c. The Parable of the Mustard Seed—The Myth of
Supremacy—Emphasis on the Dispensational
Aspect (13:31-32)
   (1) What the Mustard Showed (13:31-32a)
        (a) A Weird Growth
        (b) A Worldly Grandeur
   (2) What the Mustard Sheltered (13:32b)
d. The Parable of the Leaven—The Mystery of
Subversion—Emphasis on the Doctrinal
Aspect (13:33-35)
   (1) The Woman (13:33)
        (a) The Activity of the Leaven
              i. The Loaf
             ii. The Leaven
                  a. Belief Corrupted by Evil
                  b. Behavior Corrupted by Evil
        (b) The Action of the Woman
   (2) The Word (13:34-35)
        (a) A Note regarding the Lord's Parables
             (13:34)
        (b) A Note regarding the Lord's Purpose
             (13:35)

          i. To Vindicate the Truth of God's
            Word (13:35a)
         ii. To Voice the Truth of God's
            Word (13:35b)

B. Parables Spoken Privately (13:36-52)
  1. An Explanation (13:36-43)
    a. The Place (13:36)
    b. The Parable (13:37-43)
      (1) The Facts (13:37-38)
        (a) The Sower (13:37)
        (b) The Soil (13:38a)
        (c) The Seed (13:38b)
      (2) The Foe (13:39a)
      (3) The Future (13:39b-c)
        (a) The End-Time Age (13:39b)
        (b) The End-Time Agents (13:39c)
      (4) The Fire (13:40-42)
        (a) The Type of the Tares (13:40)
        (b) The Truth of the Torment (13:41-42)
      (5) The Faithful (13:43)
  2. An Expansion (13:44-52)
    a. The Parable of the Hidden Treasure—A National
       Postponement—The Hebrew People (13:44)
      (1) A Place (13:44a)
      (2) A Plan (13:44b)
      (3) A Price (13:44c)
    b. The Parable of the Costly Pearl—A New
       Possession—The Heavenly People (13:45-46)
      (1) The Great Quest (13:45-46a)
        (a) What the Merchant Desired (13:45)
        (b) What the Merchant Discovered (13:46a)
      (2) The Great Question (13:46b)
    c. The Parable of the Great Net—A Necessary
       Process—The Heathen Peoples (13:47-50)
      (1) What Was Sought (13:47a)
      (2) What Was Caught (13:47b)
      (3) What Was Wrought (13:48)
      (4) What Was Taught (13:49-50)

        (a) The Angels of the Lord (13:49)

        (b) The Anguish of the Lost (13:50)

     d. The Parable of the Wise Householder—A Needful Perception (13:51-52)

        (1) Truth Must Be Discerned (13:51)

        (2) Truth Must Be Dispensed (13:52)

III. THE MURDER OF JOHN (13:53–14:36)

  A. Home and Its Critics (13:53-58)

    1. The Home Scene (13:53-54)

     a. The Surroundings (13:53-54a)

     b. The Synagogue (13:54b-c)

        (1) The Authority of Christ's Teaching (13:54b)

        (2) The Astonishment of Christ's Townsfolk (13:54c)

    2. The Hostile Setting (13:55-58)

     a. The Reason for the Hostility (13:55-57a)

        (1) Small-Town Reasoning (13:55-56a)

        (2) Small-Town Resentment (13:56b-57a)

     b. The Result of the Hostility (13:57b-58)

        (1) A Sobering Observation (13:57b)

        (2) A Sad Observation (13:58)

  B. Herod and His Conscience (14:1-12)

    1. A Wrong Deduction (14:1-2)

     a. What Herod Heard (14:1)

     b. What Haunted Herod (14:2)

        (1) His First Supposition (14:2a)

        (2) His Further Supposition (14:2b)

    2. A Wicked Determination (14:3-12)

     a. A Crime Postponed (14:3-5)

        (1) The Infuriated Herodias (14:3-4)

           (a) Why John Suffered (14:3)

           (b) What John Said (14:4)

        (2) The Indecisive Herod (14:5)

           (a) What He Desired (14:5a)

           (b) Why He Delayed (14:5b)

      b. A Crime Proposed (14:6-8)
        (1) The Day (14:6a)
        (2) The Dance (14:6b)
        (3) The Dilemma (14:7-8)
           (a) The Foolish Pledge (14:7)
           (b) The Fateful Plea (14:8)
      c. A Crime Perpetrated (14:9-12)
        (1) John Beheaded (14:9-11)
           (a) The King's Cowardice (14:9)
           (b) The King's Command (14:10-11)
        (2) John Buried (14:12)
C. Humanity and Its Cares (14:13-36)
   1. Compassion for the Hosts of Mankind (14:13-14)
      a. The Deep Need of the Master (14:13a)
      b. The Deep Need of the Multitude (14:13b-14)
        (1) How It Was Manifested (14:13b)
        (2) How It Was Met (14:14)
           (a) The Heart of Jesus Revealed (14:14a)
           (b) The Healing of Jesus Resumed (14:14b)
   2. Compassion for the Hunger of Mankind (14:15-21)
      a. The Problem (14:15-18)
        (1) The Answer of Logic (14:15)
           (a) What the Disciples Saw (14:15a)
           (b) What the Disciples Said (14:15b)
        (2) The Answer of Love (14:16-18)
           (a) What the Disciples Heard (14:16)
           (b) What the Disciples Had (14:17-18)
             i. A Limited Supply (14:17)
             ii. A Limitless Savior (14:18)
      b. The Provision (14:19-21)
        (1) A Blessed Supply (14:19)
           (a) The Multitude (14:19a)
           (b) The Miracle (14:19b-c)
             i. Its Spiritual Dimension (14:19b)
             ii. Its Supernatural Dimension (14:19c)
        (2) A Bountiful Supply (14:20-21)
           (a) A Note about Needs (14:20)

          i. No Want (14:20a)
          ii. No Waste (14:20b)
        (b) A Note about Numbers (14:21)
  3. Compassion for the Helplessness of Mankind
      (14:22-33)
      a. Tranquility (14:22-25)
        (1) Desired (14:22-23)
          (a) The Method (14:22-23a)
            i. Jesus Sent His Men Away (14:22a)
            ii. Jesus Sent the Multitudes Away
                (14:22b-23a)
          (b) The Motive (14:23b)
        (2) Disturbed (14:24-25)
          (a) The Coming of the Storm (14:24)
          (b) The Coming of the Savior (14:25)
      b. Terror (14:26)
        (1) What the Disciples Saw (14:26a)
        (2) What the Disciples Supposed (14:26b)
      c. Trust (14:27-31)
        (1) The Basis of Peter's Trust (14:27)
        (2) The Boldness of Peter's Trust (14:28-29)
        (3) The Breakdown of Peter's Trust (14:30-31)
          (a) The Reason (14:30)
          (b) The Remedy (14:31)
      d. Truth (14:32-33)
        (1) The Sudden Calm (14:32)
        (2) The Sublime Confession (14:33)
  4. Compassion for the Hurts of Mankind (14:34-36)
      a. The Arrival of the Master (14:34)
      b. The Arrival of the Multitudes (14:35-36)
        (1) The News (14:35a)
        (2) The Need (14:35b-36)
          (a) No End to Their Problems (14:35b)
          (b) No End to His Power (14:36)

I. THE MALICE OF THE PHARISEES (12:1-50)

A. Restoring the Sabbath (12:1-14)

The resistance to the Lord became increasingly prominent and Matthew piled up the evidence against his own people, the Jews. The malice of the Pharisees centered on their disagreement with the Lord over the sabbath. Indeed it was the sabbath question that brought the Jewish authorities to their decision to get rid of Jesus.

The sabbath and circumcision were the most important and sacred of institutions; they made a Jew a Jew. The sabbath particularly was a distinctive of Judaism. No other people set apart one day in seven for worship of God, enjoyment of rest, and cultivation of the spiritual side of life. The rabbis hedged the sabbath around with a thousand restrictions.

1. A Matter of Hunger on the Sabbath (12:1-8)

a. Aggravation (12:1)

The Pharisees were now dogging Jesus' footsteps, looking for things to criticize. They pounced the moment the disciples began to pluck, husk, and eat corn on the sabbath. The Pharisees did not accuse the disciples of stealing, because such gleaning was legal (Deuteronomy 23:25); they accused them of breaking the sabbath. According to the rabbis, plucking corn constituted reaping, and rubbing corn in the hand was threshing. In their view both activities were illegal. The Lord's disciples, evidently with His approval, had violated the sabbath. This was the aggravation.

b. Accusation (12:2-5)

(1) Its Foundation (12:2)

The accusation followed at once: "Thy disciples do that which is not lawful to do upon the sabbath day." But the Lord kept every jot and tittle of the law. Never once in thought, word, or deed did He ever break a single commandment in letter or in spirit. Evidently then it was not a violation of the sabbath to do what the disciples were doing. The problem was not that they were breaking the sabbath, but that they were breaking the sabbath rules of the rabbis. The rabbis elevated their traditions above God's Word. In answering the charge, the King took responsibility for what the disciples had been doing. If they had broken any of God's laws, He would have restrained them.

(2) Its Folly (12:3-5)

The Lord skillfully parried the accusation. "Have ye not read...?" He asked (12:3). Jesus asked this question on six different occasions and referred to six different books of the Old Testament and seven different passages: Matthew 12:3 (Leviticus 24:6-9; 1 Samuel 21:6); Matthew 12:5 (Numbers 28:9-10); Matthew 19:4 (Genesis 1:27); Matthew 21:16 (Psalm 8:2); Matthew 21:42 (Psalm 118:22); Matthew 22:31-32 (Exodus 3:6). This is a significant illustration of our Lord's attitude toward the Word of God. He believed it, quoted it as authoritative, appealed to it without hesitation, knew it perfectly, and put His divine imprimatur on it in all its parts.[1] Those who detract from the Word of God are strangers to Christ.

(a) As to the Deed—The Shewbread (12:3-4)

The Lord drew the attention of the Pharisees to an incident in the life of David (1 Samuel 21:6). David and his followers were in flight from King Saul. They were hungry so they appealed to the high priest for bread. The only bread available was the sacred shewbread, which was placed on the table in the holy place of the tabernacle once a week. The bread was to be eaten by the priests and their dependents exclusively. However, the high priest (with a certain amount of hesitation) gave the twelve loaves to David and his men, and God's wrath did not descend. That took care of the Pharisees' objection to the disciples' eating what tradition said was unlawful food.

David's need was more important than a ritual, however authoritative. If God could thus set aside His ceremonial law, how much more could the Lord set aside rabbinic traditional law, which had no authority!

(b) As to the Day—The Sacrifices (12:5)

Again we read the Lord's cutting question, "Have ye not read...?" The Pharisees had read the law all right, but they had never understood it. "Have ye not read in the law," Jesus asked, "how that on the sabbath days the priests in the temple profane the sabbath, and are blameless?" The duties of the priests in the temple entailed hard work. The sabbath was the busiest day of the week for them.

They had to bake the shewbread and perform the sabbath day sacrifices (Numbers 28:9). Two lambs were added to the daily sacrifice on the sabbath. Think of what was involved in physical labor alone. First the priests had to inspect the animals to make sure they were without blemish. Then, paying special attention to the rituals involved, the priests had to slaughter the animals. The wood had to be brought to the tabernacle and placed on the altar. The animals had to be flayed and lifted upon the flames. In the sanctuary the lamps had to be trimmed, the table had to be tended, and the incense had to be burned on the golden altar. Evidently the Mosaic law of the sabbath did not forbid all work, only work for gain.

c. Affirmation (12:6-8)

The Lord followed up this logical reasoning with two astounding statements. He claimed to be greater than both the sanctuary and the sabbath.

(1) Jesus Greater Than the Jewish Sanctuary (12:6-7)

Looking the Pharisees in the eye, knowing what their reaction would be, aware that they wanted to get rid of Him and that they would seize on His words, Jesus said, "In this place is one greater than the temple" (12:6). The Jews had an almost idolatrous veneration for the temple. They stoned Stephen for what they considered to be an attack on it (Acts 7:47-51). They fought with the utmost fanaticism to protect it during the war with Rome in A.D. 70. To hear Jesus claim to be greater than the temple left them speechless.

The Lord's point was that if the temple service justified the priests for working on the sabbath, then the Lord's service justified the disciples because He was the true temple of God. The shekinah had long since departed from the temple. The Holy Spirit, God's true shekinah, now abode in and on the Lord. So He affirmed that He was greater than the sanctuary.

The sanctuary was the scene of endless ritual sacrifices. The Lord now swept aside the ritual law in an anticipatory statement founded on an Old Testament insight. Referring the Pharisees to Hosea 6:6, He dismissed centuries of erroneous rabbinical teaching and tradition: "If ye had known what this meaneth, I will have mercy, and not sacrifice, ye would not have condemned the guiltless" (Matthew 12:7).

The rabbis had made the sabbath a burden instead of a blessing.

They had heartlessly heaped on the longsuffering people, who were almost wholly dependent on them for Biblical teaching, a thousand requirements over and above the law. Content with the outward form—whether it had to do with the sabbath, the sanctuary, or the sacrifices—the rabbis had conveyed false ideas about God. Their God was meticulous, a stickler for details. But the true God—the One who instituted the sabbath, provided the sacrificial system, and once abode in their sanctuary—was merciful. The rabbis and Pharisees had missed the point and that was why they criticized the disciples, who were guiltless.

(2) Jesus Greater Than the Jewish Sabbath (12:8)

As if His claim to be greater than the temple were not enough fuel for the fire, the Lord added another: He affirmed that He was also greater than the sabbath. "The Son of man is Lord even of the sabbath day," He said. Jesus was Lord of the sabbath because He intended to set the whole system of sabbath-keeping aside.

He did not claim to be Lord of the sabbath as Son of God, but as Son of man, for "the sabbath was made for man" (Mark 2:27). The institution of the sabbath was a merciful provision of God for the welfare of His people. In the Old Testament the Jews found their sabbath rest in a day, the seventh day of the week in commemoration of God's creation rest (Genesis 2:1-3; Exodus 20:8-11). God's sabbath rest, however, had been broken by sin.

The Jewish sabbath was only a picture; it anticipated a rest based on the finished work of Christ (John 17:4; 19:30). So in the new covenant, our rest, like that of God, is in a person: Jesus, the Lord of the sabbath.[2]

2. A Matter of Healing on the Sabbath (12:9-14)

a. The Case (12:9-10)

Shortly after claiming to be greater than the sabbath, the Lord proved it by healing on the sabbath. This time the King took the battle into enemy territory. He entered "their synagogue" (12:9), where a spirit of criticism and hate reigned. In their synagogue on that sabbath sat a man with a withered hand, a case beyond medical help.

The Pharisees unconsciously paid the Lord a compliment by instantly linking the King in His power and the poor man in his sad condition. Perhaps the Pharisees saw the Master looking at the man; the Lord's eyes would have been alight with love and with the wondrous mercy to which He had recently referred (Matthew 12:7; Hosea 6:6).

The Pharisees had a trap ready for the Lord. We can feel sorry for those narrow-minded men, so parochial in their outlook on life and so warped in their understanding of what God is like and what the Bible is all about. How mean and petty they were when confronted with the mind of omniscient genius, the heart of infinite compassion, and the will of unyielding resolve in the person of the Lord Jesus. Baiting their trap, they asked, "Is it lawful to heal on the sabbath days?" (Matthew 12:10). Their little plot was so transparent!

b. The Comment (12:11-12)

They thought they had Him, but the Lord was ready for the Pharisees. Easily and lovingly the Lord turned the tables on them. "What man shall there be among you," He asked, "that shall have one sheep, and if it fall into a pit on the sabbath day, will he not lay hold on it, and lift it out? How much then is a man better than a sheep? Wherefore it is lawful to do well on the sabbath days." The Pharisees were silenced.

In effect the Lord had said to them, "You care for that sheep because it is *yours* and you set a high value on it." The King was now claiming to own the afflicted man as well as the sabbath! That man was *His*, His sheep. The poor man with the useless, unsightly hand was of great worth in the sight of the Savior; he was infinitely more valuable than a sheep.

c. The Cure (12:13)

Before another word could be spoken, the Lord commanded the man to stretch forth his hand, and in obeying he was healed— instantly. Christ had demonstrated His sovereignty over the sabbath. The cure was proof of His deity.

d. The Council (12:14)

"Then the Pharisees went out, and held a council against him, how they might destroy him." Such is the incorrigible wickedness of the unregenerate but religious heart. This council of Christ's enemies was the first organized meeting to plan to get rid of Him. Mark 3:6 tells us that they even went so far as to plot with the

Herodians, the adherents of Herod Antipas. The Pharisees hated all that the Herodians stood for, but their hatred of Jesus was greater.

B. Reaffirming the Scriptures (12:15-24)

In the previous passage we saw the Lord restoring the sabbath, giving it back its simple dignity until such time as all sacrifices, sanctuaries, and sabbaths would become part of an obsolete religion; they would be rendered redundant by the cross and revitalized on a higher plane and in a spiritual dimension for a new dispensation and a new covenant. Now in 12:15-24 we will see the Lord, still in an ever-growing conflict with His enemies, reaffirming the Scriptures. This passage culminates with the Pharisees' committing the unpardonable sin and is followed by the first of the denunciations of the Jewish people that would lead to the destruction of Jerusalem, the dissolution of their nation, and an age-long dispersal.

1. The Path the Lord Followed (12:15-16)

The Lord left the synagogue where He had just healed the man with the withered hand. This is the first time He made the *choice* to withdraw Himself in order to escape from His enemies. Deliberate avoidance became characteristic of the Lord until the time came for Him to be crucified. Then He set His face as a flint (Isaiah 50:7), deliberately went to Jerusalem, and allowed events to take their inevitable course. The time for Him to die, however, was not yet, not there in Capernaum, and not by the Pharisees' method of stoning.

At this time the Lord still had mass popular support. Great throngs followed Him. Mark 3:7-8 tells us that "a great multitude from Galilee followed him, and from Judaea, And from Jerusalem, and from Idumaea, and from beyond Jordan; and they about Tyre and Sidon." His *charge* to them was that "they should not make him known" (Matthew 12:16).

2. The Prophecy the Lord Fulfilled (12:17-21)

Matthew showed that the Lord fulfilled Isaiah 42:1-4. That prophecy is particularly significant from the apostle's point of view because of its reference to the Gentiles. Matthew's introduction of Gentiles at this crisis in the Lord's ministry clearly shows that the Lord was about to terminate His efforts to win the whole Jewish nation. Henceforth He would minister to the small believing remnant in Israel and look forward to a great response among the Gentile nations.

The small believing remnant of the Jews were likened by the prophet Isaiah to "a bruised reed" that the Messiah in His tenderness would not break and to "smoking flax" that He would not quench (Matthew 12:20). This prophecy marvelously foretold the gentle character of the Lord Jesus.

If the hollow cylinder of a reed is bruised, the reed can no longer stand erect. Since a reed is weak to begin with, a bruised reed is weakness further weakened. It is a fitting picture of the poor broken specimens of humanity whom the Lord comforted and healed.

Smoking flax represents something that has lost its usefulness. In Bible times flax was used for wicks in shallow earthen oil lamps; flax allowed light to shine. But when it smoldered instead, it produced fumes that caused eyes to smart. The Pharisees and religious leaders were like smoking flax, and so were their teaching and example. The Lord was patient even with them. Some of their number did indeed become disciples; Nicodemus is the outstanding example.

In His ministry the Lord cared for the believing remnant, but He was already looking ahead to the other side of the cross and the inrush of Gentiles into the church. "In his name shall the Gentiles trust," Isaiah had foretold (Matthew 12:21). By the time Matthew wrote his Gospel for the Jews, the Gentile tide had already begun to rise. That wondrous tide is running still.

3. The Prejudice the Lord Fought (12:22-24)

a. The Miracle of the Lord (12:22-23)

(1) The Action of the Master (12:22)

A demoniac who was both blind and mute was now brought to Jesus. Imagine not being able to see or speak! Here was a broken reed indeed. The man's affliction was caused by a possessing evil spirit. The Lord "healed him, insomuch that the blind and dumb both spake and saw." The cure was instantaneous and complete.

(2) The Acclaim of the Multitude (12:23)

When the Lord performed the miracle, the common people were amazed. "Is not this the son of David?" they said. In other words, "This has to be the Messiah. How could anyone else do more?"

b. The Malice of the Leaders (12:24)

The Pharisees had a different explanation. They said, "This fellow doth not cast out devils, but by Beelzebub the prince of the devils." This was the second time they had said such a dreadful thing. The first time, the Lord ignored them, but warned His disciples against them (9:34; 10:25). Now the Pharisees were becoming bolder, more contemptuous, more hardened in unbelief. They did not know it, but this time they had crossed the mysterious boundary line between God's mercy and His wrath.

There are various explanations of the blasphemous title assigned to the Lord Jesus. One is that *Beelzebub* ("lord of the flies") was the god of the Ekronites (2 Kings 1:2); the name was changed out of contempt by the Hebrews to *Baalzebel* ("lord of the dunghill") and used as an epithet for the prince of demons.[3] No more insulting thing could have been said of God's beloved Son than to ascribe His glorious works to such a source.

Edersheim saw a different play on words. (According to him *Beelzebul* is the correct reading, not *Beelzebub*.) *Zebhul,* in rabbinic usage, referred to the temple, so Beelzebul would be master of the temple. On the other hand, the phonetically similar word *zibbul* had two meanings. Its primary meaning was "manuring with dung" and it took on the additional meaning of "sacrificing to idols." Hence *Beelzebul* could mean "the lord of those sacrificing to idols," that lord being "the worst and chiefest of demons, who presided over, and incited to, idolatry."[4] In other words, the Pharisees attributed the Lord's wondrous works to the devil. Beel*zebul* (lord of the temple) was to them no better than Beel*zibbul* (lord of idolatrous worship).

The Pharisees' blasphemous lie sealed the eternal doom of those who spoke it and the fate of the nation whose false shepherds they were. Their blasphemy also marked the turning point in the life of the Lord. All events now trended toward Calvary.

C. Refuting the Scorners (12:25-37)

This time the Lord refuted the scorners. Note His calm and deliberate response to their terrible blasphemy. Here we have no angry retort, no hot and hasty denunciation. What we have is a methodical exposure of their folly and a sad statement of their doom.

1. What the Pharisees Said Was Unfounded (12:25-30)

Verse 25 begins with an affirmation of the Lord's omniscience: "Jesus knew their thoughts." He *read their thoughts* and He *rejected their theory.*

In repudiating the Pharisees' blasphemy, the Lord did something He rarely did. He answered an attack on Himself by presenting an argument. Usually if someone challenged Him, He left them to themselves or answered in a brief, authoritative, unanswerable word stamped with the genius of omniscience. The fact that here He developed a more extended answer, one based on logic and the law of cause and effect, underlines the seriousness and solemnity of the occasion. He argued that what the Pharisees had just said in their jealous rage was inconceivable, inconsistent, and incongruous.

Their accusation was inconceivable because if the Lord cast out demons by the power of Beelzebub, Satan's kingdom was in a state of civil war. A kingdom divided against itself cannot stand. Note that the Lord Jesus recognized the fact that there was an organized kingdom of evil in the unseen world, that it was directed with malice toward the human race, that it was ruled by a malevolent and personal prince, and that Satan's kingdom was united and not torn into warring factions. Satan would not proceed against the human race in the manner stated by the Pharisees. Their claim was absurd.

It was also inconsistent. The Pharisees' disciples practiced exorcism (12:27). If the Lord cast out demons by the power of the prince of demons, how did the Pharisees' "children" do it? By the prince of demons? "You be the judge," He said in effect. We read in Acts 19:13 of Jews practicing exorcism, but certainly not with the power and authority of Christ. He used no incantations or other common methods that were only indifferently successful. He cast out demons with absolute authority, by direct command, and with convincing power.

The Pharisees' disciples did not cast out demons by demonic power, and neither did the Lord. Satan's kingdom was not divided against itself. Therefore, given the ample proofs of His authority to tear up Satan's kingdom, it was obvious that what the Pharisees had said was incongruous. Jesus added, "If I cast out devils by the Spirit of God, then the kingdom of God is come unto you" (12:28). What other conclusion could there be?

Satan was "the strong man" of verse 29. He kept "his goods" (the demoniacs in his power) tenaciously, but now One had come who was stronger than he, and this One was spoiling Satan's "house." There seems to have been an unprecedented surge of demonic activity in Palestine during the period of Christ's ministry. Satan had marshaled his forces, but all in vain.

2. What the Pharisees Said Was Unforgivable (12:31-37)

a. The Nature of Their Sin Exposed (12:31-32)

The Lord exposed the nature of His enemies' sin. It was the unpardonable sin. Other sins, even speaking against Christ Himself, can be forgiven. But to attribute the gracious works of God's Beloved to the power of Satan when those works were done in cooperation with the Holy Spirit was unforgivable.

The Holy Spirit can convict people of other kinds of sin and lead them to repentance. But blasphemy against the Holy Spirit betrays a state of soul beyond hope of redemption. The people who saw so many mighty miracles, signs, and wonders in the presence of incarnate goodness and grace, and attributed it all to the foul fiend of the pit, could only be abandoned by God. They were equating the Holy One of God with the prince of demons. The Lord called this unpardonable sin "blasphemy against the Holy Ghost" (12:31).

b. The Nature of Their Souls Exposed (12:33-37)

(1) The Source of What We Say (12:33-35)

(a) A Tree and Its Vintage (12:33)

The Lord also exposed the nature of His enemies' souls. Their words revealed their inner nature, and our words reveal ours. In the first of three illustrations, Jesus said, "The tree is known by his fruit." He challenged the Pharisees to be honest and judge Him by His works. Were they or were they not good works? Was it good work to heal the sick, cleanse lepers, feed the hungry, raise the dead? If so, let His enemies acknowledge the tree because of its fruit.

(b) A Tongue and Its Venom (12:34)

In the second illustration the Lord said, "O generation of vipers, how can ye, being evil, speak good things?" The Pharisees had accused Him of being in league with Beelzebub. He accused them of being the serpent's seed. Jesus' works proved Him to be good; their words, so full of deadly poison, proved them to be of their father the devil.

(c) A Treasure and Its Value (12:35)

In the third illustration the Lord said, "A good man out of the good treasure of the heart bringeth forth good things: and an evil man out of the evil treasure bringeth forth evil things" (12:35). The reason was given in 12:34: "Out of the abundance of the heart the mouth speaketh." We are exposed by the things we say, and the Pharisees were exposed by their blasphemy of the Holy Ghost. They had made bare their hearts and displayed to all the world that they were rotten to the core. By the terrible things they had said about God's dear Son, they had revealed the evil that they treasured.

(2) The Seriousness of What We Say (12:36-37)

(a) The Everlasting Nature of Our Words (12:36)

Like the Pharisees, we will be judged by our words. Every articulate person uses thousands of words a day, enough to fill a fair-sized volume—enough in the course of a lifetime to fill a college library. Our thoughts are expressed in our words. We are accountable for every idle word. When a person is arrested, he is warned that anything he says will be used against him; similarly the Lord warns us that our words will rise up against us.

(b) The Evidential Nature of Our Words (12:37)

Today we have devices that record words and play them back. The air around us is alive with unheard noise; radio and TV stations, CB transmitters, and the like are filling the world with words. A receiver, tuned to the right wavelength, can pull them out of the air and make them audible. If man can thus capture words, God can do it better. Nothing ought to trouble us more than the fact that our every word is recorded. We need the Lord to draw the magnet of His finished work across that record. We need to have our incriminating words blotted out. We need God to say, "I will remember them no more." If He doesn't destroy the evidence, we will stand condemned by our words.

D. Refusing the Sign (12:38-50)

1. The National Folly (12:38-45)

a. The Impertinence of Israel's Peers (12:38-42)

As if they had not provoked Him enough, the scribes and Pharisees demanded that Jesus give them a sign. Their demand was swiftly and categorically denied. What more could He have done to convince them? Mark 8:11 says that they demanded "a sign from heaven." Could He make the sun stand still? Of course He could! Could He turn the moon to blood? Yes indeed! They wanted a sensational sign, the kind of sign He never gave. The sign from heaven they demanded had already been given. When Jesus was born, as Matthew had already reminded the Jews, He put a new star in the sky and wise men from the East followed that star to His feet.

The Lord castigated those who demanded a sign. He called that Christ-rejecting generation "evil" and "adulterous" (Matthew 12:39). That generation had sinned against God in the spiritual realm in the way an adulterous wife sins against her husband in the carnal realm. Such a comparison to adultery was a common figure of speech in the Old Testament (Jeremiah 3:9; Ezekiel 23:27; and particularly the prophecy of Hosea).

In denying the demand for a sign, the Lord Jesus discussed the kind of sign that that generation could expect. The discussion introduced *a new factor: the final rejection of Jesus by the Hebrews.* The Lord referred to the story of Jonah to expose the Jews' refusal to repent. By referring to Jonah, the Lord was also putting His authoritative stamp on the Scriptures. He did this consistently, never questioning their accuracy.

Jesus gave that generation "the sign of the prophet Jonas: For as Jonas was three days and three nights in the whale's belly; so shall the Son of man be three days and three nights in the heart of the earth" (Matthew 12:39-40). The experience of Jonah was a sign of the Lord's forthcoming death, burial, and resurrection. Note the words "as" and "so" in His statement; that formula usually indicates an exact parallel. Some disagree, but it seems likely that Jonah actually died in the belly of the great fish that swallowed him, and subsequently he was resurrected. Jonah 2:2 says he was in "the belly of hell."

Jonah 1:17 says that he was in the belly of the fish "three days and three nights." Drawing an exact parallel, the Lord said that He would be buried "three days and three nights." The words "three days" alone could be taken to mean any portion of a day, the view usually taken by those who insist that the Lord was crucified on a Friday. But the added words "and three nights" make that view untenable.

The Lord promised that as in the case of Jonah, His own death, burial, and resurrection would bring great blessing to the Gentiles. Thus His discussion of signs introduced *a new focus: the forthcoming reception of Jesus by the heathen.* The Jews were being given a sign that was quite out of the ordinary after all.

The Lord provided two Old Testament illustrations of Gentiles who, without Israel's light and privilege, responded when given the opportunity. The first illustration grew naturally out of the reference to Jonah: "The men of Nineveh...repented at the preaching of Jonas" (Matthew 12:41). The prophet marched through their streets, his message echoed throughout their city, and revival broke out. The historical record says that "the people of Nineveh believed God" (Jonah 3:5). They avoided God's wrath and experienced His mercy.

But Israel would not repent even though "a greater than Jonas" was in their midst. Jesus said that the despised Ninevites would "rise in judgment with this generation, and...condemn it." The word translated "rise" in Matthew 12:41 means "stand up." The reference is to a custom in both Jewish and Roman law courts that required a witness to stand when testifying in a criminal case.

After the Lord's resurrection, God stayed His hand for nearly forty years, but in the end that evil and adulterous generation, impervious to the Lord's miracles and to the signs and wonders wrought by the apostles, was handed over to judgment. Jonah had preached, "Yet forty days, and Nineveh shall be overthrown" (Jonah 3:4). And in effect Jesus was saying to the scribes and Pharisees, "Yet forty years, and Jerusalem shall be overthrown." He would declare that truth with greater clarity later (Matthew 23:36-38).

The second Old Testament illustration concerned the queen of Sheba, who "came from the uttermost parts of the earth to hear the wisdom of Solomon" (12:42). She had ventured a long, tiring, and dangerous journey to sit at the feet of Solomon, but the scribes and Pharisees had to make no such effort. The Lord, "a greater than Solomon," was in their midst.

Solomon's divinely inspired wisdom, which overawed the queen of Sheba, was in the end spoiled by his worldliness, carnality, and extravagance. That fact was attested to by the historical books of Scripture, by the book of Ecclesiastes, and by Israel's demand for redress immediately after Solomon's death. The Lord Jesus, far wiser than Solomon, not only preached a higher ethic and called for a holier life; He also lived an impeccable life.

Jesus said that the queen of Sheba "shall rise up [rise up in resurrection—not the same Greek word as in 12:41] in the judgment with this generation, and shall condemn it." Witnesses will be assembled from all over. From Tyre, Sidon, Sodom, Nineveh, and Ethiopia they will come. From the past will come Gentiles who were instantly responsive to the claims of Christ, or who would have been responsive, had He done for them what He did for obdurate, unbelieving Israel.

b. The Impenitence of Israel's People (12:43-45)

(1) A Disturbing Parable (12:43-45a)

The Lord next told a parable about a demon who had inhabited the body of a man. Having been cast out of the man, the evil spirit was restless. Craving embodiment, it "[walked] through dry places, seeking rest, and [found] none" (12:43). Its disembodied condition was as depressing to the demon as a desert is to people. Finally the demon said, "I will return into my house," still claiming as its own the body from which it had been expelled (12:44). Finding the body untenanted, it rounded up seven other spirits worse than itself and repossessed the wretched victim, so that "the last state of that man [was] worse than the first" (12:45).

(2) A Dreadful Parallel (12:45b)

Jesus added these solemn words: "Even so shall it be also unto this wicked generation." Obviously the story, quite apart from the light it shed on the character and condition of demons, has an application to the nation of Israel.

The indwelling evil spirit of idolatry that had plagued the nation of Israel from the days of the judges to the fall of the monarchy was exorcised by the Babylonian captivity. The house was "swept, and garnished [decorated]" (12:44). The Pharisees and rabbis cleaned the house and embellished it with their formalities and traditions, but they had sought no new tenant. They did not ask God to restore the shekinah glory, to send His Holy Spirit to indwell the temple and fill the land and the people with His presence, so eventually the evil spirit will return.

Idolatry will be reinstated in Israel after the rapture. The rebuilt temple in Jerusalem will be turned into a new world center for the worship of the beast, the antichrist (Revelation 13). The evil spirit will return with seven other spirits worse than itself. Thus the last state of the Jews will be worse than the first.

The Jews rejected the holy One of Israel when He was in their midst and accused Him of being in league with "the lord of those sacrificing to idols." The day will come when the majority of Jews will fall down and worship the man of sin and will praise and adore the dragon, "that old serpent, which is the Devil, and Satan" (Revelation 20:2). Today, in the rebirth of the Christ-rejecting nation of Israel, the stage is being set for such end-time events (Isaiah 28:15; Daniel 9:27; 2 Thessalonians 2).

2. The New Family (12:46-50)

a. The Old Ties Dissolved (12:46-47)

At this point there was an interruption. The Lord was given the news that His mother and brothers had arrived. That opportune event gave Him a natural way of introducing the new family.

"One said unto him, Behold, thy mother and thy brethren stand without, desiring to speak with thee" (12:47). Their stated purpose was to speak with Him, but Mark 3:21,31 makes it clear that their real purpose was "to lay hold on him" because "they said, He is beside himself." It is evident that the Lord's mother and brothers had heard of His ceaseless activity and had heard that He was on a collision course with the authorities. They had concluded that He was out of His senses, virtually insane, and they had come to put Him under some kind of restraint.

Mary must have known better. She knew that Jesus was God manifest in the flesh. Perhaps her protective maternal instinct overcame her and doubtless she was under considerable pressure from her other four sons. We do not know how much Jesus' brothers knew about the circumstances of His birth, but it seems improbable that Mary and Joseph would not have told them. However, they certainly did not believe in Jesus and they might have been fearful that official hostility toward Him would spread to them. It was not that far from Capernaum to Nazareth.

In the Gospel record of the ministry of Jesus there are only two occasions (prior to the crucifixion) when Mary appears (here and in John 2:1-4). Both times she seeks to have a say in His affairs and both times she is reproved by Him. Thus there is no basis for prayer to her on the ground that since she is the Lord's mother, He will listen to her and do as she says. Such passages as these in Matthew 12 and John 2 anticipate and repudiate Roman Catholic dogmas that exalt Mary to the status of deity, teach the bodily assumption of Mary into Heaven, and make Mary coredemptrix with Jesus.

b. The New Truth Disclosed (12:48-50)

"Who is my mother?" Jesus replied when told of the mission of Mary and her sons. "Who are my brethren?" (12:48). Note that the Lord here acknowledged only three human relationships—mother, sister, brother—an affirmation of the fact that He had no human father. But even these acknowledged relationships were deliberately distanced from Him. He had not lost affection for His human family; He was simply putting them in their proper place.

By interrupting the Lord, His relatives had inferred that their business with Him was more important than His business with the multitudes. He had to reprove them for their presumption in thinking that they could take Him home and out of harm's way. The whole incident must have been a trial to the Lord. It is easier to deal with the mistaken ideas of one's foes than those of one's family.

Having rebuked His human family members, the Lord pointed to His disciples and acknowledged them and all who would believe in Him to be His "brother, and sister, and mother" (12:50). There is now a new family in which the ties are spiritual, not natural. The Lord's brothers eventually found their way into that family. The last view we have of Mary is in the upper room where, with other believers in the Lord Jesus, she had taken her place as one of His disciples (Acts 1:12-14).

With the introduction of the new family, Matthew concluded this phase of his description of the Lord's rejection. Israel's probation had ended in failure. The Jews had rejected the King; the King had rejected them. The offer of the heavenly kingdom to Israel as a nation had finally been withdrawn. The heavenly kingdom would be offered to a new people, a heavenly people. The Jewish nation would have to suffer a new and longer exile among the Gentiles, a new and greater dispersal. Then, not forgetting His promises to Israel, the Lord would regather the scattered people and fulfill the ancient promises of the millennial kingdom, in which the Jews would have to be content with an earthly rather than a heavenly heritage (Daniel 7:27).

II. THE MYSTERIES OF THE KINGDOM (13:1-52)

A crisis in Israel's history had arrived, similar but far more serious than the crisis that resulted in the handing over of the city of Jerusalem to Nebuchadnezzar.

There are two periods in Israel's history that we must be aware of if we are to understand God's dealings with Israel. The first is "the times of the Gentiles" (Luke 21:24). This period marks Israel's loss of political ascendancy over the nations. During this time all world power is in Gentile hands. The period began with Nebuchadnezzar and will end with the reign of the antichrist. "The times of the Gentiles" will be terminated upon the personal return of Christ at Armageddon, at which point He will set up the millennial kingdom centered in Jerusalem. That kingdom is now officially postponed by Christ because of Jewish unbelief.

The second period is "the fulness of the Gentiles" (Romans 11:25), which marks Israel's loss of religious ascendancy over the nations. "The fulness of the Gentiles" began at Pentecost and will end at the rapture. For two thousand years before Pentecost, when God had anything to say, He said it for the most part to a Jew and in *Hebrew*. If a Gentile wanted the truth of God, he had to become a Jewish proselyte and submit to circumcision. But all that was set aside at the beginning of the second period ("the fulness of the Gentiles"). Now custodianship of God's truth is entrusted to the church (predominantly Gentile in character). After Pentecost, when God had anything to say, He said it for the most part in *Greek*.[5] After the rapture God will restore religious ascendancy to the Jews (the revivals of the apocalypse are all led by Jews), just as at the final return of Christ to reign, God will restore political ascendancy to the Jews.

Because the Jews had now rejected their King, all plans for the immediate visible manifestation of the kingdom were postponed. That postponement has already lasted nearly two thousand years. During this long period God has been at work, calling out members for His church; the affairs of the kingdom have been subordinated. The kingdom has gone underground, so to speak. It is not visible to men. It is here in mystery.

The kingdom is the theme of the mystery parables of Matthew 13, even though the period they cover parallels that of the church age ("the fulness of the Gentiles"). The church is involved in the parables because the church age and this phase of the kingdom overlap. In a coming day the kingdom will be manifest in two realms, Heaven and earth. The church will reign in the heavenlies, and Israel will reign on earth. The mystery parables show how things are developing now, during the time of the King's absence.

In other words, these parables deal with the present age. They tell us something of God's secret plans and purposes for our age. Today everything is marked by seeming failure. God's purposes are opposed at every turn; instead of visibly triumphing, they are continuously resisted. Truth is ever on the scaffold and wrong is ever on the throne. Yet in spite of outward appearances, God's purposes are prospering; His goals are being attained. Much that mystifies thoughtful people about the present age is made clear in the mystery parables. The first four were spoken publicly because they emphasize the outward aspect of the age.

A. Parables Spoken Publicly (13:1-35)

1. The Multitudes (13:1-2)

The same day that the Lord was formally rejected by the Jews, He went down to the seashore and addressed the multitudes who still gathered around Him. We can picture the scene: the calm blue waters of the lake of Galilee sparkling in the sun; the Lord with His back to the lake; crowds standing on a nearby hill in their colorful robes.[6]

The moment the Lord opened His mouth it was evident that the character of His teaching was changed. He spoke about the kingdom, but it was no longer "at hand." Just as considerable time lapses between seedtime and harvest, considerable time would lapse before the kingdom would be visible. The "field" was different too. It was no longer Israel; it was the world. Furthermore the Lord couched His teaching in parables of a new kind, designed to conceal as much as to reveal truth. He would explain the parables to His disciples, but blindness would be Israel's lot.

2. The Mysteries (13:3-35)

a. The Parable of the Sower (13:3-23)

The first of these mystery parables emphasizes how the message of salvation goes forth to all. The soil symbolizes the human heart and man's dispositional attitude toward the gospel. The importance of this parable is underlined by Jesus in Mark 4:13: "Know ye not this parable? and how then will ye know all parables?"

(1) The Introduction of the Parable (13:3-9)

The introduction is simply the story itself. So true to life, it tells of the scattering of the seed over a widespread area, of the seed's natural enemies (the fowls of the air, the inhospitable wayside soil, the stony places, the thorn-infested ground), and of the varying harvests of the seed that fell into good ground. Having told the story, the Lord challenged the multitudes: "Who hath ears to hear, let him hear" (13:9).

(2) The Interruption of the Parable (13:10-17)

(a) A Word about the Parables (13:10-13)

The disciples, as mystified as everyone else, asked for an explanation for this new kind of teaching. The Lord's answer clearly revealed His change of attitude toward the Jews since their blasphemy of the Holy Spirit. "Because it is given unto you to know the mysteries [secrets] of the kingdom of heaven, but to them it is not given," He said (13:11). The Lord had closed the door on Israel as a nation.

Individual Jews can still be enlightened by exercising personal faith in Christ. These believers become members of the church (the multinational, mystical body of Christ) and heirs of the heavenly kingdom. Unregenerate Jewry to this day is devoid of understanding and blind to the mystery truths of the kingdom.

The Lord added a comment about His method: "Whosoever hath, to him shall be given, and he shall have more abundance: but whosoever hath not, from him shall be taken away even that he hath" (13:12). The disciples were a case in point. As time went on, especially after Calvary and Pentecost, their eyes were opened to all truth. Israel became more and more blind, rejecting the Son of God in the Gospels and the Spirit of God in Acts, thus sealing their doom for the entire church age.

(b) A Word about God's Prophet (13:14-15)

Referring to the ominous prophecy of Isaiah 6:9-10, the Lord said:

> In them [the Jews] is fulfilled the prophecy of Esaias, which saith, By hearing ye shall hear, and shall not understand; and seeing ye shall see, and shall not perceive: For this people's

heart is waxed gross, and their ears are dull of hearing, and their eyes they have closed; lest at any time they should see with their eyes and hear with their ears, and should understand with their heart, and should be converted, and I should heal them.

This prophecy, given to Isaiah at the time of his call, sealed the doom of the northern kingdom of Israel. Soon thereafter that nation was handed over to the Assyrians for dismemberment and deportation. The Lord's quotation of the prophecy formally handed the Jews over to an even sorer dispersion.[7]

(c) A Word about the Disciples' Privilege (13:16-17)

i. The Discernment That Was Theirs (13:16)

In contrast to unbelieving Israel were the Lord's disciples. He told them how blessed they were. They had seeing eyes and hearing ears.

ii. The Dispensation That Was Theirs (13:17)

Many Old Testament saints and seers had longed to see the Messianic era. The disciples were living in a thrilling time: a time when prophecy was being fulfilled, a time when the Christ had come, a time of divine visitation unparalleled in history. Our time is equally exciting, for all around us are obvious preparations for the coming again of the Lord from glory.

(3) The Interpretation of the Parable (13:18-23)

The parable has three aspects: the sower, the seed, and the soil. First let us consider the sower. "Behold, a sower went forth to sow," said Jesus (13:3). In the next parable (the parable of the tares), the sower is said to be the Son of man, the Lord Jesus; John the Baptist plowed and prepared the soil, and the Lord Jesus sowed the seed. In the parable of the sower, however, the Lord did not restrict the sowing to Himself. It seems that the sowing in the story represents the constant sowing of the gospel seed from His day to ours.

Almost nothing is said about the sower. We know nothing about his personality or whether he was an old hand at his task. We know nothing about his method. The Lord evidently wanted to keep the sower in the background. As someone has said, a child can drop a seed as effectively as the most experienced farmer.

Not much is said about the seed either, except that it is the Word of God, according to the Lord's interpretation of the parable. That is all we need to know about the seed. It is the best kind of seed in the world; we can sow nothing better than the inspired, infallible, inerrant, inimitable Word of God. It is infinitely superior to the philosophies and theories of man.[8] Like any other seed, the Word of God has life.

Because seed is imprinted with a genetic code, a supply of seed can turn into a field of flax or a barnful of barley. Once the seed is sown, that imprinted law of life goes to work. The Word of God is the same. It carries within it the genetic code of eternal life and when it is planted in the right kind of soil, it germinates and produces life. Let us consider an example:

When James Chalmers set sail for the cannibal isles, he was the idol of Britain. His friend Robert Louis Stevenson said he was "bigger than a house and far bigger than a church." Years later when news was brought back to Britain that he had been eaten by cannibals, Joseph Parker of London's City Temple said, "I can't believe it. I don't want to believe it."

Called the "Greatheart of New Guinea," Chalmers was a national hero. He devoted thirty years to sowing gospel seed among the cannibals, often with great success. Over 130 mission stations in New Guinea alone bore witness to the fruitfulness of his labors. As a result of his ministry, more than three thousand natives of all ages gathered monthly to break bread in a communion service. Many of them Chalmers had known as wild man-eaters, but they had been radiantly transformed by the mighty power of the Word of God. Many of them still bore on their breasts the tattoos that marked those who had achieved manhood by murder. Now they quietly took their places as regenerated men at the table of the Lord.

How can we account for these transformations? Socialism, moral rearmament, and political reform can produce no such fruits. Only sowing the precious seed of the gospel can transform lost people. Down into the hearts of poor wicked men goes the seed; up it springs in new life, the very life of God germinating and growing in the soul.

The Lord, in His interpretation of the parable of the sower, concentrated on the soil—that is, those who actually hear the gospel. The different kinds of soil show the different kinds of hearts people have, which is the purpose of the parable. The two main kinds are (1) those who receive the truth of God and (2) those who receive it only partially or reject it altogether. In other words, there are productive soils and there are problem soils. Problem soils are found in the hearts of those who are wayward, weak, or worldly. Productive soil is found in the hearts of those who are willing.

(a) The Waywardness of Some (13:18-19)

i. The Word Superficially Received (13:18-19a)

The Lord began His interpretation by referring to the wayside soil, which symbolizes the waywardness of some people. We can write the words *no results* across this type of soil. Preachers are only too familiar with it.

Some people listen to the good news of the gospel, but what they hear makes no impression on their souls. The words go in one ear and out the other. It is hard to say what such people think of as they sit in church and are exposed to the most magnificent truths ever expounded. We only know that they get up and walk away. They might as well have been watching a football game or standing at the kitchen sink or closing a business deal.

ii. The Word Satanically Removed (13:19b)

Jesus explained what happens in those wayward hearts. As soon as the seed touches the soil of their souls, the "fowls" come and devour it (13:4). The "wicked one" or one of his demons snatches it before it can take root (13:19).

Such hearts are hard to begin with. They were likened by Jesus to the wayside, which is hardened by being constantly trodden down. People with hard hearts hear the message and say to themselves, "I don't believe that. I don't agree with that. I never heard such nonsense." They have their own philosophies, their own religions, their own ideas. They say, "If I accept what I'm hearing, I'll have to give up this or that. I'm not at all interested in this kind of preaching."

Before people who receive the Word superficially have gone a dozen steps, Satan has snatched away the seed. The message is dismissed from their minds as soon as they hear a joke, a piece of gossip, the latest football score, or a crying baby. An invitation to lunch or a chance to talk about business comes, and the Word is completely gone, just as if it had never been heard.

(b) The Weakness of Some (13:20-21)

The weakness of some people's profession of faith is represented by the soil in what 13:20 calls "stony places." There is a shallow layer of soil, but just beneath the surface lies a rocky shelf. Seed dropped in the shallow soil gives initial promise, but since no roots can penetrate the rocky shelf, and since no moisture can be retained in the soil, the seed has no chance to develop completely. The sun comes out, the soil and the seed are scorched, and the early promise withers away. We can write the word *no roots* over this kind of soil and the kind of people that the stony places represent.

Preachers know this kind of soil as well. They are familiar with people who are stirred, enthusiastic, and overjoyed by a message and make immediate professions of faith. There is an initial response; everything is bright with promise. But then hard times come; as soon as these shallow people discover what it is going to cost to maintain a testimony for Christ, they give up. Jesus described one of them in 13:21: "[He has no] root in himself, but dureth for a while: for when tribulation or persecution ariseth because of the word, by and by he is offended." There is no root, so of course there can be no fruit.

High pressure evangelism often produces this kind of shallow "conversion." Professions of faith are unsubstantial and worthless. People who respond to the gospel on this level have awakened souls, but they are not regenerated in spirit.

(c) The Worldliness of Some (13:22)

Thorny soil depicts the worldliness of some people. They too show initial promise, but no lasting results. Over them we can write the words *no resistance.*

Thorny soil is infested with the emblem of the curse (Genesis 3:18). Life is choked out of seed that falls there. The Lord described three kinds of thorns that destroy the seed: "the care of this world," "the deceitfulness of riches," and "the lusts of other things" (Matthew 13:22; Mark 4:19).

"The care of this world" refers to the problems of life. When a person becomes a Christian, he is not given blanket protection against common disasters. The homes of believers are just as subject to tornadoes, earthquakes, and hurricanes as the homes of unbelievers. Prayer sometimes changes the path of an oncoming storm, but it is a delusion to think that Christians are exempt from problems. Fire, theft, accident, harm, and danger are the common lot of man. Poverty and ill health can come to anyone. Christians get sick, grow old, and die. Problems knock at the doors of both pagans and believers.

Christians of course do have advantages. They have a Father in Heaven and the mighty Spirit of God to be their comforter. God is their refuge and strength, their very present help in time of trouble (Psalm 46:1). The Lord Jesus is their Great High Priest, who is able to minister to them when problems come and to make "all things work together for good" for those who love Him (Romans 8:28). For true believers, problems become a means of growth and grace. Shallow professors of faith soon wither when choked by the cares of life. They think God has let them down, that there's nothing to Christianity after all.

The second kind of thorn, "the deceitfulness of riches," refers to the prosperities of life. Wealth can be as much a snare as poverty. Many people have seemed to say *yes* to Christ, only to lose sight of spiritual things when worldly advancement beckons. Perhaps a promised promotion at work cuts right across a dawning conviction that one should become a missionary. Or business booms at the cost of neglecting the gatherings of the Lord's people. When prosperity arrives, it brings the entanglements of luxury and ease. The gospel seed can be choked out by success.

The third kind of thorn, "the lusts of other things," refers to the pleasures of life. Often pleasures that are legitimate in themselves take up time that should be devoted to the Lord's work. Or sinful pleasures allure and choke the seed. Some people amount to nothing for God because they refuse to give up some destructive, dominating habit that gives them temporary pleasure. The Lord Jesus warned that the pleasures of life can strangle the seed; it has little chance in souls filled with such thorns. Pleasure-seekers may profess to be saved, but their lives betray them. Their profession is not real because there is no evidence that the Word of God is bearing spiritual fruit in their lives.

(d) The Willingness of Some (13:23)

Having described the problem soils, the Lord turned His attention to the productive soil, which represents the willingness of some to bear fruit. In introducing the story He had said that "other [seed] fell into good ground, and brought forth fruit, some an hundredfold, some sixtyfold, some thirtyfold" (13:8). A genuine conversion is evidenced by fruit. However, not all truly saved people realize their full potential in bearing fruit.

Moderate development can be seen in some lives. They love the Lord, they love His people, and they love the Bible. They are genuinely saved and take the initial steps toward fruitfulness, yet certain areas of their lives somehow remain untouched by the Word of God and the Spirit of God.

Marked development can be seen in other lives. They become the backbone of a local church. They are helpful, cooperative, and zealous members of the family of God. They teach in Sunday school, witness to others about Christ, give conscientiously to the Lord's work, maintain an interest in missions, and stand behind the local leadership. Their lives give evidence that they love the Lord and are seeking to grow in grace and increase in the knowledge of God.

Marvelous development can be seen in a few lives. They go all the way with God. They are Spirit-filled, Christlike, soulwinning Christians. The fruit of the Spirit—love, joy, peace, long-suffering, gentleness, goodness, faith, meekness, and self-control—can be seen developing in their lives (Galatians 5:22-23).

The parable of the sower underlines what can be expected during this age: seeming failure and at the same time marvelous fulfillment of God's purpose. The visible kingdom is in abeyance and forces are operating to hinder the work of God in the world, yet that work goes on. Souls are being saved, fruit is appearing, and here and there astonishing fruitfulness is bringing wonderful glory to God.

b. The Parable of the Tares (13:24-30)

The mystery inherent in the previous story had been explained publicly. In fact the parable of the sower had already been demonstrated by the Pharisees and the multitudes that thronged the lakeside. There were those who rejected Christ and His claims outright; demonic influence urged the Pharisees on to the ultimate sin of hardness, the accusation that the holy One of Israel was in league with the prince of demons. There were those who were shallow; they would shout their hosannas one day and their hatred the next. There were those who gave the Word an initial warm response, but would throw it over at the first breath of hardship. And there were the Lord's disciples and others who in time would produce the harvest. That so few would really respond remained a mystery, but the main point of the parable could hardly be missed, even by the densest.

The parable of the tares, however, was not explained to the masters of Israel or the multitudes. The deeper meaning was expounded later to the disciples in private. The story itself is deceptively simple, but it deals with the mystery of iniquity and the malice of Satan.

The parable of the tares and the remaining parables spoken publicly are introduced by the words "another parable" (13:24,31,33). The word translated "another" is *allos,* which means "another of the same kind." The indication is that they are the same kind as the parable of the sower. In the parable of the sower the Lord taught that the gospel is not going to convert the world in this age. From the human standpoint, the success of the gospel is limited, for even where God's Word does take root, more often than not it produces only partial fruit. In the three parables introduced by "another," the Lord taught that God's work in the world in this age will be opposed, hindered, and countered with tireless persistence.

In the parable of the tares the theme is *confrontation* and the emphasis is on the diabolical; the activity of Satan is stressed. Then comes the parable of the mustard seed, where the theme is *confusion* and the emphasis is on the dispensational; a state of affairs emerges that is contrary to the New Testament purpose of God. The parable of the leaven concludes the trilogy; the theme of the parable is *corruption* and the emphasis is on the doctrinal problem of error being deliberately introduced into New Testament truth.

The parable of the tares revolves around *the sowing* of both good and bad seed. In the story the bad seed was sown by a malicious and unscrupulous enemy under cover of darkness. During *the growing* of the seed it became obvious that all was not well with the field. A poisonous weed, in its early stages similar in appearance to the wheat, was growing alongside the wheat. At *the mowing* time the noxious weed stood exposed for what it was. It was bundled for the flames even as the wheat was garnered safely into the barn.

Since the Lord reserved His explanation of the mystery in this parable until later (13:36-43), we will wait until we arrive at His explanation before attempting an exposition.

c. The Parable of the Mustard Seed (13:31-32)

Of the seven parables in the series in 13:3-50, five are left unexplained. The parable of the mustard seed is the first of those that the Lord did not interpret. All seven parables relate to the mysteries of the kingdom of Heaven and all seven are in the process of fulfillment today, for this is the age when the kingdom is in its mystery or hidden form.

The Old Testament prophets had a clear vision of the future millennial kingdom of Christ. They saw the kingdom in manifestation. They saw it as it will be one of these days: a glorious worldwide empire stretching from Jerusalem to earth's remotest bounds; a kingdom from which the curse will have been largely removed so that the lion will lie down with the lamb, the desert will blossom as the rose, and men will dwell together in peace.

Those Old Testament prophets, however, never saw the kingdom in mystery. They never saw the gospel age. That is why Paul called the gospel "the mystery which hath been hid from ages and from generations, but now is made manifest to his saints" (Colossians 1:26). And that is why the Lord Jesus referred His disciples to Psalm 78 when in explaining the mystery parables He said: "I will utter things which have been kept secret from the foundation of the world" (Matthew 13:35).

We must bear all this in mind when interpreting the mystery parables. If an interpretation simply elaborates a truth known to the Hebrew prophets in previous ages, it cannot be the proper interpretation. The popular view of the parable of the mustard seed is that it envisions Christianity spreading far and wide as some kind of spiritual extension of the nation of Israel until it overshadows the earth as a mighty, visible kingdom. Such an interpretation overlooks the mystery factor in the parable. It is a mistake to equate the church with Israel and to say that what is happening in the church is an outworking of millennial prophecy. The glory of the church in this age is like the glory of her Lord. It is "not of this world" (John 8:23).

The Old Testament prophets clearly saw the glory of a coming kingdom in which world power would be invested in the nation of Israel. They did not see the church or the church age, for that was not revealed to them (Romans 16:25; Ephesians 3:4-5). The parable of the mustard seed is a mystery parable, so it does not teach that Old Testament prophecies regarding the kingdom are being fulfilled today.

The parable of the mustard seed and the parable of the leaven are a pair. The former deals with the outward development of error in the church; the latter deals with the secret and inward development of error. As in the parable of the sower and the parable of the tares, something seems to have gone wrong, something foreseen and foretold by Christ.

The obedience of living things to the code of their kind is a fixed law of nature. That is why the Lord seemed puzzled, casting about in His mind for a suitable illustration to depict the truth He wanted to convey. Both Mark and Luke prefaced their record of the parable of the mustard seed with the Lord's question: "Whereunto shall we liken the kingdom of God? or with what comparison shall we compare it?" (Mark 4:30; also see Luke 13:18) The Lord wanted to compare the kingdom to something in nature that defied the law of its being. Had He wished to liken the kingdom to something that kept within the boundaries of its nature, He could have found a thousand illustrations. But where could He find an animal or a plant that so violated the code of its kind that it deliberately set out to be something its Maker never intended?

Every living thing carries within its structure its own particular genetic code; it reproduces and develops in accordance with the orders contained in that code. Likewise the church and Christianity were to be planted in the world with certain fixed characteristics assigned to them by God; for them to become something different was monstrous, something at which all nature would be appalled. Yet that is what happened, as the parable of the mustard seed shows.

The mustard in the parable refused to remain an herb; instead it became a tree. Herbs and trees are entirely different kinds (Genesis 1:11-12); one kind never becomes the other kind (James 3:12). The mustard seed in the parable showed two things: a weird growth and a worldly grandeur.

(1) What the Mustard Showed (13:31-32a)

(a) A Weird Growth

The mustard grows wild in Israel. In its natural state it attains considerable height and from a distance sometimes has the appearance of a small tree. However, it is a pot herb. It grows from an insignificant seed and becomes a considerable plant, but it does not become "a great tree" (Luke 13:19). The law of growth for a tree is different from that of an herb. A tree grows slowly, taking years to come to its full stature and maturity. Once it has grown, it is able to rear its mighty form for many years. An herb like the mustard grows swiftly. It develops without acquiring the strong woody tissue characteristic of a tree and lives only long enough to produce flowers and seed. For an herb to become a tree suggests a growth and development foreign to its nature.

The mustard seed in this parable represents the doctrine of Christ's kingdom. Jesus said, "The kingdom of heaven is like to a grain of mustard seed, which a man took, and sowed in his field" (Matthew 13:31). As in the previous parables, the sower is Christ and the field is the world. By saying that the sower "took" the mustard seed, the Lord indicated that He "took" the truths that He taught; He implied that His teachings were given to Him. In John 7:16 He said, "My doctrine is not mine, but his that sent me."

The truths the Lord came to sow were humble, unpretentious, and simple. His teaching was "the least of all seeds" (Matthew 13:32). No other kingdom set up on this planet ever had such lowly principles as those He enunciated for His. Think of the kingdoms of this world. Think of their principles, their pomp and power, their prosperity and pride. Think of the emblems nations employ to depict their real or fancied national spirit: lions, eagles, bears, birds and beasts of prey. Jesus set all this aside. His kingdom embraced love and meekness. If Jesus had wanted a symbol to depict His empire, He would have chosen a dove or a lamb.

Think of what Jesus taught about His kingdom. On one occasion He took a child, set the little one in the midst of the disciples, and said, "Whosoever therefore shall humble himself as this little child, the same is greatest in the kingdom of heaven" (Matthew 18:4). Who would ever dream of a kingdom like that but Him? From Matthew 7:14 we learn how He conceived His kingdom numerically. "Strait is the gate," He said, "and narrow is the way, which leadeth unto life, and few there be that find it."

Such was the seed and such was to be the plant. The Lord never envisioned His work in the world during this age as amounting to anything more than a shrub. If the Christian community had remained true to the principles of the Lord Jesus, it would have remained small, despised, and poor in the eyes of men. Instead the church has become a tree. A tree has a massive trunk and great branches that keep subdividing into smaller and smaller branches until they dwindle into twigs. In other words, a tree is an impressive symbol of organization; it is an emblem of power that is derived from a central authority and through its various administrative arms reaches down to the lowly rank and file. It is in this sense that the Bible uses a tree as a symbol. Nebuchadnezzar was likened to a tree (Daniel 4:10) and so was the nation of Israel (Judges 9:8-15).

Israel was a tree. The church is an herb. The mustard, by aspiring to become a tree, denied the law of its being and sought to raise itself above the level of its kind and vie with the trees of the forest.

Similarly the visible church has aspired to become a worldly, hierarchical system—a superpower established around a central authority that delegates its authority by thorough-going organizational means. That was not what the Lord had in mind for His church.

(b) A Worldly Grandeur

Besides a weird growth, the mustard seed in the parable also showed a worldly grandeur. In Israel the mustard plant grows to a height of twelve to twenty feet, which shows that even as a shrub it is of princely growth. And although the church was never intended to set up a worldly empire, it certainly was intended to be something that would stand out. A tree, however, soars far higher than a shrub.

Few things in nature are grander than a mighty tree with its roots driven deep into the soil and its massive head combing the clouds, Some trees grow thirty stories high; some live for hundreds, even thousands of years. With spreading branches, verdant foliage, massive strength, and splendid appearance, trees are the picture of majesty and grandeur. It was this that the mustard plant in the parable aspired to be.

The mustard that became a tree was something foreign to what its Creator intended, something to which it never could have aspired without some mysterious denial of its nature. That is the mystery of the parable. The application is that the church, which should have remained true to the humble teachings of the Savior, has become something He never intended. It has become an imperial power in the world. It has grown and developed into a vast, organized system of religion. It has become "rich, and increased with goods" (Revelation 3:17). It has made treaties, formed alliances with kings, and employed courtiers, veritable "princes of the church." It has hired armies, meddled in the affairs of nations, dabbled in politics, and ruled like a sovereign in the world. That was something the Lord Jesus never planned for His church. He foresaw it and foretold it in His parable, but He never planned it and He never sanctioned it.

The Roman church is by no means the only fulfillment of this prophecy, but it is the supreme example. So let Rome be our illustration. The Roman church is, to borrow a phrase, "the ghost of the Roman empire," its continuation in history. The ecclesiastical structure of that church is an extension of Roman imperial administration in the West. If all our histories of the Roman empire were destroyed, we could still reconstruct its organization by tracing the organization of the Roman Catholic Church and the Vatican in the Middle Ages. What pagan Rome was, papal Rome became.

The Vatican, with its own standing army, police force, law courts, prison, coinage, and stamps, has all the outward trappings of sovereign power. A thousand years after the birth of Christ, Pope Gregory gave voice to the spirit of the papacy and arrogated supreme worldly power to the pontiff:

> It is laid down that the Roman Pontiff is universal bishop, that his name is the only one of the kind in the world. To him alone it belongs to depose or reconcile bishops; and he may depose them in their absence, and without the concurrence of a Synod....He alone may use the ensigns of empire; all princes are bound to kiss his feet; he has the right to depose emperors, and to absolve subjects from their allegiance. He holds in his hands the supreme mediation in questions of war and peace, and he alone may adjudge contested successions to kingdoms....The Roman Church has never erred, and, as the Scripture testifies, never will err. The Pope is above all judgment....The Church was not to be the handmaid of princes but their mistress.[9]

The Vatican has never renounced his haughty statement of imperial power. The history of the Roman church shows that it has modeled itself on his edicts and that the achievement of those edicts has been that church's ambition.

That the Roman church is not able to exert its former power today is a tribute to the good sense of an enlightened age that refuses to grovel before such arrogance. There has not, however, been any change of heart on the part of the papacy. It has been said of Rome that in defeat she is a lamb, in equality she is a fox, and in power she is a tiger. Our history books give us scores of proofs that this assessment is true.

The Vatican power structure is that of a pyramid with the pope at the top. He dwells in grand isolation far above his subordinates and the rank and file of his church. As one Catholic put it when a terrorist tried to assassinate Pope John Paul II, "It's like trying to shoot God." Directly beneath the pope is the college of cardinals, and under the college the congregations, offices, and Roman curia (boards and courts designed to carry out the judicial program of the Vatican). All key personnel are appointed and controlled by the pope.[10]

The top congregation is the Holy Office, which achieved infamy during the Middle Ages by inaugurating the Inquisition. The very name of the Holy Office would send chills down the spines of rich and poor, learned and ignorant, prince and peasant. It maimed, tortured, and burned at the stake countless thousands of men, women, and children. John foresaw the Roman religious system as "drunken with the blood of the saints, and with the blood of the martyrs of Jesus" (Revelation 17:6). In describing the horrors of the Inquisition, one historian commented, "The annals of the Church became the annals of Hell." The Inquisition did not die easily. It was not abolished in Spain until Napoleon conquered the country in the late eighteenth century.

In recent years many independent-thinking priests and nuns have questioned the claim of the pope to rule by divine right and have objected to some of the Vatican's pronouncements on social issues. Some Catholic theologians have even challenged Rome's dogmas, but the system remains the system. The papacy would like nothing more than a return to the good old days when rank and file members throughout the world accepted the myth of supremacy and accepted papal pronouncements as God-breathed and beyond question.

The church of Rome is the kind of religious system the Lord foresaw in His parable of the mustard seed. He saw a church that had become a worldly kingdom.

(2) What the Mustard Sheltered (13:32b)

Coming back to the parable, we see what the mustard sheltered. Jesus said, "The birds of the air come and lodge in the branches thereof." In the parable of the sower the Lord had used birds to depict evil spirits snatching away seed that fell by the wayside. Birds were used in the same sense in the parable of the mustard seed. They represent evil spirits.

Some commentators say that here the birds symbolize converts flocking into the church, but that interpretation is inconsistent with the other publicly spoken parables. The stories told to the multitudes on the seashore uniformly underline the seeming failure of God's purposes in the world during this age.

In keeping with the thorns, the rocks, the leaven, the woman who hid the leaven, and the bad fish, the birds represent that which is evil. They symbolize evil spirits and the tree symbolizes the false church. The abnormal growth of the mustard makes it possible for the birds to lodge in its branches. Mark, in his account of the parable emphasized the branches of the mustard: "It…shooteth out great branches; so that the fowls of the air may lodge under the shadow of it" (4:32).

The birds represent a kind of evil that inhabits the heavens. Satan is described by the Holy Spirit as "the prince of the power of the air" (Ephesians 2:2). In describing Satanic forces that lurk in the unseen world and hinder the work of God, Paul told us of principalities, powers, rulers of this world's darkness, and wicked spirits "in high places" (Ephesians 6:12). So the birds, which were the enemy of the sower in the first parable, took up their abode in the mustard tree.

We can find evil spirits lurking in all branches of the church as it is represented by Christendom. They hide in the branches of the three primary divisions of the professing church: Protestantism, Greek Orthodoxy, and Romanism. The evil spirits lurk wherever there is an outward grasping for material structure and power, wherever the church is distorted into something it was never intended to be. We find them in the cults with weird, Bible-distorting, Christ-denying doctrines. We find the evil spirits in new churches, old churches, seemingly sound churches.

Some years ago I was scheduled to hold meetings in a church that I had every reason to believe was fundamental, Bible-believing, and sound in doctrine and practice. However, I discovered that there were people in positions of authority in that church who believed and taught a doctrine that attacked the deity of Christ. When I confronted the church leaders, they hedged as long as they could, and only when they were driven into a corner did they admit that their sympathies were with the false teaching. Here was a branch of the professing church where one would have thought that no error could be found, yet the doctrine of demons had silently flown in and was now roosting comfortably in its new nest. (I did not conduct the meetings!)

If false doctrine can penetrate a church always considered impeccably sound in the faith and true to the Word of God, how much more easily can evil spirits reside in branches of Christendom where the Bible was abandoned long ago as the sole authority and rule of belief and behavior?

There is an almost endless supply of illustrations of the way in which Christendom has become something that Christ never intended—vast, worldly, imperial, powerful. It has become something to rival kings and empires, something to give shelter to evil spirits.

Of all the parables of Christ, the mystery of the mustard seed is probably the best example of His ability to foretell the future. What He depicted has literally come to pass. The sweep and scope of what we call Christendom is proof of the inerrant foreknowledge of Christ.

d. The Parable of the Leaven (13:33-35)

The popular explanation of the parable of the leaven is that it depicts the gradual, silent, and unobtrusive permeation of society by the saving and sanctifying work of the Lord Jesus Christ. Once it has begun its beneficial work, it goes on tirelessly working away until the whole world is leavened with the gospel. That interpretation sounds good, but it is wrong because the Bible does not teach the gradual conversion of mankind.

The Bible teaches the opposite. Paul said, "Evil men and seducers shall wax worse and worse" (2 Timothy 3:13). Jesus implied the same when He gave this challenge to His disciples: "When the Son of man cometh, shall he find faith on the earth?" (Luke 18:8) The whole tenor of Bible prophecy leads to the conclusion that the world will be in a state of armed rebellion against Christ at the end, a rebellion led and motivated by a Satanic trinity.

The parable of the leaven is a companion to the parable of the mustard seed, where we saw the outward display of the professing church. In the parable of the leaven we see the inward decay of the professing church. The subject of the parable is the mystery of subversion, the emphasis is doctrinal, and the story itself revolves around the activity of the leaven and the action of the woman.

(1) The Woman (13:33)

(a) The Activity of the Leaven

i. The Loaf

"The kingdom of heaven is like unto leaven, which a woman took, and hid in three measures of meal." The three measures of meal remind us of Abraham's hospitality to his heavenly visitors. He told Sarah to take three measures of meal and prepare cakes for their guests (Genesis 18:6). We are also reminded of the meal offering required under the Mosaic law. The usual amount was three measures (Numbers 15:9; 28:12,20,28; 29:3,9,14).

Some consideration of this important Old Testament offering will give us an idea of what three measures of meal was intended to symbolize in the parable. The meal offering was made of fine flour because it symbolized Christ in the purity and evenness of His life on earth. He was always the same, never flustered, never in a hurry, never at a loss, never anxious, never afraid, always in control. He stood apart from the greatest of His followers. Peter was impetuous, John was known as a "son of thunder," and Paul lost his temper on more than one occasion. So the fine flour of the meal offering prefigured the matchless life of the Lord Jesus.

Over the fine flour was poured an unspecified amount of oil. No amount was stipulated because oil represents the Holy Spirit, and the Spirit was not given "by measure" to Christ, the Lord's anointed (John 3:34). His filling and anointing were limitless and without end.

No honey was to be added to the meal offering because honey speaks of natural sweetness, which is corruptible (Leviticus 2:11). Honey can ferment and turn sour. The sweetness of our Lord's character was not just natural; it was supernatural.

Frankincense, the most precious of perfumes, was sprinkled on the flour of the meal offering because the life of the Lord Jesus would be full of fragrance (Leviticus 2:15). Salt was also added to point to the pungency and flavor that would help make His life among men, His teaching, and His miracles so distinctive (2:13).

No leaven was to be put in the meal offering because leaven symbolizes evil (Leviticus 2:11). The offering spoke of the Lord Jesus and there was no sin or corrupting influence in Him. He was "holy, harmless, undefiled, separate from sinners" (Hebrews 7:26). Satan tried to corrupt Him, but failed because nothing in His nature would respond to temptation. It was not just that He would not sin; He could not sin. There was no leaven anywhere in His life.

Finally, the three measures suggested a life in which all the fullness of the godhead dwelt bodily (Colossians 2:9). This and all other aspects of the Old Testament meal offering spoke of Christ.

At the feast of pentecost a different kind of meal offering was presented by the Hebrew people (Leviticus 23:15-21). Instead of offering fine flour, they took the flour and made it into two loaves. While the usual offering of fine flour symbolized Christ in His material body, the loaves of pentecost symbolized Christ's mystical body. The two loaves prefigured Jew and Gentile made one in the church, the mystical body of Christ. The Lord has continued His work on earth since Pentecost through this mystical body.

The offering of the two loaves was quite different from the regular meal offering of the everyday sacrifices, for the Hebrews were told to put leaven in the offering they made at the feast of pentecost. This use of leaven symbolized an important truth: the church is not yet free from sin. Believers in the Lord Jesus make up the church. Through the miracle of the new birth they have become partakers of the divine nature (2 Peter 1:4), but they still have their old natures too and will continue to have both natures until they are called home to glory. So although the church is Christ's mystical body and will one day be perfect, it is not perfect yet. The flour is mixed with leaven.

At the feast of pentecost two things were done to deal with the presence of the leaven in the loaf: (1) a sin offering was presented to the Lord and (2) the loaves were put in the oven and baked. Note that it was a sin offering, not a trespass offering. The difference is important, for types are as accurate as mathematics.

The trespass offering dealt with sin in practice. Since we still fall into sin, the trespass offering was not part of the ritual of pentecost. Something else was required to deal with the actively working leaven in those loaves. The sin offering was needed to deal with sin in principle. The trespass offering was related to what a person did; the sin offering related to what a person was. I do what I do because I am what I am. I am not a sinner because I sin; I sin because I am a sinner. Christ died on the cross not only *for* me, but also *as* me. He became the sin offering for me. The mystical body of Christ, made up of members who still fall into sin, can function only because Christ has put away that sin in the sacrifice of Himself at Calvary.

So God dealt with the leaven in the sin offering. He also dealt with the leaven when the pentecostal loaves were put into the oven and baked. The action of the fire stopped the action of the leaven. The flame killed it. Likewise the sin in the members of the mystical body of Christ is dealt with by the action of fire. The Holy Spirit descended at Pentecost as "cloven tongues like as of fire" (Acts 2:3).

We who are believers have sin in us, but we do not have to allow sin to be operative in our lives. John wrote: "My little children, these things write I unto you, that ye sin not. And if any man sin, we have an advocate with the Father, Jesus Christ the righteous" (1 John 2:1). The Spirit of God indwells us and the Son of God upholds us so that we have all we need to cancel out the active working of sin in our lives. Although none of us this side of Heaven will ever be able to say, "I am not able to sin," all of us can say, "I am able not to sin."

One other consideration calls for our attention as we think of those three measures of meal. They prefigured the pure, unadulterated, unleavened truth that the Lord Jesus left with His church, the teaching we now find incorporated in the New Testament. The inerrant word of the Father, which became the incarnate word of Christ, is now in our hands as the inspired Word of the Spirit. That is the pure meal and it is this aspect of the meal that predominates in the parable of the leaven.

The church formed at Pentecost "continued stedfastly in the apostles' doctrine" (Acts 2:42). It was this body of teaching that gave the church its life. Jesus said, "The words that I speak unto you, they are spirit, and they are life" (John 6:63). These teachings were not to be diluted or distorted, but were to become the charter and constitution of the church.

However, in the parable leaven was introduced into the meal. Jesus foresaw that almost at once an adulterating, corrupting process would begin its deadly, permeating work in the church. The pure teaching of Christ and His apostles would be corrupted by active evil.

ii. The Leaven

a. Belief Corrupted by Evil

The leaven in the parable symbolizes belief corrupted by evil. In the Gospels Jesus spoke of three kinds of leaven: the leaven of the Pharisees (Luke 12:1); the leaven of the Sadducees (Matthew 16:6,12); and the leaven of Herod (Mark 8:14-15). These three kinds of leaven seem to be all-inclusive. They symbolize the various kinds of false teaching that have permeated the church during this age.

The leaven of the Pharisees spoke of *separatism.* Jesus frequently denounced the Pharisees because of their legalism, their dogmatic hairsplitting, and their corruption of divine truth.

A new breed of expositors surfaced when the Jews returned from Babylon. Ezra and the scribes sought to help the people understand the Scriptures (Nehemiah 8:5-8) and this was meaningful; but it was not long before volumes of commentaries filled with human opinion began to spring up. Soon the Jews had commentaries on the commentaries. What was to become the Talmud was taking root.

The rabbinical teaching about the sabbath, for instance, was a corruption of divine truth. The Lord intended the sabbath to be a day of rest, a blessing to His people, a time when they could relax and enjoy the Lord together. But the scribes and Pharisees turned the day into a burden. The simple and adequate statement in Exodus 20:9, "Six days shalt thou labour, and do all thy work," became the foundation on which they built a towering and threatening edifice.

They accused the Lord's disciples of breaking the sabbath because they broke off some ears of corn, husked them, and ate the corn on the sabbath day (Matthew 12:1-8). By plucking the corn the disciples violated the prohibition against reaping and by husking the corn they violated the prohibition against threshing. The rabbinical sabbath restrictions multiplied and in the end went to extraordinary lengths. When Jesus swept all this kind of nonsense into the rubbish heap, He brought down on His head the wrath of the Pharisees.

The whole system based on human opinion became known as the oral law and the Pharisees gave it far more weight than the Scriptures themselves. Similar reverence for the traditions and teachings of "the Fathers" found its way into the church. The Roman church places its tradition on a par with Scripture and has historically claimed that no one can interpret Scripture apart from the unanimous consent of the fathers. There is no such thing as unanimous consent, but the myth was used to keep the Bible out of the hands of the common people for centuries.

The Lord denounced the Pharisees not only for their hair-splitting but also for their hardness. Anyone who dared challenge their handling of the Scriptures was excommunicated (John 9:22, 26-38). The Pharisees became the open enemies of Christ because He violated their sabbath laws and because with the greatest of ease He tore to shreds their traditional interpretations of truth.

The Pharisees were the separatists, the fundamentalists, the traditionalists of Christ's day. They were rigid in their views and strict in their demand that all the outward trappings of religion be observed. Jesus called them "whited sepulchres...full of dead men's bones" (Matthew 23:27). The leaven of the Pharisees was the mistaken idea that they had some kind of monopoly on divine truth and that anyone who wanted to know God must come to Him through them.

The Pharisees added to Scripture; the Sadducees took away from it. The Sadducees were not numerous, but they formed a powerful aristocratic group within the nation. Their leaven spoke of *skepticism*. The Sadducees were the agnostics, the humanists, the theological liberals of their day. They denied the existence of angels, the existence of any kind of spirit, and the resurrection of the dead.

We have the leaven of the Sadducees in the professing church today. Liberals masquerade as Christians while denying such miraculous and supernatural essentials as the inerrancy of Scripture, the virgin birth of Christ, His miracles, His atoning death, His bodily resurrection, His ascension, and His literal coming again.

The leaven of Herod spoke of *secularism.* Herod Antipas was a licentious and unprincipled individual who seduced his brother's wife and persuaded her to marry him. He was so cruel and crafty that Jesus called him "that fox" (Luke 13:32). Herod arrested John the Baptist because John had publicly denounced him for his adultery. Later Herod murdered John, and when Herod (who was a superstitious man) heard of the miracles of Jesus, he thought that Jesus was John raised from the dead. Conscience made Herod a coward. When Jesus refused to perform a miracle for him or even talk to him, he made public mockery of His claim.

But Herod was a king. He represented Rome. He stood for imperial power. One party of Israelites known as the Herodians believed it was best to work through him and the powerful secular establishment to gain their religious ends. The party was probably founded during the reign of the infamous Herod the Great. As someone said, the Herodians were more than a religious party and something less than a political party.

Secularism like that of the Herodians has been with the church for a long time. Constantine taught the church to get on in the world by courting the throne. The supreme embodiment of secularism in Christendom is the Roman Catholic Church, but adherents of secularism can be found everywhere, even in evangelical circles. But God has not told us to use the system to get what we want, even when what we want is right and good for society as well as for the church. God has told us to use spiritual weapons, which He says are "mighty through God to the pulling down of strong holds" (2 Corinthians 10:4).

So in Scripture leaven is used as a symbol of worldly philosophies and principles corrupting the pure doctrine of Christ. Leaven is also used as a symbol of behavior corrupted by evil.

b. Behavior Corrupted by Evil

Paul saw this leaven at work in the church at Corinth. In that fellowship was a man guilty of gross moral sin. Paul told the others to excommunicate the man before the whole church became contaminated by his wickedness. "Purge out therefore the old leaven," the apostle wrote, "that ye may be a new lump, as ye are unleavened. For even Christ our passover is sacrificed for us: Therefore let us keep the feast, not with old leaven...of malice and wickedness; but with the unleavened bread of sincerity and truth" (1 Corinthians 5:7-8). Paul recognized the danger of behavior being corrupted by evil.

(b) The Action of the Woman

The activity of the leaven, the corrupting of truth and testimony by evil, was all foreseen by the Lord. He also knew how the leaven would get into the loaf. It was by the action of a woman. "The kingdom of heaven," He said, "is like unto leaven, which a woman took, and hid in three measures of meal." The Lord was not speaking of a literal woman. The woman in the parable represents a system.

Three mystical women appear in the New Testament. One is the earthly Jerusalem of Galatians 4:25. She is not the woman in the parable of the leaven, for the woman in the parable acted secretively, and earthly Jerusalem made no secret of her opposition to Christ. Neither did she try to introduce error into the truth of Christ; she rejected it out of hand.

The second mystical woman is the heavenly Jerusalem of Galatians 4:26 and Revelation 21:2. Since she is called "the *holy* city" (italics added), she cannot be the same as the woman in the parable. Moreover the heavenly Jerusalem has nothing to do with this age.

The other mystical woman is Babylon (Revelation 17:5)—not the literal city of Babylon on the Euphrates, but a mystical religious system located at Rome (Revelation 17:9,18). This is the woman who put the leaven into the meal. She represents the ancient Babylonish system that eventually took over the church, turned it into Christendom, and left its leaven everywhere.

Whenever we read in Scripture of a woman taking the lead and acting in a religious role, it is nearly always in an evil way. In the parable of the leaven the woman clandestinely introduced her corrupting doctrines into the pure meal of Christ's teaching. Then she sat back and watched it go to work. No one protested; people took no notice of what was happening. Besides, the popular thought was that leaven was a good thing to have in a loaf. Likewise the corrupting doctrines that have subtly taken over Christendom were introduced almost unnoticed and many innovative but evil ideas have been popularly accepted as improvements.

Ordinarily leaven in dough is thought to be desirable. When sourdough is added to meal, the result is appetizing. Flour by itself has little taste, but when yeast is added, the dough becomes light and savory. Christianity, however, was never designed to delight the flesh any more than unleavened bread at Passover was supposed to be tasty. On the contrary, God called that bread "the bread of affliction" (Deuteronomy 16:3).

The gospel is anything but appealing to the natural man, even though it is offered to us by a loving God. It begins with the assertion that people are lost in their sins and that they are hurrying on to lasting punishment in Hell. The gospel continues by telling people that their own righteousness and imagined good works are filthy rags in God's sight. It affirms that lost people are wholly incapable of producing anything morally or spiritually acceptable to God. The gospel goes on to insist on personal repentance from sin. It tells people they must believe the gospel, accept Christ by faith, and be born again from above. Once they have been regenerated, they must mortify the deeds of the flesh and live holy lives in the power of the indwelling Holy Spirit.

No wonder the gospel is unpalatable to lost people! What this representative woman has done is make it more consumable by introducing old Babylonian ideas that appeal to the religious side of the natural man. Her doctrines are a corruption of the faith, but they certainly appear to be more congenial.

(2) The Word (13:34-35)

The people listening to the parables spoken publicly must have been completely mystified. Those earthly stories with heavenly meanings went over their heads. The stories were easy enough to understand, but their deeper meanings eluded the multitude. The disciples themselves were mystified, so the Lord took them into the house where He was staying to interpret one more of the stories and to tell a few more parables privately.

Matthew pointed out that the psalmist had prophesied that the Lord would teach with parables. The apostle quoted from Psalm 78:2: "I will open my mouth in parables; I will utter things which have been kept secret from the foundation of the world" (Matthew 13:35). Note that the Holy Spirit exercised His divine prerogative to change the wording in the quotation: He changed "dark sayings of old" to "things kept secret from the foundation of the world." The obdurate hardness, blindness, and unbelief of the chosen people were foreknown by God from the beginning, but have been overruled to bring in the church and the mysteries of Christ's cross, His church, and His coming again.

B. Parables Spoken Privately (13:36-52)

1. An Explanation (13:36-43)

a. The Place (13:36)

After telling the parable of the leaven to the multitude, Jesus dismissed the crowds and retired to Peter's house. The disciples, still greatly perplexed by Christ's new form of teaching and still unable to unravel the mystery inherent in each parable, asked about the meaning of the story of the wheat and the tares. We can be grateful that they did, because we learn from the Lord's explanation that the seed in the parable of the tares is quite different from the seed in the parable of the sower. We always need to keep in mind that Bible symbols may have more than one meaning.[11]

b. The Parable (13:37-43)

(1) The Facts (13:37-38)

(a) The Sower (13:37)

There is no question about the sower's identity in the parable of the tares. He is "the Son of man." The sower is the Lord in His relationship to earth. He is God's "second man" (1 Corinthians 15:47), the Lord Jesus, who has been down here on earth and is coming back to claim Adam's lost domain for God.

(b) The Soil (13:38a)

In Matthew 13:24, where the parable itself begins, we read, "The kingdom of heaven is likened unto a man which sowed good seed in his field." Some people believe that the field symbolizes the church. Others think the field is the religious world. But the Lord said in 13:38, "The field is the world [*kosmos*]." He was referring to the created world, the planet Earth. The Lord looked out over Jerusalem, Judea, Samaria and the uttermost parts of the earth (Acts 1:8) and saw the wide world of lost men. He saw all lands where human beings dwell and made the world the setting of the parable of the tares.

(c) The Seed (13:38b)

In the parable of the sower the seed is the gospel; Scripture is sown into the hearts of men. In the parable of the tares, sons are sown into the world. The Lord Himself indicated this change in symbols.

In the parable of the tares there are two kinds of seed: "good seed" and "tares." There are two kinds of sowing: divine sowing and diabolical sowing. According to the Lord Jesus, "the good seed are the children of the kingdom," and "the tares are the children of the wicked one."

The good seed and the "wheat" (13:25) symbolize the same thing in the parable of the tares. Wheat seems to have been designed by the Creator to illustrate the people of God in the world in this age. Israel's symbol is a tree—a fig tree for instance or an olive tree or a vine. Since a tree strikes its roots deep into the earth, it is a fitting symbol for God's earthly people Israel. Israel's promises and hopes are often earthly. By deliberate contrast, the church's symbol is wheat. Wheat is a hardy annual with shallow roots that do not go deeply into the soil. Wheat is not deeply anchored to this world. Its destiny is to pass rapidly from this scene in successive harvests.

Wheat dies downward as it ripens upward; the stalk and root are dead when the grain is ripe. Just so, the Christian believer is to die to this world as he ripens for Heaven. There are other similarities: A ripened field of wheat is a field of bowed heads. The grain ripens into sweetness as the sun shines down day after day, and by some mysterious process the wheat absorbs the light.

God has His wheat in the world today. Ever since Pentecost the Lord has been sowing generation after generation of His saints into the world. They are scattered everywhere. They take root, flourish, and bear golden witness to the fact that God is at work. They ripen and are garnered home to glory. God buries His workers and carries on with His work. Even when the kingdom's prospects seem unpromising, even when days are dark and storm clouds gather, even when the atmosphere of the world is polluted by sin, God sees to it that His work goes on. Notice that the enemy in the parable could sow tares, but he could not tear up the wheat.

Here is how God's work goes on: Martin Luther for example read the Epistle to the Romans and his life was changed. John Wesley read the preface Luther wrote to his commentary on Romans, and Wesley's life was changed. C. H. Spurgeon attended a chapel of the Primitive Methodists, a group founded by Wesley, and Spurgeon was converted. Spurgeon in turn touched the life of a young man named Henry Morehouse. Morehouse came to America and transformed the preaching of D. L. Moody. C. T. Studd attended one of Moody's meetings in Britain and was transformed. Studd in turn made an impact on a group of college men known as "the Cambridge seven" and their influence on college campuses in Britain and on the missionfield can never be measured. And so it goes on. The good seed is sown as the Lord scatters His people to all parts of the world where they live for Him, reproduce, and touch other lives.

(2) The Foe (13:39a)

In keeping with the process of evil in the other parables, the foe in the parable of the tares seemed to be all-successful—at first. The "enemy came and sowed tares among the wheat" (13:25). The tares apparently were darnel, a poisonous rye grass which so resembles wheat that while the two are growing, the closest scrutiny will barely distinguish one from the other. As soon as the ears are formed, however, even a child can tell the difference. Naturalists tell us that the inner coats of darnel often harbor fungus growths and that the seeds, if eaten, can cause dizziness, vomiting, and even death. Often the roots of tares and wheat get intertwined so that any attempt to uproot the false will also uproot the true.

In the parable we see Satan's deliberate, stealthy introduction of unregenerate men and women into the Lord's harvest field. Satan sows those who closely resemble true believers in that they profess the faith. However, they are only imitation Christians; they have never been saved. They sing and preach and witness; they are religiously active, but they are strangers to the Holy Spirit. They talk about the Lord, but do not know Him. They are unconverted and lost.

Jesus called these people "the children of the wicked one" (13:38) and accounted for them by saying, "An enemy hath done this" (13:28). The Lord was not referring to the rank and file of the ungodly or even to unsaved church members in general. The people He described as tares are a special class of religious people, deliberately selected by Satan to mingle silently and subtly with the true people of God.

Church history gives us scores of examples of Satan sowing deception alongside every vital working of the Holy Spirit. The Lord sows His people into the world and then Satan comes right behind them and sows his people. They look like the real thing. The counterfeit is so clever that even saved people often cannot distinguish between the true and the false. Satan is a deceiver.

Not all unsaved people are "children of the wicked one." All unsaved people are lost and they all lie in wickedness (1 John 5:19), but they are not all sons of the devil. The parable of the tares deals with three groups of people: the children of God, the children of the devil, and lost humanity among whom they are sown.

Tares do not become wheat, nor do Satan's sons become Christians. Satan sows his own kind into the world, those who in a special sense have become partakers of his nature. All lost people have a sin nature, but Satan's children have something else—they have his nature. Both Judas and the antichrist are called the "son of perdition" (John 17:12; 2 Thessalonians 2:3), for both men were partakers of the Satanic nature. It was to the religious leaders of the day, those who had rejected Jesus and wanted to see Him crucified, that He said, "Ye are of your father the devil" (John 8:44). He did not say that of everybody, just of a special group of people.

So Satan sows his sons into the world to deceive. Wherever the Son of man sows, Satan sows. The wheat and the tares have been in the world from the beginning and they are in the world today, both growing until the harvest.

In the parable it was "while men slept" that the enemy came and did his dreadful work (Matthew 13:25). We always need to stay awake to the danger, and perhaps never more so than in times of revival when the Spirit of God is gloriously at work. For instance Simon Magus was able to deceive Philip in a time of revival: People were being saved and baptized. The city of Samaria was aflame. Then came Simon Magus, professing to be saved, willing to be baptized, wanting to join the fellowship of believers. He deceived Philip, but Peter saw right through him. "Thou has neither part nor lot in this matter," Peter said to Simon, "for thy heart is not right in the sight of God....I perceive that thou art in the gall of bitterness, and in the bond of iniquity" (Acts 8:21-23). Historians believe that Simon Magus went on to become a true apostate and one of the bitterest enemies of the early church.

(3) The Future (13:39b-c)

(a) The End-Time Age (13:39b)

After identifying the foe, the Lord directed the disciples' attention to the future. In the parable the Lord of the harvest, not at all surprised by what had happened, remained calm. He knew where the tares had come from and who was responsible. "The servants said unto him, Wilt thou then that we go and gather [the tares] up? But he said, Nay; lest while ye gather up the tares, ye root up also the wheat with them" (13:28-29). His *immediate plan* was to do nothing. How like God and how unlike us! The Lord has been exercising patience for nearly two thousand years. He waits with the knowledge that once He rises up to deal with this diabolical sowing, He will make an end of it once and for all.

Men in their folly have sought to uproot the tares, or what they considered to be tares. That was Rome's policy for centuries; she bruised, crushed, and burned all those she considered unfit for the kingdom of God. The Protestant church, as soon as it was able, responded in kind. In this dreadful process many a true child of God was broken on the wheel, tortured on the rack, and burned at the stake.

In the parable the Lord warned against any such inquisition. He silenced the suggestion of His servants that they attempt to root out the tares immediately. With one of His rare point-blank *Nos,* He forbade such efforts. "Let both grow together until the harvest," He said (13:30). Patience until the end of the age was His immediate plan.

(b) The End-Time Agents (13:39c)

The Lord also had an *impending plan:* "In the time of harvest I will say to the reapers, Gather ye together first the tares, and bind them in bundles to burn them: but gather the wheat into my barn" (13:30). He explained to the disciples, "The harvest is the end of the world; and the reapers are the angels" (13:39). The end-time agents are the angels.

The expression translated "the end of the world" is important. It means "the end of the age" or "the end of the dispensation." The expression occurs six times in the New Testament (Matthew 13:39,40,49; 24:3; 28:20; Hebrews 9:26). The word translated "end" is *sunteleia,* which means "closing time." It denotes the joining of two ages, the closing of one age leading on to the beginning of the next. (In Matthew 24:13-14 another word, *telos,* is translated "end." It means "actual and final end.")

The work of separating the true from the false is not left to us; it is reserved for the angels. It is not an age-long process; it will happen swiftly as our age draws to a close. We have no business damning people to Hell. The Lord reserves to Himself the right to take the initiative in this process. Nothing short of divine omniscience working through supernatural agency can make the proper separation of the false from the true.

(4) The Fire (13:40-42)

(a) The Type of the Tares (13:40)

Solemnly the Lord drew attention to the fire. First comes the bundling; afterward the burning. The process of bundling is going on already. Unbelievers are being gathered together in various false cults.

(b) The Truth of the Torment (13:41-42)

More terrible is the fire. The angels "shall cast them into a furnace of fire: there shall be wailing and gnashing of teeth" (13:42). The Lord referred to weeping and grinding of teeth seven times (Matthew 8:12; 13:42,50; 22:13; 24:51; 25:30; Luke 13:28). Each instance points to the end of the age.

Both Heaven and Hell are realities. But in the four Gospels the Lord Jesus, the kindest and most compassionate One who ever lived on earth, the all-knowing Son of the living God, spoke more about Hell than He did about Heaven. The Bible tells us that the ultimate destiny of the lost is the lake of fire. Again and again Scripture reveals that anguish beyond anything we can conceive is to be the final and conscious condition of those who reject Christ. Our minds cannot visualize what Hell will be like. Poets like Milton and Dante have tried to depict the torment, as have artists and preachers. Much of the result is grotesque and unreal, but the fact remains that the Word of God repeatedly warns about fire.

(5) The Faithful (13:43)

In the parable the Lord said He will command the reapers, "Gather the wheat into my barn" (13:30). In His explanation of the parable He added, "Then shall the righteous shine forth as the sun in the kingdom of their Father" (13:43).

The harvest will herald the end of the present age, during which the kingdom is in its mystery phase. The wheat will be gathered into Heaven at the rapture and the end-time judgments will descend upon the earth. Left behind, standing in the empty harvest field, will be the bundles of worthless tares, ripe and ready for the end-time judgment fires and the eternal flames that will follow.

Christ concluded His explanation of the parable of the tares by saying, "Who hath ears to hear, let him hear" (13:43). The expression implies that many who read will not understand and many who hear will not heed. It was designed to draw attention to the urgency of certain of His utterances. In this case the Lord wanted to warn us against Satanic teachers who pose as Christian preachers and missionaries. We would do well to pay heed.

2. An Expansion (13:44-52)

The next three parables form a trilogy. They are separated from the first four parables by the introduction in 13:36 and by the Lord's interpretation of the parable of the tares in 13:37-43. The Lord now had deeper mysteries to expound, mysteries for the ears of the disciples alone.

These three parables concern a hidden treasure, a costly pearl, and a great net. The parable of the hidden treasure and the parable of the costly pearl give us in broad outline the purposes of God for the present age and thus they introduce a new element of success; they show what the Lord is really doing in this time of mystery. The parable of the great net takes us on to the end of the age; the element of failure reappears, but only to show how everything will be brought to a fitting conclusion.

The trilogy depicts the future of three classes of people: the Hebrew people, the heavenly people, and the heathen peoples. In 1 Corinthians 10:32 Paul called them the Jews, the Gentiles, and the church of God.

a. The Parable of the Hidden Treasure (13:44)

(1) A Place (13:44a)

The future of the Hebrew people is depicted in the parable of the hidden treasure. The treasure was hidden in a field. We know from previous parables in Matthew 13 that the field is the world. That is the place, the scene of action in 13:44. This parable concerns God's royal purposes for this world of ours, which has become a colossal graveyard because of sin. God has not abandoned this world; on the contrary He sees a treasure in it.

It is God's great secret, partially revealed in the Old Testament, that planet Earth is to be the seat of His universal government. There is a hint in the first verse of the Bible, where the Holy Spirit uttered, "In the beginning God created the heaven and the earth."

God's secret gives cosmic significance, undreamed of by astronomers, to our best-known, best-loved text: "God so loved the world..." (John 3:16). There are much bigger orbs in space and much brighter and more imposing planets in our solar system. Yet of all the splendid worlds that whirl and dance and rush through space, God has selected our planet to be the center of everything.

On this planet God intends to display His royalty. His kingdom is to be located here by deliberate design, as part of His eternal plan. That is why the Lord will say to the sheep who are separated from the goats, "Inherit the kingdom prepared for you from the foundation of the world" (Matthew 25:34). The kingdom was planned when the planet was planned. No wonder Satan saw this world as a prize to be seized, garrisoned, and held at all costs against any intruder from the courts of bliss.

God's plans for our planet have centered in the nation of Israel ever since the days of Abraham (Genesis 12:1-3). God selected the children of Israel to be His people, put them in the land He is pleased to call His land (Joel 2:18), and gave them a capital city He calls the city of the great King (Psalm 48:2; Matthew 5:35). For a brief while the planned kingdom became openly visible as God raised up David, placed him on an everlasting throne (2 Samuel 7:8-17), and crowned him with glory and honor.

The early promise of the Davidic kingdom withered as David fell into sin and as his illustrious son Solomon debased the throne with pagan marriages and rank idolatries. Thereafter the kingdom was rent asunder and two rival kingdoms pursued their downward drift toward apostasy. The Assyrians made short shrift of the northern kingdom, and the Babylonians finished off the southern kingdom. Thereafter the monarchy was temporarily set aside and the nation was handed over to Nebuchadnezzar to be "trodden down of the Gentiles" (Luke 21:24). By the time Jesus arrived, the Romans ruled the land and an Edomite king sat on what passed for the throne of David. Every trace of the visible kingdom had vanished.

The Old Testament kingdom had at best been a shadowy picture of the ultimate Messianic kingdom and by the time Jesus came, even the shadows had passed away. Most Hebrews lived in voluntary exile and they were scattered all the way from Parthia to Spain. In the mind of God, however, the kingdom still existed and with the advent of Christ it could have come into its own. Thus John the Baptist and Jesus began their ministries with the cry, "Repent ye: for the kingdom of heaven is at hand" (Matthew 3:2; 4:17).

The treasure of God's kingdom on earth was here all the time, but it was *quite unsuspected* by most. It was hidden in the field. All roads led to Rome, not to Jerusalem. Roman legions marched across the promised land. Roman roads linked the little towns of Bethlehem, Nazareth, and Jerusalem to the great cities of Alexandria, Antioch, Carthage, Corinth, Ravenna, and Rome. But the treasure was still intact. It was seen only by Jesus and His forerunner John, but it was there.

Then the treasure was *quietly uncovered.* The man in the parable who finds the treasure represents Christ. He came to the land of the oppressed and downtrodden Jew, to the land where He knew the treasure lay interred. Judea was the spot where God's kingdom plans were focused, the spot that was to be glorified and brought into the spotlight by Jesus. So the Lord became a man and entered the world at Bethlehem of Judea. Note that it was a man, not an angel, who uncovered the treasure, "for unto the angels hath he not put in subjection the world to come" (Hebrews 2:5).

The devil was greatly alarmed at the coming of Christ; he knew that Jesus was a threat to his empire. Satan tried to murder Him (Matthew 2:16), but having failed that, he tried a different approach: he offered Him counterfeit treasure. The devil took Him up into a high mountain, showed Him all the kingdoms of the world in a moment of time, and promised Him all of them—for a price (4:8-10). Jesus knew that that was not the treasure He had come to find.

(2) A Plan (13:44b)

No sooner is the treasure discovered than it is hidden again: "The kingdom of heaven is like unto treasure hid in a field; the which when a man hath found, he hideth." By the time the Lord Jesus told this story, He had already hidden the treasure again. The kingdom had been offered to Israel, but since Israel had no use for the King, a second concealment took place. Shortly afterward Jesus wept over Jerusalem. "If thou hadst known," He cried, "even thou, at least in this thy day, the things which belong unto thy peace! but now they are hid from thine eyes" (Luke 19:42). From the moment the Jewish leaders blasphemed the Holy Spirit, the Lord changed His approach. At that turning point in His ministry He buried the treasure again.

Thus Israel, reborn as a nation after the Babylonian captivity and brought back to the land in preparation for the coming of the Messiah, was buried in a vaster, longer, and more terrible exile and captivity. The promised land, the place where the treasure was located, was passed from hand to hand by a succession of strangers. Romans, Crusaders, Muslims, and Britons all held the land for a while. But then, that was the plan: the treasure was to be buried out of sight. The promise of the kingdom was to be recalled; everything was to enter a new mystery phase; and Israel, the custodian of the part of the field where the treasure lay, was again to be dispersed among the nations.

(3) A Price (13:44c)

Far from being discouraged, the Lord knew exactly what He would do. "He hideth [the treasure], and for joy thereof goeth and selleth all that he hath, and buyeth that field."

Note the word "joy." On only one occasion in the Gospels is the Lord said to have rejoiced. It was when the seventy returned after He had sent them out to the cities of Israel with sample treasures of the kingdom—samples of the miracles and of the messages Jesus offered to men. The seventy returned in triumph, thrilled that demons, disease, and even death had been laid low before them. "In that hour Jesus rejoiced in spirit, and said, I thank thee, O Father, Lord of heaven and earth, that thou hast hid these things [the treasure of His sovereignty over the earth] from the wise and prudent, and hast revealed them unto babes" (Luke 10:21). The writer of Hebrews told his Jewish readers that it was "for the joy that was set before him" that Christ "endured the cross, despising the shame" (Hebrews 12:2).

The parable teaches us that He uncovered the treasure and hid it again with joy because He knew it was only a matter of time before the whole field and the treasure it contained would be His. The Lord simply enlarged His plans. Soon not only Israel but the entire world would be blessed.

In Matthew 13:44 there is a going, a selling, and a buying. The text implies that the man who finds the treasure "goeth *back*." Remember, the Lord Jesus was away from home. The world is man's natural home, not His. Heaven is His home. From the moment that the Jewish leaders blasphemed the Holy Spirit, the Lord set His face to go back home. From that moment, the treasure of God's royalty and His kingdom purpose was buried again and would not be unearthed until Christ's return. From that moment the Lord Jesus began to teach in mysteries.

Thereafter we see Him retracing His steps, wending His way back to His Father's home in Heaven. At last we see Him step off the brow of Olivet and back into the glory. The treasure is still in the field, for there can be no visible kingdom without the King. The Lord was homeward bound even as He told this story to His disciples.

There was a going back and there was also a selling. In the parable the Lord "selleth all that he hath"—and He possessed much. Paul told us that "he was rich" and that He gave His all (2 Corinthians 8:9). Think of who this royal treasure hunter was. By birth He was of the seed of Abraham and therefore the land belonged to Him. By birth He was the seed of David, so the throne belonged to Him. All that He might have claimed for Himself He gave up because of the broader purpose He now had in mind, that of buying the whole field and thus securing the treasure by means of His purchase.

We catch a remarkable glimpse of the purchase in the book of Ruth, where we read of Boaz's buying of Ruth's person and her property. The first time we meet Boaz, we are told that he was "a mighty man of wealth" (Ruth 2:1). We are not told how much he had to pay, but the Spirit's note that he was wealthy implies that his work of redemption was costly. He needed to be rich.

In the parable the buying is emphasized. The Lord "selleth all that he hath, and buyeth that field." Jesus bought the field in which lay the treasure of God's kingdom purposes, especially as they relate to the nation of Israel.

The world belonged to Him by right of *creation,* for He made every stick and stone, every rock and rill. Now the world belongs to Him by right of *Calvary;* He purchased the planet with His blood. Was there ever so enormous a price paid for a piece of real estate? He bought it with what the Holy Spirit calls "precious blood" (1 Peter 1:19). Thus in the Apocalypse we see Christ standing forward, when all other voices are reduced to silence or sobs, to claim the seven-sealed scroll, the title deeds of earth (Revelation 5:6-7). One day He is coming back to make the world His by right of *conquest.*

The time between Calvary and the conquest is a period of waiting. We are living in that time, that period of mystery when the kingdom is not being manifested to the world. But there are signs of change. The Jews are going back to their land and the focus of the world is on that significant spot in which treasure is hid. The owner is still away, but He is coming back. Israel must be back in the land, ready for the treasure to be revealed when He returns.

All attempts to establish the kingdom without the King are bound to fail. Imperialism, communism, attempts to Christianize the world will all come to nothing. The treasure is here in the world all right, but only the owner can uncover it. This He will do when He comes back to claim His purchased possession and establish the kingdom of God visibly on earth.

b. The Parable of the Costly Pearl (13:45-46)

While the parable of the hidden treasure depicts the future of the Hebrew people, the second parable in the trilogy—the story of the costly pearl—depicts the future of the heavenly people. The treasure has to do with Israel; the pearl with the church. Throughout the Bible the earth is a consistent symbol for Israel, and the sea is an equally uniform figure for the Gentiles. Thus the treasure was hidden in a field, while the pearl was buried in the sea. In the Apocalypse two beasts emerge, one from the sea to be the final caesar, and one from the earth to be the great deceiver, especially of the Hebrew people (Revelation 13).

The treasure relates to God's earthly people and His sovereign purposes on earth. The pearl relates to His heavenly people and His saving purposes on earth. The last glimpse of the pearl in Scripture confirms this interpretation, for in Revelation 21:21 we see the pearl associated forever with the heavenly Jerusalem, the celestial city. During the millennial reign there will be two Jerusalems. The earthly Jerusalem, the capital city of Christ's world empire, will be the joy and pride of the Hebrew people (Psalm 87:3-5). The heavenly Jerusalem, the wondrous eternal home of the redeemed, will blaze like a diamond in the sky (Revelation 21:1–22:5).

So the parable of the hidden treasure focuses on Israel and God's secret plan to unearth the buried treasure of the kingdom on earth. The parable of the costly pearl concentrates on the church—its origin, its worth, and its destiny.

The most popular interpretation of the parable of the costly pearl is that the pearl represents Christ. This view misses the mark for two reasons. First, it takes the story out of harmony with the other mystery parables in Matthew 13. The sower, the man who found the treasure, and the merchant seeking for pearls are all the same person. They all represent Christ. If the merchant is Christ, the pearl cannot be Christ.

Second, the popular view leads to the impossible conclusion that the sinner sacrifices his all in order to possess Christ. Such a conclusion is inconsistent with the teaching of Scripture. It is not the sinner who seeks Christ; it is Christ who seeks the sinner (Luke 19:10).

(1) The Great Quest (13:45-46a)

"The kingdom of heaven is like unto a merchant man, seeking goodly pearls: Who, when he had found one pearl of great price, went and sold all that he had, and bought it."

(a) What the Merchant Desired (13:45)

The merchant was seeking "goodly pearls." Those words must have astonished the disciples because Jews in those days did not count pearls as precious gems. They are never mentioned in the Old Testament. Gentiles, however, prized pearls and associated them with the wealth of kings. To impress Mark Antony, Cleopatra took from her ears a pair of pearls valued at nearly half a million dollars, dissolved them in vinegar, and drank them. The fact that the pearl was a Gentile treasure helps explain the parable. The Jews despised the Gentiles and wanted to have as little to do with them as possible. But the merchant was seeking something precious in the Gentile world, something almost foreign to Old Testament values.

The parable says that the merchant was "seeking" good pearls. The word "seeking" implies that he was going from one place to another. It implies an actual departure from one place and a corresponding arrival at another. The word depicts the Lord Jesus leaving Heaven for earth to look for those who in His eyes were of great worth and who, once found, would adorn His diadem forever. We now know what it was He came to purchase. It was His church.

(b) What the Merchant Discovered (13:46a)

The merchant found a costly pearl. By geological standards the pearl is nothing. The lowly oyster can make one in three to five years, while it takes millions of years of fierce heat and pressure to create a diamond. Crush a pearl and all you have is a little heap of lime dust. This Gentile treasure is made of calcium carbonate, the same substance we find in ordinary chalk. Yet modern man, for all his skill and genius, cannot take calcium carbonate and turn it into a pearl.

Man can no more capture the living miracle of a pearl than he can capture a sunbeam and turn it into a star. He can make artificial pearls, cultured pearls as we call them, by implanting smooth beads of mother-of-pearl into oysters so that they can grow the imitation. The counterfeit is so close to the natural that only experts can tell the difference, but there is no comparison in their value. One is real; the other is fake.

The merchant in the parable was looking for real pearls, not fakes. The church, of which the costly pearl speaks, is unique and cannot be duplicated by human means. Man has produced a counterfeit church; Christendom is a clever fraud, but it has no value in the eyes of the divine expert. The Lord came to seek the real thing. It has no intrinsic value—it is just human calcium carbonate, dust of the earth—but when it is made into a pearl, it is beyond pricing.

(2) The Great Question (13:46b)

Having discovered a costly pearl, the merchant had to decide what it was worth, how much he would pay for it. Then he "went and sold all that he had, and bought it." That is how the Lord procured the church; He bought it at the cost of Calvary.

There is only one costly pearl in the parable because the church is unique. It is one separate, individual, and incomparable entity in God's dealings with mankind. The church is not merely spiritual Israel. The church is distinct from all else and so highly esteemed on high that for the sake of this pearl the heavenly merchant paid His all. Thus the church is what Paul called "the purchased possession" (Ephesians 1:14).

It will be helpful for us to review how a pearl is created in nature. The gem is the answer of the oyster to something that has injured it. A foreign object pierces the oyster, whereupon the little creature buries the irritation under layer after layer of secretion until at last it has produced a pearl. The pearl cannot be obtained until the oyster is dead. In other words, the pearl is found in an oyster's grave. This process points us directly to Calvary. There men injured God's Son and put Him, sorely pierced, in His grave. Yet out of that suffering and death God has produced the church. The church is God's answer to Calvary.

Other facts about the costly pearl point us to the church. A pearl is silky white in color and time cannot rust or tarnish it. In the days of the Lord, pearls were the special treasure of kings and were destined for the throne. It seems that Christ had all this in mind when he selected a pearl to be a vehicle for conveying mystery truth to His disciples. He had set His heart on a rare, unique, and priceless pearl. He had counted the cost and was about to pay the price. Before long He bought it. And as an oyster's pearl is salvaged from the stormy sea, so the church was taken from the restless sea of the Gentile world. Destined for the throne, the church will be exhibited eternally as the prime example of God's sovereign grace (Ephesians 2:7).

The heavenly merchant bought the pearl with His all and that is what gives inestimable value to the church. Christ considered it of such worth that He came from afar to seek it and gave His life to possess it.

The church was a mystery, an entity undreamed of at the time the Lord spoke the parable of the costly pearl. The Jewish people knew nothing about the church since it was not revealed in the Old Testament. The truth would soon be revealed to the disciples (Matthew 16:17-18; 18:15-20), but at the time they were listening to the parable, they were as ignorant as everyone else. Not until after Pentecost would the full truth about the church be revealed. What was made plain later in the New Testament was embodied in mystery in Matthew 13. Of course when Matthew wrote, the church was well established on earth and the nation of Israel was about to be dissolved by the armies of Rome.

c. The Parable of the Great Net (13:47-50)

The parable of the great net, the last of this trilogy, depicts the future of the heathen peoples. Difficulties surround this parable and will continue to do so as long as people insist on reading the church into it. The mysteries in Matthew 13 primarily concern kingdom truth, not church truth. There is an inevitable degree of overlap between the church and the present mystery phase of the kingdom, but the two are not the same. The parable of the great net touches on God's kingdom purposes during the age in which we live, but its real focus is the end-time climax of those purposes.

(1) What Was Sought (13:47a)

The parable begins, "The kingdom of heaven is like unto a net, that was cast into the sea." Here again the sea is the symbol of the Gentile world into which the gospel net is lowered. Once in the sea, the net swings back and forth under the influence of the waters and the tides. Gentiles are being sought for the kingdom and in the present age that also involves them in the church.

But the full meaning of the parable is broader and more general. It corresponds to Romans 11 where the primary theme is not the church at all, though it is of necessity in the background. The theme of that much misunderstood chapter is not the church, but the sphere of blessing and the relationship of Jew and Gentile to that sphere of blessing. Romans 11, like the parable of the great net, has to do with the gathering in of Gentiles, as Gentiles, into the sphere of God's sovereign purposes in government and grace. Paul said in Romans 11:13, "I speak to you Gentiles."

(2) What Was Caught (13:47b)

The dragnet "gathered of every kind." There are all sorts of fish in the sea, an almost infinite variety—some good, some bad, some of use, some worthless (Leviticus 11:9-12). Like other parables in Matthew 13, the story of the great net depicts the inescapable mixing of the good with the bad in the mystery phase of the kingdom.

We see this mixture in our churches, where there is often an unhappy mingling of the saved and the lost, a mingling of the merely religious and the truly regenerate. God's work in the world draws in both kinds, the genuine and the false. Jesus had His Judas; Philip his Simon Magus. In every evangelistic campaign the gospel net draws in those who merely profess to be saved and those who are genuinely born again. There is no such mixture in the true church, for it is composed only of saved people baptized by the Holy Spirit into the mystical body of Christ. But there is a mixture in Christendom and in the kingdom during this age.

(3) What Was Wrought (13:48)

"When [the net] was full, they drew to shore, and sat down, and gathered the good into vessels, but cast the bad away." There is to be a time of judgment when the good will be separated from the bad. As far as the church is concerned, the separation will take place at the rapture when the Lord will take "the good" and leave "the bad" behind. The Lord warned the Laodicean church, "I will spue thee out of my mouth" (Revelation 3:16). The bride will go to be with Him in Heaven, but the apostate professing church will be left behind as the harlot church of Revelation 17.

The church and the rapture, however, are only incidental in the focus of the parable. Its theme is the kingdom and the ultimate separation of the good and the bad at the final return of Christ to earth. The place of this separation is plainly revealed, for the net is drawn to the shore. As we have seen, the shore (the earth) refers to Israel. Joel 3:11-13 tells us that the place is the valley of Jehoshaphat in the land of Israel.

After Armageddon the Lord will divide the good Gentiles from the bad Gentiles according to what they have done to His people (Matthew 25:31-46). This separation is a necessary prelude to the setting up of the millennial kingdom. The mystery phase of God's kingdom purposes will then be over and the kingdom will be displayed in power and glory.

(4) What Was Taught (13:49-50)

"So shall it be at the end of the world: the angels shall come forth, and sever the wicked from among the just, And shall cast them into the furnace of fire: there shall be wailing and gnashing of teeth."

(a) The Angels of the Lord (13:49)

This present age is not the age of angels, but the age of the Holy Spirit. It is true that angels have an intense interest in what is happening on earth (1 Peter 1:12), that they are active on behalf of God's people (Hebrews 1:14), and that they seem to have some kind of guardian relationship to the church (Revelation 2:1; 1 Corinthians 11:10). But since this is primarily the age of the Holy Spirit, angels remain invisible and in the background today.

During the age of the apocalypse, angels will again come to the fore. In Scripture we read of their active engagement in all of God's judgments on this planet. In the book of Revelation angels appear in all but three of the twenty-two chapters (chapters 4, 6, and 13). Of the three chapters where angels do not appear, one mentions beings of a different order (the cherubim, chapter 4) and another mentions the dragon himself (chapter 13). In some chapters of Revelation angels appear many times. They administer God's judgments on the planet and act as messengers from the throne. The renewed burst of angelic activity will be heralded at the rapture by "the voice of the archangel" (1 Thessalonians 4:16).

(b) The Anguish of the Lost (13:50)

The final separation of the good from the bad prior to the millennium will be entrusted to the angels. The wicked will have no part in that kingdom and will be banished to a lost eternity. Christ's millennial reign will begin with a nucleus of regenerated Jews and Gentiles who love the Lord.

d. The Parable of the Wise Householder (13:51-52)

(1) Truth Must Be Discerned (13:51)

The Lord now turned to His disciples. He had one more parable for them (see 13:52), a plain and simple parable in contrast to the mystery parables that make up the bulk of Matthew 13. But first He asked, "Have ye understood all these things?" The word translated "understood" is *suniēmi,* which has the primary meaning of "to bring together" (as foes are brought together for battle) or "to collect together" (as single features of an object are collected into a corporate whole). Thus *suniēmi* means "to collect, grasp, comprehend"—that is, to be earnestly occupied with a matter, to reflect on it, to ponder it, to take it to heart. The word implies mental activity; it has to do with knowledge acquired by thinking and pondering.

Suniēmi differs from *ginōskō* ("to know"), which implies immediate knowledge. The Lord did not expect His disciples to have an immediate grasp of all the aspects of the mystery. This kind of understanding would come later. But He did expect them to give careful attention to the subject and they assured Him that they were doing so.

The discourse recorded in Matthew 13 contained an entirely new revelation. It was something "kept secret from the foundation of the world" (13:35). Matthew, who recognized the importance of the parables and wrote them down in an orderly way because of their implications for the Jewish people, said that Christ fulfilled prophecy in delivering the new revelation. We are frequently reminded in the New Testament that the church and the church age had been kept secret until disclosed by the Lord and His disciples (Romans 16:25-26; 1 Corinthians 2:7; Ephesians 3:5-9; Colossians 1:26).

(2) Truth Must Be Dispensed (13:52)

In the parable of the wise householder the Lord taught His disciples that they must teach things both new and old. God had not canceled His millennial promises to Israel; He had just postponed them. Those promises were the subject of many Old Testament prophecies and the disciples were to teach them, as Paul did in Romans 9–11. But there was a new truth for a new dispensation. They would best understand how the old and the new are related by grasping the mystery parables.

At the beginning of the next passage of Scripture we will read, "Jesus had finished these parables" (13:53). The expression shows that the parables of Matthew 13 are a special collection, an organic whole. The only place where a similar expression is used is Matthew 19:1, where reference is made to the teaching of chapter 18, which contains a comprehensive statement on the functions of the (yet future) local church.

III. The Murder of John (13:53–14:36)

John the Baptist and Jesus, the messenger and the Messiah, marched in step across the conscience of their age. John's ministry came to a sudden end with his arrest. Then he died a violent death, a harbinger of what would be the portion of his Lord. Matthew introduced John's murder as another terrible sign of the rejection of Christ. Thus the resistance to Jesus is still the focus in Matthew 13:53–14:36. The solemn story of the death of John the Baptist is prefaced with an account of the Lord's visit to the synagogue in His hometown and is followed by an account of the Lord's unwearying concern for His disciples and for the thoughtless crowds who continued to throng Him.

A. Home and Its Critics (13:53-58)

1. The Home Scene (13:53-54)

a. The Surroundings (13:53-54a)

"When Jesus had finished these parables, he departed thence" (13:53). The Lord left Simon's home and headed for Nazareth, His boyhood home. Jesus' journeys did not cover vast distances. The whole length of Galilee was less than sixty-five miles and its extreme width only thirty-three.

Had it not been for Jesus, we would never have heard of Nazareth. Its lack of importance is indicated by several facts: (1) Nazareth is not mentioned in the Old Testament; (2) Nazareth was not mentioned by Josephus, who named 244 towns and cities in Galilee; (3) Nazareth is not mentioned in the Talmud.

b. The Synagogue (13:54b-c)

We know from Mark 6:1-6 that the disciples accompanied Jesus to Nazareth and that on the sabbath He followed His usual custom of going to the local synagogue. As the Lord embarked on His last period of intensive public ministry, the first place He went was Nazareth and its synagogue.

Many adults who have been away from their hometowns for years and have gone back to visit find that things look smaller and often shabbier than they remembered, especially if their childhood years were spent in unimportant places. Picture someone returning to his local church and sitting in his family pew where his earliest spiritual memories were formed. No doubt he is reminiscing. *There's where Dad sat. There's where Willie carved his initials, and what a thrashing he received for that, but the initials are still there! There's the pulpit where the preacher stood so stern and solemn. It's not nearly so awesome now. It's badly in need of new varnish. Over there is where Susie sat. I always adored Susie and I intended to marry her. Now she's the living image of her mother and has six children of her own.*

So the Lord went home and entered the synagogue He had known as a boy. He knew every stone and timber. Thirty years of memories were associated with that synagogue. It was a small place in a small town made up of small people, but Jesus loved them. That is why He went back. At the outset of His Galilean ministry He had preached in their synagogue and they had tried to stone Him to death (Luke 4:16-30). Now He would give them a chance to change their minds.

The Lord took the scroll and taught and they were astonished. This was not the boy they had known! This was not the man who had made their furniture and mended their plows! This was not the lad who had attended the synagogue school taught by the local rabbi! They had never heard teaching like His before. Here was One who spoke with authority and not as the scribes (compare Matthew 7:29). Beginning at Moses and all the prophets He showed them from the Scriptures the things concerning Himself (compare Luke 24:27). "Never man spake like this man" (John 7:46).

The people of Nazareth said, "Whence hath this man this wisdom, and these mighty works [*dunamis*, 'works of power']?" (Matthew 13:54) In other words, they were asking, "How can Jesus know anything? He has not graduated from our universities. He has no earned doctorate. He never sat at the feet of Hillel or Gamaliel. Where does He get this wisdom? How can He do such mighty works?" Evidently the Lord had performed some miracles in their midst, although Matthew did not say what they were.

2. The Hostile Setting (13:55-58)

a. The Reason for the Hostility (13:55-57a)

(1) Small-Town Reasoning (13:55-56a)

The people thought that Jesus was just the carpenter's son. How wrong they were! He was not the carpenter's son at all. He was Mary's Son, but not the carpenter's son. But that is how they viewed Him. They thought of Joseph, they thought of Jesus, and they thought they were just the same—an interesting sidelight on the thorough humanity of the Lord Jesus.

"Is not his mother called Mary?" (13:55) There was no argument about that. The local folk knew her as only small-town people can know each other. There had been some nasty gossip years ago about her hasty marriage to Joseph, but that was long forgotten. She had been an exemplary wife and mother, a good neighbor and friend, a religious and zealous believer. But she was only Mary, Jesus' mother. She was nobody. How did He get to be somebody?

None of the other children in Joseph and Mary's home were out of the ordinary. Jesus' sisters were just village girls. We would like to know more about them. His brothers—James, Joses, Simon, Judas—were nobodies too. In the end He won them all (Acts 1:12-14). James and Judas wrote books that found their way into the New Testament. James also became the leading elder of the Jerusalem church.

It is difficult for us to picture those brothers and sisters growing up in the same family as the sinless Son of God and being so blind as not to see who He really was. He was so human. He played with them, went to the synagogue school with them, watched over them, protected them, helped them, wept with them, laughed with them, sang with them, prayed with them, and dearly loved them. After the resurrection the Lord personally appeared to James, maybe in the workshop at Nazareth (1 Corinthians 15:7). In any case, His resurrection blew away the cobwebs from their eyes.

(2) Small-Town Resentment (13:56b-57a)

The townsfolk of Nazareth were not impressed with Jesus. "They were offended in him" (13:57). The word translated "offended" here is *skandalizō,* which means "to be stumbled." They had never heard such Bible exposition. They had never seen such miracles. But they were stumbled because He had grown up among them and they were too blind to see beyond His humanity to His deity.

b. The Result of the Hostility (13:57b-58)

The Lord made the sad observation, "A prophet is not without honour, save in his own country, and in his own house" (13:57). Many have proved this comment true. Often the hardest people to reach with the gospel are the members of one's own family and social circle.

The Lord "did not many mighty works there because of their

unbelief" (13:58). He did some, but not many. The loss was theirs. Unbelief stifles even the working of God.

B. Herod and His Conscience (14:1-12)

1. A Wrong Deduction (14:1-2)

The fame of Jesus had reached the royal palace at Machaerus. Herod Antipas had more than one royal residence, but the site of John the Baptist's imprisonment is believed to have been Machaerus, where a boundary fortress secured the southeast part of Herod's domains facing Arabia.

The approach to the fortress looped its way in a series of spirals over one of the frowning mountains of the east side of the Dead Sea. The way ran through a deep gorge where ten hot springs rose through a crack in the volcanic rock. The springs were reputed to have magical healing powers, and Herod the Great had gone there to bathe his diseased body. Three hours of hiking through the mountains would bring a traveler from the springs to Machaerus, which the Arabs call *El Mashnaka,* "the hanging place." The name doubtless preserves a haunting memory of one or another of Herod the Great's atrocities.

The fortress at Machaerus had been built by Alexander Janneus and restored by Herod the Great, who had also built a town on the hills behind the fortress. Josephus considered even the natural location to be impregnable, for all around Machaerus rose the bleak mountains of Moab. He wrote:

> Now when Alexander, the king of the Jews, observed the nature of this place, he was the first who built a citadel here, which afterwards was demolished by Gabinius, when he made war against Aristobulus; but when Herod came to be king, he thought the place to be worthy of the utmost regard, and of being built upon in the firmest manner, and this especially because it lay so near to Arabia; for it is seated in a convenient place on that account, and hath a prospect towards that country; he therefore surrounded a large space of ground with walls and towers, and built a city there, out of which city there was a way that led up to the very citadel itself on the top of the mountain; nay, more than this, he built a wall round that top of the hill, and erected towers at corners, of a hundred and sixty cubits high; in the middle of which place he built a palace, after a magnificent manner, wherein there were large

and beautiful edifices. He also made a great many reservoirs for the reception of water, that there might be plenty of it, ready for all uses.... Thus did he, as it were, contend with the nature of the place, that he might exceed its natural strength and security (which yet itself rendered it hard to be taken) by those fortifications which were made by the hands of men. Moreover, he put a large quantity of darts and other machines of war into it, and contrived to get everything thither that might any way contribute to its inhabitants' security under the longest siege possible.[12]

The fortress stood 3,800 feet above the Dead Sea and commanded an awesome view. From their rocky aerie, the garrison could look down on the Dead Sea and the winding Jordan river. Across seemingly endless mountains, far away in the west, on the edge of the horizon, crowning a distant ridge, could be seen a few smudges—the brow of Olivet. To the south was the rugged Judean wilderness bounded by the hills of Hebron. To the north was the gorgeous oasis of Jericho and the cleft of the Jordan valley where John had baptized.

But deep within the citadel were a well, a cemented cistern, and two dungeons. It was down in the darkness of this terrible place that John the Baptist, son of the wide-open spaces and bold herald of the Christ, had spent his last days. John's lot had been to remain in the deep dungeon in the citadel while the adulterous Herod Antipas and his murderous wife enjoyed a giddy round of pleasure in the luxurious palace. No wonder John had asked if he had made a mistake about the identity of the Messiah.

Now John was dead, but Jesus was alive, preaching and performing miracles. When news of Jesus' activities reached Herod Antipas, he had an immediate explanation: John the Baptist had risen from the dead. The thought smote his guilty conscience and haunted him in the still night hours. Matthew used Herod's wrong deduction as a bridge to recount the murder of John.

2. A Wicked Determination (14:3-12)

a. A Crime Postponed (14:3-5)

The Herods were a serpent's breed. Herod the Great was savage, but a clever statesman nonetheless. One by one he murdered the sons chosen to succeed him on the throne. The luckless Antipater was killed by his disease-ridden father only five days before the monster's own death.

After Herod the Great died, his kingdom was divided among three of his surviving sons: Archelaus, Philip, and Antipas. Archelaus was deposed before Jesus came to manhood. He inherited all his father's vices and nothing of his greatness. Philip, the son of the beautiful Cleopatra of Jerusalem, fell heir to the poorest part of the kingdom, the desert region northeast of Galilee and south of Damascus.

Antipas, who inherited Galilee and Perea, was the Herod who murdered John and mocked Jesus. Antipas was not a violent man like his brother Archelaus, but he was sly. It was Antipas who founded Tiberias, a city considered unclean by the Jews because it was built partly over a cemetery. (The city is not mentioned in the Gospels and there is no record that Jesus ever went there.)

On a visit to Rome, Antipas stayed with another of his half brothers, a man named Herod Philip (not Philip the tetrarch, but another son of Herod the Great). Herod Philip had retired from the Herodian jungle in Palestine and had moved to Rome, where he lived as a wealthy citizen. His wife Herodias, a woman of great beauty and ambition, was the granddaughter of Herod the Great. The marriage was therefore consanguineous, as were so many of the marriages within the Herodian family.

Herodias's brother Agrippa was a close friend of Caligula. When Caligula became emperor, he gave the spendthrift Agrippa the Palestinian estates left by Philip the tetrarch upon his death. The emperor also gave Agrippa the right to wear a crown and be called a king. This preferment stirred the fury and jealousy of Herodias.

While Antipas was visiting Herod Philip at Rome, Herodias entered into an intrigue with him. She had long since tired of the life of a wealthy Roman matron, and she saw in Antipas an opportunity for excitement and advancement. So she ran away with him to Galilee. Antipas divorced his legal wife, the daughter of Aretas, king of Petra, and married Herodias. Thereby Antipas made an enemy of the Nabateans, made the fortress of Machaerus more necessary than ever, and made himself guilty of entering into a marriage that was both adulterous and consanguineous.

John the Baptist denounced the whole affair and consequently earned the implacable hatred of Herodias. Herod Antipas, spurred on by his vengeful wife, arrested John and imprisoned him at Machaerus. But Herod vacillated. On the one hand was the goading of Herodias to get rid of John; on the other hand was the power of John's personality. Herod also hesitated because he did not want to make John a martyr, for he was still popular with the masses.

b. A Crime Proposed (14:6-8)

Herodias bided her time. The occasion she chose to force her husband's hand was his birthday. At the celebration Salome performed a dance. Salome, the daughter of Herodias and her former husband Philip, was most likely in her teens at the time. The dance was probably provocative, for we cannot expect that a daughter of Herodias would be much restrained by modesty. The guests, who were doubtless already inflamed by drink, responded enthusiastically. Herod, swept beyond the reach of caution, blurted out a pledge to give her anything she might like to ask for. Moreover he confirmed the rash promise with a solemn oath.

Off the girl went to inquire of her mother what she should request. Matthew said Salome was "instructed" (*probibazō*) by Herodias to demand the head of John the Baptist in a dish. The word *probibazō* implies that Salome would not have thought of such a thing herself and that her reluctance had to be overcome. Back to Herod she came. We can imagine that everyone in the banqueting hall was focusing their attention on her response and that her request exploded like a bombshell: "Give me here John Baptist's head in a charger" (14:8). Thus for one brief moment the young woman danced on the stage of history as the gruesome tool of an evil mother.

c. A Crime Perpetrated (14:9-12)

(1) John Beheaded (14:9-11)

(a) The King's Cowardice (14:9)

"The king was sorry," says the Holy Spirit. But sorry or not, he committed the terrible crime. The guests, no doubt suddenly sobered by the drama now being enacted, watched the struggle recorded on the weak ruler's countenance. Uppermost in Herod's mind was pride, the desire to save face before his guests. He had given a promise and supported it with an oath. If the promise had been given in private, the outcome might have been different. But Herod was conscious that every eye was on him. Would he revoke his pledge in view of the terrible demand now made on him? Would he dare scorn Herodias? Would he brave the ridicule of those sitting at his table?

Herod had neither the character nor the courage nor the conviction to confess that he had made a mistake. He had taken a reckless position, but was not going to climb down now. Like many weak men, he preferred the easy way out. His conscience, quickened by the boldness and bluntness of John, had troubled him for a long time. Now he trampled it underfoot and seared it with a hot iron forever.

(b) The King's Command (14:10-11)

Herod looked into the challenging faces of his lords, his high captains, and the chief men of Galilee (Mark 6:21). He thought of his oaths (one translator used the plural, indicating he had repeated his oath, as a drunken man often will). Herod looked into the face of the young woman daring him, and he gave orders for the murder of John. We see in Antipas a man intimidated by his evil companions, a man whose moral fiber had been sapped by his dissolute way of life.

John, in his lonely dungeon, heard the tramp of soldiers' feet. He looked up and saw the executioner. This was the end of his career, the place to which he had come by being faithful to his calling and his God. With one flash of the ax, John was on the shore beyond death and he knew that his labors had not been in vain.

(2) John Buried (14:12)

His disciples gathered up the mortal remains of their master and buried them "and went and told Jesus." What a lovely expression! Where else could they go? Who would better understand and advise? How often we have done the same! We are not told what Jesus said to John's disciples, but we can be sure that they went away comforted and assured. No one ever goes to Jesus in vain.

C. Humanity and Its Cares (14:13-36)

Matthew 14:13-36 shows us the Lord Jesus, in spite of His own needs, taken up with humanity and its cares. We see the sermon on the mount in action.

1. Compassion for the Hosts of Mankind (14:13-14)

a. The Deep Need of the Master (14:13a)

The news of John's murder did not take Jesus by surprise. Nothing ever took Him by surprise. But it brought into focus the certainty of His own impending death and He felt the need to get away from the crowds. "When Jesus heard of it, he departed thence by ship into a desert place apart." He went to the northeastern corner of the lake near the town of Bethsaida Julias. But He was not to rest for long.

The Lord probably set sail from Capernaum. The multitudes saw Him go and followed Him. Evidently they ran along the northern shore of the lake, arrived at His landing place before He did, and were there awaiting Him when He landed.

b. The Deep Need of the Multitude (14:13b-14)

The Lord's need to be alone was swallowed up in the deep need of the multitude. His heart went out to them. Matthew said He was "moved with compassion toward them" (14:14). Mark said that He was moved "because they were as sheep not having a shepherd" (6:34). Luke added, "He received [welcomed] them" (9:11).

The Lord was not irritated over the fact that they had broken in on His seclusion. He did not tell the multitude to go home and leave Him alone. He embraced them in the arms of love. They were poor lost sheep and their scribes and rabbis were no shepherds. The religious leaders had a dog-in-the-manger attitude toward the common people. Those leaders did not care for the people or even like them, but they did not want Jesus to shepherd them either.

The Lord Jesus pitied the people, so He taught them and "healed their sick" (Matthew 14:14). He practiced what He preached.

2. Compassion for the Hunger of Mankind (14:15-21)

It is not enough to feed men's souls. We must also pay attention to their physical needs. In the past evangelicals have so reacted against the "social gospel" of the liberals that they have often neglected the physical needs of those to whom they minister. It is true that some missionaries make "rice Christians" of nationals by dazzling them with the material things we at home take for granted. People will always come for the loaves and fishes. But the Lord was not deterred by that. He did His good works anyway. He had compassion for the hunger of mankind.

a. The Problem (14:15-18)

(1) The Answer of Logic (14:15)

The disciples were getting hungry. Everyone else was hungry too and there were no shops or provisions in that wilderness. Moreover it was long past time to get rid of the crowd. The immediate solution suggested by the disciples was simple: "Send the multitude away." The idea was pragmatic, but unfeeling. It was the answer of logic. The disciples knew that they could not feed the crowd, and they had forgotten that Jesus could.

(2) The Answer of Love (14:16-18)

The Lord's response to the disciples' logic was the answer of love: "They need not depart; give ye them to eat" (14:16). If He were to send the multitude away hungry, there would be a tremendous scramble to be first at whatever stores were still open. The women and children among that vast crowd would suffer most. Jesus refused to let them go and fend for themselves.

The word "evening" occurs in both 14:15 and 14:23. The Jews had two evenings. The first was from the ninth to the twelfth hour (between 3:00 p.m. and 6:00 p.m.). The second was a period of thirty to forty minutes after sunset or from sunset until three stars were visible. In 14:15 the reference is evidently to the first evening. It was late afternoon and soon all the markets would be closed. The disciples had their eyes on the clock, but the Lord had His eyes on the crowd. "Give them something to eat," He said in effect. But that was the problem. The disciples had nothing to give. That is our problem too.

b. The Provision (14:19-21)

(1) A Blessed Supply (14:19)

(a) The Multitude (14:19a)

The disciples said, "We have here but five loaves, and two fishes" (14:17). They were concerned about the law of supply and demand, one of the most basic principles of economics. The multitudes represented the demand. John 6:7 tells us that Philip said, "Two hundred pennyworth of bread is not sufficient for them, that every one of them may take a little." He was looking at the demand.

Andrew was looking at the supply. John 6:9 tells us what he said: "There is a lad here, which hath five barley loaves, and two small fishes." It would have been faith of the highest order if Andrew had stopped there, but he didn't. He spoiled everything by continuing, "But what are they among so many?" Everyone was looking everywhere except to Jesus.

Jesus "commanded the multitude to sit down on the grass" (Matthew 14:19). Mark added that the people sat in orderly groups of fifty and one hundred. God is a God of order. All creation proclaims that fact; all science is predicated on that fact. The Lord Jesus, God manifest in the flesh, was devoted to order. So He had the people sit down "by companies" (Mark 6:39).

The meager meal was now in Jesus' hands. The five pieces of eastern pocket bread were made of barley, the poor man's fare. The fish were probably not much bigger than sardines. There was not enough food to fill a hungry boy, still less a hungry multitude. But there was quite enough for the One who holds the grain-rich prairies in His hands.

(b) The Miracle (14:19b-c)

First there was an acknowledgment of Heaven as the source of all that meets men's needs, and then the miracle began. The five loaves and two fish multiplied miraculously in Jesus' hands. He "gave the loaves to his disciples, and the disciples to the multitude." With ever fresh supplies, the busy disciples ran to this group and that. And although Matthew never mentioned him, somewhere in that crowd was a little boy with eyes big with wonder.

What a marvelous little boy he was! Did you ever stop to think that the Lord Jesus, the Creator and Sustainer of the universe, might have gone to sleep hungry if that lad had not given Him his lunch? But Jesus took what was offered to Him (as He does to this day) and blessed it and worked wonders with it. With it He performed the only one of His miracles that is recorded in all four Gospels.

What a story that little boy had to tell when he arrived home that night! He would never tire of telling it. We can picture him as an old man with grandchildren on his knee: they say, "Tell us a story, Grandpa," and he says, "I'll tell you about the time I gave my lunch to Jesus."

The secret of the feeding of the multitude was simple. The lad made himself available to Jesus. The Lord Jesus made Himself available to His Father in Heaven. And a miracle took place.

(2) A Bountiful Supply (14:20-21)

There was *no want.* There was plenty for everyone. The Lord performed the miracle, then made that miracle available to all through His disciples. The disciples did not perform the miracle; they were the channel through which the blessing flowed. The Lord always blesses a needy world through His own.

What if the disciples had run back and forth with the Lord's bounty just to the first few rows in the nearest groups? When those people had eaten enough, they would have begun to fill their pockets and squabble with their neighbors over the food. Soon some would have stopped speaking to each other. Some would have exchanged angry words and blows. Some would have thrown food at each other. Behind those first few rows would have been thousands of people unfed, unreached, uncared for. Those up front would have been demanding more for their growing stockpiles while those farther back would have been perishing with hunger.

There is a lesson in Matthew 14:15-21 about how the Lord's work should be done. The miracle recorded here, like many other miracles, can become a parable about how the good news of God's bountiful provision in Christ should be made known to all mankind.

The church for the most part has concentrated on a few favored corners of the earth. The bulk of Christian work is done among a small minority of people. There are some six billion people in the world, most of whom have never heard the gospel, yet we keep ministering to the same few rows. As a result professing Christians squabble and fight among themselves, hurling portions of the bread of life at one another and stockpiling their knowledge of the truth. While untold millions remain untold, there is "bread enough and to spare" (Luke 15:17). If we would go to where the starving millions are, there would be no want.

There was *no waste* at the feeding of the multitude. "They took up of the fragments that remained twelve baskets full" (Matthew 14:20). Here is a simple, incidental, but pointed lesson on frugality. We are a wasteful society. Manufacturers want to stimulate sales, so they make their products with built-in obsolescence. A car is supposed to wear out so that its owner will have to buy another one. As a result the world's nonrenewable resources are being consumed by the industrial nations at an alarming rate.

In the average American home the amount of food thrown into the garbage can daily would sustain whole families in underprivileged nations. The old adage "Waste not, want not" sounds to many like an incantation from another world. Yet one of the collateral lessons we learn from 14:20 is not to waste.

Matthew concluded his account of the feeding of the multitude with a note about numbers, something dear to evangelicals in many places today. He wrote, "They that had eaten were about five thousand men, beside women and children" (14:21).

3. Compassion for the Helplessness of Mankind (14:22-33)

a. Tranquility (14:22-25)

(1) Desired (14:22-23)

(a) The Method (14:22-23a)

i. Jesus Sent His Men Away (14:22a)

The disciples had urged the Lord to send the multitudes away (14:15) and now He was about to do what they wanted Him to do. As for the disciples, He sent them away—Jesus "constrained" them to cross over the lake to Bethsaida, a suburb of Capernaum (14:22).

ii. Jesus Sent the Multitudes Away (14:22b-23a)

Matthew did not tell us why the Lord was so insistent now on sending the multitudes away. John told us it was because Jesus "perceived that they would come and take him by force, to make him a king." They were convinced by the miracle that they had just seen that Jesus was "that prophet that should come into the world," the Prophet foretold by Moses (John 6:14-15; Deuteronomy 18:15). They realized that a greater than Moses was among them. Moses had fed their fathers with manna in the wilderness, but before their own eyes Jesus had miraculously fed five or six thousand people with a little lad's lunch.

The miracle appealed to the multitude's materialistic concept of the Messiah. In John's Gospel the Lord's sermon on the true Bread of Life follows soon after this miracle; in that sermon He made it clear that He thoroughly rejected any kingship that depended on materialism.

(b) The Motive (14:23b)

It was no small feat for the Lord to dissuade the excited people, to refuse their offer of a worldly crown, to cause them to disband quietly and go on home. Left alone at last, He "went up into a mountain apart to pray: and when the evening was come, he was there alone." Here is an example of the second of the two evenings (see page 293), that peaceful hour when the sun sets and the first stars appear; the world has ceased from the rush and bustle of the day, the children are on their way to bed, and the home settles down for the night.

The Lord wanted to be alone so that He could pray—so that He could open up His heart to His Father in Heaven. The shadow of the cross had come a little nearer and loomed a little darker with the murder of John. The Lord needed to commune with the One in whose likeness He was; He needed to be alone with the One whose will He had come to do on earth. The time for the crown had come and gone; it would not return for some two thousand years. The time for the cross was drawing near.

There is something awesome in the Lord's desire for tranquility, something that rebukes our neglect of the place of prayer. Robed in humanity, the uncreated Son of God—self-existing, possessed of all the attributes of deity, Creator of the universe— poured out His heart in prayer. If He needed to pray, how much more do we!

(2) Disturbed (14:24-25)

The Lord's tranquility was soon to be disturbed by the coming of a storm. At this point Matthew 14 takes us back to the boat carrying the disciples to the other side of the lake. Sudden squalls engendered in the surrounding mountains can sweep across the lake and turn its calm surface into dangerous billows. One such unexpected and furious storm now burst on the disciples. They knew well the temper of the lake when it was in this kind of mood.

The disciples' vessel was "tossed with waves." It was lurching violently, threatening to capsize and sink. "The wind was contrary," Matthew said, meaning that it blew directly in their faces (14:24). They were about halfway across the lake and the sensible thing to do would have been to turn the boat around and let it run before the wind back to the shore from which they had come. But the Master had told them to go to the other side and there could be no turning back. Come what may, with what little strength they had, they would do what He said. They had no warrant to give up just because the wind was contrary. What a fine lesson in obedience!

b. Terror (14:26)

The wind and the waves were frightening. The experienced fishermen among them understood the imminent peril of drowning in the tumultuous waves. But now came another terror, one that made scalps creep and hair stand on end. Suddenly the disciples saw something that looked like a ghost. Some terrible phantom appeared to be pursuing them across the tempestuous sea.

Mark's account takes us back to the mountain where Jesus was wrapped in darkness and alone with His Father. In the fourth watch of the night (between 3:00 a.m. and 6:00 a.m.) the Lord saw the disciples "toiling in rowing" out there in the grip of the storm (Mark 6:48). He knew about the difficulties that overwhelmed them and responded immediately. He came down the mountain, sovereignly stepped out on the sea, and strode after the disciples. The boisterous waves were submissive to His tread.

Thus the phantom was no ghost at all. It was simply the disciples' loved Lord hurrying to their aid, moved by their helplessness in the grip of forces beyond their control. But when they saw Him drawing nearer, "they supposed it had been a spirit, and cried out" (Mark 6:49). The rowers, we can be sure, tugged frantically at the oars, trying to outdistance the uncanny apparition now stalking them from behind.

William Cowper was familiar with terror. A poor, often demented poet, he was in and out of insane asylums in an era when few greater horrors could beset a man than to be committed to a madhouse. It was that struggling saint of God who wrote:

> Ye fearful saints, fresh courage take;
> The clouds ye so much dread
> Are big with mercy, and shall break
> In blessings on your head.[13]

And so it was on the sea of Galilee. It was no ghost that haunted those dark and heaving waves and called to the disciples over the howl of the storm. It was Jesus.

c. Trust (14:27-31)

The disciples heard a familiar voice saying, "Be of good cheer; it is I; be not afraid" (14:27). Peter with his usual impulsiveness proposed a test. If it really was the Lord, then let Him summon Peter to come to Him. The Lord answered in a word: "Come" (14:29). That word, the most wonderful word in the Bible, was the *basis of Peter's trust*. He dared to put his trust in the naked word of the Christ of God.

All around Peter, the world was being torn apart. The wind was screaming in his ears and the boat was tossing like a piece of driftwood. But the surging billows were already beneath the Lord's feet. Jesus had walked some three and a half miles across the lake to reach the boat, which according to John 6:19 was twenty-five or thirty furlongs from its starting point. (All the circumstances that we are unable to cope with are also already beneath the Lord's feet.) The things that were beneath His feet, the Lord was going to put under Peter's feet as well.

Peter was going to walk on water because he had faith, the vital link to the source of power. "Faith," according to Romans 10:17, "cometh by hearing, and hearing by the word of God." Peter had heard the one word he needed: "Come." Upon it he could rest his faith and dare his all.

Picture the scene. Peter lifted one foot over the side of the boat and as the waves soaked his leg up to his waist, he was reminded that there was water out there and man cannot walk on water. But Peter pondered the word of God in Christ—"Come"—and lifted his other leg over the side. However, Peter still had an iron grip on the boat. He would not be exercising real faith until he let go. It was when he fixed his eyes on Jesus that everything came into focus and he let go. Then the impossible happened. He was no longer being ruled by circumstances; he was triumphing over them. Faith was operating in his life.

Just outside our front door we have a thermometer. The mercury in that thermometer reflects the ups and downs of the temperature outside the house. That is all a thermometer can do: respond to the influence of the temperature. Inside the house, on a wall in the hallway, we have a thermostat. It too functions in relation to the temperature. During the winter when the temperature in the house falls to a certain point, the thermostat orders the furnace to bring the temperature back to the set number of degrees. During the summer when the temperature in the house rises to a certain point, the thermostat orders the air conditioner to bring the temperature back down again. The thermometer only reacts to the temperature, but the thermostat controls the temperature. The thermostat rules because it is connected by an unseen wire to a source of power.

Every believer is either one or the other. He can be a thermometer going up or down with every change of circumstance. Or he can be a thermostat, influenced by the ups and downs of life, but instantly triumphing over them because faith links him to a wondrous source of power.

So Peter was triumphing over circumstances. "He walked on the water," said Matthew (14:29). Peter was doing what the Lord told him to do. Step by step he was walking the life of faith, walking in implicit, moment-by-moment obedience. His whole world was filled with the vision of Christ; he had his eyes fixed steadfastly on the Master.

Peter was doing just what Jesus was doing; he was doing the impossible. Peter's faith in Christ enabled the power and authority of Christ over every circumstance to operate in his life; in terms of what he was able to do at that moment and in that situation, there was absolutely no difference between Peter and Christ. Peter had not mastered the theory of whatever dynamic was involved in walking on water, but his trust in Christ at that moment so linked him with Christ that Christ's mastery was transmitted to him. Peter's faith was the switch that turned on the power in his life.

We note the *boldness of Peter's trust* during those few glorious moments when the treacherous waves were as solid as dry land beneath his feet. But there was a sudden *breakdown of Peter's trust* as he became aware of the angry wind and sea. He took his eye off the Lord and fastened it on his circumstances. Faith died and fear rose. The vital link to the source of power was severed and Peter began to sink.

But all was not lost. The Lord had not challenged Peter to try this new kind of life only to let him perish when he failed. Jesus came alongside him. Peter fixed his eye once more on the Master and cried out, "Lord, save me" (14:30). Faith took hold once more and the Lord took hold. That mighty arm was outstretched to save. That hand, able to contain in its hollow the waters of the seven seas, caught the sinking disciple. "O thou of little faith," He said, "wherefore didst thou doubt?" (14:31)

Peter's faith was little, but it was better than no faith. Peter had been given an experience of victorious living that no one else in the boat had been given, an experience he would remember to his dying day.

d. Truth (14:32-33)

(1) The Sudden Calm (14:32)

Peter and the Lord climbed into the boat and instantly "the wind ceased." The only circumstance that mattered now was that Christ was in the vessel. That took care of everything else.

(2) The Sublime Confession (14:33)

The sudden calm on top of all the other miracles of that extraordinary day and night overwhelmed the disciples. "They that were in the ship came and worshipped him, saying, Of a truth thou art the Son of God." The miracles had been performed to bring them to this grand realization of the true identity of their loved Lord. All had been designed to bring them to His feet in adoring worship. And any storm He sends to us will be worth it if it brings us to His feet.

4. Compassion for the Hurts of Mankind (14:34-36)

a. The Arrival of the Master (14:34)

The boat finally docked at Gennesaret, a plain on the western side of the lake. The disciples had started out for Capernaum, but the Lord had changed their destination, for they landed near Magdala on the northwest end of the lake but south of Capernaum. From that point they proceeded by land along the road home.

b. The Arrival of the Multitudes (14:35-36)

News that Jesus was in the area was flashed throughout the district. Seeing an opportunity too good to miss, the residents came to Him in droves, bringing their sick. The story of the woman healed by touching just the hem of His garment was evidently well known, for the crowds begged for permission to do what she had done. "And," noted Matthew, "as many as touched were made perfectly whole" (14:36).

The word translated "made perfectly whole" here is *diasōzō,* which means "completely saved or healed." *Diasōzō* occurs eight times in Scripture (Matthew 14:36; Luke 7:3; Acts 23:24; 27:43,44; 28:1,4; 1 Peter 3:20) and in all these instances is used in connection with bodily deliverance.

THE RESISTANCE FACED

(15:1–16:12)

I. A CONTRADICTION (15:1-20)
A. A Quibble (15:1-6)
   1. The Pharisees' Challenge to Christ regarding Rabbinical Tradition (15:1-2)
     a. The Place (15:1)
     b. The Problem (15:2)
   2. Christ's Challenge to the Pharisees regarding Revealed Truth (15:3-6)
     a. The Approach (15:3)
     b. The Appraisal (15:4-6a)
       (1) The Demands of the Law (15:4)
       (2) The Distortion of the Law (15:5-6a)
     c. The Application (15:6b)
B. A Quotation (15:7-11)
   1. A Denunciation (15:7-9)
     a. A Plain Statement about the Pharisees' Hypocrisy (15:7)
     b. A Prophetic Statement about the Pharisees' Hypocrisy (15:8-9)
   2. A Declaration (15:10-11)
     a. An Exhortation (15:10)
     b. An Explanation (15:11)
C. A Question (15:12-20)
   1. The Blindness of His Foes (15:12-14)
     a. Described (15:12)
     b. Denounced (15:13-14)

(1) Its Seriousness (15:13)
(2) Its Sadness (15:14)
2. The Blindness of His Friends (15:15-20)
a. How It Was Displayed (15:15-16)
b. How It Was Dispelled (15:17-20)
(1) The Food That Goes In (15:17)
(2) The Filth That Comes Out (15:18-20)
(a) The Source of Our Defilement (15:18)
(b) The Substance of Our Defilement (15:19-20)

II. A CONTRAST (15:21-39)
A. The Needy Heathen Mother—How Jesus Praised Her (15:21-28)
1. How Desperate She Was (15:21-23a)
a. Her Place (15:21-22a)
b. Her Plea (15:22b-e)
(1) The Mercy She Sought (15:22b-c)
(a) Her Appeal to the Lord's Sympathy (15:22b)
(b) Her Appeal to the Lord's Sovereignty (15:22c)
(2) The Mistake She Made (15:22d)
(3) The Miracle She Wanted (15:22e)
c. Her Plight (15:23a)
2. How Determined She Was (15:23b-27)
a. A Tragedy Revealed (15:23b)
b. A Truth Revealed (15:24)
c. A Triumph Revealed (15:25-27)
(1) Hope beyond Despair (15:25)
(2) Humility beyond Compare (15:26-27)
(a) The Crisis That Confronted Her (15:26)
(b) The Crumb That Consoled Her (15:27)
3. How Distinguished She Was (15:28)
a. What Jesus Thought of Her (15:28a)
b. What Jesus Wrought for Her (15:28b)

B. The Needy Heathen Multitude—How They Praised Jesus
   (15:29-39)
   1. His Great Compulsion (15:29-31)
      a. The Mountain (15:29)
      b. The Multitudes (15:30-31)
         (1) Their Woes (15:30)
         (2) Their Wonder (15:31a)
         (3) Their Worship (15:31b)
   2. His Grand Compassion (15:32-34)
      a. His Heart's Desire (15:32)
      b. His Hard Disciples (15:33-34)
         (1) What They Had Forgotten (15:33)
         (2) What They Had Found (15:34)
   3. His Gracious Command (15:35-39)
      a. What He Demanded (15:35)
      b. What He Did (15:36-39)
         (1) The Components of a Miracle (15:36-37)
             (a) The Simple (15:36a)
             (b) The Sublime (15:36b)
             (c) The Sensible (15:36c-37)
                 i. A Natural Channel (15:36c)
                 ii. A Notable Challenge (15:37)
         (2) The Computation of a Miracle (15:38)
         (3) The Completion of a Miracle (15:39)

III. A CONFRONTATION (16:1-12)
   A. The Sign Demanded (16:1)
      1. Why the Jews Wanted It (16:1a)
      2. Where the Jews Wanted It (16:1b)
   B. The Sign Denied (16:2-4)
      1. Readable Signs in the Sky Discerned by the Jews
         Daily—They *Could* Reason from Effect to Cause
         (16:2-3)
      2. Remarkable Signs of the Times Displayed by the Lord
         Daily—They *Should* Reason from Effect to Cause
         (16:4)
         a. His Denunciation (16:4a-b)

(1) The Sin of Their Generation (16:4a)

(2) The Sign for Their Generation (16:4b)

b. His Departure (16:4c)

C. The Sign Discussed (16:5-12)

1. The Disciples and Their Unbelief (16:5-10)

a. How Forgetful They Were (16:5-7)

(1) A Dilemma (16:5)

(2) A Discussion (16:6-7)

(a) What the Master Said (16:6)

(b) What the Men Supposed (16:7)

b. How Foolish They Were (16:8-10)

(1) In Their Minds—For Not Appreciating His Point (16:8)

(2) In Their Memories—For Not Appropriating His Power (16:9-10)

2. The Disciples and Their Understanding (16:11-12)

a. The Lesson Spelled Out (16:11)

b. The Light Turned On (16:12)

The opposition to Jesus, centered in the religious leaders and particularly in the Pharisees of Jerusalem, became increasingly pronounced. This resistance, which the Lord resolutely faced, becomes more and more prominent in Matthew's Gospel. At the beginning of this section the Pharisees make an accusation and are at once contradicted by Christ.

I. A CONTRADICTION (15:1-20)

A. A Quibble (15:1-6)

1. The Pharisees' Challenge to Christ regarding Rabbinical Tradition (15:1-2)

The Lord, we must remember, had just fed the five thousand in the wilderness. Thousands of people had eaten bread with unwashed hands, and with the Lord's evident blessing. The small-minded Pharisees did not care about the miracle. All they cared about was that the Lord had broken one of their religious taboos. Moreover they had probably seen the disciples eating some of the leftovers without first going through the ritual ceremony of washing hands.

We must also remember that these Pharisees were from Jerusalem. The authorities in the capital were already disturbed by news of Christ's continuing activity and popularity in Galilee. Their purpose in making the journey to observe Him was to find some cause of offense in Him.

"Why do thy disciples transgress the tradition of the elders?" the Pharisees quibbled, "for they wash not their hands when they eat bread" (15:2). This challenge to Christ was no small incident. His scorning of the Jews' traditions was one of the major reasons for their leaders' determination to get rid of Him. A second reason was that He ignored their sabbath laws and was therefore "not of God" and consequently a deceiver and a sinner (John 9:16,18,24). A third reason was that, according to them, He was a blasphemer in that He claimed to be God's equal. The Pharisees had already written off His miracles as being the work of Satan.

From the days of Ezra, the Jews had begun to amass explanations and traditions that they added to the law and regarded as more important than the law. They claimed that the additions had been delivered orally by Moses and handed down from generation to generation. This so-called oral law was already voluminous; in time it would become as large as the *Encyclopedia Britannica* and be known as the Talmud with its Mishna (text) and Gemara (commentary). For centuries, however, the oral law was preserved solely in the remarkably capacious memories of the rabbis.[1]

The Pharisees from Jerusalem were experts in these additions to the law. They did not accuse the disciples of breaking a specific Mosaic command. There were commands in Leviticus 11 about uncleanness and washings, but these were not at issue here. Here it was a case of breaking traditions added to the law by the religious leaders.

Not long before, as Edersheim pointed out, the two leading rabbis of the age, Hillel and Shammai, "rival teachers and heroes of Jewish traditionalism," had fixed the ordinance about washing hands. Their schools, which differed about almost everything else, agreed that water had to be poured on the hands and allowed to run down to the wrist. This and similar rules, which were "intended to separate the Jew from all contact with Gentiles," were "of the most violently anti-Gentile, intolerant, and exclusive character."[2]

There could be no modification of the rule for hand washing. Any rabbi who disregarded this tradition was excommunicated. The Pharisees regarded this and other ordinances of the scribes to be "more precious, and of more binding importance than those of Holy Scripture itself."[3] The rabbis taught that tradition was weightier than the words of the Law and the Prophets.

2. Christ's Challenge to the Pharisees regarding Revealed Truth (15:3-6)

The Lord countered the accusation of the Pharisees with a challenge. They asked Him a question; He asked them a question. "Why do ye also transgress the commandment of God by your tradition?" He said (15:3). Note the word "your." The Lord was denying their claim that Jewish tradition went back to Moses when He bluntly called it *their* tradition.

The Lord did not deny that the disciples had transgressed the Pharisees' tradition; He simply swept it aside and vindicated the disciples for ignoring it. Not only was the tradition worthless; it violated the law of God.

The Lord referred the Pharisees to the fifth commandment of the Decalogue: "Honour thy father and mother" (15:4). Ephesians 6:2 says it is "the first commandment with promise." The word translated "honour" includes the idea of supporting aged parents, as in 1 Timothy 5:3. It is not enough to give verbal respect to parents. Honoring them means providing for their physical needs where necessary.

The rabbis, however, had come up with an evasion of the demands of the law (Matthew 15:5-6). To get out of this obligation a Jew simply had to say the word "Corban" over all that he possessed (Mark 7:11). The word meant that he had dedicated his possessions to God. He could vow for instance that upon his death his savings would go to the temple. That vow absolved him from the present duty of helping his parents. He had put his material possessions under a sacred umbrella, so to speak, and the claim of the fifth commandment was superseded by the vow.

However, he could still use his material means for his own personal enjoyment. Edersheim explained: "By simply saying '[Corban], that by which I might be profited by *thee*' [the rabbinic formula for such a vow], a person bound himself never to touch, taste, or have anything that belonged to the person so addressed. Similarly, by saying '[Corban], that by which thou mightest be profited by *me*' [a corresponding rabbinic formula], he would prevent the person so addressed from ever deriving any benefit from that which belonged to him" (italics added).[4]

Thus the rabbis, in the name of the most punctilious regard for religious duty, voided God's clear-cut law. The Lord's thrust went home.

B. A Quotation (15:7-11)

1. A Denunciation (15:7-9)

a. A Plain Statement about the Pharisees' Hypocrisy (15:7)

The Lord was not through. He followed up His challenge with a quotation from Isaiah 29:13. The Pharisees said that their tradition was weightier than Scripture, but the Lord authoritatively referred them to Scripture and bluntly called them hypocrites.

b. A Prophetic Statement about the Pharisees' Hypocrisy (15:8-9)

The quotation was particularly appropriate, as were all the Lord's references to Scripture, for it ruled out tradition. Isaiah of course prophesied long before the Babylonian captivity, long before the days of Ezra and the scribes, long before the beginning of the system of traditional teaching that in the end produced the Talmud.

2. A Declaration (15:10-11)

Having thrust the sword of the Scripture at the Pharisees, the Lord turned to the multitudes who were listening in astonishment to this discussion. "Hear, and understand," He said, "Not that which goeth into the mouth defileth a man; but that which cometh out of the mouth, this defileth a man." In one sweeping statement He had denounced the entire structure by which the rabbinical schools, the scribes, the Pharisees, and the religious leaders secured their hold on the multitudes. He labeled their religious rules and regulations, their exegesis, and their spirit-stifling, God-dishonoring, Bible-contradicting, man-enslaving, soul-destroying, ego-building, Satan-serving traditions as worthless.

Based on what the disciples said next, it is doubtful that the multitudes fully understood the Lord's remark. The Jerusalem Pharisees, however, were smart enough to know that they had been checkmated by the One whom they had come to call to account.

C. A Question (15:12-20)

1. The Blindness of His Foes (15:12-14)

"Knowest thou that the Pharisees were offended, after they heard this saying?" (15:12) the disciples asked. The Lord's reply showed how little He cared about the opinion of these false teachers. "Every plant, which my heavenly Father hath not planted, shall be rooted up," He said (15:13). The disciples perhaps were more than a little alarmed at the Lord's fearless exposure of these powerful men. These were no local rabbis who had been offended. They were a deputation from Jerusalem.

The Lord never made room for error, no matter who was teaching it. His Father had not planted the noxious weed of traditional religion, a religion more concerned with human opinion and outward conformity than with truth and reality. "They be blind leaders of the blind," He said. "Let them alone" (15:14). Jesus was fully aware of their hostility, but because of the ditch into which they were leading the blind people who followed them, He spoke out against them.

2. The Blindness of His Friends (15:15-20)

The disciples did not seem to understand. They had been raised in a religion that placed emphasis on ritual cleanness. So the Lord explained that food in itself did not defile, even if it did happen to be ceremonially unclean or even if it did happen to be eaten with unwashed hands. It was only food and could have only a physical effect.

Before long, Peter (who raised this issue) would be taught once and for all that Judaism was obsolete and its Levitical restrictions about diet were lifted (Acts 10). There was such a thing in the Old Testament as *ritual* uncleanness, as Daniel recognized (Daniel 1:8), but it was only of limited value and that mostly of a picture-book nature. Far more important was *real* uncleanness, the defiling things that came out of a man's innermost being: evil thoughts resulting in murder, adultery, fornication, theft, lying, and blasphemy.

II. A CONTRAST (15:21-39)

A. The Needy Heathen Mother—How Jesus Praised Her (15:21-28)

After His brush with the Jerusalem Pharisees the Lord left the lake and headed to the coast, then north to the region of Tyre and Sidon. These two Phoenician cities had a history of seafaring, commerce, colonization—and vile religion. There the Lord met a pagan woman noted by Matthew for her desperation and determination.

We must remember that Matthew was writing for Jews and he was now tracing the movement of Jesus away from the Jewish people, whose leaders were actively rejecting Him, and toward the lost world of the Gentiles. There was something symbolic and prophetic in this deliberate move to the sea. He left the small Jewish inland lake and went to a representative of a people to whom the sea was a highway to the world. The desperate woman who now met Him represented the countless millions from the Gentile world who for centuries now have filled up the ranks of the church.

The Jerusalem delegation had locked horns with Jesus and had doubtless gone home filled with indignation. So He sought out a Gentile to whom to manifest His grace. His spirit was longing for that faith which He could not find in Israel but which He knew was waiting for Him in lands where darkness ruled.

The pagan woman introduced in 15:22 was not just a Gentile. She was a Canaanite, a member of the accursed race whom God had commanded Joshua to exterminate. Her story hinges on the thrice-repeated words, "But he answered." Underline them in 15:23,24,26 and the word "then" in 15:28.

1. How Desperate She Was (15:21-23a)

The woman had a demon-possessed daughter. Demon possession was probably not at all uncommon among those involved in the demonic religious system of the Canaanites.

The fame of the wonder-working Prophet from Nazareth had reached this mother. She had heard of His great heart of love. Perhaps she had also heard rumors that He was the promised Messiah of the Jews, for she appealed to Him as the "son of David" (15:22).

David's name was known in her part of the world. The Holy Spirit recorded that Hiram, a king of Tyre during the reigns of David and Solomon, was "ever a lover of David" (1 Kings 5:1). That may account for the way the woman addressed the Lord Jesus and cried to Him to have mercy on her and heal her child. She cried, "O Lord, thou son of David...But he answered her not a word" (Matthew 15:22-23). He said nothing, but He bathed His soul in her expression of faith, which was so different from the critical unbelief of the rulers of His own people.

2. How Determined She Was (15:23b-27)

The disciples soon tired of her persistence. "Send her away," they said (15:23). A short while before, they had said, "Send the multitude away" (14:15). That was their solution to a problem. It was not His. The fact that He did not send her away spoke volumes about His compassion for the poor soul. It evidently spoke to her, for she persisted in her pleas. The Lord was moved by her determination, but He put her to the test, and a very severe test it was. His first words were chilling enough. "But he answered and said, I am not sent but unto the lost sheep of the house of Israel" (15:24).

The woman had none of the religious antecedents of the Jews; she was not raised on the Scriptures; she had no roots in Abraham and David. She was only a lost pagan who had heard of Jesus and had no hope apart from Him. Her ignorance was evident in her original plea, for a Gentile had no claim on the "son of David." Then she dropped the title "son of David" and said, "Lord, help me" (15:25). It was a better plea—to Him an irresistible plea. True, His earthly mission was confined to the nation of Israel. But His heart went out to this woman as it had already gone out to those "other sheep...not of this fold" (John 10:16).

Reveling in her marvelous courage and determination, He tested her faith one more time. She was like a pagan Jacob, clinging desperately to God and saying, "I will not let thee go, except thou bless me" (Genesis 32:26). The Lord, who "knoweth our frame" (Psalm 103:14), knew how far He could try this woman whose mother-love and majestic faith drove her to cling to her only hope.

"But he answered and said, It is not meet to take the children's bread, and to cast it to dogs" (Matthew 15:26). Perhaps the Lord was thinking of the recent miracle when the multitude was fed and there was "bread enough and to spare." The Jews had been offered everything and believed nothing. This Gentile was offered nothing and believed everything. The test was severe, but behind the winter's cloud shone the sunshine of eternal summer. It sounded as if God loved only Jews, but the woman was not to be put off.

"Truth, Lord," she said, "yet the dogs eat of the crumbs which fall from their masters' table" (15:27). It was only a scrap she wanted. She would be content with the dog's portion. The logic of love took His heart by storm.

3. How Distinguished She Was (15:28)

"Then Jesus answered," beaming on her now, "O woman, great is thy faith: be it unto thee even as thou wilt." She did not doubt for a moment that the pandemonium had gone from her home. With joy in her heart, she returned to find that "the peace of God, which passeth all understanding" (Philippians 4:7) now reigned in its place. The peace of Israel's rejected Messiah had descended for the first time on a home in a Gentile land.

B. The Needy Heathen Multitude—How They
Praised Jesus (15:29-39)

1. His Great Compulsion (15:29-31)

a. The Mountain (15:29)

The Lord headed north to Sidon, then eastward to the head-waters of the Jordan near Damascus, then south to the eastern side of the lake of Galilee. Somewhere on the mountains of its eastern shore He paused to rest.

We learn from Mark 7:31 that His journey on the east of Jordan embraced Decapolis, a territory sandwiched between the tetrarchy of Philip and the jurisdiction of Herod Antipas. The name *Decapolis* means "ten cities" (there were actually fourteen in the district). These cities are said to have been colonized by veterans of the army of Alexander the Great and formed into a confederacy by the Roman general Pompey, so the population of the area was largely Gentile. There were Jews living in the district, but their religious ardor had been cooled by their daily contact with the heathen inhabitants. The mountain retreat in Matthew 15:29 was probably in Decapolis.

b. The Multitudes (15:30-31)

The Lord's rest was soon ended as multitudes from round about flocked to Him with their sick. The phrase "cast them down at Jesus' feet" suggests that the people brought their sick hastily, dropped them off, and hurried back home for more. Jesus' great compulsion was to heal the "lame, blind, dumb, maimed." It made no difference what their afflictions were. "He healed them" (15:30).

From all over that semi-Gentile district the multitudes came, went, and came again, bringing more and more needy ones to Christ and watching closely as He healed them. They were overwhelmed and they "glorified the God of Israel" (15:31).

The authorities might be brewing mischief in their cauldrons of jealousy and hate, and the Lord's ministry in Galilee might be over, but already He was feeling a refreshing breeze blowing from the Gentile and semi-Gentile world. Not long after Pentecost that breeze would become the mighty wind that is still blowing from Gentile lands.

2. His Grand Compassion (15:32-34)

a. His Heart's Desire (15:32)

After three days the crowds ran out of food. The Lord was about to discontinue this latest outpouring of miraculous power, but He wanted to feed the multitudes before He sent them away. Just as His Galilean ministry had ended with a feast for the five thousand, so His Decapolis ministry would end with a table spread in the wilderness. "I will not send them away fasting," He said, "lest they faint in the way."

b. His Hard Disciples (15:33-34)

(1) What They Had Forgotten (15:33)

The disciples said, "Whence should we have so much bread in the wilderness, as to fill so great a multitude?" It would seem incredible that the disciples would again demur if our own unbelief and forgetfulness did not furnish us with sufficient firsthand proof of the sinful skepticism of the human heart, even a believer's heart.

(2) What They Had Found (15:34)

As if to remind them of the former occasion, the Lord asked how much food they had. They did not have much—just seven loaves a few little fish—but it was enough.

3. His Gracious Command (15:35-39)

"He commanded the multitude to sit down on the ground" (15:35) and then it was the same wondrous story all over again. The Lord who had taught the disciples to pray, "Give us this day our daily bread" (6:11), proved once again His ability to answer that prayer. As Paul would later put it, "My God shall supply all your need according to his riches in glory by Christ Jesus" (Philippians 4:19).

The fact that in Decapolis the Lord fed people of largely heathen origin, making no difference between the four thousand who were outside the covenant and the five thousand Hebrews He had fed before, shows that more and more, as Jewish opposition was increasing, His eye was on the Gentile world. Matthew kept on reminding his Jewish readers of this trend.

Campbell Morgan noted Matthew's careful use of the Greek words translated "baskets." At the end of the feeding of the five thousand, the disciples gathered "twelve baskets full" of leftovers (14:20). In 14:20 the Greek word is *kophinos,* which signifies a small wicker basket in which a traveling Jew would have kept his food. At the end of the feeding of the four thousand, the disciples gathered "seven baskets full" of leftovers (15:37). In 15:37 the word is *spuris,* which signifies a large "platted and woven"[5] basket in which a Gentile would have kept his wares. Luke used *spuris* to refer to the kind of basket in which the Christians of Damascus lowered Paul down over the wall (Acts 9:25).

The same distinction was made later in Matthew when the Lord chided the disciples for their lack of faith. He said, "Do ye not yet understand, neither remember the five loaves of the five thousand, and how many baskets [*kophinos*] ye took up? Neither the seven loaves of the four thousand, and how many baskets [*spuris*] ye took up?" (16:9-10)

This careful discrimination between the Hebrew lunch basket and the Gentile merchant's hamper is significant because it supports the view that the feeding of the four thousand was a miracle performed for Gentiles rather than Jews. The sandglass of opportunity for the Jews was fast running out.

Having ministered to the Gentiles and having given them a foretaste of good things to come, the Lord sent them away and crossed back over the lake to Magdala.

III. A CONFRONTATION (16:1-12)

The Lord was still determinedly facing the mounting opposition of His foes. He had stirred up popular (though unreliable) support among the masses by the miraculous feeding of the four thousand, but now He was back at Magdala for a confrontation. The Pharisees were there waiting for Him, this time holding hands with their old enemies the Sadducees. They were united now—against Him.

A. The Sign Demanded (16:1)

The Lord's bitter enemies, the Pharisees, had closed ranks against Him with the Sadducees. Together they demanded a sign from Heaven. All His other mighty miracles they rejected out of hand. According to their blasphemous opinion, the Lord had performed them in league with Beelzebub. They wanted an incontrovertible sign, a sign that only God in Heaven could give. They wanted Him to make the sun stand still, or send the shadow on the sundial back a dozen degrees, or turn the moon to blood, or pull down a star. Noah, Joshua, Elijah, and Hezekiah had been given signs such as these. Why not the Pharisees and Sadducees?

This was the last time the rulers came to Him before He made a final break with them, with the nation, and with the multitudes in order to devote Himself entirely to preparing His disciples for the cross. After Caesarea Philippi (16:13) the Lord's attitude toward His enemies was one of judgment.

The demand for a sign was made by a group of men who were tempting the Lord. The Pharisees, being ritualists, believed that a sign could be given, but not by Him. The Sadducees, being rationalists, believed that a sign could not be given at all. So they were deliberately putting Him to the test; they were looking for something to use against Him.

B. The Sign Denied (16:2-4)

The Pharisees and Sadducees wanted a sign in the sky, so the Lord pointed them to the sky. The Lord's answers were always marvelously appropriate and opportune. He said, "When it is evening, ye say, It will be fair weather: for the sky is red. And in the morning, It will be foul weather to day: for the sky is red and lowring" (16:2-3). They *could* read the signs of the sky. They *could* argue from effect to cause. And they *should* argue from effect to cause. "O ye hypocrites," He continued, "ye can discern the face of the sky; but can ye not discern the signs of the times?"

The times were alive with signs. Day after day, week after week, month after month, the Lord had performed signs and wonders and miracles without number. He had healed the sick, opened the eyes of the blind, made the dumb speak and the lame walk, cleansed lepers, and cast out demons. He had turned water into wine, stilled the storm, walked on waves, and fed hungry multitudes. No case had been too hard for Him. He had even raised the dead. When in all of history had there been so many marvelous signs?

He would not give the Pharisees and Sadducees a sign from Heaven above, but He would give them a sign from Hell beneath. He would give them the sign of the prophet Jonah. To the *rationalists* it was a sign that they were wrong and blind and culpable. It was a sign of resurrection, for a man buried in a whale's belly had come back as from the dead. To the *ritualists* it was a sign that they were wrong and blind and culpable. It was a sign of rejection, for Jonah had come back from what he called "the belly of hell" (Jonah 2:2), not to preach revival to Israel, but to carry a message to the Gentiles that resulted in the conversion of many.

With this parting denunciation the Lord turned His back on the Pharisees and Sadducees and walked away. Never again did He talk publicly or work a miracle in those parts.

C. The Sign Discussed (16:5-12)

The Lord and His disciples crossed over to the northeast shore of the lake. He was now on His way to Caesarea Philippi at the utmost limit of the land.

The Lord seems to have been silent during the voyage. His heart was heavy and His mind was full of His recent encounter with official Jewish unbelief and all that it portended for Israel. Already on the way was a day that would be "red and lowring" (16:3). The hills He could see from the boat, the city of Jerusalem, the whole land would know war and bloodshed and atrocity. The Lord knew the signs of the sky. Foul weather was on the way.

1. The Disciples and Their Unbelief (16:5-10)

a. How Forgetful They Were (16:5-7)

(1) A Dilemma (16:5)

The minds of the disciples were occupied with more mundane things. When they unloaded the boat, they saw that the provision baskets were empty. They had forgotten to bring enough bread. Mark 8:14 says that they had only one loaf with them.

(2) A Discussion (16:6-7)

(a) What the Master Said (16:6)

The Lord's attention was drawn to the discussion about the dilemma. He was concerned with the spiritual aspect. Breaking in on their talk, He said, "Beware of the leaven of the Pharisees and of the Sadducees." Each sect in its own way had leavened and corrupted the holy Bread of Scripture, the ritualists by what they had added to it and the rationalists by what they had taken away from it.

(b) What the Men Supposed (16:7)

This unexpected remark of the Lord provoked further discussion among the disciples. "It is because we have taken no bread," they said. Here they were at cross-purposes with the Lord. He wanted to teach them a spiritual lesson; they were taken up with their failure to buy bread.

b. How Foolish They Were (16:8-10)

(1) In Their Minds—For Not Appreciating His Point (16:8)

Note the disciples' failure to grasp the spiritual and their inclination to emphasize the material on this and similar occasions when the Lord spoke of food in a symbolic sense. At Capernaum they failed to grasp His meaning when He spoke of Himself as the Bread of Life (John 6). At Jacob's well they did not appreciate His point when He spoke of having meat to eat of which they knew nothing (John 4).

To this day the Roman church does the same thing. It takes the

Lord's metaphor concerning the communion loaf ("This is my body") with materialistic literalism and claims that a few Latin words pronounced by one of its priests can turn the wafer into the actual body of Christ. The error arises from a failure to understand that the Lord was speaking in metaphors in order to draw a spiritual lesson from a material source.

(2) In Their Memories—For Not Appropriating His Power (16:9-10)

The Lord dealt first with the material issue: the lack of bread. He reminded the disciples of His recent miracles. Twice He had spread a table for the multitudes in the wilderness and given them "bread enough and to spare." Had they forgotten so soon? Did they think He would let them starve? Could He not multiply their one loaf as He had multiplied the little lad's five loaves? Had He not taught them to pray, "Give us this day our daily bread"? They must learn to trust Him for their material needs.

2. The Disciples and Their Understanding (16:11-12)

As for the spiritual issue, the disciples needed to learn to discern truth. They had failed to understand the Lord's warning, so He spelled it out for them once more. He was not speaking of mere bread. He was speaking of leaven—not literal leaven, but leaven as a symbol of the doctrine of the Pharisees and Sadducees.

We still need to beware of this leaven, for it permeates so much of Christendom. The leaven of the Pharisees is present in the wrong interpretation of the Scriptures. The leaven of the liberals is present in the fatal intolerance of the Scriptures. We must understand the Lord's warning.

PART THREE

The King Is Rejected
Matthew 16:13–27:66

THE SHADOW OF HIS REJECTION

(16:13–25:46)

I. THE PRIVATE DISCUSSIONS (16:13–20:34)
   A. Milestones of the Kingdom (16:13-28)
      1. Peter and the Christ (16:13-20)
         a. The First Question (16:13-14)
            (1) The Question Asked (16:13)
               (a) Where It Was (16:13a)
               (b) What It Was (16:13b)
            (2) The Question Answered (16:14)
               (a) The Disciples Thought of His Message
                   and Said "John" (16:14a)
               (b) The Disciples Thought of His Miracles
                   and Said "Elias [Elijah]" (16:14b)
               (c) The Disciples Thought of His Ministry
                   and Said "Jeremias [Jeremiah], or one of
                   the prophets" (16:14c)
         b. The Further Question (16:15-20)
            (1) The Question Asked (16:15)
            (2) The Question Answered (16:16-20)
               (a) Peter's Insight (16:16)
               (b) Peter's Investiture (16:17-20)
                   i. The Revelation (16:17)
                   ii. The Rock (16:18)
                      a. The Challenge (16:18a)
                      b. The Christ (16:18b)
                      c. The Church (16:18c-d)
                         1. The Foundation (16:18c)
                         2. The Future (16:18d)
                   iii. The Responsibility (16:19-20)

b. The Father's Voice (17:5)
  (1) The Cloud (17:5a)
  (2) The Comment (17:5b)
  (3) The Command (17:5c)
c. The Familiar Voice (17:6-8)
  (1) Why Jesus Spoke (17:6)
  (2) What Jesus Said (17:7)
  (3) Whom the Disciples Saw (17:8)
4. The Valley (17:9-23)
  a. Descending into the Valley (17:9-21)
    (1) The Discourse (17:9-13)
      (a) Truth Concealed (17:9)
      (b) Truth Revealed (17:10-13)
          i. The Question Asked (17:10)
          ii. The Question Answered (17:11-13)
          a. The Prophetic Aspect (17:11)
          b. The Present Aspect (17:12-13)
            1. Truth Underscored (17:12)
              (a) The Rejection of the
                   Heaven-Sent Messenger
                   (17:12a)
              (b) The Rejection of the
                   Heaven-Sent Messiah
                   (17:12b)
            2. Truth Understood (17:13)
    (2) The Demoniac (17:14-18)
      (a) The Situation in the Valley (17:14-16)
          i. The Father of the Lad (17:14-15)
          a. The Father's Place (17:14)
          b. The Father's Plea (17:15a)
          c. The Father's Plight (17:15b)
          ii. The Followers of the Lord (17:16)
      (b) The Savior in the Valley (17:17-18)
          i. A Word of Protest (17:17)
          ii. A Word of Power (17:18)
    (3) The Disciples (17:19-21)
      (a) The Question of Power (17:19-20)
          i. Their Lack of Power Exposed (17:19)

            ii. Their Lack of Power Explained (17:20)
               a. Measuring Faith in Terms of a
                   Mustard Seed (17:20a)
               b. Measuring Faith in Terms of a
                   Mountain Site (17:20b)
         (b) The Question of Prayer (17:21)
            i. Its Activity (17:21a)
            ii. Its Accompaniment (17:21b)
     b. Discerning beyond the Valley (17:22-23)
        (1) The Second Forecast of the Lord (17:22-23a)
        (2) The Saddened Followers of the Lord (17:23b)
C. Members of the Kingdom (17:24–18:35)
  1. Secular Relationships (17:24-27)
     a. Tax Money Demanded (17:24-25a)
     b. Tax Money Discussed (17:25b-27)
        (1) What the Lord Anticipated (17:25b)
        (2) What the Lord Asked (17:25c-26a)
        (3) What the Lord Argued (17:26b)
        (4) What the Lord Accepted (17:27)
          (a) A Moral Principle (17:27a)
          (b) A Miraculous Provision (17:27b)
  2. Spiritual Relationships (18:1-35)
     a. Receiving Believers (18:1-11)
        (1) The Greatness of a Child (18:1-5)
          (a) The Quest for Greatness (18:1)
          (b) The Quality of Greatness (18:2-5)
             i. Illustration (18:2)
             ii. Illumination (18:3-5)
               a. New Birth (18:3)
               b. New Behavior (18:4)
               c. New Bonds (18:5)
        (2) The Goodness of a Child (18:6-9)
          (a) The Offense (18:6)
             i. Its Substance (18:6a)
             ii. Its Seriousness (18:6b)
          (b) The Offender (18:7-9)
             i. The Woe (18:7)

         a. The Way the World Is Now Constituted (18:7a)

         b. The Way the Woes Are Now Caused (18:7b)

      ii. The Warning (18:8-9)

         a. Against Wrong Deeds (18:8)

         b. Against Wrong Desires (18:9)

   (3) The Guardians of a Child (18:10-11)

     (a) God Sees (18:10)

       i. The Administrators of God's Purposes in This World (18:10a)

       ii. The Advocates in God's Presence in That World (18:10b)

     (b) God Saves (18:11)

b. Restoring Backsliders (18:12-14)

   (1) The Lost Sheep (18:12a-b)

     (a) The Sheep That Were Safely in the Fold (18:12a)

     (b) The Sheep That Was Straying from the Fold (18:12b)

   (2) The Loving Shepherd (18:12c-14)

     (a) His Expedition (18:12c)

     (b) His Exultation (18:13)

     (c) His Explanation (18:14)

c. Reconciling Brethren (18:15-35)

   (1) A Principle (18:15-20)

     (a) The First Step—Christian Love Rules (18:15)

     (b) The Further Step—Common Law Rules (18:16)

     (c) The Final Step—Christian Leaders Rule (18:17-20)

       i. The Executive Power of the Local Church (18:17a)

       ii. The Excommunicating Power of the Local Church (18:17b-20)

         a. Where It Works (18:17b-18)

                       1. What the Offender Becomes (18:17b)

                       2. Where the Offender Is Bound (18:18)

                  b. Why It Works (18:19-20)

                       1. Because of the Prayer of Conviction by the Church (18:19)

                       2. Because of the Presence of Christ in the Church (18:20)

            (2) A Proposal (18:21-22)

               (a) Magnanimity in Forgiveness beyond the Normal (18:21)

               (b) Magnificence in Forgiveness beyond the Natural (18:22)

            (3) A Parable (18:23-35)

               (a) The Man and His Debt (18:23-27)

                  i. His Plight (18:23-25)

                     a. The Day of Reckoning (18:23-24)

                       1. Something That Is Completely Inescapable (18:23)

                       2. Someone Who Was Completely Insolvent (18:24)

                     b. The Day of Ruin (18:25)
His lost condition embraced:

                       1. His Future (18:25a)

                       2. His Family (18:25b)

                 ii. His Plea (18:26a)

                iii. His Pledge (18:26b)

                iv. His Pardon (18:27)

               (b) The Man and His Deed (18:28-30)

                  i. What He Demanded (18:28)

                    a. His Search (18:28a)

                    b. His Severity (18:28b)

                 ii. What He Discovered (18:29)

                iii. What He Did (18:30)

               (c) The Man and His Doom (18:31-35)

        i. The Story (18:31)
       ii. The Summons (18:32-33)
          a. The Man's Wickedness Exposed (18:32)
          b. The Man's Wickedness Expanded (18:33)
      iii. The Sentence (18:34)
      iv. The Summary (18:35)

D. Marriage in the Kingdom (19:1-15)
  1. The Salient Factors in the Case of Divorce (19:1-12)
    a. The Context of the Lord's Teaching on Divorce (19:1-2)
      (1) The Place (19:1)
      (2) The People (19:2a)
      (3) The Power (19:2b)
    b. The Content of the Lord's Teaching on Divorce (19:3-12)
      (1) The Lord and His Foes—He Restated the Divine Ideal (19:3-9)
        (a) The First Challenge and the Appeal to Adam (19:3-6)
        (b) The Further Challenge and the Appeal to Moses (19:7-9)
      (2) The Lord and His Friends—He Realized the Difficulties Involved (19:10-12)
        (a) The Pragmatic Response of His Men (19:10)
        (b) The Pragmatic Response of the Master (19:11-12)
          i. On Being Receptive (19:11)
          ii. On Becoming Remarried (19:12)
  2. The Silent Factor in the Case of Divorce (19:13-15)
    a. Little Children Brought to Jesus (19:13)
      (1) The Purpose (19:13a)
      (2) The Problem (19:13b)
    b. Little Children Blessed by Jesus (19:14-15)
      (1) The Great Fact (19:14)
      (2) The Gracious Act (19:15)

E. Motives in the Kingdom (19:16–20:16)
   1. A Proposal (19:16-22)
      a. What the Man Desired (19:16)
      b. What the Man Discovered (19:17)
         (1) The Claim of the Lord (19:17a)
         (2) The Claim of the Law (19:17b)
      c. What the Man Demonstrated (19:18-19)
         (1) His Question (19:18a)
         (2) His Quandary (19:18b-19)
            (a) The Individual Commandments covering Human Relationships (19:18b-19a)
            (b) The Inclusive Commandment covering Human Relationships (19:19b)
      d. What the Man Declared (19:20)
         (1) His Good Life (19:20a)
         (2) His Great Lack (19:20b)
      e. What the Man Discerned (19:21-22)
         (1) The Test (19:21)
         (2) The Tragedy (19:22)
            (a) His Departure (19:22a)
            (b) His Dismay (19:22b)
   2. A Problem (19:23-30)
      a. The Lord's Assertion (19:23-24)
         (1) The Principle Revealed (19:23)
         (2) The Principle Repeated (19:24)
      b. The Disciples' Astonishment (19:25-26)
         (1) The Incredible (19:25)
         (2) The Impossible (19:26)
      c. The Lord's Assurance (19:27-30)
         (1) Peter's Question Asked (19:27)
         (2) Peter's Question Answered (19:28-30)
            (a) A Promise (19:28-29)
               i. For the Twelve Disciples, Millennial Blessing (19:28)
               ii. For All True Disciples, Multiplied Blessings (19:29)
            (b) A Principle (19:30)

    3. A Parable (20:1-16)
      a. Recruiting the Laborers (20:1-7)
        (1) Those with the Law as Their Guarantee (20:1-2)
          (a) The Time (20:1)
          (b) The Terms (20:2)
        (2) Those with the Lord as Their Guarantee (20:3-7)
            Those entering His service:
          (a) With the Dawn of Childhood upon Them
             (20:3-4)
          (b) With the Dew of Youth upon Them
             (20:5a)
          (c) With the Drive of Manhood upon Them
             (20:5b)
          (d) With the Decrepitude of Age upon Them
             (20:6-7)
      b. Recompensing the Laborers (20:8-16)
        (1) The Order (20:8-12)
          (a) The Last Who Are Now First—The
             Loving Reward of Those Who Dared
             to Trust in His Benevolence (20:8-9)
          (b) The First Who Are Now Last—The
             Legal Remuneration of Those Who Desired
             to Trust in Their Bargain (20:10-12)
             i. What They Supposed (20:10)
             ii. What They Said (20:11-12)
        (2) The Owner (20:13-15)
          (a) His Government (20:13-14a)
          (b) His Grace (20:14b)
          (c) His Greatness (20:15a)
          (d) His Goodness (20:15b)
        (3) The Observation (20:16)
F. Ministry in the Kingdom (20:17-34)
  1. The Price Revealed (20:17-19)
    a. The Way (20:17)
    b. The Warning (20:18-19)
      (1) The Lord's Destination (20:18a)
      (2) The Lord's Decease (20:18b-19c)

(a) His Treatment at the Hands of the
Hebrews (10:18b-c)
  i. The Fearful Treachery He Would
     Face (20:18b)
  ii. The False Trial He Would
      Face (20:18c)
(b) His Treatment at the Hands of the
Heathen (20:19a-c)
  i. He Would Be Mocked (20:19a)
  ii. He Would Be Mutilated (20:19b)
  iii. He Would Be Murdered (20:19c)
(3) The Lord's Deliverance (20:19d)
2. The Path Revealed (20:20-28)
  a. The Quest of the Two Disciples (20:20-23)
    (1) Their Mother (20:20-21)
      (a) Her Devout Worship (20:20a)
      (b) Her Dearest Wish (20:20b-21)
    (2) Their Mistake (20:22-23)
      They were ignorant of:
      (a) The Price of the Throne (20:22-23a)
        i. What They Contended (20:22)
        ii. What the Lord Conceded (20:23a)
      (b) The Principle of the Throne (20:23b-c)
        i. The Question of Propriety (20:23b)
        ii. The Question of Priority (20:23c)
  b. The Quarrel with the Ten Disciples (20:24-28)
    (1) An Explosion (20:24)
    (2) An Explanation (20:25-27)
      (a) Concerning Secular Power—The
          Worldly Concept (20:25)
      (b) Concerning Spiritual Power—The
          Wondrous Contrast (20:26-27)
        i. A Spirit of Service (20:26)
        ii. A Spirit of Servitude (20:27)
    (3) An Example (20:28)
3. The Power Revealed (20:29-34)
  a. The Men (20:29-30)

   (1) Where the Blind Men Sat (20:29-30a)
    (a) The Heedless Crowds (20:29)
    (b) The Hopeless Case (20:30a)
   (2) What the Blind Men Said (20:30b-c)
    (a) They Sensed Their Opportunity (20:30b)
    (b) They Seized Their Opportunity (20:30c)
  b. The Multitude (20:31)
   (1) They Were Indignant (20:31a)
   (2) They Were Ignored (20:31b)
  c. The Master (20:32-34)
   (1) His Call (20:32)
   (2) His Compassion (20:33-34a)
   (3) His Converts (20:34b)

II. THE PUBLIC DISPUTES (21:1–23:39)
 A. Crises (21:1-22)
  1. The Sign of the Foretold Triumph (21:1-17)
   a. The Heralding of the Messiah of Israel (21:1-7)
    (1) The Place (21:1)
    (2) The Plan (21:2-3)
    (3) The Prophecy (21:4-5)
     (a) His Majesty (21:4)
     (b) His Meekness (21:5)
    (4) The Presentation (21:6-7)
   b. The Hosannas of the Multitudes of Israel (21:8-14)
    (1) Jubilation (21:8-9)
     (a) Spontaneous Activity (21:8)
     (b) Spontaneous Acclamation (21:9)
    (2) Jerusalem (21:10-11)
     (a) Its Ignorance Revealed (21:10)
     (b) Its Ignorance Removed (21:11)
    (3) Judgment (21:12-13)
     (a) The Sanctuary Cleansed (21:12)
     (b) The Scriptures Confirmed (21:13)
    (4) Jesus (21:14)
   c. The Hostility of the Masters of Israel (21:15-17)
    (1) Displeasure (21:15-16)

(a) What They Saw (21:15)

(b) What They Said (21:16)

(2) Departure (21:17)

2. The Sign of the Fruitless Tree (21:18-22)

a. The Lord's Coming to the Tree (21:18-19a)

(1) When It Was (21:18a)

(2) Where It Was (21:18b)

(3) Why It Was (21:18c)

(4) What It Was (21:19a)

b. The Lord's Cursing of the Tree (21:19b-20)

(1) The Action of the Messiah (21:19b)

(2) The Astonishment of the Men (21:20)

c. The Lord's Comment on the Tree (21:21-22)

(1) The Unlimited Scope of Our Power (21:21)

(a) The Operating Principle (21:21a)

(b) The Overwhelming Potential (21:21b-c)

i. The Simple Meaning of This Word (21:21b)

ii. The Symbolic Meaning of This Word (21:21c)

(2) The Ultimate Source of Our Power (21:22)

B. Causes (21:23–22:14)

1. A Parable of Responsibility (21:23-32)

a. The Context of the Parable—The Lord's Authority (21:23-27)

(1) The Demand of the Temple Authorities (21:23)

(2) The Dilemma of the Temple Authorities (21:24-26)

(a) The Proposal (21:24-25a)

(b) The Problem (21:25b-26)

(3) The Decision of the Temple Authorities (21:27)

b. The Content of the Parable—The Leaders' Accountability (21:28-32)

(1) How Appropriate the Parable Was (21:28-31a)

(a) The Two Sons (21:28-30)

i. The Final Position of the First Son (21:28-29)

ii. The False Profession of the Second Son (21:30)

(b) The True Sin (21:31a)

(2) How Applicable the Parable Was (21:31b-32)

(a) The Contrast with the Harlots (21:31b-32a)

(b) The Condemnation of the Hypocrites (21:32b)

2. A Parable of Retribution (21:33-46)

a. The Lord and His Vineyard (21:33-39)

(1) The Householder (21:33a-c)

(a) The Vineyard Planted (21:33a)

(b) The Vineyard Protected (21:33b)

(c) The Vineyard Provisioned (21:33c)

(2) The Husbandmen (21:33d-39)

(a) Their Trust (21:33d)

(b) Their Treachery (21:34-39)

i. How They Treated Their Lord's Servants (21:34-36)

a. The First Group (21:34-35)

b. The Final Group (21:36)

ii. How They Treated Their Lord's Son (21:37-39)

a. The Expectation (21:37-38)

1. The Plan (21:37)

2. The Plot (21:38)

b. The Execution (21:39)

b. The Lord and His Vengeance (21:40-46)

(1) The Appeal (21:40-41)

(a) The Question Asked (21:40)

(b) The Question Answered (21:41)

(2) The Application (21:42-46)

(a) A Solemn Revelation (21:42-44)

i. From the Scriptures (21:42)

ii. From the Savior (21:43-44)

a. Justice (21:43)

b. Judgment (21:44)

(b) A Swift Reaction (21:45-46)

i. The Leaders' Concern (21:45)

ii. The Leaders' Caution (21:46)

3. A Parable of Rejection (22:1-14)

a. The King's Exclusive Invitation to the Hebrew Race (22:1-7)

(1) The King's Announcement (22:1-6)

(a) Sent (22:1-3a)

i. The Wedding Declared (22:1-2)

ii. The Workers Dispatched (22:3a)

(b) Scorned (22:3b-6)

i. The First Refusal (22:3b)

ii. The Further Refusal (22:4-6)

a. Fresh Details Are Revealed by the King (22:4)

b. Fatal Defiance Is Returned to the King (22:5-6)

1. Carelessly Neglecting the Invitation (22:5)

2. Callously Rejecting the Invitation (22:6)

(2) The King's Anger (22:7)

b. The King's Expanded Invitation to the Human Race (22:8-14)

(1) The Quest for the Wedding Guests (22:8-10)

(a) The Turning Point (22:8)

(b) The Tremendous Plan (22:9-10)

i. The Great Commission Given (22:9)

ii. The Great Company Gathered (22:10)

a. Their Coming (22:10a)

b. Their Composition (22:10b)

(2) The Question of the Wedding Garment (22:11-14)

(a) A Swift Exposure (22:11-13)

i. The Neglectful Man's Sin (22:11-12a)

        ii. The Neglectful Man's Silence
           (22:12b)
        iii. The Neglectful Man's Sentence
           (22:13)
      (b) A Solemn Example (22:14)

C. Cases (22:15-46)
  1. The Plan Devised (22:15)
  2. The Plan Developed (22:16-45)
    a. The Royalists Try to Trap the Lord (22:16-22)
      (1) Their Guile (22:16)
        (a) Flattering Him about His Convictions
           (22:16a)
        (b) Flattering Him about His Courage
           (22:16b)
      (2) Their Goal (22:17-18)
        (a) The Trap Set (22:17)
        (b) The Trap Seen (22:18)
      (3) Their Government (22:19-21b)
        (a) The Caesar's Coin (22:19-21a)
          i. Delivered to Him (22:19)
          ii. Described by Them (22:20-21a)
        (b) The Caesar's Claim (22:21b)
      (4) Their God (22:21c-22)
        (a) His Worship (22:21c)
        (b) Their Wonder (22:22)
    b. The Rationalists Try to Trap the Lord (22:23-33)
      (1) Their Unbelief Explained (22:23)
      (2) Their Unbelief Expressed (22:24-28)
        (a) The Command They Cited (22:24)
          i. Its Authenticity (22:24a)
          ii. Its Authority (22:24b-c)
            a. The Need for the Law (22:24b)
            b. The Nature of the Law (22:24c)
        (b) The Case They Cited (22:25-28)
          i. Aimed at Discrediting God's
            Revelation (22:25-27)
            a. As Foolish (22:25-26)
            b. As Futile (22:27)

ii. Aimed at Discrediting Man's Resurrection (22:28)
(3) Their Unbelief Exposed (22:29-33)
  (a) Their Ignorance Rebuked (22:29-30)
    i. Ignorance of the Nature of God's Revelation (22:29)
      a. It Reveals God's Mind (22:29a)
      b. It Reveals God's Might (22:29b)
    ii. Ignorance of the Nature of Man's Resurrection (22:30)
      It effects a fundamental change in:
      a. Man's Needs (22:30a)
      b. Man's Nature (22:30b)
  (b) Their Ignorance Revealed (22:31-33)
    i. To These Learned Men (22:31-32)
      a. The Case the Lord Cited (22:31)
      b. The Conclusion the Lord Cited (22:32)
    ii. To the Listening Multitude (22:33)
c. The Religionists Try to Trap the Lord (22:34-45)
  (1) The Pharisees' Question concerning the Commandments (22:34-40)
    (a) The Question Asked (22:34-36)
      i. It Was a Loaded Question (22:34-35)
      ii. It Was a Legal Question (22:36)
    (b) The Question Answered (22:37-40)
      i. The Two Great Basics of the Old Testament Statutes (22:37-39)
        a. The Supreme Commandment (22:37-38)
        b. The Supplementary Commandment (22:39)
      ii. The Two Great Basics of the Old Testament Scriptures (22:40)
  (2) The Lord's Questions concerning the Christ (22:41-45)

      (b) Their Full Measure (23:32-36)
         i. How the Lord Described Them (23:32-33a)
        ii. How the Lord Damned Them (23:33b-35)
           a. They Were Destined for Hell (23:33b)
           b. They Were Deserving of Hell (23:34-35)
              1. Their Terrible Activity Revealed (23:34)
              2. Their Terrible Accountability Revealed (23:35)
        iii. How the Lord Doomed Them (23:36)
    2. The Lord's Rejection of Jerusalem (23:37-39)
      a. His Rejection Described (23:37)
      b. Its Ruin Declared (23:38)
      c. His Return Decreed (23:39)

III. THE PROPHETIC DISCOURSE (24:1–25:46)
  A. The Lord's End-Time Perception (24:1-3)
    1. The Impressive Setting (24:1a)
    2. The Impulsive Saying (24:1b-2a)
    3. The Important Statement (24:2b-3)
      a. What the Lord Asserted (24:2b)
      b. What the Lord Asked (24:3)
  B. The Lord's End-Time Prophecy (24:4-51)
    1. The Nations of the World (24:4-14)
      a. End-Time Problems (24:4-8)
        (1) National Disasters (24:4-7a)
          (a) Deceptive Creeds (24:4-5)
          (b) Dreadful Conflicts (24:6-7a)
        (2) Natural Disasters (24:7b-8)
          (a) They Will Be Prevalent (24:7b)
          (b) They Will Be Preliminary (24:8)
      b. End-Time Persecutions (24:9-10)
        (1) Those Marked by Terror (24:9)
        (2) Those Marked by Treachery (24:10)

            c. End-Time Prophets (24:11-14)
            (1) False Prophets (24:11-12)
                (a) Their Number (24:11)
                (b) Their Nature (24:12)
            (2) Faithful Prophets (24:13-14)
                (a) Their Endurance (24:13)
                (b) Their Evangelism (24:14)
        2. The Nation of Israel (24:15-31)
        a. Israel's Coming Ruin (24:15-26)
            (1) The Flight of the Saints at That Time
                 (24:15-20)
                (a) Their Comprehension (24:15)
                (b) Their Compulsion (24:16-18)
                (c) Their Complications (24:19-20)
            (2) The Fury of the Storm at That Time
                 (24:21-22)
                (a) The Severity of the Great Tribulation
                     (24:21)
                (b) The Shortness of the Great Tribulation
                     (24:22)
            (3) The Folly of the Sinners at That Time
                 (24:23-26)
                (a) In Receiving the Lie (24:23-24)
                (b) In Rejecting the Lord (24:25-26)
        b. Israel's Coming Redeemer (24:27-31)
            (1) The Speed with Which He Will Return
                 (24:27)
            (2) The Slaughter with Which He Will Return
                 (24:28)
            (3) The Signs with Which He Will Return
                 (24:29-30)
                (a) The Ruination of This World's System
                     (24:29)
                (b) The Revelation of This World's Savior
                     (24:30)
            (4) The Sound with Which He Will Return
                 (24:31)
        3. The Nationals of Heaven (24:32-51)

    a. Two Kinds of Confirmation (24:32-39)
      (1) The Sign of the Fig (24:32-36)
        (a) A Comparison (24:32-33)
        (b) A Confirmation (24:34-35)
        (c) A Caution (24:36)
      (2) The Sign of the Flood (24:37-39)
        (a) An Appeal (24:37)
        (b) An Appraisal (24:38-39a)
        (c) An Application (24:39b)
    b. Two Kinds of Christians (24:40-51)
      (1) The First Warning (24:40-44)
        (a) Those Received by Christ at the Rapture
           (24:40-42)
        (b) Those Rejected by Christ at the Rapture
           (24:43-44)
      (2) The Further Warning (24:45-51)
        (a) The Wise Servant—The One Taken
           (24:45-47)
        (b) The Wicked Servant—The One Left
           (24:48-51)
          i. His Deeds (24:48-49)
         ii. His Doom (24:50-51)
C. The Lord's End-Time Parables (25:1-46)
  1. For the Nation of Israel:
    Parable of the Virgins (25:1-13)
    a. The Marriage Call (25:1-5)
      (1) The Heavenly Groom (25:1)
      (2) The Holy Ghost (25:2-5)
        (a) Neglecting the Spirit of God (25:2-4)
        (b) Neglecting the Son of God (25:5)
    b. The Midnight Cry (25:6-10)
      (1) The Guests Aroused (25:6-9)
      (2) The Groom Arrives (25:10)
    c. The Mistaken Claim (25:11-13)
      (1) The Appeal (25:11-12)
        (a) What Was Desired (25:11)
        (b) What Was Discovered (25:12)
      (2) The Application (25:13)

2. For the Nationals of Heaven:
Parable of the Talents (25:14-30)
   a. The Time of Responsibility (25:14-18)
      (1) The Trust Bestowed (25:14-15)
      (2) The Trust Believed (25:16-17)
      (3) The Trust Betrayed (25:18)
   b. The Time of Reckoning (25:19-30)
      (1) The Worthy Servants (25:19-23)
         (a) Reviewing Their Stewardship (25:19-22)
         (b) Rewarding Their Stewardship (25:23)
      (2) The Worthless Servant (25:24-30)
         (a) His Excuse (25:24-25)
         (b) His Exposure (25:26-30)
            i. His Denunciation (25:26-29)
            ii. His Destiny (25:30)
3. For the Nations of Earth:
Parable of the Sheep and Goats (25:31-46)
   a. A Throne (25:31)
   b. A Throng (25:32-33)
      (1) The Hebrew Saints (25:32)
      (2) The Hebrew Survivors (25:33)
   c. A Thrill (25:34-46)
      (1) The Happiness of Those Redeemed
          (25:34-40)
         (a) Their Standing (25:34-36)
         (b) Their Surprise (25:37-39)
         (c) Their Salvation (25:40)
      (2) The Horror of Those Rejected
          (25:41-46)
         (a) Their Curse (25:41-43)
         (b) Their Complaint (25:44)
         (c) Their Condemnation (25:45-46)

In Part Three of the Gospel of Matthew the King is rejected. In the first section, which ends with the Olivet discourse, we see the lengthening shadow of that rejection. Israel's folly in refusing to acknowledge the Messiah looms over private discussions, public disputes, and prophetic discourses. In the second section, two terrible chapters show the rejection taking final shape.

I. THE PRIVATE DISCUSSIONS (16:13–20:34)

A. Milestones of the Kingdom (16:13-28)

This passage brings the Christ, the cross, and the church into focus. The Lord's Galilean ministry was finished. He was now facing the active opposition of the nation's religious leaders led by the Pharisees of Jerusalem. Herod, who had murdered John the Baptist, was turning his evil thoughts toward John's apparent successor. The masses were displaying growing indecision and inability to grasp anything beyond the material. The dullness of Jesus' disciples added to the picture as the Lord moved away from the nation of Israel and toward the cross, the upper room, and the birthday of the church.

The time had come when the Lord must bluntly announce to His disciples the impending events of His death, burial, and resurrection. He had prepared for this important step by secret prayer (Luke 9:18). Up to now it had seemed to His disciples that He would sweep away all opposition. Indeed the common people had been ready to take Him by force and crown Him King. He was the kind of King they could understand, One who could heal their hurts and put bread on the table. If the Lord had not sent the disciples away before He sent the multitudes away (Matthew 14:22-23), the twelve would doubtless have joined them in this impulsive move.

The disciples were certainly expecting a speedy manifestation of the kingdom, the power, and the glory of the promised Messiah. They had probably taken little or no notice of His announcement that the Bridegroom must soon go away, and that then they would fast and mourn (9:15). The time had come to tell them plainly what lay ahead.

There could be no literal kingdom on earth until the second coming of Christ. Moreover the spiritual kingdom would not be found in the nation of Israel; it would be found in the church.

1. Peter and the Christ (16:13-20)

a. The First Question (16:13-14)

(1) The Question Asked (16:13)

(a) Where It Was (16:13a)

We now cross the "great divide" of Matthew's Gospel. A conversation results in a great confession and the first revelation of the church. The scene, described so well by Edersheim, is far from Galilee and Israel; far from Judea and Jerusalem; far from the temple, the synagogue, and the priests; far from the scribes, the Pharisees, the Herodians, and the Sadducees. We find Jesus and His disciples "in the lonely grandeur of the shadows of Hermon," in a land that is mostly Gentile. Matthew identified the area as "the coasts of Caesarea Philippi."

When the Lord and His disciples left the area of Magdala, they crossed the sea of Galilee and then headed straight north to Caesarea Philippi (capital of the tetrarch Philip). According to Edersheim it was about a two-day journey. As they traveled, they could see in the distance mount Hermon with its twin snow-clad peaks and beyond that the majesty of Lebanon.

About ten miles north of the sea of Galilee they neared the waters of Merom. Doubtless they skirted the swamp and tangle of vegetation by lake Merom. Perhaps they recalled that here Joshua had broken the northern coalition and fought the last decisive battle in the conquest of Canaan. To the northwest was Kadesh Naphtali, an ancient city of refuge that had been the home of Barak. Taking the Roman road farther on, they passed through the plain in which all the springs of the Jordan join. To the west of the road were Jordan's lower springs, the main source of the river.

Finally they arrived at Caesarea Philippi, 1,147 feet above sea level, a lush spot hidden amid three valleys. Nearby on the western side of a steep mountain were the upper sources of the Jordan. There the river burst out of an immense cavern, which in olden times had been dedicated to the pagan god Pan. When Philip had received the tetrarchy from Augustus, he had changed the name of the nearby town of Paneas to Caesarea Philippi in honor of the emperor. Not far from the town was Philip's castle, which like Machaerus was virtually impregnable, having been built on sheer walls of rock.[1]

In the neighborhood of Caesarea Philippi, the Lord tarried with His disciples for about a week. Here He received Peter's confession and began to speak plainly about a cross and a church. I have taken the time to describe the setting because of its significance. In this distant and obscure spot on the boundary line between Jewish and Gentile territory, the Lord in thought and intent, in spirit and in direct prophecy, turned His back on a Jewish kingdom and embraced a mostly Gentile church.

(b) What It Was (16:13b)

Before He spoke plainly, He tested His disciples to see if they were ready for the great revelation. He asked two questions. The first was of a general nature: "Whom do men say that I the Son of man am?"

(2) The Question Answered (16:14)

People were saying various things. Some, like Herod, said He was John the Baptist risen from the dead. Others, basing their opinion on the closing verses of the last of the Old Testament prophets, thought Jesus was Elijah (Malachi 4:5).

Because of a legend preserved by the Jews, some people thought that Jesus was Jeremiah.[2] According to the legend Jeremiah, by God's command, had hidden the tabernacle, the ark, and the altar of incense in a cave on mount Pisgah. This cave would not be located until the time came for God to restore glory to Israel. Appended to the legend was a prophecy that Jeremiah would rise from the dead to reveal this cave and its contents.

The last group mentioned by the disciples were those who, having no certain view at all, suspected that Christ was "one of the prophets." The disciples took no cognizance of the blasphemous view of the leaders of Israel who simply wrote the Lord off as an impostor.

Such were the various opinions men had of Jesus. The common people ranked Him with the holiest and greatest individuals in the nation's history, but that would never do. To rank the Lord with other human beings, however honored, was to do Him grave dishonor. He is not to be compared with other men at all.

b. The Further Question (16:15-20)

(1) The Question Asked (16:15)

The Lord ignored the answer to the first question and asked His disciples the second question: "Whom say ye that I am?"

(2) The Question Answered (16:16-20)

(a) Peter's Insight (16:16)

Peter rose to the occasion. "Thou art the Christ, the Son of the living God," he said. The answer was marvelous in its conciseness and comprehensiveness. Peter acknowledged Jesus to be both human and divine; he recognized that the Son of man is the Son of God. By saying, "Thou art the Christ," Peter put Him on the throne of Israel as the Lord's anointed Prophet, Priest, and King. By saying, "Thou art...the Son of the living God," Peter put Him on the throne of the universe.

Peter's great confession is the cardinal creed of the church. Jesus is the Christ. He is God's own Son. He is the Messiah. He is God incarnate. He is truly man; He is God in essence and in substance.

(b) Peter's Investiture (16:17-20)

i. The Revelation (16:17)

The Lord instantly acknowledged Peter's confession and identified the source of his inspiration: "Blessed art thou, Simon Barjona: for flesh and blood hath not revealed it unto thee, but my Father which is in heaven." *Bar-jona* means "son of Jona." The Lord called Peter "Bar-jona" to illustrate how true his confession was—the Lord was as truly the Son of God as Peter was the son of Jona.

ii. The Rock (16:18)

Then came the memorable words, "Thou art Peter [*petros*], and upon this rock [*petra*] I will build my church; and the gates of hell shall not prevail against it." The two Greek words are distinct. *Petros* is in the masculine gender and denotes a loose stone or pebble. *Petra* is in the feminine gender and denotes a rock or a cliff, firm and immovable. (The rocky Edomite stronghold of Seir is called

Petra to this day.) *Petra* in 16:18 refers to Christ. The church is not built on Peter, but on Christ.

We must remember that the Lord was talking to His disciples who as Hebrews were rooted and grounded in the Old Testament Scriptures. They would have known that in the Old Testament the word "rock" is never used symbolically of man; it is used figuratively only of God and Christ. Christ is the foundation stone (Isaiah 28:16) and the rejected stone (Psalm 118:22). The Lord Jesus did not trifle with symbols. He took up the well-understood Hebrew symbol of deity, the rock (Deuteronomy 32:31), and declared, "Upon this rock [upon God, upon Himself as God] I will build my church."[3]

Peter understood the Lord's utterance correctly (1 Peter 2:6-8). The view that Peter is the rock on which the church is built is false. Peter was simply a stone—the first stone perhaps, but just a stone, one of many to be built up on that Rock (1 Peter 2:4-5).

What was to be built on that Rock? Something new, something never before revealed: what the Lord called "my church [*ecclesia*]." The word *ecclesia* was familiar to both Jews and Greeks.[4] The Hebrews used it to describe themselves as a selected people, as a theocracy, as a people governed by God rather than by politics or human kings. The Greeks used the word to describe an assembly of free men, a town meeting; no slave could be a member of such a group. The Lord used *ecclesia* to denote His own assembly in this world, His own believing people, those who have made the great confession, those who uphold His authority in their lives individually and collectively. His followers would be neither Jews nor Greeks, but (as they later came to be called) Christians.

"I will build," the Lord said. He, through His Holy Spirit, quarries stones out of nature's dark mine, shapes and fashions them, makes them "lively [living] stones," and places them shoulder to shoulder with others of "like precious faith" in that "habitation of God through the Spirit" that is being erected in this day and age (1 Peter 2:5; 2 Peter 1:1; Ephesians 2:22).

"And the gates of hell [Hades] shall not prevail against it." Hades is the realm of the dead, and the gates perhaps symbolize the entrance to that realm. The Lord was declaring that death will not triumph over His church. We read His triumphant shout in Revelation 1:18: "I am he that liveth, and was dead; and, behold, I am alive for evermore, Amen; and have the keys of hell and of death." Death can no more hold the Christian than it could hold the Christ. One day the dead in Christ will rise shouting, "O grave, where is thy victory?" (1 Corinthians 15:55)

Another view is that since "the gate" was the place where the rulers of an oriental city met (Genesis 19:1; Ruth 4:1), the "gates of hell" symbolize the place where Satan and his fallen angels take counsel against the church. But neither Satan nor all his hosts are a match for the Spirit-born, Spirit-built church. The Lord Jesus "spoiled" the Satanic hosts at the cross (Colossians 2:15) and He has equipped us to war victoriously against them (Ephesians 6:11-12).

Putting the two thoughts together, we conclude that Christ has promised that neither the power of death nor the power of the devil can prevail against the church which He is building.

iii. The Responsibility (16:19-20)

a. Prospective Responsibility (16:19)

At this point the Lord entrusted Peter with "the keys of the kingdom of heaven." The idea was easily understood by the disciples. Among the Hebrews the symbol of keys did not refer to the priests; it referred to the scribes, the teachers of the law whose duty it was to unlock the truth of God. The scribes had failed miserably in their office and now the Lord committed the keys to Peter.

After telling the parables of the kingdom, the Lord had said, "Every scribe which is instructed unto the kingdom of heaven is like unto a man that is an householder, which bringeth forth out of his treasure things new and old" (Matthew 13:52). When Peter made His inspired confession of faith (16:16), he became a scribe "instructed unto the kingdom of heaven." When the Lord said to him, "I will give unto thee the keys of the kingdom of heaven" (16:19), He was saying in effect, "You are my scribe."

Because Peter was the first to utter the great confession of the church age, he was to be the first to open the church's previously locked doors to both the Jews and the Gentiles. He was the first to preach the gospel to the Jews on the day of Pentecost and to the Gentiles in the home of Cornelius. As soon as Peter had thus unlocked the doors of the church, his primacy, as far as keys or any other function was concerned, was finished. He had received the reward of his prompt and bold confession.

Greek scholars point out the force of the grammatical construction in the statement translated, "Whatsoever thou shalt bind on earth shall be bound in heaven." In the Greek a simple future is followed by a perfect participle passive. If the Lord had intended to say simply, "Whatsoever you bind on earth will be bound in Heaven," He would have used the simple future passive instead of a perfect participle passive. The meaning of the original Greek is that the disciples would be so led by the Spirit that they would follow the divine or heavenly format. That is, what they would "bind" or "loose" on earth would be consistent with the divine pattern. If the Lord had used the simple future passive, He would have implied an automatic heavenly endorsement of the church's action on earth, which is something else altogether and certainly not what He meant.

In a similar passage in John's Gospel (20:22-23) it is evident that the Holy Spirit would be the One who would make it possible for people on earth to forgive or not forgive sins, a prerogative that belongs to God alone.

b. Present Responsibility (16:20)

The conversation concluded with the Lord charging His disciples to keep these great truths to themselves and not to tell anyone that He was the Christ. He had already put the Jewish nation to the test and the Jews had not received Him. It was useless to proclaim Himself to them anymore (at least not before Pentecost). Their doom was sealed and there was no point in increasing their guilt any further.

2. Peter and the Cross (16:21-28)

Peter had wholeheartedly responded to the truth about the Christ. The truth about the cross was something else. Peter could not accept that. The man who triumphed gloriously when faced with the deity of Christ, fell flat on his face when faced with the death of Christ. Godhead was possible to understand; Golgotha was impossible.

a. The Challenge of the Cross (16:21-23)

(1) The Cross Foretold (16:21)

(a) The Significant Timing of This Revelation (16:21a)

Peter's great confession along with the Lord's revelation concerning the church is one of the major watersheds of the Gospel of Matthew. "From that time forth," the Lord spoke more and more about the cross and gave further revelation concerning the church. The disciples had scaled the heights; now they must scan the depths. From now on they must prepare themselves for His final rejection at the hands of the authorities and for His death, which was as certain as the sunset. Matthew said that the Lord "began" to talk about these things. He would go on talking about them in the days ahead, adding more details.

(b) The Startling Truth of This Revelation (16:21b-d)

He began by concentrating on two aspects of the revelation, one full of hate and the other full of hope. He indicated that the rulers would conspire against Him and kill Him, but they would not have the last word, for He would rise from the dead.

The disciples hardly heard the hopeful part. The part that shook them to the core of their being was this: "He must go unto Jerusalem, *and* suffer many things of the elders *and* chief priests *and* scribes, *and* be killed" (italics added). Perhaps they caught the cadence of the *and*s. And! And! And! It was a deliberate drumbeat marking out each step in the onward march of the Son of God. But they missed the last *and*, which was just as deliberate, just as decisive: "*and* be raised again the third day."

Note the word "must" in 16:21. It is stated once, but implied throughout. We could state the thought this way: "The One you have just confessed as Son of God *must* go to Jerusalem and *must* suffer many things and *must* be killed and *must* be raised again." The point of danger was Jerusalem, but Jesus could not stay away from Jerusalem because that "must" came thundering out of eternity. Christ's death was decided before the foundation of the world, before the beginning of time. He had come into the world to die.

Events must take their course. Men would kill Him; God would resurrect Him. The cross would become God's instrument for providing salvation to men. The "must" came out of the past and blazed the way into the future ages of eternity. The "must" of the resurrection was an integral part of the divine plan.

(2) The Cross Forbidden (16:22-23)

(a) How Peter Rebuked the Lord (16:22)

No doubt all the disciples were stunned by this revelation. Peter was the first to recover. Matthew said, "Peter took him, and began to rebuke him." The words translated "took him" mean "took Him aside." Peter intended to give the Lord a little pep talk. Evidently the Lord did not allow him to finish, for Matthew said that Peter "began" to remonstrate with Him. The word translated "rebuke" here literally means "to chide." Peter was angry with Him and said, "Be it far from thee, Lord: this shall not be unto thee."

(b) How the Lord Rebuked Peter (16:23)

The Lord, it seems, turned His back on Peter, faced the other disciples, and said to Peter, "Get thee behind me, Satan: thou art an offence [*skandalon*, 'a stone of stumbling'] unto me: for thou savourest not [you do not regard] the things that be of God, but those that be of men." Behind Peter lurked Satan. The voice was the voice of Peter; the words were the words of Satan. A few moments before, Jesus in effect had said to Simon, "You are Peter; you are a stone." Now He was saying, "You are a *skandalon*, a stone of stumbling."

b. The Choice of the Cross (16:24-28)

(1) The Principle Involved (16:24-25)

"Then said Jesus unto his disciples, If any man will come after me, let him deny himself, and take up his cross, and follow me. For whosoever will save his life shall lose it: and whosoever will lose his life for my sake shall find it." This paradox is often worked out in the history of the church. The cross was not only for Him; it is also for us.

The world looks on this principle, the logic of the cross, as folly. But as Jim Elliot, one of the five young men martyred by the Indians in Ecuador, wrote in his diary, "He is no fool who gives what he cannot keep to gain what he cannot lose."[5] C. T. Studd, who gave up fame and fortune to take the gospel to pagan tribes, wrote:

> Some wish to live within the sound
> Of Church or Chapel bell,
> I want to run a Rescue Shop
> Within a yard of hell.[6]

Doubtless Studd was considered a fool by his socialite contemporaries. The history of the church is full of the annals of such people. Some became heroes in their lifetimes or were made such by their deaths. Others unknown and unsung down here are counted over yonder as the aristocracy of Heaven.

(2) The Priorities Involved (16:26)

"For what is a man profited, if he shall gain the whole world, and lose his own soul? or what shall a man give in exchange for his soul?"

The disciples had been thinking in terms of a material kingdom, one that would begin at Jerusalem and conquer the world. Satan had once offered such a kingdom to Christ. But now, in the light of Calvary, there could be no thought of a worldly kingdom, at least not until God's purposes in grace had been accomplished in the creation, development, and rapture of a church.

The Lord was saying that in His own disciples there must be no desire for the world in its present state of sinfulness. The carnal Messianic hopes of the Jews could have no part in the lives of those who had been to Calvary. The Lord pointed to the price that would have to be paid if it were possible to gain the world.

It has been well said that the first question that comes to a soul is "Heaven or Hell?" When that question is settled in favor of Heaven, the second question that comes to a soul is "Heaven or earth?" We must settle the second question at the foot of the cross and in the light of the value of a soul.

(3) The Prophecies Involved (16:27-28)

(a) The Return of the Lord Foretold (16:27)

The Lord prophesied, "The Son of man shall come in the glory of his Father with his angels; and then he shall reward every man according to his works." There is a cross for the Christian in this age, but the present age will end. In the next age there will be a crown.

The kingdom foreseen by the Old Testament prophets—the literal millennial kingdom, the world-empire of the Christ—has not been canceled by Jewish intransigence and unbelief. It has merely been postponed. It will come. The Lord Jesus is coming again, coming in glory, coming with the hosts of Heaven, coming to reward, coming to reign. So let us take up the cross and be rewarded one day with a crown.

(b) The Revelation of the Lord Foretold (16:28)

The Lord's next words must have caused a considerable stir: "There be some standing here, which shall not taste of death, till they see the Son of man coming in his kingdom." There is little doubt that He was referring to the forthcoming experience of

Peter, James, and John on the mount of transfiguration. The connection would be even more clearly seen if the chapter divisions were eliminated.

B. Manifestations of the Kingdom (17:1-23)

We are going to consider the vision, the visitors, and the voices in the story of the transfiguration. This manifestation of the kingdom was followed by another in the valley.

1. The Vision (17:1-2)

Six days had passed since Peter's confession, time enough for the truth to sink in that there was to be a cross before there was to be a crown. We can picture the Lord and three of His disciples (Peter, James, and John) ascending the heights of mount Hermon, which towers some 9,400 feet above sea level. The shaggy foothills gave no hint of the awesome desolation that awaited the climbers. They would soon be standing amid snow.

Mount Hermon! Below were the sources of the Jordan and the beautiful but almost pagan city of Caesarea Philippi. Beyond the summit lay the great lands of the Gentiles. To the south were Galilee, Samaria, Decapolis, Perea, and Judea. The location had been sacred to the terrible Baal cults of ancient times, but from now on it would be sacred to the followers of Jesus. Peter would one day call it "the holy mount" (2 Peter 1:18).

Matthew, Mark, and Luke all recorded the incident on the mount of transfiguration, but John did not—although he was the only one of them present. Why was he silent about it? John wrote to demonstrate the deity of Christ, and the transfiguration was not the proof of Christ's deity. The apostle found abundant proofs elsewhere.

On the surface it seems that this revelation of glory was the greatest of all proofs of Christ's claim to be God, that the transfiguration was the greatest demonstration of the soundness of Peter's confession, "Thou art the Christ, the Son of the living God" (16:16). But that was not the case. The transfiguration was the climax of Christ's *human* life.

Matthew wrote that the Lord was "transfigured" (17:2). The word translated "transfigured" is *metamorphoomai*, which literally means "to change form." The Lord was changed so that the glorious magnificence of His perfect, sinless, holy humanity could be displayed. That was the purpose of the transfiguration and that was why John did not record it in his Gospel.

Campbell Morgan pointed out that the Lord's human life was expressed in three stages: "innocence, holiness, perfected glory."[7] The process began with innocence; He was born with a sinless nature. We are not. Childhood's innocence is soon swept away before the manifestation of the inherent sin nature. A baby will have temper tantrums before he is old enough to walk or talk. A child will lie, steal, and disobey. Jesus never did. He was absolutely sinless in thought, word, and deed. He was born innocent and He maintained that innocence throughout His early life.

Then came the temptation. Human nature eventually comes up against allurement and incitement from without, so Jesus was tempted by the devil. The arch-tempter himself was allowed to assail the sinless humanity of Jesus. The fierce heat of temptation was turned up, but in vain. He was not only innocent; He was holy.

On the mount of transfiguration the process was carried forward to completion. The perfect humanity of Jesus, which had been displayed in innocence and impeccable holiness, was there manifested in glory. The Lord was seen in all the glory of His humanity. He was man as God had always intended man to be. We know nothing of that glory, for there is sin in us. But one day we will be like Him and we will be glorified too. In God's sight we already are (Romans 8:30).

2. The Visitors (17:3)

Seven persons were present on the mount. They were gathered in three groups: (1) Peter, James, and John; (2) Moses and Elijah; (3) Jesus and the Father. Two of the seven came out of the past (Moses and Elijah); three were from the present (Peter, James, and John); two came out of eternity (Jesus and the Father). The Old Testament was represented by Moses, who stood for the Law, and by Elijah, who stood for the Prophets. The New Testament was represented by Peter, James, and John. James, the first of the apostles to die, was the church's martyr; John was the church's mystic; Peter was the church's messenger, commissioned to fling wide its gates to Jew and Gentile alike.

3. The Voices (17:4-8)

Luke 9:31 tells us what Moses and Elijah talked about with Jesus on this remarkable occasion: "his decease which he should accomplish at Jerusalem." The word translated "decease" here really means "exodus." Moses had made his exodus by dying alone in the arms of God on Nebo's solitary heights, and by being buried by the angels. He represented all those who depart this life by way of death. Elijah had made his exodus by way of a chariot of fire. He had been caught up into Heaven without dying, so he represented all the living saints who will be caught up in the rapture.

These two representative men talked to Jesus about His exodus. His forthcoming death would fulfill all the sacrifices of the law so closely linked with Moses, and all the sayings of the prophets, of whom Elijah was the supreme representative. What a conversation it must have been!

a. The Foolish Voice (17:4)

Matthew recorded three voices. The first was the foolish voice of Peter. He blurted out, "Lord, it is good for us to be here: if thou wilt, let us make here three tabernacles; one for thee, and one for Moses, and one for Elias." Note the procession of *and*s by which Peter linked all three persons, as if to put Moses, Elijah, and Jesus on the same footing.

b. The Father's Voice (17:5)

Peter was still bumbling on with his irresponsible nonsense when the brow of Hermon was suddenly wrapped with a cloud. That in itself was not unusual. A thick mantle of cloud often enfolds the summit of that mountain within minutes, only to disperse and disappear just as quickly. But this cloud was different. The text says it was "a bright cloud" and the implication is that it was the shekinah glory cloud. In Old Testament times that cloud once reposed on the mercy seat on the sacred ark within the holy of holies behind the veil. The shekinah was the visible token of God's presence.

When the queen of England moves from Buckingham Palace to Windsor Castle, Sandringham, or Balmoral, the royal standard goes with her. When the flag flies over one of these residences, it means that the queen is there in person. In the same way the shekinah proclaimed God's presence among His people. That glory had long since departed from Israel, but it appeared now to honor Jesus and to proclaim God's personal presence on the mount.

Then came the Father's voice putting an immediate end to Peter's blundering remarks: "This is my beloved Son, in whom I am well pleased; hear ye him" (17:5). The same voice had said the same words at Jesus' baptism (3:17). At that time the voice had endorsed the hidden years spent in private. Now it endorsed the years spent in public. God's all-seeing eye had been on His Son night and day. The Father had rejoiced over Him and now proclaimed Him once more to be His well-beloved Son. Thus in the transfiguration the glory of Christ's humanity was owned by God in the proclamation of Christ's deity.

c. The Familiar Voice (17:6-8)

The disciples were overcome with terror at the sight of the cloud and the sound of the voice, but "Jesus came and touched them, and said, Arise, and be not afraid" (17:7). Already He assumed the great work of mediation that would be His throughout the present age. He would be the sole Mediator between God and man.

"And when they had lifted up their eyes, they saw no man, save Jesus only" (17:8). Moses was gone; Elijah was gone; Jesus remained. The Old Testament dispensation was thus typically removed to make room for the New Testament era in which the Lord Jesus alone is the Great High Priest, our Mediator and Advocate with the Father.

4. The Valley (17:9-23)

a. Descending into the Valley (17:9-21)

(1) The Discourse (17:9-13)

On the way down from the mount of transfiguration the disciples asked the Lord about Elijah. Although they had no doubt at all that they had just seen the Messiah as no one else had ever seen Him, they still did not have things in perspective. They failed to grasp that the offer of the kingdom to Israel had been withdrawn and that long ages would pass before it would be offered again at the Lord's second coming. The sight of Elijah on the mountain had added to their bewilderment, for the Old Testament told of the coming of Elijah prior to the coming of the Messiah.

The Lord then plainly declared that Elijah would come to "restore all things" (17:11) prior to the ultimate installation of the kingdom. Jesus also made it clear that the nation was by no means ready for such a visitation. John the Baptist had already come in the spirit and power of Elijah, and he had been rejected. It would be many a long day before Elijah would come to herald the Lord's return.

John the Baptist had been put to death by Herod, but not before being rejected by the leaders of Israel. They had stood back and allowed Herod to arrest and assassinate John, and they were now taking active measures to put the Son of man to death also.

(2) The Demoniac (17:14-18)

While Jesus, Peter, James, and John were on the mount, a father brought his demoniac son to the disciples who were left behind. The description of the scene, taken as a whole rather than verse by verse, gives us a fascinating composite picture of the closing days of the present age.

The disciples in the valley portray a dispirited church. Christ was absent, having gone on high to enter into His glory. Some of His own had gone to be with Him. Down below, the believers were powerless in the face of crisis and they seemed resigned to their powerlessness. They evidently had not thought of prayer and fasting. The real power of God seemed to have departed from His people. "Why could not we cast him out?" was their wretched cry (17:19). One reason was that they had not availed themselves of the spiritual weapons of the believer's warfare. Another reason was their unbelief.

The demented boy is a picture of the people in the world today who are in the grip of evil spirits and enslaving, tormenting lusts. The boy was possessed by a callous, fierce demon. Luke 9:38 tells us that he was his father's only son, a fact mentioned perhaps to remind us of the heavenly Father's only Son, who had just been acknowledged on high. The boy's father felt that the disciples (representing the church) ought to be able to help and of course he was right.

The world ignores the church partly because of its evident lack of power in the face of the ever-worsening crises in human affairs. One reason the charismatics have so much influence is that they profess to have power. But when that power doesn't work in the way they expect it to or in the way many charismatics teach it should, the inevitable result is distress of mind. People who drink of their water thirst again.

Like drifting crowds today, the spectators milled around, pulled this way and that. The throng, with no conviction, concern, or conscience of its own, looked at the debacle, pointed fingers at the helpless believers, and no doubt secretly enjoyed the disciples' inability to speak with authority or act with power.

The religious leaders who were there portray the dead religion of the present age. Mark 9:14 tells us that the scribes, who professed to be experts in Bible matters, were questioning the disciples. These leaders were set in their opposition to Christ and were putting the Lord's disciples on the defensive. Doubtless the scribes too were finding secret satisfaction in the miserable failure of the disciples to do anything in this hour of crisis. The religious leaders had no power themselves and it probably made them feel good to see these evangelicals in the same condition.

Then Jesus came back, bringing the absent disciples with Him. In the wondrous company of saints from other ages, they had been gazing on the Lord in glory. With the return of Jesus, all was instantly changed. The evil one was cast out and sanity was restored to the boy. Only Jesus can eject the prince of the power of darkness from the world and bring peace on earth.

(3) The Disciples (17:19-21)

At the earliest possible moment the defeated disciples asked the Lord the reason for their failure. "Because you have such little faith," He said in effect. How much faith did they need? Only as much as a mustard seed. But they had forgotten their dependence on God as the only source of spiritual power. The proof of their forgetting was their neglect of prayer and fasting.

b. Discerning beyond the Valley (17:22-23)

Once more the Lord reminded the disciples of His impending death. This time He added the detail that He would be betrayed. Now the terrible tidings began to sink in. Instead of opposing the announcement, they plunged into sorrow.

C. Members of the Kingdom (17:24–18:35)

1. Secular Relationships (17:24-27)

a. Tax Money Demanded (17:24-25a)

The disciples were back in Capernaum and the question of relationships and relative loyalties was suddenly sprung on Peter. He was confronted by the people who were responsible for collecting the annual half-shekel tax that was levied against all Jews for the maintenance of the temple and its services. "Doesn't your Master pay His taxes?" they asked in effect.

The Jerusalem temple was very costly to maintain, so the temple officials used Exodus 30:13 as their authority to levy a temple tax on all male Jews over twenty years of age. A half-shekel was the equivalent of two or three days' pay. Theoretically the tax was obligatory, although the Pharisees and Sadducees argued about that issue, just as they did about everything else. On the first of the month Adar (March) the authorities made a public announcement that it was time to pay the tax. On the fifteenth of Adar, collection booths were set up throughout the country. Payment could be made at the booths until the twenty-fifth of the month; after that payment had to be made directly to the temple in Jerusalem.

We must remember that this was a Jewish tax, not a Roman one, and that it was a tax with Scriptural warrant. The half-shekel that was paid was regarded as given to God.

So the tax collectors accosted Peter. There can be little doubt that the question was asked in a hostile manner and with malicious intent. The revenue officers could easily have asked Jesus directly since He was back in town and available. Doubtless they were hoping that Jesus would refuse to pay the tax or that Peter would make an incriminating statement. Peter, however, knew that the Lord kept the Mosaic law in letter and in spirit. Never had he known Him to do anything else. So he answered with a brief *yes* and walked away.

b. Tax Money Discussed (17:25b-27)

The Lord did not wait for Peter to bring up the subject. Being omniscient, He knew all that had happened. Jesus put a question of His own to Peter: "Of whom do the kings of the earth take custom or tribute? of their own children, or of strangers?" (17:25) The Lord was reminding Peter of his confession at Caesarea Philippi and of what he had heard on the mount of transfiguration. The Lord's question could be expressed as follows: "Peter, you said I was the Son of God. Now you are saying that I have to pay this half-shekel. How can that law have any claim on Me as the Son of God?"

The Lord, however, recognized another side of the issue. "Notwithstanding," He said in effect, "lest we should be a stumbling block in the way of these men, we will pay this tax." Jesus told Peter to take a fishing line, cast the hook into the lake, take the first fish that came to hand, and open its mouth. There he would find enough money to pay the tax for both the Lord and himself. What a display of the lordship of Christ over creation! He deliberately paid the tax in a way that would show that the realm of nature was tributary to Him. (This is the only place in the New Testament where this kind of fishing is mentioned.)

We can assume that Peter went back to the tax collector and said, "Sir, come with me, if you please," and then did what Jesus had told him to do. I would like to think that after Peter took the coin from the fish's mouth and paid the tax, he gave the collector the fish for his supper!

The Lord's willingness to pay the tax is another demonstration of His submission to the law of God. "Give unto them for me and thee," He said (17:27). Note that He made a difference between Himself as the tax-exempted Son and Peter as the unexempted subject. At the same time He did include Peter in the "we"—"lest *we* should offend them" (italics added). There is perhaps a hint here that the time would soon come when the Lord's disciples would be emancipated completely from Jewish obligations. He was already calling them out of the Jewish fold.

2. Spiritual Relationships (18:1-35)

The Lord continued His more or less private discussion on the subject of members of the kingdom. His comments anticipated the spiritual relationships within the kingdom during the present age. After this talk with His disciples, He left Galilee, never to return until after His death and resurrection.

Matthew 18 is an important chapter. In itself it forms an organic whole, but it is linked with chapter 16 by the Lord's prophetic references to His church. It is true that Matthew is the Jewish Gospel, but it is far more than that. It not only emphasizes the Lord's rejection by the Jews and the consequences of that rejection for the Jewish nation; Matthew also anticipates the church, and it is the only Gospel that does bluntly mention the church. The Gospel of Matthew mentions the church by name twice, by implication in the parable of the pearl, and by allusion in the prophetic discourse on the mount of Olives. To rule the church out of Matthew 13, 24, and 25 is to be overzealous for the Jewishness of the Gospel.

In Matthew 16 we have the first direct mention of the church; in Matthew 18 we have the second. These two references form a pair. In chapter 16 we find the church in its universal aspect; in chapter 18 we find the church in its local aspect.

The Lord set before us the universal church when He said, "Upon this rock I will build my church; and the gates of hell shall not prevail against it" (16:18). The church was still future when He spoke, while the nation of Israel was a very present reality. The church is an entity separate and distinct from Israel. To equate Israel with the church confuses clearly defined groups.

The church age is a parenthesis inserted into time and marking out the period of God's sovereign displeasure with the nation of Israel because of its murder of His Son. The church was supernaturally injected into history on the day of Pentecost; it will be supernaturally ejected out of history at the rapture. In this present church age the specific promises of God to the nation of Israel are suspended. God will resume His direct dealings with Israel after the rapture of the church. The fact that Israel has now been reconstituted as a sovereign nation and is back in the promised land is a clear indication that God is about to remove the church and pick up His promises and prophecies to the Hebrew people.

In the church age salvation is offered to Jews on the same basis that it is offered to Gentiles. Jews and Gentiles alike are saved by personal faith in Christ. A Jew who trusts Christ becomes a Christian and is added to the church in the same way as anyone else, no matter what his nationality or former religion is. This topic is discussed by Paul in Romans 9–11, where the apostle takes up God's past, present, and promised dealings with the Jewish people.[8]

The church in its local aspect is directly mentioned in Matthew 18:17 and it is the general theme of the chapter. The Lord reviewed the threefold function of a local church: the reception of believers (18:1-11); the restoration of backsliders (18:12-14); and the reconciliation of brethren (18:15-35). Of course when Matthew wrote his Gospel, the universal church and local churches were already well established on earth. All was still in the future, however, when the Lord spoke.

a. Receiving Believers (18:1-11)

(1) The Greatness of a Child (18:1-5)

(a) The Quest for Greatness (18:1)

Mark 9:34 tells us that the disciples had been arguing among themselves about which of them would be greatest in the coming kingdom. They were still laboring under the false impression that the Lord was about to set up the Messianic kingdom. They were quite sure that the establishment of the kingdom would mean great power and glory for them. The plain warning of the Lord that He was soon to be crucified, that millennial hopes for Israel were now indefinitely postponed, had fallen on deaf ears.

To settle their argument about who would be greatest, the disciples appealed directly to the Lord. While answering their question, He revealed the first function of the local church in the age that was about to dawn: that of receiving believers into its midst.

(b) The Quality of Greatness (18:2-5)

The Lord opened this new line of teaching about the church by the use of an object lesson. "Jesus called a little child unto him, and set him in the midst of them" (18:2). He said, "Except ye be converted, and become as little children, ye shall not enter into the kingdom of heaven" (18:3). We are not to be childish, but childlike.

The only way into the kingdom is by means of a new birth. Those who are born again take their place among God's people as little children. There is no sophistication, no struggle for caste, no self-seeking ambition, no pride in a little child. A small child is a lesson in simplicity, a model member of the church.

Mark 9:36 tells us that Jesus took the child "in his arms." The Lord set him in the midst of the disciples to illustrate that in the local church we are to receive those whom the Lord has received. The picture is one of love, life, and lowliness.

(2) The Goodness of a Child (18:6-9)

A child has great value in the sight of God. We are not to offend any of His little ones or cause one of them to stumble. No greater crime can be committed than to harm a child, especially one who believes in Christ.

Let teachers in our schools and colleges who deliberately set out to corrupt the minds and beliefs of the young with humanistic and hurtful philosophies beware. Let those who exploit little children for the sake of lust and personal gain beware. Let all those who abuse children beware. Jesus, the kindest and most tender of men, said of such a one that "it were better for him that a millstone were hanged about his neck, and that he were drowned in the depth of the sea" (18:6). The word translated "millstone" refers to a great stone requiring the strength of a mule to move it.

Going beyond this primary lesson, we note that we are not to offend babes in Christ either. The Lord's warning was addressed to those who cause "one of these little ones which believe in me" to stumble. New Christians are to be nurtured and nourished and brought along in their new life in Christ. Woe to those who corrupt them with false doctrines or bad example.

Offenses will come. Given the depravity of man, sin is inevitable. But woe to the person who tempts one of those who are under the special protective care of the living God. There are two woes in 18:7. The first is the woe of *a great compassion,* the lamentation of the Man of Sorrows over the offenses of the world. The second is the woe of *a great curse.* The Lord warned that those whose sin causes others to stumble should beware. They would be better off to mutilate themselves than to continue in a course that puts them in danger of Hell fire. The Lord made no apology for preaching about the terrible reality of Hell. He spoke about it frequently, and always as a place of eternal torment. Here the Lord specifically referred to "everlasting fire" (18:8) and "hell fire" (18:9).

(3) The Guardians of a Child (18:10-11)

(a) God Sees (18:10)

As our Lord concluded this warning, He cast a fascinating flash of light on the mysteries of the world beyond our natural sight. "Take heed that ye despise not one of these little ones," He said, "for I say unto you, That in heaven their angels do always behold the face of my Father which is in heaven."

When Jacob was at Bethel his eyes were opened to see a constant stream of angelic traffic "ascending and descending" a celestial stairway (Genesis 28:12). They were not descending and ascending; they were ascending and descending. The angels had been assigned duties on this planet and they were going up that shining ladder to give their reports to the One above (Genesis 28:13). They were coming back down to execute the divine will. The Lord Himself made reference to the "ascending and descending" of angels (John 1:51).

Angels are busy in this world. For example we all have attendant angels. Peter did (Acts 12:7-10) and so did Paul (Acts 27:23). Angels carried the soul of Lazarus to "Abraham's bosom" when he died (Luke 16:22). We learn from Revelation 1:20 and from the letters to the seven churches in Revelation 2–3 that each local church has its angel. The Holy Spirit tells us that the good angels are "ministering spirits" who serve the "heirs of salvation" (Hebrews 1:14). The Apocalypse shows us angels actively engaged in the closing judgments. The Lord's birth was heralded by angels. His temptation in the wilderness and His agony in the garden were both followed by a special ministry of angels to His needs (Matthew 4:11; Luke 22:43). Angels attended His resurrection.

In Matthew 18:10 the Lord clearly indicated that little children have guardian angels. Woe betide those who get the young hooked on drugs or ruin their impressionable minds with Satanic philosophies. Their angels make personal reports to God the Father in Heaven about all such crimes against His throne.

The Soviets were guilty of despising little ones. Having invaded Afghanistan, they found themselves unable to subdue the freedom fighters in that country and resorted to a particularly diabolical form of terror that was aimed at children. Testimony poured in from the United Nations Commission on Human Rights and from physicians who served the young victims. A seven-year-old was maimed by a blast from what looked like a harmless tin can; a child of twelve lost three fingers when she picked up a pen loaded with explosives; a tiny tot was maimed by a bomb that looked like a doll. It is estimated that thousands of children were harmed by brightly colored bombs concealed in toy trucks, dolls, and balls.[9] We can be sure that the angels of those children besieged the throne of God.

God's answer to their guardian angels had already been written. He had said of the Soviet Union that its day of reckoning would come. To some extent that day has already come with the demise of the Soviet Union and the disarray of Russia and some of the other former Soviet republics. But God is by no means through with Russia. She has yet a role to play in end-time events (Ezekiel 38–39). In a day to come Russia will spearhead a massive onslaught on Israel, and God will respond. "My fury shall come up in my face," He said (Ezekiel 38:18).

(b) God Saves (18:11)

Matthew 18:11 brings us back to the underlying spiritual lesson in 18:1-11 about receiving believers. The Lord said, "The Son of man is come to save that which was lost." Only saved people can be received into the fellowship of a local church. Unsaved people can be welcomed to attend the services of the church, but only saved people can share its life.

b. Restoring Backsliders (18:12-14)

The function of the local church is not only to receive new believers into its fellowship; the church is also responsible to restore backsliders.

The story of the lost sheep is told more fully in Luke 15, where the context is different. There, where the emphasis is on human lostness, the Lord told a three-part story about a lost sheep, a lost piece of silver, and a lost son. Human beings are lost as sheep are lost by wandering astray from God. People are lost as coins are lost by a sudden fall. And people are lost as the prodigal son was lost by deliberate choice.

(1) The Lost Sheep (18:12a-b)

In Matthew, in the immediate context, the Lord was talking about the loss of a child who has been seduced from the protection of the fold by unscrupulous and wicked people. If not sought and found, the child will become hardened by sin and will perish.

In the broader context of chapter 18, the story of the lost sheep is more related to the restoration of one of God's sheep who has strayed from the protection of the Christian community.

(2) The Loving Shepherd (18:12c-14)

The story shows that the Lord exercises the same love and concern for a wandering backslider as He does for a lost sinner. The restoration of a backslider brings as much joy to His heart as the salvation of a sinner does.

The church has a responsibility to seek those who are lost in trespasses and sins; it also has a responsibility to seek out and restore those who are lost to its fellowship. There should be as much rejoicing in the local church over the restoration of a backslider as there is over the reception of a new believer.

When Jesus was speaking of receiving new believers in terms of receiving a little child, He spoke of "*my* Father which is in heaven" (18:10, italics added). Now, speaking of restoring backsliders in terms of seeking lost sheep, He said, "It is not the will of *your* Father which is in heaven, that one of these little ones should perish" (18:14, italics added). His use of the word "your" introduces the factor of *our* responsibility.

Note too what 18:14 says about God's will. It is not the will of our Father in Heaven for any of His little ones to perish. His will should be our will. Just as our Lord Jesus Christ sought those astray from the fold, whether they were lost sinners or wayward saints, so should we. Seeking lost sheep is one of the functions of the local church.

It is not accidental that in the New Testament those who would be leaders of God's people are called shepherds or pastors. Those who would lead God's people must have a shepherd heart for the flock.

c. Reconciling Brethren (18:15-35)

(1) A Principle (18:15-20)

(a) The First Step—Christian Love Rules (18:15)

An attempt to reconcile a brother involves three steps. In the first, Christian love rules. "If thy brother shall trespass against thee," Jesus said, "go and tell him his fault between thee and him alone: if he shall hear thee, thou hast gained thy brother."

The words translated "against thee" are the subject of some debate. We do not necessarily have to wait until a brother sins against us personally before we take the initiative and talk to him about what is going on. The purpose of going to him is not to condemn or criticize or add fuel to the fire, but to "gain" him. The word translated "gained" in 18:15 is *kerdaino,* a commercial term associated with profit and loss (see Acts 27:21). A brother who has sinned is in certain ways lost to the fellowship and he has set himself up to be a tragic loser at the judgment seat of Christ. It is possible to have a saved soul and a lost life. So Christian love takes the initiative and starts a move toward reconciliation.

(b) The Further Step—Common Law Rules (18:16)

In the second step toward reconciliation, common law rules. "But if he will not hear thee," Jesus said, "then take with thee one or two more, that in the mouth of two or three witnesses every word may be established." He was referring to the principle established in the law of Moses (Deuteronomy 19:15).

While the first attempt at reconciliation is secret, the second is formal. It is more satisfactory to settle an issue in a quiet one-on-one conversation, but when the sinning brother is obdurate, he makes the more formal step necessary. The mission is the same: to convince the brother of his fault. Witnesses are taken along so that impartial observers can weigh the issues involved, apportion blame, lend their voices in persuasion, and become partners in prayer. More than personal interest is involved.

(c) The Final Step—Christian Leaders Rule (18:17-20)

i. The Executive Power of the Local Church (18:17a)

When steps one and two fail, the problem becomes far more serious. The sin and stubbornness of the erring one now affects the testimony of the local church. So in the third step, Christian leaders rule. The local church is here envisioned as a visible body of believers who have a corporate testimony and who are endowed with the power and authority to exercise discipline.

ii. The Excommunicating Power of the Local Church (18:17b-20)

a. Where It Works (18:17b-18)

When the problem is told to the church, there is still the opportunity for a quiet and peaceable restoration. However, if the offending brother refuses the reconciling ministry of the local church, his case is desperate indeed, for the church has the power to excommunicate.

Once a believer is excommunicated by the local church—acting properly under the leading of the Holy Spirit, in accordance with the Scriptures, and through its properly recognized leaders—he becomes an outsider. "Let him be unto thee as an heathen man and a publican," Jesus said (18:17). Traditional Jewish law forbade a Hebrew to associate, eat, or travel with a heathen; and if a Jew became a publican, he was excommunicated. Christian love modifies this restriction, for the attitude of a believer toward a heathen or a publican is that of concern for the person's spiritual welfare.

We do not treat lost people as lepers; we try to win them to Christ. We do not treat excommunicated believers as pariahs; we seek their repentance and restoration. At the same time, we do deny them the means of grace that are linked by the Holy Spirit with the communion of the local church. We do deny them access to the Lord's table and any active part in the assembly's fellowship and services.

b. Why It Works (18:19-20)

Christ has pledged that He will be present whenever the members of a local church meet. When the second member of the fellowship arrives at a gathering of that church, the Lord Himself arrives. There is no meeting at which He is not present. We may forget that fact; we may act as though it were not true; but it is. The Lord is always present when church members come together—and it takes only two to make a quorum. It is this divine presence that endows the church with its unique dignity. How gracious, how glorious, that the Creator of the universe, the risen Christ of Calvary, gathers with His people, be they many or few! To be excommunicated by the local church on Scriptural grounds is a serious matter, for it means that the offending one is cut off from all this.

The whole matter of church discipline is to be bathed in prayer. If prayer leads to the excommunicating step, prayer must pursue the outcast in his terrible vulnerability. Prayer must seek his repentance and restoration. Jesus promised, "If two of you shall agree on earth as touching any thing that they shall ask, it shall be done for them of my Father which is in heaven" (18:19). That verse, so often quoted out of context, is not a blank check enabling us to demand anything we want of God; the context is the excommunication of an offending and unrepentant brother.

Nowadays church discipline is rarely administered and even when it is, the person excommunicated by one church simply runs over to another church and joins himself to that fellowship, or imagines that he does. But if he has been legitimately disciplined, he cannot escape the penalty that easily, for Jesus said that what is bound on earth is bound in Heaven and what is loosed on earth is loosed in Heaven (18:18). Of course there are many instances where church leaders, through ignorance of the Scriptures, act out of the will of God. Their edicts have no value at all and are not binding.

If the excommunication is legitimate—if it is based on a sound grasp of the issues and of Scripture—it will not do any good for the excommunicated believer to join another congregation, which may or may not know he is under discipline, and which may not even care. The offender is still under discipline. God's blessing does not rest on him. God's Spirit within him is a grieved Spirit. The offender is vulnerable to Satan. He cannot escape the binding power of the local church acting under the guidance of the Holy Spirit.

The outward evidence of God's displeasure may not be seen at once. The excommunicated brother may appear to be prospering, but he is under interdict. The church has consulted the will of God. It has arrived at the truth both as to the offence and as to what Scripture says. It has gathered in the name of the Lord Jesus and its decision is final, authoritative, and binding. The offender will remain an outsider, no matter how many churches he joins or Christian organizations he serves, until he comes back in repentance and seeks the forgiveness of those he has wronged, until he is "loosed" from his bondage by that church and restored to its fellowship. Such is the principle.

(2) A Proposal (18:21-22)

(a) Magnanimity in Forgiveness beyond the Normal (18:21)

Peter had been impressed by the Lord's teaching on reconciliation. He realized that if he were the injured party, he would have to exercise a forgiving spirit. But how often would one be called on to forgive? The rabbis had decided that three times would be forbearance and forgiveness enough. Peter, with a great show of magnanimity, suggested that he forgive seven times. He was reducing love to logic, mercy to mathematics, a matter of spirituality to a matter of arithmetic.

(b) Magnificence in Forgiveness beyond the Natural (18:22)

The Lord swept all such carnal considerations aside. He did not just demand forgiveness beyond the norm; He demanded forgiveness beyond nature. That is how God forgives us. God does not say, "I'll forgive you seven times." We would all be in a sorry plight if He did.

There is an interesting use of the number "seventy times seven" in Daniel 9:24, which gives a preview of the future of the Jewish people. The prophecy reads, "Seventy weeks are determined upon thy people and upon thy holy city, to finish the transgression, and to make an end of sins, and to make reconciliation for iniquity, and to bring in everlasting righteousness, and to seal up the vision and prophecy, and to anoint the most Holy."

The seventy "weeks" were seventy sevens (of years), which produce the number "seventy times seven." The resulting period of 490 years was to be interrupted after a span of 483 years, at which time the coming Messiah would be "cut off [crucified]," thus making atonement for sin (Daniel 9:25-26). The final seven-year period would bring iniquity to a head in the person of the antichrist (9:27). Thereafter Christ would return and bring in the millennial reign of righteousness.

In other words, God promised the Jews that He would forgive and forgive and forgive for this perfect number of times ("seventy times seven"). We know of course that He has inserted the church age between the sixty-ninth and seventieth seven and has gone on forgiving and forgiving and forgiving in spite of the crime of Calvary. He will go on forgiving until time will be no more.

(3) A Parable (18:23-35)

(a) The Man and His Debt (18:23-27)

The Lord answered Peter's proposal with a parable. The down-to-earth story tells of a man who owed an oriental ruler an incalculable debt, stated to be "ten thousand talents" (18:24). It is hard to translate Bible money into present-day equivalents because of fluctuating values. It is best to draw parallels, and to point out that a talent was the heaviest unit of weight used by the Hebrews and the number "ten thousand" was the highest round number.[10] By all standards, the man's debt was beyond computation.

The day of accounting came; the man was brought before the king and found to be bankrupt. The king commanded that such assets as the man had be liquidated. He was to be sold, along with his wife and family. Even so, his indebtedness to the throne would not be totally satisfied.

The man's condition illustrates our state before God. We are all ten-thousand-talent debtors. God has lavished on us life, skills, and opportunities. In return, we have misappropriated His investment, abused His gifts, wasted our substance, despised His laws, ignored His claims, sinned constantly and with a high hand. We have accumulated an incalculable debt.

The man's only hope, as is ours, was to cast himself on the mercy of the king, who was willing to forgive the debt. The debtor, however, had no grasp of the principle of grace; he only understood law. He appealed not for grace, but for more time. "Lord, have patience with me," he said, "and I will pay thee all" (18:26). He asked for patience; he received pardon. The lord was "moved with compassion" and loosed him from his debt (18:27).

(b) The Man and His Deed (18:28-30)

The man's indebtedness was canceled, but his nature was unchanged. He was the same harsh, cruel man he had always been. He was forgiven, but he was neither justified nor regenerated. The gospel goes beyond forgiveness. We can be forgiven, yet go on to aggravate God's throne and make judgment inevitable. Forgiveness, when properly received, results in a change of behavior that reflects genuine conversion.

At this point we need to turn to an actual incident recorded in Luke 7:36-50. The Lord was invited to the home of Simon the Pharisee. When the Lord arrived, Simon showed the Lord none of the common courtesies usually extended to a guest. Then a sinful woman came in and outraged the host by washing the feet of Jesus with her tears. When the Lord read Simon's heart, He told the Pharisee a story and asked him a question:

> There was a certain creditor which had two debtors: the one owed five hundred pence, and the other fifty. And when they had nothing to pay, he frankly forgave them both. Tell me therefore, which of them will love him most?

Simon grudgingly answered, "I suppose that he, to whom he forgave most." The Lord then applied the story to Simon and the woman. Jesus ended the incident by turning to the woman and saying, "Thy sins are forgiven." The spectators asked, "Who is this that forgiveth sins also?" Then Jesus sent the woman away with these parting words: "Thy faith hath saved thee; go in peace." She was not only forgiven, but also saved.

The man in the parable in Matthew 18 was forgiven, but the forgiveness was really contingent on a further work of grace being done in his heart. We can conclude that he experienced no such work, for instead of demonstrating the characteristics of a truly saved man, he at once went out and exhibited all the harshness and ruthlessness of his unregenerate heart.

One of his fellow servants owed him "an hundred pence" (the equivalent of about three months' wages for a laborer), a mere pittance compared with the ten-thousand-talent debt he had owed. The man seized his fellow servant, "took him by the throat," and demanded instant repayment (18:28). "Have patience with me, and I will pay thee all," the fellow servant pleaded, using the same words the forgiven debtor had used when appealing to his lord (18:29, compare 18:26). But the man who had received mercy was adamant. He cast his fellow servant into the debtors' prison. The poor man's pleas made no impression whatsoever on the creditor's hard heart.

(c) The Man and His Doom (18:31-35)

When the evil man's wickedness was brought to the attention of his lord, the king had him arrested at once. "O thou wicked servant," he said, "I forgave thee all that debt, because thou desiredst me: Shouldest not thou also have had compassion on thy fellowservant, even as I had pity on thee?" (18:32-33) The word translated "wicked" here is *ponēros*. *Ponēros* and its synonyms are used in the New Testament to refer to human depravity and the wicked working of our evil nature. The wicked behavior of the unforgiving man revealed his unregenerate heart.

He was forced to face the consequences of his wickedness. The man had no plea, for he knew his case to be hopeless. The new sentence was far worse than the one that had been rescinded. Before he was to have been sold; now "his lord was wroth, and delivered him to the tormentors, till he should pay all that was due unto him" (18:34).

In human courts of law, previous conviction increases the penalty for a further transgression. The man in the parable was arrested, arraigned, tried, and sentenced not because of his ten-thousand-talent debt, but because of his wicked behavior toward his fellow servant; however, his punishment was made commensurate with what he had once owed. Because of his new sin, he would not be eligible for parole until he paid the equivalent of his former debt. Mercy had been replaced with wrath.

In applying the parable, the Lord showed the seriousness of an unforgiving spirit. "So likewise shall my heavenly Father do also unto you," Jesus said, "if ye from your hearts forgive not every one his brother their trespasses" (18:35). Peter had asked how often he must forgive, and Jesus in effect said to him and us, "You must go on forgiving and forgiving because that is how the heavenly Father forgives." After all, the transgressions we are called on to forgive are relatively petty when compared with the enormous transgressions we have asked God to forgive.

The parable shows that an unforgiving spirit reveals an unregenerate heart, and an unregenerate heart eventually lands a person in the place of torment. Why would the Lord tell such a parable to His disciples? One of them had an unregenerate heart; he was a mere pretender and he ended up in perdition. His name was Judas. And why should the parable be told in the local church? The ranks of church members often include some who have never been truly regenerated.

D. Marriage in the Kingdom (19:1-15)

1. The Salient Factors in the Case of Divorce (19:1-12)

a. The Context of the Lord's Teaching on Divorce (19:1-2)

"When Jesus had finished these sayings [the sayings recorded in Matthew 18], he departed from Galilee" (19:1). He did not return to Galilee until after the resurrection. Matthew omitted many incidents that happened between the conclusion of the Lord's Galilean ministry and the beginning of the events that led rapidly to the cross. The omitted incidents are recorded in Luke 9:51–17:11 and John 7:2–11:54.

Matthew 19 places us in the land "beyond Jordan" called *Perea,* a name that simply means "beyond." Perea extended from Pella in the north to Machaerus in the south. It began on the Jordan opposite the southern boundary of Galilee and continued to Moab, about halfway down the eastern shore of the Dead Sea. Perea was part of the area ruled by Herod Antipas. In Bible times it was a fertile land containing numerous towns and many fine buildings. The people were essentially farmers and less influenced by the hostility of the Pharisees than city folk were.

It was in this farming area that the Lord gave His one full-length and definitive teaching on the vexing subject of divorce. This teaching was prompted by a loaded question directed to Him by the Pharisees.

b. The Content of the Lord's Teaching on Divorce (19:3-12)

Great multitudes had assembled. "The Pharisees also came unto him, tempting him, and saying unto him, Is it lawful for a man to put away his wife for every cause?" (19:3) This was a deliberate attempt to catch the Lord on the horns of a dilemma, to embroil Him in a controversy that already existed between the two rival schools of Hillel and Shammai. The school of Hillel maintained that a man could divorce his wife for all sorts of reasons: he no longer loved her, or he had found someone he liked better, or she had burned his dinner, or she went into public places with an uncovered head, or she spoke disrespectfully about his parents, or she was childless. Shammai was stricter and permitted divorce only for fornication, adultery, or some other form of unchastity.

The Lord's teaching on divorce is complex. When dealing with a complex portion of Scripture, especially one that is highly controversial (Matthew 24 for instance or the warning passages of Hebrews), it is best to begin with a careful and thorough structural analysis. So let us first look at the structure of Matthew 19:3-12. The outline provides the analysis:

> (1) The Lord and His Foes—He Restated the Divine
>   Ideal (19:3-9)
>   (a) The First Challenge and the Appeal to Adam
>   (19:3-6)
>   (b) The Further Challenge and the Appeal to Moses
>   (19:7-9)
> (2) The Lord and His Friends—He Realized the Difficulties
>   Involved (19:10-12)
>   (a) The Pragmatic Response of His Men (19:10)
>   (b) The Pragmatic Response of the Master (19:11-12)
>   i. On Being Receptive (19:11)
>   ii. On Becoming Remarried (19:12)

Looking at this structural analysis, we can see at a glance that the Lord dealt with two classes of people. He was inflexible when dealing with His foes, but He made concessions when dealing with His friends.

(1) The Lord and His Foes—He Restated the Divine
     Ideal (19:3-9)

(a) The First Challenge and the Appeal to Adam (19:3-6)

It seems that the Pharisees hoped to get the Lord embroiled in the lively controversy that was raging in the theological circles of the day. The Lord simply sidestepped the arguments and took His questioners back to the Bible and back to the beginning. He repainted the picture of the idyllic situation in the garden of Eden where a loving couple lived in sinless perfection in a perfect environment.

Marriage was God's idea. It was instituted by Him at the beginning of human history when He made the first two human beings. (Incidentally, by referring to the Genesis account of creation, Jesus gave the lie to the theory of evolution and endorsed the literal truth of the Bible history of Adam and Eve.) God ordained marriage to be the fundamental principle of order in society, and the marriage relationship to be even more binding than the child-parent relationship. According to God's plan, when a man marries, he establishes a bond with his wife of such a nature that she is as much a part of him as his own body is.

The Lord carried these Scriptural truths to their logical conclusion: God intended marriage to be permanent. There was no room in the original arrangement for polygamy or divorce. The one man (Adam) was married by God to the one woman (Eve). She was not created by a separate fiat of the divine will; God took her directly from Adam's side so that she was literally bone of his bone and flesh of his flesh. The original intent was that one man would be married to one woman until death dissolved the relationship. So the Lord made His own authoritative decree: "What therefore God hath joined together, let not man put asunder" (Matthew 19:6).

Thus Christ went back to the original eternal principle and ignored Hillel, Shammai, and the teachings of the rabbis. The Lord's answer did not satisfy the Pharisees, for it concentrated on conditions prior to the fall, so His challengers tried again.

(b) The Further Challenge and the Appeal to Moses (19:7-9)

In the context of the sinless perfection that prevailed at the beginning, there could be no question of divorce. The need for it would never arise. But man is no longer living in paradise. We dwell in a sin-cursed world and we have fallen Adamic natures. Even believers, who are indwelt by the Holy Spirit, feel the pressure of temptation. All kinds of evil can lurk within the marriage relationship. The Pharisees therefore responded to Christ's idealistic statement by appealing to Moses.

"Why did Moses then command to give a writing of divorcement, and to put her away?" the Pharisees asked. They were referring to Deuteronomy 24:1, which reads, "When a man hath taken a wife, and married her, and it come to pass that she find no favour in his eyes, because he hath found some uncleanness in her: then let him write her a bill of divorcement, and give it in her hand, and send her out of his house." The divorce dissolved the marriage. The law went on to say that the woman thus legally divorced was *free to be another man's wife.* Her first husband was not allowed to remarry her under any condition. It is significant that this legislation is found in Deuteronomy, which was written in the eleventh month of the fortieth year after the exodus (Deuteronomy 1:3), just prior to the death of the great lawgiver. The ruling was not part of the original legislation given at Sinai.

In answering this second challenge of the Pharisees, Jesus said,

"Because of the hardness of your hearts [Moses] suffered you to put away your wives" (Matthew 19:8). The basic cause of divorce is the hardness of the human heart.

Moses was faced with this hardness. If he had codified the primeval marriage rule given in Eden at the time of creation when the world was young and man's heart was not yet sullied by sin, the Israelites would have reacted by refusing to marry. As in our own permissive and lawless society, they would have preferred to live in illicit liaisons rather than run the risks of an indissoluble tie. If a man did marry and his wife turned out to be incompatible, he might have abused her or even murdered her.

Therefore Moses, under the guidance of God, appended a divorce clause to the law. He did not command divorce, as the Pharisees claimed; he allowed it under certain circumstances. What he did command was that if a marriage were to be dissolved, it must be done legally, with due formality, and in a way that would protect the woman. Moreover the divorce was to be permanent. The "*writing* of divorcement" was what Moses commanded (19:7, italics added). A woman could not be dismissed from her husband's home by word of mouth or by forcible expulsion. A written document was required.

Moses refused to grant divorce on two grounds: (1) A man who falsely accused his wife of uncleanness was forbidden by law ever to divorce the woman (Deuteronomy 22:13-19). (2) If a man seduced a woman and the case against him was proven, he was compelled by law to marry her and was denied the right ever to divorce her (Deuteronomy 22:28-29).

The Mosaic law then was an accommodation to the hardness of the human heart. Divorce was a lesser evil than wife abuse or lawless liaisons. Moses could not hope to change men's hearts. He could only try to mitigate the hardness by allowing divorce and regulating its practice.

The Lord continued, "But from the beginning it was not so" (Matthew 19:8). The original institution of marriage contained no provision for divorce. Initially marriage was not a civil contract made by man. Marriage was God's plan for the human race. It was not something that man could repeal or dissolve.

The concept of marriage here restated by the Lord was the divine ideal. It is still the divine ideal. Marriage is for the benefit of man and woman, for the sanctifying of the most intimate of all human relationships, for the protection of the children resulting from the marriage, and for the health of society.

The divine ideal is basic, but what happens when the divine ideal is broken beyond repair by the immorality of one of the partners? The Lord addressed that issue with one of His resounding "I say unto you" statements: "I say unto you, Whosoever shall put away his wife, *except it be for fornication* [*porneia*[11]], and shall marry another, committeth adultery: and whoso marrieth her which is put away doth commit adultery" (19:9, italics added). The immoral behavior of one of the marriage partners dissolves the marriage bond. In a modern action for divorce on the ground of adultery, it is not the law that annuls the marriage bond; the law merely gives legal effect to the annulment already brought about by the adultery.

Note that in the sermon on the mount, where the Lord set forth the highest of all moral codes, He dealt with divorce as He did in Matthew 19. He made the same provision for the innocent party in a broken and violated marriage: "But I say unto you, That whosoever shall put away his wife, *saving for the cause of fornication,* causeth her to commit adultery: and whosoever shall marry her that is divorced committeth adultery" (Matthew 5:32, italics added). The Lord thus graciously provided a way of escape for the innocent party. He or she is allowed an unencumbered divorce and is free to remarry—in contrast to one who seeks to end a marriage on other and frivolous grounds. Adultery breaks the marriage bond and the consequent divorce sets the injured partner free to marry again. No one has any right to cast stones at such an individual or to treat the innocent party as though he or she were the guilty party.

Some Christians hold a particularly harsh and tyrannical view that ignores the Lord's escape clause for the innocent victim of a broken marriage. If the innocent party is a woman and she remarries, they cast stones at her in a particularly nasty way. They accuse her of having two living husbands. Their accusation comes close to being a libelous statement, for it practically calls her a bigamist. Besides the fact that there is no truth in their statement, it is heartless.

Here is an example: A woman suffers for years because of the infidelity of her husband. In the end he is publicly exposed and sued for molesting young teens. The woman seeks refuge in divorce and begins to pick up the shattered fragments of her life. At this point her husband abandons her and leaves her to get along as best she can. Eventually she meets a man who proposes marriage. He is an itinerant servant of the Lord, a man she honors and respects. The woman, according to the Lord's own rule, is an innocent victim; she has Scriptural grounds for fifty divorces. So the marriage takes place. Almost at once the man receives a letter from a group of professing Christians to whom he has ministered on many occasions; he is told that he will no longer be welcome as a speaker in their church because his wife has two living husbands. The poor woman now has a new cross to carry. She is made to feel that she is some kind of pariah. Such heartlessness is not the spirit of Christ.

(2) The Lord and His Friends—He Realized the Difficulties Involved (19:10-12)

(a) The Pragmatic Response of His Men (19:10)

The disciples reacted at once: "If the case of the man be so with his wife, it is not good to marry." Faced with the divine ideal—one man, one woman, one body, no divorce—they instantly voiced an objection that illustrated both the hardness of the human heart and the wisdom of the Mosaic law in including legislation pertaining to divorce.

The disciples were ordinary, pragmatic men. They were not priests of an ascetic order; they were alive to everyday life in the workaday world. The disciples could think of a score of situations where the marriage yoke was intolerable. So can we if we are at all familiar with the world about us. There are spouses who are unfaithful to their partners, sometimes promiscuously so. What is a woman to do if she is married to a man who frequents harlots, or to a man who is a homosexual? Does she have no protection? Does her marriage vow bind her to him regardless of his disgusting lifestyle and regardless of the risk of contracting some communicable disease from him? What should a man do if his wife uses mind-altering, soul-destroying drugs, or tries to get him to become an addict? What should a woman do if her husband is a drunkard who habitually abuses her or beats her or tries to force her to sell her body?

These are not hypothetical questions. Many a partner is bound by a marriage vow to a situation that is a living hell. A happily married individual may find it easy to pontificate the divine ideal in such cases, but he would not be nearly so dogmatic if the ill-fitting shoe were on his foot or if the one being constantly abused were his beloved child.

(b) The Pragmatic Response of the Master (19:11-12)

i. On Being Receptive (19:11)

So the disciples objected. And the Lord immediately came down from the high plateau to the lower ground on which they stood. He refused to do this with His foes. There could be no lowering of the standard for them; He knew their hearts only too well. He upheld before them the counsels of perfection: according to the divine ideal, divorce is not an option.

The Lord's response to His disciples was swift and to the point. Aware of the fact that not all people can live up to His teaching on marriage and divorce, the Lord said to His friends, "All men cannot receive this saying, save they to whom it is given." The Lord recognized two things: (1) the absolute sanctity of marriage, including the importance of safeguarding it from any attempt to tear it down or devaluate it; and (2) the sad but undeniable fact that, apart from God's special grace, not all people, not even all His own people, can accept the disciplines demanded by the ideal. Certainly we are not to force those disciplines, as a rule of faith, on other people. The Lord did not slight those who do not have what it takes to receive His teaching. Nor did He give us authority to sit in judgment on those who find His standards too high.

ii. On Becoming Remarried (19:12)

Verse 12 is related to the question of remarriage of divorced persons. The issue is simple: Must a divorced person be forced to remain celibate?

The Lord pointed out that there are three ways a person can be steered into a celibate life, either before marriage or as a result of a disastrous marriage. He said, "There are some eunuchs, which were so born from their mother's womb: and there are some eunuchs, which were made eunuchs of men: and there be eunuchs, which have made themselves eunuchs for the kingdom of heaven's sake."

So there are three kinds of celibacy. The first kind is based on *constitution*. Some people are so constituted physically, emotionally, or psychologically as to be naturally celibate. The opposite sex does not attract them. There is no particular virtue in having such a nature. Such people might find release from marriage a positive relief and have no desire to contract another marriage. They would have no difficulty with a teaching that banned remarriage.

The second kind of celibacy is based on *compulsion*. Some people are "made eunuchs of men." In oriental society men who served in harems were castrated, often against their will. The practice was cruel, but as in the case of constitutional eunuchs, compulsory celibacy was not necessarily an indication of virtue.

We do not make physical eunuchs nowadays in our society, but many churches impose celibacy on divorced persons by forbidding remarriage, even when there were Scriptural grounds for the divorce. These churches ignore the anguish caused by the unnatural lifestyle they enforce. For all practical purposes, they make divorced people eunuchs. A church that takes a hard line on divorce virtually forces a divorced person to remain single or else face excommunication or some other form of church displeasure. There is something harsh and impractical about a rule that tells a young divorced person, "You can never marry again." Such a ruling inflicts great hardship on a normal healthy person, exposes him to fierce temptation, and often drives him out of the church and into the arms of the world. Or he may seek fellowship in another less rigid church.

The third kind of celibacy is based on *conviction*. Some people make themselves eunuchs "for the kingdom of heaven's sake." This kind of celibacy is voluntary. An individual deliberately mortifies his natural desires and impulses at the cost of much personal pain and loss. By means of the special grace of God, he upholds the divine ideal to further the cause of Christ. Such a vow of celibacy may be taken by an unmarried person or a divorced person. The purpose is to free himself from the distractions of married life in order to devote the remainder of his time on earth to the things of God. This was the kind of life that Jesus lived.

The Lord concluded His teaching on celibacy with these words: "He that is able to receive it, let him receive it." Obviously He was referring to His statement in 19:11, where He had told His disciples that not everyone could receive His divine ideal.

2. The Silent Factor in the Case of Divorce (19:13-15)

a. Little Children Brought to Jesus (19:13)

It surely was no accident that at this point Matthew introduced the subject of children, for when parents divorce, the chief losers are the children. He wrote, "Then were there brought unto him little children." The word translated "little children" is the plural of *paidion,* which means "young child." Luke in his account used the word *brephos,* which means "newborn baby" (Luke 18:15).

Parents were so drawn to Jesus that they wanted His blessing on their children. But the disciples were outraged that people would waste the Master's time by bringing little children and babes in arms to Him so that He might pray for them. The Lord was "much displeased" with the disciples, for He loved to bless little children (Mark 10:14). Mark meant that He was indignant. Very rarely in the

Gospels do we read of Jesus being angry, and this was one of those occasions.

b. Little Children Blessed by Jesus (19:14-15)

The Lord said, "Suffer little children, and forbid them not, to come unto me: for of such is the kingdom of heaven" (19:14). He gathered the little ones in His arms and blessed them. His heart still goes out to all the children of the world. Happy are they who seek to bring little ones to Him.

Parents who squabble, cheat on each other, and turn their home into a living hell must be hardhearted and selfish indeed. How the Lord's heart must ache over the children in that home! The sad fact is that many such parents are professing Christians. But by their behavior they damage the little ones whom Jesus would take into His arms. The fighting of husbands and wives can turn their children away from the Lord, perhaps for eternity. What an accounting there will be one day!

E. Motives in the Kingdom (19:16–20:16)

1. A Proposal (19:16-22)

a. What the Man Desired (19:16)

The subject of motives in the kingdom is introduced by an interruption. A young man came to Jesus with a proposal. Luke 18:18 says he was a "ruler"; that is, he was a ruler of the synagogue. He desired eternal life and he proposed to do some good thing in order to attain it. The desire was good, but the proposal was wrong.

Hoping to earn eternal life, people have performed incredible feats, just as Naaman was quite prepared to pay a great price for his cleansing or do some great thing (2 Kings 5:5,13). A religion reveals itself to be false when it requires its followers to do something in order to gain bliss in the life to come. False religion stresses payment, penance, pilgrimages, fasts, floggings, deeds, and self-denial.

b. What the Man Discovered (19:17)

(1) The Claim of the Lord (19:17a)

First the Lord challenged the man's use of the word "good." When the young ruler addressed the Lord as "Good Master,"[12] He responded, "Why callest thou me good? there is none good but one, that is, God." Jesus was challenging the young man to own Him as God. The Lord was saying in effect, "What do you mean by calling Me good? Do you mean that I am relatively good, as a man can be good in comparison with other men? Or do you mean that I am absolutely good, as God is good? Are you saying that I am just a good man, or are you saying that I am God?" There is all the difference in the world. Even many unbelievers are prepared to say that Jesus was a good man.

(2) The Claim of the Law (19:17b)

Then the Lord challenged the young man's goodness. "If thou wilt enter into life," He said, "keep the commandments." The ruler had made his appeal on the ground of goodness, and Jesus answered him on the same ground. The Lord said in effect, "If you want to earn eternal life, live a perfect life." To keep the commandments of God perfectly is an impossible task for a sinful man.

The ten commandments had been expanded into 613 separate pieces of legislation covering all aspects of one's duty to God and his fellow man. In order to merit eternal life, it would have been necessary for the ruler to keep all those commandments all the time. That was and is Heaven's irreducible minimum. God can and will accept nothing less than perfection.

So the Lord challenged the man about whether he thought Christ was perfect and whether he thought of himself as perfect.

c. What the Man Demonstrated (19:18-19)

The young ruler found himself in a quandary. When he hedged, the Lord recited five of the ten commandments, choosing those that emphasized man's duty to man and the outward aspects of personal morality (commandments six to nine and five). He did not recite the first four, which demand absolutely unwavering love for God, or the tenth commandment, which deals with inner desire. The fifth commandment was a duty godward,[13] but it also enshrined a duty manward (duty to parents); so the Lord substituted it (possibly because it was easier to keep) for the devastating tenth commandment, which forbids evil desires.

The Lord added a statement that bound commandments six

through nine and five together: "Thou shalt love thy neighbour as thyself" (19:19). That summary statement went beyond the letter of those commandments to the spirit behind them. He took goodness out of the realm of law and placed it in the realm of love. He moved goodness from a system of outward compliance to a sphere of inward compulsion.

d. What the Man Declared (19:20)

The young man's reply revealed the depths of his self-deception. "All these things," he said, "have I kept from my youth up." He had kept the commandments as far as the letter of the law went, but he was overlooking the summary statement that dealt with the spirit of the law. He missed the point.

True, he had not killed anyone. He had not been guilty of a sordid affair with someone else's wife. He had not stolen. He had not destroyed anyone's reputation with lies. He had honored his parents. He had kept the letter of the law. So he said in effect, "I have always loved my neighbor as myself, ever since I reached the age of accountability."

We may say the same, but we do not love our neighbors as we love ourselves. A. P. Gibbs used to illustrate this fact in his own inimitable style. "You are coming home from town," he would say, "and you see smoke ahead, near where you live. A house is on fire. The fire engines roar past with howling sirens and clanging bells. You quicken your pace and round a corner. The fire is on your street! You break into a run. Then you heave a sigh of relief. You say, 'I'm so glad! It's *my* house! I'm glad it's not my neighbor's.'" Whoever said such a thing as that?

e. What the Man Discerned (19:21-22)

The man claimed to have done all that needed to be done to merit eternal life, but note what he discerned when Jesus put him to the test. The Lord said, "If thou wilt be perfect, go and sell that thou hast, and give to the poor, and thou shalt have treasure in heaven: and come and follow me" (19:21). The young ruler now saw the point. Jesus had proved to him that he did not love his neighbor as himself, that he had not kept the spirit of the law, that he had not earned eternal life. He was rich in this world's goods, but bankrupt in good works. Matthew 19:22 tells us that "he went away sorrowful."

2. A Problem (19:23-30)

a. The Lord's Assertion (19:23-24)

(1) The Principle Revealed (19:23)

The encounter with the young ruler introduced a problem connected with wealth. The Lord told His disciples that it was very difficult for a rich man to enter the kingdom of heaven. Riches give a person entrance to most places down here, but they do not open the gates of Heaven. Wealth translates into power; power generates pride; and pride slams the gates of the kingdom shut. It is difficult for a rich man to be "poor in spirit" (5:3).

(2) The Principle Repeated (19:24)

In 19:24 the Lord gave an illustration of the principle He had revealed in 19:23. He said, "It is easier for a camel to go through the eye of a needle, than for a rich man to enter into the kingdom of God." The "eye of a needle" evidently refers to the small door in the gate of a walled eastern city. When the main gates were closed for the night, a merchant arriving late was forced to enter through the small postern gate. Usually he had to unload his camels so that they could get through.

b. The Disciples' Astonishment (19:25-26)

(1) The Incredible (19:25)

Riches are a problem because people tend to trust in them, but the Lord made it clear that money cannot buy salvation. The disciples were amazed at the teaching because rich men often get what they want just because they are rich. Riches seem to smooth the way through this life. Moreover almost everyone would like to be rich. "Who then can be saved?" the disciples asked.

(2) The Impossible (19:26)

It is impossible for men, in their own strength, relying on their own resources, to win the favor of God. The rich young ruler's wealth was a millstone around his neck. In his case the best thing to be done with his wealth was to give it away.

Since it is impossible for men to save themselves, the saving rests with God. He is the God of the impossible, the God who can work on the most obdurate human heart so that at last it capitulates to the grace that alone can save. "With God all things are possible," Jesus said.

c. The Lord's Assurance (19:27-30)

(1) Peter's Question Asked (19:27)

Peter as usual was the spokesman for the disciples. Having heard the Lord's promise to the rich young ruler (19:21), Peter asked in effect, "What about us?" He was not thinking about salvation. He was thinking about what reward the apostles would have in the promised kingdom.

(2) Peter's Question Answered (19:28-30)

(a) A Promise (19:28-29)

i. For the Twelve Disciples, Millennial Blessing (19:28)

Jesus replied, "Verily [Truly] I say unto you, That ye which have followed me, in the regeneration when the Son of man shall sit in the throne of his glory, ye also shall sit upon twelve thrones, judging the twelve tribes of Israel." The Lord's answer leaped over the church age. What the Lord called "the regeneration" looks ahead to the millennial age—the time of making all things new, the coming golden age when the curse will be largely removed from the earth, men will learn war no more, deserts will blossom as the rose, and a centenarian will be a youth.

During the millennium the Lord will rule over the whole world. Jerusalem will be the world's capital and Jews will administer the earthly empire.[14] The twelve apostles will have authority over the twelve reconstituted tribes of Israel. Each apostle will control tremendous wealth and wield enormous power. The rich young ruler forfeited his place in the millennial kingdom for the sake of his puny purse. Judas would throw away his reward for the sake of thirty pieces of silver. Both might have helped rule an empire.

ii. For All True Disciples, Multiplied Blessings (19:29)

Besides the dispensational reward, there is a chance for all to win eternal wealth. Jesus said, "Every one that hath forsaken houses, or brethren, or sisters, or father, or mother, or wife, or children, or lands, for my name's sake, shall receive an hundredfold, and shall inherit everlasting life." What bank on earth can guarantee a return as great as "an hundredfold [10,000 percent]"? The Lord enumerated the things on which people most often set their hearts. He began with houses and ended with lands. In between He listed the most cherished members of the family circle. All who give up anything for Christ will one day reap enormous rewards.

Although the promise doubtless has millennial and eternal overtones, many a servant of God who has given up the comforts of home and the security of wealth for the Lord's sake, has found himself mothered by hundreds of God's saints and has been the recipient of countless deeds of kindness in this life. Thus in Romans 16:13 Paul could write, "Salute Rufus chosen in the Lord, and his mother and mine." Dan Crawford once said that the mother of Rufus was claimed by Paul as one of his ten thousand mothers in Christ.

(b) A Principle (19:30)

The Lord concluded His discussion of motives in the kingdom with a warning (19:30) and a parable (20:1-16). He warned, "Many that are first shall be last; and the last shall be first." In other words, we cannot trust human estimates about who is first or last, greatest or least. At the judgment seat of Christ there will be many surprises. It is likely that the Lord had Judas in mind when He gave this warning. Judas was counted as one of the foremost of the disciples. He was in charge of the finances of the apostolic company—and he fell through covetousness. The Lord also intimated that Peter should beware of a spirit of pride as he smugly compared himself with the rich young ruler.

3. A Parable (20:1-16)

By telling the parable of the laborers in the vineyard, the Lord illuminated the principle behind the warning in 19:30: Some who are first will be last and some who are last will be first. A gifted preacher I once knew was greatly troubled by this parable in his unconverted days. Before his conversion he was a skillful speaker for the British Labour Party and the cause of trade unionism. His crowd-swaying oratory could have enabled him to become prime minister if he had not dedicated his gift to a higher cause. Before he was saved, he considered this parable to be an affront to the labor movement and the principle of equal pay for equal work. He overlooked the fact that the workers who had a contract were scrupulously dealt with according to the terms of the contract.

The Labour Party spokesman missed the point of the story. The parable was designed to rebuke Peter's self-seeking spirit that had prompted him to ask in effect, "What are we going to get out of all this?" The subject matter is not salvation truth but kingdom truth, not eternal life but reward for service.

a. Recruiting the Laborers (20:1-7)

Early in the morning the first recruits were hired *with the law as their guarantee.* They had a contract, one they considered fair. At the third, sixth, and ninth hours the lord of the vineyard recruited more laborers. They were hired *with the lord as their guarantee.* He promised to give them what was right when the time of reckoning came. At the eleventh hour he hired additional workers who were even more dependent on the generosity of the owner of the vineyard.

Throughout the day when the lord went to the marketplace, he saw men "standing idle" (20:3). He asked why they were idle when there was so much work to be done. They expressed a willingness to work if they were given the opportunity, and they did work when the call came. All who were sent, went. Note that they were standing in the marketplace, the place where opportunity could find them. They were not off pursuing pleasure or wasting time lazing around at home.

All this is true to spiritual life. There is inequality of opportunity for service. Some people are not saved when they are young. Some are not called to work in the vineyard immediately after conversion. Some are not called to preach to thousands or pastor great churches. Some do not see revival follow their ministry. Among the Lord's servants there is inequality in length of service and talent.

The "day" in the parable seems to represent the span of human life. We recall the Lord saying elsewhere, "I must work the works of him that sent me, while it is day: the night cometh, when no man can work" (John 9:4).

So we are beginning to apply the parable to our lives, but we have not yet reached its bottom line. The point of the parable comes out in Matthew 20:8-16.

b. Recompensing the Laborers (20:8-16)

(1) The Order (20:8-12)

(a) The Last Who Are Now First (20:8-9)

The late starters dared to trust in the owner's benevolence. They had no contract and struck no bargains. They did not say, "We will serve you on these terms." Nor did they have Peter's spirit, for they did not say, "What will we get?"

To these laborers' astonishment they received a full day's wage, just as if they had been called early in the morning. The owner rewarded them, not for the length of their service, but for their willingness, faithfulness, and trust. Similarly the Lord measures the way we seize and employ the opportunities we have, not just the length of our service.

(b) The First Who Are Now Last (20:10-12)

The early starters desired to trust in their bargain. Their spirit was wrong from the beginning. These laborers wanted to know up-front what they would get out of working in the vineyard and they received just what they bargained for: legal remuneration instead of loving reward.

At the end of the day their spirit was still wrong. They saw those who had served in the vineyard for a shorter time receiving a full day's reward, and the early starters put two and two together. If one hour's work earned a "penny," twelve hours' work should be worth twelve pennies. They received exactly what they had bargained for, but they were envious and furious. Their spirit of jealousy was evident. They did not have the gracious, compassionate spirit of the one for whom they worked.

We learn from this parable that as long as we do not neglect the opportunity given to us, the amount of time we spend in the Lord's service is not nearly so important as the spirit in which our service is rendered. Perhaps if the laborers in the parable had shown the same spirit as the lord, their reward would have been increased twelvefold.

(2) The Owner (20:13-15)

(a) His Government (20:13-14a)

In answering the disaffected workers, the owner (who obviously represents the Lord) said to their spokesman, "Friend, I do thee no wrong" (20:13). He was not angry, for he called the man "friend." It was not too late for them to adopt a different attitude. The owner was not unfair either. The workers received a just reward—no more, no less than they had bargained for. They were recompensed according to a firm agreement.

(b) His Grace (20:14b)

The owner added, "I will give unto this last, even as unto thee." The late starters were getting far more than they expected because they did not bargain. The lord said in effect, "They trusted me and because they trusted me and served me faithfully, I will deal with them according to my grace."

(c) His Greatness (20:15a)

The owner asked, "Is it not lawful for me to do what I will with mine own?" He was absolute, undisputed sovereign over all that was his. He could do what he liked with it. What he did with it was his own business. Likewise our Lord is undisputed Lord and owner of the universe. He is well able to recompense adequately those who trust and obey.

(d) His Goodness (20:15b)

Finally the owner claimed to be good. He asked, "Is thine eye evil, because I am good?" Because he was good, he struck a fair bargain with those who demanded a contract. He gave them generous terms that they were glad to accept. Because he was good, he gave "good measure, pressed down, and shaken together, and running over" (Luke 6:38) even to those who came into his service late in the day. Likewise our Lord is absolutely good and good to all who trust Him.

(3) The Observation (20:16)

"So *the* last shall be first, and *the* first last" (italics added). Note the definite articles here and the word "many" in 19:30. The Lord did not use the word "all." Some who are first will still be first, and some who are last will still be last when the day of reckoning comes. Let us make sure then that in our service we do not try to bargain with our Lord; instead let us trust Him and serve Him with the spirit in which He serves us.

F. Ministry in the Kingdom (20:17-34)

1. The Price Revealed (20:17-19)

Here we read the Lord's most comprehensive statement so far regarding His impending crucifixion. Crucifixion was to be the price of our salvation, a terrible price indeed. In His statement He piled up detail after detail in an awesome display of divine foreknowledge. According to the law of compound probabilities, the chances against a prediction coming true increase enormously with each specific detail added to it. And of course the more unlikely the detail, the more unlikely the fulfillment.

Suppose I had said to my wife, "I am going to Chicago. While I am there I will be arrested and falsely accused of a crime. I will be humiliated in the court by the judge. I will be condemned to death and executed. But don't worry. Don't sell anything. Don't give away my books. Don't probate my will. I will be back three days after my funeral." I would not have made such a statement unless I had access to some extraordinary information, or I was insane, or I was trying to perpetrate a bizarre practical joke.

The Lord Jesus certainly was not insane, nor was He setting the stage for the greatest hoax in history. But He did have access to information that belonged to God only, information about the future.

What the Lord foretold about His approaching death did happen. He did die in Jerusalem. He was betrayed to the chief priests and scribes. He was condemned to death by the leaders of the Hebrew people. They did hand Him over to the Gentiles for execution. He was mocked by the Gentiles, for Herod and his men of war "set him at nought" (Luke 23:11). The Lord was scourged and He did die by crucifixion. Above all, and contrary to all the odds against the prophecy, He did rise from the dead. Moreover He did rise on the third day. Detail after detail was fulfilled, furnishing convincing proof that Jesus could do something that no one else could do: He could foretell the future accurately, infallibly, minutely.

The most famous of the soothsaying oracles of ancient times was the Delphic oracle. People came from all over to drink from the fountain of satanically inspired prophecy given by a pythoness. However, the prophetic utterances of the Delphic oracle were known to be of a cryptic, ambiguous nature. When Croesus, king of Lydia, was contemplating war with Persia, he consulted the Delphic oracle and was told, "If Croesus wars with Persia he will destroy a great nation." He took the prophecy to mean that he would destroy Persia, but the nation he destroyed was his own. Too bad he did not know Daniel, who could have told him that Persia would be victorious! (Daniel 7:5)

2. The Path Revealed (20:20-28)

a. The Quest of the Two Disciples (20:20-23)

(1) Their Mother (20:20-21)

What a contrast: the Lord talking to His disciples about a cross, and two of them approaching Him about a crown! Their mother was their spokeswoman. Matthew 20:20 calls her "the mother of Zebedee's children"; in other words she was the mother of James and John. Her name was Salome (Matthew 27:56; Mark 15:40; 16:1). Some have assumed that she was now a widow. She is thought to have been the sister of Mary, the Lord's mother (John 19:25), in which case James and John would have been the Lord's cousins. Perhaps it was their family ties that made them think they stood a better chance than the others of securing a favored position for themselves in the coming kingdom.

Evidently the disciples still thought the Lord was about to set up an earthly kingdom. It is extraordinary how thoroughly they ignored all the Lord's warnings of His coming death. Even when His death occurred in exact conformity to His repeated prophecies, they disbelieved His promise of resurrection.

Salome's prayer that her two sons be allowed to sit on the Lord's right hand and left hand was a mistake, but it did not altogether displease the Lord. At least she believed that He was the Messiah and that He was going to set up a kingdom. Would that the desire of all mothers and fathers were that their children might achieve greatness in the Lord's kingdom! Her ambition was more laudable than that which motivates many parents.

(2) Their Mistake (20:22-23)

Salome's sons were fired by a similar goal, but they did not know what they were asking. The Lord swiftly revealed their mistake. True, Jesus had talked about all twelve apostles sitting on thrones in the distant day when His kingdom would come (Matthew 19:28). But they did not know the price of a throne or the principle of securing one in His kingdom.

There was a cup to be drained, a cup of anguish and sorrow (Matthew 26:39,42). The contemplation of that cup would bring beads of blood to His brow in Gethsemane (Luke 22:44). There was to be a baptism of suffering in the chill waters of death. The tomb would come before the throne. There would be no crown without a cross. Could the two disciples participate in the cup and the baptism? They claimed that they could.

Behind their request and their reply was faith. They still believed that Jesus was a King. No one asks to be elevated to the side of a man who is going to the gallows. They had not yet grasped the fact that He was going to die. Even when He put the cross before them in terms of the two ordinances He later left with the church (the cup symbolizing His death for us, and baptism symbolizing our death with Him), they took His prophecy in their stride. They were sure they could endure any test that might come their way. "We are able," they said (20:22).

"Ye shall drink indeed of my cup, and be baptized with the baptism that I am baptized with," He said (20:23). And James and John did drink of His cup, but not to its fullness. They were immersed in the chill waters of death, but the waters were not nearly so icy as His. James was the first apostle to die and he died a martyr's death. John was the last of the apostles to die.

There is a place to be filled at the Lord's side "in the crowning day that's coming by and by."[15] But the right to that place is not His to give. It has to be earned. Although God gives unmerited salvation, He never gives unmerited reward. That reality ought to grip our souls.

b. The Quarrel with the Ten Disciples (20:24-28)

(1) An Explosion (20:24)

When the other disciples heard about Salome's request, their indignation knew no bounds. They felt that James and John had taken unfair advantage of their kinship to Jesus. They all aspired to the seats of supreme power in the kingdom, which they still imagined was just around the corner. They all had their eyes on self. How the Lord's heart must have been pained! He had just been setting the cross before them when, as Matthew recorded it, all this fuss broke out over positions in the kingdom. The disciples must not have been listening to a word He said. With His ominous words about the cup and the baptism still reverberating in their ears, they began their wrangling.

(2) An Explanation (20:25-27)

The Lord's patience with His people is marvelous. He did not scold the disciples. He accepted the implied tribute that they still believed Him to be a King. The Lord understood that they had not yet received the Holy Spirit and were spiritually handicapped. Gently He explained to them the difference between secular power as exercised by the Gentiles, and spiritual power as it would be entrusted to the disciples and exercised by them.

(a) Concerning Secular Power—The Worldly Concept (20:25)

"Ye know," Christ said, "that the princes of the Gentiles exercise dominion over them, and they that are great exercise authority upon them." The word translated "exercise authority" implies harsh use of authority. At that time half the known world was under the iron heel of Rome, so the Jews knew how severe Gentile rulers could be. The Romans exercised authority to increase their power, minister to their pride, and gain their own ends. Such ambition is contrary to the spirit of the Lord Jesus.

(b) Concerning Spiritual Power—The Wondrous Contrast (20:26-27)

In Christ's kingdom, whether in the purely spiritual realm of the church or in the more secular realm of the millennial empire, power and authority belong to those who have a humble serving spirit, not a haughty selfish spirit. Jesus said, "Whosoever will be great among you, let him be your minister [*diakonos*]; And whosoever will be chief among you, let him be your servant [*doulos*]."

I know a brother in Christ who has caught the spirit of these verses. He is not an eloquent preacher or the pastor of a great church. Rather, he is a successful businessman whose quiet influence for God is felt in the marketplace. He is also a wise and tender shepherd to a small flock of God's people. I will always remember my visits to his home. He invariably gives me the most comfortable chair in the house and contents himself with any corner he can find. Now he is getting on in years and uses a cane, but quietly and firmly and with the grace of a courtier he installs his visitor in the seat of honor, his own easy chair.

At bedtime he says, "Let me have your shoes." The first time I was in his home I was startled and asked, "Why do you want my shoes?"

"I am going to clean and polish them," he answered.

"They don't need it," I objected.

"Yes they do," he replied. "Besides, that's what I do for the Lord."

No matter how many guests he has, none can escape. Refusing to give up one's shoes makes no difference. The first thing that greets the visitor next morning is the sight of his shoes beside his bed, gleaming as if new. My friend has a serving spirit.

Years ago when I first joined the staff of Moody Bible Institute, the radio pastor was Robert Little. Bob was a gifted expositor and conducted a number of daily and weekly broadcasts over the Moody network. In addition he spoke at churches and conferences all over the country. His radio parish extended to millions and reached into city after city. People would come to see him or call in with their problems, great and small, so his study time was continually interrupted. His workload was overwhelming, but somehow Bob had time for them all.

Once when we were having coffee break together on campus, he told me this story: One day the telephone rang and a voice said, "Is this Pastor Little?"

"Yes, it is," Bob replied. "Can I help you?"

"Will you bury my dog?"

"I beg your pardon?"

"Will you come and bury my dog? My dog has just died. It's my only friend and I want it to have a Christian burial. I listen to you over WMBI. I live here in Chicago. I don't know any other ministers. Will you come and bury my dog?"

I asked Bob how he had responded to this unusual request. He said, "Of course I went. Look at it like this. Here was a man who had only one friend in the world, his dog. When his dog died, he wanted to treat its mortal remains with respect. So he turned to the only other friend he had—me."

"What did you do?" I asked.

"Well, we put his dog in a box. He went out to the garden, dug a hole, and put the box in the hole. Then I took off my hat and prayed for the man." Bob paused. "You know," he said, "that man will now go on listening to me on the radio. Who knows? One day he may turn to Christ."

Bob Little had learned the secret of true greatness. He had learned to be a servant.

(3) An Example (20:28)

Jesus concluded His explanation by using Himself as an example of serving: "The Son of man came not to be ministered unto, but to minister, and to give his life a ransom for many." There it was again—the cross. The Lord's words here remind us of Paul's magnificent christological passage in which he explained that even though Christ Jesus was equal with God, He humbled Himself by becoming a man, by becoming a servant (*doulos,* "a slave"), and by becoming "obedient unto death, even the death of the cross." Because He humbled Himself, He is now exalted and has a name above all other names. One day every knee will bow before that name and every tongue will confess Him to be Lord (Philippians 2:5-11).

Are we following the Lord's example? Do we want to be ministered to or do we want to minister? Jesus came to give His life in service every moment of every day for over thirty-three years. He came to give His life in sacrifice on a cross of shame. Such is the path of ministry in the kingdom.

3. The Power Revealed (20:29-34)

a. The Men (20:29-30)

Great crowds were on the road going to Jerusalem. They were pilgrims on the way to celebrate the Passover. Apparently the Lord was somewhat ahead of the crowd as He came from the Jordan and entered Jericho by its eastern gate. He was soon to perform another of His gracious miracles.

Matthew said that there were two blind men and that the miracle took place as Jesus was leaving Jericho. Mark in his parallel account mentioned the principal blind man, Bartimaeus, indicated that the miracle took place as Jesus was leaving Jericho, and also referred to the Lord's entry into Jericho (Mark 10:46-52). Luke in his parallel account mentioned the principal blind man and indicated that he "sat by the way side begging" as Jesus drew near to Jericho (Luke 18:35).

What probably happened was that Bartimaeus and his companion were begging near the eastern gate of the city. Jesus, ahead of the crowd, passed them by. Then came the crowd, and Bartimaeus learned that the multitude was hard on the heels of Jesus. Bartimaeus had missed the opportunity of a lifetime. The Lord had passed by on His way to Jerusalem and would never come that way again. Jesus and the excited crowds had now gone into Jericho and the blind men, having no sure hope of catching up to Him in the city, hurried around the wall to the southern gate through which Jesus would eventually emerge.[16]

In the city the Lord sought out and saved Zacchaeus (Luke 19:1-10).

Meanwhile the two blind men had settled themselves in a good location and were determined not to waste their last opportunity to receive their sight. In due time they heard the crowd coming out of Jericho and raised their voices in urgent cries, "Have mercy on us, O Lord, thou son of David" (Matthew 20:30). "Son of David" was a popular Jewish title for the Messiah.

The two blind men were aware of their desperate need for Christ. One reason people resist the gospel today is that they do not recognize themselves as blind and lost. We need more Holy Ghost-inspired preaching on sin and its consequences. We need to teach the ten commandments to lay a moral foundation for the gospel. Probably no one is truly converted who is not first thoroughly convicted (John 16:8-11). It was when people were "pricked in their heart" that they cried out, "Men and brethren, what shall we do?" (Acts 2:37)

The reason we have so many false professions in our churches is that people are talked into "accepting Christ" without first being made aware of their lostness. The old Puritans used to say that in working on souls, it was necessary to put in the sharp needle of conviction before trying to pull through the thread of salvation. Jesus said much the same in Matthew 9:12: "They that be whole need not a physician, but they that are sick."

b. The Multitude (20:31)

Beggars were a common sight. They were an annoyance even when they kept their place and quietly asked for alms, but when they loudly called out to Christ, the multitude had no sympathy. The people tramping past the blind men bluntly told them to be quiet. But the two men knew they needed Christ and, crowd or no crowd, opposition or no opposition, they were not going to be silenced. They were not intimidated by the heartless throng. The blind men ignored their critics. Matthew wrote, "They cried the more, saying, Have mercy on us, O Lord, thou son of David."

How easily people are kept from Christ by fear of their particular crowd! Even when it is part of a popular movement that for the moment applauds the Master and His men, the crowd is no friend to a genuinely seeking soul. The crowd, when all is said and done, is the crowd. It will congratulate today and crucify tomorrow.

The crowd does not like to be disturbed. Think of those who make up your crowd—your professional peers, perhaps the kids at school, the gang, the members of your club. If you lift up your voice to express some heartfelt need to come to Christ, and if you do it in a way that makes your crowd feel ill at ease, they will try to silence you. Someone will make a cutting remark.

The two blind men were made of sterner stuff than to be silenced or kept from Christ by those in the crowd who rudely told them to "hold their peace." Their sense of need was stronger than any desire to be at peace with the multitude who blocked their way to Jesus. So "they cried the more."

c. The Master (20:32-34)

(1) His Call (20:32)

"Jesus stood still." He knew the blind men were there of course; He knew all about them. By standing still He made it possible for them to come to Him at last. We can imagine that the milling multitudes stood still too. It was one of those moments when the universe holds its breath. Two men were coming to Christ.

The Lord gave the blind men a chance to express their need. Often the over-eager soulwinner puts words into the mouth of the one he is bringing to Jesus. It would be far better to ask questions so that the lost one can express both need and faith in his own words. "What do you want me to do?" Jesus asked in effect.

(2) His Compassion (20:33-34a)

The blind men turned in the direction of that kind, compelling voice. Revealing their hearts' hunger and hope, they said, "Lord, that our eyes may be opened" (20:33). The Lord's heart went out to them. "Jesus had compassion on them," Matthew said (20:34). Their desperation and determination moved Him and He "touched their eyes."

The enormity of their demand was no deterrent to the Lord. As John Newton wrote, "Jesus loves to answer prayer"; he continued:

> Thou art coming to a King;
> Large petitions with thee bring;
> For His grace and power are such,
> None can ever ask too much.[17]

(3) His Converts (20:34b)

The astonishing miracle took place: "Immediately their eyes received sight." Blind eyes were made to see and the first thing they saw was Jesus. Imagine coming out of darkness into the light of day, seeing nothing but blackness and then seeing Him! "They followed him," Matthew concluded. Of course they did. With such a vision before their newly opened eyes, of course they did.

They saw plenty of other things that they had never seen before: the beauty of nature, the walls of Jericho, the expression on a human face, color, the moving pageant of constantly changing crowds. But they had eyes only for Jesus. Ten thousand new sensations were being recorded in their brains. A new world had opened up before them. They saw themselves, but they followed Jesus. That is what happens when a person has a genuine encounter with God's beloved Son.

II. THE PUBLIC DISPUTES (21:1–23:39)

We have come to another turning point in Matthew's Gospel: here the private discussions give way to the public disputes, which are precipitated by the Lord's triumphant entry into Jerusalem. With this event the Lord's last crowded week on earth begins. He initiates the action, for since the nation of Israel has rejected Him, He now rejects the nation.

A. Crises (21:1-22)

1. The Sign of the Foretold Triumph (21:1-17)

a. The Heralding of the Messiah of Israel (21:1-7)

A short time before the triumphal entry, Jesus had raised Lazarus from the dead. That miracle had convinced the Sanhedrin of the urgent need to get rid of Him once and for all, lest popular enthusiasm for this unwanted Messiah spark Roman intervention (John 11:47-54). After resurrecting Lazarus, Jesus had left Bethany, but evidently He had subsequently returned. Now He left that happy, peaceful home again and headed toward Jerusalem to force a confrontation on the Jews.

According to Edersheim "it was a bright day in early spring."[18] Matthew 21:2 tells us that the Lord sent a couple of His disciples to "the village over against you" (just off the high road), presumably Bethphage, to gain possession of the ass's colt.[19]

(1) The Place (21:1)

There is some uncertainty about the location of Bethphage. *Bethphage,* which means "house of figs," was an appropriate designation for a region that abounded in luxurious fig trees. The name seems to have been attached to the district in general, and in particular to a little village within the boundaries of the outskirts of Jerusalem. Those boundaries are sometimes said to have been two thousand cubits (about a mile) beyond the city walls. So Bethphage may have been halfway between the city walls and Bethany.

(2) The Plan (21:2-3)

The two disciples found the animal as directed, were challenged as forewarned, and obtained the use of it as instructed.

We must keep in mind that at this time of the year enormous crowds came to Jerusalem for the Passover feast. Visitors filled the city to capacity and overflowed to every available accommodation in nearby villages. News spread swiftly among the crowds that Jesus was coming, that He had commandeered the use of an ass's colt, and that He was about to march in triumph into Jerusalem. Expectation was fanned to a fever pitch and a great multitude went forth to meet Him. Many of them were anxious to see the One who had just raised a man from the dead, but among the multitude were a number of Pharisees whose hearts were filled with bitterness, jealousy, and hatred.

In the meantime, somewhere along the road,[20] Jesus and His companions met the two disciples with the colt.

(3) The Prophecy (21:4-5)

The Lord's purpose was extraordinary, unlike that of His usual low-key entrances into Jerusalem and His normal practice of discouraging popular demonstrations. Matthew told us that He deliberately provoked this demonstration to fulfill the prophecy of Zechariah 9:9. The Lord did not just yield to the clamor of the crowd; He actually caused the clamor—for the purpose of fulfilling prophecy.

The prophecy, as Matthew quoted it, said, "Behold, thy King cometh unto thee, meek, and sitting upon an ass, and a colt the foal of an ass" (21:5). There was a breed of swift asses used by kings in the East (Judges 10:4; 1 Kings 1:33), but the animal in Matthew 21:5 was bred to be a beast of burden. There was little in this scene to disturb Roman officialdom. Men like Pilate were familiar with an emperor's triumphal entry with chariots, war horses, marching legions in gleaming armor, heralds, weapons, and long lines of captives. There was nothing of interest in this procession of excitable Jews accompanying a man in a peasant's homespun robe as He rode a beast of burden into Jerusalem. There was nothing to pose a threat in a cavalcade of rude countrymen and fishermen waving palm branches and chanting Psalms.

(4) The Presentation (21:6-7)

But the Lord's entry was triumphal just the same. Through all the centuries following, the world has celebrated it on Palm Sunday. Almost forgotten are the proud pageants of emperors, but remembered to this day is the procession of the meek King who sat on an ass and used old clothes for a saddle and palm fronds for a carpet.

Combining meekness and majesty, the Lord came into the city. His triumphant entry was His last appeal to Jerusalem to recognize its King.

b. The Hosannas of the Multitudes of Israel (21:8-14)

(1) Jubilation (21:8-9)

We can retrace the journeys of the multitudes. Some followed Jesus from Bethany and others came to meet Him from Jerusalem. And we can picture the two crowds merging and forming a procession. Edersheim described the scene:

> The long procession swept up and over the ridge where first begins "the descent of the Mount of Olives" towards Jerusalem. At this point the first view is caught of the southeastern corner of the City. The Temple and the more northern portions are hid by the slope of Olivet on the right; what is seen is only Mount Zion....At that time it rose, terrace upon terrace, from the Palace of the Maccabees and that of the High-Priest, a very city of palaces, till the eye rested in the summit on that castle, city, and palace, with its frowning towers and magnificent gardens, the royal abode of Herod, supposed to occupy the very site of the Palace of David....It may have been just as the precise point of the road was reached, where "the City of David" first suddenly emerges into view, "at the descent of the Mount of Olives," "that the whole multitude of the disciples began to rejoice and praise God with a loud voice for all the mighty works that they had seen" [Luke 19:37].[21]

The song the multitude raised was from the hallel that was sung at every Passover: "Hosanna [Save now!] to the son of David:

Blessed is he that cometh in the name of the Lord; Hosanna in the highest" (Matthew 21:9; see Psalm 118:25-26). Jewish tradition says that Psalm 118:25-28 was chanted antiphonally as the people of Jerusalem welcomed pilgrims coming for the feast. The citizens of Jerusalem chanted the first clause of each verse and the pilgrims answered with the second clause. When they reached the last verse of the Psalm (118:29), both groups blended their voices to sing it in unison and then added Psalm 103:17 as a conclusion.

However, more than an ordinary pilgrim-welcome was extended to Jesus. The shouts rang out across the valley. Luke's Gospel tells us that the clamor infuriated the Pharisees, who demanded that Jesus silence His disciples. The Lord refused. "I tell you," He said, "if these should hold their peace, the stones would immediately cry out" (Luke 19:40).

The procession continued on its way. The road dipped and for a moment the city vanished behind a ridge of Olivet. But soon the path rose again and climbed over rugged terrain until it reached an outcropping of smooth rock where the whole city burst into view. Straight ahead was the Kidron valley, here seen at its greatest depth where it joined the valley of Hinnom. From this point Jerusalem seemed to be a city "rising out of a deep abyss."[22]

(2) Jerusalem (21:10-11)

At last the Lord arrived in Jerusalem. Matthew said, "All the city was moved, saying, Who is this?" (21:10) From the Greek word translated "moved" we have derived our English word *seismic*. The Lord's triumphal entry shook Jerusalem morally and spiritually from end to end. We can be sure that although the Roman authorities were not alarmed because they were used to Jewish demonstrativeness, they kept a watchful eye on all this popular clamor. The Jewish authorities were enraged. Jews from all over the diaspora (they were in Jerusalem for the Passover) were astonished and wanted to know who the man was whose entrance into the city had caused such a stir. The answer was, "Jesus the prophet of Nazareth of Galilee" (21:11).

(3) Judgment (21:12-13)

The activities of this Messiah were not yet over. Jesus went into the temple courts,[23] as He had done once before (John 2:13-16), with the express purpose of cleansing them. The Lord's ministry thus began and ended with a cleansing of the temple. When the

Jewish authorities, who profited from the temple trade, immediately went back to their profaning of the temple, Jesus announced the fact that the whole edifice would be pulled down (Matthew 24:1-2).

The part of the temple that had become "a den of thieves" (21:13) was the court of the Gentiles. It was separated from the environs of the sanctuary by a stone partition. The general Jewish contempt for Gentiles led the priests to sanction the commercialization of their court and doubtless added to the Lord's wrath. The granting of concessions to merchants and money-changers was financially rewarding to the Jewish authorities.

Oxen, sheep, and doves were in constant demand for the general offerings. As Passover time drew near and each family required a lamb, the demand for lambs increased. According to Josephus it was not unusual for two hundred thousand lambs to be required for the Passover feast. Even if we allow for exaggeration, this figure gives some idea of the kind of traffic that had overtaken the court of the Gentiles.

Then too, on the twenty-fifth day of the month Adar (eighteen or nineteen days before Passover), tax officers set up business in that court to collect the annual half-shekel temple tax. Coins bearing a heathen inscription or a heathen monarch's image could not be paid into the temple treasury, so money-changers also set up business to convert foreign money or other coins into half-shekels— at a price. Every Israelite who had not already paid the tax in his hometown had to pay the collector in the temple, so business was brisk. The money-changers profited from converting secular money into sacred money and perhaps from arranging loans for the poor.

(a) The Sanctuary Cleansed (21:12)

The Lord's sudden appearance in the temple court was part of His planned confrontation with the nation of Israel. His all-seeing eyes must have noticed many other social abuses in the city, but He went straight to the temple, to the heart of the city, for "judgment must begin at the house of God" (1 Peter 4:17). If the temple was wrong, everything was wrong.[24] Political reformers invariably make the mistake of thinking that they can cleanse society by attacking the social ills of mankind. What is needed is not reformation but regeneration. Society will be changed automatically if human hearts are changed. That is why Jesus went to the temple; that was the place to begin. Israel needed radical heart surgery, not just a band-aid. With true insight, Jesus passed over social abuses for the time being and dealt with spiritual abuses.

In the Apocalypse, John saw a city without a temple (Revelation 21:22); the whole city had become a temple. The day will come when the world will be filled with the knowledge of God as the waters now cover the sea (see Isaiah 11:9), but not until the second coming of Christ.

In the temple the Lord cast out those who bought and sold. There was something so authoritative about Him, something so awesome, that they fled from Him. With magnificent contempt He "overthrew the *tables* of the moneychangers," and their coins rolled and rattled far and wide; with sublime restraint He threw over "the *seats* of them that sold doves" (Matthew 21:12, italics added). Not for a moment would He think of harming the unoffending birds by turning over the tables on which their cages stood. The temple authorities did not dare to interfere.

(b) The Scriptures Confirmed (21:13)

Then in a scathing denunciation of the whole commercial scheme sponsored by the chief priests, the Lord said, "It is written, My house shall be called the house of prayer; but ye have made it a den of thieves." His words were a composite quotation from Isaiah 56:7 and Jeremiah 7:11. Jesus was likening the temple, as run by the chief priests, to a robber's cave. They had turned the hallowed courts into an unholy cavern where brigands squabbled over their ill-gotten gains.

(4) Jesus (21:14)

There is a lovely footnote to the story of the cleansing of the temple. Amid all the debris—overturned tables and chairs and coins of a score of nations scattered over the floor—Jesus healed the blind and lame who came to Him in the temple.

In quoting from the prophet Isaiah, the Lord had used only one sentence, but the temple authorities were versed enough in the Scriptures to know the whole context: "Mine house shall be called an house of prayer for all people [all nations]. The Lord God which gathereth the outcasts of Israel saith, Yet will I gather others to him, beside those that are gathered unto him" (Isaiah 56:7-8). And so He did. Then and there in that cleansed Gentile court, the Lord gathered to Himself the outcasts of Israel, as in the millennial age He will gather all nations to worship in the rebuilt temple.

c. The Hostility of the Masters of Israel (21:15-17)

(1) Displeasure (21:15-16)

The chief priests, rebuked publicly and shamed before all the people, were boiling inwardly with impotent rage. They were "sore displeased," as Matthew put it (21:15). At the moment they were powerless to stop the Lord, but they did venture a remonstrance. "When the chief priests and scribes saw the wonderful things that he did, and the children crying in the temple, and saying, Hosanna to the son of David; they were sore displeased, And said unto him, Hearest thou what these say?" Of course He did. True, the children were picking up the words of their elders, but it delighted the soul of the Savior. It was like the music of Heaven in His ears. He might well have cast the question right back at the priests: "Hearest *thou* what these say?"

The children were saying, "Hosanna." As we have seen, the word literally means "save now." In other words, they were singing, "Save now the Son of David"—the Hebrew version of the British slogan "God save the king!"

What can we say about the abysmal wickedness of these chief priests and scribes who were supposed to be the spiritual leaders of Israel? "They saw the wonderful things that he did" and they were angry! As Campbell Morgan said, "We do not want to know anything more about them."[25]

Jesus answered the masters of Israel, as He so often did, by quoting Scripture. Matthew 21:16 says, "Jesus saith unto them, Yea; have ye never read, Out of the mouth of babes and sucklings thou hast perfected praise?" (see Psalm 8:2). The chief priest and scribes were as much afraid of the Lord's Bible as they were of Him.

(2) Departure (21:17)

With that parting shot the Lord turned His back on the religious leaders. He went back to Bethany and spent the night there. In so doing He circumvented both a popular uprising in His favor and a nocturnal attack on Himself.

2. The Sign of the Fruitless Tree (21:18-22)

a. The Lord's Coming to the Tree (21:18-19a)

Mark's account (Mark 11), which is more chronological than Matthew's, indicates that the incident involving the fig tree also took place on the day after the triumphal entry but before the cleansing of the temple.

In the Holy Land fig trees were considered so valuable that a person who cut one down, even if it yielded meager crops, was thought to be deserving of death at the hand of God. Normally a fig tree was prolific. In a suitable location a tree bore three crops a year and ripe figs hung on it for ten months of the year. It was barren for two months (April and May) before the first crop ripened. The first crop ripened toward the end of June; the second crop ripened in August; the third crop, often small and of little commercial value, ripened in September and hung all winter on the tree.

Although it was considered a crime among the Jews to destroy a fruit-bearing fig tree, there was no such protection for a barren tree. Not only did a barren tree yield no fruit; it also occupied valuable space that could have been given to a good tree. Moreover its roots depleted the soil of nutrients.

The incident involving the fig tree took place in April. A tree would not normally be bearing new fruit that early, but it might well have had some of the previous year's figs on it. Moreover at least two varieties of fig trees were found in the Holy Land, and one variety (mentioned in Isaiah 28:4) produced what was called "the first ripe fig before summer"; one of the features of this variety was that its fruit appeared before its leaves.

The tree in Matthew 21:19 was in full, luxuriant foliage and evidently enjoyed an unusually favorable location. It was standing alone by the wayside in a conspicuous place. When the Lord, who could not have been mistaken as to various fig seasons, saw the tree, He expected it to live up to its promise and provide Him and His hungry disciples with fruit. The leaves made an outward profession of vigorous life, but their boast was barren. The branches bore neither a remnant of the previous year's fruit nor "the first ripe fig before summer." The tree had nothing to offer its Creator.

b. The Lord's Cursing of the Tree (21:19b-20)

Jesus said to the tree, "Let no fruit grow on thee henceforward for ever [*eis ton aiōna,* 'to the end of the age']." Matthew reported, "Presently the fig tree withered away" (21:19). The word translated "presently" is *parachrēma,* which means "at once" or "on the spot." The disciples were astonished. "How soon is the fig tree withered away!" they exclaimed.

The miracle of the fig tree is unique in the ministry of Jesus because it was His only judgment miracle. His cursing of the fig tree was a symbolic act, not a vindictive act. The fig tree represented the highly favored nation of Israel, which should have had so much to offer God and the world. Jesus had come looking for fruit, but had found nothing but leaves. Just the day before, the religious leaders had given Him further evidence of the nation's barrenness in their carping criticism of the innocent praise of children in the temple. Now in this symbolic act He officially withdrew His blessing from the nation. Soon Israel would wither and die and then remain bereft of national life and spiritual fruit until the end of the age.

In Matthew 23 this symbolic cursing is replaced by specific cursing of the nation that had so terribly debased its mission.

c. The Lord's Comment on the Tree (21:21-22)

The Lord did not at this time explain the symbolic significance of the cursing of the fig tree. Instead He made a practical application. Picking up on the disciples' comment about the swift death of the barren tree, He gave them a lesson in faith.

Behind the symbolic cursing of the nation of Israel was Jewish intransigent unbelief, but the Hebrew nation had been founded on faith (Genesis 12:1-4; 15:6) and nurtured on faith (Hebrews 11). The Lord taught the disciples not to falter in faith, for faith can move mountains; faith can remove all obstacles.

The Lord was not speaking of faith in the abstract or faith as a vague sentiment. Even the unsaved glibly say, "Just have faith." In what or in whom do they have faith? Faith alone does nothing. Faith must be in the Lord. Faith is only the link, only the power line that puts us in touch with the need at one end and the power at the other.

Jesus said, "All things, whatsoever ye shall ask in prayer, believing, ye shall receive" (Matthew 21:22). His statement is of course conditioned by His will (1 John 5:14-16). In Matthew 21:22 we have the broad general rule for prayer. The rule is liberal, gracious, and awesome in potential, but it is qualified by just and reasonable limitations expounded elsewhere in the Scriptures (James 4:2-3; 2 Corinthians 12:7-9; Luke 22:42).

B. Causes (21:23–22:14)

1. A Parable of Responsibility (21:23-32)

The public disputes began in earnest as the Lord told three parables directed at the sin and rejection of the nation of Israel.

The first parable was given in response to a demand by an official delegation from the Sanhedrin who challenged His right to do what He did and teach as He taught.

a. The Context of the Parable (21:23-27)

(1) The Demand of the Temple Authorities (21:23)

The Lord had dealt the authorities a direct and devastating blow by ridding the temple of its profitable trade, one in which members of the Sanhedrin had vested interests. He had called the whole conglomeration a "den of thieves" (21:13).

The populace had seen the difference in the Lord's style of teaching. "He taught them as one having authority, and not as the scribes" (7:29). The Jewish leaders were up in arms but they were afraid of Him, afraid of His wisdom and power, afraid of His influence over the people. They decided that the best strategy was to discredit Him in the eyes of the people; if that failed, they would catch Him saying something wrong and use His own words against Him; if that failed, they would move secretly and swiftly to have Him put to death.

The day after the cleansing of the court of the Gentiles, the Lord was back in the temple. He was poaching on the Sanhedrin's preserve and challenging their authority (or so it seemed to them, for the Lord always upheld constituted authority, if not the way it was wielded). He was teaching an appreciative audience who hung on His words in a way they never hung on the words of the scribes. The leaders felt that their power base was being eroded, and power was what mattered to them—power and money.

It was evident that the delegation that came to Jesus was official. Matthew wrote, "The chief priests and the elders of the people came unto him." Mark and Luke indicated that scribes (teachers of the law) also came (Mark 11:27; Luke 20:1), so all segments of the Sanhedrin were present. This seems to be the first time this governing body took formal notice of the Lord's claims and actions.

The leaders had witnessed the triumphal entry into Jerusalem, the loud *hosanna*s of the people, the cleansing of the temple, the miracles of healing in its courts, and teaching unlike any that had ever before fallen from mortal lips. Yet instead of crowning Him, the leaders confronted Him. "By what authority doest thou these things? and who gave thee this authority?" they asked. That was the problem. He was not part of the system; He had not graduated from their schools; He acted outside the establishment; He had not asked for their permission to teach in the temple courts; He had acted in what they considered to be a highhanded way against their interests. Who did He think He was? What right had He to do what He did? How dare He challenge them and the things they sanctioned?

Well, to begin with, He was the Son of David. That was something they could check for themselves in the temple archives. Moreover He was the Son of God. That is where His authority came from, although He did not tell them so. His response was a marvelous demonstration of His wisdom.

(2) The Dilemma of the Temple Authorities (21:24-26)

(a) The Proposal (21:24-25a)

The Lord countered the Sanhedrin's question with another question. "Jesus answered and said unto them, I also will ask you one thing, which if ye tell me, I in like wise will tell you by what authority I do these things. The baptism of John, whence was it? from heaven, or of men?" The Lord's authority derived from the same source as John's: Heaven. Christ's question really answered their question, but He had them on the horns of a dilemma.

(b) The Problem (21:25b-26)

The Sanhedrin had not accepted John the Baptist's ministry. In fact John had denounced the religious leaders of Israel as a "generation of vipers" (3:7). But the common people held John in high esteem as a martyr prophet; for the moment they were convinced that Christ was a prophet too (21:11) and they were enthusiastically supporting Him. With the temple courts crowded with such people, the leaders did not dare to say that John was *not* "a man sent from God" (John 1:6). On the other hand if they admitted that John was God-sent, they would have to acknowledge Jesus too because John had identified Jesus as the Christ. John merely claimed to be the forerunner of Christ.

(3) The Decision of the Temple Authorities (21:27)

Faced with the Lord's question, the leaders took refuge in an evasion—and here in the King James version we find a masterful play on words. "We cannot tell," they said. "Neither tell I you by what authority I do these things," Jesus replied.

Why did the Lord not reveal the source of His authority? Because it would not have done any good. The last light God had sent to the leaders was that of John and they had rejected that light. If they were deliberately blind to the source of John's authority, they would be equally blind to the source of Christ's authority. God only gives us more light when we respond to the light we have.

b. The Content of the Parable (21:28-32)

We must always remember that Jesus loved the members of the Sanhedrin. They were lost, blind, bitter, worldly, unscrupulous, and self-seeking, but He loved them. He was going to die for them. His parable, while pointed in its truth, was spoken with love for their deluded souls.

Both this parable (21:28-32) and the next one (21:33-46) related to the vineyard. Both parables were about the nation of Israel, for the vine represents Israel up to the time the nation rejected Christ. (The fig represents Israel in the present age, and the olive represents Israel as it will be in a coming day when at last the nation turns to Christ; see Romans 11). Parables of the vineyard are all based on Isaiah's song of the vineyard (Isaiah 5).

(1) How Appropriate the Parable Was (21:28-31a)

The first parable was about responsibility and accountability. A man told his two sons to go and work in his vineyard. The first son refused to go, but afterward repented and went. The second son promised to do as he was told, but never did so. The first son, who seemed to be rebellious, proved to be righteous. The second son, who seemed to be righteous, proved to be rebellious.

After telling the story the Lord forced the leaders, who had just refused to commit themselves publicly about the authority of John's ministry, to commit themselves anyway. He simply asked them which of the two sons did the will of his father. The answer was obvious. They had no option but to say "The first" (21:31).

(2) How Applicable the Parable Was (21:31b-32)

The Lord's application was devastating. There was no question that John the Baptist had come "in the way of righteousness" (21:32). His lifestyle should have appealed to the Jewish leaders, for he had exhibited what they thought righteousness was all about: prayer, fasting, almsgiving. But they had rejected John's ministry.

They appeared to be righteous, but they proved to be more rebellious than publicans and harlots.

Publicans and harlots would not have been expected to respond to John's call for repentance, but they acted like the son in the parable who was initially defiant and later repentant. They appeared to be rebellious, but they proved to be righteous. Jesus said to the leaders:

> Verily I say unto you, That the publicans and the harlots go into the kingdom of God before you. For John came unto you in the way of righteousness, and ye believed him not: but the publicans and the harlots believed him: and ye, when ye had seen it, repented not afterward, that ye might believe him.

Thus the religious leaders, having rejected John's authority and now rejecting Christ's authority, stood condemned by the repentance and obedience of the publicans and harlots, the people they despised most. How great and terrible was the leaders' responsibility before God!

The Lord gave these spiritually blind rulers of the nation of Israel no opportunity to reply. Even while the sword of the parable of accountability was twisting in their souls, He told them another vineyard story. The first parable had emphasized the character of their unbelief. The next one, dealing with retribution, would reveal the criminality of their unbelief.

2. A Parable of Retribution (21:33-46)

a. The Lord and His Vineyard (21:33-39)

(1) The Householder (21:33a-c)

The householder, who was the owner of the vineyard, cultivated the soil, planted the vines, provided hedges and a watchtower for protection, and dug a winepress for processing the fruit. He did all that care and forethought could suggest for the good of the vineyard.

The householder represents God, and the vineyard represents the unique nation of Israel. Israel owes its existence to the direct planting of God. Its founding father Abraham was called by God and told that a nation would spring from his seed (Genesis 12–13). The vine of Israel was nurtured in Egypt and then transplanted to a prepared and promised land. The land is small today, but when the full scope of God's promise is fulfilled, it will stretch from the Euphrates to the Nile (Genesis 15:18).

The land God gave to Israel was central to all the great nations of antiquity. Three continents (Europe, Africa, and Asia) spread out like spokes from its hub. Recognizing Israel's strategic location, the empires of Egypt, Assyria, Babylon, Persia, Greece, and Rome coveted its land. Versatile and varied, the land of Israel had four seasons and was astonishingly productive—"a land flowing with milk and honey."

Israel is protected by mountains and deserts, yet its chief bulwark is God. Of all the nations in the world, Israel alone exists in treaty relationship with God. He is its owner; the land is called His land. More than once God has warned other nations against any ill-treatment of the Jews (Genesis 12:3; 15:13-14). In preparing Israel for its role as His ambassador to the rest of the world, God gave the nation not only His promises, but also His precepts and a succession of great and gifted men to write the sacred pages of its unique Book.

(2) The Husbandmen (21:33d-39)

The husbandmen in the parable represent Israel's priests, rulers, and elders, to whom God entrusted the care of the vineyard of Israel. What a miserable crowd they were! They treated the vineyard as though it belonged to them. The Lord graphically portrayed their persistent rebelliousness: "[The householder] sent his servants to the husbandmen, that they might receive the fruits [of the vineyard]. And the husbandmen took his servants, and beat one, and killed another, and stoned another" (21:34-35). This happened again and again. The long history of the ill-treatment of Israel's prophets is a commentary on this part of the parable (1 Kings 18:13; 22:24-27; 2 Kings 6:31; 2 Chronicles 24:19-22; 36:15-16; Hebrews 11:35-38).

The Lord then brought the story up to date: "Last of all [the householder] sent unto [the husbandmen] his son, saying, They will reverence my son" (Matthew 21:37). This final messenger was of quite a different caliber and character from the householder's servants. Likewise there was all the difference in the world between Moses and Jesus (Hebrews 3:3-6); between John the Baptist and Jesus there was a great gulf fixed. Between the greatest of the prophets and Jesus was a difference not only of degree but also of kind. He was the owner's Son. The implication was unmistakable: Jesus was claiming to be God's Son.

b. The Lord and His Vengeance (21:40-46)

(1) The Appeal (21:40-41)

(a) The Question Asked (21:40)

The Lord showed Israel's religious leaders where their wickedness was leading them. Instead of giving reverence to (standing in awe of) God's Son, they were plotting His death. With majestic finesse, the Lord forced them to act as their own judge and jury and pass sentence on themselves. He asked, "When the lord therefore of the vineyard cometh, what will he do unto those husbandmen?" The story was so gripping and it was told with such realism that those men were carried along by it. Forced for the moment to forget their hatred of Jesus, they blurted out the truth.

(b) The Question Answered (21:41)

They said, "[The householder] will miserably destroy those wicked men." The rulers were so caught up in the spirit of the story that they employed an unusual but vivid figure of speech known as *paronomasia* ("the repetition of words similar in sound, but not necessarily similar in sense").[26] The words they used were *kakous kakōs,* so their answer could be rendered, "He will *miserably* destroy those *miserable* men" or "He will put those *wretches* to a *wretched* death."

(2) The Application (21:42-46)

(a) A Solemn Revelation (21:42-44)

i. From the Scriptures (21:42)

There was no need for the Lord to say any more. The religious leaders had pronounced judgment on themselves, as they soon realized. However, we read in Mathtew 21:42 that He added a solemn revelation: "Did ye never read in the scriptures, The stone which the builders rejected, the same is become the head of the corner: this is the Lord's doing, and it is marvellous in our eyes?" (a quotation from Psalm 118:22-23). Thus the Lord brought home to them their folly.

Those men were eager enough to set up the Messianic kingdom. Nothing would have pleased them more than to have a militant Messiah who would smash the power of Rome and make Jerusalem the capital of a new world empire and themselves the chief administrators of it all. But in their blindness they were rejecting the very Messiah who was the cornerstone of the kingdom.

ii. From the Savior (21:43-44)

Israel was about to lose everything. Jesus said to its leaders, "Therefore say I unto you, The kingdom of God shall be taken from you, and given to a nation bringing forth the fruits thereof. And whosoever shall fall on this stone shall be broken: but on whomsoever it shall fall, it will grind him to powder."

Christ is the stone. Even the religious leaders recognized that. They did not, however, catch all the implications of the symbolism. To Israel, then and there, Christ was a stumbling stone and a rock of offense (Isaiah 8:14-15; Romans 9:32-33; 1 Corinthians 1:23; 1 Peter 2:8) because He did not come as a militant Messiah in pomp and splendor, but as a humble workingman from Nazareth. The nation stumbled over such a Christ.[27]

Because of Israel's unbelief, the kingdom of God was about to be taken away from the Jews. When Nebuchadnezzar rose to world power, Israel lost its political ascendancy over the nations and will not get it back "until the times of the Gentiles be fulfilled" (Luke 21:24) when Christ returns to reign.[28] Because of Calvary, Israel lost its spiritual ascendancy over the nations and will not get that back "until the fulness of the Gentiles be come in" (Romans 11:25) at the time of the rapture of the church. Then God will again speak to mankind through the Jews, as we discover in the book of Revelation.

For almost two thousand years God has been using the church[29] as His instrument in the world. The Jews are in the backwaters and the flood tides flow in Gentile lands. But this age is only a parenthesis in God's dealings with the human race. When His present purposes are fulfilled, "the kingdom of God shall be…given to a nation bringing forth the fruits thereof." This nation will be the new nation of Israel that will come into being at Christ's return. The Jews as a people will at last turn to Him and become the heart of the millennial kingdom on earth. Isaiah foretold such a new nation of Israel (Isaiah 66:7-14). The new nation cannot be the church, for the church is not a nation; it transcends all nations.

The prophecy of the stone in Matthew 21:44 was one of mercy and judgment for those listening to Christ that day. "Whosoever shall fall on this stone shall be broken," Jesus said. But a broken man can be healed. The nation of Israel fell over Christ when, assembled before Pilate, it cried for His death. But in God's mercy many Jews were healed on the day of Pentecost and thereafter, and many found their way into the church.

"But," Jesus added, "on whomsoever [this stone] shall fall, it will grind him to powder." From such a judgment, brought on by continuing unrepentance, there could be no recovery. For unrepentant people there remains nothing but utter ruin.

(b) A Swift Reaction (21:45-46)

i. The Leaders' Concern (21:45)

"When the chief priests and Pharisees had heard his parables, they perceived that he spake of them." However, they did not show any signs of repentance. Presumably Matthew mentioned the Pharisees here because they carried a lot of weight in the Sanhedrin. Before Calvary, it was the Pharisees who predominated in Israel's enmity toward Jesus; after the resurrection and Pentecost, it was the Sadducees.

ii. The Leaders' Caution (21:46)

If they dared, the Sanhedrin would have arrested Jesus right then and there in the temple court. Prudence and fear of the multitude held them back. They decided to bide their time, for the day would soon come when the fickle mob, who now "took him for a prophet," would be howling for His death.

3. A Parable of Rejection (22:1-14)

Matthew said, "And Jesus answered" (22:1). He knew what those chief priests and Pharisees were thinking and He answered what was in their hearts by telling another parable. In this story the rejected son of the owner of the vineyard is now the king's son for whom a marriage feast is being prepared.

This was the last parable in a trilogy about the nation of Israel and the national consequences of rejecting the King. As we have noted, the first was a parable of responsibility; the second was a parable of retribution. The last was a parable of rejection.

In this third story we see the nation of Israel being set aside and, for the present age, the church being called to take its place. The first part of the parable deals with Israel's rejection. The second part deals prophetically with the call of the Gentiles to the gospel feast.

The Lord was nearing the end of His earthly sojourn. Indeed He was in Jerusalem to die. He was also there to cast the Jews out from the unique place of privilege that had been theirs for some two thousand years, to confront the Sanhedrin, and to expose and ultimately expel the rulers of the nation. So He told this prophetic parable that is far-reaching in its scope.

a. The King's Exclusive Invitation to the Hebrew Race (22:1-7)

(1) The King's Announcement (22:1-6)

Three invitations are envisioned in the parable, the first two being extended to Israel. At the time Jesus told the story, the first invitation (22:1-3) had already been given. It had been issued to the Jewish people by John the Baptist, the Lord Himself, and His commissioned disciples. There was probably not a nook or cranny of the Holy Land where that invitation had not been heard. The Jews had been willing enough to eat the loaves and fishes and benefit from the Lord's healing miracles, but they had been unwilling to accept Him as Messiah on His terms. Had they responded, the joyous wedding day would have come quickly.

The second invitation (22:4-6) was issued to the Jews on and immediately after the day of Pentecost. Throughout the book of Acts the rule for presenting the gospel invitation was "to the Jew first," in the homeland and then in the diaspora. But the vast majority of Jews still would not come. Some were indifferent, being more concerned with their merchandise than with the message. Some were actively hostile, as in the parable "the remnant took his servants [the apostles], and entreated them spitefully, and slew them" (Matthew 22:6; see Acts 4:1-3; 5:40-41; 7:54-60; 8:1; 11:19; 12:2-5).[30]

(2) The King's Anger (22:7)

In the parable the behavior of "the remnant" in 22:6 provoked the anger of the king. "He sent forth his armies, and destroyed those murderers, and burned up their city" (22:7). And when Israel rejected the second invitation, God's patience was exhausted; the Roman armies were sent to destroy Jerusalem, uproot the nation, and bring down His wrath on the temple. The destruction of Jerusalem took place in A.D. 70 and the final expulsion from the land took place in A.D. 135 after the failure of the Bar Kokhba rebellion.

b. The King's Expanded Invitation to the Human Race (22:8-14)

(1) The Quest for the Wedding Guests (22:8-10)

Those who had received the first two royal invitations had refused to come, so the King sent His messengers into the highways of life with the gospel. The appeal was no longer confined to the house of Israel, as it had been during the period covered by the Gospels. During that time the Lord had rebuffed the Syrophoenician woman with the words, "I am not sent but unto the lost sheep of the house of Israel" (15:24). Now He could say, "Other sheep I have, which are not of this fold: them also I must bring" (John 10:16).

In the parable no expense had been spared to provide the feast and now no effort was spared to invite people to it. "And the wedding was furnished with guests." An assortment of people responded, "both bad and good" (Matthew 22:10). The word translated "bad" here is *ponēros,* which refers to the natural depravity of mankind, the wicked behavior of our evil nature. The gospel reaches "bad" people. It also reaches "good," moral, upright, religious people. All kinds of people are called and many kinds of people respond.

The parable parallels the Lord's program for world evangelism. The apostles were to begin "in Jerusalem, and in all Judaea." Then they were to go to Samaria. After that they were to reach out to "the uttermost part of the earth" (Acts 1:8). For nearly two thousand years the inviting has been going on and the banquet hall is filling up quickly now. But still there is room.

(2) The Question of the Wedding Garment (22:11-14)

It is not enough to make an outward response to the gospel invitation. Among the multitudes of people who have come forward in evangelistic campaigns and made professions of being saved when urged to do so by zealous soul-winners, there are thousands who have never been saved at all. Each of these people who have not been genuinely converted has perhaps responded intellectually or emotionally to the gospel, but his conscience has never been quickened, his heart has never been cleansed, his will has never been touched, and his spirit has never been regenerated. In other words, he has never put on the wedding garment.

In olden times, often when a king hosted a royal feast, he would present each guest with a festive robe to be worn on that occasion. The king in the parable no doubt followed that custom. The wedding garment he provided (now called a caftan) symbolizes the seamless robe of the righteousness of Christ, which is given to all who truly trust in Him for salvation, all who are genuinely saved. That robe is the only garment that will be accepted by the King. The garment of our own righteousness is unacceptable to God. To appear at the wedding feast in such a covering is an insult to His holiness. Love spreads the feast, but not love at the expense of holiness. There is no excuse for appearing in the wrong garment because the required robe is God's gift to His guests.

(a) A Swift Exposure (22:11-13)

i. The Neglectful Man's Sin (22:11-12a)

The man in the parable who was not wearing a wedding garment represents those who profess salvation, but do not possess salvation. They have responded in some inadequate way to the gospel. They imagine that their own goodness is good enough for God.

Note that two different Greek words are translated "not" in 22:11-12: "When the king came in to see the guests, he saw there a man which had *not* [*ou*] on a wedding garment: And he saith unto him, Friend, how camest thou in hither *not* [*mē*] having a wedding garment?" (italics added). Vincent pointed out that *ou* was always used when the reference was to a matter of fact. The fact was that the man did not have on the garment that would make his presence acceptable at the marriage feast. *Mē* was always used when the reference was to a matter of thought. The man did not have on the wedding garment because he had, with deliberate thought, not put it on.

The man thought that his own garment was as good as the one that had been offered to him. The problem was not that no wedding garment was available to him. And he had not forgotten to put it on. This was a case of conscious omission. Whatever his reason was—and who can fathom the excuses people make for not donning the righteousness of Christ?—the man had the audacity to try to make himself acceptable while refusing the one thing that would make him acceptable.

Note that in 22:12 the king called the man "Friend," a translation of *hetairos*. Only Matthew recorded the Lord's use of this word. It is also found in the context of 11:16-17: "Whereunto shall I liken this generation? It is like unto children sitting in the markets, and calling unto their fellows [*hetairos*], And saying, We have piped unto you, and ye have not danced; we have mourned unto you, and ye have not lamented." So the word was used to describe those who are so self-willed that nothing pleases them. It is also found in 26:50;

right after being kissed by Judas, the Lord said to the traitor, "Friend [*hetairos*], wherefore art thou come?" True, the word is one of comradeship, but in the New Testament it is used in association with those who rejected the goodness and salvation of God.

ii. The Neglectful Man's Silence (22:12b)

The man in the parable did not despise the feast. He came forward in response to the invitation to be a wedding guest. But he did despise the condition on which he would be acceptable. The king detected him at once, but was not hasty in judgment. He walked with awesome majesty to the place where the man sat and suddenly every eye was on this miserable guest. The king addressed him in moderate terms, but demanded an explanation.

It was the man's judgment day. He was "speechless," as all neglectful men will be when God asks them to explain why they insulted His glory and grace by refusing to put on the garment of salvation provided at such infinite cost at Calvary.

iii. The Neglectful Man's Sentence (22:13)

The judgment of the neglectful man was swift and sure, just and terrible. He had insulted the king by rejecting "so great salvation" (Hebrews 2:3). For the man, as for all his kind, there could be nothing but "outer darkness" and "weeping and gnashing of teeth."

(b) A Solemn Example (22:14)

This remarkable parable applied to those who first heard it—that is, the Jews and their leaders who would not believe the Lord. It also applies to those who down through the entire gospel age have heard the royal invitation. The Lord's last word on the subject is solemn: "Many are called, but few are chosen." We are thus warned to make our own calling and election sure.

C. Cases (22:15-46)

1. The Plan Devised (22:15)

The Lord's enemies had heard more than enough. Far from being repentant, they were deliberate in plotting His death—just as deliberate as the man in the Lord's last parable who decided he could get along without the king's wedding garment. The Jewish authorities decided they could get along without a Messiah like Jesus and without a kingdom like the one He represented.

While the Lord was still in the temple, the Pharisees, Sadducees, and Herodians readied traps for Him. Their despicable plot, which seems to have been instigated by the Pharisees, was intended to "entangle [trap] him in his talk." However, they were up against incarnate omniscience. Few chapters in the Bible give us a better glimpse of the Lord's wisdom than Matthew 22.

2. The Plan Developed (22:16-45)

a. The Royalists Try to Trap the Lord (22:16-22)

(1) Their Guile (22:16)

The first attack was made by the Herodians, a group we will call the royalists. They tried to trap the Lord with flattery: "Master," they said, "we know that thou art true, and teachest the way of God in truth, neither carest thou for any man." They put their question in honeyed terms, but they did not deceive the Lord for a moment.

The Herodians, really a political party among the Jews, supported the dynasty of Herod. A Herod occupied Jesus' throne and the Herodians had come to terms with the fact that an Edomite sat on the throne of David as Rome's puppet king. They had also come to terms with Roman occupation of their country. In matters of religion the Herodians leaned more toward the Sadducees than the Pharisees. Normally there was little love lost between the Pharisees and the Herodians, but opposition to Christ gave them a common cause.

Rather than identify themselves too closely with the Herodians whom they hated, the Pharisees probably sent some of the younger men of their sect (men who, like Saul of Tarsus, were training in the rabbinical schools such as the one run by Gamaliel) to stand with the Herodians in this new confrontation with Christ. Perhaps the Pharisees thought that Christ would fall for the young men's ingenuous, civil questions asked in apparent sincerity. If the Jews thought they could thus deceive the Christ of God, they were mistaken.

(2) Their Goal (22:17-18)

(a) The Trap Set (22:17)

The question was politically loaded. "Is it lawful to give tribute unto Caesar, or not?" If He said *yes,* He would be abdicating His

Messianic claims. The Messiah, they thought, would never agree to pay tribute to a Gentile power, especially one so ruthless and rapacious as Rome. He was to be a deliverer. He was to set up the glorious global empire that was the theme of so many Old Testament prophets. Jesus had been heralded in those temple courts as the Son of David, but if He said *yes,* He would be discredited as the Messiah.

If He said *no,* the Herodians would report Him to the Romans as a traitor, as a dangerous man who was advocating resistance to Roman occupation of the land.

(b) The Trap Seen (22:18)

The Lord saw through the question and He saw through the men. "Why tempt ye me, ye hypocrites?" He asked. He was not afraid of them. They thought they had Him, but how little they knew Him!

He could read their thoughts. Matthew wrote, "Jesus perceived their wickedness." The word translated "wickedness" here is *ponēria* (akin to *ponēros*). Their pretense at sincerity covered corruption and deception underneath. The word translated "perceived" here is *ginōskō,* which means "to know by experience." The Lord had been up against their kind before. He was more than a match for them. They thought He was an ignorant peasant from a crude background and backward village, but He had the keenest mind in the universe.

(3) Their Government (22:19-21b)

(a) The Caesar's Coin (22:19-21a)

i. Delivered to Him (22:19)

"Shew me the tribute money," the Lord said. He made the Herodians produce a Roman coin, the kind of money in which tribute was paid to Rome. Hebrew taxes were paid in shekels, the old Jewish coin. No doubt the men thought that the Lord was hedging and did not see where He was leading them, so they instantly delivered a denarius to Him. The denarius, a sample of Roman coin, was the equivalent of a workingman's daily wage.

ii. Described by Them (22:20-21a)

The Lord held up the denarius and asked, "Whose is this image and superscription?" (22:20) The small silver coin was stamped with the head of the Roman emperor and with the letters TICAESARDIVIAVGFAVGVSTVS. The letters represented the Latin phrase, *Tiberius Caesar, Divi Augususti Filius Augustus,* which means "Tiberius Caesar, August Son of the Divine Augustus." The words themselves were offensive to Jews. On the back of the coin were engraved a seated female figure and the inscription PONTIF MAXIM, which proclaimed the caesar to be the sovereign pontiff of Rome's pagan religious system.

That such an offensive coin was in circulation among the Jews of the promised land was evidence of their subjection to Rome. The right of coinage, even in the rabbinic view, belonged to the head of state and was proof of de facto government, which it was unlawful to oppose. The use of the denarius in ordinary transactions showed that the Jewish nation was a dependency of Rome. The Jews were under Rome and ruled by Rome, and they acquiesced in this status by using Roman money. By promptly producing a denarius, the Herodians gave a vivid demonstration of the political situation.

(b) The Caesar's Claim (22:21b)

Instead of being entangled by His enemies, Jesus gave them an answer at which people have marveled ever since: "Render therefore unto Caesar the things which are Caesar's." They were using the caesar's coins, so let them give the caesar his due. The Lord Jesus upheld the established government of the land, for the government was of God. The Romans were imperial successors to the Babylonians, Persians, and Greeks, whose rule was part of God's judgment on the land. The times of the Gentiles were in force and those times were not yet fulfilled (Luke 21:24).

Romans 13:1 tells us that "the powers that be are ordained of God." Above all human thrones is the throne of God. We must be law-abiding citizens, rendering to those who govern the state that which they have a constitutional right to demand. We do not have the right to disobey lawful authority, even when, as in the case of the Jews, the authority is a kind that we naturally detest.

(4) Their God (22:21c-22)

(a) His Worship (22:21c)

But there was more. Jesus said, "Render...unto God the things that are God's." The Lord does not make us independent of the state or a law unto ourselves, but we have a duty that transcends all civil duty, a duty to God. We are to pay our taxes and obey the law if doing so does not conflict with our obedience and loyalty to God. In such matters of conscience, no one has the right to tell another person where his duty lies. But in most cases, our duty to the rulers of our land is in no way incompatible with our duty to God.

(b) Their Wonder (22:22)

Matthew added, "When [the royalists] had heard these words, they marvelled, and left him, and went their way." The wisdom of Jesus transcended that of any other teacher they had heard. He had answered their question without embroiling Himself in the party strife of the Herodians and Pharisees. The Herodians departed having detected nothing treasonable in His answer. The Pharisees retreated having detected nothing unpatriotic in His answer. He had left the caesar on his throne and God on His throne. "Never man spake like this man" (John 7:46).

b. The Rationalists Try to Trap the Lord (22:23-33)

Jesus was still in the temple court and it was now the turn of the Sadducees, the rationalists, to challenge the authority of Christ. The problem with them was their unbelief. They challenged Biblical inerrancy and authority. They brought the Bible to the bar of human reason instead of bringing human reason to the bar of Holy Writ.

(1) Their Unbelief Explained (22:23)

"The same day came to him the Sadducees, which say that there is no resurrection." The Sadducees were the skeptics. Although they were religious and accepted much of what was in the Bible, they repudiated the supernatural. They had no patience with the Pharisees' beloved traditions and rejected traditional interpretations of the Scriptures. The Sadducees denied the validity of the concept of a bodily resurrection.

The Sadducees were also the materialists of that day and saw all poverty as evidence of God's disfavor. In their view, to relieve the poor was to interfere with God's government. The Sadducees were wealthy, aristocratic, and powerful as a religious group; they held the high priesthood in their hands. And because they bowed to foreign rule and pagan custom, they had the favor of Rome. Liberal in both religion and politics, the Sadducees were a group to be feared.

Yet they were afraid that this poor Galilean peasant with His ragtag and bobtail following might do something to bring about a sharp Roman reaction and the loss of the civil and religious liberties that they still possessed. The attitude of the Sadducees toward Christ was summarized by one of their number, Caiaphas, the current high priest (A.D. 18–36). To rouse the Sanhedrin to take action against Jesus, he said to the council: "Ye know nothing at all [You have no sense], Nor consider that it is expedient for us, that one man should die for the people, and that the whole nation perish not" (John 11:49-50). Expediency was his law of life.

The Sadducees were quite willing to sacrifice this unwanted Messiah in order to secure their own ends, but in the time frame of Matthew 22:23 it was not expedient to do so because He was popular with the multitude. To arrest Him might spark an uprising that in turn might provoke the Roman reprisals they feared. Under the circumstances the best thing to do was to discredit Him. So they came to Him with a typical liberal theological argument.

(2) Their Unbelief Expressed (22:24-28)

(a) The Command They Cited (22:24)

The Sadducees cited the well-known Mosaic law about a childless widow (Deuteronomy 25:5). This commandment required the brother of a deceased man to marry the widow. The firstborn son of this union was legally regarded as the son of the deceased. The purpose of the command was to protect the widow and also to keep her late husband's property in the family. (This is the law that underlies the story of the book of Ruth.)

(b) The Case They Cited (22:25-28)

The Sadducees told a story that they thought exposed the folly of believing in bodily resurrection. The story revolved around a woman who was widowed seven times. One by one, seven brothers married the ever-childless woman, only to die and leave the poor widow to be taken by the next in line. In the end the woman died too, having been married, according to Mosaic law, to all seven of the brothers. None of them had been able to "raise up seed unto his brother" (22:24). Now the barren woman herself had joined all seven men in death. One can almost sense the smugness with which the Sadducean questioner produced the punch line: "In the resurrection whose wife shall she be of the seven? for they all had her" (22:28).

(3) Their Unbelief Exposed (22:29-33)

The Lord was not impressed with their philosophical argument. He brought them right back to the Scriptures, which He considered to be inspired, infallible, authoritative, and the one safe guide in matters of faith and morals.

(a) Their Ignorance Rebuked (22:29-30)

i. Ignorance of the Nature of God's Revelation (22:29)

"Ye do err," Jesus said, "not knowing the scriptures, nor the power of God." All those who are ignorant of the Scriptures are in error; they deceive themselves. There was no excuse for the Sadducees' not knowing the Scriptures. They were not unable; they were unwilling to know them. It was their unwillingness that the Lord rebuked.

Note the Lord's threefold condemnation of theological liberalism and rationalism. He condemned (1) self-deception (Romans 1:21-22); (2) ignorance of the spiritual content of the Scriptures (Acts 13:27); and (3) unwillingness to accept the fact of God's powerful sovereign intervention in the natural order of events. The problem of rationalists is not that they cannot believe, but that they will not believe. If they would admit that God is omnipotent and omniscient, all difficulties would vanish. The Sadducees, like all their kind, were blind to the Word of God and the power of God.

ii. Ignorance of the Nature of Man's Resurrection (22:30)

The Sadducees' hypothetical case was a classic example of their ignorance. They assumed that life after death is the same as life before death. That is not so. All relationships are changed in the resurrection. "In the resurrection they neither marry, nor are given in marriage, but are as the angels of God in heaven."

The Lord ignored, as wholly irrelevant and not worth discussing, the Sadducean denial of the existence of angels and spirits. They did exist. The Old Testament Scriptures spoke of them frequently. He made no concession to the Sadducees' unbelief.

In the resurrection we will be like the unfallen angels. They have no need or desire for marriage. We will be as immortal as the angels. Being immortal, they have no need or desire to propagate their kind. Marriage, ordained of God for the propagation of the species down here, will no longer be a part of life in the resurrection. We will no longer be subject to human wants or passions. We will never get tired, never get hungry, never grow old, never be tempted. The age-long conflict of spirit and flesh will be over forever.

In the resurrection we will certainly know each other and love each other, but the marriage relationship and all that it implies will be no more. Thus the Sadducees' silly story was based on ignorance rooted in willful unbelief.

It was unnecessary for Jesus to prove the actual fact of resurrection, for He had already raised three people from the dead (Luke 7:12-15; 8:49-55; John 11:43-44). The case of Lazarus, the last of them, was of recent vintage and was common knowledge in Jerusalem, as the Sadducees knew (John 11:46-53; 12:9-11). Moreover the Old Testament Scriptures affirmed the doctrine of bodily resurrection (Job 19:26) and gave three examples of it (1 Kings 17:17-23; 2 Kings 4:32-37; 13:21).

(b) Their Ignorance Revealed (22:31-33)

i. To These Learned Men (22:31-32)

The Lord further rebuked the ignorance of the Sadducees. Again referring them to the Bible that they disbelieved, He quoted from a passage written by Moses: Exodus 3:6. By quoting this Scripture He affirmed that it was divinely inspired, the very Word of God. "As touching the resurrection of the dead," He said, "have ye not read that which was spoken unto you by God, saying, I am the God of Abraham, and the God of Isaac, and the God of Jacob? God is not the God of the dead, but of the living." In other words, death does not bring about a cessation of being.

The Sadducees believed that when a man died, he ceased to exist; he was annihilated. Jesus wrote an authoritative "Nonsense" over that rationalistic belief. According to that view, in Exodus 3:6 God had announced Himself to be the God of nonexisting persons! Rationalism always leads to absurd positions.

God spoke those words to Moses when He called him to become Israel's kinsman-redeemer. By that time Jacob, Isaac, and Abraham had been dead for centuries. But since "God is not the God of the dead, but of the living," those men were still alive. God has so fashioned man that he is incomplete without his body, but he can and does continue to exist after death as a disembodied spirit. Man's need for a resurrection body is met by God's power, ability, and purpose to provide such a body.

All this the Sadducees could have deduced for themselves if they had not been blinded by willful ignorance and unbelief. We are not told what the Sadducees replied in private, but from their continued hostility to Christ we gather that they rejected His teaching out of hand. As the couplet says,

> A man convinced against his will,
> Is of the same opinion still.

We do know that in public Jesus "had put the Sadducees to silence" (Matthew 22:34).

ii. To the Listening Multitude (22:33)

The general public "were astonished at his doctrine." The Lord had opened up to them unimagined depths in the Scripture and affirmed its divine inspiration and absolute authority.

Luke added the comment that some of the scribes present, doubtless those who belonged to the Pharisaic party, were delighted with the public discomfiture of their old enemies, the Sadducees. "Master, thou hast well said," they exclaimed (Luke 20:39).

c. The Religionists Try to Trap the Lord (22:34-45)

Now it was the turn of the Pharisees, the religionists. Matthew called their champion "a lawyer" (22:35). He was a scribe, a teacher of the law. This man was put forward by the Pharisees in the hope that his legal training would make him a more formidable adversary than the Herodians and Sadducees had been.

(1) The Pharisees' Question concerning the Commandments (22:34-40)

(a) The Question Asked (22:34-36)

The Pharisees' representative asked, "Which is the great commandment in the law?" (22:36) Matthew exposed his motive: he was "tempting" Christ (22:35). There was plenty of room in the lawyer's question for wrangling. The rabbis had divided the law into 248 affirmative and 365 negative commands. Some of these commands were spoken of as light and others as heavy. There were 613 altogether (the number of letters in the Decalogue). No matter which command the Lord picked, it would be possible to challenge Him.

The rabbis were great at splitting hairs, and they made all kinds of subtle refinements to the law. They would argue for years over a simple statement like "Thou shalt not seethe a kid in his mother's milk." How would this Teacher weigh in against all the ponderous opinions propounded in the rabbinic schools?

(b) The Question Answered (22:37-40)

i. The Two Great Basics of the Old Testament Statutes (22:37-39)

a. The Supreme Commandment (22:37-38)

The Lord simply took the lawyer back to Deuteronomy 6:4-5; 10:12; 30:6, back to the creed of the Hebrew people, back to words every Jew repeated in his devotions, back to his confession of faith. "Hear, O Israel: The Lord our God is one Lord: And thou shalt love the Lord thy God with all thine heart, and with all thy soul, and with all thy might" (Deuteronomy 6:4-5). The word translated "one" here is important, for it signifies a compound unity, not a single one. In the Hebrew text of verse 4, the last letter of the word translated "hear" is majuscular (larger than the other letters) and the last letter of the last word is also majuscular to emphasize "the first and great commandment" (Matthew 22:38).[31]

The Lord thus sidestepped the Decalogue and chose one well-known and all-embracing commandment. Nine of the ten commandments of the Decalogue are stated in the negative, but Jesus summed them all up in the positive. Instead of emphasizing the things we have done that we ought not to have done, "the first and great commandment" emphasizes the thing we have not done that we ought to have done. Who apart from Jesus has ever loved God with every beat of his heart, with all the faculties and endowments of his soul, and with all the strength and dynamic of his might? God is to be loved with all our being, and nothing is to be preferred before Him.

b. The Supplementary Commandment (22:39)

The Lord did not stop there, for some might consider "the first and great commandment" to be a theoretic abstraction. He added a concrete reality based on Leviticus 19:18. "And the second is like unto it," He said. "Thou shalt love thy neighbour as thyself"

(Matthew 22:39). In nature and extent, in universal application and personal implication, the second great commandment grows out of the first. Duty to God and duty to man—both are summed up in the word *love.*

ii. The Two Great Basics of the Old Testament Scriptures (22:40)

"On these two commandments," Jesus said, "hang all the law and the prophets." The two commandments were basic, touching all of life's relationship. The precepts of the law and the preaching of the prophets were simply expositions of the two basics. The tedious tomes of the teachers of the law and of the inventors of tradition could be swept aside. One does not need lawyers to understand God's law. One needs only love. Everybody understands the law of love.

(2) The Lord's Questions concerning the Christ (22:41-45)

(a) The Question concerning the Pedigree of the Messiah (22:41-42)

i. The Question Asked (22:41-42a)

The Lord had silenced the religionists. In the sudden stillness He asked a question. It was directed primarily to the Pharisees, the ones who were in the forefront of the attack on His claims to be the Christ. He broached what was perhaps the most familiar subject in their theology: the descent of the Messiah. "What think ye of Christ?" He said. "Whose son is he?" (22:42)

The answer of any church, sect, cult, or religion to that question will expose the group for what it is. The question is the touchstone of truth. If the group is wrong about the person of Christ, its teaching is false.

ii. The Question Answered (22:42b)

The Pharisees had a ready answer: "The son of David."[32] That is how the multitude had hailed the Lord during His triumphal entry. And the children in the temple had cheered Him as the Son of David. The Lord had brought the Pharisees around full circle.

But they were too blind to see that the One now questioning them was the Son of David. If they balked at linking that title to Jesus, how would they react to His claim to be the Son of God?

(b) The Question concerning the Priority of the Messiah
     (22:43-45)

i. The Implication—The Lord's Ancestor Confessed Christ's Deity (22:43-44)

The Pharisees' answer was true, but inadequate. The Messiah was much more than the Son of David. The Lord had their answer about the human descent of the Messiah; now let them state the truth concerning the divine descent of their Messiah. Jesus referred the Pharisees to Psalm 110:1. They would have readily acknowledged Psalm 110 to be both Davidic and Messianic. He said, "How then doth David in spirit call him Lord, saying, The Lord said unto my Lord, Sit thou on my right hand, till I make thine enemies thy footstool?"[33]

ii. The Application—The Lord's Adversaries Confronted Christ's Deity (22:45)

No one had challenged the fact that the Messiah was to be David's Son. And no one in Christ's day would have challenged the fact that David, speaking by divine inspiration, had called the Messiah "Lord." Yet no man calls his son "lord," so here was a seeming contradiction. The Messiah was to be both David's Son and David's Lord. The explanation lies in the deity of Christ. The Pharisees were silent.

3. The Plan Defeated (22:46)

"No man was able to answer him a word, neither durst any man from that day forth ask him any more questions." The Pharisees rejected Jesus as David's Son and as God's Son. They were His enemies and now they await the day when they will be made His footstool.

D. Curses (23:1-39)

Jesus was still in the temple court with His disciples gathered around Him, the multitudes spread out before Him, and the national leaders of Israel in the background. The leaders were still smarting at being so effectively silenced by the Lord. Already infuriated, they were willing to pay any price to get rid of Him. Now His scathing denunciation of their hypocrisy would sign His death warrant.

In Matthew 23 the Lord rejected rabbinic Judaism and, by extension, all false religion. His pronouncement of woe on the leaders of Judaism was followed by His rejection of Jerusalem.

1. The Lord's Rejection of Judaism (23:1-36)

a. The Position of Honor (23:1-3)

The position of honor was occupied by the scribes and Pharisees. The scribes were interpreters of the law. As an order, they arose in the days of Ezra in a natural way. The remnant who had returned from the Babylonian exile desperately needed to have their Hebrew Scriptures expounded to them, especially since the majority of the repatriates no longer understood the Hebrew language. Ezra and his colleagues filled this need (Nehemiah 8:1-8) and from that humble beginning, the order of scribes developed. With the passing of time, however, their interpretations evolved into a vast mixture of truth and error that became known as the Talmud.[34] In the New Testament we never see the priests acting as teachers, for their teaching function had been completely taken over by the scribes.

The scribes in Matthew 23:2 evidently belonged to a Pharisaical sect because the Lord linked them with the Pharisees. "The scribes and the Pharisees sit in Moses' seat," Jesus said. Campbell Morgan rephrased the statement this way: "The scribes and Pharisees have seated themselves on Moses' seat."[35] They seated themselves and falsely claimed to speak ex cathedra (the Greek word translated "seat" in 23:2 is *kathedra*). The calling of a Levite or a priest had divine sanction, but the calling of a scribe had no such direct divine authorization.

Insofar as the scribes taught or commanded what was in the Mosaic Law, they were to be honored and obeyed. They had once been true expositors of that Law, but through the years they had added to the Law a large number of useless traditions, glosses, evasions, injunctions, and wrong interpretations. Elsewhere (16:11-12 for instance) the Lord had warned against their errors and He set an example by ignoring extrabiblical traditions such as those concerning the sabbath and ceremonial washings.

Now He warned His listeners not only to draw the line between God's Word and man's traditions, but also to avoid the hypocrisy of the scribes and Pharisees. "They say, and do not," He explained (23:3). No one should be so foolish as to follow their example. And although they had a position of honor, no one should be so blind as to accept their teachings uncritically, swallowing the ten thousand things they had added to the Word of God.

b. The Practice of Hypocrisy (23:4-36)

The Lord elaborated on that warning in a long exposure of the downright hypocrisy of those religious leaders. In denouncing them He was also exposing all religious hypocrisy and the uselessness of empty outward form in religion. Let us beware of being hypocritical, for His eye penetrates all of life's little disguises.

(1) What the Leaders Sought (23:4-12)

(a) The Adherence of Men (23:4)

"They bind heavy burdens and grievous to be borne, and lay them on men's shoulders." For example the rabbis converted the sabbath from a day of rest to a wearisome observance of endless regulations.[36]

According to the scribes an ordinary sabbath-day's journey was limited to two thousand cubits (about one thousand yards); however, on Friday a man could place enough food for two meals at the boundary of that distance, thus theoretically extending his house that far so that on Saturday he could continue walking for another two thousand cubits. On the sabbath a tailor was not permitted to go out with his needle; neither was a scribe permitted to go out with his pen. No ingredients could be added to a solution unless they would be completely dissolved before the sabbath. Wool was not to be dyed unless the whole process could be completed before the sabbath. Rabbis argued over how much guilt a person would incur if in blowing out a candle on the sabbath its flame happened to light another one. One rabbi forbade a man to throw hot water over himself on the sabbath in case the floor were to be cleaned as a result. A person could not drag a chair on the sabbath since he might create a rut in the ground. A woman was not permitted to look in a mirror on the sabbath because she might see a gray hair and pull it out, which would be work. Likewise a person could not put in false teeth on the sabbath. It was considered work to tie a knot, undo a knot, sew two stitches, sow two seeds, pluck a blade of grass, or pick a piece of fruit on the sabbath. To write two letters of the alphabet or to change one into another on the sabbath was sinful, but to write one big letter in the space of two smaller ones was not. To climb a tree or clap hands was to break the sabbath.

The rabbis endlessly debated such issues. According to Edersheim, twenty-four chapters of the Babylonian Talmud (156 double pages of folio) are devoted to the sabbath laws. He wrote, "Matters are seriously discussed as of vital religious importance, which one would scarcely imagine a sane intellect would seriously entertain."[37] Far from accepting the Lord's rebuke, the scribes and rabbis went on adding intolerable burdens for centuries.

(b) The Admiration of Men (23:5)

Jesus said of the religious leaders, "They make broad their phylacteries, and enlarge the borders [fringes] of their garments." Phylacteries were small, square, leather-covered cases containing small scrolls of parchment on which were written the texts of Exodus 13:1-10,11-16 and Deuteronomy 6:4-9; 11:13-21. They were fastened by long leather straps to the forehead and also worn on the left arm near the heart. In time, superstitious reverence was attached to the phylacteries and they were regarded as amulets or charms. The fringes (Numbers 15:37-41; Deuteronomy 22:12), fastened to the corners of the garments of devout Jews, were made up of white and blue threads and came to represent the 613 precepts of the law.

The Mosaic injunction that excerpts from the law be worn was originally intended to remind the Jews of God's claims on them; the fringes were intended to remind them of their separation from the world. Now the phylacteries and fringes had become mere ostentatious trappings of religion. The Pharisees wore them "to be seen of men," to impress people with their superior piety.

(c) The Advancement of Men (23:6)

The religious leaders wanted the best places at feasts and the most important seats in the synagogues. They are not alone in this desire for advancement. Today there are people who want to be pastors of big churches because of the position, power, and preferments such offices often bestow. There are people who want to be deacons or elders for the same reasons. In all spheres of Christian work there is often intense competition for promotion and position.

(d) The Adulation of Men (23:7-12)

i. The Leaders' Worldly Goal Described by the Lord (23:7)

The scribes and Pharisees wanted to be greeted as rabbi, father, and master (leader). They loved to be saluted with such titles in the marketplace, to be publicly recognized, to be given what they considered their proper place.

ii. The Leaders' Worldly Goal Dismissed by the Lord (23:8-12)

We can imagine how these men, standing in the background, must have cringed beneath the lash of the Lord's denunciation. Everyone in the temple court would have looked at them, not with the usual fawning respect, but with eyes suddenly opened to their pompous show. How the scribes and Pharisees must have boiled inwardly when the Lord used them as object lessons when teaching His disciples how *not* to serve God. "Neither be ye called masters," He said, "for one is your Master, even Christ" (23:10).

We have no right to set ourselves up as masters, as the final authority on matters of faith and morals. We have no right to direct the conduct of another person's life, to intrude ourselves between him and Christ. He must go directly to Christ, for we are not able, by ritual or any other way, to impart spiritual life to his soul.

(2) What the Leaders Taught (23:13-22)

Just as the public ministry of the King began with eight beatitudes (Matthew 5:1-12), so it closed with eight curses poured out on the nation that had rejected Him. We need only run our eyes down the eight woes in Matthew 23 to see how thorough His rejection of Israel was to be. He called the leaders "hypocrites," "fools and blind," "whited sepulchres," and "a generation of vipers." The Lord did not speak out of personal vindictiveness—in a moment He would weep for them. He was simply summarizing the state of a people who could reject such a One as He and the fate of a people who would reap the inevitable reward of their deeds.

(a) The Hypocrisy of Their Preaching (23:13)

The Lord denounced the hypocrisy of their preaching. They prevented people from accepting Him by barring and bolting the kingdom of Heaven. The leaders had no intention of entering in themselves and they did all in their power to prevent anyone else from going in. When the day of Pentecost arrived and the church was born, they continued to "shut up the kingdom of heaven" by dogging the steps of the apostles. The leaders of Judaism stirred up opposition to the gospel, instigated riots, denied Christ's resurrection, and slandered those who proclaimed it.

(b) The Hypocrisy of Their Prayers (23:14)

The Lord said: "Woe unto you, scribes and Pharisees, hypocrites! for ye devour widows' houses, and for a pretence make long prayer." A prayer is measured not by its length but by its depth. Widows and orphans deserve the compassion and protection of those who profess to love God, but (in ways not told) those leaders exploited the weakness of widows—in spite of commands from God to deal kindly with them (Deuteronomy 10:18; 27:19; Psalm 68:5).

In Luke's Gospel this woe is followed by the story of the widow's mite (Luke 20:47–21:4). The Lord had no use for the prayers of those who used prayers as a cloak to cover their own wickedness and greed.

(c) The Hypocrisy of Their Proselytes (23:15)

The Jews had two classifications of proselytes: (1) those who were circumcised and were called "proselytes of righteousness"; and (2) those who were not yet circumcised and were called "proselytes of the gate." (The root of the word *proselyte* means "to come over.") Jesus said that the scribes and Pharisees would "compass sea and land," go to any lengths, to make a convert. But what was the result? They made him "twofold more the child of hell" than themselves. Literally translated, the phrase reads "twice as much a son of Gehenna." It often happens that a convert to a religion is twice as zealous as those born and raised in it. When a person is converted to something false, it is a double tragedy.

The Lord was not denouncing Israel's mission to mankind. It was Israel's destiny to witness to the world about the true and living God; and that will be Israel's mission in the millennium. Jesus was denouncing proselytizing people to Pharisaic, rabbinic Judaism.

(d) The Hypocrisy of Their Precepts (23:16-22)

i. Their Folly Expressed (23:16-19)

The Lord then poured His scorn on the artificial values of the leaders. If a man swore an oath by the temple, the Pharisees said, "It is nothing" (23:16). The oath was not binding. But if he swore by the gold of the temple, the Pharisees said, "He is a debtor." He was obliged to keep his oath. The presumption was that it was a religious oath. Similarly it meant nothing to swear by the altar, but everything to swear by the sacrifice on the altar. The Pharisees graded oaths according to such foolish and artificial distinctions. If a man swore by an object that was not graded as sacred, he was not considered guilty of oath-breaking if he failed to keep his pledge.

ii. Their Folly Exposed (23:20-22)

The Lord showed the abysmal folly of the leaders' precepts. The temple was sacred because it was God's dwelling place on earth. That was what made anything in the temple sacred. The gold derived whatever sanctity it had from the temple and was nothing without the temple. Similarly the altar was what consecrated the sacrifice. The Pharisees had so twisted the truth that they had everything backwards. Jesus pointed out that to swear by the temple or the altar was to swear by God.

The Pharisees and their kind affirmed that to swear by Heaven was not binding either. Writing His authoritative "nonsense" across all such notions, the Lord said, "He that shall swear by heaven, sweareth by the throne of God, and by him that sitteth thereon" (23:22).

How the leaders must have bristled at being exposed! All their puerile evasions of keeping promises rendered them culpable. Their carefully woven fabric of precepts was full of holes.

(3) What the Leaders Wrought (23:23-28)

(a) A Show of Religion (23:23-24)

i. Developing Minor Matters of the Law (23:23a)

Continuing, the Lord denounced the leaders' show of religion as worthless. He ridiculed the burdensome traditions of the scribes and Pharisees in the matter of tithing. What should have been the overflow of a joyful and grateful heart was made drudgery by them. The minute rabbinic rules required that even the smallest products of the soil, like mint and anise and cumin, had to be tithed. In practice the Mosaic law of tithing extended to corn, wine, oil, and the firstborn of herds and flocks (Deuteronomy 14:23), but the Pharisees seized on Leviticus 27:30 and rigorously applied the law of tithing to everything.

ii. Devaluating Major Matters of the Law (23:23b-24)

a. The Seriousness of Their Behavior (23:23b)

The Lord upheld the law of tithing, but took His scalpel to the Pharisees' satisfaction with outward compliance with the law.

"What about the weightier matters of the law?" He demanded in effect. "What about judgment, mercy, and faith?" The Lord's words echoed Micah 6:8. Making such an issue over tithing while neglecting the moral issues of the law was (and is) the essence of Pharisaism.

b. The Senselessness of Their Behavior (23:24)

The Lord graphically summed up the Pharisees' love of minutiae. "Ye blind guides," He said, "strain at a gnat [habitually filter out a gnat], and swallow a camel." How foolish to be so careful with little things while being so careless with big issues!

(b) A Show of Respectability (23:25-26)

The leaders' show of respectability was also worthless. In their outward conformity to all the rules of religion while being inwardly corrupt, they were like someone who washes the outside of a cup but not the inside. They were careful about appearances, but the Lord, who read their hearts, declared that inwardly they were "full of extortion and excess" (23:25). "Thou blind Pharisee," said Jesus, using the singular to add emphasis to the charge (23:26). How terrible to have one's secrets so glaringly exposed!

(c) A Show of Righteousness (23:27-28)

The leaders' show of righteousness was likewise worthless. The Lord likened them to "whited sepulchres" (23:27). They looked beautiful on the outside, but inside they were "full of dead men's bones." In effect Jesus said to the Pharisees, "You put on a good outward show." But He had to add, "Within ye are full of hypocrisy and iniquity" (23:28). External purity should result from inward purity. Unless inward purity comes first, outward ceremonial cleanness amounts to nothing.

Take a moment to picture the scene again. There is the Lord, whose kind but searching glance is able to see the wounds that shame would hide. Every word He speaks is another nail in His coffin, so to speak. He knows that He is on His way to the cross.

There are the disciples, aghast at the Lord's frontal attack on the powerful religious leaders of the nation.

There are the multitudes. They have thought vaguely about the pretensions of the leaders, but have never been able or willing to put their thoughts into words. Never in all their experience had anyone else spoken so succinctly, bluntly, and boldly about hypocrisy.

And there are the scribes and Pharisees in their fine raiment. They are stunned, shocked, and stabbed to the heart, for they have been thoroughly exposed by the preacher from Nazareth. Will they *repent?* No. *Revenge* is their word. They will have this man who claims to be their King dead and in His tomb before the week is out.

(4) What the Leaders Thought (23:29-36)

(a) Their Foolish Mistake (23:29-31)

In Jerusalem tombs were sometimes dug out of the rock in the sides of hills or cliffs. The entrances to such tombs were often decorated, but what was the use of honoring the prophets of the past by adorning their tombs? The only real way to honor a prophet was to obey him.

In 23:29 we note one more woe, a woe to those who gilded the tombs of the prophets and shook their heads over the stubbornness and unbelief of those who had slain the prophets. It was national pride, not repentance, that motivated the scribes and Pharisees to "garnish the sepulchres." Their hearts were filled with the same pride, rebellion, unbelief, and hatred that had caused their fathers to persecute and martyr the prophets and righteous men of old. The leaders of Jesus' day were the spiritual heirs not of the prophets, whose tombs had become national shrines, but of their murderers. The scribes and Pharisees were in fellowship not with the prophets, but with those who had killed them. The same seething hatred that had led the ancestors of the scribes and Pharisees to kill the prophets, would now lead them to murder Christ.

Yet those hypocritical leaders said, "If we had been in the days of our fathers, we would not have been partakers with them in the blood of the prophets" (23:30). Such was their foolish mistake! The scribes and Pharisees were soon to dye their hands crimson in richer blood drawn from nobler veins. Their fathers had martyred God's saints; they would murder God's Son.

(b) Their Full Measure (23:32-36)

i. How the Lord Described Them (23:32-33a)

The Lord described their full measure of guilt. He called the scribes and Pharisees "serpents" and "generation of vipers" (23:33). They were a venomous breed indeed, true children of that old serpent the devil (John 8:44). What an assessment of their character! Remember, these were the religious leaders of the day, men who had a reputation among the people for piety and set the norms for faith and morals. They were spiritual descendants of Cain, who murdered Abel, the first martyr of the true faith.

ii. How the Lord Damned Them (23:33b-35)

a. They Were Destined for Hell (23:33b)

The Lord asked them, "How can ye escape the damnation of hell [Gehenna]?" Note that He did not say there was no escape. There was a way of escape, but they would refuse that new and living way into the holiest through the blood of Jesus (Hebrews 10:19-20). How rare it is for a Pharisee of whatever persuasion to accept God's means of grace! The Lord was talking to men who refused the conditions of salvation. The great white throne judgment and the flames of eternal fire are the inevitable end of unrepentant behavior such as theirs.

b. They Were Deserving of Hell (23:34-35)

1. Their Terrible Activity Revealed (23:34)

"Fill ye up then the measure of your fathers," Jesus had said (23:32). And indeed the scribes and Pharisees would fill up the measure of their fathers. The Lord would send them prophets, for that was what the apostles were. The prophetic gift was revived in Israel after Pentecost for the inauguration of the new dispensation, for the introduction of the church, and for the writing of the New Testament.

The Lord would send wise men like Stephen and Philip the evangelist (Acts 6:3-5; 7:1-60). Such men would be full of wisdom and the Holy Ghost. Before these wise men, even a brilliant Pharisee like Saul of Tarsus would not be able to stand.

The Lord would send a new order of scribes, interpreters instructed in the law of love and in all the mysteries of the kingdom of Heaven (Matthew 13:52).

The Pharisees would treat these prophets, wise men, and interpreters as their fathers had treated God's messengers in their day. The leaders would chase them from city to city and kill some, as the book of Acts bears witness.[38]

2. Their Terrible Accountability Revealed (23:35)

Here we have the statement of consequence: "That upon you may come all the righteous blood shed upon the earth, from the blood of righteous Abel unto the blood of Zacharias son of Barachias, whom ye slew between the temple and the altar."

Opinions differ about who "Zacharias" was. One unsupported view is that he was the father of John the Baptist. Another view is that he was the prophet Zechariah, who was the son of Berechiah (Zechariah 1:1); this Zechariah was one of the last of the Old Testament prophets, but nothing is said in the Old Testament to indicate that he was martyred.

The most probable view is that the martyr of Matthew 23:35 was Zechariah, the son of the godly priest Jehoiada. Jehoiada was the man who hid baby Joash from Athaliah's murderous hate and eventually put the young prince on the throne of David. It was not at all uncommon for a man to have two names, so it is likely that Zechariah's father Jehoiada had two names, one of them being Barachias.

Joash repaid Jehoiada's kindness by murdering his son after Zechariah denounced the king for his lapse into idolatry. As Zechariah was dying he said, "The Lord look upon it [his martyrdom], and require it" (2 Chronicles 24:22). Thus his blood cried from the ground for vengeance just as Abel's did. According to a Jewish legend recorded by Edersheim, the blood of Zechariah did not dry up, but continued to bubble on the pavement for two and a half centuries until the Babylonians came and avenged it.[39]

Zechariah was killed in the open space in the court of the priests, between the holy place of the temple and the great brazen altar of sacrifice. The fact that one of God's servants was murdered on such a sacred spot aggravated the crime. Since the Jews placed the book of Chronicles at the end of their Canon, in the Jewish Bible Abel was the first martyr and Zechariah was the last; the order of the books thus added weight to the Lord's words.

What the Lord was saying to the stubborn and unrepentant men of His day was solemn indeed. He was telling them that if God were to take all the innocent blood shed in Old Testament times and heap it on their heads, if God were to hold them accountable for all the murders and massacres of former times, they would still be less guilty than they now were, because they were about to shed the blood of God's beloved Son.

iii. How the Lord Doomed Them (23:36)

Jesus added, "All these things shall come upon this generation." Mark the expression "this generation," for we will find it again in 24:34. There can be little doubt that it referred to a literal generation. In 23:37-39 the Lord went on to describe the coming judgment and fall of Jerusalem, which took place in A.D. 70, well within the lifetimes of some who heard Him say the words recorded in 23:36. Theirs was the generation that would see "these things" happen.

The term "generation" is somewhat elastic. We cannot pinpoint exactly when a generation begins or when it ends. It is generally thought of as a time span of thirty or forty years. In the context of 23:36 a generation could last a hundred years. The Lord spoke these words of judgment around A.D. 33, and the final dissolution of Jewish national life did not come until the time of the Bar Kokhba rebellion in A.D. 135.

It is of passing interest to note that in the terrible struggles that marked the doom of Jerusalem, another "Zacharias" was martyred. He was called Zacharias the son of Baruch and he was slain by the Zealots in the temple.[40]

2. The Lord's Rejection of Jerusalem (23:37-39)

a. His Rejection Described (23:37)

Jerusalem had rejected its King. For a thousand years since David, Israel's hope had been focused on the coming of great David's greater Son. And He had come. The people of Jerusalem, on a wave of euphoria, had shouted their *hosannas*, but He knew better than to trust the passing plaudits of the crowd. Within a day or so the same mindless multitude would be shouting for His death.

Now the King rejected Jerusalem. He mourned its inevitable doom: "O Jerusalem, Jerusalem, thou that killest the prophets, and stonest them which are sent unto thee, how often would I have gathered thy children together, even as a hen gathereth her chickens under her wings, and ye would not!" That was the root problem: "Ye would not."

b. Its Ruin Declared (23:38)

In His mind's eye the Lord could see the coming siege. He could see the hills around the city black with crosses and on every cross a Jew. And it broke His heart.

The siege of Jerusalem was one of the most terrible in history. The Romans first systematically subdued Galilee in a series of fierce battles, at times massacring all the inhabitants of a city, especially if it had put up a particularly stubborn defense. Meanwhile in Jerusalem, instead of preparing for the coming siege by uniting under a common leader, various factions savagely fought one another.

One faction was led by the fierce John of Gischala, another by the more moderate Ananus, the eldest of the chief priests. John of Gischala was welcomed to the ranks of the Zealots, who were led by Eleazar and had been driven into the temple by the more law-abiding citizens. John suggested to the Zealots that they make common cause with the Idumeans, men of Arab stock who had been pillaging the countryside. John and his confederates infiltrated the Idumeans into Jerusalem, where they added to the internal strife. Terrible scenes of carnage and atrocity took place. The Idumeans then abandoned the Zealots and departed. First, however, they opened the prison doors and released thousands of inmates. The prisoners fled to join the ranks of Simon the son of Gioras, the head of another band of lawless ruffians who were settled at Masada.

The state of anarchy was known to the Roman general Vespasian. He simply bided his time, allowing the Jews to weaken themselves with all this internal strife. At length, however, the vast Roman army moved through Samaria, advanced toward Jerusalem, and camped in the valley of Thorns, about three miles from Jerusalem. From the neighboring heights they could see the towers and walls of the city.

Then the order came to march, and with its impressive might the army of Vespasian overcame all resistance and camped before the wall of the doomed city. The battle swayed back and forth, but relentlessly and inevitably the Romans took one section of Jerusalem after another amid scenes of both courage and carnage.

Famine stalked the stricken streets and the ruffian soldiers defending the city were merciless in their hunt for food. They seized people they suspected of concealing food and tortured them, demanding they disclose secrets they often did not have regarding food stores. Natural affection and generous sentiment vanished before the plague of hunger. People ate offal and filth and some even became cannibals and devoured their own children. A measure of wheat was worth its weight in gold.

When Titus took charge of the campaign, he added new horrors. He crucified Jewish prisoners, as many as five hundred at a time. The prisoners were brought in nightly and the soldiers fastened the victims to the crosses in all sorts of ludicrous positions. Soon the places chosen for the crucifixions were covered with crosses, and the Romans ran out of wood. The Zealots pointed to the terrible sight to check any desire on the part of the hapless population to desert.

Meanwhile in the city treacheries went on. The high priest Matthias was slain on the charge of holding correspondence with the Romans, but not until his three sons were massacred before his eyes. People started to desert. The Arabian and Syrian allies of the Romans seized a large party of deserters and cut them open alive, looking for gold and jewels they were suspected of swallowing.

At length the Romans took the tower of Antonia. The temple cloisters became the scene of more carnage and fires. On the tenth of August (the date Solomon's temple was destroyed by Nebuchadnezzar) Titus, who wanted to preserve Herod's magnificent temple, issued orders that the fires around it be extinguished. But in the heat of battle one enraged legionary climbed on the shoulders of a comrade and threw a lighted torch through the small gilded door into the porch. Soon the whole building was in flames.

When the siege was all over, the Romans had 97,000 captives on their hands. The number of those who had been slain or who had died of famine has been estimated at 1,300,000. The tallest and strongest-looking of the captives were selected to grace Titus's triumphal return to Rome. A vast number, including the old and the sick, were put to death. Thousands were dispatched to the mines in various parts of the empire or distributed among the provinces for the amusement of the populace in the arenas.

Thus Jerusalem fell. Foreseeing the event in all its horror, Jesus said, "Behold, your house is left unto you desolate" (23:38). How desolate only time would tell. After the Bar Kokhba rebellion (A.D. 132–135) the Romans were thoroughly fed up with Judea; they banished all Jews from the land, posted the country out of bounds to them, changed its name to Palestine in honor of their old foes the Philistines, and changed the name of Jerusalem to Aelia Capitolina.

c. His Return Decreed (23:39)

Before He walked out of the temple, the Lord said, "Ye shall not see me henceforth, till ye shall say, Blessed is he that cometh in the name of the Lord." He could not leave without a parting word of hope, so to His "Woe! Woe! Woe!" He added that word "Blessed." Then He withdrew His presence from the multitude. Never again would He walk those temple courts. In a few days He would be separated from them by death, for after His resurrection He would appear only to His own.

But beyond the centuries, in ages then unborn, He would come again. Then Israel too will say, "Blessed is he that cometh in the name of the Lord." The Jewish nation still is not ready to say that. The time has not yet come, but the day draws near.

III. THE PROPHETIC DISCOURSE (24:1–25:46)

The private discussions and public disputes were over. The King had passed final judgment on the nation of Israel. All that remained was the cross. But first, in an astonishing prophetic discourse, the King gave His disciples a sketch of the general tenor of the new church age that was about to be inserted into time, and then went on to speak of the end-time events that would herald His coming again. This important prophetic statement gathers together the main threads of Old Testament end-time prophecy and the threads of New Testament prophecy, weaves them into an imposing fabric of eschatology, and embroiders the fabric with flashes of insight from the Lord's omniscient foreknowledge.

Matthew bracketed the Lord's public ministry between two sermons: the sermon on the mount, in which the emphasis was practical; and the Olivet discourse, in which the emphasis was prophetical. In one sermon we read of the rules of the kingdom; in the other we read of the return of the King. Before giving the sermon on the mount, the Lord was baptized; after giving the Olivet discourse, the Lord was buried. Prior to the first sermon He proved that the tempter could not conquer Him; after the last sermon He proved that the tomb could not conquer Him.

The Olivet discourse can be divided into two parts: the Lord's end-time prophecy in Matthew 24 and the Lord's end-time parables in Matthew 25. The prophecy deals with the course of this age, and the parable with the climax of this age. The prophecy is concerned with God's judicial dealings with mankind; the parables deal with God's judgmental dealings with mankind. Both prophecy and parables are concerned with the last days as they affect the Jews, the Gentile nations, and the church.

Many cannot see the church in the Olivet discourse. They claim that the Gospel of Matthew is the Gospel of the Jew and therefore all its prophecy is Jewish. But the essential Jewishness of Matthew's Gospel does not preclude truth concerning the church. Indeed this Gospel mentions the church twice, showing in a most emphatic way both its universal and local aspects (Matthew 16; 18). Moreover the church is clearly implied elsewhere, as in the parable of the pearl. It would be strange indeed if in the Olivet discourse, the Lord's most comprehensive prophetic statement, He had nothing to say about the church, for it is nearest and dearest to His heart.

A. The Lord's End-Time Perception (24:1-3)

The prophecy was prompted by the disciples' pride in the temple. Herod the Great was a villain, but he was a villain with a flare for architecture. The temple built in the days of Cyrus by the Jews who had been repatriated from Babylon was a modest structure, but Herod set out to make it and its surroundings magnificent. Work on it was still going forward in Christ's day. In fact the finishing touches were not added until A.D. 64.

The Lord was not impressed. He had wept over what was going to happen to the land, the city, and the temple. "There shall not be left here one stone upon another, that shall not be thrown down," He prophesied (24:2). And in A.D. 67, three years after the completion of Herod's temple, the Jewish war with Rome broke out. Titus issued orders to his soldiers to spare the temple, but his word was of no avail against the prophetic word of Christ. The war ended with the temple going up in flames.

Matthew's account of the Olivet discourse (24:4–25:46) is not concerned with the coming destruction of the temple. Matthew concentrated on what the King had to say about the end-time events that would climax in His coming again.

B. The Lord's End-Time Prophecy (24:4-51)

The prophetic discourse in Matthew 24 was a topical sermon and in it the Lord dealt with end-time events under three headings: topic number one, the Gentile nations; topic number two, the Jews; and topic number three, the church.

First He looked at end-time events as they will concern the Gentile nations (24:4-14). Since His dealings with the nations will go right on to the end, His comments embraced the great tribulation as well as the events leading up to that time of terror, as those events involve the nations.

The Lord then dropped that topic and dealt with end-time events as they will affect the Jewish people (24:15-31). Since the great tribulation will be pre-eminently "the time of Jacob's trouble" (Jeremiah 30:7), and since it will be the most dreadful period in all of Jewish history, and since it will drive the surviving remnant of the Jewish people to Christ, the Lord emphasized the tribulation primarily in this part of the prophetic sermon.

Finally the Lord talked about end-time events as they will affect the church (24:32-51). The church is not named, but it is clearly implied. Actually the church will be raptured before any of the events concerning the Gentile nations and Israel come to a head. The church comes last in the discourse only in sermonic order. Anyone who has preached topical sermons understands that three subjects relating to the same general theme cannot always be in strict chronological sequence, although the items under each subject might well be in chronological order.

The Lord dealt with His three topics in the order of history. For the first two thousand years of Bible history, God dealt solely with the nations. After the call of Abraham, He dealt supremely with the Jews; the nations were still there, but the divine focus had changed. That period of history also lasted for about two thousand years. For the two thousand years since Pentecost, He has been focusing on the church.

Critics of this interpretation say that when we relate the end of Matthew 24 to the church, we imply that the church has to go through the great tribulation. This objection is invalid because the sermon is topical in nature. Each of the three topics is a separate sermonic entity. In dealing with the church, the Lord made no reference to the tribulation at all, and for a very good reason. The tribulation will affect the nations and Israel, and thus it is in the first two sections of the sermon that the Lord dealt with the subject. Since it has nothing to do with the church, the tribulation is not mentioned in the third section.

1. The Nations of the World (24:4-14)

a. End-Time Problems (24:4-8)

(1) National Disasters (24:4-7a)

(a) Deceptive Creeds (24:4-5)

The Lord began the prophecy with a warning: "Take heed that no man deceive you" (24:4). He was focusing on end-time Messianic movements that center around cultic personalities such as Hitler and Marx. The abandonment by the West of its traditional Christian-Judaic heritage has opened the door for countless opportunistic cults. False oriental religions have taken fresh root; false "Christian" creeds run wild; and Islam, backed by the vast resources of the oil-rich Arab states, is on the march. After the rapture diabolical philosophies will flourish. The devil's messiah will arrive and deceive most of the world.

(b) Dreadful Conflicts (24:6-7a)

"Ye shall hear of wars and rumours of wars," Jesus said, "but the end is not yet" (24:6). The word translated "end" here is *telos*, which means "the very end." In that statement the Lord took in the endless conflicts of the age. Then He focused on a new kind of war: "Nation shall rise against nation, and kingdom against kingdom" (24:7). Up until World War I, wars were between armies, but now wars are between nations. In the past wars were often persistent and savage, but with the twentieth century came "total war." All the resources of whole nations are committed to the conflict. Think of how much of our gross national product and national budget is related to armaments. Wars between nations will continue until they culminate at Armageddon.

(2) Natural Disasters (24:7b-8)

"There shall be famines, and pestilences, and earthquakes," the Lord warned (24:7), and these have become so common and widespread as to be almost taken for granted. Many parts of the world are in the grip of famine. The problem of the world's starving millions is aggravated by the fact that the densest populations are to be found in the world's poorest countries.

Gone are the optimistic days when we thought that medical science was going to eliminate disease. Terrible new viruses have appeared. Until recently no one had heard of AIDS. When it first surfaced in the early 1980s, it was restricted to male homosexuals, intravenous drug abusers, Haitians, and hemophiliacs. Now millions are believed to be infected with HIV, the virus that causes the disease. Originally the curse of the sodomite (or so it seems), this fearful scourge is affecting the rest of society as part of an expanding judgment on promiscuous lifestyles and disregard of God's moral laws. Other infectious diseases such as tuberculosis and malaria, as well as ordinary viruses can thrive in the bodies of those whose immune systems have been destroyed by AIDS.

Far worse are the viruses now known to be lurking in the hot zones and equatorial jungles of the earth. One of these viruses is ebola, which dissolves its victims' internal organs, is highly infectious, and has no cure. All these pestilences are but the harbinger of terrible plagues to come.

Earthquakes seem to be on the increase, or at least our awareness of them. We now know what areas of the world are most earthquake-prone. One major geological fault runs through Palestine and the Middle East. Many of America's great cities are built on high-risk fault lines.

b. End-Time Persecutions (24:9-10)

(1) Those Marked by Terror (24:9)

Along with end-time problems will come persecutions. The twentieth century has witnessed a resurgence of savage persecution on a scale never before known. Whole races have been marked for liquidation. The Nazis exterminated six million Jews under conditions of unbelievable barbarity. The communists in their worldwide drive for power are said to have eliminated the equivalent of the entire Spanish-speaking population of all of Latin America. The heartless persecutions of unwanted peoples in such places as Vietnam, Cambodia, and Ethiopia are so commonplace that we simply turn blind eyes and deaf ears to the horrors. And the worst is yet to be.

The holocaust of the great tribulation will eclipse all previous persecutions in a blood bath that will be universal in scope, ruthless in character, deliberate in purpose, and heartless in operation. Although its chief focus will be the world's Jews, it will embrace all Gentiles who refuse to wear the mark of the beast and who help or harbor a Jew.

(2) Those Marked by Treachery (24:10)

The Lord underlined the fact that end-time persecutions will be marked by betrayals. Betrayers have always been common enough. The communists for example became experts in using brainwashing techniques to elicit betrayals. During the great tribulation many will betray neighbors, friends, and family in the hope of buying some measure of immunity for themselves by such a show of loyalty to the beast.

c. End-Time Prophets (24:11-14)

The Lord drew attention to both the false and the true prophets of the endtime. "Many false prophets shall rise," He said (24:11). There will also be true prophets, for God will not leave Himself without a witness, even in the tribulation age. We learn from the Apocalypse that He will raise up two great witnesses (Revelation 11), who will win 144,000 witnesses (Revelation 7; 14), who in turn will win a multitude that no man can number. "This gospel of the kingdom shall be preached in all the world [*oikoumenē,* 'the inhabited world'] for a witness unto all nations," Jesus said, "and then shall the end [*telos,* 'the very end'] come" (Matthew 24:14). The "gospel of the kingdom" to be preached in the tribulation age is the special postrapture, end-time message of the imminence of Christ's coming kingdom.

The beast will turn on these witnesses in fury. All who will not receive his mark and worship his image will be savagely tormented and slain. "But he that shall endure unto the end [*telos*], the same shall be saved" (24:13)—saved in the sense of "delivered," as in 1 Thessalonians 1:10. Those who base a falling-away doctrine on Matthew 24:13 do violence to the context. The verse has nothing to do with losing salvation in the age of grace; it has everything to do with being delivered out of the great tribulation by the second coming of Christ to set up His millennial kingdom.

2. The Nation of Israel (24:15-31)

The Lord's reference to *telos* and "enduring to the end" forms a natural bridge from the first topic (the nations of the world) to the second topic (the nation of Israel). By far the most dramatic and terrible end-time events for Israel will be the coming of the antichrist, the great tribulation, and the battle of Armageddon. These national disasters will prune the fig tree of all its bad fruit and prepare the remnant for the return of Christ.

The second topic of the prophetic sermon is based on the assumption that Israel, reconstituted as a nation, will be back in the land and as Christ-rejecting as ever. The Lord assumed that His listeners had a working knowledge of Old Testament prophecies, particularly those of Daniel. Jesus quoted him with every confidence that he was a genuine, Spirit-inspired, accurate, and authoritative guide to the future. For instance the Lord started with a mention in 24:15 of "the abomination of desolation, spoken of by Daniel the prophet," a clear reference to Daniel 9:27; 11:31; 12:11.

The order of prophesied events is as follows:[41] Shortly after the rapture of the church, a dynamic leader will arise in Europe. He will unite ten key European nations under ten "kings" and revive the Roman empire. As part of his overall strategy for world domination, he will sign a seven-year treaty with the nation of Israel. Under cover of this treaty the religious Jews will rebuild their temple in Jerusalem; their enemies will be held back by the overwhelming military might of this ruler (called the beast in the Apocalypse and the antichrist elsewhere). The Islamic nations will appeal to Russia. Seeing its global position being eroded by the dynamism and determination of the revitalized West (led by the beast), Russia will make the fatal decision to invade Israel. A military disaster of unprecedented magnitude will overtake the combined antisemitic forces (Ezekiel 38–39). This will create an enormous geo-political vacuum, which will make it possible for the beast to assume global rule.

The beast will now have no more use for Israel. He will seize the rebuilt temple, put an image of himself in the inner sanctuary, and command that universal worship be given to him and his image. Then he will launch an all-out pogrom against the Jews; he will set out to exterminate them along with all those who refuse to receive his mark and worship his image. It is this image that is referred to by both Daniel and Jesus as the abomination of desolation.

a. Israel's Coming Ruin (24:15-26)

(1) The Flight of the Saints at That Time (24:15-20)

In discussing the coming reign of terror, the Lord emphasized that believers will need to flee from Jerusalem. Once the beast has desecrated the temple, it will be folly to tarry for any reason at all. Nothing must impede their flight to the mountains. Woe to those who are hindered by a physical condition such as pregnancy or by religious scruples if news of the desecration comes on a sabbath. Many think the ultimate place of hiding and security for these refugees will be the ancient rock city of Petra.

(2) The Fury of the Storm at That Time (24:21-22)

(a) The Severity of the Great Tribulation (24:21)

Alluding to Daniel 12:1, the Lord said, "Then shall be great tribulation, such as was not since the beginning of the world to this time, no, nor ever shall be." God's people have always been persecuted in this sin-cursed world, but we must not confuse ordinary persecutions with the great tribulation. It will be a special period of three and a half years (1,260 days) during which Satan will be allowed to do his worst against God's people in particular and mankind in general. It will be a time when God will pour out His wrath on this planet, and the Jewish people will finally be brought to the end of their Christ-rejecting self-reliance and pride.

(b) The Shortness of the Great Tribulation (24:22)

The Lord added, "Except those days should be shortened, there should no flesh be saved: but for the elect's sake those days shall be shortened." This is another of those statements in Scripture that show how much the careless and unbelieving world owes to the presence of God's people in its midst.

(3) The Folly of the Sinners at That Time (24:23-26)

At that time Satan will lure people by dazzling them with spectacular miracles, signs, and lying wonders. There will be rumors that Christ has returned and even the elect will have moments when they almost succumb to the seemingly convincing proofs. Many of the "signs" will be wrought by the false prophet, who is the second beast of Revelation 13. The false prophet along with the antichrist and the great red dragon make up the Satanic trinity. The false prophet will not be alone, for "there shall arise false Christs, and false prophets" here, there, and everywhere (24:24). Each one will have some great sign or deceiving wonder. The Lord warned His people not to be deceived, not to be lured out of hiding, for His return would be very evident.

b. Israel's Coming Redeemer (24:27-31)

(1) The Speed with Which He Will Return (24:27)

The Lord said His return will be "as the lightning cometh out of the east, and shineth even unto the west." The angry storm clouds will have been building up for months and then with a flash like lightning the Lord will come. There will be no time for repentance or remorse. Men will be caught red-handed wherever they are and whatever they are doing—whether they are gathering on the plains of Megiddo, or storming the city of Jerusalem, or murdering God's people, or worshiping the beast, or displaying his mark to close some commercial deal.

(2) The Slaughter with Which He Will Return (24:28)

The Lord's return will be accompanied by a wholesale slaughter of the multiplied millions massed in their might at Megiddo. The entire period of terror will culminate at that battlefield, to which the armies of East and West will be drawn. Not least among the horrors of Armageddon will be the assembling of thousands of birds of prey who will be summoned to be God's undertakers. They will fly over the assembled hosts and knell the doom of the wicked.

Centuries before Jesus was born, God had asked Job, "Doth the eagle mount up at thy command?…She seeketh the prey, and her eyes behold afar off. Her young ones also suck up blood: and where the slain are [that is, on the field of battle], there is she" (Job 39:27-30). The description of Armageddon in Matthew 24:28 is similar: "Wheresoever the carcase is, there will the eagles be gathered together."

(3) The Signs with Which He Will Return (24:29-30)

The signs of the Lord's return will not be lying signs such as those produced by the beast and his wizard prophet. There will be awesome signs, shaking heaven above and earth beneath, "and then shall appear the sign of the Son of man in heaven: and then shall all the tribes of the earth mourn, and they shall see the Son of man coming in the clouds of heaven with power and great glory" (24:30).

Too late the truth will dawn on all the branded dupes of the devil. They will admit to each other: "The Bible, which we have despised, was right all the time. The prophecies were not allegories, but literal actualities. The One whose peerless name we have customarily used as a curse word is the eternal, uncreated Son of the living God. Here He is, coming back as He said, not as a carpenter but as a conqueror, not with His glory veiled, but with that glory dimming the brightness of the noonday sun."

(4) The Sound with Which He Will Return (24:31)

At His return the Son of man "shall send his angels with a great sound of a trumpet, and they shall gather together his elect from the four winds, from one end of heaven to the other." Moses anticipated the judgmental scattering of Israel into all parts of the

earth because of national sin; he also foresaw the end-time ingathering of all the remaining outcasts of Israel. In Deuteronomy
30:3-5 he prophesied that national repentance would be followed
by national regathering:

> Then the Lord thy God will turn thy captivity, and have
> compassion upon thee, and will return and gather thee from
> all the nations, whither the Lord thy God hath scattered thee.
> If any of thine be driven out unto the outmost parts of heaven
> [the four points of the compass from whence the winds of
> heaven blow], from thence will the Lord thy God gather thee,
> and from thence will he fetch thee: And the Lord thy God will
> bring thee into the land which thy fathers possessed, and thou
> shalt possess it.

The rebirth of the state of Israel in our day and the regathering
of the Jewish people to their ancestral homeland do not completely
fulfill the prophecy of Moses. The ingathering of exiles is only
partial and it is being accomplished in unbelief. Israel, still rejecting Christ, is not yet the olive branch being grafted back in to its
former spiritual privilege (Romans 11); it is the fig tree barren of
all that could minister to Christ, but putting forth its end-time
leaves. Israel is being regathered today not in anticipation of the
coming of Christ to reign, but in anticipation of the coming of the
antichrist to ruin.

The Lord concluded the second topic of this sermon with the
sound of a trumpet. The sounding of the trumpet will herald the
fulfillment of the prophetic aspect of Israel's annual feast of
trumpets (Leviticus 23:23-25). The feast of trumpets is the forerunner of the feast of atonement and the joyous millennial feast of
tabernacles. The sign of the fig tree in Matthew 24:32 is a natural
bridge to the third topic, the church.

3. The Nationals of Heaven (24:32-51)

In terms of chronology the Lord now goes back in time. The
rapture of the church, which is the subject matter of this passage,
will precede the events described in the two previous passages,
which dealt with the consummation of God's end-time purposes in
regard to the Gentile nations and Israel. Topically, end-time truth
concerning the church comes last because the church came upon
the scene last; indeed it was not even born when the Olivet
discourse was given. Chronologically, end-time truth concerning

the church comes first and precedes most of what the Lord revealed in His discussion of the first two topics.

In 24:3 the disciples had not asked a question about the Lord's coming and the church; at that time they had no real concept of the church, although truth concerning it had been given to them. They had asked a more general question about end-time events, especially Jewish end-time events. The Lord answered their immediate questions first, then went on to speak of what was closest to His heart: His coming for the nationals of Heaven prior to His judgmental dealings with Israel and the other nations.

a. Two Kinds of Confirmation (24:32-39)

The use of the fig tree as a symbol of Israel can be traced back to a time when there was no church on earth (Judges 9:10-11). In Matthew 24, however, the fig tree is used as a sign of the approaching rapture, a sign for the church, a sign based on the nation of Israel and its unbelief. The sign of the flood was derived from a time when there was no nation of Israel on earth. The flood too is a sign of the rapture, a sign for the church, a sign based on the Gentile nations and their unbelief. The fig tree points to a significant *political* sign: the rebirth of the state of Israel. The flood points to a significant *moral* sign.

(1) The Sign of the Fig (24:32-36)

The sign of the fig tree will be given to make it clear when "summer is nigh" (24:32), when springtime is here and the long winter of Christ's absence is about to end, when the Lord's return is more than imminent.

(a) A Comparison (24:32-33)

Just a day or two before, the Lord had performed the "miracle" of the fig tree (21:18-20). Now the Lord presented a "parable" of the fig tree (24:32). The budding of the fig tree is *the* sign that we have arrived at the endtimes.

In Scripture three trees symbolize the nation of Israel. The vine represents the nation of Israel from the time it becomes a nation until the time it rejects Christ (Matthew 21:33-44; Isaiah 5:1-7). In the upper room the Lord told His disciples that henceforth He was the true vine and His Father was the husbandman (John 15:1-6). Israel's national failure was complete.

The olive tree represents Israel after the return of Christ and the national repentance of Israel (Romans 11). During our present age the Jews have been broken off from the place of religious privilege that was theirs in Old Testament times. The Gentiles (the wild olive branches) have been grafted in and now occupy the place forfeited by the Jews when they rejected Christ.

The church is predominantly Gentile in composition. However, in a coming day God will graft the Jewish people back in to the place of religious privilege, so Gentiles should not boast about the rich spiritual things they now enjoy. Paul said in effect, "If the breaking off of the natural branches has been such a blessing to the Gentile world, what will it be like when they are grafted back in, when Israel finally manifests the enormous spiritual potential that is rightfully hers?" Well, we know what it will be like; it will be the millennium!

The fig tree represents Israel from the time the nation rejects Christ to the time when Israel as a nation accepts Christ. The cursing of the literal fig tree by Israel's rejected King was a symbolic act. It was a parable as well as a miracle. The symbolic cursing (Matthew 21) was followed by the actual cursing of the nation that the tree symbolized (Matthew 23).

"Now," said the Lord, "learn a parable of the fig tree" (24:32). The fig tree (the nation of Israel) that died under its Creator's curse will come back to life. The tree will again have an abundance of leaves—not fruit, but leaves. In other words, the nation of Israel, which began to disintegrate in A.D. 70 and was finally evicted from the promised land in A.D. 135 at the time of the Bar Kokhba rebellion, is to come back to life as a nation just prior to the consummation of end-time events. The reconstitution of the nation will be in unbelief; Israel will still be rejecting Christ. Accordingly the Lord did not indicate that the fig tree would bring forth fruit when it came back to life.

That is exactly what has happened. The Zionists had no thought of fulfilling prophecy in their crusade for a revived state in Palestine. The leaders of the movement were secularists and they conceived a secular state. Theodore Hertzl, the founder of Zionism, was a thoroughly secularized pragmatist and visionary.[42] Just the same, the rebirth of the state of Israel in our lifetime is an extraordinary miracle; it is the sign that the church age has about run its course, that the rapture is imminent, and that God is about to begin His end-time dealing with the Jewish people. He will pick up where He left off when the church-age parenthesis was inserted into His dealings with mankind.

(b) A Confirmation (24:34-35)

The Lord confirmed, "This generation shall not pass, till all these things be fulfilled" (24:34). We have already seen that in 23:36 the expression "this generation" refers to a literal generation. If the expression means a literal generation in 23:36, it must mean a literal generation in 24:34—in spite of well-meaning attempts to soften the impact of the verse by making the expression refer to something else.

Note also that the word "not" in 24:34 is a translation of the Greek *ou mē,* a very strong term that can be literally rendered "by no means." The expression translated "be fulfilled" can be rendered "begin to be." So the Lord was saying, "This generation shall by no means pass, till all these thing begin to be."

Which generation did the Lord mean? Obviously He did not mean the generation *to* which He was speaking. That was the generation of 23:36, the generation that witnessed the cursing of the fig tree. They lived to see the Roman war, the destruction of Jerusalem and the temple, and the beginning of the end of Jewish national life. If in 24:34 it was not the generation *to* which He was speaking, then surely it had to be the generation *of* which He was speaking—the generation that would witness the rebirth of the state of Israel, the budding of the fig tree, and the beginning of the end of "all these things."

As we have already noted, the question arises, How long is a "generation"? The expression was deliberately chosen by the Lord because of its elasticity. A generation can stretch all the way from the time of one's birth to the time of one's death and the deaths of one's contemporaries. Or it could be the relatively brief period when one's generation is in charge of the things that are happening. In any case no hard and fast lines can be drawn where a generation begins and ends because of the endless flow of births and deaths. One generation very gradually merges into another generation.

(c) A Caution (24:36)

By using the yardstick of a generation the Lord evidently intended to guard against date-fixing, for He cautioned, "Of that day and hour knoweth no man, no, not the angels of heaven, but my Father only." This verse is a clear reference to the rapture of the church, which is always set before us as an undated event.

The Lord's return to set up His kingdom at the very end is, by contrast, a dated event. God consistently set dates for His Old Testament people (Genesis 15:13-16; Daniel 9:24-27). Biblically literate Jews could have computed the time of the exodus and the actual date of the crucifixion. Similarly Jews living at the time of the setting up of the abomination of desolation will be able to do a countdown to the return of Christ. The length of the intervening period is given as forty-two months in Revelation 13:5; as "a time, and times, and half a time" (three and a half years) in Revelation 12:14; and even more specifically as 1,260 days in Revelation 11:3. Dates are given for Jewish events because Israel is God's earthly people. No dates are given for church events because the church is God's heavenly people; the church is rooted in eternity.

So although the Jews could set dates, we are not to make any attempt to set a date for the rapture. That date is secret. However, we know from the rebirth of the state of Israel that "summer is nigh" (Matthew 24:32).

(2) The Sign of the Flood (24:37-39)

(a) An Appeal (24:37)

The flood is another sign that end-time events and the rapture of the church are at hand. In appealing to the story of Noah, the Lord drew our attention to Genesis 4–6, which He endorsed as inspired, authoritative, and historical. Any attack on these chapters is an attack on the deity of Christ.

(b) An Appraisal (24:38-39a)

The Lord declared that conditions on earth at the time of His return will parallel conditions on earth in the days of Noah. (Luke 17:28-32 indicates that the days before the Lord's return will also parallel the days of Lot. Noah lived in a pornographic society; Lot lived in a perverted society. Both are hallmarks of our day.)

The days of Noah were marked by seven characteristics: spiritual decline, social dilemma, shameless depravity, scientific development, some devotion, strong delusion, and sudden destruction. To illustrate His point the Lord picked up just one of these characteristics: strong delusion. They "knew not," he said (Matthew 24:39). Of all the things Jesus could have underlined, He chose to emphasize the fact that the people of the endtimes will be deluded by the secular humanism and gross materialism that dominated Noah's age.

Before the flood there was no excuse for not knowing that God was about to intervene directly in human affairs, for Noah was "a preacher of righteousness" (2 Peter 2:5). God never leaves Himself without a witness. The more degenerate the times, the more definite the testimony.

Day by day Noah labored on the ark; night by night he preached to a careless world. But he won not a single convert outside the members of his immediate family. He was simply ignored. People went about their business. They planned meals and marriages as nonchalantly as though there were no such man as Noah, no such person as God, and no such prospect as judgment. Jesus mentioned their "eating and drinking, marrying and giving in marriage" (Matthew 24:38), but He did not dwell on the gross sins referred to by the Holy Spirit in Genesis 6. Indeed eating and drinking were necessities. And in an age when God's primeval law of marriage was being set aside by society, the people who married must have been better than average. But because they "knew not," they were just as lost as the prostitutes, perverts, and pornographers who abounded in their world.

Noah's contemporaries were held accountable by the court of Heaven for their ignorance of God, their ignorance of the salvation He had provided, their ignorance of their lostness, and their ignorance of the signs of the times. The word translated "knew" in Matthew 24:39 is *ginōskō*, which means "to acquire knowledge, become acquainted with, learn, perceive." The same word is used in 24:32 in connection with the budding of the fig tree: "Ye *know* that summer is nigh" (italics added).

(c) An Application (24:39b)

"So shall also the coming of the Son of man be." This crucial statement indicates that the days prior to the Lord's return will be marked by the same careless inattention to faithful preaching and fulfilled prophecy. Judgment was looming in the days of Noah, and it is looming now.

b. Two Kinds of Christians (24:40-51)

So then, the Lord used the illustrations of the fig tree and the flood to set the stage for what He had to say about what we call the rapture of the church. At this point we must distinguish between Christians who, being genuinely saved, will be caught away at the rapture to be with Christ, and those who, merely professing to be saved, will be left behind at the rapture (spewed out of His mouth, Revelation 3:16).

(1) The First Warning (24:40-44)

(a) Those Received by Christ at the Rapture (24:40-42)

The Lord warned, "Then shall two be in the field; the one shall be taken, and the other left. Two women shall be grinding at the mill; the one shall be taken, and the other left" (24:40-41). These words refer to the rapture. People who disagree with this interpretation point to the context and etymology.

Appealing to context, they claim that the reference cannot be to the rapture because the warning comes *after* prophecies related to the great tribulation. In their view, to say that the warning refers to the rapture is to say that the church will go through the tribulation. Not so! The structure of the chapter shows it to be a three-part topical sermon, with each topic treated as a separate entity. That the church does not go through the great tribulation is clear from 1 Thessalonians 4:13–5:11 and 2 Thessalonians 2:6-8. The latter reference makes it clear that during the great tribulation the Holy Spirit will no longer restrain and the church will no longer be here. It is the removal of the restrainer (the Holy Spirit in the church) that will enable the antichrist to come, and the tribulation cannot start until the antichrist comes.

The argument from etymology hinges on the word "took" in Matthew 24:39: "The flood came, and took them all away." The argument is that the taking away in 24:39 is a taking away in judgment, so the taking away in 24:40-41 has to be a taking away in judgment; at the time of the Lord's actual return to reign, one will be taken in judgment and the other will be left to go into the millennial kingdom. This interpretation sounds plausible enough until we examine the actual words used by the Lord.

In 24:39 the word translated "took" is *airō,* which suggests a taking away in violence, as in the flood. If the Lord had wanted to suggest a similar taking away in judgment in 24:40-41, He surely would have used *airō* again. Instead He used *paralambanō.* This word can be used in a negative sense, but it is often used in a very tender way in the New Testament. It can mean "to take from one's side in peace and blessing." James Strong's definition is "to associate with oneself (in any familiar or intimate act or relation)."[43] It certainly seems that the Lord deliberately introduced a different thought by introducing a different word, one that frequently has the opposite sense.

For instance the word is used for the taking of a bride, as in the first use of this word in the New Testament: "Fear not to *take* unto thee Mary thy wife" (Matthew 1:20, italics added). It is used in connection with the choosing of certain disciples to share in the transfiguration experience: "Jesus *taketh* Peter, James, and John" (Matthew 17:1, italics added). It is used to describe the Lord's taking His disciples away for a rest after their return from their evangelistic mission: "He *took* them, and went aside privately into a desert place" (Luke 9:10, italics added). Above all, the word is used to describe the Lord's return for His own: "I will come again, and *receive* you unto myself" (John 14:3, italics added).

Those who refuse to see the rapture of the church in Matthew 24:40-41 make much of the Jewish nature of Matthew's Gospel. No doubt the book of Matthew is the most Jewish of the Gospels, but it is also the only Gospel that mentions the church. As we have already seen, the church is mentioned both directly and indirectly. It is hard to imagine the Lord giving us His one full-length exposition of the endtimes without making reference to the church and its rapture, which are near and dear to His heart.

In view of the suddenness and solemnity of the rapture, the Lord warned His people to work and watch. "Watch therefore," He said, "for ye know not what hour your Lord doth come" (24:42). This is another reference to the rapture as an undated, secret event.

(b) Those Rejected by Christ at the Rapture (24:43-44)

Again the Lord warned His listeners about being watchful and ready. "In such an hour as ye think not the Son of man cometh," He said (24:44).

Much has been made of the use of the title "Son of man" here. It is essentially a title associated with Christ's relationship to the earth. The title occurs eighty-four times in the Gospels, which contain the record of His coming for the special purpose of reclaiming this earth for God. As a result of the fall, dominion over this earth was seized from the first man by Satan; Jesus came as Son of man to reclaim that dominion. To Him alone belongs the right to rule the earth (Ezekiel 21:27).

The title is rarely used outside the Gospels. It occurs in Acts 7:56, where Stephen saw the Lord standing at God's right hand to welcome home the first martyr of the church, in anticipation of the day when He will bring the church back with Him when He comes to reign. There is a reference to the "son of man" in Hebrews 2:6, which really is a quotation from Psalm 8:4; the writer of Hebrews was referring to the first man Adam and only by application to the Lord. The title does not occur again until the Apocalypse, where it is used twice (Revelation 1:13; 14:14) and anticipates the Lord's coming to overthrow the usurper and reign in righteousness over a renovated planet.

We can see then that "Son of man" is not a title associated with the true church. In the church age we use the title "Son of God." The use of "Son of man" in Matthew 24:39 shows that the rapture of the church will bring the Lord's earthly goals into focus once more. The use of "Son of man" in 24:44 shows that those addressed will be left behind in a world that is about to be convulsed by the usurper, a world that can anticipate the final coming of Jesus as Son of man to consummate God's purposes on this planet.

The use of the title "Son of man" points to the postrapture earth. We learn from 2 Thessalonians 2 the fate of those who are left behind, who only profess to know Christ, who do not belong to the true church. They will be totally deceived by the man of sin. Hence the warning and the pointed use of His pre-Pentecostal and postrapture title in Matthew 24:44.

(2) The Further Warning (24:45-51)

In this segment of the Olivet discourse the emphasis on being busy in the Master's service is even more pronounced. In 24:40-41 two were in the field and two were grinding at the mill; in each pair nothing outward distinguished the one taken in the rapture from the one left behind for judgment. In 24:45-51 the difference between the two servants is obvious. (Note the emphasis on the title "lord" in these verses.)

(a) The Wise Servant—The One Taken (24:45-47)

This servant is busy, diligently fulfilling the task the Lord has entrusted to him. Because he is "faithful and wise" (24:45), he is guaranteed a reward at the judgment seat of Christ. The Lord called him "blessed" (24:46), for in the millennial age he will be made a ruler.

(b) The Wicked Servant—The One Left (24:48-51)

This man proves himself to be no true servant at all. Jesus described him as "that evil servant" (24:48). The word translated "evil" here is *kakos*, which means "depraved, bad in nature." The wicked servant is a man with a vicious disposition. He has no conviction about the coming of the Lord. He abuses his authority; he abuses those under him; he finds his fellowship with drunkards. The Lord's coming will take him completely by surprise. He will end up at the great white throne and he will be sent with the hypocrites to the place of "weeping and gnashing of teeth." In spite of all his pretensions of being a Christian, he has never been saved at all.

C. The Lord's End-Time Parables (25:1-46)

Matthew 25 is a parabolic supplement to the prophetic teaching of Matthew 24. Like the prophecy, the parables cover the three divisions of the human race: the Jews, the Gentiles, and the church. The first parable has to do with Israel, the second with the church, and the third with the Gentile nations. The order is different, but the subjects are the same.

1. For the Nation of Israel: Parable of the Virgins (25:1-13)

The parable of the wise and foolish virgins is well known, but much abused. The coming of the groom for the bride is an obvious reference to the rapture of the church, but from that point on, the church is out of the picture and the focus is on the people of Israel. This is a postrapture parable and must be understood in that light.

After the rapture God will revert to His Old Testament ways of dealing with Israel and the other nations. The church age is a clearly marked parenthesis in God's dealings with the human race, a parenthesis that began with the day of Pentecost and will end with the rapture. The unique feature of the parenthetical age is the baptizing work of the Holy Spirit.

a. The Marriage Call (25:1-5)

The scene is Israel in the period immediately following the rapture. The Lord comes on stage, as do ten virgins. The number *ten* denotes completeness, as in the ten commandments. (In the church the controlling number is not ten, but "two or three," as in Matthew 18:20.) The ten virgins (the friends of the Bridegroom) go forth to meet the Bridegroom. They do not represent the church; the bride represents the church. Nor were the virgins in the rapture, but they are invited to the reception.

(1) The Heavenly Groom (25:1)

In Bible times a bridegroom would first go to his bride's house and then conduct her to his home. Along the way they would be joined by various friends until the procession was complete. Then they would all go to the wedding feast. In the parable the heavenly groom has come for His bride, the church, and the call is going forth to Israel to join the procession. A company is being formed of those willing and ready to go forth to meet the groom and the bride when the time comes. The groom of course is Christ. He is referred to as "Lord" by the foolish virgins (25:11) and as "the Son of man" by Jesus Himself (25:13).

Many people will be saved after the rapture (Revelation 7). They will not be in the church of course because the church will be in Heaven, but they will be in the kingdom. During the tribulation age they will be looking ardently for the coming back of the King—at least the wise ones will. Many other people will profess to be saved.

(2) The Holy Ghost (25:2-5)

(a) Neglecting the Spirit of God (25:2-4)

In the parable, some of the virgins neglect the oil, which is symbolic of the Holy Ghost. In many ways all ten virgins are alike. They all have lamps; they all set out to meet the Bridegroom; they all fall asleep. Outwardly all the virgins are the same; what distinguishes them is their supply of oil. The wise virgins have oil in their lamps and in their vessels. The foolish virgins have oil in their lamps, but not in their vessels. That is the crucial difference.

The *lamps* symbolize the Word of God (Psalm 119:105), the only source of spiritual light in this dark world of sin. Each virgin has a lamp and knows it is necessary to use it as a guide in the darkness. Oil in the lamp suggests that each of them has the Word of God illuminated for them by the Spirit of God, for only by the operation of the Spirit of God does the Word of God cast its light (1 Corinthians 2:14). Each virgin has benefited from the initial illuminating work of the Holy Spirit.

The *vessels* represent individuals' personal lives (Psalm 31:12; Acts 9:15; 1 Peter 3:7). Concerning God's work in our lives, we are reminded that "we have this treasure in earthen vessels, that the excellency of the power may be of God, and not of us" (2 Corinthians 4:7).

In the parable all ten virgins start out with oil in their lamps. All ten allow the lamps to go out through neglect. All are initially enlightened, but later neglect the truth of the Word of God. Five of the virgins, however, also have oil in their vessels. In other words, five have the Holy Spirit in their lives and five do not. Outwardly they are the same, but inwardly they are different. Some are genuinely saved. Others are not. They have neglected the all-important step of receiving the regenerating Holy Spirit who has shone through the Word into their lives.

(b) Neglecting the Son of God (25:5)

All ten virgins fall asleep when the groom's coming is seemingly delayed. The proneness of the flesh to dull spiritual perception asserts itself.

b. The Midnight Cry (25:6-10)

(1) The Guests Aroused (25:6-9)

At midnight something happens to wake everyone up—some quickening of end-time events, some clarion call of God. Right at the last moment the cry is heard: "Behold, the bridegroom cometh; go ye out to meet him" (25:6). At this point the foolish virgins discover their tragic mistake: they have no oil in their vessels. The wise virgins are able to relight their lamps; they have what it takes to grasp Bible truth once again. The foolish virgins want the wise virgins to share their oil, but no one can be saved on the strength of someone else's spiritual experience. Only God can impart the Holy Spirit. The foolish virgins have waited until it is too late to fill their vessels; they stumble off in a vain quest for oil.

(2) The Groom Arrives (25:10)

While the foolish virgins are away, the Bridegroom comes. Those who are ready go in with him to the marriage, and the door is shut (ominous words). The foolish virgins not only miss the rapture; they miss the reception as well. They are shut out from everything.

c. The Mistaken Claim (25:11-13)

(1) The Appeal (25:11-12)

When the foolish virgins return, they knock on the door and say, "Lord, Lord, open to us," but He answers, "I know you not." They have the language of a believer, but not the life of a believer. The Bible does not say what happens to them. It simply says that the door is shut. They are on the wrong side, and they are repudiated by the Lord whose name they speak so insincerely.

(2) The Application (25:13)

The parable ends with a warning: "Watch therefore, for ye know neither the day nor the hour wherein the Son of man cometh." The warning applies to all in the postrapture, sin-dominated, satanically-ruled world. They are cautioned not to neglect the divine light and the possession of divine life. No doubt many will have been aroused by the rapture of the church and by the dawn of a new spiritual awakening pioneered by the "two witnesses" and the "hundred and forty and four thousand" (Revelation 11:3; 7:4). But there will be numbers of people who—though awakened to postrapture, tribulation, and kingdom truth—will neglect the all-important step of accepting Christ personally. They will fall asleep, never to waken again until it is too late. They will be dead to the signs of the times and the rapid 1,260-day countdown to the Lord's return.

2. For the Nationals of Heaven: Parable of the Talents (25:14-30)

This is clearly a parable for the church. The period between the nobleman's departure and return represents the period between the Lord's ascension and the rapture. The parable is one of accountability and it applies to us who are living in this age while the Lord is away. It concerns two days: the day of responsibility (the present age) and the day of reckoning (at the judgment seat of Christ).

a. The Time of Responsibility (25:14-18)

When the kingdom age dawns, the Lord will need many people to administer His affairs. In the present age of probation we are given talents and trusts, and the way we handle them will determine our positions in the millennial kingdom. Talents are the spiritual gifts bestowed sovereignly by God on all believers.

The "talent" was the heaviest weight in use among the Hebrews. It weighed as much as a man could lift. So even the servant who received one talent received something of incalculable worth. The greatness of the trust must not be minimized. Our Lord has handed over to each of us awesome responsibility.

Two of the three servants in the story went immediately to work. The third servant hid his talent. The master, a shrewd judge of men, knew that the third servant had some ability, even if it was less than that of the others. There was no excuse for him to bury his talent. He should have done all he could to secure a word of commendation at the Lord's return. By neglect he became an unprofitable servant.

b. The Time of Reckoning (25:19-30)

"After a long time the lord of those servants cometh, and reckoneth with them" (25:19). This one statement fixes the interpretation of the parable to our own age. The Lord will be away during the great tribulation too, but those days are to be shortened (24:22). It is the present age that is marked by the prolonged absence of the Lord.

The day of reckoning is coming when "we shall all stand before the judgment seat of Christ" (Romans 14:10; also see 2 Corinthians 5:10). The judgment seat is for believers, not unbelievers.

(1) The Worthy Servants (25:19-23)

The first two servants were commended for faithful service and rewarded by being made rulers "over many things." A crown (2 Timothy 4:8), a throne (Revelation 3:21), and a kingdom (Matthew 25:34) are held out to us as incentives for faithful service. What we gain in the church age, we will enjoy in the kingdom age.

(2) The Worthless Servant (25:24-30)

Much more is said about the third servant. Let us note carefully his standing. The Lord, who normally commits His work to the saved, entrusted all three men with talents. All three were called "his own servants" (25:14), so the third servant, like the first two, was owned by the Lord as one of His. The word translated "servant" in this parable means "slave," so the third man was one the Master had bought. He was judged at the same time as the others—an important point because the unsaved will not be judged at the judgment seat of Christ, but later at the great white throne (Revelation 20:11-15). He was judged as a servant—and what will be in view at the judgment seat of Christ is service, not sonship. All three men were judged on the basis of their performance, not their persons.

(a) His Excuse (25:24-25)

Adding insult to injury, the worthless servant said, "Lord, I knew thee that thou art an hard man…and I was afraid." His excuses were disavowed.

(b) His Exposure (25:26-30)

i. His Denunciation (25:26-29)

He was not guilty of gross sin. He was not a murderer or a thief or a drunkard, as in 24:49. He was simply charged with neglect. At the judgment he could show only the one talent that had been entrusted to him, so he was condemned. He was pronounced "wicked" (25:26; the word translated "wicked" here is *poneros,* which is often used to describe the malignancy of wrong behavior). The man had a saved soul and a lost life. He was stripped of his talent, which was then given to the more able of the first two servants.

ii. His Destiny (25:30)

After being told what he should have done with his talent, He was cast into "outer darkness," where there is "weeping and gnashing of teeth." This verse is certainly the most difficult statement in the parable because it implies that the servant was not saved at all, a conclusion that is contradicted by the rest of the parable.

What else could the statement mean? It does not refer to some kind of purgatory, for the Bible knows of no such place; purgatory is the invention of Catholic theologians. The statement cannot mean that the man was once saved and somehow lost his salvation, for such an idea is contrary to the tenor of the whole New Testament, which denies that salvation is in any way dependent on our works.

To avoid the difficulty inherent in this verse, some have envisioned the place of "outer darkness" as some remote spot, in the kingdom but far removed from the central glory in Jerusalem. But the Bible speaks of no such place. And this theory does not explain the "weeping and gnashing of teeth," an expression used elsewhere to refer to the misery of the lost in Hell.

What then do we know about the destiny of the worthless servant? We do know that the question of personal salvation will not be raised at the judgment seat of Christ. We know too that rebukes and rewards will be commensurate with neglect or service, as the case may be. Since this servant was one of the Lord's own people, we cannot envision him suffering personal anguish in the flames of a lost eternity. But may it not be that such faithless servants as he will be taken to that place of "outer darkness" not to suffer but to see? May it not be that they will be taken to where there is "weeping and gnashing of teeth" not to be punished or purged, but to see souls they might have reached—to see the result of their sinful failure and neglect? It may well be.

Then in grace the Lord will wipe away their tears, and the judgment will be over. The church will be forever free from blemish. Those rewarded will reign with Christ. Others, like the faithless servant in the parable, will enter the kingdom "saved; yet so as by fire" and, at least for the millennial age, suffering loss (1 Corinthians 3:12-15).

3. For the Nations of Earth: Parable of the Sheep and Goats (25:31-46)

In this passage, for the first and last time the Lord Jesus referred to Himself as a King. Immediately after telling the parable He went on His way to be crowned with thorns by a mocking world. The cross was only three days ahead.

a. A Throne (25:31)

When the great tribulation and the battle of Armageddon are over, what is left of the human race (after the wars, famines, earthquakes, pestilences, and persecutions of the Apocalypse) will be summoned to the valley of Jehoshaphat near Jerusalem to be judged (Joel 3:2,12). In the valley the Lord will set up a throne, "the throne of his glory." There will be something eminently right about the Lord Jesus being seated in power and glory on this planet.

This judgment of the nations will be separate from other judgments mentioned in Scripture. Its purpose will be to decide who among those still living on earth are to be allowed to enter the millennial kingdom.

b. A Throng (25:32-33)

Three separate groups will gather at the throne: those called "sheep," those called "goats," and those whom the Lord called "my brethren" (25:40). Which brethren did He mean? We can trace three "family circles" in the New Testament: (1) those who are the

Lord's brethren because they have been born again and God is their Father (Hebrews 2:11); (2) those who belonged to the same human family when Jesus lived on earth, the natural children of Mary and Joseph (Matthew 12:47); and (3) members of the Hebrew nation, who always enjoyed a strong sense of national brotherhood (Deuteronomy 17:15-20). It was this third circle that the Lord referred to in the parable when He spoke of "the least of these my brethren." They were Jews; they belonged to the same nation as He.

The survivors of the nations, the remnant of mankind who are gathered at the throne, will be divided into two classes: sheep and goats. The sheep the Lord will own as His; the goats He will repudiate. It is interesting to note that a goat is a naturally quarrelsome, lascivious, destructive, and evil-smelling creature, often associated with Satanism and witchcraft.

The background of this judgment will be the great tribulation. The beast will have been on the rampage for three and a half years, ruthlessly stamping out all vestiges of worship of the true God. Raw savagery and terror will have been the instruments of his policy; the special target of his hate, the Jews. Here and there some bold Gentile will have offered refuge to a fleeing Jew and by God's grace survived the holocaust. Such "righteous Gentiles," as the Jews call them, will be but few. The majority will have been too intimidated by the beast's gestapo to dare to help.

The criterion of this judgment will be simple. The Judge will ask, "What did you do to My brethren? What did you do to the Jews? Did you shelter them or did you persecute and betray them? Did you turn a blind eye to what was going on?" The criterion will not be "What did you do with Jesus?" but "What did you do to the Jews?" This will be God's test. At the judgment of the nations the Lord will accept the individual's attitude toward the Jews as the token of what his attitude would have been toward Him if he had heard of Him. What the individual did to the Jews will be evidence of what he would have done with Jesus. The worldwide dispersion of the persecuted Jews will give everyone the opportunity to make a gesture of goodwill toward the Jews.

So the survivors of the planet will be drawn to Jerusalem and the valley of Jehoshaphat for this great assize. The Jews who are still alive, all believers now, will stand with Christ; they will hardly dare to believe that the nightmare is over. The motley, ragtag and bobtail crowd of Gentiles, speaking a thousand tongues, will be assembled before the King; they will have outlived the seven-year rule of the beast, but many of them will be branded for eternity with his festering mark. "They shall look on him whom they pierced" (John 19:37).

c. A Thrill (25:34-46)

The valley of Jehoshaphat (called the Kidron valley in Jesus' day) lies between Jerusalem and the mount of Olives. The garden of Gethsemane across from Jerusalem will bear sober witness to the sufferings of the King at the hands of men.

At the great assize, those described as sheep will be made to stand on the right hand of the King—toward Jerusalem. Those described as goats will be made to stand on His left hand—toward the ominous Tophet valley of Hinnom. There will be a thrill of happiness for those who are selected for life, and a thrill of horror for those weeded out for judgment.

(1) The Happiness of Those Redeemed (25:34-40)

The "sheep" will take up their stand with wonder and the King will say, "Come, ye blessed of my Father, inherit the kingdom prepared for you from the foundation of the world: For I was an hungred, and ye gave me meat..." (25:34-36) In joy and amazement they will reply, "When saw we thee an hungred...?" (25:37-39)

The "goats" will respond the same way: "When...?" (25:44). Neither class will have known the King personally. They will have had no idea that their behavior was an advertisement of an attitude toward God in which Omniscience could see potential faith or adamant unbelief.

The Holy Spirit calls those who will be chosen to stand on Christ's right hand "righteous" (25:37), so they will have had at least the germ of faith in their hearts. Romans 4:3 tells us that "Abraham believed God, and it was counted unto him for righteousness." These Gentiles with the germ of faith in their hearts will come into the blessing of Abraham: God promised him, "I will bless them that bless thee, and curse him that curseth thee: and in thee shall all families of the earth be blessed" (Genesis 12:3).

In Matthew 25:40 the Lord stated the principle that will be the basis of the acceptance of these "righteous" Gentiles: "Inasmuch as ye have done it unto one of the least of these my brethren, ye have done it unto me." He who reads all hearts and whose own heart is free from all narrowness, will accept what the "sheep" have done for a Jew as having been done for Him. As the poet wrote, "There's a wideness in God's mercy / Like the wideness of the sea."[44]

(2) The Horror of Those Rejected (25:41-46)

Those assembled on His left hand will have no hope. Many will have been branded with the mark of the beast. All will be able to remember cursing or kicking a Jew, or betraying a Jew to the tormentors, or refusing to give a Jew a cup of cold water. The Lord will not be able to find anything of value in their lives. He will not accuse them of murder, gross sexual sin, or robbing the poor. Their damning sins will be sins of omission, not what they have done but what they have not done. They will not have given Him meat or drink or clothing.

These "goats" will complain bitterly about their sentence. They will say, "Lord, when saw we thee an hungred, or athirst, or a stranger, or naked, or sick, or in prison, and did not minister unto thee?" (25:44) Back will come the answer: "Inasmuch as ye did it not to one of the least of these, ye did it not to me" (25:45). There will be no further discussion. "These shall go away into everlasting punishment; but the righteous into life eternal" (25:46).

There the Olivet discourse ended—on a solemn note indeed. The Lord's destiny would now lead Him to the cross, the tomb, and the glory of His Father's throne on high.

THE SHAPE OF HIS REJECTION

(26:1–27:66)

I. THE TRAP (26:1-5)
    A. The Savior's Warning (26:1-2)
        1. The Conclusion of His Olivet Discourse (26:1)
        2. The Closeness of His Own Decease (26:2)
            a. The Coming Passover (26:2a)
            b. The Coming Passion (26:2b)
    B. The Sanhedrin's Wickedness (26:3-5)
        1. The People (26:3a)
        2. The Place (26:3b)
        3. The Plan (26:4-5)
            a. To Employ Craftiness (26:4)
                (1) To Ensure the Lord's Capture (26:4a)
                (2) To Ensure the Lord's Crucifixion (26:4b)
            b. To Employ Caution (26:5)

II. THE TRUTH (26:6-13)
    A. The Woman's Coming (26:6-7)
        1. Where She Sought the Lord (26:6)
        2. What She Brought the Lord (26:7)
            a. The Costliness of Her Act (26:7a)
            b. The Conspicuousness of Her Act (26:7b)
    B. The Woman's Critics (26:8-9)
        1. They Described Her Act of Worship as Wasteful (26:8)
        2. They Described Her Act of Worship as Wicked (26:9)

473

C. The Woman's Commendation (26:10-13)
The Lord praised:
1. Her Splendid Devotion (26:10)
2. Her Spiritual Discernment (26:11-12)
   a. As to the Poor (26:11)
   b. As to His Person (26:12)
3. Her Special Distinction (26:13)

III. THE TRAITOR (26:14-16)
A. His Fellow Conspirators (26:14)
B. His Fearful Crime (26:15)
   1. His Proposal (26:15a)
   2. His Price (26:15b)
C. His Future Conduct (26:16)

IV. THE TABLE (26:17-29)
A. The Past—The Lord and the Passover (26:17-20)
   1. The Site Was Selected (26:17-19)
      a. The Observation of the Disciples (26:17-18)
         (1) What the Men Requested (26:17)
         (2) What the Master Revealed (26:18)
      b. The Obedience of the Disciples (26:19)
   2. The Stage Was Set (26:20)
B. The Present—The Lord and His People (26:21-25)
   1. The Bomb Exploded (26:21-22)
      a. The Revelation (26:21)
      b. The Response (26:22)
   2. The Betrayal Exposed (26:23-25)
      a. What Jesus Said (26:23-24)
         (1) A Despicable Deed Exposed (26:23)
         (2) A Damnable Deed Exposed (26:24)
      b. What Judas Said (26:25)
C. The Prospect—The Lord and His Purpose (26:26-29)
   1. The Sacred Covenant (26:26-28)
      a. The Lord's Body (26:26)
      b. The Lord's Blood (26:27-28)
         (1) The Type (26:27)
         (2) The Truth (26:28)
   2. The Second Coming (26:29)

      a. The Fruit of the Vine (26:29a)
      b. The Faith of the Victor (26:29b)

V. THE TEARS (26:30-46)
  A. The Plan (26:30-32)
    1. A Final Hymn (26:30)
    2. A Further Hurt (26:31)
    3. A Future Hope (26:32)
  B. The Pledge (26:33-35)
    1. Peter's Promise Made (26:33-35a)
      a. The Boast Recited (26:33)
      b. The Boast Rebuked (26:34)
      c. The Boast Repeated (26:35a)
    2. Peter's Promise Multiplied (26:35b)
  C. The Place (26:36-38)
    1. Jesus and His Closest Followers (26:36)
      a. The Arrival (26:36a)
      b. The Arrangement (26:36b)
    2. Jesus and His Closest Friends (26:37-38)
      a. His Sorrow (26:37-38a)
      b. His Supplication (26:38b)
  D. The Plea (26:39-45a)
    1. The First Plea (26:39-41)
      a. The Prayer (26:39)
        (1) Distance (26:39a)
        (2) Desolation (26:39b)
        (3) Devotion (26:39c)
      b. The Protest (26:40-41)
        (1) What He Saw (26:40a)
        (2) What He Said (26:40b-41)
          (a) Peter's Failure (26:40b)
          (b) Peter's Folly (26:41)
    2. The Further Plea (26:42-43)
      a. Back to His Father (26:42)
      b. Back to His Followers (26:43)
    3. The Final Plea (26:44-45a)
      a. The Same Words (26:44)
      b. The Same Weakness (26:45a)
  E. The Plunge (26:45b-46)

B. The Arraignments (26:57–27:26)
  1. Before the Religious Rulers of the Jews (26:57-75)
    a. Where Peter Sat (26:57-58)
      (1) The Inner Court Where Jesus Was Tried (26:57)
      (2) The Outer Court Where Peter Was Tested (26:58)
    b. What Peter Saw (26:59-68)
      (1) The False Witnesses (26:59-63a)
        (a) Those Who Brought What the Sanhedrin Considered to Be Inconclusive Testimony (26:59-60a)
          i. Searching for Them (26:59)
          ii. Sifting through Them (26:60a)
        (b) Those Who Brought What the Sanhedrin Considered to Be Incriminating Testimony (26:60b-63a)
          i. The Two Who Pleased the Court (26:60b)
          ii. The Testimony That Pleased the Court (26:61-63a)
            a. The Saying of Jesus Was Distorted (26:61)
            b. The Silence of Jesus Was Disconcerting (26:62-63a)
      (2) The Faithful Witness (26:63b-68)
        (a) The Oath (26:63b-64)
          i. Administered to Christ (26:63b)
          ii. Answered by Christ (26:64)
            a. I Am the Son of God, As Your Statement Asserted (26:64a)
            b. I Am the Son of Man, As Your Scriptures Affirm (26:64b)
        (b) The Outcome (26:65-68)
          i. The Death Sentence Decreed by the Sanhedrin (26:65-66)
            a. The Rending of His Vesture by Caiaphas (26:65)

    (d) Where He Stood (27:5)
       i. What He Did in the Temple Court (27:5a)
       ii. Why He Departed from the Temple Court (27:5b)
  (2) The Traitor's Money (27:6-10)
    (a) How the Chief Priests Fondled the Silver (27:6-8)
       i. Their Religious Scruples (27:6)
       ii. Their Rationalistic Solution (27:7-8)
          a. The Nature of the Field They Purchased (27:7)
          b. The Name of the Field They Purchased (27:8)
    (b) How the Chief Priests Fulfilled the Scriptures (27:9-10)
       i. The Prophecy Was First Proclaimed by Jeremiah, a Pre-Exilic Prophet (27:9a)
       ii. The Prophecy Was Finally Penned by Zechariah, a Postexilic Prophet (27:9b-10)
b. The Sentencing of Jesus (27:11-26)
  (1) The Charge (27:11-14)
    (a) The Matter of the Sovereignty of Jesus (27:11)
       i. The Question Asked (27:11a)
       ii. The Question Answered (27:11b)
    (b) The Mystery of the Silence of Jesus (27:12-14)
       i. Before the Jews (27:12)
       ii. Before the Judge (27:13-14)
          a. Extreme Provocation (27:13)
          b. Extreme Perplexity (27:14)
  (2) The Choice (27:15-26)
    (a) The Malefactor (27:15-18)
       i. A Convenient Custom (27:15)
       ii. A Convenient Convict (27:16)

       iii. A Convenient Contrast (27:17-18)
         a. What Pilate Pointedly
           Underlined (27:17)
         b. What Pilate Perfectly
           Understood (27:18)
     (b) The Message (27:19)
       i. When It Came (27:19a)
       ii. What It Claimed (27:19b)
     (c) The Multitude (27:20-25)
       i. The True Culprits (27:20)
       ii. The Tremendous Clamor (27:21-23)
         a. The Decision (27:21)
         b. The Dilemma (27:22-23)
           1. What Should I Do? (27:22)
           2. What Has He Done? (27:23)
       iii. The Terrible Curse (27:24-25)
         a. The Judge and His Professed
           Innocence (27:24)
         b. The Jews and Their Provoking
           Insistence (27:25)
     (d) The Murder (27:26)
       i. The Criminal Freed by Pilate
         (27:26a)
       ii. The Crime Formalized by Pilate
         (27:26b)

VII. THE TREE (27:27-56)
  A. The Soldiers (27:27-31)
    1. Their Company (27:27)
    2. Their Contempt (27:28-30)
      a. Of the Lord's Messianic Position (27:28-29)
        (1) How They Robed Him (27:28-29a)
        (2) How They Ridiculed Him (27:29b)
      b. Of the Lord's Majestic Person (27:30)
        (1) Their Vileness (27:30a)
        (2) Their Violence (27:30b)
    3. Their Course (27:31)
      a. The Last Joke (27:31a)
      b. The Last Journey (27:31b)

B. The Site (27:32-38)
  1. The Man Who Carried the Cross
     (27:32)
  2. The Men Who Committed the Crime
     (27:33-37)
     a. The Vinegar (27:33-34)
        (1) Golgotha (27:33)
        (2) Gall (27:34)
     b. The Victim (27:35a)
     c. The Vesture (27:35b)
     d. The Vigil (27:36-37)
        (1) A Finished Work (27:36)
        (2) A Final Word (27:37)
  3. The Men Who Were Condemned with the Christ
     (27:38)
C. The Scoffers (27:39-44)
  1. The Rabble (27:39-40)
     a. Who They Were (27:39)
        (1) How Transient Their Character (27:39a)
        (2) How Terrible Their Conceit (27:39b)
     b. What They Wanted (27:40)
        (1) To Prove the Lord Wrong (27:40a)
        (2) To Prove the Lord Right (27:40b)
  2. The Rabbis (27:41-43)
     a. Their Ranks (27:41)
     b. Their Ridicule (27:42-43)
        They ridiculed His claim to be:
        (1) Their Savior (27:42a)
        (2) Israel's Sovereign (27:42b)
        (3) God's Son (27:43)
  3. The Robbers (27:44)
D. The Signs (27:45-54)
  1. The Sun (27:45-50)
     a. Darkness such as Was Never Known Before
        (27:45)
        (1) When It Commenced (27:45a)
        (2) When It Concluded (27:45b)
     b. Despair such as Was Never Known Before
        (27:46-49)

(1) The Anguished Cry (27:46)
    (a) The Time (27:46a)
    (b) The Terror (27:46b)
(2) The Anxious Crowd (27:47-49)
    (a) The More Compassionate Ones
        (27:47-48)
        i. Their Inference (27:47)
        ii. Their Interference (27:48)
    (b) The More Critical Ones
        (27:49)
c. Death such as Was Never Known Before
    (27:50)
    (1) The Loud Voice (27:50a)
    (2) The Last Victory (27:50b)
2. The Sanctuary (27:51a)
3. The Stones (27:51b)
4. The Sepulchers (27:52-53)
    a. The Remarkable Sight (27:52a)
    b. The Resurrected Saints (27:52b-53)
        (1) The Focal Point of Their Appearances
            (27:52b-53a)
        (2) The Factual Proof of Their Appearances
            (27:53b)
5. The Sentries (27:54)
    a. Where They Stood (27:54a)
    b. What They Saw (27:54b)
    c. What They Said (27:54c)
E. The Sympathizers (27:55-56)
    1. Where They Were (27:55)
    2. Who They Were (27:56)

VIII. THE TOMB (27:57-66)
    A. The Tomb Given (27:57-61)
        1. The Intercession of Joseph (27:57-58)
            a. His Great Wealth (27:57)
            b. His Great Work (27:58)
        2. The Interment of Jesus (27:59-61)
            a. The Last Loving Gift (27:59-60)

       (1) The Clean Linen (27:59)

       (2) The Clean Location (27:60)

          (a) Completely Surrendered (27:60a)

          (b) Carefully Secured (27:60b)

     b. The Last Lingering Gaze (27:61)

B. The Tomb Guarded (27:62-66)

    1. The Sanhedrin's Predicament (27:62-64)

     a. What Was Remembered (27:62-63)

     b. What Was Requested (27:64)

       (1) The Patrolling of the Sepulcher of This
Supposed Redeemer (27:64a)

       (2) The Prevention of a Story of a
Supposed Resurrection (27:64b)

    2. The Sanhedrin's Precaution (27:65-66)

     a. The Permission of the Governor (27:65)

     b. The Posting of the Guard (27:66)

In Matthew 25 we caught a glimpse of the King crowned, sitting on the throne of His glory, judging the nations, and about to rule the earth. In chapter 27 we will see the King crucified, dying in agony and shame amid two thieves. In between is chapter 26, in which the plot thickens and events move rapidly toward the cross.

I. THE TRAP (26:1-5)

A. The Savior's Warning (26:1-2)

1. The Conclusion of His Olivet Discourse (26:1)

What grips our attention in 26:1 is the word "finished." We read, "And it came to pass, when Jesus had finished all these sayings…" There are similar statements in Matthew 7:28; 11:1; 13:53; 19:1. These verses mark turning points in the Lord's public ministry. At the turning point in 26:1, the Lord had no more to say to the Jews. The next time He speaks to them, they will hear Him refer to them as "these my brethren," as in the closing parable of the Olivet discourse. By then the nation will have been thoroughly pruned in the great tribulation and purged by His return.

2. The Closeness of His Own Decease (26:2)

a. The Coming Passover (26:2a)

Two events lay ahead for the Lord and His disciples. The Lord mentioned first the coming Passover: "Ye know that after two days is the feast of the passover." The Passover, one of the highlights of the year, was one of His earliest childhood memories, one of His most fascinating subjects at school. But now He spoke knowing that this year He was the paschal Lamb. This was the last year the feast would be kept in the will of God. That Passover had a terrible attraction for Him; it has a tremendous attraction for us. Edersheim wrote:

> Everyone in Israel was thinking about the Feast. For the previous month it had been the subject of discussion in the Academies, and, for the last two Sabbaths at least, that of discourse in the Synagogues. Everyone was going to Jerusalem.…It was a gathering of universal Israel, that of the memorial of the birth-night of the nation.[1]

b. The Coming Passion (26:2b)

The Lord mentioned too the coming passion: "The Son of man is betrayed to be crucified." He was underlining the greatest of all betrayals, the crime beyond all crimes.

Judas's first bright hopes, which had been fanned by the preaching of John the Baptist, increased by the Lord's miracles, and cheered on by His growing popularity, were beginning to fade. The betrayer was disillusioned by the Lord's refusal to capitalize on the enthusiasm of the crowd, by His repeated withdrawals, and by His unwillingness to show Himself openly in Jerusalem and come to terms with the existing establishment. *What kind of a King*, he wondered, *would avoid all the normal paths to power?*

Judas became an active traitor the first time he put his hand into the bag to divert funds intended for the poor to his own secret bank account (John 12:6). *I might as well salvage something for myself,* he thought. Each succeeding misappropriation became easier until in the end he could even put a price tag on Jesus.

When did Judas cross the great gulf between being a disciple and being a betrayer? Some think it was right after the Lord's discourse on the Bread of Life, when Christ said that anyone expecting to share His life must eat His flesh. That hard saying turned many people against Him—so much so that Jesus challenged His disciples, "Will ye also go away?" (John 6:67)

B. The Sanhedrin's Wickedness (26:3-5)

1. The People (26:3a)

"The chief priests, and the scribes, and the elders of the people" assembled. The heads of the priesthood were there, as were the temple officials, the leading Sanhedrists (scribes and elders), and all the leaders of the Jewish nation—the men who were supposed to be the religious elite. All were united in a common hatred of God's beloved Son.

2. The Place (26:3b)

They were gathered in "the palace of the high priest," which was not their usual meeting place. Jewish law ruled that in all criminal cases, sentence must be passed in the regular meeting place of the

Sanhedrin. The gathering in the palace was essentially a meeting of the ruling religious authorities with the captain of the temple guard and his officers. They had convened to discuss ways and means of trapping, arresting, and killing the unwanted Messiah. Caiaphas, the high priest, presided over the session.

3. The Plan (26:4-5)

They planned to employ both craftiness and caution. Cunning by nature, they decided to "take Jesus by subtilty [guile]" (26:4). The word translated "subtilty" here is *dolos,* which was also used by Paul when he addressed Elymas the sorcerer: "O full of all subtilty [*dolos*] and all mischief, thou child of the devil, thou enemy of all righteousness, wilt thou not cease to pervert the right ways of the Lord?" (Acts 13:10) More appropriate words could not have been found to describe those religious leaders of Israel who were gathered at the home of Caiaphas.

Exercising caution, they said, "Not on the feast day, lest there be an uproar among the people" (Matthew 26:5). The recent demonstration of popular support for Jesus during His triumphal entry into Jerusalem gave those wicked men pause. They were afraid of a riot, afraid of Pilate's penchant for violent revenge. The Jewish leaders were still determined to get rid of Jesus; they just wanted to avoid the feast.

But God had already decreed that Jesus would be taken on the feast day. Christ was to die as the Passover Lamb. Jesus had said, "After two days is the feast of the passover, and the Son of man is betrayed to be crucified" (26:2). From the beginning, the Passover had been set as the date for the crucifixion, just as Pentecost had been set as the date for the birthday of the church. Those wicked men, for all their power and plans, could no more alter the divine decree than they could reverse the spin of the world on its axis in space.

The coming of Judas changed their plans. They suddenly saw a way through their difficulties. Now they could proceed. Judas would keep in touch with them as to the whereabouts of Jesus; then in a suitably secluded spot, at a conveniently quiet hour, they could seize Him and have Him arraigned, tried, and sentenced before anyone could drum up effective opposition.

Matthew would write about the betrayal, but first he described an idyllic scene and a lovely act of devotion by one who understood what lay ahead for Him.

II. THE TRUTH (26:6-13)

A. The Woman's Coming (26:6-7)

1. Where She Sought the Lord (26:6)

The incident took place in the home of Simon the leper, evidently a man Jesus had healed. Tradition has it that he was either the father of Lazarus and his sisters, or the husband of Martha. In any case, Simon seems to have had some close relationship with the much-loved family at Bethany.

2. What She Brought the Lord (26:7)

John identified the woman as Mary, the sister of Lazarus.[2] She had in her hand an alabaster flask of costly ointment. Mark 14:3 tells us it was spikenard, which contained myrrh and nard and was found in Syria, India, and the Himalayas. The strong-scented ointment was imported at great cost and sold for a small fortune.

Slipping into the room where Jesus was reclining at table, Mary made her love offering. She broke the seal on the flask and poured the fragrant perfume on the head of the Lord, anointing Him and thereby filling the room with the lovely fragrance. The beautiful and meaningful gesture was an expression of enlightened devotion and personal love.

When had Mary purchased the spikenard? How long had she saved up for it? Had she originally bought it with her own wedding day in mind? Had she deliberately withheld it from Lazarus at the time his body was anointed for burial? All we know is that Mary had invested a large sum in this ointment and that she poured it out as an act of worship for the Lord she loved.

B. The Woman's Critics (26:8-9)

1. They Described Her Act of Worship as Wasteful (26:8)

The disciples broke out in an indignant storm of protest. Spurred on by Judas, they asked, "To what purpose is this waste?" John 12:5 tells us that Judas priced out the spikenard at "three hundred pence." Since a penny was a working man's daily wage, that ointment represented the best part of a year's earnings. To pour it out over the head of Jesus seemed to the dull disciples to be reckless extravagance. But love is always prodigal. Love never counts the cost. Love is always eager to give, and give unstintingly.

We can have little doubt that behind much of the discord among the disciples was the pernicious influence of Judas. We can almost see the disappointment on his face when he was not one of those selected to climb the mount of transfiguration. In all those disputes along the way about who would be the greatest, in all those petty misunderstandings among the disciples, can we not hear the echo of his voice? Can we not discern the deadly leaven of his presence? When Mary brought her gift to Jesus, the traitor was unmasked.

2. They Described Her Act of Worship as Wicked (26:9)

Implying that Mary's act was wicked, the disciples said, "This ointment might have been sold for much, and given to the poor." There is much need in this world, there are many poor, and there are always those who call it a wicked waste when money is given to spiritual rather than social ends. But it is dangerous to put the physical plight of the poor in the driver's seat and neglect ministering to their spiritual needs.

To many people, the most outrageous waste of all is to give money to something that will minister to Christ alone, something that will have no secondary utilitarian use at all. Few people grasp the burnt offering side of giving. Even some well-meaning Christians called it a waste when five young men "threw away" their lives in an Ecuadorian jungle in an effort to open a bridgehead for the gospel among a wild Indian tribe.

C. The Woman's Commendation (26:10-13)

Jesus leaped to Mary's defense. The words He used suggest that she was covered with embarrassment or overwhelmed with anxiety over the caustic criticism of her love gift. Her act of worship was "a good work upon me," Jesus said (26:10). As for the poor, there would never be a time when the Lord's people would not have occasion to minister to them. However, He would soon be gone. She had seized her opportunity; her critics, we can infer, had missed theirs.

"She hath poured this ointment on my body...for my burial," Jesus said (26:12). There it is, out in the open at last: The Lord was soon to die and be buried.

We do not find Mary at the cross. We find some of the other New Testament Marys there, but not Mary of Bethany, for she had already anticipated Calvary. We do not find her at the tomb either, for she had already made her contribution to the Lord's burial. Moreover she had no need to go to the tomb, for having grasped the truth of the Lord's death and burial, Mary went on to believe that He would rise again.

It seems that at this point she alone, of all His followers, grasped the truth of the Lord's resurrection. No wonder Jesus accepted Mary's love gift, defended her against her critics, extolled her, and promised that her fame would reach into all the world, as indeed it has. Hers is no memorial of marble upon which time at last will do its relentless work. Hers is a memorial in the deathless shrine of Scripture. Mary's story is read in a thousand tongues, and the earth is a richer place because of her act of worship.

III. THE TRAITOR (26:14-16)

A. His Fellow Conspirators (26:14)

The "waste" of the spikenard was enough to spur Judas on. We can imagine what he said to himself: "If I could have gotten my hands on those three hundred pence, what a generous commission I could have skimmed off! Well, I'll find a way to make some money out of this debacle, this foolish charade of King and kingdom. I'll cash in on this business by selling this Messiah to His foes. If He extricates Himself, as He did several times in the past when His enemies made an overt move, well and good. I'll be the richer and no one will be the wiser. If He does not escape, that will prove Him to be a phony and I'll be better off out of this business. It won't hurt me to have made some money and some friends in high places at the same time."

The Lord's enemies had already decided to keep a strict watch on Christ's movements. "The chief priests and the Pharisees had given a commandment, that, if any man knew where he were, he should shew it, that they might take him" (John 11:57). Thus Judas could pose as a patriot in betraying Christ. So it is recorded in Matthew 26:14 that "one of the twelve, called Judas Iscariot, went unto the chief priests." They were now partners in the crime of the ages.

B. His Fearful Crime (26:15)

1. His Proposal (26:15a)

"What will ye give me, and I will deliver him unto you?" That was the traitor's diabolical proposition. It was the measure of the meanness of Judas's soul. He would sell Jesus for cold cash. It was the price of infamy.

The members of the Sanhedrin must have been delighted. Here was an end to their difficulties in "taking" Jesus. They were not going to let this opportunity slip through their fingers; it might never come again. But they did not regard Judas as an equal coconspirator. They kept him at arm's length and treated him as a common informer, a spy.

Judas made his proposal and they pondered their man. They would give as little as they thought he would take. He was selling himself as well as Jesus.

2. His Price (26:15b)

"They covenanted with him for thirty pieces of silver," Matthew said. The word translated "covenanted" here is *histēmi,* which literally means "to place in the balances, to weigh." Thus Matthew's statement could be rendered, "They weighed unto him thirty pieces of silver." In so doing they were fulfilling a prophecy that they evidently had forgotten: "So they weighed for my price thirty pieces of silver" (Zechariah 11:12).

The thirty pieces of silver were the shekels of the sanctuary, money that was supposed to have been used for the purchase of sacrifices. The amount was the price paid when an ox gored someone else's servant (Exodus 21:32); it was the market value of a slave. This was the Sanhedrin's contemptuous evaluation of the worth of One who had healed their sick, their blind, their lame, their demon-possessed; who had raised their dead and fed their multitudes. Judas must have considered it a poor enough reward for his crime. But now he was their tool. They had bought him as well as the Lord.

C. His Future Conduct (26:16)

"From that time he sought opportunity to betray him." The Sanhedrin no longer deemed it necessary to wait for the termination of the feast. From then on, Judas kept his eyes open, looking for a favorable opportunity to earn his terrible "wages of unrighteousness" (2 Peter 2:15).

IV. THE TABLE (26:17-29)

A. The Past—The Lord and the Passover (26:17-20)

As we consider the Lord's last Passover, we need first to look to the past, for all the roots of the feast are there. Fitfully for some fifteen hundred years the Jewish people had thus celebrated their great redemption by the blood of the lamb and their exodus from the land of Egypt (Exodus 12; Leviticus 23:5-8).

The Passover lamb was slain on the fourteenth day of Nisan. The feast of unleavened bread began on the fifteenth day of Nisan and lasted for seven days (Numbers 28:17). It was common for the Jews to blend the slaying of the Passover lamb, the Passover feast, and the feast of unleavened bread and to look on the whole celebration as one great festival. They used the names *Passover* and *unleavened bread* more or less interchangeably to describe the entire eight-day period. It was the practice of the Jews to remove all leaven from their houses on the night between the thirteenth and fourteenth of Nisan, to eat the Passover feast on the evening of the fourteenth, and to observe the "high sabbath" on the fifteenth.

One of the complicating factors in determining the sequence of events day by day in Matthew 26–28 is that the Jewish day began at sunset rather than in the morning. And considerable disagreement exists as to whether the Lord was crucified on a Wednesday or a Friday. Edersheim expressed his view that the Passover "began on the 14th Nisan, that is, from the appearance of the first three stars on Wednesday evening (the evening of what had been the 13th), and ended with the first three stars on Thursday evening (the evening of what had been the 14th day of Nisan)."[3]

Another complicating factor is the sabbath question. The first day of each of the three predominant annual feasts (Passover, Pentecost, and tabernacles) was "a holy convocation," a sabbath on which no work was to be done (Leviticus 23:7,24-25; Exodus 12:16). The first day of the feast completely overshadowed the ordinary weekly sabbath. The sabbath or high day of John 19:31 was one such holy convocation. This high sabbath has often been mistaken for the ordinary weekly sabbath, thus confusing the dating of events surrounding the crucifixion.

The Lord said He would be "three days and three nights in the heart of the earth" (Matthew 12:40), a statement that leaves no room for hedging. It is true enough that the Jewish idiom "three days" (or "three years") could be taken to mean parts of three days (or years). But that is not the case here where the Lord so definitely spoke of three nights in addition to three days. Any attempt to trace the sequence of events must allow for the Lord's body to be in the tomb for three full days and nights.

The chronology is full of difficulty and all kinds of positions are taken. The view taken here is that, tradition to the contrary notwithstanding, the Lord was crucified and buried on the fourteenth day of Nisan (Tuesday sunset to Wednesday sunset), which was also the preparation day. All four Gospels affirm that He was buried on the preparation day (Matthew 27:62; Mark 15:42; Luke 23:54; John 19:31). It would have been unthinkable to allow bodies of the crucified to be exposed during the sabbath (the high sabbath of the Passover, not the ordinary weekly sabbath).

If this view is correct, the last supper commenced on the evening of Tuesday, the fourteenth of Nisan. After supper and the inauguration of the new covenant, the Lord went to Gethsemane. He was arrested and His various trials continued throughout the night. About the sixth hour (our Tuesday midnight) Pilate pronounced his historic statement, "Behold your King!" (John 19:14). The Lord was crucified at the third hour (nine o'clock) Wednesday morning.

At the sixth hour darkness descended (Wednesday noon). This is a crucial point in time, for the daily sacrifice was killed at the sixth hour. The sacrifice was offered at the seventh hour as the Lord hung on the cross as the sin-bearer. Right after the offering of the daily sacrifice, the killing of the Passover lambs began throughout the country.

The Lord gave His final cry at the ninth hour (three o'clock in the afternoon) and died. He was buried in haste before sunset— that is, before the high day (the first day of the Passover feast) began (before six o'clock on Wednesday).

Although this view allows for three full days and nights of entombment and a resurrection on the third day, "the first day of the week" (Matthew 28:1-10; Mark 16:1-18; Luke 24:1-49; John 20:1-23), this interpretation is not without problems of its own. The major problem is that if the Lord was on the cross when the Passover lambs were being slain, it is difficult to see how He celebrated the Passover. Some take the view that the Lord kept an anticipatory feast.[4] Some say He celebrated without a regulation lamb, since He Himself was the Lamb that was to be slain.

However we work the chronological problems out, in Matthew 26:17 Passover time had come. This great feast, so rooted in Israel's significant past, was uppermost in everyone's mind. It was "the first day of the feast of unleavened bread" and the disciples wanted to know where arrangements should be made to eat the Passover. Their question shows that the day was the fourteenth of Nisan.

Evidently someone in the city had a large upper room that was at the Master's disposal. The Lord sent Peter and John to make the arrangements (Mark 14 and Luke 22 furnish the details), thus keeping the location secret from Judas until the last moment. The room was furnished, doubtless with couches arranged around a table. We are not told to whom the house with the upper room belonged. Some have speculated that John Mark lived there with his parents. Mark's mother was a sister of Barnabas (Colossians 4:10) and certainly her home was large (Acts 12:12).

So it was the preparations were made and the disciples, with Jesus in the midst, took possession of the upper room, the room where Passover was replaced by the Lord's table and where seven weeks later the church was born. "When the even was come, he sat down with the twelve" (Matthew 26:20).

B. The Present—The Lord and His People (26:21-25)

There is little in the Biblical accounts to show that the Lord observed the details of the paschal feast; for instance there is no mention of a lamb. We know from rabbinical authors that under conventional circumstances the head of the family took a cup of mixed wine and water, blessed it, tasted it, and passed it to the guests. He then washed his hands and the dishes were placed on the table. A special benediction was pronounced over the bitter herbs, which were then taken by one and all, dipped in a sauce, and eaten. Next a piece of unleavened bread was broken and raised with a ritual formula. A second cup was then filled and the history of the Passover recounted. Psalms 113 and 114 were sung and the cup was drunk. The paschal meal itself was then celebrated. Hands were washed, the lamb was cut up, and a portion was given to everyone, along with some unleavened bread and bitter herbs dipped in sauce (the "sop" of John 13:26). At the end of the meal the third cup was drunk (the "cup of blessing" of 1 Corinthians 10:16) and the feast was concluded with a solemn grace.

We can be sure that everything in the upper room was proceeding as the Lord had planned. John 13:1-17 tells us that He washed the disciples' feet, but Matthew told us little or nothing of what actually went on. His memory of the occasion was dominated by the betrayal of Judas and the solemn substitution of a new feast of remembrance for the age-old Passover.

1. The Bomb Exploded (26:21-22)

a. The Revelation (26:21)

"As they did eat," the Lord dropped a bombshell. He had spoken of it repeatedly before, but now He detonated the bomb. Right when everyone was enjoying the feast, He suddenly declared, "One of you shall betray me [deliver me up]."

b. The Response (26:22)

Instantly joy turned to sorrow. Each disciple searched his heart, desperate lest some unsuspected treachery might lurk within. "Is it I?" Peter asked. "Lord, is it I?" Thomas asked. One and all, they voiced their self-doubt.

2. The Betrayal Exposed (26:23-25)

On one side of the central figure, John "was leaning on Jesus' bosom" (John 13:23). Judas, perhaps sitting next to Jesus on the other side, was stricken and stabbed to the depths of his soul by this unexpected announcement. He too stammered, "Is it I?" He had the blood money in his purse as he spoke. "Thou hast said," Jesus replied (Matthew 26:25).

The other evangelists tell us more, but Matthew said enough. He showed us Jesus looking Judas through and through and bluntly telling him in effect, "Thou art the man." Then without a further word Matthew turned his back on Judas and dismissed him from the scene.

C. The Prospect—The Lord and His Purpose (26:26-29)

1. The Sacred Covenant (26:26-28)

a. The Lord's Body (26:26)

The Lord again interrupted the meal to institute a new feast for a new dispensation. "As they were eating," Matthew said, "Jesus took bread, and blessed it, and brake it, and gave it to the disciples, and said, Take, eat; this is my body." The bread of course was a metaphor, but what a vivid one!

The bread represented the Lord's body. The bread was broken to represent the breaking of His body. How amazing it is that Jesus blessed the bread and gave thanks for it (1 Corinthians 11:23-24)! Jesus, Son of the living God, with full knowledge of the torture that lay ahead of Him, actually gave thanks for the breaking of His body. Just a few hours hence His enemies were going to hammer His holy hands to a tree—yet He gave thanks. They were going to take His feet, which had walked many weary miles in the service of the sons of men, and nail them to a cross—yet He gave thanks. His bruised and broken body was to be bowed beneath the weight of the whole world's sin—yet He gave thanks.

b. The Lord's Blood (26:27-28)

"And he took the cup, and gave thanks, and gave it to them, saying, Drink ye all of it: For this is my blood of the new testament, which is shed for many for the remission of sins." The prophet Jeremiah had foretold the enacting of this new covenant and spelled out its provisions (Jeremiah 31:31). It contained two kinds of clauses. Its eschatological clauses belong exclusively to Israel and are guaranteed by the shed blood of Calvary's Lamb. The soteriological clauses belong inclusively to both the nation of Israel and the church, and provide for the salvation of all those who believe, salvation by the shed blood of the Lord Jesus Christ.

Royal blood was to be drawn from Prince Emmanuel's veins. The cost was enormous; His agony would be beyond human comprehension—still He gave thanks. He gave thanks because He could see beyond the tears, beyond the torment, beyond the anguish and pain to the great multitude, which no one can number, from all the races of mankind and from all the ages of time. He could see them ransomed, healed, restored, forgiven, washed in His blood, saved from their sins, forever like Him. He could see them singing His praise, worshiping God, and indwelt by His Spirit for eternity. So He sealed the sacred covenant.

2. The Second Coming (26:29)

Speaking of the second coming, the Lord added, "I will not drink henceforth of this fruit of the vine, until that day when I drink it new with you in my Father's kingdom." Thus He led His disciples through the dark valley that lay ahead into the sunshine that lies beyond. As the old order was crumbling, He anticipated the glories of the millennial age and the indescribable wonders of the eternal ages.

V. THE TEARS (26:30-46)

The shadows lengthened. Already the gloom of night was heavy in that upper room. Judas had gone out into a darkness from which he would never return. The next stop on the journey to Calvary would be Gethsemane.

A. The Plan (26:30-32)

1. A Final Hymn (26:30)

The Passover was a time for singing the Great Hallel, the Hallelujah Psalms. Psalms 113 and 114 were sung before the emptying of the second cup. They tell of God humbling Himself, of the tramp of Israel's marching feet, of the shaking of the earth. At the conclusion of the paschal supper the rest of the Hallel was sung: Psalms 115–118 and possibly Psalm 136.

We can picture the Lord lingering for those last precious moments in the company of His dearest friends in the quiet of the upper room. In a short while all Hell was to be let loose, but for the moment all was still and He raised His voice in song. We can hear the words that echoed around those walls:

> "I will take the cup of salvation, and call upon the name of the Lord" (Psalm 116:13).

> "I will pay my vows" (Psalm 116:14). This was Jonah's final pledge when he was in the "belly of hell" (see Jonah 2:2,9).

> "I called upon the Lord in distress: the Lord answered me, and set me in a large place. The Lord is on my side; I will not fear: what can man do unto me?" These words from Psalm 118:5-6 spoke so accurately of the Lord's purpose and prospect.

> "The stone which the builders refused is become the head stone of the corner." The Lord had quoted these words from Psalm 118:22 to His enemies just a short while before.

> "This is the day which the Lord hath made; we will rejoice and be glad in it" (Psalm 118:24). It is astonishing that the Lord was able to sing this verse on that dark night before the day of the cross, the darkest day ever to disgrace the unhappy history of this world.

> "Blessed be he that cometh in the name of the Lord" (Psalm 118:26). Less than a week earlier, this triumphal note had rung through the streets of Jerusalem. The Lord knew that it will one day ring through those streets again.

> "O give thanks unto the Lord; for he is good: for his mercy

endureth for ever" (Psalm 118:29). This final doxology led naturally into Psalm 136 (the great song of the exodus) with its refrain (repeated twenty-six times), "For his mercy endureth for ever."[5]

The Lord took one last look around and then went out into the night. But He had garrisoned His heart with those reassuring words, "His mercy endureth for ever."

2. A Further Hurt (26:31)

As the Lord and the eleven disciples trooped down the outer stairway and headed through the gloom toward the garden of Gethsemane, He again warned them of what lay ahead. He went from quoting the poet to quoting the prophet and reminded His friends that the Shepherd was to be smitten; the sheep were to be scattered (Zechariah 13:7). One and all, the disciples would abandon Him. He knew; He understood; He forgave. God was still on the throne.

3. A Future Hope (26:32)

The Lord told the disciples that when it was all over, He would meet them in Galilee. That was the plan. Death was a small matter, a mere incident, wholly unable to hinder His proposed meeting! They would forget and need to be reminded, but He would not forget. The appointment was made.

B. The Pledge (26:33-35)

1. Peter's Promise Made (26:33-35a)

The idea of being offended (stumbled) that night because of Christ was too much for Peter. He vowed that even if all other men were stumbled, he would not be offended. He was a rock—or so he thought. He did not know his own heart. Jesus knew him better than he knew himself. The Lord even knew the details. "This night," He said, "before the cock crow, thou shalt deny me thrice" (26:34). Remaining unimpressed, Peter insisted, "Though I should die with thee, yet will I not deny thee" (26:35).

2. Peter's Promise Multiplied (26:35b)

The other disciples, carried away by Peter's earnestness and not to be outdone, pledged the same. The Lord did not argue the point. He knew the terrible weakness of the flesh. They would find out in time what He already knew.

C. The Place (26:36-38)

1. Jesus and His Closest Followers (26:36)

The moon was full and its silvery light bathed the way to Gethsemane. Edersheim wrote, "The streets could scarcely be said to be deserted, for from many a house shone the festive lamp, and many a company may still have been gathered; and everywhere was the bustle of preparation for going up to the Temple, the gates of which were thrown open at midnight."[6]

Jesus and His disciples made their way out of Jerusalem by the gate to the north of the temple and descended toward the Kidron, which at that time of year would have been swollen into a torrent. They crossed the stream and turned left where the road ran toward the mount of Olives. Soon they went off the road to the right and arrived at *Gethsemane* ("the oil-press"), a small enclosed garden where olive trees doubtless grew. Edersheim speculated that it belonged to Mark's father.

2. Jesus and His Closest Friends (26:37-38)

The Lord left eight of His disciples and took Peter, James, and John into the garden, where He "began to be sorrowful and very heavy," full of anguish and distress (26:37). He confided in His three dearest human friends: "My soul is exceeding sorrowful, even unto death" (26:38). The thought is that He was crushed with anguish. The shadow of Calvary had now begun to fall on His soul.

He charged the three disciples, "Tarry ye here, and watch with me" (26:38). He wasn't asking much, but that was all they could do. The human side of Jesus longed for the comfort of knowing that at least there were a few who cared enough to watch. They needed to watch not just for His sake, but for the sake of their own souls as well.

When the Lord began His ministry, great crowds thronged Him, but as time went on, they dwindled. After His discourse on the Bread of Life, even many of His followers left Him, but then He still had the twelve. Now one of them was a traitor; somewhere out there Judas was placing himself at the head of a mob. Jesus still had eleven disciples, but eight were back at the gate. He was reduced to three.[7]

In effect Jesus said to the three, "If you can do nothing else, you can watch." He rarely spoke of His sorrow, but now He placed it before them. The surging seas of the sorrows of a world of sin were rolling in from the mighty deep and breaking in a thunderous surf on His soul. He had indeed become "a man of sorrows, and acquainted with grief" (Isaiah 53:3).

D. The Plea (26:39-45a)

"He went a little farther," Matthew said (26:39). We need to think how far He had already come. He had come all the way from glory to Galilee—by way of a virgin's womb; by way of Bethlehem, Egypt, Nazareth; by way of a manger; by way of a carpenter's bench. He had come all the way from Galilee to Gethsemane—by way of Jordan; by way of Capernaum; by way of many a long mile, as a man on many a mission of mercy and miracle. Now He would go from Gethsemane to Gabbatha, from Gabbatha to the grave, and from the grave back to glory.

Luke said He went a little farther, "about a stone's cast" into the garden (Luke 22:41). Remember that Luke knew all about the Jewish mode of death by execution. It was he who told of the stoning of Stephen. It was Luke who told of the stoning of Paul by an infuriated mob at Iconium who were incited by angry Jews from Pisidian Antioch. "A stone's cast" was the distance of death. The Lord took His place in death's dark vale.

Utter desolation broke over His soul and He began to pray. Luke 22:44 tells us that "being in an agony he prayed more earnestly: and his sweat was as it were great drops of blood." He pleaded, "O my Father, if it be possible, let this cup pass from me: nevertheless not as I will, but as thou wilt" (Matthew 26:39).

Satan had come to Jesus in the wilderness years ago and offered Him the crown without the cross. Satan, using Peter's voice, had come to Him again at Caesarea Philippi; when He had first broached the subject of the cross to His disciples, Peter had said, "Be it far from thee, Lord" (16:22). Now Satan was back again, lurking in the dark shadows beyond the moonlight. He was whispering, "Not the cross!" Jesus, as man, shrank from the cross, but the horror of what lay ahead was eclipsed by "that good, and acceptable, and perfect, will of God" (Romans 12:2).[8]

And what was it that filled His cup with horror? Was it the cross? Any man would shrink from the cross, for it was a dreadful way to die. But many had died that way and many more would. No, it was not the physical means of death that caused Him to sweat blood. It was our sin. It was the thought of being made sin, of dying for sin, of being accursed of God. It was the thought of being alone with no eye to pity Him and no hand to save.

The Lord soon had a bitter taste of that appalling loneliness, for He found Peter, James, and John all sound asleep. To boastful Peter He said, "What, could ye not watch with me one hour?" (26:40) So He added to their task. "Watch and pray," He said (26:41). He had made His last appeal to men, to three special men, to those who, of all men, should have stood by Him.

Now the disciples needed to pray, not for Him but for themselves. "Pray," the Lord said, "that ye enter not into temptation." Watching sights the enemy; praying fights the enemy. The old serpent of Eden was back in a garden, the garden of Gethsemane. Being unable to touch Him, he would attack them. Jesus added a word of understanding and compassion for His weary disciples: "The spirit indeed is willing, but the flesh is weak."

He went back to pray again that some other way might be found, and to pledge again to do His Father's will. Thus the terrible night wore on. Three times in all He went away to pray; three times He submitted to the will of His Father. Likewise Paul in later years prayed three times for some relief from his "thorn in the flesh," but submitted at last, like his blessed Master, to God's will (2 Corinthians 12:7-9). Paul was given grace. Jesus could look forward to wrath.

Jesus came back to the sleeping disciples to watch and pray over them. "Sleep on now," He said, "and take your rest" (Matthew 26:45).

E. The Plunge (26:45b-46)

Doubtless it was a while later when He heard the voices of the mob, saw the lanterns amid the trees, and announced: "Behold, the hour is at hand, and the Son of man is betrayed into the hands of sinners. Rise, let us be going: behold, he is at hand that doth betray me." In less than twenty-four hours He would be dead.

VI. THE TRIALS (26:47–27:26)

A. The Arrest (26:47-56)

1. The Conspirators (26:47-49)

a. The Mob (26:47)

Matthew devoted considerable space to the arrest and arraignment of the Lord Jesus. Beginning with the arrival of the mob, he described them as "a great multitude with swords and staves, from the chief priests and elders of the people." Evidently the conspirators were quite willing to let someone else do their dirty work. And evidently they were not sure whether this Messiah would put up a fight at the last minute. They knew that He had eleven men with Him and that at least two of them were armed (Luke 22:38,49-50). Besides, this noted Galilean had mysterious powers they did not understand, although they were willing enough to ascribe them to the devil. They feared what would happen if He turned those powers loose against them. The chief priests and elders decided it would be safest to send Judas and a mob of armed men on ahead.

b. The Man (26:48)

Matthew 26:47 calls Judas "one of the twelve" to underscore his infamy. Now in 26:48 he is described as "he that betrayed him." All the evangelists labeled Judas thus, speaking of him, when they must, with an epithet of shame.

Judas had given the crowd at his back a sign: "Whomsover I shall kiss, that same is he: hold him fast"—as though He who upholds all things by the word of His power (Hebrews 1:3) could be held by the likes of them against His will! It seems that Judas intended to skip out of the way as soon as He had given the terrible sign that now brands him, as soon as his dark deed was done. He would let others take the risk if this meek and lowly Messiah were suddenly to show some spark of fire.

c. The Master (26:49)

"Forthwith [Judas] came to Jesus, and said, Hail, master; and kissed him." Jesus simply stood there and let him do it, just as he had done a thousand times before. The word translated "kissed" in 26:49 is *kataphileō*, which means "to kiss fervently." The traitor's shameful kiss, now implanted on the Savior's cheek, was more demonstrative than the usual kiss of salutation. It was an ostentatious kiss—ten thousand times worse than a slap in the face.

2. The Confrontation (26:50-54)

a. A Last-Minute Word of Reclamation to Judas (26:50)

"Friend," Jesus said to Judas, "wherefore art thou come?" We have already seen how Jesus used this word "friend [comrade, fellow]" before (11:16; 20:13; 22:12). Of course Jesus knew why Judas had come. The comment was more of an exclamation than a question. It was the Lord's last appeal to whatever was left of conscience in Judas. Nothing could reverse the onward march of events as far as Jesus was concerned, but there might be mercy yet for Judas. The Lord knew what lay ahead for this man if he was not reclaimed: death by suicide and eternal torment in Hell's hottest flames.

The moment was gone as fast as it came. The mob surged in according to plan and Judas was swept aside—his lips still sealed, his soul now a prey to second thoughts.

b. A Last-Minute Word of Revelation to Peter (26:51-54)

(1) The Sword (26:51-52)

(a) How It Was Used (26:51)

Fully awake now and impetuous as ever, Peter hurled himself to Christ's defense. Sword in hand, he slashed out and sliced off the right ear of one of the servants of the high priest. Evidently the victim was one of those who had seized Jesus. But not thus was the Lord to be defended, as Peter might have known if he had spent the past few hours watching and praying instead of sleeping. Elsewhere we are told that Jesus tenderly healed the smitten servant of the high priest (Luke 22:51).

(b) How Useless It Was (26:52)

This incident is not without its lesson. In seeking to defend the Savior, many an overzealous disciple of Christ has cut off an unbeliever's ear and made him even harder to reach. The unsaved person can only think of the un-Christian words and deeds of the one who has hurt him or the crass way some truth has been forced down his throat. It takes a special miracle of grace for such an unbeliever to have his spiritual hearing restored so that he will be willing to listen again to Jesus. How careful we should be not to misrepresent Him!

The Lord, however, had a different lesson for Peter. Jesus told him to put away his sword. The cause of Christ was not to be advanced by such means. "All they that take the sword shall perish with the sword." Resorting to violence only results in a violent response.

(2) The Sovereign (26:53)

The Lord did not need Peter's sword. Jesus could see what Peter could not see. Up yonder in Heaven were twelve legions of angels (seventy-two thousand of them) in battle array, straining over the battlements of the celestial city. A single word could unleash them. In a moment they could be ready to disband the mob, sweep away the Sanhedrin, execute summary vengeance on mankind, and usher in the battle of Armageddon. The word never came, for "as a sheep before her shearers is dumb, so he openeth not his mouth" (Isaiah 53:7).

It is worth noting that the revelation of Matthew 26:53 was given to Peter, not Pilate. It was intended to inform, not to intimidate.

(3) The Scripture (26:54)

"But," asked Jesus, "how then shall the scriptures be fulfilled, that thus it must be?" Note the word "must." Doubtless this was the answer He had received in His agonizing times of prayer an hour or two before: "Thus it must be." Why? Because the Scriptures said so. Old Testament types—such as Isaac on mount Moriah, the Levitical offerings, the Passover, the ark of Noah, Jonah—had to be fulfilled. Direct prophecies—such as Isaiah 53, Psalm 22, Psalm 69—had to be fulfilled. Divinely inspired, infallible Scripture had to be fulfilled. In His hour of agony the Lord placed His own imprimatur on the authority of God's holy Word.

3. The Cowards (26:55-56)

a. The Followers of Judas (26:55-56a)

(1) What Jesus Asked (26:55)

We can see the mob huddled in the background, armed with swords and clubs, waiting to see what would happen. The Lord dragged them out into the open. "Am I a robber?" He demanded in effect. The word translated "thief" in 26:55 is the same word that is used to describe the two men who were crucified with Jesus (27:38).

There were other questions implied: Why do you come armed as if I were dangerous? Why do you come in the night? The Lord reminded the mob how accessible He had made Himself in the temple. But their plot depended, or so they imagined, on a show of force sprung on Him in a lonely place under cover of darkness.

(2) What Jesus Accepted (26:56a)

The party that came to arrest the Lord was large. John described part of it as a "band" (John 18:3,12). The word translated "band" is *speira,* the name of a cohort, a division of the Roman army. It is not likely that a whole cohort was present, but evidently there were enough men to enforce the arrest. Luke 22:52 says that besides the multitudes, the chief priests, captains of the temple, and elders were present too. Evidently the Sanhedrin was afraid that Jesus would defend Himself. If He had done so, no armies in the world could have stood against Him. But that was not the divine purpose. As Matthew commented, "All this was done, that the scriptures of the prophets might be fulfilled."

b. The Followers of Jesus (26:56b)

We look sadly at the cowardly followers of Jesus. "All the disciples forsook him, and fled." He had told them again and again that He was to be taken and slain, but His warnings did not fortify them against the overwhelming terror that seized them at His arrest. The misery of loneliness, betrayal, and abandonment entered the Savior's soul.

B. The Arraignments (26:57–27:26)

1. Before the Religious Rulers of the Jews (26:57-75)

The next events were recorded against the background of the Lord's arraignments before the Jews and Gentiles. The record of Christ's appearance before the Jewish religious leaders is continually punctuated in Matthew's account by references to Peter. So we can look at the tragic trial as through Peter's eyes and listen to it as through Peter's ears.

a. Where Peter Sat (26:57-58)

(1) The Inner Court Where Jesus Was Tried (26:57)

The court of the high priest was entered by a porch in which was a gate. Beyond the gate and porch was a raised and columned pavement that formed an audience chamber. Flanking the two sides of the courtyard were the palaces of Annas and Caiaphas, the former and present high priests. The Lord would have been arraigned in the audience chamber. Not far away Peter lurked at a point from which he could see the Lord. We learn from John 18:18 that the night was cold and that some of the people in the courtyard made a small fire of coals.

(2) The Outer Court Where Peter Was Tested (26:58)

"Peter followed him afar off." That was Matthew's reticent way of describing the behavior of his friend and fellow disciple. As we trace Peter's downfall, we see him acting in defiance of the Lord's counsel in the first Psalm. We see him walking in the counsel of the ungodly, standing in the way of sinners, and sitting in the seat of the scornful.

b. What Peter Saw (26:59-68)

(1) The False Witnesses (26:59-63a)

(a) Those Who Brought What the Sanhedrin Considered to Be Inconclusive Testimony (26:59-60a)

In the face of the many who came clamoring to make some detrimental and incriminating remarks against Heaven's Beloved, our Lord maintained a studied and simple silence. He knew that in the minds of the religious leaders He was already convicted and condemned. To contradict the false and flimsy fables now being concocted and paraded as evidence was useless. The Sanhedrin had only one goal: to put Him to death. He answered the charges with majestic silence.

> "Hearest Thou not?" the accusers cry,
> No answer was the stern reply.

(b) Those Who Brought What the Sanhedrin Considered to Be Incriminating Testimony (26:60b-63a)

i. The Two Who Pleased the Court (26:60b)

Jewish law required the agreeing testimony of at least two witnesses before judgment could be passed. Many false witnesses came; Matthew recorded that sad fact twice. At last came two false witnesses whose inaccurate testimony was united enough and close enough to the truth to be admitted by the high priest as evidence.

ii. The Testimony That Pleased the Court (26:61-63a)

The false witnesses testified, "This fellow said, I am able to destroy the temple of God, and to build it in three days" (26:61). No such words ever passed His lips. He had not said that He would destroy the temple. He had said, "Destroy this temple," not "I will destroy." Moreover the authorities had misunderstood His words. He had been referring to His body, God's true temple on earth, not Herod's temple (John 2:19-22).

The Sanhedrin, however, cared little for the accuracy of the reporters or the symbolism of the Savior. They were only interested in securing a conviction that could be whitewashed with some show of legality. They had found their two witnesses and so had satisfied the legal code (Deuteronomy 17:6; 19:15).

"But Jesus held his peace" (Matthew 26:63). Unruffled and calm, He suffered this travesty of justice.

(2) The Faithful Witness (26:63b-68)

(a) The Oath (26:63b-64)

i. Administered to Christ (26:63b)

The high priest knew Christ's claims. He knew too how he could use those claims against Him, use them to whip up a religious frenzy. Why should he bother with false witnesses when he could create a courtful of witnesses? There was no way the prisoner could remain silent when adjured by God. His silence would be as damning as an affirmative statement (Leviticus 5:1). So Caiaphas deliberately forced Christ to answer a question that in a technical sense was illegal. It was the kind of question for which, under American law, provision is made in the Fifth Amendment to the Constitution. It was a question that required a self-incriminating answer.

Caiaphas put the Lord under oath. "I adjure thee by the living God," he said, using the legal terminology for administering an oath. The Lord was in effect being sworn in, just as in our courts a witness is asked to affirm that he will tell "the truth, the whole truth, and nothing but the truth." Then Caiaphas put the question—two questions really: "Are you the Messiah? Are you the Son of God?"

ii. Answered by Christ (26:64)

A claim under oath to be the Messiah would damn Jesus in the eyes of the Romans; a claim to be the Son of God would damn Him in the eyes of the Jews. One claim could earn Him capital punishment as a traitor; the other, capital punishment as a blasphemer. But the Lord deliberately refrained from appealing to His constitutional rights under Hebrew law. His answer was immediate, explicit, unequivocal: "Thou hast said"—in other words, "It is as you have said." The Lord's response was an affirmation pure and simple.

But the Lord was not finished. He added a direct answer to the rage and unbelief written all over the face of the high priest: "Nevertheless [in spite of your unbelief] I say unto you, Hereafter shall ye see the Son of man sitting on the right hand of power, and coming in the clouds of heaven." Caiaphas did not see the deity of Christ then, but he will see it in a coming day. When Christ comes, he will call on the rocks and hills to fall on him and hide him from the wrath of the Lamb. One day he will look on Him whom he pierced.

Caiaphas had a foretaste of things to come when a few days later the terrified guard came rushing in from the open tomb with the tidings of a resurrection. The high priest had a further foretaste when along with his guilty colleagues he was confronted by a group of apostles. They were filling Jerusalem with the tidings of a risen Christ and resolutely resisted all attempts to bully and beat them into silence. "You'll see," said Jesus, not in arrogance, but in sorrow for the state of the man's soul.

(b) The Outcome (26:65-68)

i. The Death Sentence Decreed by the Sanhedrin (26:65-66)

The outcome was inevitable. Far from being convinced that Jesus was the Son of God, the high priest rent his garment and cried, "He hath spoken blasphemy; what further need have we of witnesses?" (26:65)

The high priest's robe was known as "the robe of the ephod" (Exodus 39:22-23). It was woven all of blue linen, the color of heaven, to remind priest and people alike of his high and holy calling. It was hemmed with pomegranates and bells of pure gold, which were reminders that he was to have a ringing testimony for God and that he was to be exceedingly fruitful in the service of God. The neck was protected with "an habergeon," literally "a coat of mail"; the Holy Spirit added, "that it should not rend." When Aaron's sons Nadab and Abihu were executed by God for profaning their ministry, Aaron, Eleazar, and Ithamar (the father and brothers of the dead men) were expressly warned not to rend their garments as an expression of dismay (Leviticus 10:6).

By tearing his garment, the wicked Caiaphas did more than he realized. He rendered the office he so terribly disgraced as null and void. God tore it up and discarded it just as definitely as the high priest ruined his robe. God had no more use for his office; He had a new Great High Priest whom He would soon install in Heaven. A few hours later God also tore the temple veil in two, making the temple, its sacrifices and services, and the Judaism it embodied obsolete and of no further use in the divine economy.

Caiaphas asked the court for a verdict. They said, "He is guilty of death" (Matthew 26:66).

ii. The Dreadful Scorn Displayed by the Sanhedrin (26:67-68)

Not content with finding Christ guilty of blasphemy and not content with passing the death sentence on Him, members of the court began to abuse Him. "Then did they spit in his face, and buffeted him; and others smote him with the palms of their hands, Saying, Prophesy unto us, thou Christ, Who is he that smote thee?"

Well might twelve legions of angels have drawn their swords at the sight; well might they have eagerly yearned to descend the skyways of the stars and make an end of the vile creatures who could so abuse God's beloved Son. But the hour of vengeance had not come. First God must display His infinite love and incredible grace in the arena of time. So the scorners slapped Him; they spit in His face; they scoffed. They revealed what man is like; they revealed what God is like. The silence of the Savior in the face of extreme provocation was the opening act in the drama of divine love.

The brutality of Israel's religious leaders in their treatment of Christ was a terrible indictment of them, their nation, and the world. Their savagery was foreseen, foretold, and permitted by God for the larger purpose of paving a highway of salvation. On that highway the guilty sons of Adam's ruined race could move from the dark paths of sin to the gates of glory and up to the throne of God.

The stage was now set for sin to be exposed. The stage was now set for God to demonstrate His love. He had revealed His wisdom and power in creation, but His love could be fully revealed only at Calvary. The events that culminated at Calvary show how far man will go in expressing his hatred for God and how far God will go in expressing His love for man.

c. What Peter Said (26:69-75)

(1) Peter's Denials (26:69-74)

(a) The First Denial (26:69-70)

First a maid, probably a female porter, challenged Peter with the statement that he was one of the followers of the Lord. "Thou also wast with Jesus of Galilee," she said (26:69). Evidently she recognized John as a disciple and because John had gained access to the courtyard for Peter, she suspected that Peter was also a disciple (John 18:16). Feeling every eye on him, Peter categorically denied his relationship with the Lord. "I know not what thou sayest," he said (Matthew 26:70).

(b) The Further Denial (26:71-72)

Comparing the four Gospels, we might conclude that Peter's second denial was a multiple denial to four different parties, but in such swift succession that they are telescoped together as one. This time Peter denied his relationship to the Lord with an oath. In a court of justice, a man taking this kind of oath invoked malediction on himself if his statement were false. "I do not know the man," Peter said. It would seem that at this point the cock crowed, but Peter did not heed the warning.

(c) The Final Denial (26:73-74)

Peter's oath silenced suspicions for the moment, but after a while (Luke 22:59 says it was about an hour later) he was accosted again. Those who were standing around queried him a third time. "Surely thou also art one of them; for thy speech bewrayeth thee," they said (Matthew 26:73). What a wonderful testimony to have: "Your speech gives you away. You have been with Jesus"!

Peter soon put an end to that impression. He continued to call down God's curse on himself if what he said were false and added profanity to his disclaimer. The people in the courtyard stopped accusing him of being a disciple of Jesus when they heard that. Nothing will more quickly annul a Christian testimony than bad language.

Such were Peter's denials. Few of us can afford to cast stones at him. Most of us have experienced cowardice in our own hearts and have seen where it leads.

(2) Peter's Desolation (26:75)

The cock crowed a second time and suddenly the words of Jesus—"Before the cock crow, thou shalt deny me thrice"—took possession of Peter's mind. "He went out, and wept bitterly."

Where did he go? We are not told. If we could have followed Peter, perhaps we would have seen him retrace his steps back to the Kidron, cross the stream, and find his way to the garden where he had fallen asleep when bidden by Jesus to watch and pray. Perhaps he would have gone that other distance, that stone's cast, to the place where a few hours earlier his beloved Master had wept and prayed. It could be that there Peter experienced his own private Gethsemane of agony and pain.

2. Before the Roman Rulers of the Jews (27:1-26)

The trial before the religious leaders was over and now came the trial before the Roman rulers, Pilate and Herod. Matthew ignored the fiasco before Herod and told us instead about the terrible end of Judas.

a. The Suicide of Judas (27:1-10)

(1) The Traitor's Misery (27:1-5)

We cannot help wondering about Judas. No doubt he had hoped to reap position, prestige, prosperity, and power in Christ's kingdom. Disappointment over Christ's failure to materialize the earthly kingdom on which he had set his sights probably played a large part in his decision to sell Christ to the Jewish authorities.

It would seem, however, that he expected Christ to extricate Himself from the snare of His enemies. Judas knew of other occasions when Jesus had been faced with mob violence and arrest. Previously He had always confounded those who sought to harm Him. The likelihood is that Judas, having pocketed his thirty pieces of silver, looked to Christ to walk away unharmed. Jesus would escape, Judas would be better off financially, and no one would be any the wiser. But things did not work out that way.

(a) What He Saw (27:1-3a)

Standing in the shadows in Caiaphas's courtroom, Judas watched the trial of Jesus. The informal night session of the Sanhedrin decided on the death of Jesus. The morning session was perfunctory; it was convened to find a satisfactory way to carry out the sentence. The hope of the court was to cast the shame and blame onto the Romans. The Romans would not be likely to consider the Jewish charge of blasphemy as a capital offense, so some other ground had to be found before presenting the case to Pilate. Cynically the Sanhedrin decided to use the Lord's claim to be Israel's Messiah and rightful King. They would pervert the claim so as to confront Pilate with a case of treason against the caesar, a case he could not afford to ignore or take lightly. Having settled the issue, the Sanhedrin bound their unresisting prisoner and handed Him over to Pontius Pilate, the Roman governor.

When Judas saw Jesus being abused by the religious authorities, bound, and led away to Pilate, remorse filled his soul.

(b) Whom He Sought (27:3b)

"Then Judas…when he saw that he was condemned, repented himself, and brought again the thirty pieces of silver to the chief priests and elders." The word translated "repented" is *metamelomai,* which literally means "to regret." It does not denote genuine repentance. It refers to the consequences of sin rather than the sin itself. There was no deep regret in the soul of Judas over what he had done; there was only regret that things had not happened the way he had hoped or expected they would. In his regret he did not go to the Savior. If he had, even at that late hour, he would have found forgiveness. Instead he went to the priests. The results were what we would expect from such godless men.

Judas brought with him the price of his infamy, the thirty pieces of silver he had received for betraying Christ. He had not spent a penny of his ill-gotten gains. The coins were like red-hot coals in his pocket; they scorched and scarred his hand; they burned like a flame in his conscience. Why did he take them back to the priests? Did he think he could buy back his honor or purchase for such a paltry sum the Savior's release? Did he think the sight of his remorse would melt those stony-hearted priests? If so, he was soon to be taught a lesson in priestly politics.

(c) What He Said (27:4)

i. Judas's Belated Remorse (27:4a)

"I have betrayed the innocent blood," Judas said to the priests. His soul was filled with the horror of the consequences of his sin.

We look at Judas and we see the terror of a lost soul. We see the spiritual blindness that sin causes. He took his sin to wicked men dressed up as God's priests. Those priests could not save his soul even if they wanted to. All they could do was seal his damnation in Hell.

ii. The Sanhedrin's Brutal Reply (27:4b)

They looked at the wretched, tormented man, eyed him up and down with distaste, and listened to his anguished confession of sin. Then they callously said, "What is that to us? see thou to that." At least they were more honest than priests who claim to have power to forgive sins. However, they were as indifferent to the guilt of Judas as they were to the innocence of Jesus. "That's your business, mister," they said in effect, "not ours."

(d) Where He Stood (27:5)

The priests were at that moment moving across the courtyard from the palace of the high priest toward the palace of the procurator. Just over the wall were the temple courts. With a final gesture of despair, Judas flung the blood money over the wall and into the sanctuary. Perhaps the priests could hear the pieces of silver rolling and rattling across the marble mosaic of the temple court. Before they could recover themselves, Judas turned on his heel, rushed blindly away, and hurled himself headlong into a lost eternity.

We need only look at the difference between Peter and Judas to see the difference between remorse or regret and true repentance. Peter "went out and wept bitterly" (26:75); Judas "went and hanged himself" (27:5).

(2) The Traitor's Money (27:6-10)

(a) How the Chief Priests Fondled the Silver (27:6-8)

The priests had less conscience than Judas, for they carefully collected the money. Some discussion followed as to what should be done with those cursed coins. Some of the men were for putting the money back in the temple treasury, but others had scruples about that because the coins represented "the price of blood" (27:6). They decided not to put the dirty money in the treasury, but to put it to some charitable use.

While committing the most lawless act in history, those priests discussed the niceties of law and conscience with regard to the blood-tainted silver coins. They decided to buy a potter's field and use it as a place in which to bury strangers. No one was fooled, however, for the people at once called the haunted spot "the field of blood" (27:8).

(b) How the Chief Priests Fulfilled the Scriptures (27:9-10)

While all this solemn religious farce was being carried on, the priests, blinded by their guilt and greed, were actually fulfilling an Old Testament prophecy. The prophecy was first "spoken" by Jeremiah and later written into the book of God by Zechariah, the Holy Spirit having inspired both men (see Zechariah 11:12-13). Matthew, with the Jews in mind, wrote the prophecy into his record to show the sovereignty of God, making even His enemies act so as to fulfill His Word.

Had those evil priests kept their wits about them, they would have recalled the prophecy and made every effort to circumvent its fulfillment. As it was, they unconsciously acted just as had been foretold. Afterward when it was too late to undo what they had done, the written Word of God rose up as a witness against them.

b. The Sentencing of Jesus (27:11-26)

(1) The Charge (27:11-14)

(a) The Matter of the Sovereignty of Jesus (27:11)

Having cleared up the collateral issue of the suicide of Judas, Matthew was ready to write about the sentencing of Jesus. As we read Matthew's account of the trial of Jesus by Pilate, we are impressed with the sovereignty of Jesus. There is no doubt about which of the two men, Jesus or Pilate, was sovereign; neither is there any doubt about who was really on trial.

Some think Pilate had risen to his high position from slavery. Certainly he had married well, for his wife was related to the caesar. But Pilate was not a popular man, even among his friends. He was hard, cold, and calculating, with a streak of brutality in his nature. Just a short while before, he had seized temple money in order to finance an aqueduct and as a result had found himself embroiled with the Jews in an insurrection, which he had crushed harshly. He knew well the temper, touchiness, and toughness of the Jews and their influence around the world. The last thing Pilate wanted at that moment was more rioting in Jerusalem.

i. The Question Asked (27:11a)

Originally the Sanhedrin wanted Pilate to accept their verdict, endorse it, and hand Jesus over to them for execution. They would then have stoned Him as a blasphemer. But it was not to be, for Jesus was sovereign in this situation. The prophecy had long ago been written: "They pierced my hands and my feet" (Psalm 22:16). The prophet was a Jewish shepherd boy who probably had never heard of death by crucifixion.

Pilate insisted on trying Jesus for himself. Since the charge of blasphemy cut little ice with Pilate (though it did excite a certain amount of superstitious dread), the Jews changed the charge to treason. Jesus had claimed to be a King and with blatant hypocrisy, which did not deceive the governor for a moment, the Jews reminded him, "We have no king but Caesar" (John 19:15). Though not deceived, the vacillating Pilate was driven into a tight corner by this subtle, supercilious remark. Matthew did not go into all the details. He simply recorded Pilate's question: "Art thou the King of the Jews?" (27:11)

ii. The Question Answered (27:11b)

Again the Lord gave a brief but adequate answer: "Thou sayest"—in other words, "It is as you say." Matthew recorded no explanations, no appeals to His ancestry (though far more noble than Pilate's)—just a bare acknowledgment of His royalty.

The Gospels are unanimous in telling us that this was the first interchange between Pilate and Jesus. To Pilate the idea of Jesus being a king was absurd. He asked the question so that the prisoner could deny the charge and the case could be dismissed. Jesus, beaten and battered, did not look like a king. He did not act like any king whom Pilate had known. It was to the governor's surprise that the dignified and quiet man before him affirmed that, all appearances to the contrary, He was indeed the King of the Jews.

(b) The Mystery of the Silence of Jesus (27:12-14)

The Lord's affirmation provoked a storm of abuse from the chief priests and elders, but Jesus "answered nothing" (27:12). The silence of Jesus baffled Pilate because he was used to the vociferous and vehement protestations of the average Jewish prisoner. "Hearest thou not how many things they witness against thee?" he asked (12:13). Matthew noted, "And he answered him to never a word; insomuch that the governor marvelled greatly" (27:14). You cannot argue with silence.

(2) The Choice (27:15-26)

The ball was now in Pilate's court and he did not like it. There was something about this King that was royal in spite of His bruises and spittle-matted beard. He was royal in the majestic silence with which He faced His accusers, those rabble priests whose demeanor and denunciations gave them away as emissaries of Hell. Jesus needed no glittering diadem, no regal purple, no ivory throne, no imperial guard, no diamond-studded scepter, no trappings of earthly monarchy to proclaim Him King. Pilate sensed that he was in the presence of a greater King than the caesar, that Jesus was more than a king.

When Matthew described the trial, he left out most of the details. He stripped the account down to the bare essentials that would prove to his Jewish readers that Jesus was their King. Pilate asked, "Are you a king?" and Jesus answered, "Yes, I am," and that was that. All the rest, as far as Matthew was concerned, was embroidery. There was one exception: Matthew did tell us how Pilate tried to disengage himself from the dilemma in which he found himself.

Pilate had to choose between two alternatives: (1) He could do the right thing and release this obviously innocent man, this King who posed no threat to the caesar of Rome. If Pilate released Jesus, he would run the risk of another uprising in Jerusalem and the dangerous possibility that the caesar would learn of his releasing a man who claimed to be King. (2) Pilate could do the wrong thing and condemn Jesus to death, and live with a gnawing conscience to the end of his days.

(a) The Malefactor (27:15-18)

Pilate knew that Jesus was innocent; King or not, he posed no threat to the caesar or anyone else. We can be quite sure that the Roman procurator had kept himself informed through his spies about the activities of this Jesus of Nazareth over the past few years. A populist teacher from the backwoods of Galilee who opposed the Jewish religious establishment and went around doing good and preaching peace was no enemy of Rome.

However, Pilate was too big a coward to release Jesus in the face of the determination of the Sanhedrin to have Him crucified. Then he remembered that it was a local custom for the governor to release a prisoner to the Jews at Passover time. Normally the people could choose whomever they wanted, but he had a brilliant idea: this year he would limit the choice. It so happened that he had "a notable prisoner" on hand, a man named Barabbas (27:16). Why not force the people to choose between Barabbas and Jesus?

Pilate remembered the *hosanna*s that had rung through Jerusalem a few days before when Jesus had come to town. What better way was there to foil the priests, please the people, and let himself off the hook than to give the masses the choice of Jesus or Barabbas? Barabbas was a rebel, robber, and rabble-rouser. Surely the people would choose Jesus, the One who had healed their sick, cleansed their lepers, exorcised their demoniacs, fed their multitudes, and raised their dead.

Barabbas, which literally means "son of the father," was a title rather than a name, and some of the ancient manuscripts give the prisoner's name as Jesus Barabbas. So the choice was clear: Jesus who was called Barabbas (a thief, brigand, murderer, and insurrectionist); or Jesus who was called Christ (the Messiah, Son of David, and Son of the Father). Pilate seems to have had little doubt about the outcome, but he had underestimated the malice of the priests.

(b) The Message (27:19)

While Pilate was sitting on the judgment seat and the priests were outside inciting the mob, Pilate's wife, who had been having nightmares, sent her vacillating husband an urgent message. "Have thou nothing to do with that just man," it said, "for I have suffered many things this day in a dream because of him."

Pilate's wife would not have been isolated from news about Jesus. Doubtless from time to time as Pilate had received information, he had talked it over with his wife. She would have heard the gossip of her servants and the jokes of the elite about this Jewish King with unworldly views and carpenter roots. Her extraordinary dream must have convinced her that Jesus was, if nothing else, a "just [righteous] man." Knowing the weakness of her husband and the craftiness of the priests, she feared for her husband and sent him her message.

The Romans were much given to premonitions, prognostications of soothsayers, dreams, and portents. According to Suetonius, both Julius Caesar and Caesar Augustus were superstitious. Pilate must have been greatly troubled by the message from his wife, but not troubled enough to save him from disaster.

(c) The Multitude (27:20-25)

i. The True Culprits (27:20)

The true culprits in what happened next were "the chief priests and elders," the religious leaders of Israel. Matthew said that these wicked men "persuaded the multitude that they should ask [for] Barabbas, and destroy Jesus."

ii. The Tremendous Clamor (27:21-23)

We can picture those priests running here and there among the people, urging them to deny Jesus and choose Barabbas. The leaders persuaded the multitude to choose a guilty man instead of a godly man, to choose one who hurt people instead of One who helped people, to choose a violent man instead of a virtuous man, to choose a robber instead of a Redeemer, to choose a godless insurrectionist instead of God incarnate.

How did the priests persuade the people? What words did they use? What arguments did they offer? Perhaps they said, "Men and brethren, what Israel needs is not a meek Messiah like this Jesus of Nazareth, but a militant Messiah like Barabbas. We need one who will teach us how to fight, not how to forgive. Barabbas is the man for us! Barabbas is our kind of king. Barabbas is a hero, a man's man. He's not afraid of Romans. Hail Barabbas!" The priests urged the crowd on until they took up the chant, "Barabbas! We want Barabbas!" Such was the tremendous clamor.

iii. The Terrible Curse (27:24-25)

a. The Judge and His Professed Innocence (27:24)

With a ceremonial but futile gesture, Pilate caved in to the crowd. He called for a basin of water and rinsed his hands, thus symbolically handing responsibility for the murder of Jesus back to the Jews. "I am innocent of the blood of this just person: see ye to it," he said. (He described Jesus the way his wife had described Him in her message: "just.")

Could washing his hands remove Pilate's guilt for condemning someone who he knew was innocent? Could a mere ritual cleanse him from the guilt of condemning One who he half believed was the Jews' Messiah, One whom he secretly feared, One whose claim to be God was credible enough to awaken his superstitions to active alarm? No, there was no washing the guilt off his hands. History has long since passed its judgment on Pilate, as the caesar did not many years after the crucifixion of Christ.

b. The Jews and Their Provoking Insistence (27:25)

"See ye to it," said Pilate, and the priests and the people responded at once. "His blood be on us, and on our children," they cried. And so it has been. For nearly two thousand years that blood and that self-pronounced curse have pursued the Jews from land to land.[9] Yet as a nation they still persist in Christ-rejecting unbelief.

(d) The Murder (27:26)

"Then released he Barabbas unto them: and when he had scourged Jesus, he delivered him to be crucified."

The Roman scourge was a terrible instrument made of thongs loaded at the tips with pieces of bone or metal. In a scourging the victim was stripped and tied to a low post in such a position that the skin of his back was stretched tight. At the first blow, blood began to flow. As the flogging proceeded, the skin on his back was torn to ribbons. Sometimes vital organs were exposed and lacerated. Often the victim died.

Perhaps Pilate hoped that the scourging of Jesus would excite some passing pity in the Lord's enemies and make a last-minute reprieve possible. If so, he was doomed to disappointment. There was no eye to pity and no arm to save.

Thus ended the trials. Jew and Gentile alike refused a fair trial to the One before whom all must stand.

"What shall I do then with Jesus which is called Christ?" was Pilate's plaintive cry when the mob chose Barabbas. Sooner or later that question must be asked and answered by all. We must either crown Him or crucify Him. As the old gospel hymn puts it:

> Jesus is standing in Pilate's hall—
> Friendless, forsaken, betrayed by all:
> Hearken! What meaneth the sudden call?
> What will you do with Jesus?

> What will you do with Jesus?
> Neutral you cannot be;
> Some day your heart will be asking,
> "What will He do with me?"[10]

VII. THE TREE (27:27-56)

A. The Soldiers (27:27-31)

1. Their Company (27:27)

The Lord had endured the agony in the garden; He had been bullied and beaten by the Sanhedrin; He had been marched to Pilate, to Herod, and back to Pilate; He had been grilled by Pilate. He was worn out and yet He survived the scourging. That says something for the Lord's physique, but by now His body must have been throbbing with pain. In this condition He was taken over by the soldiers for further insults, torments, and brutal horseplay before being led away to Calvary.

First the soldiers brought Him into "the common hall," the praetorium, and there "the whole band of soldiers" abused Him—that is, the entire cohort.

2. Their Contempt (27:28-30)

Matthew concentrated on the way the soldiers ridiculed the Lord's claim to be King of the Jews. They arrayed Him in mock royal robes, threw a scarlet mantle over His lacerated shoulders, placed a crown of thorns on His head, thrust a reed into His hand for a scepter, knelt before Him, and cried, "Hail, King of the Jews!" (27:29) Little did the soldiers know how suitable was the crown of thorns. Thorns are the symbol of the curse (Genesis 3:17-18) and Jesus bore the curse for us so that the curse might be removed, including the curse on the world of nature (Romans 8:19-22).

We can hear the coarse jests, ribald laughter, and jeering mockery of the Roman soldiers. In such a close-knit band, there would have been ringleaders, regimental clowns who would have sharpened their wits on this man delivered to their hands. Even the more refined soldiers in the ranks would have been unable to resist a grin at some of their humor. There would also have been bullies in the band, who would not have been able to refrain from taking advantage of a helpless man. Matthew said that they brutally "smote

him on the head" (27:30). The word translated "smote" here means
"kept on beating."

Adding special spite to the mimicry and raucous laughter was an
underlying antisemitism, a hatred and scorn nurtured by Gentiles
against Jews. To the Roman soldiers there was something outra-
geously funny about the Jews having a King.

3. Their Course (27:31)

But all things come to an end. A word of command ended the
cruel horseplay and Roman discipline took over. The Lord's own
seamless robe was thrown back over His shoulders and the order
was given to march Him to Calvary.

B. The Site (27:32-38)

1. The Man Who Carried the Cross (27:32)

Staggering beneath the weight of the wooden beams of the cross,
the Lord emerged from the common hall. His face was now set
toward Golgotha. At last even His great strength failed and the
soldiers, recognizing His sheer physical inability to proceed another step, commandeered the services of a man in the crowd.

The man's name was Simon and he was from the city of Cyrene
in north Africa. Some think he was a black man. If so, he was
probably a proselyte, for he had a Jewish name. Cyrenian Jews had
several synagogues in Jerusalem (Acts 2:10; 6:9). After Pentecost
Cyrenians were active in spreading the gospel (Acts 11:20; 13:1),
and it is possible that Simon was one of them. Mark 15:21 mentions
Simon's sons Alexander and Rufus and it is likely that Rufus was the
same one referred to by Paul in Romans 16:13. If so, the encounter
in Matthew 27:32 was a providential meeting and we can imagine
that in later years Simon, Alexander, Rufus, and their mother never
tired of talking about it. At the time of the crucifixion, however,
Simon may have shrunk from carrying that cross. He may have
resented the shame and compulsion associated with bearing the
cross, but somehow Jesus won his heart.

2. The Men Who Committed the Crime (27:33-37)

a. The Vinegar (27:33-34)

Matthew used the Hebrew word for the site of the crime:
Golgotha, "the place of the skull." When Jesus arrived at the ghastly

place, the soldiers "gave him vinegar to drink mingled with gall" to deaden consciousness (27:34). Having tasted it and realized its character and purpose, He refused to drink it. He was not going to bear our sins in His body on the tree in a drugged condition. Every nerve, every fiber of His body must be awake to endure the pain. He was to meet death in full possession of the faculties of body and soul.

b. The Victim (27:35a)

Like all the evangelists, Matthew barely touched on the crucifixion itself. All he said was, "And they crucified him." We are driven to other sources for information about the horrible details of a death by crucifixion.[11]

First the upright beam of the cross was planted firmly into the ground. It was high enough to elevate the victim about two feet above the ground and allow room over his head for an inscription. Next the transverse beam was laid on the ground, the victim was thrown down, and his arms were stretched out and bound to that piece of wood. Then two long, sharp nails were driven through his hands into the wood. Next the victim was hauled up by ropes, perhaps by means of ladders, and the transverse beam was either nailed or bound to the upright beam. A support for the body was usually provided. Last of all, the feet were placed against the upright beam and firmly nailed to it. The victim was left to die, not from loss of blood, but from exhaustion.

Crucifixion made death as painful and slow as fallen human ingenuity and Satanic inspiration could make it. The process of dying could last for several days. The agonies endured by the victim from cramping, thirst, wounded hands and feet, and swollen arteries defy description. Thus man treated the Lord of glory.

> For such a cruel death He died,
> He was cast out and crucified;
> Those loving hands that did such good,
> They nailed them to a cross of wood.

c. The Vesture (27:35b)

Matthew hurried on to another aspect of the scene. He described how the soldiers "parted his garments, casting lots: that it might be fulfilled which was spoken by the prophet." Matthew added a quotation from Psalm 22:18, a portion of Scripture that the soldiers neither knew nor had any intention of fulfilling.

A quarternion, which is a detachment of four soldiers, did the actual work of crucifixion. Roman law gave them the garments of the victim as their loot. So the Lord's sandals, girdle, outer robe, and headdress were quickly divided among the four soldiers, after lots were cast to determine who was to receive what. There remained the inner robe, a tunic that reached from the shoulders to the knees. Ordinarily this garment was made of two pieces, which were fastened at the shoulders. But Christ's inner robe, like the one worn by the high priest, was without seam. Probably it was woven for Him by loving hands. Rather than tear this seamless robe, the soldiers cast a special lot for it.

d. The Vigil (27:36-37)

(1) A Finished Work (27:36)

"And sitting down they watched him there," wrote Matthew of the men who committed the crime. Theirs was a finished work. Never in all the annals of the universe was such a terrible work done. Man's wickedness could extend no further. Here is the end result of sin: men nailing their Maker to a cross and sitting down to watch Him die. And their work was done with carpenter's tools!

(2) A Final Word (27:37)

The soldiers sitting there beneath the shadow of the cross could read Pilate's inscription at its head: "THIS IS JESUS THE KING OF THE JEWS." We are told elsewhere that the words were written in Latin, Greek, and Hebrew. An inscription was customarily written on a board and carried before the prisoner to the place of execution to proclaim to the world the crime for which the condemned man was to be put to death. Pilate made the Lord's inscription as provocative and as insulting to the Jews as he could. The Jewish leaders were offended and outraged. John 19:21 tells us that they tried to persuade Pilate to soften the wording of the accusation, but Pilate refused to change it.

Pilate's inscription was correct. Jesus *was* the King of the Jews, the last rightful claimant to the throne of David. Two separate royal lines ran from David to Christ. One line ran from Solomon down through the kings of Judah to Joseph. But, as we have previously noted, a curse rested on that line, a curse centering on Jehoiachin (also called Jechonias, Jeconiah, and contemptuously Coniah). "Write ye this man childless"—so ran the divine decree in Jeremiah

22:30. Actually Jehoiachin had a number of sons (1 Chronicles 3:17-18), but no son or descendant of his was ever to ascend David's throne. No natural-born son of Joseph (a lineal descendant of Jehoiachin) could be the Messiah; the curse forbade it.

But David and Bath-sheba had another son besides Solomon. He was called Nathan, doubtless in honor of God's faithful prophet. Nathan's royal line also pursued its way through history, though it ran down the back alleys and was overlooked by all except the sacred historian. Mary was a direct lineal descendant of David through this line. Jesus was the virgin-born Son of Mary and thus a direct lineal descendant of David. He was adopted by Mary's husband Joseph and by adoption became legal heir to the Davidic throne. Thus the curse on Jehoiachin was both enforced and circumvented. Only in the person of the Lord Jesus could this have happened. He was David's Son by birth and David's heir by adoption. In Him the royal line terminated fully, finally, and forever.

Jesus was indeed the King of the Jews. Pilate stubbornly insisted on proclaiming that fact, and Jewish objections to his inscription were overruled by God.

3. The Men Who Were Condemned with the Christ (27:38)

Setting one event against another in glaring contrast, Matthew reported, "Then were there two thieves crucified with him, one on the right hand, and another on the left." This too seems to have been a deliberate attempt on the part of Pilate to annoy the Jews. It was bad enough that he should proclaim Jesus to be their King, but then to crucify Him between thieves, as though He were just another common criminal, was the final insult—an insult to the priests, to the people, and to the Prince of glory.

C. The Scoffers (27:39-44)

1. The Rabble (27:39-40)

"They that passed by reviled him, wagging their heads" (27:39). "They that passed by" were the idle throng, the passing strangers, the people of Jerusalem. Jesus had performed countless miracles for them, had loved them, had shown them the kindness of God; and they thanked Him by scoffing Him. Nodding at Him knowingly, they threw in His face the statement of the false witnesses: "Thou that destroyest the temple, and buildest it in three days, save

thyself. If thou be the Son of God, come down from the cross"
(27:40).

The Lord's public ministry ended as it had begun—with a
Satanic "If thou be the Son of God" ringing in His ears (27:40;
4:3,6). He was the Son of God, but God remained silent. Although
we talk about the problem of pain and silence of God and the
mystery of iniquity, the greatest and most unanswerable questions
about sin and suffering and silence are all brought into focus at
Calvary. There they are solved for us—and if not there, than
nowhere. God remained silent in the face of this provocation
because had He answered, it would have been with bolts of wrath.
As it was, God was in Christ, reconciling the world to Himself. The
silence was not one of callous indifference, but one of love,
compassion, grace, and forbearance of a supernatural order and
infinite degree.

2. The Rabbis (27:41-43)

a. Their Ranks (27:41)

It was bad enough for the careless rabble to hurl insults at the
dying Savior, but what can we say about the chief priests, the scribes,
and the elders? The great among the people, the intelligentsia, the
elite, the cream of Jewish society, the leaders of the Sanhedrin, the
nobility of Israel, the social, secular, and spiritual heads of the
nation scoffed Him. What blindness! What abysmal abuse! What
Satanic darkness! What Hellish hate!

b. Their Ridicule (27:42-43)

"He saved others," they sneered. "Himself he cannot save. If he
be the King of Israel, let him now come down from the cross, and
we will believe him. He trusted in God; let him deliver him now, if
he will have him: for he said, I am the Son of God."

"He saved others." What a statement! That is how Luke presented Him in his Gospel—as the Savior of sinners. "The King of
Israel." That is how Matthew presented Him from beginning to
end. "He trusted in God." That is how Mark presented Him—as the
divine Servant, who trusted in God in utter dependence and
obedience. "The Son of God." That is how John portrayed Him. So
the Gospels of Matthew, Mark, Luke, and John, all taken together,
give us the matchless story of this amazing One. And lo, the
unbelieving, God-defaming religious leaders of Israel, in utter

ignorance and with malicious intent, proclaimed Him to be all that He ever claimed to be. Truly God makes even the wrath of man to praise Him.

3. The Robbers (27:44)

"The thieves also, which were crucified with him, cast the same in his teeth." Even the robbers felt superior to the Savior and, following the example of the religious leaders, hurled their blasphemous insults at Him. Here were two sin-laden men, dying in agony. They were about to be flung into eternity, but they were so blind, so lost, that they could abuse the Son of God with their expiring breath. We can perhaps find some excuse for them, crazed as they were with pain and tormented by the thought of approaching death. But it added another bitter drop to our Lord's cup of suffering that these criminals could see Him as beneath them, as worthy of their imprecations, as a fitting object for their foul-mouthed scorn.

D. The Signs (27:45-54)

1. The Sun (27:45-50)

a. Darkness such as Was Never Known Before (27:45)

At high noon an unearthly darkness suddenly descended to wrap the whole land in a midday midnight for three hours. No human eyes were allowed to gaze on the Lord's last hours. Of what happened in those dreadful hours we know nothing. The Lord entered into a darkness of body, soul, and spirit, into a mystery of suffering that defies description and into which we must not probe.

b. Despair such as Was Never Known Before (27:46-49)

(1) The Anguished Cry (27:46)

All we are permitted to know is that just as the three hours of darkness ended, the Lord cried out, "Eli, Eli, lama sabachthani," which means, "My God, my God, why hast thou forsaken me?" The Lord was quoting Psalm 22:1 and thus with almost His last breath He was endorsing the Old Testament. He tasted the ultimate horror of a lost soul: to be abandoned by God. In that mysterious loneliness He who knew no sin was made sin for us and experienced the torment of a soul in Hell.

An Old Testament type gives us a vivid picture of Christ's despair. One of two goats taken on the day of atonement was known as the scapegoat. Over its head the high priest recited the sins of the children of Israel. When the long catalog was finished, the goat was handed over to "a fit man," who led it away into the desert, to "a land not inhabited" (Leviticus 16:21-22). There, far from human haunts, far from its kind, it was abandoned amid scenes of appalling desolation. There, with never a drop of water, never a blade of grass, in indescribable loneliness and isolation, it raised its plaintive cry—which was answered with total and awful silence. Thus our Savior suffered. His orphan cry rang up to Heaven and the only answer in the darkness was impenetrable, imponderable, complete silence.

(2) The Anxious Crowd (27:47-49)

Some of those who stood by the cross misinterpreted the Lord's cry and thought he was calling for the prophet Elijah. With a belated surge of compassion, one of them ran for a sponge dipped in vinegar, which he lifted to the Lord's parched lips on a reed. In full possession of His senses, the Lord recalled a prophecy that still awaited fulfillment—"In my thirst they gave me vinegar to drink" (Psalm 69:21)—and accordingly accepted the sour drink.

c. Death such as Was Never Known Before (27:50)

Jesus "cried again with a loud voice [and] yielded up the ghost." He died not as a victim, but as a victor. No man took His life from Him; He laid it down Himself (John 10:18). When all was done that had to be done, with sublime dignity He dismissed His Spirit into the keeping of His Father. Redemption's work was finished.

2. The Sanctuary (27:51a)

The other signs followed in swift succession. Most significant to the Jews to whom Matthew was writing was the sign in the sanctuary. The veil of the temple was torn in two from top to bottom, an ominous sign heralding the end of Judaism and its ritual religion, the end of the Old Testament economy. Edersheim said the veil was sixty feet long, twenty feet wide, as thick as a man's hand when measured right across the palm, and enormously heavy.[12] A yoke of oxen could not have rent that veil. The fact that it was torn in two from the top indicated the divine nature of this symbolic catastrophe.

We are not told what the Jews did about the veil. Presumably they sewed it back up again and went about their business of serving a now-dead religion as though nothing had happened. If so, it was not to be for long. Even as Matthew wrote, God was preparing to pull the entire temple down.

3. The Stones (27:51b)

Accompanying the sign of the veil was the sign of the stones. There was a terrible earthquake. Breaking rocks, drenched with the Savior's blood, lifted their voice in protest against men's murder of their Maker.

4. The Sepulchers (27:52-53)

Another sign was the opening of graves, the subsequent resurrection of those entombed, and the appearance of those saints to many in Jerusalem. Speaking in later years to King Agrippa, Paul could truthfully say, "This thing was not done in a corner" (Acts 26:26). The ushering of the Lord Jesus into the realm of death and back out again was accompanied by signs and wonders calculated to impress all but the most adamant and stony hearts.

5. The Sentries (27:54)

Not least among the signs of that day was the conversion of the sentries, "the centurion, and they that were with him." Watching Jesus, they had seen a man dying with dignity and grace, forgiving His foes, giving a thief who moments before had been cursing Him the promise of paradise, making final arrangements for the well-being of His mother, talking to God as Father, and crying out in thirst of body and unfathomable throes of spiritual torment. They had seen the orchestrated outrage of nature as darkened sky and rending rocks protested His death.

These Roman legionnaires, who had witnessed many a scene of horror in that callous age, "feared greatly." Their harsh training in the Roman army, their iron discipline, and their reputed courage in the face of danger, all conspired to make them men who were fearless, but they "feared greatly." What sent shudders through these soldiers was the fact that the One whom they had crucified was the Son of God. They had heard the rabble scoff at Christ's claim, they had heard the rabbis deride it, and they had heard the robbers make fun of it, but these Romans believed it.

We decry the totally unwarranted efforts of those who try to dilute the confession of the centurion and those who were with him. They did not say, "This was *a* son of the *gods*." They said, "This was the Son of God." They were the first fruits among the vast army of Gentiles who have since made the same confession. Matthew emphasized their conversion to set in greater contrast and condemnation the unbelief of the Jews.

E. The Sympathizers (27:55-56)

Except for John, the men among the Lord's sympathizers were conspicuously absent. The women came to the cross and stood through it all. Three of them were identified by Matthew: (1) There was Mary Magdalene, one who had owed much, been forgiven much, and loved much. (2) There was Mary, the wife of Cleopas and mother of Joses and James the Less. (She is thought to have also been the mother of Lebbaeus and Simon Zelotes. Edersheim thought that Cleopas was the brother of the Joseph who was the husband of the Lord's mother.[13]) (3) There was Salome, the mother of Zebedee's children (James and John) and sister of the virgin Mary.

Thus two of the Lord's aunts were at the cross and they were accompanied by a woman out of whom the Lord had cast seven demons. These women appear to have stood close to the cross at first. With them were the Lord's mother and John (John 19:25-27). When John took the Lord's mother away from the scene to his own home, the other women seem to have withdrawn to some distance away (perhaps fearing for their own safety), leaving the Lord Jesus to endure His agonies alone.

VIII. THE TOMB (27:57-66)

And so the Lord of life died. He who had flung the stars into space, who had made the worlds out of nothing, who had stooped down to fashion Adam's clay, who had breathed into his nostrils the breath of life, was dead. The Lord had suffered every indignity that mankind could devise. He had taken on the hosts of Hell. He had bowed beneath the load of the wrath and curse of God. Now He was dead and, being dead, required a tomb.

A. The Tomb Given (27:57-61)

1. The Intercession of Joseph (27:57-58)

It is interesting that God had on hand a Joseph to provide protection for the Lord when He was born, and a Joseph to provide protection for Him when He was buried. One Joseph was a carpenter; the other was a counselor. One was poor; the other was prosperous. Both men were described as "just" (Matthew 1:19; Luke 23:50). Both blazed for a moment on the sacred page and then disappeared into obscurity.

It was Joseph of Arimathea who went to Pilate to request permission to take custody of the dead body of Jesus. This Joseph was a member of the Sanhedrin, one of the few who dissented from the policy of Annas and Caiaphas in regard to Jesus. Like other pious wealthy Jews, Joseph had been building a sepulcher in Jerusalem for himself and his family.

It is not unlikely that Joseph had read Isaiah 53:9, which prophesied that the Messiah would be buried with the rich and, being convinced that Jesus was the Messiah, had purposefully set about preparing his own tomb for Jesus in order to fulfill the prophecy. If so, Joseph had probably concealed his allegiance to Jesus in order to prevent the authorities from interfering with his project. But when Jesus died, Joseph resolutely threw off his cloak of secrecy to act as the evangelists said he did.

2. The Interment of Jesus (27:59-61)

a. The Last Loving Gift (27:59-60)

In any case, the tomb that Joseph had hewn was ready and available for the burial of the Lord's body. Matthew said it was "his own new tomb" (27:60). The word translated "new" here is *kainos*, which means "freshly made," so Matthew was saying that the tomb was unused, undefiled by any dead body.

Matthew told us very little about the interment of Jesus. He simply said that Joseph wrapped the body "in a clean linen cloth" (27:59). John added other details, telling how Joseph's colleague Nicodemus brought a large amount of myrrh and aloes, aromatic spices used for burying the dead (John 19:39). Because of the impending sabbath, haste characterized all that was done. A partial embalmment was all that time allowed. The stone was rolled in place and the men left.

b. The Last Lingering Gaze (27:61)

"Mary Magdalene, and the other Mary" remained behind. They could not tear themselves away. The burial seemed so final. If they had left the tomb and gone to visit Mary of Bethany, she would have told them otherwise. She had stayed away from the cross and the funeral, not because she did not care, but because she knew that Jesus was going to rise again. That is why she had given her precious spikenard to Jesus while He was still alive instead of saving it for His burial (John 12:1-7). She had no need to wait and watch and weep at the tomb. She was waiting at home for the rest of the story to unfold.

B. The Tomb Guarded (27:62-66)

1. The Sanhedrin's Predicament (27:62-64)

a. What Was Remembered (27:62-63)

We wonder what the leaders of the Sanhedrin thought when that strange darkness fell over the land; when the earthquake, like the crack of doom, heralded our Lord's departure from this life; when news came of the rending of the temple veil to match the rending of the high priest's robe. We wonder what they thought when it was reported that, contrary to customary expectations of a slow death, Jesus had simply dismissed His spirit and died. If the soldiers had had to hasten His death by breaking His legs, He would have been proven to be a false Messiah (Exodus 12:46; Numbers 9:12). But instead of breaking His legs, the Romans had pierced His side. We wonder what the leaders of the Sanhedrin thought when they heard that pagan soldiers of Rome had confessed Jesus to be the Son of God. We wonder what they thought when they were told that two of their number, the greatly respected Nicodemus and the enormously rich Joseph of Arimathea, had boldly gone to Pilate, received from him the body of Jesus, and given it an honorable burial.

Now it was the day following the preparation day. It was the first day of the feast, the high day, the fifteenth of Nisan, and a terrible thought belatedly gripped the leaders of the Sanhedrin: Jesus had said that He would rise again. It seems that with the exception of Mary of Bethany, none of His friends remembered that prophecy, but His enemies did.

b. What Was Requested (27:64)

The chief priests and Pharisees rushed off to Pilate and urged "that the sepulchre be made sure until the third day." They offered a glib explanation of what might happen if the tomb were not secured: the disciples might under cover of night raid the tomb, steal the body, and spread the story of a resurrection. "So the last error shall be worse than the first," the religious leaders said. What the first error was they refrained from saying. I presume it was the colossal mistake of crucifying Jesus in the first place.

Evidently these evil men judged the Lord's disciples to be as devious and crafty as they were. In actual fact, the disciples were so thoroughly demoralized that they were incapable of even thinking up such a scheme. In their state of mind they could not have executed that kind of plan even if they had been bent on somehow carrying on the Master's cause.

2. The Sanhedrin's Precaution (27:65-66)

Pilate saw their point. "Ye have a watch [guard]," he said (27:65). The Greek can be interpreted as the imperative "Have ye a guard," or as the indicative "Ye may have a guard." The word translated "watch" is *koustōdia,* which refers to a guard of four soldiers. Clearly Pilate provided the Sanhedrin with such a guard. So off the leaders went, armed with a seal for the sepulcher and soldiers to keep intruders away. No one was going to tamper with that tomb. Their precautions render the subsequent resurrection of Christ all the more unassailable as historical fact.

So the world spun on through space. People settled down to the daily routine of their lives. The Lord's disciples hid themselves. The women made preparations for completing the embalming. The soldiers paced up and down or cast dice to while away the time. The lifeless body of the Lord lay still and cold. The moments ebbed away.

It seemed that death was reigning supreme, but try as it might, it could not corrupt that immortal clay lying swathed and bound in the inner darkness of the tomb. Heaven above and Hell beneath watched that sepulcher with baited breath, and angels gathered in the shadows.

PART FOUR

The King Is Raised
Matthew 28:1-20

THE KING IS RAISED

(28:1-20)

I. THE LIGHT BROKE THROUGH (28:1-10)
A. The Angel of the Lord (28:1-8)
   1. A Change (28:1-4)
      a. In the National Order of Things (28:1)
      b. In the Natural Order of Things (28:2-4)
         (1) The Ground Convulsed (28:2a)
         (2) The Grave Conquered (28:2b)
         (3) The Guard Confounded (28:3-4)
   2. A Challenge (28:5-6)
      a. What the Angel Shared with the Women (28:5)
         (1) God's Peace—To Still Their Fears (28:5a)
         (2) God's Power—To Stir Their Faith (28:5b)
      b. What the Angel Showed to the Women (28:6)
         (1) By Way of Proclamation (28:6a)
         (2) By Way of Proof (28:6b)
   3. A Charge (28:7-8)
      a. A Revelation (28:7)
         (1) The Announcement (28:7a)
         (2) The Appointment (28:7b)
      b. A Response (28:8)
B. The Appearing of the Lord (28:9-10)
   1. The Meeting (28:9-10a)
      a. When He Met the Women (28:9a)
      b. Why He Met the Women (28:9b-10a)
         (1) To Banish All Doubt (28:9b-c)
            (a) As to His Resurrection from the Dead
               (28:9b)

(b) As to the Reality of His Deity
(28:9c)
(2) To Banish All Dread (28:10a)
2. The Message (28:10b)

II. THE LIE BROKE DOWN (28:11-15)
  A. The Need for the Lie (28:11-12)
    1. The Official Report of the Resurrection (28:11)
    2. The Official Reaction to the Resurrection (28:12)
      a. The Meeting Convened by the Sanhedrin (28:12a)
      b. The Money Conveyed to the Soldiers (28:12b)
  B. The Nature of the Lie (28:13-14)
    1. Its Inherent Weakness (28:13)
    2. Its Incidental Weakness (28:14)
      a. From the Point of View of the Men Who
          Disseminated the Lie (28:14a)
      b. From the Point of View of the Men Who
          Devised the Lie (28:14b)
  C. The News of the Lie (28:15)
    1. The Financial Bribe Accepted by the Men
        (28:15a)
    2. The Fraudulent Belief Accepted by the Masses
        (28:15b)

III. THE LORD BROKE IN (28:16-20)
  A. To Confront the Disciples with the Glory of His
      Passion (28:16-17)
    1. The Appointment (28:16)
    2. The Appearing (28:17)
      a. The Happiness of the Disciples (28:17a)
      b. The Hesitation of the Doubters (28:17b)
  B. To Convince the Disciples of the Greatness of His
      Purpose (28:18-20)
    1. His Power (28:18)
    2. His Plan (28:19-20)
      a. Go! (28:19-20a)
        (1) Reaching the Nations (28:19)

        (a) The Best of News (28:19a)
        (b) The Best of Names (28:19b)
    (2) Teaching the Nations (28:20a)
  b. Lo! (28:20b-c)
    (1) His Presence to Be Personally Experienced
         by His Own (28:20b)
    (2) His Presence to Be Permanently Experienced
         by His Own (28:20c)

I. The Light Broke Through (28:1-10)

The light broke through, dispelling the darkness of the tomb, banishing the gloom and unbelief of the apostles, and flooding the ages with radiance and new truth. The three days and three nights of darkness, heralded by the mysterious darkness that was wrapped around our Lord's last three hours on the cross, were over. Never again will a believing child of God go out into the dark when death comes. Now "the path of the just is as the shining light, that shineth more and more unto the perfect day" (Proverbs 4:18).

A. The Angel of the Lord (28:1-8)

1. A Change (28:1-4)

a. In the National Order of Things (28:1)

"The end of the sabbath." Thus begins Matthew's account of the resurrection of Christ in the Gospel that is directed specifically toward the nation of Israel. Some scholars want to retranslate that first phrase as "late on the sabbath," but let the King James rendering stand. It is an eloquent, profound, and startling commentary on a change in the national order of things. Judaism was finished. The Jewish sabbath was rendered obsolete by the Lord's resurrection, just as the temple was made obsolete by the tearing of the veil, and the priesthood by the rending of the high priest's robe. "The end of the sabbath," Matthew wrote. To his Jewish compatriots and to those within the ranks of the professing Christian church who were still bemused by questions concerning the sabbath, he was crying, "It is finished!"

It was on the sabbath that the Lord of life and glory, the incarnate Creator of the universe, the Lord of the sabbath, lay silent and still in death. The sabbath was rooted and grounded in a law that could not save, a law that at best was a schoolmaster to bring people to Christ.

In creation God rested on the seventh day (Genesis 2:1-2). In revelation God set apart the seventh day for His people's rest (Exodus 20:8-11). In resurrection all that is changed. Thus the Lord Jesus replied to His critics who accused Him of breaking the sabbath, "My Father worketh...and I work" (John 5:17). In the Old Testament God's rest was in a day, but His sabbath rest was broken by the entrance of sin. Now His rest is in a person. God rests in the person of Christ and in His finished work, and so do we. The resurrection spelled "the end of the sabbath" and all that it represented.[1]

In Matthew 28:1 it was not only "the end of the sabbath." We also read that "it began to dawn toward the first day of the week." With spiritual instinct and insight the infant church turned away from the sabbath as a day of rest to the first day of the week as a day of worship (Acts 20:7; 1 Corinthians 16:1-2). Uncluttered with Mosaic prohibitions and rabbinical rules, the first day was observed in commemoration of the consummation of our redemption in Christ's conquest over death.

When Mary Magdalene and "the other Mary" (the wife of Cleopas and the mother of James the Less) went "to see the sepulchre," they had no idea of the enormous change that had transpired. That tomb was the grave of all their hopes. It contained the mortal remains of One whose life and love had conquered their hearts. They expected to see nothing else. In their sorrow they came to see the sepulcher, but instead they saw the Savior. Oh happy day! What hope for all in Christ!

b. In the Natural Order of Things (28:2-4)

(1) The Ground Convulsed (28:2a)

The women did not know it yet, but there had been a change in the natural order of things. Matthew wrote, "Behold, there was a great earthquake."

The ground shook with palsy when its Creator died; it shook with pleasure when He rose again. The ground convulsed when Jesus descended into the underworld; with His pierced feet, Jesus marched resolutely into Hades and then out again, causing the bedrock granite of the earth to tremble like a bowl of jelly beneath His tread.

(2) The Grave Conquered (28:2b)

"The angel of the Lord descended from heaven, and came and rolled back the stone from the door, and sat upon it." The angel did not come to let Christ out of the tomb; He had already come out. The angel came to show the world the evidence of the resurrection: an open and empty tomb.

With magnificent disregard for the governor's imperial seal, the angel rolled back the stone. With majestic disdain for priest and procurator, the angel sat on the stone. Let Jerusalem and Rome try to interfere with him! What did he care about the machinations of the Sanhedrin or the might of the caesar? What did the angel care about priestly courts or princely cohorts? One angel in one night overthrew all of Sennacherib's hosts (2 Kings 19:35). The angel at the Lord's tomb was only one of the twelve legions that the living Christ could call down from on high (Matthew 26:53).

We can imagine the hosts of Heaven challenging the opposition: "Ho there Caesar, bring on your shock troops. Summon your soldiers; bring them back from Britain, from Greece and Gaul, from the Euphrates river and the Euxine sea. Throw them in, wave after wave, against that lone angel, if you dare. And reduce your empire to ruins before its time!"

No power on earth could roll back that stone in order to close the tomb again. No Jewish Sanhedrin or Roman sovereign could re-wrap the empty graveclothes around the incarnate clay that linen had bound for a few short days.

(3) The Guard Confounded (28:3-4)

In 28:3 we find one of the rare Biblical descriptions of angels: "His countenance was like lightning, and his raiment white as snow." The angel was panoplied in blinding glory, bathed in the unapproachable light of another world. Or so the keepers saw him. In mortal fear they shook in their shoes and fell headlong, as though dead, at the angel's feet.

2. A Challenge (28:5-6)

The angel presented his terrifying countenance to the women. Reading their natural fear, he hastened to disarm their apprehension by offering a comforting word: "Fear not ye: for I know [*oida*, 'know by intuition, without effort'] that ye seek Jesus, which was crucified. He is not here: for he is risen, as he said. Come, see the place where the Lord lay." The women had come "to see the sepulchre," and with gentle irony the angel said in effect, "Well, come and see it!"

The empty tomb, the great apologetic of the resurrection, separates Christianity from the world's other religions. None of the false faiths has a true answer to the terrible reality of death. Christianity invites the world to come and look at an empty tomb.

The first to extend the invitation was an angel. Angels heralded the incarnation when Christ came down from above, and angels (Luke 24:4) heralded the resurrection when Christ came up from below. They are intensely interested in the process of redemption because their Beloved is involved in it from beginning to end.

Think what Peter missed because of his denial of Christ. Think what Matthew and the other disciples missed because of their unbelief. Had they taken seriously the Lord's repeated statements about His impending betrayal, trials, death, burial, and resurrection, they would have been bold enough to be present at the courts to give their testimony and at Calvary to protest the crime. They would have been keeping vigil outside the tomb on resurrection morning, eager to be the first to welcome the risen Lord back from the dead. They might have been able to give eyewitness reports of the greatest event in history. Instead news of the empty tomb was first announced by angels, and the glorious evangel was carried first by those faithful women who, in spite of their unbelief, went early to the tomb.

That vacated sepulcher became the cornerstone of apostolic preaching. The young church invited Jew and Gentile, Greek and barbarian, bond and free, rich and poor, great and small to ponder an empty tomb, a risen Christ. Paul preached the resurrection on Mars hill and to King Agrippa. Peter preached it on the day of Pentecost. "God hath raised him from the dead" is at the heart of Paul's great gospel treatise (Romans 10:9).

The angel's announcement was light in the darkness, life from the dead, hope for the hopeless, assurance of salvation, the essence of the gospel. The bold preaching of this news sent shudders through the Sanhedrin.

Hardened unbelievers, those who will not believe, go away in a rage from the empty tomb. They invent untenable theories to account for it. The sad truth is that people remain unbelievers, not because they *cannot* believe (for the proof of Christ's resurrection is overwhelming), but because they *will not* believe. Nowhere is that unwillingness more evident than in the Sanhedrin's attempt to explain away the hard and inconvenient evidence of Christ's triumph over death.

Wavering believers hear the words "Come, see," and the evidence of an empty tomb and a risen Christ puts new conviction in them, just as Pentecost put new courage in the disciples. A Christ up from the grave and a Comforter down from the glory gave birth to the church and a new dispensation.

3. A Charge (28:7-8)

a. A Revelation (28:7)

The angel charged the women, "Go quickly, and tell his disciples that he is risen from the dead; and, behold, he goeth before you into Galilee; there shall ye see him: lo, I have told you."

Galilee was where it had all begun. That was where the Lord had grown up, where He had called His disciples, where most of His miracles had been done, where His greatest messages had been preached. He would meet the disciples in Galilee.

The apostolic band was in disarray. One of the disciples was dead; one was still bowed by the burden of denial; all were living in fear; all were confused. The Lord intended to reconstitute the group and recommission it. He would meet them on a mountain and forge them anew into the nucleus of the church that was soon to be born.

b. A Response (28:8)

With their great news, the women rushed off on their happy mission. Fear and joy must have fought for mastery in their souls—fear because of the messenger (in spite of his assurances) and joy because of the message. They were overwhelmed with the revelation that the Lord had risen.

B. The Appearing of the Lord (28:9-10)

1. The Meeting (28:9-10a)

a. When He Met the Women (28:9a)

Then the women met Jesus Himself. Matthew recorded the meeting with astonishing brevity.

It was "as they went to tell his disciples" that the Lord met them. There is no substitute for prompt obedience to the revealed will of God if we want more and greater revelation.

The Lord had no intention of letting the tidings rest merely on hearsay, even if the source was a shining angel. Angelic appearances are worthy of notice, but our gospel does not rest on the word of an angel, no matter how bright his countenance or how bold his confidence. The Lord wants no such intermediaries. Our faith must rest on something more solid than "a vision of angels" (Luke 24:23). It must rest on a personal encounter with the Lord Himself. Still, it was as the women were obeying the light they had that they were given more. That is always God's way.

b. Why He Met the Women (28:9b-10a)

The reason the Lord appeared to the women was to banish all doubt and dread. Angels may leave us with a residue of fear, but the Lord never will, if we love Him. "Perfect love casteth out fear" (1 John 4:18). "Be not afraid," the Lord said (Matthew 28:10).

"Jesus met them, saying, All hail. And they came and held him by the feet, and worshipped him" (28:9). "All hail" means "Rejoice!" The women were overwhelmed with joy. Recognizing Him instantly, they went down at His feet. They gazed at the nail prints, reverently clasped His feet in their hands, felt the solid reality of His resurrection body, bowed in adoring wonder, and worshiped with hearts too full for words. The angel's words were true—gloriously, wonderfully true. The Lord was risen indeed!

2. The Message (28:10b)

After dispelling the women's doubt and fear, the Lord repeated the instructions of the angel. They were to tell the disciples to meet Him in Galilee. The disciples needed to get away from Jerusalem for a while, for it was a cauldron of hate and malice.

"Go tell my brethren," He said. For the first time the Lord called the disciples "brethren." In spite of their faults and failures, in spite of their doubts and disarray, He called them "my brethren." Such is His grace. Death, burial, and resurrection had not changed His heart. He was the same loving, patient, forgiving, encouraging Jesus. "There shall they see me" was His last cheerful word.

II. THE LIE BROKE DOWN (28:11-15)

Two groups hurried into the city: the women and the watchmen. The women were overwhelmed with triumph; the watchmen were overwhelmed with terror. The women were about to confront the world with the most tremendous fact in history; the watchmen would soon confront the world with the most tremendous falsehood in history. With the skill of an artist and the genius of inspiration, Matthew brought the two together: "Now when they [the women] were going [in obedience to Christ], behold, some of the watch came into the city" (28:11).

A. The Need for the Lie (28:11-12)

1. The Official Report of the Resurrection (28:11)

The report that the terrified guards brought to the Sanhedrin threw those religious leaders of the Jews into a state of consternation. The incredible had happened. In an hour or two the news would be all over Jerusalem. They had half feared a resurrection claim and had secured the guard from Pilate to render the sepulcher tamper-proof. There was no doubting the genuineness of the watchmen's report; something of a supernatural nature had happened and the tomb was now empty.

2. The Official Reaction to the Resurrection (28:12)

The Sanhedrin had made a colossal blunder in interfering with Jesus of Nazareth, but they were committed to the course on which they had embarked. They certainly were not going to admit the claims of Christ or confess themselves guilty of the greatest crime in all the annals of time. No, they must concoct a story. But first they must secure the silence and cooperation of the guard. The Sanhedrin had been able to buy Judas for the price of a slave. It was going to take "large money," a large sum to buy those watchmen. "Every man has his price" is the cynical saying of the world. Those men certainly did, and their price was high.

B. The Nature of the Lie (28:13-14)

1. Its Inherent Weakness (28:13)

The watchmen were paid to propagate the story that while they slept, the Lord's disciples came and stole His body. What a weak and foolish lie it was! Can you imagine a witness appearing in a court of law to announce to judge and jury, "Sirs, I consider myself a credible witness to the event I am about to describe because I was sound asleep when it happened"? The story was ludicrous. If the guards were asleep, how could they know what happened?

2. Its Incidental Weakness (28:14)

a. From the Point of View of the Men Who Disseminated the Lie (28:14a)

The watchmen were Roman soldiers. For a soldier of Rome to sleep while he was on duty or to lose what he was guarding was a capital offense. If the story had been true, the guards would have been the first to deny it. As it was, they were filled with alarm lest any such report should reach the ears of the governor. It took all the persuasive power of the priests to assure those men that they would come to no harm, that Pilate would acquiesce in the deception, and that the Sanhedrin would make sure that he did.

b. From the Point of View of the Men Who Devised the Lie
   (28:14b)

If the disciples stole the body, why did not the Sanhedrin or the Roman governor arrest the disciples, bring them to trial, cross-examine them as to the whereabouts of the body, and convict them of grand larceny, tampering with the governor's seal, and grave-robbing? Nothing would have put a swifter end to the report of the resurrection than a body identified as Jesus of Nazareth. There was of course no body to produce.

The members of the Sanhedrin were nobody's fools. They were clever, crafty men. But the best they could do was to launch a propaganda offensive against the truth. In the face of growing reports of the risen Christ having been seen and handled, all the Sanhedrin could do to avoid a public hue and cry over that empty tomb was to concoct a foolish lie. The fact that their propaganda cannot stand five minutes' serious investigation shows to what extremes the religious leaders were driven by the resurrection of Christ. He was alive and they could not deny it.

C. The News of the Lie (28:15)

Writing many years later, Matthew said, "So they took the money, and did as they were taught: and this saying is commonly reported among the Jews until this day." Yes, and until our day too. People are gullible, especially when religious beliefs and prejudices are involved. To the relief of the Sanhedrin the thoughtless multitudes accepted the lie. As a maxim of propagandists says, "If a lie is repeated often enough, people will believe it." The "news" of the theft of the body became part of Jewish anti-Christian teaching from the beginning. Repeating the lie has been a popular rabbinic way of refuting the fact of the resurrection ever since.

III. THE LORD BROKE IN (28:16-20)

No amount of falsehood could alter the fact that Jesus had been seen alive. He showed Himself to the disciples in Jerusalem repeatedly (Acts 1:3), but Matthew did not dwell on those appearances. Instead he described a meeting in Galilee. This was the last scene painted by Matthew.

The Lord broke in to confront the disciples with the glory of His passion and to convince the disciples of the greatness of His purpose.

A. To Confront the Disciples with the Glory of His Passion (28:16-17)

1. The Appointment (28:16)

They met on a mountain in Galilee by prior appointment. We are not told which mountain it was, but perhaps it was the one where the Lord had given His sermon on the mount. In that no-man's land of Galilee situated between the thriving Gentile world and the dying Jewish world, in peaceful surroundings and amid scenes filled with memories of His ministry, the Lord sought to remove any lingering doubts in the minds of His followers.

Matthew only mentioned "the eleven disciples," but perhaps others were present. If the occasion was the same one as that mentioned by Paul in 1 Corinthians 15:6, more than five hundred people witnessed this appearance of the Lord.

2. The Appearing (28:17)

"They saw him," said Matthew. "They worshipped him." Would that no more could have been said! However, Matthew had to add, "But some doubted." The word translated "doubted" is *distazō*, which occurs only in Matthew—here and in 14:31, where it is used in reference to Simon Peter when he walked on the water, then lost his nerve, looked away from Jesus to the angry elements, and began to sink. After rescuing Peter, the Lord said to him, "O thou of little faith, wherefore didst thou *doubt* [waver, hesitate]?" (italics added).

It seems incredible that anyone faced with the overwhelming evidence of a risen Christ could still have hesitated, but some did. The only explanation for such incorrigible unbelief is found in our own stubborn hearts.

B. To Convince the Disciples of the Greatness of His Purpose (28:18-20)

1. His Power (28:18)

The Lord set before the disciples a vision of His power. "All power is given unto me in heaven and in earth," He said. The word translated "power" here is *exousia*, which refers to authority or delegated power along with the right to use it. In this context neither "power" nor "authority" is an adequate translation. As the

Lord used it in 28:18, *exousia* means "all the right of absolute authority and all the resources of absolute power."

Christ wields absolute authority in Heaven. Cherubim and seraphim, thrones and dominions, unfallen angels, sinless sons of light—from the highest to the lowest they gladly own His sway. As they hover over little children, ascend and descend Jacob's ladder, superintend the affairs of local churches in the unseen world, minister to those who are the heirs of salvation, battle Satan's hordes, or stand by in the hour of death, they rejoice in His authority and power.

Principalities and powers, rulers of this world's darkness, wicked spirits in high places, fallen angels, demon bands, Satan himself—all are circumvented, held in check, by Christ. Whether they are overruling the affairs of nations or empires, disseminating Satanic creeds, tormenting children, inciting men to war, spreading famine and woe, inciting people to lust, binding youth with drugs, blinding adults with delusions, hindering God's work, or sowing tares among the wheat, at length they are curbed by the Lord. They gnash their teeth in rage, but they bow before the authority and power of the One who says to them, "Thus far, and no farther."

Christ wields absolute authority on earth too. Kingdoms wax and wane, empires rise and fall, nations come and go, generations appear and vanish, but nothing happens on earth outside of His permissive will. Being limited in our understanding, we often shake our heads over what appears to be the power and triumph of the foe. We cannot explain many of the things His omniscience permits, things we would expect His omnipotence to hinder. All we know is that He is on the throne, wielding all power and authority on earth as in Heaven, let come what may.

2. His Plan (28:19-20)

a. Go! (28:19-20a)

The Lord also set before His disciples, and us, a vision of His plan. It can be summed up in two words, "Go" and "Lo." First He said, "Go ye therefore, and teach all nations, baptizing them in the name of the Father, and of the Son, and of the Holy Ghost" (28:19). Note the word "therefore." It links our authority—our authority to invade the nations of mankind with the saving gospel of Christ—to His authority as Lord of Heaven and earth. Our authority could not come from a higher source. The unbelieving may challenge our right to take the gospel to other lands, but we have every right. We have a mandate that transcends that of any human political, religious, or economic power. We are commissioned to go, and go we must, for Satan holds the nations in darkness. Millions are blinded by communism, humanism, Buddhism, Hinduism, Confucianism, Islam, and false cults of apostate Christianity.

(1) Reaching the Nations (28:19)

It took the apostles a long time to come to grips with that compelling word "Go." But by the time Matthew was writing down his reminiscences of Christ's appearance on the mountain in Galilee, the marching orders of Christ had been taken seriously, especially by Paul, the latecomer to the apostolic band. The frontiers of the church were already expanding far and wide under his driving ambition, towering example, and quenchless zeal.

The work of reaching the nations is still far from finished. Thousands of tribes do not even have a page or two of the Bible in their native tongue. Untold millions are still untold. In spite of our ability to use mass communication and high technology in reaching the nations, we are not keeping pace with the birthrate.

(2) Teaching the Nations (28:20a)

The work of teaching the nations is even farther from completion. The call is to evangelism, enlistment, enlightenment, and discipleship. We are to teach our converts to "observe all things whatsoever I have commanded you." That takes time, patience, knowledge, and commitment, all backed by the eloquent example of a Christ-filled life.

Having taught the nations the gospel, we are to baptize them in the name of the triune God. Baptism is the outward expression of an inward experience, the bold and often dangerous confession of Christ before a Christ-rejecting world. In many countries baptism is the final break with the past and invites persecution, discrimination, and death.

b. Lo! (28:20b-c)

We are not called to go alone to city slums, arctic wastes, equatorial jungles, college campuses, or our own neighborhoods. The task would be impossible if "Go" were the only word, so the

Lord added "Lo." He promised, "Lo, I am with you alway, even unto the end of the world."

Many proofs of the trustworthiness of this pledge could be produced from the roll call of God's missionaries and martyrs down through the ages, but we will only consider the testimony of one of them here. The testimony is that of Paul, the greatest of all apostles and ambassadors, or as Shakespeare would say, "the noblest Roman of them all." We will glean his testimony from four scenes in Scripture.

In the first scene we see the apostle in Corinth in the midst of his missionary career. Already he bears in his body the slave brands of Jesus Christ, the telltale scars of many a beating and privation. In Europe he has been thrashed and tortured in the prison stocks at Philippi, assaulted at Berea and Thessalonica, and scoffed at in Athens. In Corinth itself he has faced the blasphemy and riotous unbelief of the large Jewish community. The doors of the synagogue have been firmly closed against him. The bright spots in the story of bitter and persistent persecution in Corinth are Crispus, the believing chief ruler of the synagogue, and Justus, with whom Paul has taken up temporary residence. In spite of the spiritual blessing that has attended his ministry, Paul seems to be filled with foreboding. He has barely recovered from the "many stripes" received at Philippi (Acts 16:23), so we can well imagine his doubts and depression. (After all, the lictor's lash would have been torture to his flesh the same as anyone else's—he was not made of iron.) Just when we wonder whether Paul can stand any more, the Lord makes good His promise. "Then [saith] the Lord to Paul in the night by a vision, Be not afraid, but speak, and hold not thy peace: For I am with thee, and no man shall set on thee to hurt thee: for I have much people in this city" (Acts 18:9-10).

In the second scene Paul is back in Jerusalem. The brethren there barely say *thank you* for the financial gift he has brought them from his Gentile converts in many lands. The elders are more concerned with asking him to prove his Jewishness by undertaking a considerable financial burden and joining in some rites in the temple. A riot ensues in the temple courts when Paul's enemies recognize him, and he is rescued only in the nick of time from the mob that would have killed him then and there. The soldiers who rescue him allow him to give his testimony to the mob, but a further riot ensues. Determined to get to the bottom of the problem, the Roman captain gives orders for Paul to be "examined by scourging" (Acts 22:24). Fortunately Paul's Roman citizenship saves him from this horror and earns him the opportunity of bearing witness before the Sanhedrin. Again there is a tumult and it is evident that the Jewish authorities are intent on killing Paul. The soldiers deliver him from the Jews and take him to the prison in the castle. "The night following the Lord [stands] by him, and [says], Be of good cheer, Paul: for as thou hast testified of me in Jerusalem, so must thou bear witness also at Rome" (Acts 23:11). The Lord has kept His promise.

In the third scene we see Paul in a ship on his way to Rome. He is still a prisoner and has appealed to caesar. A terrible storm is threatening Paul's life and the lives of all on board. The vessel is at the mercy of wind and wave. All bearings are lost and all hope is gone for both passengers and crew. But Paul has a word of encouragement. He tells them, "There stood by me this night the angel of God, whose I am, and whom I serve, Saying Fear not, Paul; thou must be brought before Caesar: and, lo, God hath given thee all them that sail with thee" (Acts 27:23-24). The Lord has again made good His promise.

In the fourth scene Nero's wickedness has erupted into a wholesale persecution of Christians. Having been acquitted and rearrested, Paul has been brought back to Rome for the last time. The great apostle is incarcerated in a terrible dungeon. (No one escaped from that dungeon and some prisoners were eaten alive by rats.) Paul is troubled by the news that heresy rages in many of the churches he founded. He is cold and his physical infirmities brought on by his frequent floggings and straitened circumstances are troubling him. Paul longs for something to read, for he is virtually alone. Some of his faithful aides are doing his errands far from Rome. Others, like Demas, have forsaken him. Paul has been abandoned by his remaining friends to face the hostile court alone. (His first hearing at court was difficult because Alexander the coppersmith had prejudiced the authorities against him.) Death is now a certainty, but the Lord has once more made good His promise. Paul is able to write, "At my first answer no man stood with me, but all men forsook me: I pray God that it may not be laid to their charge. Notwithstanding the Lord stood with me, and strengthened me" (2 Timothy 4:16-17). Shortly afterward Paul is taken out of the dungeon, beheaded (tradition says), and "promoted to glory."

Jesus promised, "Lo, I am with you alway, even unto the end of the world." As David Livingstone was fond of saying, "It is the word of a gentleman of the most sacred and strictest honor, and there is an end on't."[2] And so it is.

NOTES

Part One, Section 1

1. See *The Companion Bible* (Grand Rapids: Zondervan, 1964) appendix 99.
2. The generations of the heavens and earth (Genesis 2:4–4:26); of Adam (5:1–6:8); of Noah (6:9–9:20); of the sons of Noah (10:1–11:9); of Shem (11:10-26); of Terah (11:27–25:11); of Ishmael (25:12-18); of Isaac (25:19–35:29); of Esau (36:1-8); of the sons of Esau (36:9-43); of Jacob (37:1–50:26); of Aaron and Moses (Numbers 3:1); of Pharez (Ruth 4:18-22).
3. See John Phillips, *Exploring the World of the Jew* (Neptune, NJ: Loizeaux, 1993) 77-89.
4. The natural-born sons of Joseph and Mary obviously came under the interdict, so could never sit on the throne of David. Only Jesus qualified. Besides, all records—apart from the Biblical records—are now destroyed, and the Jews must either have Jesus as their King or have no king at all.
5. From the hymn "The Great Physician" by William Hunter.
6. See Alfred Edersheim, *The Life and Times of Jesus the Messiah* (Peabody, MA: Hendrickson, 1993) 148.
7. F. W. Boreham, *My Christmas Book* (Grand Rapids: Zondervan, 1953) 72-79.
8. Ibid., 78.
9. See *The Scofield Reference Bible* (New York: Oxford University Press, 1945). Bullinger took issue with this view. He maintained that there is a figure of speech involved here (historical hysteresis) by which the Holy Spirit in later and subsequent Scriptures added supplementary details not given in the history itself. Sometimes the details were historical facts of which no mention had before been made. Here is his comment:

   > Matt. ii.23.—"And he came and dwelt in a city called Nazareth: that it might be fulfilled which was spoken by the prophets, He shall be called a Nazarene."
   >
   > Through missing this *Hysteresis,* the commentators have created a difficulty of their own.
   >
   > First, they cannot find such a prophecy in any of the prophets.
   >
   > Then, they try and make a connection between *netzer,* a branch, and *Nazarene;* and, as there is none, the difficulty is only increased.
   >
   > Even if the connection could be established, the difficulty would not be removed: for it says "prophets" (*plural*), and the word *netzer* is

used of Christ in only one prophet, Isaiah. So the difficulty is further increased.

But there is really no difficulty at all. It is absolutely created. It is assumed from the outset that it says "which was *written*." But it does not say so! It says "which was SPOKEN." The fact is, some prophecies were written down and never spoken; some were both written and spoken; while others were spoken and never written. This is one of the latter class: and there is all the difference in the world between τὸ ρηθέν, *which was spoken*, and ὅ γέγραπται, *which standeth written!*

Thus, this beautiful *Hysteresis* reveals to us the historical fact that several prophets had declared by the Holy Spirit that the Messiah should be called a Nazarene. But for this *Hysteresis* we should never have known it.

See E. W. Bullinger, *Figures of Speech Used in the Bible* (London: Eyre and Spottiswood, 1898) 710-711.

10. An exposition of all these parables will follow in due course, but it will be helpful at this point to summarize the mystery parables of Matthew 13 as follows:

   1. THE MYSTERY OF GOD'S PERMISSIVE WILL
      God's purposes in the world during the present age will be marked by
      a. Distractions
         The Parable of the Sower
         Only a small percentage of the seed sown produces fruit and only a percentage of that is top quality.
      b. Deceptions
         The Parable of the Tares
         Satan sows his own false ministers in among God's true people to confuse and deceive.
      c. Distortions
         The Mustard Tree
         The professing church assumes the role of a world imperial power and harbors many evil spirits.
      d. Defilements
         The Parable of the Leaven
         Doctrinal error permeates all of Christendom.

   2. THE MYSTERY OF GOD'S PERFECT WILL
      a. His people during the continuation of this age
        (1) His original people
           The Parable of the Hid Treasure
           The Jewish people are buried in the world, but are still the objects of God's watchful care and will one day be reconstituted as a nation in God's purpose and time.
        (2) His other people
           The Parable of the Pearl
           The church, not named by the Lord here but the evident subject of the parable, is the special object of the absent King's affection.
      b. His people during the consummation of this age
         The Parable of the Dragnet

The present mystery phase of the kingdom, containing so much of a mixture of good and evil, will be terminated by divine intervention.

11. The church is not Israel; neither is it the kingdom, although it is not totally unrelated to the kingdom. The church is a separate entity in the purposes of God. It was foreseen (as many Old Testament types make clear) as a clear-cut parenthesis in God's Old Testament kingdom purposes. The church was injected supernaturally into history on the day of Pentecost and will be supernaturally ejected back out of history at the rapture. At that time God will resume His direct dealings with Israel. The Jews are now being regathered in the promised land as foretold in preparation for postrapture events. The kingdom of the heavens will then be set up as promised.

12. The omissions are important. For instance the parable of the wheat and tares and the parable of the dragnet are exclusive to Matthew. They are omitted by Mark and Luke; in the kingdom of God there are no tares and no bad fish. The parable of the leaven, however, is not exclusive to Matthew because even the true doctrines of the kingdom can be adulterated by saved people.

13. The baptism of the Spirit is mentioned directly only seven times in the New Testament. The first five references are *prophetical* (Matthew 3:11; Mark 1:8; Luke 3:16; John 1:26,33; and Acts 1:5). All five foretell something that was going to happen consequent to the coming of the Christ. The first four have to do with John the Baptist's prophecy. The fifth records what the Lord said to his disciples on the way to the mount of Olives and His ascension. He told them that the baptism of the Spirit would occur "not many days hence"; it took place ten days later in the upper room on the day of Pentecost. The sixth reference is *historical* (Acts 11:16) and has to do with the adding of Gentiles to the Christian church. The only other reference is *doctrinal* (1 Corinthians 12:13). It explains exactly what the baptism of the Spirit does: This ministry of the Holy Spirit takes an individual believer in the Lord Jesus and adds him to the mystical body of Christ (the church) so that between him and the Christ and all other Christians exists a mysterious oneness so unique that it can be likened only to the organic oneness of a human body.

Part One, Section 2

1. Paraphrase of Julia Ward Howe's "Battle Hymn of the Republic."
2. Edersheim, *The Life and Times of Jesus the Messiah*, 84. Other great cities with large Jewish populations also had numerous synagogues. In Alexandria they were in all quarters. The great central synagogue was like a basilica. It had a double colonnade and was so large that special signals were necessary to alert people in the remote sections as to when responses were required. The various trade guilds sat together in the central synagogue so that visitors would be able to find potential employers or workmen. The choir of this Jewish cathedral held seventy chairs encrusted with precious stones, where sat the Alexandrian elders, whose constitution was modeled after the great Sanhedrin in Jerusalem (Edersheim, 42).

The synagogues bonded the Jews of the world together in a common form of worship. They were a natural platform for the spread of the gospel and were used as such by both Christ and His apostles as long as opportunity afforded. The ruler of the synagogue often invited distinguished visitors to address the worshipers, an ideal situation as long as it lasted.

3. There are only five brief periods in the Bible with a concentration of miraculous activity: (1) at the time of the exodus and the conquest of Canaan; (2) in the days of Elijah and Elisha; (3) in Babylon in the days of Daniel; (4) at the time of Christ and the early days of apostolic witness; and (5) during the coming age of the great tribulation. The first four of these periods ended with the giving of the written Word. The last will end at the return of the living Word. Each period is a transitional period. In between there are hardly any miracles at all. Obviously the use of miracles is common only at critical junctures in God's dealing with men, and miracles are intended as a sign of a coming change. The overwhelming majority of Bible miracles have some Jewish context.

4. Unger listed the cities embraced as Scythopolis, Hippos, Gadara, Pella, Philadelphia, Gerasa, Dion, Canatha, Raphana, and Damascus. See Merrill F. Unger, *Unger's Bible Dictionary* (Chicago: Moody Press, 1957) 257.

5. Edersheim, *The Life and Times of Jesus the Messiah*, 363.

6. Shakespeare, *The Merchant of Venice*, 4.1, Portia to Shylock.

7. Compare Exodus 32:15-20 where we read that Moses deliberately broke the original tablets of stone on which the law had been engraved by the finger of God, because the people could not look on the unbroken law and live in their sin. The second tablets of the law were put unbroken into the ark as soon as it was made (Exodus 25:21) and were therefore out of sight to all except God. That is why the impious men of Beth-shemesh were instantly smitten by God when they presumed to look inside the ark (1 Samuel 6:19). The sacred ark was of such christological significance that it is mentioned by ten different names in the Old Testament a combined total of 185 times.

8. J. B. Phillips, *The New Testament in Modern English* (New York: Macmillan, 1972) 10.

9. From the hymn "Abide with Me" by Henry F. Lyte.

10. See John Phillips, *Exploring Revelation* (Neptune, NJ: Loizeaux, 1991) 12-13.

11. From the hymn "Abide with Me" by Henry F. Lyte.

12. G. Campbell Morgan, *The Gospel According to Matthew* (London: Oliphants, 1946) 75.

13. The argument that "that which is perfect" refers to the second coming of Christ is obviously wrong. The phrase is a rendering of one Greek word: *teleios,* literally translated "the perfect" and derived from the word *telos,* which means "finished." The word is neuter, so cannot refer to Christ. It has to refer to a thing. *Teleios* conveys the idea of the completion or finishing of something that has been going through a process of development and has now arrived at the conclusion of that process. Christ's second coming is not a process, but an instantaneous event resulting in immediate and radical changes.

14. Edersheim, *The Life and Times of Jesus the Messiah,* 69.
15. See Edersheim, *The Life and Times of Jesus the Messiah,* 74.

Part One, Section 3

1. In the Bible, water for drinking invariably symbolizes the Holy Spirit, and water for cleansing symbolizes the Word of God, the Holy Spirit's active agent for accomplishing His will.
2. See Edersheim, *The Life and Times of Jesus the Messiah,* 379-380.
3. Of the eighty-eight occurrences of the title in the New Testament, eighty-four are in the Gospels. They are all used by the Lord Himself. He is called the Son of man once in the book of Acts (7:56), where Stephen sees Him standing at God's right hand; once in the Epistles (Hebrews 2:6, which quotes from Psalm 8:4 and refers to Adam and, by application, to the Lord); and twice in the book of Revelation (1:13; 14:14). See *The Companion Bible,* appendix 98:XVI.
4. God gave to the first man, Adam, dominion over the earth (Genesis 1:26). This dominion was surrendered to Satan in the fall. No one man of Adam's race has succeeded in achieving universal dominion, though Satan has tried repeatedly to bring in such an individual. Satan will succeed briefly with the antichrist. His triumph will be short-lived because Jesus as the second man, the last Adam (1 Corinthians 15:45-47), will come, put an end to the beast's vile rule, and establish the kingdom that is such a prominent theme in Matthew's Gospel.
5. From the hymn "Master, the Tempest is Raging" by Mary A. Baker.
6. See G. H. Pember, *Earth's Earliest Ages* (London, Pickering and Inglis, n.d.) 72.
7. Edersheim, *The Life and Times of Jesus the Messiah,* 347.
8. Those who deny the existence of demons are like people in Britain during the time of the great plague. Attributing the terrorizing epidemic to bad air, they sealed up their houses, stopped up their chimneys, and burned foul-smelling messes on their hearths until they choked on the fumes. They relied on the imagined virtues of posies and nosegays to offset the menace of the air. They lived in filth and flung their offal into the streets. The kennel was the sewer and it ran down the middle of the narrow road, a place given over to scavenger dogs and rats. People lived in an environment infested with fleas. Little did they know that the plague was caused by an invisible bacterium carried by fleas that infested the rats. They knew nothing about germs, bacteria, or viruses and would not have believed anyone who told them that their bodies could become hosts to millions of invisible germs.

    Modern men, scoffing at the idea of demons, are also like the doctors who gave wrong advice during the plague because they were ignorant of bacteria and the causes of infection. Their ignorance made them vulnerable and in no way altered the facts.

Part Two, Section 1

1. Note the quote from the Old Testament (Isaiah 28:11) in 1 Corinthians 14:21 and its application to the Hebrew people. The cessation of sign

gifts was foretold in 1 Corinthians 13:8. They became redundant when Israel as a nation finally rejected the apostolic preaching. With the completion of the New Testament canon and the fall of Jerusalem in A.D. 70 and the final dispersion of the Jews in A.D. 135, the sign miracles came to an end.

2. If the Jews had accepted Christ then, possibly Judas would have betrayed Jesus to the Romans. His crucifixion, burial, and resurrection would have followed, making possible the spiritual redemption of mankind. Probably Nero would have become the antichrist. The nations would have been stirred up against Jerusalem. Armageddon would have been precipitated and the triumphant Lord would have set up His millennial kingdom. In any case, Old Testament prophecies would have been fulfilled in rapid sequence and the glory age would have come.

3. Traditional rendering of statement by Tertullian.

Part Two, Section 2

1. Edersheim produced some cogent reasons for his view that the Pharisees had a hand in Herod's arrest of John the Baptist. See Edersheim, *The Life and Times of Jesus the Messiah,* 452-453.

2. The expression "the kingdom of heaven" is a technical one used only by Matthew. It is not essentially the same as the expression "the kingdom of God" used by the other evangelists. The expression "the kingdom of heaven" refers to the mystery phase of the kingdom and relates to the fortunes of the kingdom during the period of Israel's rejection of Christ. Truth concerning this phase of the kingdom is developed in Matthew 13. It overlaps with the church age, the great secret of God, known to Him from a past eternity, a hidden mystery throughout the age of the Old Testament kingdom (Ephesians 3:4-12).

3. W. E. Vine, *An Expository Dictionary of New Testament Words* (Old Tappan, NJ: Revell, 1940) III:208, IV:189.

4. *The Companion Bible,* appendix 142.

Part Two, Section 3

1. *The Companion Bible,* appendix 143.

2. This theme is developed further in Hebrews 4:1-11, a warning passage dealing with creation rest, Canaan rest, covenant rest, and Calvary rest. See John Phillips, *Exploring Hebrews* (Neptune, NJ: Loizeaux, 1992) 55-61.

3. See *The Companion Bible,* 1329.

4. Edersheim, *The Life and Times of Jesus the Messiah,* 446.

5. That, incidentally, is the real significance of the sign gift of tongues. It was a judgment sign to the nation of Israel. God was warning Jewish unbelievers that if the nation did not repent, it would be again scattered among the nations, and the Hebrew people would be forced to speak the languages of the Gentiles (1 Corinthians 14:21-22; Isaiah 28:11-12). The fall of Jerusalem, the completion of the New Testament Canon, and the cessation of the sign gifts were all more or less contemporaneous events.

6. While I was in the British army and stationed in Palestine, I took a week's

leave to tour Galilee. The tour was conducted by a military chaplain who knew all about the region. When we were on the shores of the sea of Galilee, he explained how Jesus could have spoken to enormous crowds in this area without the use of a public address system. Jesus, he said, selected His site with care when He chose to speak from the shores of this lake. The hills surrounding the lake form a basin, and the lake itself is a natural sounding board. If a man standing on the edge of the lake and facing the people on the slopes speaks in a conversational tone of voice, his voice is picked up by the still waters and relayed to any number of people on the hillside. The chaplain asked for a volunteer to put his explanation to the test. I volunteered. I stood at the lakeside where Jesus once stood, faced the scores of men seated on the hillside a hundred yards or so up the slopes, opened a New Testament, and read to them the parable of the sower. I did not shout or raise my voice; I spoke in an ordinary tone of voice, as I would to a friend standing by my side. The men heard every word clear as a bell. The lake was the Lord's amplifier.

7. This prophecy is of the deepest import in Israel's history. It is written down seven times (Isaiah 6:9-10; Matthew 13:14-15; Mark 4:12; Luke 8:10; John 12:40; Acts 28:25-27; Romans 11:8). It is solemnly quoted in Matthew 13:14-15 as coming from God on the day counsel was taken by the Jews to destroy Him. It is quoted in John 12:40-41 as coming from the Son of God after the raising of Lazarus, which resulted in further counsel being taken by the Jews to put Him to death. It is quoted by Paul as coming from the Holy Spirit when after a whole day's conference with the great apostle, the Jews of Rome "believed not" (Acts 28:25-27).

8. Some years ago evangelist Harold Wildish stood on a street corner in a busy part of London intending to have a street meeting. Finding it difficult to attract a crowd, he took off his hat, slipped something beneath it, put it on the sidewalk, and accosted the next man who passed by. "Excuse me," he said in his gentlemanly way, "there's something alive under that hat." The man stopped and stared, and soon Wildish had gathered a considerable crowd. He then said, "Stand back, if you please, ladies and gentlemen. I'm going to reach down and take the live thing out from under my hat." The crowd backed off and formed a circle. In a twinkling Wildish reached under his hat, pulled out what was hidden underneath, and held it up for people to see. It was a Bible! Before the crowd could recover, he put in a few pointed words for the Lord. Wildish was right of course. The Bible is alive. It is the living Word of the living God.

9. Andrew Miller, *Miller's Church History* (Fincastle, VA: Scripture Truth) 335.

10. All power in the Roman church comes down from the top. Under the cardinals are the bishops and archbishops, who rule Rome's dioceses around the world. Below these are the priests, nuns, and brothers, who do the ordinary work of the church. Forming the lowest level of all are the laity.

11. See John Phillips, *Bible Explorer's Guide* (Neptune, NJ: Loizeaux, 1987) 61-68.

12. Josephus, *Wars of the Jews*, 7.6.2. Also see Edersheim, *The Life and Times of*

Jesus the Messiah, 453-454, and H. V. Morton, *In the Steps of the Master* (London: Rich & Cowan, 1934) 272-291.

13. From the hymn "God Moves in a Mysterious Way" by William Cowper.

Part Two, Section 4

1. See John Phillips, *Exploring the World of the Jew,* 55-76.
2. Edersheim, *The Life and Times of Jesus the Messiah,* 482-485.
3. Ibid., 485.
4. Ibid., 489.
5. Morgan, *The Gospel According to Matthew,* 200.

Part Three, Section 1

1. See Edersheim, *The Life and Times of Jesus the Messiah,* 523-525.
2. 2 Maccabees 2:1-8.
3. See Morgan, *The Gospel According to Matthew,* 211.
4. See Morgan, *The Gospel According to Matthew,* 212.
5. Elisabeth Elliot, *Shadow of the Almighty* (New York: Harper, 1958) 247.
6. Norman P. Grubb, *C. T. Studd, Cricketer & Pioneer* (London: Religious Tract Society, 1933) 166.
7. Morgan, *The Gospel According to Matthew,* 222.
8. See John Phillips, *Exploring Romans* (Neptune, NJ: Loizeaux, 1991).
9. See John Barron, "From Russia with Hate," *Reader's Digest* (November 1985) 127:106-109.
10. Thus we read in the Apocalypse of there being "ten thousand times ten thousand" around the throne (Revelation 5:11). And in 1 Samuel 18:7 we read that Saul slew "his thousands," but David, by slaying Goliath, had slain "his ten thousands."
11. Much discussion centers around *porneia,* the word translated "fornication" in Matthew 19:9. Some claim that the word was only used to describe premarital sex, which was a ground for divorce in some cases. Illicit sex after marriage was punishable not by divorce, but by death (Deuteronomy 22:13-24). Those who believe that *porneia* refers only to premarital sex say that no divorce is permissible except when the wife is proved to have been unchaste before marriage. Other Bible students claim that *porneia* is not restricted to the sin of unmarried people. Those who hold this view say that it cannot be proven that the discovery of previous immorality in a wife automatically annulled her marriage; they point to Hosea as a classic example to the contrary (Hosea 1:2). It seems hard to support the view that *porneia,* as used by the Lord in Matthew 19:9, simply means premarital uncleanness. As used in this verse, the word points directly to the sin of adultery.
12. In spite of some textual criticism, the title must be retained if the sense of the context is to be maintained. Both Matthew and Luke agree (Matthew 19:16; Luke 18:18).
13. The fifth commandment by structural arrangement really belongs with the first four. Note the phrase "the Lord thy God," which links the first five commandments in Exodus 20.

14. The age-long sojourn during the diaspora in all Gentile lands will well equip the Jews to be administrators of all nations in the Lord's great kingdom.
15. From the hymn "The Crowning Day" by D. W. Whittle.
16. Some take the view that there were two healings, one on the way into Jericho and one on the way out.
17. From the hymn "Come, My Soul, Thy Suit Prepare" by John Newton.
18. Edersheim, *The Life and Times of Jesus the Messiah*, 725.
19. Matthew 21 refers to an ass and a colt. *The Companion Bible* (page 1355) explains, "Here the *two* are sent for, because Zech. 9.9 was to be fulfilled. In Mark, and Luke, only *one* (only one being necessary to fulfil the part of Zechariah quoted by John 12.14,15)."
20. They would have picked up the well-known caravan road that extended from Jericho to Jerusalem.
21. Edersheim, *The Life and Times of Jesus the Messiah*, 727-728.
22. Ibid., 729.
23. From Mark we learn that this event probably took place the next day. Matthew often grouped his material without regard to chronology in order to produce a cumulative effect and to convince the Jews of the claims of Christ.
24. See Morgan, *The Gospel According to Matthew*, 251.
25. Morgan, *The Gospel According to Matthew*, 252.
26. *The Companion Bible*, appendix 6.
27. To the church He is the headstone of the corner, the foundation stone (1 Corinthians 3:11; Ephesians 2:20-22; 1 Peter 2:4-7). To the nations at the end of the age, at the second coming, He will be the smiting stone "cut out without hands" (Daniel 2:34). C. I. Scofield noted that Israel stumbled *over* Him, the church is built *on* Him, and the nations will be broken *by* Him. See notes on Matthew 21:44 in *The Scofield Reference Bible*, 1029-1030.
28. The fact that the Jews never actually ruled the nations does not detract from this thought. They would have, had they been obedient to God. Similarly Nebuchadnezzar, the "head of gold," never ruled the globe, but he could have (Daniel 2:37-38). Israel's political ascendancy was implied in both the Abrahamic and Davidic covenants (Genesis 15; 2 Samuel 7:9-11). The "times of the Gentiles" did not begin until Israel's (Judah's) cup of rebellion was full. From then until now the Hebrew people have been conquered, persecuted, driven from land to land, and until recently exiled from the promised land. That the Jews lost their political ascendancy is what the "times of the Gentiles" is all about. Global empire, as God planned, will be given to the Jews by Christ during the millennium after the "times of the Gentiles" has been terminated with the overthrow of the antichrist.
29. The church is mostly Gentile in composition, but really neither Jewish nor Gentile; it is something new, unique, and unforeseen by the prophets.
30. See John Phillips, *Exploring Acts* (Neptune, NJ: Loizeaux, 1991).
31. See *The Companion Bible*, 247.
32. This is the last of nine occurrences of this title in Matthew's Gospel.

33. For a full exposition of Psalm 110, see John Phillips, *Exploring the Psalms, Volume Two* (Neptune, NJ: Loizeaux, 1988).
34. See John Phillips, *Exploring the World of the Jew,* 55-76.
35. Morgan, *The Gospel According to Matthew,* 272.
36. See Edersheim, *The Life and Times of Jesus the Messiah,* appendix 17.
37. Edersheim, *The Life and Times of Jesus the Messiah,* 1046.
38. Some of these things anticipate the postrapture age when the gospel of the kingdom will be preached and many Jews will persecute those who preach it before they in turn are persecuted by the antichrist.
39. Edersheim, *The Life and Times of Jesus the Messiah,* 759.
40. Josephus, *Wars of the Jews,* 4.5.4.
41. For a fuller discussion see John Phillips, *Exploring Revelation.*
42. For a fuller discussion see John Phillips, *Exploring the World of the Jew,* 133-148.
43. James Strong, "Greek Dictionary of the New Testament" in *The Exhaustive Concordance of the Bible* (New York: Abingdon, 1890) 55.
44. From the hymn "There's a Wideness in God's Mercy" by Frederick W. Faber.

Part Three, Section 2

1. Edersheim, *The Life and Times of Jesus the Messiah,* 805.
2. Some think that the incidents recorded in Matthew 26:6-13 and John 12:2-8 are not the same.
3. Edersheim, *The Life and Times of Jesus the Messiah,* 805.
4. H. D. M. Spence and Joseph S. Exell, eds., *Matthew* in *The Pulpit Commentary,* 23 vols. (Grand Rapids: Eerdmans, 1963) 15:519.
5. For a verse-by-verse exposition of these Psalms, see John Phillips, *Exploring the Psalms, Volume Two.*
6. Edersheim, *The Life and Times of Jesus the Messiah,* 842.
7. See Morgan, *The Gospel According to Matthew,* 302.
8. See Morgan, *The Gospel According to Matthew,* 303.
9. For a further discussion of this sad fact, see John Phillips, *Exploring the World of the Jew.*
10. From the hymn "What Will You Do with Jesus?" by Albert B. Simpson.
11. See Edersheim, *The Life and Times of Jesus the Messiah,* 879-880.
12. Edersheim, *The Life and Times of Jesus the Messiah,* 894.
13. Ibid., 888-889.

Part Four

1. Rest is the theme of Hebrews 4, where creation rest, covenant rest, Canaan rest, and Calvary rest are all brought into review. For a further discussion see John Phillips, *Exploring Hebrews.*
2. W. Garden Blaikie, *The Personal Life of David Livingstone* (New York: Revell, n.d.) 197.